788 Rapid Recipes In a Single Source

WHEN the first issue of *Quick Cooking* magazine was published in early 1998, thousands of busy cooks across the country breathed a sigh of relief and said, "It's about time!"

"It's about time...we sit down with our family for home-cooked meals again," they confided. *"It's about time...we spend quality family time together preparing quick and easy dishes,"* they told us. *"It's about time...someone realized a magazine filled with fast recipes is greatly needed."*

We heard that timely message loud and clear. As a matter of fact, saving you time is what this *1999 Quick Cooking Annual Recipes* book is all about, too.

Complete Collection of Rapid Recipes. This one-of-a-kind book gathers every rapid recipe from the first six issues of *Quick Cooking* magazine—*788 recipes in all*—into one classic collection. And each year, we'll publish a brand-new volume with all the recipes from the previous six issues of *QC*.

So you no longer need to clip out recipes from each issue and file them in your own recipe card box. And if you can't stand the thought of cutting up your issues, you'll never have to worry about dog-earring their pages again. You'll always have the recipes right at hand, handsomely displayed on your kitchen bookshelf!

Convenient Chapters for Busy Cooks. This big book's 356 pages are divided into 21 handy chapters that correspond to favorite features in *QC*. So it's easy to find just the right recipe for your time and tastes.

For example, when the clock is already ticking close to dinnertime as you walk in the front door, turn to "30 Minutes to Mealtime" for 12 complete meals that will put a halt to your family's hunger in a hurry. Or when you do have some time to spare, make a few "Freezer Pleasers" that can be frozen for no-fuss future meals. (A complete list of chapters can be found on page 5.)

Easy-to-Use Indexes. We've listed all 788 recipes in *three different indexes* to make each and every one fast to find. (The indexes begin on page 338.) The comprehensive general index lists every recipe by food category and/or major ingredient, while the alphabetical listing of recipes is perfect for folks who are looking for a specific family favorite. The third index designates all recipes that use less sugar, salt and fat and include Nutritional Analysis and Diabetic Exchanges.

Large Print and Color Photos. For easier reading while cooking, we've used large print throughout the book (even the index!). And each recipe is complete on a page...there's no stopping and turning the page to finish a dish. What's more, big full-color photos let you easily see what the finished foods will look like *before* you begin cooking.

Sturdy Cover Stands the Test of Time. Unlike so many other cookbooks, this timeless collection is printed on high-quality coated paper that will stand up to common kitchen spills and splatters for years to come. (Yet you can still jot down the glowing compliments you'll receive after serving a newfound family favorite!) Plus, the book lies open *and stays open* as you cook.

What's on the Menu? To make meal planning extra easy, our food editors "grouped" several recipes from various chapters to create *57 around-the-clock suggested menus*. (You'll find this time-saving tool on page 6.)

Best of all, every recipe, procedure and kitchen tip in this *1999 Quick Cooking Annual Recipes* collection was specifically selected with the busy cook's lack of time in mind. So this book will never go "out of date". Year after year, you can treat your loved ones to comforting, wholesome home cooking—the kind that tends to bind families together...and spend less time (and money) doing it than you would making a side trip to stop for costly containers of pre-cooked "takeout"!

1999 Quick Cooking Annual Recipes

Editor: Julie Schnittka

Art Director: Maribeth Greinke

Food Editor: Coleen Martin

Associate Editor: Kristine Krueger

Assistant Art Directors: Ellen Lloyd,
Stephanie Marchese, Jim Sibilski

Production: Claudia Wardius

Cover Photography: Scott Anderson

Taste of Home Books
©1998 Reiman Publications, L.P.
5400 S. 60th St., Greendale WI 53129

International Standard Book Number:
0-89821-258-8
International Standard Serial Number:
1522-6336

PICTURED ON THE COVER: Chicken in Basil Cream (p. 39), Garlic Angel Hair Pasta (p. 238), Lemon Asparagus (p. 287) and Microwave Cherry Crisp (p. 289).

For additional copies of this book or information on other books, write: *Taste of Home* Books, P.O. Box 990, Greendale WI 53129. **Credit card orders call toll-free 1-800/558-1013.**

Taste of Home's QUICK COOKING

Executive Editor: Kathy Pohl

Food Editor: Coleen Martin

Associate Food Editor: Corinne Willkomm

Senior Recipe Editor: Sue A. Jurack

Managing Editor: Julie Landry

Senior Editor: Bob Ottum

Associate Editors: Henry de Fiebre, Ann Kaiser, Faithann Stoner, Kristine Krueger, Sharon Selz

Test Kitchen Home Economist: Sue Draheim

Test Kitchen Assistants: Judith Scholovich, Sherry Smalley, Suzi Hampton, Sue Hampton

Editorial Assistants: Barb Czysz, Sarah Grimm, Ursula Maurer

Design Director: Jim Sibilski

Art Director: Julie Wagner

Food Photography: Scott Anderson, Glenn Thiesenhusen

Food Photography Artist: Stephanie Marchese

Photo Studio Manager: Anne Schimmel

Production: Ellen Lloyd, Claudia Wardius

Publisher: Roy Reiman

⏱ *Contents*

What's on The Menu?

GRAB A MENU from the best "fast food" place in town—your kitchen! The price is right, the atmosphere is relaxing, and the service couldn't be friendlier nor the guests more appreciative. And with the *1999 Quick Cooking Annual Recipes* book in your hands, you've already given yourself a generous tip!

Here's how to use the menu ideas featured here: Our food editors screened all the recipes that appear in this book, then "grouped" several from various chapters to make up menus for everyday and special-occasion family meals. Plus, you can mix and match recipes to make up menus of your own.

For even more complete meals, turn to the following chapters: The Busiest Cooks in the Country (p. 8), 30 Minutes to Mealtime (p. 22), Thinking Up a Theme (p. 40) and Company's Coming! (p. 304).

Six Breakfast Choices

Eighteen Lunch Choices

Thirty-Three Dinner Choices

Chapter 1

BETWEEN work, school and a slew of other activities, you probably pack more than possible into a typical day.

So you likely think there's little time left over to prepare a delicious down-home dinner for your famished family. But this chapter pleasantly proves that memorable family mealtimes are within reach!

Six fellow frenzied cooks share their time-saving tricks, menu-planning pointers and reliable rapid recipes that are guaranteed to put you on the meal-making fast track in no time!

DINNERS IN A DASH. Clockwise from lower left: Cantaloupe Salad, Chicken Fingers, Dressed-Up Cucumbers, Oven Potato Wedges and Walnut Brownies (all recipes on pp. 16 and 17).

Our Food Editor Shares Time-Saving Secrets

WHEN she's not in our offices supervising a staff of trained home economists, sorting through *hundreds* of recipes a week, and testing and editing them, Food Editor Coleen Martin is often cooking up a storm in her own kitchen.

She, husband Andy and their two young children—David and Sara—live in Brookfield, Wisconsin. "I've always felt at home in the kitchen," smiles Coleen. "My mom and grandma were both great cooks. I have fond memories of spending time with them in the kitchen when I was growing up."

Following her mom's "recipe" for organization, Coleen constantly plans ahead to make sure she can fit wholesome homemade meals into her family's hectic lifestyle.

"When I walk out the door in the morning, I always know what we'll be having for dinner that night," she reports. "I'll take something out of the freezer—a cut of meat that's quick to prepare, a casserole or potpie I've made from leftovers—so it can thaw in the fridge during the day.

"If I'm planning a stir-fry, I'll often chop up the veggies the night before. Little steps like that save time. I've learned never to leave things to the last minute because there might not *be* a last minute."

Two of the kitchen "tools" Coleen relies on to get meals on the table in short order are her microwave and her freezer (see her tips for organizing a freezer below left). "I use the microwave to reheat foods and cook vegetables," she details. "And I keep my freezer well-stocked."

Quality Time in the Kitchen

Coleen was happy to share one of her favorite fast meals, complete with appetizer. "To take the edge off the kids' (and our!) hunger, Southwestern Cheese Dip can be whipped up in no time," she advises. "It's great with vegetables or chips.

"For the Crispy Chicken, I use boneless chicken breasts—one of my favorite quick-cooking cuts of meat. David helps me crumble cereal for the coating. (Some of our best 'quality time' is spent in the kitchen.)

"Vegetable Rice Medley combines rice with frozen vegetables. The veggies are small enough for Sara to handle easily. The same's true of the rice, which she can pick up with her fingers.

"For dessert, One-Bowl Chocolate Cake mixes up quickly and bakes while we eat. David loves to help decorate it."

Freezer's Key to Fast Meals

- I keep a grocery list in a handy kitchen drawer. As soon as we run out of anything, Andy or I add that item to the list.
- I also keep a freezer list in that drawer. It has two columns—one for uncooked foods, the other for precooked ones (browned ground beef, containers of soup, etc.). That way, I can tell at a glance what I have in my freezer...and when the time's arrived for me to restock certain items.
- Everything in my freezer is labeled and dated. Every 3 months, I take out each item, check for freezer burn and use up any little odds and ends or small amounts of leftovers.
- I keep precooked foods on the top shelf of the freezer and uncooked foods on the bottom shelf, so I know right where to reach when I'm in a hurry.

—*Coleen Martin*

Southwestern Cheese Dip

1 pound plain *or* Mexican-flavored process American cheese, cubed
1 jar (8 ounces) process cheese spread
1 pound sliced bacon, cooked and crumbled
1 bunch green onions with tops, sliced
1 can (4 ounces) chopped green chilies
Raw vegetables *or* tortilla chips

Place cheeses in a 1-1/2-qt. microwave-safe bowl. Top with bacon, onions and chilies. Microwave at 50% power for 6-8 minutes or until cheese is melted, stirring every 2 minutes. Serve with vegetables or chips. **Yield:** 3 cups.

Crispy Chicken

1-1/2 cups crisp rice cereal, coarsely crushed
2 tablespoons all-purpose flour
1/2 teaspoon salt
1/4 teaspoon dried thyme
1/4 teaspoon poultry seasoning
1/4 cup butter *or* margarine, melted
4 boneless skinless chicken breast halves (about 1 pound)

In a shallow bowl, combine cereal, flour and seasonings. Place butter in another bowl. Dip chicken in butter, then into cereal mixture. Place in a greased 11-in. x 7-in. x

2-in. baking pan. Drizzle with remaining butter. Bake, uncovered, at 400° for 20-25 minutes or until juices run clear. **Yield:** 4 servings.

One-Bowl Chocolate Cake

2 cups all-purpose flour
2 cups sugar
1/2 cup baking cocoa
2 teaspoons baking soda
1 teaspoon baking powder
1/2 teaspoon salt
1 cup vegetable oil
1 cup buttermilk
2 eggs
1 cup hot water
Frosting of your choice
Colored sprinkles, optional

In a large bowl, combine dry ingredients. Stir in oil, buttermilk and eggs. Add water and stir until combined. Pour into a greased 13-in. x 9-in. x 2-in. baking pan. Bake at 350° for 35-38 minutes or until a toothpick inserted near the center comes out clean. Cool completely. Frost (see three frosting recipes on page 326). Decorate with sprinkles if desired. **Yield:** 12-16 servings.

Vegetable Rice Medley

1 cup uncooked long grain rice
2-1/4 cups water
2 to 3 tablespoons onion *or* vegetable soup mix
1/4 teaspoon salt
2 cups frozen corn, peas *or* mixed vegetables

In a saucepan, combine the rice, water, soup mix and salt; bring to a boil. Add the vegetables; return to a boil. Reduce heat; cover and simmer for 15 minutes. Cook until the rice and vegetables are tender. **Yield:** 4-6 servings.

On-the-Go Grandma's Ahead Of Her Time

IT'S EASY TO see how Ruth Taylor became such an excellent juggler. This bustling grandmother from Greeneville, Tennessee constantly has her hands full.

As president of her church women's circle, a service club member and community volunteer, Ruth wears numerous hats. And for this wife, mother of four, grandma of three, and day-care "nana" for neighborhood youngsters, a chef's hat is among them.

"I learned my way around the kitchen from an expert—my mother, known as the best cook in our county," Ruth notes.

"When I was growing up, Mom, Dad and my brother handled farm chores while I took on meal-making duties. In my teen years, Mom managed several restaurants. That's when I discovered the importance of efficient cooking and food with a personal touch."

Nowadays, Ruth puts that experience to good use cooking up fuss-free meals.

"Two key ingredients in most all my recipes are economy and speed," Ruth explains. "I plan many dishes that I can prepare ahead by slicing vegetables or precooking meat. Others use convenience foods or mixes and call for basic on-hand ingredients.

Ready to Reheat

"Our family's schedules vary, so I like meals that can be easily reheated. I also plan menus that leave leftovers for soups or casseroles that taste good the second time around," she adds.

Ruth shares a favorite meal that's sufficiently fast for any action-packed day.

"Skillet Steak and Corn combines canned vegetables and meat in a savory sauce. Cut into thin strips, the steak cooks quickly. When your family eats in shifts, skillet dishes like this are a breeze to warm up. Poultry lovers can substitute chicken for the beef.

"Fruited Lettuce Salad is a colorful and refreshing combination that wakes up the taste buds with its tangy dressing," Ruth says.

"For dessert, Strawberry Sponge Cake uses pur-chased sponge cakes. So there's no need for baking.

"To showcase its pretty strawberry-red layer, I dish it up in clear dessert glasses or dishes like a trifle."

Skillet Steak and Corn

✓ Nutritional Analysis included

      1 pound boneless round steak, cut into strips
      1 medium onion, cut into 1/4-inch wedges
  1/2 teaspoon dried thyme
      2 tablespoons vegetable oil
  3/4 cup red wine *or* beef broth
      1 can (14-1/2 ounces) diced tomatoes, undrained
      2 cans (11 ounces *each*) Mexicorn, drained
Hot cooked rice

In a skillet or wok over medium-high heat, brown steak, onion and thyme in oil. Add wine or broth; simmer for 10 minutes or until liquid has evaporated. Stir in tomatoes; cover and simmer 15 minutes longer. Add corn; heat through. Serve over rice. **Yield:** 4 servings. **Nutritional Analysis:** One serving (prepared with low-sodium broth and no-salt-added tomatoes; calculated without rice) equals 386 calories, 975 mg sodium, 70 mg cholesterol, 36 gm carbohydrate, 32 gm protein, 12 gm fat. **Diabetic Exchanges:** 3 lean meat, 2 starch, 1 vegetable.

Fruited Lettuce Salad

      6 cups torn salad greens
      1 can (11 ounces) mandarin oranges, drained
      1 cup green grapes
  1/4 cup finely chopped onion
  2/3 cup sliced almonds
  1/3 cup orange juice

Pre-Planned Menu Saves Minutes

- I pre-plan 14 menus for a 2-week period, including a lunch and dinner for each day. That way, I don't waste time wondering what to fix, and I can buy my ingredients ahead.
- After the 2-week plan is complete, I put needed items on my grocery list.
- I write my menus on a legal pad and save meal plans from previous weeks so I don't repeat dishes.
- By going through cookbooks before I start my plan, I easily incorporate three new recipes every 2 weeks. To save time, I write the cookbook name and the recipe page on my menus.
- If I have soon-to-expire coupons for a certain item or hear of an upcoming special, I incorporate that ingredient into one or more meals.
- I decide how to weave a certain fruit or vegetable into meals when it's in season and reasonably priced.
- I plan meals that provide leftovers for microwavable brown-bag lunches.
- Every morning, I review my menu plan and decide what to serve that day. I figure out how long the meal will take to fix, when I need to start and in what order to prepare each recipe. —*Ruth Taylor*

1/3 cup vegetable oil
3 tablespoons vinegar
1-1/2 teaspoons celery seed

In a large bowl, toss the greens, oranges, grapes, onion and almonds. Combine remaining ingredients in a jar with tight-fitting lid; shake well. Pour over salad and toss to coat. Serve immediately. **Yield:** 4-6 servings.

Strawberry Sponge Cake
(Not pictured)

1 quart fresh strawberries, diced
1 carton (13-1/2 ounces) strawberry glaze

9 individual cream-filled sponge cakes
1 package (8 ounces) cream cheese, softened
1 can (14-1/2 ounces) sweetened condensed milk
1 carton (12 ounces) frozen whipped topping, thawed

Combine the strawberries and glaze; set aside. Slice the cakes in half lengthwise; place in an ungreased 13-in. x 9-in. x 2-in. dish. In a mixing bowl, beat cream cheese and milk until smooth; fold in the whipped topping. Spread over cakes. Spoon strawberry mixture over top. Cover and refrigerate for 30 minutes or until ready to serve. Spoon into individual serving dishes. Refrigerate any leftovers. **Yield:** 16 servings.

Busy Mom Has A Ball in The Kitchen

BEING A good sport comes naturally to Maribeth Edwards of Follansbee, West Virginia. Wife and mother in an athletic family, she's come up with a game plan for quick, easy meals.

Depending on the season, Maribeth must keep track of swim meets, volleyball, basketball and baseball games for Jessica and Travis. And her own schedule doesn't allow for "extra innings" in the kitchen. "Like many busy couples, my husband, David, and I find mealtime is the perfect time to touch base with the kids and each other," she says.

"David works swing shifts in a local steel mill and may get home in the afternoon, evening or at the crack of dawn. So I look for flexible meals that can be warmed up for a late supper or even for breakfast.

"On Saturday, when our grocery store flyers arrive, I plan a 7-day menu," Maribeth continues. "I try to include sales and coupon items into my once-a-week shopping list. I also check David's work schedule and our family's activity calendar. That way, I know how many reheatable meals I'll be needing.

Convenience Is a Blessing

"I also like to precook meats in my slow cooker for 'emergency meals'. I keep sliced roast beef and ham in the freezer. When I'm in a rush, I layer cold cuts into sandwiches, toss them into salads or sizzle them into stir-fries.

"I find convenient meals like these are a real blessing on Sundays," adds Maribeth, also a Bible school teacher. "After services, we can get lunch ready in minutes and relax as we're eating.

"My favorite time-saving appliance is my bread machine—it's perfect for turning out old-fashioned loaves, no-fuss pizza crusts and sweet breads in a jiffy. Frequently, it's a lifesaver when a bake sale comes up for school, church or Little League."

When her brood's in the mood for snappy, informal dining, Maribeth provides a tasty at-home meal that stacks up to fast food...in no time.

"Super Supper Hero is so versatile. You can serve it with the works or just your family's favorite meats, vegetables and cheeses," she recommends. "As a hearty in-hand meal, youngsters love it.

"Seasoned Fries are always popular with my meat-and-potatoes bunch. The cheesy seasoning can easily double as a flavorful baked potato topper, too.

"For dessert, Almond Ice Cream Cups can't be beat," Maribeth attests. "The recipe is a fun and delicious way to dress up plain vanilla ice cream.

Snack Scores Points

"It's easy to leave room for these light, refreshing muffin-sized treats. They also score points when the kids invite their hungry teammates home for an after-game snack."

Maribeth's play-by-play meal plan assures everything's ready in a snap. "I make the dessert first and place it in the freezer while I fix the rest of the meal," she reveals. "Next I make the vegetable topping for the hero, then prepare the fries. I assemble the sandwich while the fries are baking."

Before games, you'll find Maribeth gathering up uniforms, caps, mitts...plus dozens of recipe clippings. "Between innings, the mothers in the bleachers often exchange menu ideas," she confides.

With the quick recipes Maribeth is pitching, many of those moms are sure to be hitting scrumptious home runs at mealtime!

Super Supper Hero

2-1/2 cups cubed eggplant
1 cup thinly sliced red onion
1 cup *each* julienned green, sweet yellow and red peppers
1/4 cup olive *or* vegetable oil
1/2 cup chopped tomato
1 teaspoon dried oregano
1/2 teaspoon salt
1/4 teaspoon pepper
1 unsliced loaf (1 pound) Italian bread
Lettuce leaves
1/2 pound sliced fully cooked ham
1/2 pound sliced cooked turkey breast
1/4 pound sliced hard salami
1/2 pound sliced mozzarella cheese

In a large skillet, saute eggplant, onion and peppers in oil for 5 minutes. Add tomato, oregano, salt and pepper. Remove from the heat and set aside. Cut bread in half lengthwise; hollow out the bottom, leaving a 3/4-in. shell (discard removed bread or save for another use). Layer with lettuce, ham, turkey, salami and cheese. Top with sauteed vegetables. Replace bread top. Secure with toothpicks; cut into slices. **Yield:** 4-6 servings.

Seasoned Fries

6 cups frozen shoestring potatoes
1/2 cup grated Parmesan cheese
2 teaspoons Italian seasoning
1/2 teaspoon salt

Place potatoes on a foil-lined baking sheet. Bake at 450° for 8 minutes. Combine remaining ingredients;

sprinkle over potatoes and mix gently. Bake 4-5 minutes longer or until the potatoes are browned and crisp. **Yield:** 4-6 servings.

Almond Ice Cream Cups

1 pint vanilla ice cream, softened
1/3 cup miniature semisweet chocolate chips
1/2 teaspoon almond extract
1 cup whipped topping
1/4 cup crushed shortbread cookies
1 tablespoon sliced almonds, toasted

In a bowl, combine ice cream, chocolate chips and extract; fold in whipped topping. Spoon into paper-lined muffin cups. Sprinkle each with cookie crumbs and almonds. Serve immediately or freeze. **Yield:** 12 servings.

Major League Time-Savers

- To save food prep time, I take out all the pantry items I'll need for a meal and put them on a tray. Later, I simply grab the tray and start cooking!
- My meal plans regularly include two dishes that bake at the same oven temperature. That way, I can have both in the oven at the same time.
- When making lasagna, I don't cook the pasta ahead of time. Instead, I add extra sauce for moisture and let the noodles cook as the lasagna bakes.
- Rather than browning meatballs, I add them uncooked directly to my sauce. As the sauce cooks, so do the meatballs. I cut one open to judge its doneness.
- Often I make an extra batch of cookie dough and spoon dollops onto waxed paper. After freezing them solid, I put a dozen in a freezer bag labeled with the cookie's name, baking time and temperature. They stay in the freezer (for up to 4 months) until we're hungry for their fresh-baked flavor.

—*Maribeth Edwards*

Serve Up Old-Fashioned Foods in a Wink

VISITORS to Maplewood Bed & Breakfast in Hinsdale, Massachusetts can't help but feel welcome. The 1770's farmhouse, decorated with antiques and filled with the aromas of fresh-baked goodies, is so warm and homey it often reminds them of Grandma's house.

But Charlotte Baillargeon, the grandmother who manages the day-to-day operations of this busy bed-and-breakfast, has a plateful of other activities.

Charlotte also works part-time as a bookkeeper for a nearby community college, pens a folksy food column for a South Boston newspaper and cares for grandson Andrew. Husband Bob is a foreman at a local manufacturer, so they're up before dawn and make every minute count.

"To save time, I try to do two things at once," Charlotte says. "For example, in the morning, I pop muffins in the oven to bake while I'm taking a shower. Then I let them cool while I take my daily walk.

"When I get back, I might peel potatoes and carrots for a slow-cooker meal or pull something out of the freezer. Since I love to make big batches of soup, I freeze the leftovers in 1-quart containers. When I need a head start on a quick dinner, I'll take a container out in the morning to thaw."

Leftovers Make Easy Weekday Meals

For weekend family get-togethers, Charlotte often prepares a big meal, such as a turkey dinner, that can later help hurry along the preparation of other dinners.

"As soon as we're done eating, I package all the leftover meat and freeze it to use in hot turkey sandwiches, potpies and casseroles. I also cook the bones right away so I'll have soup stock before the night is over," she says.

Like many mothers, Charlotte lets family members celebrating birthdays choose a favorite meal for her to make. "Almost everyone requests my tender breaded Chicken Fingers," she adds.

"I begin marinating the chicken strips early in the day to cut down on last-minute fuss.

"Later, the nicely seasoned Oven Potato Wedges bake in the oven while I fry the chicken."

Charlotte's Cantaloupe Salad, with its fresh-tasting dressing, is great with most any meal. And tasty Dressed-Up Cucumbers are amazingly easy. "I just add chopped green pepper and onion from our garden and bottled dressing," she explains.

To top off a meal on a moment's notice, Charlotte often stirs up her fudgy Walnut Brownies. "I ran out of boxed brownie mix once and experimented with cake mix instead. The result was so yummy my family thought I'd made brownies from scratch!" she recalls.

Try Charlotte's quick-to-please menu in your own kitchen—it's sure to simplify your busy life.

Chicken Fingers

- 6 boneless skinless chicken breast halves
- 1 egg, beaten
- 1 cup buttermilk
- 1-1/2 teaspoons garlic powder
- 1 cup all-purpose flour
- 1 cup seasoned bread crumbs
- 1 teaspoon salt
- 1 teaspoon baking powder
- Oil for frying

Cut the chicken into 1/2-in. strips; place in a large resealable plastic bag. Combine egg, buttermilk and garlic powder; pour over chicken. Seal and refrigerate for 2-4 hours. In another large resealable plastic bag, combine flour, bread crumbs, salt and baking powder. Drain chicken, discarding buttermilk mixture. Place chicken in the bag with the flour mixture; seal and shake to coat. In an electric skillet, heat oil to 375°. Fry the chicken in batches for 4-5 minutes or until golden brown. Drain on paper towels. **Yield:** 6 servings.

Oven Potato Wedges

- 2 pounds red potatoes, cut into small wedges
- 1 large onion, chopped
- 3 tablespoons olive *or* vegetable oil
- 1 teaspoon garlic powder
- 1/2 teaspoon salt
- 1/2 teaspoon dried oregano

In a large bowl, combine all ingredients; stir to coat. Place in a single layer in an ungreased shallow baking pan. Bake, uncovered, at 425° for 30-35 minutes or until the potatoes are tender and lightly browned. **Yield:** 6 servings.

Cantaloupe Salad

- 1 large cantaloupe, peeled
- 3 tablespoons orange juice
- 3 tablespoons honey
- 1 cup halved red seedless grapes
- 3 kiwifruit, peeled, quartered and sliced
- Lettuce leaves
- Shredded coconut

Cut six rings, about 1/2 in. wide, from the center section of the cantaloupe. Remove seeds and set rings aside. Cube the remaining cantaloupe. In a bowl, combine orange juice and honey. Add grapes, kiwi and cubed cantaloupe; stir gently to coat. Place cantaloupe rings on lettuce; top with fruit and sprinkle with coconut. **Yield:** 6 servings.

She Shares Supermarket Savvy

- We try to be very frugal shoppers. I look over the grocery store flyers first and make my shopping list according to what's on special. I shop to stock the pantry and freezer, then plan daily menus using items I have on hand.
- We buy fresh fruits and veggies each week, choosing seasonal produce because it's less expensive.
- When something we use often is on sale, we buy a lot and freeze it or store it. But I'm careful not to buy so much that the item gets stale or freezer-burned before we're able to use it.
- To save time later, I repackage bulk items into smaller servings before storing. I label the packages with the date so the oldest items are used first.
- I buy convenience items to save minutes. For example, I add chopped tomatoes and extra spices to prepared spaghetti sauce for "from scratch" flavor. And I top a simmering kettle of chicken soup with refrigerator biscuits and cover it. In just 15 minutes, I have "dumplings" that taste homemade.

—*Charlotte Baillargeon*

Dressed-Up Cucumbers

3 large cucumbers, cut into 1/4-inch slices
1/4 cup chopped green pepper
1/4 cup finely chopped onion
1 cup Italian salad dressing

Combine all ingredients in a bowl. Cover and refrigerate until serving. **Yield:** 6 servings.

Walnut Brownies

1 package (18-1/4 ounces) chocolate cake mix
1/4 cup vegetable oil
1/4 cup water
2 eggs
1/2 cup chopped walnuts
1/2 cup semisweet chocolate chips

In a mixing bowl, combine cake mix, oil, water and eggs; beat until smooth (batter will be thick). Stir in walnuts and chocolate chips. Spread into a greased 13-in. x 9-in. x 2-in. baking pan. Bake at 325° for 25-33 minutes or until the top springs back when lightly touched in the center. Cool on a wire rack. Cut into bars. **Yield:** 3 dozen.

Ranch Wife Rounds Up Rapid Recipes

IT'S NO exaggeration to say that Judie Anglen is at home on the range. Life on a busy farm and ranch at Riverton, Wyoming provides the former caterer with plenty of opportunities to put her cooking skills to good use.

"Summer and fall are busy times here," Judie reports. "Husband Earl and the men are cutting and cubing hay and irrigating the corn, barley and oats.

"I enjoy fixing hearty, home-style meals whenever I can," she adds. "Most every day I cook for Earl, our son-in-law and a local teen we've hired who lives and works on the ranch.

"Often I feed several more people—seasonal work like branding cattle brings as many as 20 men to the table. So I've become really good at stretching meals and being creative. I have an 'emergency' shelf in the pantry well-stocked for these occasions."

Judie keeps on hand a variety of pastas, jars of prepared spaghetti and Alfredo sauce and other convenience products that help her put a good meal on the table fast.

Welcome to the West

Judie's a fine example of Western hospitality. As the local hostess for Western Welcome Service, she greets newcomers to the area. She also operates Cottonwood Ranch Bed & Breakfast in her 13-room home.

What with work crews, bed-and-breakfast guests and the couple's six children and 12 grandchildren, you can usually find Judie in the kitchen cooking up the simple supper she shares here.

"Our son is a world-record-holding fisherman who keeps us well-supplied with fresh fish," Judie relates. "So I make my Fast Baked Fish often. It's moist, tender and flavorful."

Snipped dill adds wonderful fresh flavor to her savory rice side dish. "It complements the fish quite nicely, and it's a snap to prepare," she comments.

Judie recalls modifying another recipe to come up with her pretty Honey-Glazed Carrots. "The original recipe called for sugar," she explains. "A local man who keeps bees on our farm shares some honey with us, so I use it instead. We love the sweet flavor."

To complete this well-rounded meal, Judie slices generous servings of her Peach Mallow Pie, a fruity dessert that's a breeze to make ahead.

Bring Judie's delicious dinner home to your range ...and round up the family for a fast feast!

Fast Baked Fish

1-1/4 pounds fish fillets*
    1 teaspoon seasoned salt
Pepper to taste
Paprika, optional
    3 tablespoons butter *or* margarine, melted

Place fish in a greased 11-in. x 7-in. x 2-in. baking dish. Sprinkle with seasoned salt, pepper and paprika if desired. Drizzle with butter. Cover and bake at 400° for 15-20 minutes or until fish flakes easily with a fork. **Yield:** 4 servings. ***Editor's Note:** Orange roughy, haddock, trout or walleye may be used in this recipe.

Honey-Glazed Carrots

☑ Nutritional Analysis included

    1 package (16 ounces) baby carrots
    1 tablespoon water
    2 tablespoons butter *or* margarine
    2 tablespoons honey
    1 tablespoon lemon juice

Place carrots and water in a 1-1/2-qt. microwave-safe dish. Cover and microwave on high for 5-7 minutes or until crisp-tender. Meanwhile, melt butter in a skillet; stir in honey and lemon juice. Cook over low heat for 5 minutes, stirring constantly. Add carrots; cook and stir for 2 minutes or until glazed. **Yield:** 4 servings. **Nutritional Analysis:** One 1/2-cup serving (prepared with margarine) equals 127 calories, 107 mg sodium, 0 cholesterol, 18 gm carbohydrate, 1 gm protein, 6 gm fat. **Diabetic Exchanges:** 1 vegetable, 1 fruit, 1 fat. **Editor's Note:** This recipe was tested in an 850-watt microwave.

Judie's Fast-to-Fix Favorites

- To start the day, I'll often whip up healthy "fruit smoothies" as a speedy breakfast for Earl and me. I blend bananas and apple juice with whatever seasonal fruit or frozen berries I have on hand to make tasty shakes.

- My favorite made-in-minutes meals are nutritious stir-fries. I stock the freezer with a variety of quick-cooking meats and mixed frozen vegetables. Then I mix and match ingredients and toss them in my wok to prepare dinner in a jiffy.

- On those days when I know I'll be working, I rely on my slow cooker for fuss-free meals. I get up early to put everything into the pot, then switch it on before I leave the house. When I get home, I have a hearty meal ready and waiting. —*Judie Anglen*

Dilled Rice

    1 cup uncooked long grain rice
    2 tablespoons butter *or* margarine
2-1/2 cups chicken broth
    1 teaspoon dried minced onion
    2 tablespoons snipped fresh dill *or* 2 teaspoons
    dill weed

In a 2-qt. saucepan, saute rice in butter until golden, stirring constantly. Add broth and onion; bring to a boil. Reduce heat to low; cover and cook for 20 minutes or until rice is tender. Stir in dill. **Yield:** 4 servings. **Nutritional Analysis:** One 3/4-cup serving (prepared with margarine and low-sodium broth) equals 253 calories, 137 mg sodium, 3 mg cholesterol, 41 gm carbohydrate, 5 gm protein, 7 gm fat. **Diabetic Exchanges:** 2-1/2 starch, 1-1/2 fat.

Peach Mallow Pie

  35 large marshmallows
  1/2 cup milk
1-1/2 cups frozen sliced peaches, thawed *or* 1
    package (10 ounces) frozen sweetened
    raspberries, thawed, undrained
  1/8 teaspoon almond extract
    1 carton (8 ounces) frozen whipped topping,
    thawed
    1 graham cracker crust (9 inches)

Place marshmallows and milk in a large microwave-safe bowl. Microwave, uncovered, on high for 1-2 minutes. Stir until smooth; set aside. Finely chop the peaches; mash lightly with a fork or pulse in a food processor until finely chopped. Add to marshmallow mixture. Stir in extract. Fold in whipped topping; pour into crust. Refrigerate for 2 hours. **Yield:** 6-8 servings. **Editor's Note:** This recipe was tested in an 850-watt microwave.

Homemade Mainstays In a Hurry

WHEN it comes to busy cooks, Deb Morrison of Skiatook, Oklahoma takes the cake. Actually, she bakes the cake, frosts it with icing and adorns it with delicate roses and beautiful borders.

"Making wedding cakes has been a hobby of mine for about 8 years now," Deb relates. "I mostly bake them for brides at my church and give them as wedding presents from our family."

Depending on the size, Deb can devote a full day to baking a wedding cake and another day to decorating it. "I spent 12 hours baking one cake that served more than 300 people," she notes. "It took 8 hours to decorate it—and that doesn't include the time needed to create the frosting roses.

"But making just a few cakes a year keeps it fun," Deb assures. It also gives her free time to spend with husband Casey and sons Caleb, Chad, and Craig.

Deb and Casey are busy working out the details of the family's upcoming move to 15 acres of land they recently purchased. Besides a catfish pond (where the boys are eager to fish), the lot has plenty of space for another of Deb's hobbies—raising golden and lynx Palomino rabbits. "I have 100 rabbits right now, and my main focus is showing them," she says.

Cooking Tops Pastimes

Deb and her family travel throughout the U.S., attending at least six rabbit shows a year. The pedigreed animals draw lots of interest, sparking sales and making Deb one of the nation's top breeders of Palomino rabbits.

When she's not grooming, feeding and conditioning her rabbits, Deb is active in her church, tends a backyard herb garden and enjoys cross-stitch projects.

But cooking for her family remains one of her favorite pastimes. "I love collecting and reading cookbooks," she comments. "I'm always learning something new or trying something new."

While most of the meals Deb serves her family are homemade, she employs different strategies to save time in the kitchen.

When baking, she might decide to knead enough dough to have a batch of dinner rolls plus cinnamon rolls for breakfast the next day. Or she might make extra when grilling chicken to get a head start on another meal.

"Cooked on the grill, it has a unique taste our kids love," Deb informs. "I use the leftovers in chicken salad, on sandwiches, over a green salad—even on crackers with cheese for a snack."

Convenience items also help shave minutes off preparation time. In fact, several are used in this quick-to-fix menu that's special enough for company.

Traditional Taste in Less Time

"When I was growing up, Lasagna Casserole was my favorite meal," Deb shares. "We had it every year for my birthday. Mother made the sauce from scratch, but I use store-bought spaghetti sauce to save time."

The hearty main dish retains the wonderful taste of the traditional favorite—without all the work. "I recently tried sausage rather than ground beef, and everyone raved about the added spiciness," she reports.

An envelope of salad dressing mix gives Deb a jump-start on her Herbed Tossed Salad. Basil from her herb garden boosts the fresh flavor of the dressing when drizzled over colorful salad fixings.

Easy Black Forest Torte couldn't be simpler—all you need is a boxed cake mix, pie filling, miniature marshmallows and whipped topping.

"I sampled this fancy-looking dessert during a visit with my grandmother," Deb relates. "The marshmallows and cherries trade places during baking, and the flavor is excellent."

The fuss-free torte is a short-and-sweet ending to an effortless meal your family is sure to enjoy!

Lasagna Casserole

1 pound ground beef
1/4 cup chopped onion

Deb's Tips for Busy Bakers

- People always look forward to eating the cakes I bake. I use convenient boxed cake mixes—even for wedding cakes—but I have a secret: I add 1/2 teaspoon vanilla and 1/2 teaspoon butter extract for "from-scratch" flavor.

- When making a cake that needs to be turned out of the pan, I grease the pan, then cut a piece of waxed paper to fit into the bottom of the pan. I pour in the batter and bake as directed. After it's cooled 10 minutes, I turn the cake onto a plate or cake board and immediately peel off the waxed paper.

- When making a chocolate cake, I coat the pan with baking cocoa instead of white flour. It works the same as flour but doesn't leave a white residue on the side of the cake. It's nice when serving bundt cakes and other desserts that won't be covered with frosting.

- No time to make homemade buttercream frosting to decorate a cake? Add between 1/2 cup and 1-1/2 cups confectioners' sugar to a can of prepared frosting. This gives it the consistency and flavor of decorator frosting.
    —Deb Morrison

1/2 teaspoon salt
1/2 teaspoon pepper, *divided*
1 pound medium shell pasta, cooked and drained
1 pound (4 cups) shredded mozzarella cheese, *divided*
1 carton (24 ounces) small-curd cottage cheese
2 eggs, beaten
1/3 cup grated Parmesan cheese
2 tablespoons dried parsley flakes
1 jar (26 ounces) spaghetti sauce

In a skillet, cook beef and onion until meat is no longer pink and onion is tender; drain. Sprinkle with salt and 1/4 teaspoon pepper; set aside. In a large bowl, combine pasta, 3 cups of mozzarella cheese, cottage cheese, eggs, Parmesan cheese, parsley and remaining pepper; stir gently. Pour into a greased 13-in. x 9-in. x 2-in. or shallow 3-qt. baking dish. Top with the beef mixture and spaghetti sauce (dish will be full). Cover and bake at 350° for 45 minutes. Sprinkle with remaining mozzarella. Bake, uncovered, 15 minutes longer or until the cheese is melted and bubbly. Let stand 10 minutes before serving. **Yield:** 6-8 servings.

Herbed Tossed Salad

8 cups torn lettuce
1 cup fresh cilantro *or* parsley, coarsely chopped
1 cup sliced fresh mushrooms
2 medium tomatoes, chopped
1 medium carrot, shredded
2 radishes, sliced
1 envelope Italian salad dressing mix
1 tablespoon minced fresh basil *or* 1 teaspoon dried basil
1 garlic clove, minced

In a large bowl, toss the lettuce, cilantro, mushrooms, tomatoes, carrot and radishes. Prepare salad dressing according to package directions; add basil and garlic. Pour over the salad and toss to coat. **Yield:** 6-8 servings.

Easy Black Forest Torte

4 to 5 cups miniature marshmallows
1 package (18-1/4 ounces) chocolate cake mix
1 can (21 ounces) cherry pie filling
1 carton (8 ounces) frozen whipped topping, thawed

Sprinkle marshmallows in a greased 13-in. x 9-in. x 2-in. baking pan. Prepare cake batter according to package directions; pour over the marshmallows. Spoon pie filling over the batter. Bake at 350° for 1 hour or until a toothpick inserted near the center comes out clean. Cool. Frost with whipped topping. Store in the refrigerator. **Yield:** 12-16 servings.

Chapter 2

WHEN your family's eyeing the table while you're eyeing the clock, turn to this lifesaving section for 12 complete meals that take 30 minutes or less to prepare.

In addition to a savory selection of full menus, you'll find 12 enticing entrees that also go from start to finish in just half an hour.

Each and every recipe is a tried-and-true family favorite from a busy country cook. So each dish is sure to earn you rave reviews in your kitchen as well!

TIMELY MAIN COURSES. Clockwise from upper left: Shrimp Monterey (p. 37), Chicken in Basil Cream (p. 39), Hearty Hamburger Supper (p. 36), Favorite Meat Loaf Cups (p. 38).

sons and go well with a hearty salad for a light lunch.)

"For a slightly different flavor, I'll sometimes replace half the mozzarella with cheddar...or whatever cheese I have in the fridge," Donna advises.

Pizza Soup

1-1/4 cups sliced fresh mushrooms
1/2 cup finely chopped onion
1 teaspoon vegetable oil
2 cups water
1 can (15 ounces) pizza sauce
1 cup chopped pepperoni
1 cup chopped fresh tomatoes
1/2 cup cooked Italian sausage
1/4 teaspoon Italian seasoning
1/4 cup grated Parmesan cheese
Shredded mozzarella cheese

In a large saucepan, saute mushrooms and onion in oil for 2-3 minutes or until tender. Add water, pizza sauce, pepperoni, tomatoes, sausage and Italian seasoning. Bring to a boil over medium heat. Reduce heat; cover and simmer for 20 minutes, stirring occasionally. Before serving, stir in Parmesan cheese. Garnish with mozzarella cheese. **Yield:** 4 servings.

Cheese Bread

1 unsliced loaf (1/2 pound) French bread
2 tablespoons butter or margarine, softened
1/2 teaspoon Italian seasoning
1/2 cup shredded mozzarella cheese
1/4 cup grated Parmesan cheese

Slice bread lengthwise; place cut side up on a baking sheet. Spread butter on cut surfaces; sprinkle with half of the Italian seasoning. Top with cheeses and remaining Italian seasoning. Bake at 350° for 20-25 minutes or until the cheese is melted. Cut crosswise into 1-in. pieces. **Yield:** 4 servings.

Peach Cake

3/4 cup cold butter or margarine
1 package (18-1/2 ounces) yellow cake mix
2 egg yolks
2 cups (16 ounces) sour cream
1 can (29 ounces) sliced peaches, drained
1/2 teaspoon ground cinnamon
1 carton (8 ounces) frozen whipped topping, thawed

In a bowl, cut butter into dry cake mix until mixture resembles coarse crumbs. Pat into a greased 13-in. x 9-in. x 2-in. baking pan. In another bowl, beat egg yolks; add the sour cream and mix well. Set aside 6-8 peach slices for garnish. Cut remaining peaches into 1-in. pieces; stir into sour cream mixture. Spread over crust; sprinkle with cinnamon. Bake at 350° for 25-30 minutes or until the edges begin to brown. Cool on a wire rack. Spread with whipped topping; garnish with reserved peaches. Store in the refrigerator. **Yield:** 12 servings.

Fast Favorite With Pizza Fans

"BUSY" is definitely the way to describe Donna Britsch of Tega Cay, South Carolina. "With all I have going on, people ask when I sleep," she chuckles.

Whether working at her home-based personnel consulting business or performing as a clown for charity, Donna relies daily on quick meals like this one she shares.

"Since the Peach Cake needs to bake, I work backward and start by assembling it," Donna reports. "The first time I made this scrumptious dessert, I was thrilled to find out how easy it was.

"Sometimes I'll scoop softened vanilla ice cream on each serving instead of spreading whipped topping over the entire cake," she adds.

Next, Donna fixes a batch of Pizza Soup. "Anyone who likes pizza will love it," she assures. Sons Nathan and Tyson help themselves to big bowls when they get home from college in the evening.

"If you have some leftover ground beef on hand, you can use that instead of sausage," she informs. "Convenient canned mushrooms work just as well as fresh. The soup can also simmer all day in the slow cooker."

Thick slices of Cheese Bread round out this fast feast. (They also make a super snack for Donna's

Quick Route To Cajun Taste

WITH a full-time receptionist job, a hobby farm, a husband and a toddler daughter, Carrina Cooper finds she never seems to have enough hours in the day.

"When I get home from work, I'm looking for ways to serve a satisfying meal without spending much time in the kitchen," she admits. So Carrina, who's from McAlpin, Florida, makes these delicious dishes often.

"I fix the Corn Bread Casserole first, so it can bake while I prepare everything else," she remarks. "It's easy to add variety by stirring in cooked crumbled bacon. Since my husband, Steve, likes spicy foods, I frequently sprinkle chopped jalapeno peppers over half of the casserole for him.

"We all enjoy the Cajun Chicken Strips," she informs. "If I happen to have only pork chops on hand, I'll use them instead."

A delightful dessert of creamy Homemade Chocolate Pudding is a snap to fix using common pantry ingredients. It's also an easy late-night snack.

"I usually top the pudding with M&M's," Carrina says. "Sometimes, Steve adds a dollop of whipped topping to his instead...and daughter Morgan loves to dip fresh strawberries in hers."

Cajun Chicken Strips

1 tablespoon all-purpose flour
1 teaspoon poultry seasoning
3/4 teaspoon garlic salt
1/2 teaspoon paprika
1/4 teaspoon pepper
1/8 to 1/4 teaspoon cayenne pepper
1-1/2 pounds boneless skinless chicken breasts, cut into 1/2-inch strips
2 tablespoons butter *or* margarine
Italian parsley and chili peppers, optional

In a large resealable plastic bag, combine the first six ingredients. Add chicken, half at a time, and shake to coat. In a large skillet, cook chicken in butter for 8-10 minutes or until the juices run clear. Garnish with parsley and peppers if desired. **Yield:** 4-6 servings.

Corn Bread Casserole

1 can (15-1/4 ounces) whole kernel corn, drained
1 can (14-3/4 ounces) cream-style corn
1 package (8-1/2 ounces) corn bread/muffin mix
1 egg
2 tablespoons butter *or* margarine, melted
1/4 teaspoon garlic powder
1/4 teaspoon paprika

In a large bowl, combine all ingredients. Pour into a greased 11-in. x 7-in. x 2-in. baking dish. Bake, uncovered, at 400° for 25-30 minutes or until the top and edges are golden brown. **Yield:** 4-6 servings.

Homemade Chocolate Pudding

✓ Nutritional Analysis included

1 cup sugar
1/2 cup baking cocoa
1/4 cup cornstarch
1/2 teaspoon salt
4 cups milk
2 tablespoons butter *or* margarine
2 teaspoons vanilla extract
M&M's, optional

In a heavy saucepan, combine the sugar, cocoa, cornstarch and salt. Gradually add milk. Bring to a boil over medium heat; boil and stir for 2 minutes. Remove from the heat; stir in butter and vanilla. Spoon into individual serving dishes. Chill until serving. Sprinkle with M&M's if desired. **Yield:** 6-8 servings. **Nutritional Analysis:** One 1/2-cup serving (prepared with skim milk and margarine and served without M&M's) equals 196 calories, 244 mg sodium, 2 mg cholesterol, 38 gm carbohydrate, 5 gm protein, 4 gm fat. **Diabetic Exchanges:** 2 starch, 1 fat, 1/2 milk.

Recipes Make Tasty Short Story

A HAPPY ENDING is what Carol Bushell of Holyrood, Ontario finds at the close of the day when she can serve a satisfying supper for herself and her father, a retired farmer, without spending hours in the kitchen.

Carol, a novelist and poet, spends most of her day putting words on paper and has little time to fuss with food on the stove.

"Still, my father and I like a hot, hearty evening meal," she says. "I'm thrilled when I can supply one without a huge production."

That's why Carol often relies on this made-in-minutes menu.

"Dad and I love moist and tender Broiled Ginger Chicken," she reports. "It's a snap to prepare, and the flavorful chicken breasts are also great in sandwiches or sliced thin and used as an appetizer."

Stir-Fried Cabbage cooks quickly so it stays crisp and keeps its bright color. "I serve economical cabbage often," Carol says. "Prepared this way, it's an excellent side dish with any entree."

A backyard rhubarb patch provides tangy stalks that Carol uses in the same mouth-watering way her mother did. "I can whip up the sauce for Rhubarb Sundaes in just 4 minutes while the chicken is broiling," she shares.

"It's fun to fix when unexpected guests drop by and also delicious served over pound cake. I freeze extra rhubarb I've picked so we can enjoy this treat anytime we like throughout the year."

Broiled Ginger Chicken

4 boneless skinless chicken breast halves (about 1 pound)
1/2 cup mayonnaise
1 tablespoon soy sauce
1/4 teaspoon ground ginger
1/8 teaspoon cayenne pepper

Flatten the chicken to 1/4-in. thickness. Place on a broiler pan rack. Broil for 3 minutes on each side. Combine mayonnaise, soy sauce, ginger and cayenne; brush over chicken. Broil 2-3 minutes longer on each side or until juices run clear. **Yield:** 4 servings.

Stir-Fried Cabbage

2 tablespoons vegetable oil
6 cups sliced cabbage
3 tablespoons water
1/2 teaspoon salt

In a large skillet, heat oil over medium. Add the cabbage, water and salt. Cook, uncovered, for 5-7 minutes or until crisp-tender, stirring occasionally. **Yield:** 4 servings.

Rhubarb Sundaes

2 cups chopped fresh *or* frozen rhubarb, thawed
2 tablespoons water
Pinch salt
1/2 cup sugar
Vanilla ice cream

In a microwave-safe bowl, combine the rhubarb, water and salt. Cover and microwave on high for 3 minutes, stirring after 1-1/2 minutes. Stir in sugar; cover and microwave 1 minute longer. Serve warm or cooled over ice cream. Store any leftover sauce in the refrigerator. **Yield:** about 2 cups sauce. **Editor's Note:** This recipe was tested in a 700-watt microwave.

Dinner Is Simply Delicious

AFTER WORKING all day cleaning houses, the last thing Felicia Johnson of Oak Ridge, Louisiana wants to do is to make a mess in *her* kitchen when she comes home at night!

"I'd rather put together a simple supper so I can relax in the evening and help my daughter, Whitney, with her homework," this busy mom remarks.

Fortunately, Felicia has a large collection of recipes handed down from her grandmother. She puts together delicious time-tested meals like the one here using recipes that are quick to fix.

Orange Blossom Lamb is a special main dish that's easily assembled. After browning, the chops simmer in a flavorful sauce.

"Lamb tastes so good cooked this way, and it's really no fuss," Felicia says. "This recipe also works well with pork chops."

Her Almond Currant Rice is Whitney's favorite side dish. "Stirring in the almonds and currants at the last minute is a snap, and we love the flavor," Felicia says. "You can substitute your favorite dried fruits and nuts if you like."

Dilly Sweet Peas, a tongue-tingling addition to the meal, gets fun flavor from chopped dill pickles and pickle juice balanced with a bit of honey. "Whitney and I always go back for seconds," assures Felicia.

Pineapple topped with sherbet and mint jelly makes a refreshing end to this easy menu. "Servings of Minty Fruit Ice go so well with lamb. We especially enjoy this combination on warm days," she notes.

Orange Blossom Lamb

    8 rib lamb chops (1 inch thick)
    2 tablespoons butter *or* margarine
    1 can (6 ounces) orange juice concentrate,
       thawed
    1 medium onion, sliced
    1 to 2 teaspoons soy sauce
    1 teaspoon salt
Dash pepper

In a large skillet, brown lamb chops in butter. Add remaining ingredients; mix well. Reduce heat; cover and simmer for 20-25 minutes or until the meat is tender, turning once. To serve, spoon sauce over the lamb. **Yield:** 4 servings.

Almond Currant Rice

    2 cups uncooked instant rice
    2 tablespoons butter *or* margarine
    1/4 teaspoon salt
    1/4 cup chopped toasted almonds
    1/4 cup dried currants

Prepare rice according to package directions, adding butter and salt. Just before serving, stir in almonds and currants. **Yield:** 4 servings.

Dilly Sweet Peas

    1 package (10 ounces) frozen peas
    1/4 cup chopped dill pickles
    2 tablespoons butter *or* margarine
    1 tablespoon dill pickle juice
    1 to 2 teaspoons honey

Prepare peas according to package directions; drain. Add remaining ingredients and toss to coat. **Yield:** 4 servings.

Minty Fruit Ice
(Not pictured)

    4 pineapple rings
    1 pint lemon sherbet
    1/4 cup mint jelly, melted

Place pineapple rings in small bowls. Top each with 1/2 cup sherbet and 1 tablespoon jelly. Serve immediately. **Yield:** 4 servings.

1 can (14-3/4 ounces) salmon, drained, flaked and bones removed
2 cups mashed potato flakes*
1 cup (4 ounces) shredded cheddar cheese

In a saucepan, melt butter over medium heat. Stir in flour and ketchup until smooth. Gradually stir in milk. Bring to a boil; cook and stir for 2 minutes. Add salmon. Prepare mashed potatoes according to package directions. Spoon half into a greased 11-in. x 7-in. x 2-in. baking dish. Top with the salmon mixture, remaining potatoes and cheese. Bake, uncovered, at 375° for 15-20 minutes or until heated through and cheese is melted. **Yield:** 6 servings. ***Editor's Note:** 3 cups leftover mashed potatoes may be substituted for the potato flakes.

Simple Coleslaw

1-1/2 cups shredded cabbage
1-1/2 cups torn salad greens
1/4 cup chopped green pepper
1/4 cup chopped celery
1 small carrot, sliced
1/2 cup mayonnaise
1/4 cup chopped green onions
1 teaspoon vinegar
1/4 teaspoon sugar
1/4 teaspoon prepared horseradish
1/8 teaspoon salt
Dash pepper

In a large bowl, combine cabbage, salad greens, green pepper, celery and carrot. In a small bowl, combine the remaining ingredients. Pour over cabbage mixture and stir to coat. Serve immediately. **Yield:** 6 servings.

Butterscotch Applesauce Cake

1/2 cup butter *or* margarine, softened
1 cup packed brown sugar
2 eggs
1 cup applesauce
2 cups all-purpose flour
1 teaspoon baking soda
1/2 teaspoon salt
1/2 teaspoon ground cinnamon
1 cup raisins
2 cups (12 ounces) butterscotch chips
1/3 cup sugar
3/4 cup chopped pecans

In a mixing bowl, cream the butter and brown sugar. Add eggs and applesauce; mix well. Combine flour, baking soda, salt and cinnamon; add to the creamed mixture. Stir in raisins. Spread in a greased 13-in. x 9-in. x 2-in. baking pan. Sprinkle with the butterscotch chips, sugar and pecans. Bake at 375° for 25 minutes or until a toothpick inserted near the center comes out clean. **Yield:** 12-15 servings.

Fast Fare for The Finish Line

LIKE so many busy cooks, Evelyn Gebhardt often has to race to put a hearty home-cooked meal on the table. But for this preschool teacher from Kasilof, Alaska, racing is a big part of her life.

"My husband, Paul, races in the 1,100-mile Iditarod Trail Sled Dog Race each March, and I'm the volunteer coordinator for a local 200-mile race," Evelyn explains.

No matter how busy the family is, Evelyn likes to have a sit-down dinner with Paul and their daughter, Kristin. That's why she favors simple, filling menus.

"My Butterscotch Applesauce Cake goes into the oven first," Evelyn notes. "Its pretty golden topping is loaded with pecans and butterscotch chips."

Next, she prepares the Speedy Salmon Casserole, which bakes at the same oven temperature as the cake.

"Simple Coleslaw, with its zippy dressing, takes just minutes to toss together," she concludes.

Speedy Salmon Casserole

1 tablespoon butter *or* margarine
1 tablespoon all-purpose flour
3 tablespoons ketchup
1/2 cup milk

Serve Up Speedy Summer Flavors

SUMMERS are a whirlwind of activity for Julie Scott of Pratt, Kansas. Although she has time off from her job as an elementary school teacher, the wife and mother still has plenty to fill her schedule.

If she's not tending the blooms in her flower garden, you might find Julie cross-stitching projects, painting country crafts or making stained glass.

She's also active in her church, volunteers as a 4-H club leader and is a member of an investment club. Since this leaves her little time in the kitchen, she relies on menus like this one for a family on the go.

"These dishes have a nice summery feel," Julie remarks. "But the ingredients are available year-round, so I sometimes serve this meal in winter when we need a change of pace from heavy meat-and-potatoes fare.

"My husband, David, loves the tasty Beef-Stuffed French Bread. Its cheesy filling goes together in a jiffy.

"While the meat is browning, I chop the vegetables for the sandwich and Easy Veggie Salad," she says.

"The light dressing whisks together in a snap and tastes better than bottled dressing.

"Our daughters, Lindsay and Sarah, love the mild orange-flavored topping on the Vanilla Fruit Dessert."

Beef-Stuffed French Bread

1 unsliced loaf French bread (1 pound)
1 pound ground beef
1 can (10-3/4 ounces) condensed cheddar cheese soup, undiluted
1 medium green pepper, chopped
1 celery rib, chopped
1 tablespoon Worcestershire sauce
1 teaspoon salt
1/2 teaspoon pepper
4 slices process American cheese, halved

Cut off top of bread. Carefully hollow out bottom of loaf, leaving a 1/2-in. shell. Cut removed bread into small cubes; set aside. In a skillet, brown beef; drain. Add soup, green pepper, celery, Worcestershire sauce, salt and pepper. Cook and stir for 3-4 minutes. Stir in the reserved bread cubes. Spread into bread shell. Top with cheese. Replace bread top. Place on an ungreased baking sheet. Bake at 350° for 6-8 minutes or until cheese is melted. **Yield:** 4 servings.

Easy Veggie Salad

1 can (16 ounces) kidney beans, rinsed and drained
1 can (14-1/2 ounces) cut green beans, drained
1 small cucumber, halved and thinly sliced
2 cups thinly sliced carrots
1/2 cup chopped green pepper
1/4 cup sliced radishes
1/2 cup cider *or* red wine vinegar
1/3 cup sugar
2 tablespoons vegetable oil
1 teaspoon ground mustard
1 teaspoon salt
Dash pepper

In a large bowl, combine the beans, cucumber, carrots, green pepper and radishes. In a small bowl, combine the remaining ingredients; mix well. Pour over vegetables and toss to coat. Serve with a slotted spoon. Refrigerate leftovers up to 2 days. **Yield:** 12-14 servings.

Vanilla Fruit Dessert

1/2 cup cold milk
1 package (3.4 ounces) instant vanilla pudding mix
1 cup (8 ounces) vanilla yogurt
1/2 cup orange juice concentrate
4 to 6 cups assorted fruit (apples, grapes, mandarin oranges, etc.)

In a mixing bowl, combine milk, pudding mix, yogurt and orange juice concentrate. Beat on low speed for 2 minutes. Serve over fruit. Refrigerate any leftover topping. **Yield:** 4-6 servings (1-3/4 cups topping).

Stovetop Meal Is a Short-Order Solution

SPEEDY skillet suppers are a real lifesaver for Eve Gauger Vargas of Prairie Village, Kansas. If her job with an international pharmaceutical company isn't keeping her on the go, her two active teenage daughters are.

Both Desi and Ariana sing in the school choir and hold down part-time jobs. "They're also involved in just about every sport known to man," Eve jokes, "including soccer, basketball and field hockey."

Often the family's meals must be fast-to-fix affairs squeezed in between work, rehearsals and practice. "We make a lot of stovetop meals because they cook more quickly than oven-baked dishes," Eve reports.

Italian Sausage Skillet, served over rice or pasta, is a hearty favorite.

"This garden-fresh dish gets extra color from a can of stewed tomatoes," Eve notes. "The Italian sausage has so many wonderful flavors you don't need to add any other seasonings."

Better yet, you'll need just four ingredients for crisp Cheese Toast.

"My mom came up with this recipe when I was growing up," Eve shares. "The tangy triangles broil to a pretty golden color in just minutes. Or you can pop them in the toaster oven."

To round out the meal, Eve serves Berry Special Pie. She developed the refreshing dessert after tasting something similar at a restaurant.

"It's light and not too sweet," she says. "Thanks to a prepared crumb crust, it goes together quickly. We love it with raspberries, but you can substitute any fresh berries."

Italian Sausage Skillet

1-1/4 pounds uncooked Italian sausage links
3 small zucchini *or* yellow summer squash, cubed
1/2 cup chopped onion
1 can (14-1/2 ounces) stewed tomatoes
Hot cooked rice *or* pasta

In a skillet over medium heat, brown the sausage until no longer pink; drain. Cut sausage into 1/4-in. slices; return to the skillet to brown completely. Add zucchini and onion; cook and stir for 2 minutes. Stir in tomatoes. Reduce heat; cover and simmer for 10-15 minutes or until the zucchini is tender. Serve over rice or pasta. **Yield:** 4-6 servings.

Cheese Toast

2 tablespoons mayonnaise
2 teaspoons prepared mustard
6 to 8 slices bread, crusts removed
1/3 cup grated Parmesan cheese

Combine mayonnaise and mustard; spread on one side of each slice of bread. Cut each slice into four triangles; place with plain side down on a lightly greased baking sheet. Sprinkle with cheese. Broil 4 in. from the heat for 1-2 minutes or until lightly browned. **Yield:** 4-6 servings.

Berry Special Pie

1/2 cup semisweet chocolate chips
1-1/2 teaspoons shortening
1 chocolate crumb crust (8 or 9 inches)
2 cups fresh raspberries
1 carton (8 ounces) frozen whipped topping, thawed

Melt chocolate chips and shortening; stir until smooth. Spread over the bottom of pie crust. Top with raspberries and whipped topping. Refrigerate until serving. **Yield:** 6-8 servings.

Flavor's Farm-Fresh—and Fun!

FAMILY get-togethers are busy occasions for Edna and Martin Hoffman of Hebron, Indiana. The couple has four children, 17 grandchildren, one great-grandchild and another on the way.

"We often get together for birthdays or when everyone is in town," Edna relates. "Quick-to-fix meals give us more time to visit."

Speed is also the key to hurry-up meals in the field. "We farm 1,700 acres with a son and a grandson, so it's helpful to have dishes that take only minutes to prepare," she says.

Edna's days are busy with farm errands, tending flower and vegetable gardens, refinishing furniture and sewing clothes and crafts. She and Martin also are actively involved in the church where their other son is pastor.

"When I make soups and casseroles, I like to prepare extra," she explains. "These freezer meals are handy for church potlucks or families in need."

The menu Edna shares here can be served as a morning meal, light lunch or simple supper.

Dilly Scrambled Eggs, with a sprinkling of cheese, have farm-fresh flavor and cook in minutes.

For a change from the usual breakfast bread, Edna toasts up a batch of English Muffins with Bacon Butter. "The hint of Dijon mustard in this hearty spread really dresses up the English muffins," she comments.

Toasted coconut adds fun flavor to Ambrosia Fruit Cups. It's a breeze to toss together in minutes, or it can be made ahead and chilled if you're serving a large group.

"You can substitute almost any kind of fruit," Edna assures. "Another good combination is kiwi, bananas and strawberries. They taste wonderful together, and they're colorful, too."

Dilly Scrambled Eggs

```
      6 eggs
  1/4 cup water
  1/2 teaspoon salt
Dash pepper
      2 tablespoons butter or margarine
  1/4 cup shredded cheddar cheese
      1 teaspoon snipped fresh dill or 1/4 teaspoon
        dill weed
```

In a bowl, beat the eggs, water, salt and pepper. Melt butter in a skillet; add egg mixture. Cook and stir gently over medium heat until eggs are almost set. Sprinkle with cheese and dill; cook until eggs are completely set and cheese is melted. **Yield:** 4 servings.

English Muffins with Bacon Butter

```
  1/2 cup butter or margarine, softened
  1/2 to 3/4 teaspoon Dijon mustard
      4 bacon strips, cooked and crumbled
      4 to 6 English muffins, split
```

In a bowl, combine butter and mustard; stir in bacon. Toast the English muffins; spread with bacon butter. Refrigerate any leftover butter. **Yield:** 4-6 servings.

Ambrosia Fruit Cups

```
      1 can (8 ounces) pineapple chunks
      2 large oranges, peeled and sliced
      2 medium bananas, sliced
      1 cup flaked coconut, toasted
      1 tablespoon orange juice
      2 drops almond extract
```

Drain pineapple, reserving 2 tablespoons of juice (discard or save the remaining juice for another use). Place pineapple and juice in a bowl; add remaining ingredients and toss lightly. **Yield:** 4 servings.

She Spices Up a Swift Supper

VARIETY is the spice of life for Mary and Wayne Malchow of Neenah, Wisconsin. Mary livens up home-cooked dishes with a pinch of this and a dash of that.

She loves to experiment with recipes, but there are days when she's too busy to make a meal from scratch. That's why she appreciates convenience items like the ones used in this made-in-minutes menu.

"I put together the Spicy Shepherd's Pie first and pop it in the oven," Mary explains. "I use taco seasoning to add zippy flavor and top it off with instant mashed potatoes."

Red radishes, tomatoes and onion rings are tossed together with contrasting green cucumbers and mixed greens to make Colorful Garden Salad.

Mary finishes off her fast feast with Apple Delight, a tart and tongue-tingling dessert that's a breeze to cook in the microwave.

Spicy Shepherd's Pie

1 package (6.6 ounces) instant mashed potatoes*
1 pound ground beef
1 medium onion, chopped
1 can (14-1/2 ounces) diced tomatoes, undrained
1 can (11 ounces) Mexicorn, drained
1 can (2-1/4 ounces) sliced ripe olives, drained
1 envelope taco seasoning
1-1/2 teaspoons chili powder
1/2 teaspoon salt
1/8 teaspoon garlic powder
1 cup (4 ounces) shredded cheddar cheese, divided

Prepare mashed potatoes according to package directions. Meanwhile, in a large skillet, cook beef and onion until the meat is browned; drain. Add tomatoes, corn, olives, taco seasoning, chili powder, salt and garlic powder. Bring to a boil; cook and stir for 1-2 minutes. Transfer to a greased 2-1/2-qt. baking dish. Top with 3/4 cup cheese. Spread mashed potatoes over the top; sprinkle with remaining cheese. Bake, uncovered, at 350° for 12-15 minutes or until cheese is melted. **Yield:** 4-6 servings. ***Editor's Note:** 4-1/2 cups hot mashed potatoes (prepared with milk and butter) may be substituted for the instant mashed potatoes.

Colorful Garden Salad

1 to 2 medium cucumbers, sliced
1 medium tomato, sliced and quartered
6 fresh mushrooms, sliced
4 radishes, sliced
4 slices red onion
4 cups torn salad greens
1/4 cup vegetable oil
5 teaspoons vinegar
5 teaspoons sugar
1/4 teaspoon salt
1/8 teaspoon pepper
2 tablespoons crumbled cooked bacon

In a large bowl, combine the first six ingredients. In a small bowl, combine oil, vinegar, sugar, salt and pepper; mix well. Pour over salad and toss to coat. Top with bacon. **Yield:** 4-6 servings.

Apple Delight

✓ Nutritional Analysis included

4 medium tart apples, peeled and sliced
4 teaspoons brown sugar
Ground cinnamon to taste
4 teaspoons butter *or* margarine
Caramel ice cream topping, optional

Divide the apples among four ungreased 10-oz. microwave-safe bowls. Top each with 1 teaspoon of brown sugar. Sprinkle with cinnamon; top each with 1 teaspoon butter. Cover and microwave on high for 10 minutes or until apples are tender. Cool slightly; drizzle with caramel topping if desired. **Yield:** 4 servings. **Nutritional Analysis:** One serving (prepared with margarine and without caramel topping) equals 124 calories, 46 mg sodium, 0 cholesterol, 23 gm carbohydrate, trace protein, 4 gm fat. **Diabetic Exchanges:** 1-1/2 fruit, 1 fat. **Editor's Note:** This recipe was tested in an 850-watt microwave.

Pineapple Chicken

✓ Nutritional Analysis included

    1/2 cup barbecue sauce
    1/2 cup orange juice
    1/4 cup packed brown sugar
      2 tablespoons vegetable oil
      2 tablespoons all-purpose flour
    1/4 teaspoon salt, optional
      4 cups cubed cooked chicken
      2 cans (5-1/2 ounces *each*) pineapple
        chunks, drained
      1 can (8 ounces) sliced water chestnuts,
        drained
    1-1/2 teaspoons ground ginger
    Hot cooked rice

In a large saucepan, combine the first six ingredients until smooth. Bring to a boil; reduce heat and simmer for 2 minutes, stirring occasionally. Add the chicken, pineapple, water chestnuts and ginger; cover and simmer for 10 minutes. Serve over rice. **Yield:** 4 servings. **Nutritional Analysis:** One serving (prepared without salt; calculated without rice) equals 349 calories, 283 mg sodium, 85 mg cholesterol, 37 gm carbohydrate, 24 gm protein, 12 gm fat. **Diabetic Exchanges:** 3 lean meat, 2 fruit, 1 vegetable, 1/2 fat.

Sweet Spinach Salad

✓ Nutritional Analysis included

    3/4 cup French salad dressing
      2 tablespoons honey
      2 tablespoons orange juice
    3/4 teaspoon paprika
      6 cups torn fresh spinach
    3/4 cup sliced green onions

In a jar with a tight-fitting lid, combine salad dressing, honey, orange juice and paprika; shake well. Place the spinach and onions in a large bowl or divide among individual plates or bowls; drizzle with dressing. **Yield:** 6 servings. **Nutritional Analysis:** One serving with 2 tablespoons of dressing (prepared with fat-free French dressing) equals 81 calories, 347 mg sodium, 0 cholesterol, 21 gm carbohydrate, 2 gm protein, trace fat. **Diabetic Exchanges:** 1 vegetable, 1 fruit.

Praline Grahams

    12 graham crackers (4-3/4 inches x 2-1/2 inches)
    1/2 cup butter *or* margarine
    1/2 cup packed brown sugar
    1/2 cup finely chopped walnuts

Line a 15-in. x 10-in. x 1-in. baking pan with heavy-duty foil. Break the graham crackers at indentations; place in a single layer in pan. In a small saucepan, combine butter and brown sugar. Bring to a rolling boil over medium heat; boil for 2 minutes. Remove from the heat; add nuts. Pour over crackers. Bake at 350° for 10 minutes or until lightly browned. Let stand for 2-3 minutes. Remove to a wire rack to cool. **Yield:** 4 dozen.

Recipes Stand The Test of Time

RETIREMENT does not always mean extra free time, especially if you are as active as Marian Platt.

Since she and husband Art retired to Sequim, Washington, Marian has devoted her days to writing, cooking and tending her garden beds. She writes a weekly food column for a local newspaper, too.

Marian and Art also squeeze other activities into their busy lives, including golf, bridge, fishing, camping and visiting their two grown children and their families.

So Marian often relies on tried-and-true dishes that can be prepared in a jiffy.

"I've been making this flavorful Pineapple Chicken since a friend gave me the recipe 30 years ago," she reports. Chunks of sweet pineapple, tender chicken and crunchy water chestnuts are coated in a tasty glaze.

Her Sweet Spinach Salad features a tangy dressing sweetened with honey. "It's a snap to stir up and drizzle over fresh spinach and green onions," she says.

You'll need just four ingredients for Praline Grahams. "Someone brought these crunchy, nutty treats to a meeting I attended, and I wouldn't leave without the recipe," Marian recalls.

Mexican Menu Warms Winter

MARRIED to a minister, Kathy Ybarra often finds her days revolving around her husband's congregation in Rock Springs, Wyoming.

Not only does she help out with many church functions, Kathy also works as the church secretary and bookkeeper.

"My husband, Jesse, and I are always on-call to help the members of our congregation in hospital emergencies and other crises," she relates. "The work is very rewarding, but occasionally it leaves me little time to plan meals."

When she does have free time, Kathy likes to try new recipes.

"Jesse and I try to sit down for a meal together at noon each day," she notes. "We love Mexican food, so I usually have the ingredients for this tasty menu on hand. The spicy meal really warms us up during the winter months.

"I start by browning the tortillas for the Mexican Cookies in the oven while I assemble the main dish.

"Then I turn the oven temperature down and pop the burritos in to bake while I put the finishing touches on these light, crunchy cookies," Kathy continues. "I love chocolate, and Jesse loves cinnamon, so these treats are perfect for both of us.

"A woman in our congregation shared the recipe for hearty Green Chili Burritos. They soon became a fast favorite in our home, and when I serve them at church potlucks, they disappear fast."

Fresh-tasting Taco Salad is the perfect accompaniment to the zippy burritos. Made with convenient canned kidney beans, bottled dressing and tortilla chips, it's quick to toss together.

"For a spicy change of pace, substitute salsa for the Thousand Island dressing," Kathy suggests.

Green Chili Burritos

> 1 can (16 ounces) refried beans
> 8 flour tortillas (6 inches)
> 1/2 pound ground beef, cooked and drained
> 1 cup (4 ounces) shredded sharp cheddar cheese, *divided*
> 1 can (4-1/2 ounces) chopped green chilies

Spread refried beans over tortillas. Top each with beef and 2 tablespoons of cheese. Fold ends and sides over filling and roll up; place seam side down in a greased 13-in. x 9-in. x 2-in. baking dish. Sprinkle with chilies and remaining cheese. Bake, uncovered, at 350° for 20 minutes or until heated through. **Yield:** 4 servings.

Taco Salad

> 6 cups chopped iceberg lettuce
> 1/2 cup finely chopped onion
> 3/4 to 1 cup kidney beans, rinsed and drained
> 1-1/2 cups (6 ounces) shredded cheddar cheese
> 1 medium tomato, chopped
> 4 cups taco-flavored tortilla chips
> 1/2 cup Thousand Island salad dressing

In a large bowl, layer the first five ingredients in order listed. Just before serving, add chips and salad dressing; toss to coat. **Yield:** 4-6 servings.

Mexican Cookies

> 4 flour tortillas (6 inches)
> 1/2 cup semisweet chocolate chips
> 3/4 teaspoon shortening
> 1/4 cup confectioners' sugar
> 1/4 teaspoon ground cinnamon

Cut each tortilla into eight wedges; place on ungreased baking sheets. Bake at 400° for 10-12 minutes or until lightly browned. Meanwhile, in a microwave or double boiler, melt chocolate chips and shortening. Stir until smooth; keep warm. In a large resealable plastic bag, combine confectioners' sugar and cinnamon. Add tortilla wedges a few at a time and shake to coat. Place on waxed paper-lined baking sheets. Drizzle with melted chocolate. Refrigerate until serving. **Yield:** 32 cookies.

TO SQUEEZE meal preparation into the busy life she leads on her family's wheat farm near Coulee City, Washington, Kim Jorgensen must be creative.

Besides teaching crafts and selling her handiwork at shows, Kim is very active in her church.

But most every night, Kim gathers husband Chris and children Ian, Conor and Fiona around the table.

The number increases to nine at harvesttime, when Kim takes turns with her mother-in-law cooking for the hungry crew.

"When I'm pressed for time, I rely on these tried-and-true recipes that everyone likes," she says.

"I make the Broccoli Cashew Salad first and put it in the fridge so the flavors of the dressing can blend."

For dessert in a hurry, Kim jazzes up pudding mix to create Eggnog Pudding. "This recipe is easy to double and serve in a no-fuss graham cracker crust."

Shrimp gives an elegant touch to rich and creamy Seafood Fettuccine.

Seafood Fettuccine

- 3/4 pound fresh *or* frozen shrimp, cooked, peeled and deveined
- 1 can (4 ounces) mushroom stems and pieces, drained
- 1/2 teaspoon garlic powder
- 1/8 teaspoon salt
- 1/8 teaspoon pepper
- 1/4 cup butter *or* margarine
- 1 package (8 ounces) fettuccine, cooked and drained
- 1/2 cup grated Parmesan cheese
- 1/2 cup milk
- 1/2 cup sour cream
- Minced fresh parsley, optional

In a large saucepan, saute shrimp, mushrooms, garlic powder, salt and pepper in butter for 3-5 minutes. Stir in fettuccine, cheese, milk and sour cream. Cook over medium heat for 3-5 minutes or until heated through (do not boil). Garnish with parsley if desired. **Yield:** 4 servings. **Editor's Note:** Scallops or crab may be substituted for half of the shrimp.

Broccoli Cashew Salad

- 6 cups broccoli florets
- 2 medium tomatoes, cut into 1/2-inch chunks
- 3 tablespoons chopped red onion
- 1 can (2-1/4 ounces) sliced ripe olives, drained
- 1 cup mayonnaise
- 1 tablespoon soy sauce
- 2 teaspoons lemon juice
- 1-1/2 teaspoons seasoned salt
- 1/8 teaspoon pepper
- 1/2 cup cashews
- Lettuce leaves

Place the broccoli in a saucepan with a small amount of water. Cover and cook for 5-8 minutes or until crisp-tender. Rinse in cold water; drain and place in a large bowl. Add tomatoes, onion and olives; toss. In a small bowl, combine mayonnaise, soy sauce, lemon juice, seasoned salt and pepper; mix well. Add to broccoli mixture and toss to coat. Just before serving, stir in cashews. Serve on lettuce. **Yield:** 4-6 servings.

Eggnog Pudding

☑ Nutritional Analysis included

- 2 cups cold milk
- 1 package (3.4 ounces) instant vanilla pudding mix
- 1/2 teaspoon ground nutmeg
- 1/4 teaspoon rum extract
- Additional nutmeg, optional

In a bowl, combine the first four ingredients. Beat for 2 minutes. Spoon into individual dishes. Sprinkle with nutmeg if desired. **Yield:** 4 servings. **Nutritional Analysis:** One 1/2-cup serving (prepared with skim milk and sugar-free pudding) equals 117 calories, 328 mg sodium, trace cholesterol, 23 gm carbohydrate, 7 gm protein, trace fat. **Diabetic Exchanges:** 1 starch, 1/2 skim milk.

30-Minute Main Dishes

BUSY weekdays call for satisfying suppers that can feed a hungry clan in a hurry. Here are 12 memorable main dishes that go from start to finish in just half an hour. Add them to your recipe collection and enjoy them soon!

Pork Chops with Apple Rings

With a fruity apricot, raisin and apple topping, these tender chops are special enough to serve to company, yet simple enough to fix anytime. The best part is that the apples don't have to be peeled—just core and slice, and you're ready to go. —Kathleen Harris, Galesburg, Illinois

      6 pork chops (1/2 inch thick)
  1/2 teaspoon celery salt
  1/2 teaspoon rubbed sage
  1/2 teaspoon salt
  1/4 teaspoon pepper
      2 tablespoons butter *or* margarine
      2 medium unpeeled Golden Delicious apples,
         cored and cut into 1/2-inch rings
  1/4 cup diced dried apricots
      2 tablespoons golden raisins
      2 tablespoons brown sugar

Sprinkle pork chops with celery salt, sage, salt and pepper. In a large skillet, brown chops in butter on one side; turn. Top with apple rings. Sprinkle with apricots, raisins and brown sugar. Cover and cook on low heat for 18-22 minutes or until meat juices run clear. **Yield:** 6 servings.

Hearty Hamburger Supper

(Pictured on page 23)

My husband and I are retired and enjoy home cooking. This hearty stovetop meal proves it need not be time-consuming. I gave this recipe to a young neighbor who tells me she uses it often since she's a nurse and is always short of time. —Georgene Remm, Wausa, Nebraska

  3/4 pound ground beef
      1 small onion, chopped
      4 cups diced cabbage
  1/4 cup all-purpose flour
1-1/2 teaspoons salt
  1/4 teaspoon paprika
      2 cups milk
Hot mashed potatoes
Additional paprika

In a large saucepan, cook the beef and onion until meat is browned and onion is tender; drain. Add cabbage;

cook and stir for 2 minutes. Sprinkle with flour, salt and paprika; mix well. Gradually add milk. Bring to a boil; boil and stir for 2 minutes. Reduce heat; cover and simmer for 10-12 minutes or until the cabbage is tender. Serve over potatoes. Sprinkle with paprika if desired. **Yield:** 4 servings.

Vegetable Oven Pancake

(Pictured below)

I clipped this recipe when I was first married, but my husband was actually first to prepare it. The puffy pancake looked beautiful and tasted even better. It wasn't until I made this dish myself that I realized how simple it really is. We like to vary the vegetables, depending on what's in season. —Mirien Church, Aurora, Colorado

      1 teaspoon butter *or* margarine
      2 eggs
  1/2 cup milk
  1/2 cup all-purpose flour
  1/2 teaspoon salt, *divided*
      2 cups broccoli florets
      1 cup chopped green pepper
      1 cup chopped tomato
  1/2 cup chopped red onion
      2 tablespoons water
  1/8 teaspoon pepper
1-1/2 cups (6 ounces) shredded cheddar cheese,
         divided

Place butter in a 9-in. pie plate in a 450° oven until melted. Remove; carefully tilt to coat bottom and sides. In a bowl, beat eggs and milk. Add flour and 1/4 teaspoon salt; mix well. Pour into pie plate. Bake for 14-16 minutes or until puffed around the edges and golden brown. Meanwhile, in a skillet, cook broccoli, green pepper, tomato and onion in water for 8-10 minutes or until crisp-tender; drain well. Add pepper and remaining salt. Sprinkle 1/2 cup cheese over pancake; top with veg-

Vegetable Oven Pancake

etables and remaining cheese. Bake 3-4 minutes longer or until cheese is melted. Cut into wedges; serve immediately. **Yield:** 4 servings.

Creamed Chicken 'n' Biscuits

(Pictured at right)

We have a dairy farm and three young children, so I'm always on the lookout for easy, hearty meals like this one. Using leftover or canned chicken, I can whip up this entree in minutes. To save even more time, I sometimes serve the hot chicken mixture on buns.
—Shari Zimmerman, Deford, Michigan

BISCUITS:
    2 cups all-purpose flour
    1 tablespoon baking powder
    1 teaspoon salt
  2/3 cup milk
  1/3 cup vegetable oil
CREAMED CHICKEN:
  1/4 cup finely chopped onion
  1/4 cup butter *or* margarine
  1/4 cup all-purpose flour
  1/4 to 1/2 teaspoon salt
  1/8 teaspoon pepper
    2 cups milk *or* chicken broth
    2 cups chopped cooked chicken
Minced fresh parsley

In a bowl, combine flour, baking powder and salt; add milk and oil. Stir until the dough forms a ball. Knead in the bowl 10 times or until smooth. Roll or pat dough into a 6-in. square about 1 in. thick. Cut into six rectangles. Place on a lightly greased baking sheet. Bake at 450° for 10-12 minutes or until golden brown. Meanwhile, in a skillet, saute onion in butter until tender. Stir in flour, salt and pepper until smooth. Gradually add milk; bring to a boil. Reduce heat; cook and stir for 1-2 minutes or until thickened. Stir in chicken and parsley; heat through. Split biscuits; top with the creamed chicken. **Yield:** 6 servings.

Bean Burritos

Main dishes like this one that can be prepared in a flash are essential for me, my husband and our two sons. I always have the ingredients for this recipe on hand. Cooking the rice and shredding the cheese the night before save precious minutes at dinnertime.
—Beth Osborne Skinner, Bristol, Tennessee

    1 can (16 ounces) refried beans
    1 cup salsa
    1 cup cooked long grain rice
    2 cups (8 ounces) shredded cheddar cheese, *divided*
  12 flour tortillas (6 to 7 inches)

In a bowl, combine the beans, salsa, rice and 1 cup of cheese. Spoon about 1/3 cupful off-center on each tortilla. Fold the sides and ends over filling and roll up. Arrange burritos in a greased 13-in. x 9-in. x 2-in. bak-

Creamed Chicken 'n' Biscuits

ing dish. Sprinkle with the remaining cheese. Cover and bake at 375° for 20-25 minutes or until heated through. **Yield:** 1 dozen.

Shrimp Monterey

(Pictured on page 22)

For a special occasion or when company's coming, this delicious seafood dish makes a lasting impression. You'll be surprised at how fast you can prepare it. A mild, fresh-tasting sauce and the Monterey Jack cheese nicely complement the shrimp. I serve it over pasta or rice.
—Jane Birch
Edison, New Jersey

    2 garlic cloves, minced
    2 tablespoons butter *or* margarine
    2 pounds uncooked medium shrimp, peeled and deveined
  1/2 cup white wine *or* chicken broth
    2 cups (8 ounces) shredded Monterey Jack cheese
    2 tablespoons minced fresh parsley

In a skillet over medium heat, saute garlic in butter for 1 minute. Add shrimp; cook for 4-5 minutes or until pink. Using a slotted spoon, transfer shrimp to a greased 11-in. x 7-in. x 2-in. baking dish; set aside and keep warm. Add wine or broth to the skillet; bring to a boil. Cook and stir for 5 minutes or until the sauce is reduced. Pour over shrimp; top with cheese and parsley. Bake, uncovered, at 350° for 10 minutes or until cheese is melted. **Yield:** 6 servings.

Chicken Tortilla Chowder

(Pictured below)

As a student attending college full-time, I find my time in the kitchen is limited. This recipe helps me have a hot meal on the table when my husband gets home. He's a real meat-and-potatoes man, but he loves this thick, creamy chowder with tortilla strips that puff up like home-made noodles. —Jennifer Gouge, Lubbock, Texas

1 can (14-1/2 ounces) chicken broth
1 can (10-3/4 ounces) condensed cream of chicken soup, undiluted
1 can (10-3/4 ounces) condensed cream of potato soup, undiluted
1-1/2 cups milk
2 cups cubed cooked chicken
1 can (11 ounces) Mexicorn
1 jar (4-1/2 ounces) sliced mushrooms, drained
1 can (4 ounces) chopped green chilies
1/4 cup thinly sliced green onions
4 flour tortillas (6 to 7 inches), cut into 1/2-inch strips
1-1/2 cups (6 ounces) shredded cheddar cheese

In a Dutch oven or soup kettle, combine broth, soups and milk. Add the chicken, corn, mushrooms, chilies and onions; mix well. Bring to a boil. Add the tortilla strips. Reduce heat; simmer, uncovered, for 8-10 minutes or until heated through. Add cheese; stir just until melted. Serve immediately. **Yield:** 8-10 servings (2-1/2 quarts).

Chicken Tortilla Chowder

Turkey Linguine

Here's a combination I concocted to use when I'm in a hurry. It's a quick, delicious and complete meal that I frequently serve to family and company. You may want to keep it a secret that you prepared this attractive, colorful skillet dish in just half an hour! —Audrey Thibodeau, Mesa, Arizona

1 pound boneless turkey breast, cut into 1/2-inch strips
1 tablespoon olive *or* vegetable oil
1/2 cup chopped onion
2 garlic cloves, minced
1 cup broccoli florets
1 cup thinly sliced carrots
1 tablespoon minced fresh basil *or* 1 teaspoon dried basil
1 teaspoon minced fresh tarragon *or* 1/4 teaspoon dried tarragon
1 teaspoon minced fresh thyme *or* 1/4 teaspoon dried thyme
1/8 teaspoon pepper
2 tablespoons cornstarch
1-1/2 cups chicken broth
8 ounces linguini *or* pasta of your choice, cooked
1/2 cup grated Parmesan cheese

In a large skillet or wok, stir-fry turkey in oil for 2 minutes. Add onion and garlic; cook and stir for 1 minute. Add broccoli, carrots, basil, tarragon, thyme and pepper; stir-fry for 3-4 minutes or until vegetables are crisp-tender. Combine cornstarch and broth until smooth; add to turkey mixture. Cook and stir until mixture comes to a boil; cook 2 minutes longer. Serve over linguine; sprinkle with Parmesan cheese. **Yield:** 4 servings.

Favorite Meat Loaf Cups

(Pictured on page 22)

My family enjoys meat loaf, but sometimes I can't spare the hour or more it takes to bake in the traditional shape. A quick alternative is to divide the meat mixture into muffin cups for individual servings that are ready in less than 30 minutes. —Sue Gronholz, Columbus, Wisconsin

2 eggs, beaten
1/4 cup milk
1/4 cup ketchup
1/2 cup crushed cornflakes
4 tablespoons dried minced onion
1 teaspoon prepared mustard
1 teaspoon salt
1/4 teaspoon pepper
2 pounds lean ground beef
Additional ketchup, optional

In a large bowl, combine the first eight ingredients. Add beef; mix well. Press into 12 foil-lined or greased muffin cups. Bake at 350° for 25 minutes or until the meat is no longer pink. Drain before serving. Drizzle with ketchup if desired. **Yield:** 6 servings.

Mexican Chip Casserole

cause it combines tender beef and nutritious vegetables in one dish. We enjoy it year-round but especially in summer, when I grow my own broccoli and onions. Plus, it doesn't heat up the kitchen while it's cooking. —Ruth Stahl
Shepherd, Montana

   3 tablespoons cornstarch, *divided*
1/2 cup plus 2 tablespoons water, *divided*
1/2 teaspoon garlic powder
   1 pound boneless round steak, cut into thin 3-inch strips
   2 tablespoons vegetable oil, *divided*
   4 cups broccoli florets
   1 small onion, cut into wedges
1/3 cup soy sauce
   2 tablespoons brown sugar
   1 teaspoon ground ginger
Hot cooked rice

In a bowl, combine 2 tablespoons cornstarch, 2 tablespoons water and the garlic powder until smooth. Add beef and toss. In a large skillet or wok over medium-high heat, stir-fry beef in 1 tablespoon oil until meat reaches desired doneness; remove and keep warm. Stir-fry the broccoli and onion in remaining oil for 4-5 minutes. Return beef to pan. Combine soy sauce, brown sugar, ginger, and remaining cornstarch and water until smooth; add to the pan. Cook and stir for 2 minutes. Serve over rice. **Yield:** 4 servings.

Mexican Chip Casserole

(Pictured above)

This satisfying casserole relies on convenient packaged ingredients to create an entree with savory Southwestern flair. There's nothing tricky about the preparation, and I have time to set the table while it's in the oven.
   —Doris Heath, Franklin, North Carolina

   1 pound ground beef
   1 medium onion, chopped
   1 garlic clove, minced
   1 can (10-3/4 ounces) condensed cream of mushroom soup, undiluted
   1 can (11 ounces) Mexicorn
   1 can (4 ounces) chopped green chilies
   1 package (10-1/2 ounces) corn chips
   1 can (10 ounces) enchilada sauce
   1 to 2 cups (4 to 8 ounces) shredded Co-Jack cheese

In a skillet, cook beef, onion and garlic until meat is browned and onion is tender; drain. Add soup, corn and chilies; mix well. In an ungreased shallow 3-qt. baking dish, layer meat mixture, corn chips and enchilada sauce; top with cheese. Bake, uncovered, at 350° for 8-10 minutes or until heated through. **Yield:** 6 servings.

Beef Broccoli Stir-Fry

My family often requests this tasty stir-fry. It's great be-

Chicken in Basil Cream

(Pictured on page 23 and on front cover)

When I first read this recipe, I thought it looked difficult. But because I had all the ingredients readily at hand, I gave it a try. Am I glad I did! Not only is it simple to prepare, it tastes wonderful. One bite and you'll agree.
   —Judy Baker, Craig, Colorado

1/4 cup milk
1/4 cup dry bread crumbs
   4 boneless skinless chicken breast halves (about 1 pound)
   3 tablespoons butter *or* margarine
1/2 cup chicken broth
   1 cup whipping cream
   1 jar (4 ounces) sliced pimientos, drained
1/2 cup grated Parmesan cheese
1/4 cup minced fresh basil
1/8 teaspoon pepper

Place milk and bread crumbs in separate shallow bowls. Dip chicken in milk, then coat with crumbs. In a skillet over medium-high heat, cook the chicken in butter on both sides until juices run clear, about 10 minutes. Remove and keep warm. Add broth to the skillet. Bring to a boil over medium heat; stir to loosen browned bits from pan. Stir in cream and pimientos; boil and stir for 1 minute. Reduce heat. Add Parmesan cheese, basil and pepper; cook and stir until heated through. Pour over the chicken. **Yield:** 4 servings.

Chapter 3

THE NEXT time you're looking to host a fun and festive get-together, don't panic! Our talented *Quick Cooking* kitchen staff has taken the guesswork out of party planning by creating six easy theme-related menus.

From an "eggstra"-special Easter dinner, a fishermen's feast and a backyard beach party to a "spooktacular" spread, a flurry of winter fun and an out-of-this-world birthday bash, you can easily create long-remembered occasions for your family and friends with just a short time spent in the kitchen.

PARTY FAVORITES. Clockwise from upper right: Flying Saucers, Little Dippers and Moonbeam Munchies (all recipes on p. 43).

Launch an Out-of-This-World Bash

BLAST OFF to birthday fun with a space-age party that's sure to please any would-be astronauts. Best of all, this simple-to-fix menu won't cause burnout for the cook. We've geared the gathering for 6- to 8-year-olds. But, with a little imagination, you can swiftly stretch that orbit to include folks of all ages. Reach for the stars...add your own creative touches!

Flying Saucers

These handy pita pocket sandwiches can be filled and served ready to eat...or you can set up a make-your-own buffet with ingredients that the guests can choose to suit themselves.

> 1/2 cup mayonnaise
> 2 tablespoons Dijon mustard
> 4 large pita breads, halved
> 8 lettuce leaves
> 16 thin slices bologna
> 8 thin slices fully cooked ham
> 16 thin slices tomato

Combine the mayonnaise and mustard; spread about 1 tablespoon into each pita half. Stuff each with one lettuce leaf, two slices of bologna, one slice of ham and two slices of tomato. **Yield:** 4-6 servings.

Little Dippers

For a galaxy of good eating, pair this creamy dip with your favorite fruits cut into star shapes. We shaped apples, kiwifruit and strawberries with small cookie cutters (you could also use a knife). Melon, pears and bananas are other possibilities. If you find fresh starfruit in your supermarket, simply slice it.

> 1 cup (8 ounces) vanilla yogurt
> 3 tablespoons orange marmalade
> 1 tablespoon confectioners' sugar
> 1 large apple, sliced 1/4 inch thick
> 5 large strawberries, halved lengthwise
> 1 large kiwifruit, sliced 1/4 inch thick

In a small bowl, combine yogurt, marmalade and sugar. Cut the apple slices with a 2-1/2-in. star cookie cutter. Cut strawberries and kiwi with a 1-1/2-in. star cookie cutter. Serve with dip. **Yield:** about 6 servings (1 cup dip).

Saturn Slush

Swirled in tall glasses, the alternating blueberry and strawberry layers in this refreshing blended beverage will remind you of Saturn's rings. Even the garnish looks "spacey"!

> 1 package (20 ounces) frozen unsweetened
>   strawberries, unthawed
> 3 cups orange juice, *divided*
> 3/4 cup confectioners' sugar, *divided*
> 2 cups frozen blueberries
> ORBITAL GARNISH:
> 6 fresh strawberries, hulled and halved
>   widthwise
> 6 unpeeled orange slices

In a blender, combine frozen strawberries, 2 cups of orange juice and 1/2 cup of confectioners' sugar. Cover and process until smooth; set aside. Rinse the blender container. Add blueberries and remaining juice and sugar. Cover and blend until smooth. Alternate layers of strawberry and blueberry in glasses; stir layers a few times to create a swirl. For garnish, thread a strawberry top, hulled side first, an orange slice and a strawberry tip, cut side first, through a drinking straw or stirring stick; place in glass. **Yield:** 6 servings.

Moonbeam Munchies

This simple from-scratch sugar cookie dough can be mixed in a flash and is easy to roll and cut. To save time the day of the party, prepare the dough the night before.

> 2 cups sugar
> 1 cup shortening
> 1 egg
> 2 teaspoons lemon extract
> 5-1/4 cups all-purpose flour
> 1 teaspoon baking soda
> 1/2 teaspoon salt
> 1 cup sour milk*
> 1/2 cup water
> 5 drops yellow food coloring

In a mixing bowl, cream sugar and shortening. Add egg and extract. Combine flour, baking soda and salt; add to the creamed mixture alternately with sour milk. Mix well. Refrigerate for 2 hours or overnight. On a lightly floured surface, roll dough to 1/4-in. thickness. Cut with a round cookie cutter. If desired, cut some circles in half and form into half moon shapes. Place on greased baking sheets. Bake at 350° for 8-10 minutes or until the edges begin to brown. Remove to wire racks to cool. Combine water and food coloring; brush over cooled cookies. Allow to dry completely. Store in airtight containers. **Yield:** 6 dozen whole moons. ***Editor's Note:** Prepared refrigerator sugar cookie dough can also be used. To sour milk, place 1 tablespoon white vinegar in a measuring cup. Add milk to equal 1 cup.

Rocket Cake

Not your ordinary birthday cake, this dessert requires almost no countdown—just start with a purchased ice cream cake roll, then frost and decorate it for takeoff. (We used construction paper to make the rocket's fins and cone.)

> 1 prepared ice cream cake roll (1-1/4 pounds)
> 1 can (16 ounces) *or* 2 cups vanilla frosting
> Blue and red construction paper

Place ice cream roll vertically on a 10-in. plate. Frost top and sides. From blue construction paper, cut out four fins about 2-1/4 in. high and 1-1/2 in. deep. Insert fins along bottom edge of cake. For the nose cone, draw an 8-in. circle on red construction paper. With a pencil, mark eight equal sections. Cut out a three-eighths section and discard; tape cut sides together to form a cone. Place on top of the cake. Serve immediately. **Yield:** 4-6 servings.

Get Hopping on Eggstra-Special Easter Meal

YOUR family will love this fast but fancy-looking Easter feast. Since preparing it won't keep you in the kitchen all day, you're sure to have a hoppy holiday!

Special Ham Slices

A taste-tempting sauce combines orange juice, brown sugar and spices to give wonderful flavor. Convenient ham steaks cook in less than half an hour.

    12 boneless ham steaks (about 3 pounds)
     1 cup orange juice
    3/4 cup packed brown sugar
     2 teaspoons grated orange peel
     1 teaspoon ground mustard
    1/4 teaspoon ground cloves

Place ham in an ungreased 13-in. x 9-in. x 2-in. baking dish. Combine remaining ingredients; pour over ham. Bake, uncovered, at 325° for 20-25 minutes or until heated through, basting occasionally. **Yield:** 12 servings.

Cottontail Carrots

Glistening with a subtly sweet glaze, these scrumptious carrots are sure to become an often-requested dish.

✓ **Nutritional Analysis included**

     2 pounds carrots, julienned
    1/4 cup apple juice
    1/4 cup butter *or* margarine
     2 tablespoons brown sugar
     1 teaspoon salt, optional
    Minced fresh parsley

In a 2-qt. microwave-safe casserole, combine carrots and apple juice. Cover and microwave on high for 10-12 minutes or until crisp-tender, stirring once. Add butter, brown sugar and salt if desired; toss to coat. Sprinkle with parsley. **Yield:** 12 servings. **Nutritional Analysis:** One 1/2-cup serving (prepared with margarine and without salt) equals 77 calories, 72 mg sodium, 0 cholesterol, 11 gm carbohydrate, 1 gm protein, 4 gm fat. **Diabetic Exchanges:** 1-1/2 vegetable, 1 fat. **Editor's Note:** This recipe was tested in a 700-watt microwave.

Tie-Dyed Easter Eggs

These brightly colored eggs are so pretty they're sure to be noticed no matter where you hide them.

    12 hard-cooked eggs
    12 cheesecloth squares* (about 8 inches)
    1/4 cup vinegar
    Liquid food coloring

Dry the eggs. Dampen cheesecloth with vinegar; wrap a square around each egg, gathering edges together and securing with a rubber band or string. Holding tied end, squeeze drops of food coloring in random patterns on wrapped eggs. Repeat with other colors. Unwrap carefully; place in an egg carton to dry complete-

ly. Refrigerate until serving. **Yield:** 1 dozen. ***Editor's Note:** Cheesecloth is available in the housewares section of most grocery stores. Cotton cloth or paper towels may be substituted for the cheesecloth.

Stuffing Baskets

These appealing "baskets" hold delectable sliced mushrooms and pecan tidbits.

     1 medium green pepper, chopped
    1/4 cup butter *or* margarine
     1 jar (4-1/2 ounces) sliced mushrooms
     1 package (6 ounces) instant stuffing mix
    1/2 cup chopped pecans

In a saucepan, saute green pepper in butter until crisp-tender. Drain mushrooms, reserving liquid; set mushrooms aside. Add water to liquid to measure 1-2/3 cups. Add to green pepper. Bring to a boil; stir in the stuffing mix. Remove from the heat. Cover and let stand for 5 minutes. Add mushrooms and pecans; fluff with a fork. Spoon into paper-lined muffin cups; pack lightly. Bake at 350° for 30-35 minutes. **Yield:** 1 dozen.

Peter Rabbit Cake

Baked and decorated ahead of time, this coconut-topped cake makes an eye-catching fitting finale.

     1 package (18-1/4 ounces) white cake mix
     1 can (16 ounces) vanilla frosting
    1-3/4 cups flaked coconut, *divided*
     2 drops red food coloring
     2 drops green food coloring
    Assorted jelly beans
     1 stick black licorice, cut lengthwise into
       1/8-inch strips

Mix and bake cake according to package directions, using two greased and floured 9-in. baking pans. Cool for 10 minutes; remove from pans to wire racks to cool. For bunny's head, place one cake on a 20-in. x 14-in. covered board. Cut remaining cake into two ears and one bow tie (see Fig. 1). Place ears 4 in. apart on top of head. Place bow tie so it fits in curve of head (see photo). Frost the top and sides of head, ears and bow tie. Sprinkle 1-1/4 cups coconut over head and ears. Divide remaining coconut between two resealable plastic bags; add red food coloring to one bag and green to the other. Seal bags and shake to coat. Place pink coconut on ears to within 1/2 in. of the edges. Place green coconut around the cake. Use jelly beans for eyes, nose and to decorate bow tie. Cut licorice into seven 2-in. pieces and seven 3/4-in. pieces. Place six 2-in. pieces next to nose for whiskers. Bend the remaining 2-in. piece into a semicircle and place 3/4 in. below nose for mouth. Connect nose to mouth with one 3/4-in. piece. Place three 3/4-in. pieces above each eye for eyelashes. **Yield:** 12 servings.

Fig. 1 Cutting cake

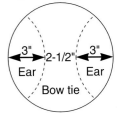

Fishermen's
Feast Reels
In Raves

HAD ANY BITES? You will when guests cast a glance at this festive fish-themed spread. It's a fun way to observe Father's Day, celebrate an angler's birthday or honor the special fisherman in your life.

Best of all, it doesn't take hours to tackle this flavorful fare...and that's no fish story. Convenience foods create an a-lure-ing meal that's both eye-pleasing and time-easing.

Catch-of-the-Day Fish

Anglers will be hooked on this clever catch of the day. Simply dress up fillets with cheesy "scales" (scalloped potatoes from a package). Lemon slices and lime wedges do double duty, adding fun finishing touches and refreshing flavor when squeezed over the fish.

> 1 package (5 ounces) cheesy scalloped
>   potatoes with skins
> 4 fresh *or* frozen fish fillets (about 1 pound),
>   thawed
> 16 lime wedges
> 2 lemon slices, halved
> 4 ripe olive slices
> 8 pimiento pieces

Prepare scalloped potatoes, following the package directions for stovetop method. Place the fish in an ungreased 13-in. x 9-in. x 2-in. baking dish. Using tongs, arrange potatoes on fish to look like scales (see photo). Cover and bake at 450° for 8-10 minutes or until the fish flakes easily with a fork. Carefully transfer to serving plates. Garnish with lime for tails and fins, lemon for heads, olives for eyes, and pimientos for eyes and mouth. **Yield:** 4 servings.

Vegetable Bobbers

A simple combination of fresh vegetables makes an irresistible "bobber" garnish, especially when placed on a bed

of herb "seaweed". You could also use celery in place of carrots, radishes rather than tomatoes, and zucchini or yellow squash instead of cucumber.

> 8 cherry tomatoes, halved
> 8 cucumber slices (about 1/4 inch thick)
> 8 carrot sticks (4 inches x 1/4 inch)
> **Fresh dill *or* tarragon sprigs, optional**

With a sharp knife, pierce a small hole in the center of tomatoes and cucumbers. Thread two tomato halves and one cucumber slice onto each carrot, forming bobbers (see the photo). Place bobbers alongside fish; add dill or tarragon sprigs for seaweed if desired. **Yield:** 8 bobbers.

Hook, Line 'n' Sinker Mix

As the name implies, your guests'll fall hook, line and sinker for this munchable mixture that features pretzel stick "fishing rods" and cheddar cheese goldfish crackers. It takes mere minutes to toss the ingredients together and zap the mix in the microwave.

> 3 tablespoons butter *or* margarine, melted
> 1 tablespoon dried parsley flakes
> 3/4 teaspoon dried tarragon
> 1/2 teaspoon onion powder
> 1/4 to 1/2 teaspoon celery salt
> 1 cup goldfish crackers
> 1 cup pretzel sticks
> 1/2 cup Cheerios
> 1/2 cup dry roasted peanuts

In a 2-qt. microwave-safe bowl, combine the first five ingredients; mix well. Add crackers, pretzels, Cheerios and peanuts; toss to coat. Microwave, uncovered, on high for 1-1/2 minutes, stirring once. Cool completely. Store in an airtight container. **Yield:** 3 cups. **Editor's Note:** This recipe was tested in a 700-watt microwave.

Bait Box Treats

WORMS FOR DESSERT? It may sound a little fishy, but trust us—anglers of all ages will save room for these tasty Bait Box Treats.

New bait containers may be purchased from your local bait and tackle store. If they're not available, use empty margarine, dip or sour cream containers. Decorate them with construction paper and markers to resemble bait containers.

Fill them with your favorite "mud" pudding and top with crushed cookie "dirt". (Here we show a prepared serving of chocolate fudge instant pudding sprinkled with crushed cream-filled chocolate sandwich cookies.)

A few colorful gummy candy worms wiggling out of the dirt add a realistic touch kids are sure to appreciate.

Rod and Reel Breadsticks

Convenient refrigerated dough is the key to these reel-y fun and reel-y easy-to-assemble breadsticks. A tasty dusting of sesame seeds, Parmesan cheese and garlic salt adds yummy flavor that seasoned fishermen are sure to enjoy.

> 1 tube (11 ounces) refrigerated breadsticks
> 2 tablespoons butter *or* margarine, melted
> 1/2 teaspoon garlic salt
> 2 teaspoons grated Parmesan cheese
> 1 teaspoon sesame seeds

Separate dough into rolls; set four aside. Unroll remaining rolls; twist each to form a 14-in. rope. Place ropes 4 in. apart on ungreased baking sheets for rods. For reels, place a coiled roll 1-1/2 in. from end of rod, with the coiled end touching the rod. Pinch rod and reel dough together to seal. Combine butter and garlic salt; brush over dough. Sprinkle with Parmesan cheese and sesame seeds. Bake at 375° for 12-14 minutes or until golden brown. Cool slightly; carefully remove from baking sheets. **Yield:** 4 servings.

Dive into This Backyard Buffet

WHEN it's time for fun in the sun, there's no better way to enjoy the lazy days of summer than with a poolside party or breezy beach bash in your own backyard. This warm-weather meal won't drown you with last-minute details, so you'll have plenty of time to soak up the sun...and bask in all the compliments!

Edible Inner Tubes

Guests can really sink their teeth into this fun "inner tube" sandwich made with a lettuce-lined bagel. Dill pickle relish gives tangy zip to the thick tuna salad filling.

　　1 can (12 ounces) tuna, drained
　　1/3 cup seasoned bread crumbs
　　1/4 cup creamy Italian salad dressing
　　2 to 3 tablespoons Dijon mustard
　　2 tablespoons dill pickle relish
　　6 plain bagels
Lettuce leaves

In a bowl, combine the first five ingredients. Cut the bagels in half horizontally. Place lettuce on the bottom halves; top with tuna mixture. Replace top halves. **Yield:** 6 servings.

Cool Waters Shakes

Ride a wave of approval when you serve this refreshing berry-flavored beverage. Kids will love its pastel blue color and sea-foamy consistency...and with just three simple ingredients, it's a breeze to whip up in the blender.

　　4 cups cold milk
　　2 packages (3 ounces *each*) berry blue gelatin
　　1 quart vanilla ice cream

In a blender, combine 2 cups of milk, one package of gelatin and 2 cups of ice cream. Cover and process for 30 seconds or until smooth. Repeat. Pour into glasses and serve immediately. **Yield:** 6 servings.

Seashell Salad

Presented in a new sand pail, this festive salad features a zesty dressing that's simple to stir together. An assortment of pasta shapes resembles seashells while red and yellow peppers add color and crunch. For an extra-special touch, you could cut the peppers with a small star-shaped cookie cutter.

　　3 cups uncooked medium shell, spiral, wagon
　　　　wheel *and/or* penne pasta
　　1/3 cup vinegar
　　1/4 cup olive *or* vegetable oil
　　1 teaspoon garlic salt
　　1 teaspoon sugar
　　1 teaspoon Italian seasoning
　　1/4 teaspoon pepper
　　1 medium sweet red pepper
　　1 medium sweet yellow pepper
　　2 tablespoons chopped green onions

Cook the pasta according to package directions until tender; drain and rinse in cold water. Place in a large bowl; set aside. In a jar with tight-fitting lid, combine vinegar, oil and seasonings; shake well. Add peppers, onions and dressing to pasta; toss to coat. Cover and refrigerate until serving. **Yield:** 6-8 servings.

Susie Sunshine Cake

This cake is so light and lemony no one will believe it starts with a boxed mix. The frosting (frozen whipped topping flavored with grated citrus peels) looks professional, but it's quite easy to blend (see pointers below). Fresh fruit garnishes provide the fun final touches.

　　1 package (9 ounces) yellow cake mix
　　1 carton (8 ounces) frozen whipped topping,
　　　　thawed
　　1 teaspoon grated lemon peel
　　1 teaspoon grated orange peel
Red and yellow liquid food coloring
　　2 medium lemons, sliced and halved
　　2 medium oranges, sliced and halved
　　2 blueberries
　　1 large strawberry

Prepare and bake the cake according to package directions, using a greased and floured 8-in. round baking pan. Cool for 10 minutes; remove from pan to a wire rack to cool completely. Transfer to a 12- to 14-in. serving plate. Combine whipped topping and lemon and orange peels. Frost top and sides of cake. Place drops of red and yellow food coloring randomly over frosting (see photo 1 below). With a spatula, blend colors randomly (see photo 2). Alternate lemon and orange slices around base of cake to form rays. Add two orange slices and blueberries for eyes. Slice the strawberry; use two center slices for the mouth, placing them on the cake with straight edges touching. Refrigerate until serving. **Yield:** 6 servings.

Frosting with Finesse

1 Place drops of red and yellow food coloring randomly over the frosted cake.

2 Blend colors randomly over frosting with a spatula.

Speedy Spread
Is Spooktacular

AS the witching hour nears, you don't have to be scared silly of Halloween entertaining. This eerily easy menu won't haunt you with complicated cooking methods or exotic ingredients.

Neighborhood goblins and ghosts will gobble up this frightful feast!

Great Pumpkin Sandwiches

Your guests might think you were visted by the Great Pumpkin when you serve this puffy layered tortilla sandwich. It's seasoned with onion and garlic and loaded with melted cheddar cheese. A celery stick with leaves makes it look like it was just picked from the pumpkin patch.

    3 cups (12 ounces) shredded cheddar cheese
    3/4 cup butter *or* margarine, softened
    3 eggs
    1/2 teaspoon garlic salt
    1/2 teaspoon onion salt
    9 flour tortillas (6 inches)
Paprika
    3 celery sticks with leaves, optional

In a food processor, blend cheese and butter. Add the eggs, garlic salt and onion salt; process for 1 minute or until creamy. Spread 1/2 cupful on each tortilla. Stack three tortillas, cheese side up, for each sandwich; sprinkle with paprika. Place on an ungreased baking sheet. Bake at 400° for 10-15 minutes or until golden and bubbly. If desired, add celery to resemble a pumpkin stem. Cut sandwiches into halves to serve. **Yield:** 6 servings.

Bat Wing Soup

Convenient stewed tomatoes are the base for this spooky soup that gets extra richness from cream. It's nicely flavored with garlic (to keep those vampires away!) and garnished with toasty bat wings. (They are a snap to cut out of white bread—see instructions below.)

    4 garlic cloves, peeled
    2 tablespoons vegetable oil
    4 cans (14-1/2 ounces *each*) stewed tomatoes
    1/2 cup whipping cream

Turn Bread into Bat Wings

 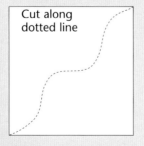

Cut along dotted line

To make bat wings to float in the soup, remove crusts from bread. Flatten with a rolling pin. Using a kitchen shears and referring to diagram above, cut each slice in half diagonally, cutting wavy lines to resemble bat wings.

    6 slices bread, crusts removed
    2 tablespoons butter *or* margarine, softened
    2 teaspoons Italian seasoning

In a saucepan, saute garlic in oil until tender. In a blender or food processor, process garlic and tomatoes in batches until smooth. Return all to the pan; bring to a boil. Reduce heat to low. Add cream and heat through. Follow directions below left to cut bat wings from bread. Place on an ungreased baking sheet. Spread with butter; sprinkle with Italian seasoning. Bake at 400° for 5-8 minutes or until golden brown, turning once. Add two wings to each bowl of soup. Serve immediately. **Yield:** 6 servings.

Frankenstein Salads

Kids of all ages will love these Frankenstein faces made from rectangles of jiggly green gelatin. Bean sprout hair, jelly bean eyes and nose, mini marshmallow bolts and a sour cream smile give this monster some playful personality.

    2 packages (6 ounces *each*) lime gelatin
2-1/2 cups boiling water
    3/4 cup bean sprouts
    12 orange jelly beans
    6 red jelly beans
    3 tablespoons sour cream
    12 miniature marshmallows
Purple kale, optional

In a bowl, dissolve gelatin in water. Pour into an 8-in. square pan that has been coated with nonstick cooking spray. Refrigerate for 4 hours or until firm. Cut into six rectangles; place each on a plate. Decorate with bean sprouts for hair, orange jelly beans for eyes and a red jelly bean for nose. Fill a small plastic bag with sour cream; cut a small hole in the corner of the bag. Pipe a jagged smile on face. Place marshmallows on side of head for bolts. Garnish plates with kale if desired. **Yield:** 6 servings.

Black Cat Cupcakes

If a black cat crosses your path, we hope it's one of these cute chocolaty creations. This time-saving recipe relies on a boxed cake mix and a can of prepared frosting jazzed up with simple cookie and candy decorations.

    1 package (18-1/4 ounces) chocolate cake mix
    1 can (16 ounces) dark chocolate frosting
    12 chocolate cream-filled sandwich cookies, quartered
    48 yellow jelly beans
    24 black jelly beans
    24 pieces black rope licorice

Prepare and bake cake according to package directions for cupcakes, using paper-lined muffin cups. Cool for 10 minutes; remove from pans to wire racks to cool completely. Frost tops of cupcakes. Insert two cookie pieces into each for ears. Add yellow jelly beans for eyes and a black jelly bean for nose. Cut each piece of licorice into thirds, then in half; place three halves on each side of nose for whiskers. **Yield:** 2 dozen.

Festive Fare
Features Frosty Fun

DON'T let cooking for holiday gatherings make you shiver. The easy shepherd's pie conveniently bakes alongside the comforting cauliflower casserole.

By assembling the snowman dessert and fir trees in advance, you'll avoid the blizzard of last-minute details. The cool shakes take just minutes to whip up.

Snowman Party Stew

Youngsters will dig right into this playful potato-topped pie, loaded with ground beef and vegetables.

    1 pound ground beef
    1 package (16 ounces) frozen vegetables for
      stew, *divided*
    1 can (10-1/4 ounces) beef gravy
    2 cups mashed potatoes (prepared with a small
      amount of milk)
   16 whole black peppercorns
  1/4 cup ketchup

In a skillet, brown beef; drain. Remove 24 peas and one carrot chunk from the stew vegetables; set aside. Add the remaining vegetables to beef. Cook until vegetables are thawed. Add gravy; mix well. Pour into an ungreased 9-in. pie plate. Top with eight mashed potato snowmen, using 1 tablespoon of potatoes for each head and 3 tablespoons for each body. Bake, uncovered, at 350° for 20 minutes. Meanwhile, with a sharp knife, cut the reserved carrot into eight strips. Insert one strip into each snowman for a nose. Place three reserved peas on each for buttons. Add peppercorns for eyes. Drizzle ketchup between head and body to form a scarf. **Yield:** 6-8 servings. **Editor's Note:** If serving small children, remove the peppercorns.

Cauliflower Snowman

A homemade white sauce seasoned with Swiss cheese and garlic salt adds great flavor to this speedy vegetable bake.

    6 cups cauliflowerets
  1/4 cup diced white onion
  1/4 cup butter *or* margarine
  1/3 cup all-purpose flour
    2 cups milk
    1 cup (4 ounces) shredded Swiss cheese
    1 teaspoon salt
  1/4 teaspoon garlic salt
  1/4 teaspoon white pepper
   10 whole ripe olives
    1 baby carrot

In a large saucepan, cook cauliflower in a small amount of water for 6-7 minutes or until crisp-tender; drain well. In a medium saucepan, saute onion in butter for 2 minutes. Stir in flour until blended; gradually add milk. Bring to a boil; boil for 2 minutes, stirring constantly. Remove from the heat; stir in cheese until melted. Add salt, garlic salt and pepper. Place half of the cauliflower in a greased 2-1/2-qt. baking dish; top with half of the sauce. Repeat. Bake, uncovered, at 350° for 20 minutes or until bubbly. Add olives for eyes and mouth and a carrot for the nose. **Yield:** 6-8 servings.

Sweet Snowman

Creating this charming snowman is even more fun than building the real thing—and you don't need mittens.

    2 tablespoons vanilla frosting
    3 Sno Balls*
    3 wooden skewers (8 inches)
    1 chocolate wafer (2-1/2 inches)
    2 chocolate cream-filled sandwich cookies
    1 piece red shoestring licorice (12 inches)
    2 brown M&M's
    1 piece candy corn
    5 miniature chocolate chips
    3 semisweet chocolate chips
  Confectioners' sugar, optional

Place 1 teaspoon vanilla frosting on top of each Sno Ball. Stack Sno Balls on a serving plate on top of each other to form the snowman. Cut skewers slightly shorter than the height of the snowman; insert through the center of Sno Balls to secure them. Place chocolate wafer on top to form hat brim. Place a dollop of frosting on top of one sandwich cookie; top with the second cookie. Attach to wafer with frosting to create the hat. Carefully tie licorice around snowman for a scarf. Use frosting to attach M&M's for eyes, candy corn for nose, miniature chips for mouth and semisweet chips for buttons. Dust confectioners' sugar around base of snowman if desired. **Yield:** 1 snowman (3 servings). ***Editor's Note:** Hostess brand Sno Balls are coconut marshmallow-covered chocolate cakes with cream filling.

Edible Evergreens

To assemble, gather the edge of a fruit roll as you wrap it around a sugar cone "trunk".

    6 green Fruit Roll-Ups,* unrolled
    2 sugar ice cream cones

With a scissors, cut roll-ups widthwise into thirds. Gather each piece, beginning with a long side, to form ruffles. Place ice cream cones on a serving plate. Starting at base of cone, attach ruffles by wrapping around cone. Pinch at top to form a point. **Yield:** 2 trees. ***Editor's Note:** This recipe was tested with Fruit Roll-Ups brand, which has fruit pieces measuring approximately 5 x 5 inches. If roll-ups have precut designs in them, place unrolled fruit between two sheets of greased waxed paper. Microwave on high for 10-15 seconds. Roll fruit flat with a rolling pin. Remove waxed paper.

Melted Frosty

(Not pictured)

This rich shake gets its unique taste from buttermilk.

    1 quart vanilla ice cream
    2 cups buttermilk
    2 teaspoons vanilla extract
    1 teaspoon ground cinnamon
  1/2 cup miniature chocolate chips, optional

In a blender, place half of the ice cream, buttermilk, vanilla and cinnamon; cover and blend until smooth. Repeat. Pour into glasses. Stir in chocolate chips if desired. **Yield:** 8 servings.

Chapter 4

NEVER has the saying "less is more" been more true than for today's time-pressed cooks. They know that fewer ingredients mean faster meals (and less mess to clean up!).

So busy cooks who steer clear of long lists of ingredients will turn to this chapter frequently. With just five ingredients—or fewer—per recipe, each delicious dish is a snap to prepare.

But while these main meals, salads, breads, soups, snacks, side dishes and desserts are short on ingredients, they're all long on flavor!

LESS IS BEST. Clockwise from upper right: Easy Baked Chicken (p. 59), Cran-Apple Salad (p. 68), Taco Puffs (p. 63) and Double Chocolate Torte (p. 58).

Orange-Topped Chops

(Pictured at far right)

This recipe has just two main ingredients, plus a few seasonings. As the chops simmer, they pick up the fruity flavor. You can substitute any canned fruit for the oranges.
—Cindy Milleson, Bozeman, Montana

✓ Nutritional Analysis included

  6 pork chops (1/2 inch thick)
  1 tablespoon vegetable oil
  1 can (11 ounces) mandarin oranges, drained
  1/2 teaspoon ground cloves
Pepper to taste

In a skillet, brown pork chops on both sides in oil. Top with oranges; sprinkle with cloves and pepper. Cover and simmer for 35 minutes or until meat juices run clear. **Yield:** 6 servings. **Nutritional Analysis:** One serving equals 167 calories, 39 mg sodium, 52 mg cholesterol, 6 gm carbohydrate, 11 gm protein, 7 gm fat. **Diabetic Exchanges:** 2 lean meat, 1/2 fruit, 1/2 fat.

Sesame Green Beans

(Pictured at far right)

For me, the most time-consuming part of preparing this side dish is picking the green beans in the garden. My family loves their fresh taste, and I love that they're fast to fix!
—Jeanne Bennett, North Richland Hills, Texas

✓ Nutritional Analysis included

  3/4 pound fresh green beans
  1/2 cup water
  1 tablespoon butter *or* margarine
  1 tablespoon soy sauce
  2 teaspoons sesame seeds, toasted

In a saucepan, bring beans and water to a boil; reduce heat to medium. Cover and cook for 10-15 minutes or until the beans are crisp-tender; drain. Add butter, soy sauce and sesame seeds; toss to coat. **Yield:** 6 servings. **Nutritional Analysis:** One 1/2-cup serving (prepared with margarine) equals 43 calories, 245 mg sodium, 0 cholesterol, 4 gm carbohydrate, 1 gm protein, 2 gm fat. **Diabetic Exchanges:** 1 vegetable, 1/2 fat.

Peanut Butter Apple Dip

At our family gatherings, I'm "required" to serve this creamy dip—so I'm thankful it mixes up so quickly! It's especially attractive served with red and green apple wedges.   —Kim Marie Van Rheenen, Mendota, Illinois

  1 package (8 ounces) cream cheese, softened
  1 cup peanut butter
  1 cup packed brown sugar
  1/4 cup milk
  3 to 4 apples, cut into wedges

In a mixing bowl, combine the first four ingredients; mix well. Serve with apples. Store in the refrigerator. **Yield:** 2-2/3 cups.

Almond Rice Pilaf

(Pictured at right)

With quick-cooking rice, this is a speedy side dish...but the almonds make it special enough to serve to company. It goes well with all kinds of meats.   —Sharon Adamczyk Wind Lake, Wisconsin

  3/4 cup chopped onion
  1/2 cup slivered almonds
  1 tablespoon butter *or* margarine
  2 cups chicken broth
  2 cups uncooked instant rice

In a saucepan, saute onion and almonds in butter until the onion is tender and the almonds are lightly browned. Add broth; bring to a boil. Stir in rice and cover. Remove from the heat. Let stand for 5-8 minutes or until the liquid is absorbed. **Yield:** 6 servings.

Tropical Bananas

(Pictured below)

Lime provides the refreshing twist to this exotic-tasting dessert that's quick, healthy and delicious. I sometimes like to serve it as a midday snack.   —Kathleen Jones Chicago, Illinois

  1 medium lime
  2 medium firm bananas, sliced
  2 tablespoons salted peanuts
  1 tablespoon honey
  1 tablespoon flaked coconut

Grate lime peel and set aside. Squeeze lime; measure 1 tablespoon juice (save remaining juice for another use). In a bowl, toss bananas with lime juice. Add peanuts and honey; mix well. Spoon into individual dishes. Sprinkle with coconut and lime peel. Serve immediately. **Yield:** 2 servings.

Tropical Bananas

Sesame Green Beans
Almond Rice Pilaf
Orange-Topped Chops

Rocky Road Fudge

With so few ingredients, this fudge stirs up in a jiffy. That's a good thing, since the chocolaty aroma is so tempting folks can hardly wait to taste it! —Marlene Corrigan
Scranton, Pennsylvania

2 cups (12 ounces) semisweet chocolate chips
1 can (14 ounces) sweetened condensed milk
2 tablespoons butter *or* margarine
3 cups salted dry roasted peanuts
1 package (10-1/2 ounces) miniature marshmallows

In a saucepan, combine the chocolate chips, milk and butter. Cook and stir over medium heat until chips are melted and the mixture is smooth. Remove from the heat; stir in peanuts and marshmallows. Spread into a greased 13-in. x 9-in. x 2-in. baking pan. Refrigerate until firm. Cut into squares. **Yield:** about 3-1/4 pounds.

Ranch Pretzels

For a fast, fun snack, start with plain pretzels and add a new taste twist. It takes just a few minutes to coat them with seasonings and pop them into the oven to bake. —Lois Kerns, Hagerstown, Maryland

1 package (20 ounces) large thick pretzels
1 envelope ranch salad dressing mix
3/4 cup vegetable oil

1-1/2 teaspoons dill weed
1-1/2 teaspoons garlic powder

Break pretzels into bite-size pieces and place in a large bowl. Combine remaining ingredients; pour over pretzels. Stir to coat. Pour into an ungreased 15-in. x 10-in. x 1-in. baking pan. Bake at 200° for 1 hour, stirring every 15 minutes. **Yield:** 12 cups.

Roasted Red Potatoes

These tender, tasty potatoes are so simple to make. There's no need to peel them—just slice, season and bake. —Kitty Hernandez, Chicago, Illinois

✓ Nutritional Analysis included

1 pound small red potatoes
1 tablespoon olive *or* vegetable oil
1/2 teaspoon salt
1/8 teaspoon pepper
2 tablespoons grated Parmesan cheese

Cut the potatoes into 1/4-in.-thick slices; toss with oil. Place in a single layer in a greased 13-in. x 9-in. x 2-in. baking pan. Sprinkle with salt, pepper and Parmesan cheese. Cover tightly with foil. Bake at 350° for 40 minutes or until tender. **Yield:** 4 servings. **Nutritional Analysis:** One serving equals 117 calories, 352 mg sodium, 2 mg cholesterol, 15 gm carbohydrate, 4 gm protein, 4 gm fat. **Diabetic Exchanges:** 1 starch, 1 fat.

Double Chocolate Torte

Double Chocolate Torte

(Pictured above and on page 54)

If you love chocolate, you won't be able to resist this rich, fudgy torte. I often make it for company because it's easy to prepare yet looks so impressive. For special occasions, I place it on a fancy cake plate and I use a can of whipped topping to decorate it. It looks and tastes awesome!
—Naomi Treadwell, Swans Island, Maine

   1 package fudge brownie mix (13-inch x 9-inch pan size)
   1 cup (6 ounces) semisweet chocolate chips, melted
 1/2 cup butter (no substitutes), softened
   2 cups whipped topping
   1 teaspoon chocolate sprinkles

Prepare brownie mix according to package directions for fudge-like brownies. Spread batter in a greased and floured 9-in. round baking pan. Bake at 350° for 38-42 minutes or until the center springs back when lightly touched. Cool for 10 minutes. Invert onto a serving plate; cool completely. In a bowl, stir melted chocolate and butter until smooth. Spread over the brownie layer; refrigerate for 30 minutes. Just before serving, top with whipped topping. Decorate with sprinkles. **Yield:** 9-12 servings.

Creamy Fruit Dip

You can whip up this three-ingredient dip in no time in a blender or with a mixer. It's yummy and smooth and goes great with any kind of fresh fruit. —Bonnie Wither
Branford, Connecticut

✓ Nutritional Analysis included

   1 package (8 ounces) cream cheese, softened
   3 tablespoons orange juice concentrate

   1 jar (7 ounces) marshmallow creme
Fresh whole strawberries
Sliced kiwifruit

In a mixing bowl, beat cream cheese and concentrate until smooth. Fold in marshmallow creme. Serve with fruit. Store in the refrigerator. **Yield:** 2 cups. **Nutritional Analysis:** One 2-tablespoon serving of dip (prepared with fat-free cream cheese) equals 56 calories, 79 mg sodium, 0 cholesterol, 12 gm carbohydrate, 2 gm protein, 0 fat. **Diabetic Exchange:** 1 starch.

Strawberry Asparagus Salad

This is my family's favorite springtime salad. The dressing is so light and refreshing, and the vivid combination of red berries and green asparagus is a real eye-catcher.
—Judi Francus, Morristown, New Jersey

✓ Nutritional Analysis included

 1/4 cup lemon juice
   2 tablespoons vegetable oil
   2 tablespoons honey
   2 cups cut fresh asparagus (1-inch pieces)
   2 cups sliced fresh strawberries

In a small bowl, combine lemon juice, oil and honey; mix well. Cook asparagus in a small amount of water until crisp-tender, about 3-4 minutes; drain and cool. Arrange asparagus and strawberries on individual plates; drizzle with dressing. **Yield:** 8 servings. **Nutritional Analysis:** One serving equals 68 calories, 1 mg sodium, 0 cholesterol, 9 gm carbohydrate, 1 gm protein, 4 gm fat. **Diabetic Exchanges:** 1 fat, 1/2 fruit.

Ultimate Cheese Bread

Loaded with mushrooms and cheese, this festive-looking garlic bread is a great party appetizer. Accompanied by soup or a salad, it's hearty enough to serve as a meal.
—Carolyn Hayes, Marion, Illinois

   1 unsliced loaf French bread (1 pound)
   1 package (8 ounces) sliced Swiss cheese
   1 jar (4-1/2 ounces) sliced mushrooms, drained, optional
 1/2 cup butter *or* margarine, melted
 1/8 to 1/4 teaspoon garlic powder

Cut bread diagonally into 1-1/2-in. slices to within 1/2 in. of bottom. Repeat cuts in opposite direction. Cut cheese into 1-in. squares. Place one cheese square and one mushroom if desired into each slit. Combine butter and garlic powder; spoon over the bread. Place on an ungreased baking sheet. Bake at 350° for 8-10 minutes or until cheese is melted. **Yield:** 10-12 servings.

Swiss Tuna Bake

My husband enjoys cooking just as much as I do. One night he tossed together this comforting casserole from meager ingredients we had in our cupboard. It turned out

to be the best-tasting tuna casserole I have ever had! Swiss cheese flavors the noodles nicely. —Joanne Callahan
Far Hills, New Jersey

4 cups cooked medium egg noodles
1-1/2 cups (6 ounces) shredded Swiss cheese
1 cup mayonnaise
1 can (6 ounces) tuna, drained and flaked
1 cup seasoned bread crumbs, *divided*

In a large bowl, combine the noodles, cheese, mayonnaise and tuna. Sprinkle 1/2 cup bread crumbs into a greased 9-in. square baking dish. Spread noodle mixture over the crumbs. Sprinkle with the remaining crumbs. Bake, uncovered, at 350° for 20 minutes or until heated through. **Yield:** 4 servings.

Nutty Peach Crisp

(Pictured below)

A co-worker brought this easy, delicious dessert to work, and I couldn't resist asking for the recipe. A moist bottom layer made with canned peaches and boxed cake mix is covered with a lovely golden topping of coconut and pecans. —Nancy Carpenter, Sidney, Montana

1 can (29 ounces) sliced peaches, undrained
1 package (18-1/4 ounces) yellow *or* butter pecan cake mix
1/2 cup butter *or* margarine, melted
1 cup flaked coconut
1 cup chopped pecans

Arrange peaches in an ungreased 13-in. x 9-in. x 2-in. baking dish. Sprinkle dry cake mix over the top. Drizzle with butter; sprinkle with coconut and pecans. Bake at 325° for 55-60 minutes or until golden brown. Let stand for 15 minutes before serving. Serve warm or cold. **Yield:** 12-15 servings.

Nutty Peach Crisp

Seafood Stuffing

Seafood Stuffing

(Pictured above)

For an easy and elegant side dish, I add canned crab and shrimp to boxed stuffing mix. When I served this to my mom as part of her birthday dinner, she said it was the best she had ever tasted. —Marcy Thrall
Haddam Neck, Connecticut

1 package (6 ounces) instant chicken-flavored stuffing mix
1 can (6 ounces) crabmeat, drained and cartilage removed *or* 1 cup imitation crabmeat
1 can (6 ounces) small shrimp, rinsed and drained *or* 1 cup frozen small cooked shrimp
1 teaspoon lemon juice

Prepare stuffing according to package directions. Gently stir in crab, shrimp and lemon juice. Serve immediately. **Yield:** 4-6 servings.

Easy Baked Chicken

(Pictured on page 55)

I was surprised when my sister-in-law told me she used just three simple ingredients to bake this tender, flavorful chicken. The pretty, crispy coating seals in the juices to keep the chicken moist and delicious. —Susan Adair
Muncie, Indiana

1 broiler/fryer chicken (3-1/2 to 4 pounds), cut up
1 cup Italian salad dressing
1-1/4 cups crushed cornflakes

Place chicken in a large resealable plastic bag or shallow glass container; add salad dressing. Seal or cover and turn to coat. Refrigerate for at least 1 hour. Drain and discard marinade. Coat chicken with cornflakes; place in a greased 13-in. x 9-in. x 2-in. baking dish. Bake, uncovered, at 350° for 1 hour or until juices run clear. **Yield:** 4 servings.

Salsa Fish

(Pictured below)

My family loves outdoor activities, especially fishing. I give their catch of the day some unexpected zip with salsa. It dresses up these golden crumb-coated fillets and keeps them moist and tender.
—Diane Grajewski
North Branch, Michigan

    2 pounds fish fillets (walleye, bass *or* perch)
    1 cup seasoned bread crumbs
    1 tablespoon vegetable oil
1-1/2 cups salsa
    8 ounces shredded *or* sliced mozzarella *or* provolone cheese

Coat fish fillets in bread crumbs. In a skillet, brown fillets in oil. Arrange in a greased 13-in. x 9-in. x 2-in. baking dish. Top with salsa and cheese. Bake, uncovered, at 400° for 7-10 minutes or until fish flakes easily with a fork and cheese is melted. **Yield:** 6 servings.

Chewy Macaroons

(Pictured below)

These coconut cookies are lightly crisp on the outside and chewy on the inside. Sometimes I make them a bit larger so I can top them with ice cream and strawberry sauce.
—Herbert Borland, Des Moines, Washington

    2 egg whites
    1/2 teaspoon vanilla extract
Pinch salt
    6 tablespoons sugar
    1 cup flaked coconut

In a small mixing bowl, beat egg whites, vanilla and salt until foamy. Gradually add sugar, beating until stiff peaks form. Fold in the coconut. Drop by tablespoonfuls 2 in. apart onto well-greased baking sheets. Bake at 300° for 25 minutes or until lightly browned. Immediately remove to wire racks to cool. Store in an airtight container. **Yield:** about 2 dozen.

Salsa Fish
Greens with Herb Vinaigrette
Chewy Macaroons

Spinach Cheese Swirls

Spinach Cheese Swirls

(Pictured above)

My family loves these super-easy sandwiches brimming with great spinach and onion flavor. Refrigerated pizza dough shaves minutes off prep time and creates a golden brown crust. The cheesy slices taste terrific warm or cold.
—*Mary Nichols, Dover, New Hampshire*

  1 package (10 ounces) frozen chopped
    spinach, thawed and drained
  2 cups (8 ounces) shredded mozzarella cheese
  1 cup finely chopped onion
  1 garlic clove, minced
  1 tube (10 ounces) refrigerated pizza crust

In a bowl, combine the first four ingredients and mix well. On a greased baking sheet, roll pizza dough into a 14-in. x 10-in. rectangle; seal any holes. Spoon filling over crust to within 1 in. of edge. Roll up, jelly-roll style, starting with a long side; seal the ends and place the seam side down. Bake at 400° for 25-27 minutes or until golden brown. Cut into slices. **Yield:** 4 servings.

Chili Chicken

For busy days, I keep convenient pantry items on hand to spice up chicken breasts. While they bake, I can do other things. —*Michael Dobrowski, Reno, Nevada*

✓ Nutritional Analysis included

  4 boneless skinless chicken breast halves (1
    pound)
  1 can (14-1/2 ounces) Italian stewed tomatoes
  1 can (15 ounces) chili with beans
  4 slices cheddar *or* American cheese

Place chicken in an ungreased 11-in. x 7-in. x 2-in. baking dish. Top with tomatoes. Bake, uncovered, at 350° for 50 minutes. Spoon chili over each chicken breast; bake 10 minutes longer. Top with cheese; return to the oven for 3-4 minutes or until cheese is melted. **Yield:** 4 servings. **Nutritional Analysis:** One serving (prepared with fat-free chili and reduced-fat cheddar) equals 311 calories, 589 mg sodium, 69 mg cholesterol, 21 gm carbohydrate, 37 gm protein, 5 gm fat. **Diabetic Exchanges:** 4-1/2 very lean meat, 1 starch, 1 vegetable.

Berry Applesauce Gelatin

Applesauce and strawberry chunks give substance to this lovely rose-colored treat. My mother-in-law shared the recipe for this refreshing gelatin salad, which is not only great-tasting, but good for you! —*Julie Bick, Lyons, Ohio*

✓ Nutritional Analysis included

  1 package (6 ounces) strawberry gelatin
  1 cup boiling water
  2 cups frozen unsweetened strawberries
  2 cups applesauce
  2 tablespoons lemon juice

In a bowl, dissolve gelatin in boiling water. Stir in the strawberries until thawed and separated. Add the applesauce and lemon juice; mix well. Pour into an 11-in. x 7-in. x 2-in. pan; chill until set. **Yield:** 8 servings. **Nutritional Analysis:** One serving (prepared with sugar-free gelatin and unsweetened applesauce) equals 48 calories, 48 mg sodium, 0 cholesterol, 11 gm carbohydrate, 1 gm protein, trace fat. **Diabetic Exchange:** 1 fruit.

Crunchy Raisin Treats

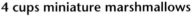

Peanuts give an extra crunch to these crispy treats dotted with raisins. As an evening snack, they are irresistible with milk.
—*Bernice Morris, Marshfield, Missouri*

  4 cups miniature marshmallows
  1/4 cup butter *or* margarine
5-1/2 cups crisp rice cereal
1-1/2 cups raisins
  1 cup salted dry roasted peanuts

In a large saucepan or microwave-safe bowl, melt marshmallows and butter; stir until smooth. Add cereal, raisins and peanuts; mix well. Pat into a greased 13-in. x 9-in. x 2-in. pan. Cool completely; cut into squares. **Yield:** 3 dozen.

Greens with Herb Vinaigrette

(Pictured at far left)

Dijon mustard adds tanginess to the light vinaigrette that coats this salad. For variety, I sometimes add minced garlic or a tablespoon of whipping cream. You can even use flavored vinegars or different types of oil. —*Sally Hook Houston, Texas*

6 to 8 cups torn salad greens
  3 tablespoons olive *or* vegetable oil
  1 tablespoon cider *or* red wine vinegar
1/2 to 1 teaspoon Dijon mustard
1/2 teaspoon Italian seasoning

Place greens in a salad bowl. Combine remaining ingredients in a jar with tight-fitting lid; shake well. Pour over greens and toss to coat. **Yield:** 6-8 servings.

Easy Pasta Alfredo

Who would believe that five simple ingredients could taste so rich and delicious? This creamy, comforting sauce can be made in a matter of minutes. —Karin DeCarlo
Milford, Pennsylvania

1/2 cup butter *or* margarine
1 cup whipping cream
1/8 teaspoon ground nutmeg
1 cup shredded Parmesan cheese
1 package (19 ounces) frozen cheese tortellini

In a saucepan, melt butter over medium-low heat. Add cream and nutmeg; heat through but do not boil. Stir in Parmesan cheese until melted. Cook tortellini according to package directions; drain. Transfer to a large serving bowl. Add the cheese sauce and toss to coat. Serve immediately. **Yield:** 4 servings.

Quick Caramel Rolls

(Pictured below)

Refrigerated crescent rolls and caramel ice cream topping make these yummy, gooey treats a snap to assemble. I used to whip up a huge panful for our kids when they were growing up...now our grandchildren love them, too.
—Jeannette Westphal, Gettysburg, South Dakota

1/4 cup butter *or* margarine
1/2 cup chopped pecans
1 cup caramel ice cream topping
2 tubes (8 ounces *each*) refrigerated crescent rolls

Quick Caramel Rolls

Place butter in a 13-in. x 9-in. x 2-in. baking pan; heat in a 375° oven until melted. Sprinkle with pecans. Add ice cream topping and mix well. Remove dough from tubes (do not unroll); cut each section of dough into six rolls. Arrange rolls in prepared pan with cut side down. Bake at 375° for 20-25 minutes or until golden. Immediately invert onto a serving plate. Serve warm. **Yield:** 2 dozen.

Sunny Apple Salad

Orange juice concentrate lends a tangy flavor to this crunchy salad. Its sunny color is sure to brighten up even the grayest day. You can stir up the remaining orange juice concentrate for breakfast the next morning.
—Tammy Neubauer, Ida Grove, Iowa

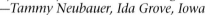

✓ Nutritional Analysis included

2 medium red apples, diced
1 medium green apple, diced
1 medium carrot, grated
1 can (8 ounces) crushed pineapple, drained
3 tablespoons orange juice concentrate

In a bowl, combine all ingredients; mix well. Cover and refrigerate until serving. **Yield:** 10-12 servings. **Nutritional Analysis:** One 1/2-cup serving equals 36 calories, 2 mg sodium, 0 cholesterol, 9 gm carbohydrate, trace protein, trace fat. **Diabetic Exchange:** 1/2 fruit.

Praline Parfaits

The recipe for this sweet, nutty ice cream sauce comes from a famous New Orleans restaurant. When we entertain, I top each pretty parfait with whipped cream and a pecan half. —Cindy Stephenson, Houston, Texas

1 bottle (16 ounces) dark corn syrup
1/3 cup sugar
1/3 cup water
1 cup chopped pecans
3 to 4 cups vanilla ice cream

In a saucepan, combine the corn syrup, sugar and water; bring to a boil, stirring constantly. Remove from the heat; stir in pecans. Cool completely. Spoon half of the ice cream into four parfait glasses or dishes. Top each with 2 tablespoons sauce. Repeat layers. Refrigerate the leftover sauce. **Yield:** 4 servings (about 2-1/2 cups sauce).

Snackers

These crisp, chewy treats pack lots of peanut flavor. They're our favorite travel snack. I always make a double batch so we have some left when we reach our destination.
—Mrs. W.H. Gregory, Roanoke, Virginia

3 cups Crispix cereal
1/2 cup salted peanuts
1/3 cup packed brown sugar
1/3 cup corn syrup
1/4 cup peanut butter

Ravioli Casserole

In a bowl, combine cereal and peanuts; set aside. In a microwave-safe bowl, combine brown sugar and corn syrup. Microwave on high for 1-2 to minutes or until the sugar is dissolved, stirring several times. Immediately stir in peanut butter until smooth. Pour over cereal mixture and toss to coat. Drop by rounded tablespoonfuls onto waxed paper. Cool. **Yield:** about 1-1/2 dozen. **Editor's Note:** This recipe was tested in an 850-watt microwave.

Broccoli Cheese Casserole

I often serve this dish to company because it's easy to make and looks so appealing. The crumb topping is very flavorful. —*Vicki Schrupp, Little Falls, Minnesota*

  1 jar (8 ounces) process cheese spread
1/4 cup butter *or* margarine, *divided*
  2 packages (10 ounces *each*) frozen chopped
      broccoli, thawed
  1 cup crushed butter-flavored crackers, *divided*

In a saucepan, combine cheese spread and 2 tablespoons butter. Cook and stir until the butter is melted and the mixture is smooth. Add broccoli and 1/2 cup of cracker crumbs. Transfer to a greased 8-in. square baking dish. Melt remaining butter; toss with remaining crumbs. Sprinkle over broccoli. Bake, uncovered, at 350° for 20-25 minutes or until bubbly. **Yield:** 6-8 servings.

No-Fuss Meat Loaf

Instant stuffing mix makes this nicely seasoned meat loaf simple enough for beginners to make. I often combine the mixture in a resealable plastic bag instead of a bowl. Then I toss the bag for easy cleanup.
  —*Betty Braswell, Elgin, Pennsylvania*

  2 eggs
1/2 cup water

1 package (6 ounces) instant stuffing mix
2 pounds ground beef
Ketchup

In a large bowl, beat eggs and water. Add stuffing mix and contents of seasoning packet; mix well. Add beef; mix well. Press into an ungreased 9-in. x 5-in. x 3-in. loaf pan. Top with ketchup. Bake, uncovered, at 350° for 1-1/4 to 1-1/2 hours or until no pink remains and a meat thermometer reads 160°. **Yield:** 6-8 servings.

Ravioli Casserole

(Pictured at left)

The whole family will love the fun, cheesy flavor of this main dish that tastes like lasagna without all the fuss. Prepared spaghetti sauce and frozen ravioli hurry the preparation along. —*Mary Ann Rothert, Austin, Texas*

  1 jar (28 ounces) spaghetti sauce
  1 package (25 ounces) frozen cheese ravioli,*
      cooked and drained
  2 cups (16 ounces) small-curd cottage cheese
  4 cups (16 ounces) shredded mozzarella cheese
1/4 cup grated Parmesan cheese

Spread 1/2 cup of spaghetti sauce in an ungreased 13-in. x 9-in. x 2-in. baking dish. Layer with half of the ravioli, 1-1/4 cups of sauce, 1 cup of cottage cheese and 2 cups of mozzarella cheese. Repeat layers. Sprinkle with the Parmesan cheese. Bake, uncovered, at 350° for 30-40 minutes or until bubbly. Let stand 5-10 minutes before serving. **Yield:** 6-8 servings. ***Editor's Note:** 4-5 cups of any style cooked ravioli may be substituted for the frozen cheese ravioli.

Taco Puffs

(Pictured on page 54)

I got this recipe from a friend years ago and still make these cheesy sandwiches regularly. I serve them for dinner along with a steaming bowl of soup or fresh green salad. —*Jan Schmid, Hibbing, Minnesota*

  1 pound ground beef
1/2 cup chopped onion
  1 envelope taco seasoning
  2 tubes (17.3 ounces *each*) large refrigerated
      biscuits
  8 ounces cheddar cheese, cut into 16 slices *or 2
      cups* (8 ounces) shredded cheddar cheese

In a skillet, cook beef and onion over medium heat until beef is browned and onion is tender; drain. Add the taco seasoning and prepare according to package directions. Cool slightly. Flatten half of the biscuits into 4-in. circles; place in greased 15-in. x 10-in. x 1-in. baking pans. Spoon 1/4 cup meat mixture onto each; top with two cheese slices or 1/4 cup of shredded cheese. Flatten the remaining biscuits; place on top and pinch edges to seal tightly. Bake at 400° for 15 minutes or until golden brown. **Yield:** 5 servings.

Strawberry Soup

This refreshing chilled soup is a lovely addition to a special brunch or luncheon. With its fruity flavor and thick frothy texture, you could even serve it as a punch!
—Lucia Johnson, Massena, New York

    1 pint fresh strawberries, hulled
1/2 cup white wine *or* apple juice
1/2 cup sugar
    2 tablespoons lemon juice
    1 teaspoon grated lemon peel

In a blender, combine all ingredients. Cover and process until smooth. Pour into two bowls; cover and refrigerate until thoroughly chilled, 1-2 hours. **Yield:** 2 servings.

Chicken Chili

(Pictured below)

My aunt gave me the recipe for this thick "instant" chili. To save time, I usually cook and cube the chicken the night before or use leftovers. The next day, it's simple to simmer the ingredients on the stovetop. —Yvonne Morgan
Grand Rapids, Michigan

    2 cans (15 ounces *each*) great northern beans,
      rinsed and drained
    2 jars (16 ounces *each*) picante sauce
    4 cups cubed cooked chicken
    1 to 2 teaspoons ground cumin
Shredded Monterey Jack cheese

In a saucepan, combine beans, picante sauce, chicken and cumin. Bring to a boil. Reduce heat; cover and simmer for 20 minutes. Sprinkle individual servings with cheese. **Yield:** 6 servings.

Chicken Chili

Pizza Chicken Roll-Ups

(Pictured at right)

I love the chicken roll-ups my mom made for special occasions, filled with spinach and cream cheese. My own kids wouldn't eat those, so I came up with this pizza-flavored variety the whole family enjoys. —Tanja Penquite
Oregon, Ohio

    4 boneless skinless chicken breast halves
  12 pepperoni slices
    8 mozzarella cheese slices, *divided*
    1 can (15 ounces) pizza sauce
Minced fresh parsley, optional

Flatten chicken to 1/4-in. thickness. Place three slices of pepperoni and one slice of cheese on each. Roll up tightly; secure with toothpicks. Place in a greased 11-in. x 7-in. x 2-in. baking dish. Spoon pizza sauce over roll-ups. Cover and bake at 350° for 35-40 minutes. Uncover; top with the remaining cheese. Bake 5-10 minutes longer or until cheese is melted. Sprinkle with parsley if desired. **Yield:** 4 servings.

Zucchini Bake

(Pictured at right)

Mushrooms, onion, cheddar cheese and a hint of basil dress up garden-fresh zucchini. I let everyone season their own servings of this side dish with salt and pepper at the table. —Jacquelyn Smith, Carmel, Maine

✓ Nutritional Analysis included

    2 cups sliced zucchini
1-1/2 cups sliced fresh mushrooms
  1/4 cup sliced onion
  1/2 cup shredded cheddar cheese
  1/2 teaspoon dried basil

In a greased shallow 1-qt. baking dish, layer zucchini, mushrooms and onion. Sprinkle with cheese and basil. Cover and bake at 350° for 20 minutes. Uncover and bake 10 minutes longer or until vegetables are tender. **Yield:** 4 servings. **Nutritional Analysis:** One 1/2-cup serving (prepared with reduced-fat cheese) equals 43 calories, 90 mg sodium, 3 mg cholesterol, 4 gm carbohydrate, 5 gm protein, 1 gm fat. **Diabetic Exchanges:** 1 vegetable, 1/2 lean meat.

Walking Salad

This speedy stuffed apple is a great snack for a family hike. In a brown-bag lunch, it's a nice change from the usual peanut butter and jelly sandwich. —Mrs. John Crawford
Barnesville, Georgia

    2 tablespoons peanut butter
    1 tablespoon raisins
    1 teaspoon honey
    1 medium apple, cored

In a small bowl, combine peanut butter, raisins and honey. Spoon into center of apple. **Yield:** 1 serving.

Savory Biscuit Bites
Pizza Chicken Roll-Ups
Zucchini Bake

Savory Biscuit Bites

(Pictured above)

These light, golden puffs are super simple to make, and their flavor is oh-so-good. Their small size makes them easy to munch, and they're wonderful warm or cold.
—Wendy Chilton, Brookeland, Texas

    1/4 cup butter *or* margarine, melted
      2 tablespoons grated Parmesan cheese
      1 tablespoon dried minced onion
1-1/2 teaspoons dried parsley flakes
      1 package (12 ounces) refrigerated biscuits

In a bowl, combine butter, cheese, onion and parsley. Cut biscuits into quarters; roll in butter mixture. Place in a greased 15-in. x 10-in. x 1-in. baking pan; let stand for 25 minutes. Bake at 400° for 8 minutes or until lightly browned. **Yield:** 40 pieces.

Feta Pitas

Toasty pitas sprinkled with tasty toppings get rave reviews from my family. These snacks are fun and filling.
—Tammy Smith, Live Oak, Texas

      6 whole pita breads
1-1/2 cups crumbled feta cheese *or* shredded
      mozzarella cheese

      1 tablespoon Italian seasoning
    3/4 cup thinly sliced red onion
      1 small tomato, thinly sliced

Place pita breads on an ungreased baking sheet. Sprinkle with cheese and Italian seasoning. Top with onion and tomato. Bake at 350° for 10-12 minutes. Cut into wedges if desired. Serve immediately. **Yield:** 6 servings.

Citrus Slush

I use convenient cans of frozen lemonade and orange juice to create the base for this sweet-tart slush. Either regular or pink lemonade—or a can of each—works fine in this great thirst-quencher.
—Janis Plourde
Smooth Rock Falls, Ontario

      2 cans (12 ounces *each*) frozen lemonade
      concentrate, thawed
      1 can (12 ounces) frozen orange juice
      concentrate, thawed
      1 cup chilled lemon-lime soda per serving
      (about 6 liters)

Combine the concentrates in a 1-1/2-qt. freezer-proof container; cover and freeze. Remove from the freezer 30 minutes before serving. For each serving, combine 3 tablespoons slush base with 1 cup soda; stir well. **Yield:** 25 servings.

Dilly Beef Sandwiches
Acorn Squash Slices
Green Beans with Almonds

Dilly Beef Sandwiches

(Pictured above)

My younger sister, Jean, shared this recipe, which puts a twist on the traditional barbecue sandwich. As a busy mother of four, Jean never has much time to cook, but she does like to entertain. This crowd-pleaser, made in a convenient slow cooker, is perfect for our large family gatherings. —Donna Blankenheim, Madison, Wisconsin

> 1 boneless beef chuck roast (3 to 4 pounds)
> 1 jar (16 ounces) whole dill pickles, undrained
> 1/2 cup chili sauce
> 2 garlic cloves, minced
> 10 to 12 hamburger buns, split

Cut roast in half and place in a slow cooker. Add pickles with juice, chili sauce and garlic. Cover and cook on low for 8-9 hours or until beef is tender. Discard pickles. Remove roast. When cool enough to handle, shred the meat. Return to the sauce and heat through. Using a slotted spoon, fill each bun with about 1/2 cup meat mixture. **Yield:** 10-12 servings.

Creamy Potato Casserole

I was in a hurry the afternoon I made up this fast-to-fix potato casserole. I just mixed the sliced spuds with the rest of the ingredients and put them in the oven. In a mild cheese sauce, the tender potatoes bake to a pretty golden brown. —Connie Clifton, Pegram, Tennessee

> 8 medium potatoes, peeled and thinly sliced
> 1 small onion, chopped
> 1 can (10-3/4 ounces) condensed cheddar cheese soup, undiluted
> 1 cup (8 ounces) sour cream
> 1 teaspoon salt

Combine all ingredients; mix well. Place in a greased 8-in. square baking dish. Cover and bake at 350° for 70-75 minutes or until the potatoes are tender. Uncover and bake 10-15 minutes longer or until lightly browned. **Yield:** 6-8 servings.

Acorn Squash Slices

(Pictured above)

Acorn squash is a favorite with my family. This recipe gets sweet maple flavor from syrup and an appealing nuttiness from pecans. It's easy because you don't have to peel the squash. —Mrs. Richard Lamb, Williamsburg, Indiana

✓ Nutritional Analysis included

> 2 medium acorn squash (about 1-1/2 pounds each)
> 1/2 teaspoon salt

3/4 cup maple syrup
2 tablespoons butter *or* margarine, melted
1/3 cup chopped pecans, optional

Wash squash. Cut in half lengthwise; discard seeds and membrane. Cut each half crosswise into 1/2-in. slices; discard the ends. Place slices in a greased 13-in. x 9-in. x 2-in. baking dish. Sprinkle with salt. Combine syrup and butter; pour over squash. Sprinkle with pecans if desired. Cover and bake at 350° for 40-45 minutes or until tender. **Yield:** 6 servings. **Nutritional Analysis:** One serving of 2 slices (prepared with sugar-free maple-flavored pancake syrup, reduced-fat margarine and pecans) equals 170 calories, 98 mg sodium, 0 cholesterol, 31 gm carbohydrate, 2 gm protein, 7 gm fat. **Diabetic Exchanges:** 1 starch, 1 fruit, 1 fat.

Green Beans with Almonds

(Pictured at left)

A touch of lemon juice gives a fresh taste to this simple side dish. Slivered almonds look so pretty with the French-style green beans.
—*Ruth Andrewson*
Leavenworth, Washington

1 package (16 ounces) frozen French-style green beans
1/2 cup slivered almonds
1/4 cup butter *or* margarine
2 teaspoons lemon juice
1/4 teaspoon salt

Place the beans in a saucepan and cover with water; cook until crisp-tender. Meanwhile, in a skillet over low heat, toast almonds in butter. Remove from the heat; stir in lemon juice and salt. Drain beans. Add almond mixture and toss to coat. **Yield:** 6-8 servings.

Scandinavian Pecan Cookies

(Pictured below)

We enjoyed these rich, buttery cookies at a bed-and-breakfast in Galena, Illinois, and the hostess was kind enough

Scandinavian Pecan Cookies

to share her simple recipe. The pretty nut-topped treats are so special you could give a home-baked batch as a gift.
—*Laurie Knoke, DeKalb, Illinois*

1 cup butter (no substitutes), softened
3/4 cup packed brown sugar
1 egg, *separated*
2 cups all-purpose flour
1/2 cup finely chopped pecans

In a mixing bowl, cream butter, brown sugar and egg yolk. Gradually add flour. Shape into 1-in. balls. In a small bowl, beat egg white. Dip balls in egg white, then roll in pecans. Place 2 in. apart on ungreased baking sheets; flatten slightly. Bake at 375° for 8-12 minutes or until edges are lightly browned. Cool on wire racks. **Yield:** 4-5 dozen.

Fruity Orange Gelatin

Pineapple and oranges add sweet fruit flavor to this attractive make-ahead salad. The addition of sherbet makes this gelatin especially refreshing.
—*Esther Miller*
Holmesville, Ohio

✓ Nutritional Analysis included

1 package (6 ounces) orange gelatin
2 cups boiling water
2 cups orange sherbet
1 can (20 ounces) crushed pineapple, undrained
1 can (11 ounces) mandarin oranges, drained

In a bowl, dissolve gelatin in water. Stir in sherbet until melted. Stir in pineapple and oranges. Pour into a 2-qt. serving bowl. Chill until firm. **Yield:** 10-12 servings. **Nutritional Analysis:** One 1/2-cup serving (prepared with sugar-free gelatin) equals 77 calories, 17 mg sodium, 2 mg cholesterol, 18 gm carbohydrate, 1 gm protein, 1 gm fat. **Diabetic Exchange:** 1 fruit.

Fish Nuggets

My family loves to camp and fish. We developed this different breading made with saltines and graham crackers for a change of pace. It fries to a tasty golden brown and has become a campground favorite.
—*Deana Brandenburg, Great Bend, Kansas*

2 pounds haddock *or* cod fillets
1 cup finely crushed graham crackers (about 16 squares)
3/4 cup finely crushed saltines (about 25 crackers)
1-1/2 to 2 teaspoons seasoned salt
Oil for deep-fat frying

Cut fish into 1-in. cubes; secure with a toothpick if necessary. Combine cracker crumbs and seasoned salt in a shallow bowl; roll fish in crumb mixture until coated. In an electric skillet or deep-fat fryer, heat oil to 375°. Fry nuggets, a few at time, for 3 minutes or until browned. Drain on paper towels. **Yield:** 4-6 servings.

Cran-Apple Salad

(Pictured at right and on page 55)

This tart and tasty salad goes so wonderfully with lots of different meals. Folks will think you slaved over it, but with four ingredients, preparation takes only minutes! Crunchy walnuts, celery and apples make it special.
—Lucille Foster, Grant, Nebraska

1 can (16 ounces) whole-berry cranberry sauce
1 medium unpeeled tart apple, diced
1 celery rib, thinly sliced
1/2 cup chopped walnuts

In a bowl, combine the cranberry sauce, apple and celery. Cover and refrigerate. Stir in walnuts just before serving. **Yield:** 4-6 servings.

Cran-Apple Salad

Creamy Baked Spinach

Cream cheese turns ordinary spinach into a side dish that's pretty enough to serve company. This casserole is a snap to stir up because it relies on convenient frozen spinach.
—Beverly Albrecht, Beatrice, Nebraska

2 packages (10 ounces *each*) frozen chopped spinach
2 packages (3 ounces *each*) cream cheese, softened
4 tablespoons butter *or* margarine, *divided*
1/4 teaspoon salt
1/2 cup seasoned bread crumbs

Cook spinach according to package directions; drain well. Stir in cream cheese, 2 tablespoons of butter and salt. Transfer to a greased 1-qt. baking dish. Melt remaining butter; toss with bread crumbs. Sprinkle over spinach mixture. Bake, uncovered, at 350° for 20 minutes or until lightly browned. **Yield:** 4-6 servings.

Almond-Topped Chicken

(Pictured at far right)

Lemon juice adds a pleasant tartness to the buttery sauce that I serve over chicken. My family loves this easy-to-make entree. I often toss in more almonds for extra crunch.
—Karen Zink, Grand Island, Nebraska

4 boneless skinless chicken breast halves
5 tablespoons butter *or* margarine, *divided*
1/3 cup slivered almonds
3 tablespoons lemon juice

In a skillet, cook the chicken in 2 tablespoons of butter until juices run clear, about 20 minutes. Transfer to a serving plate and keep warm. Add almonds and remaining butter to skillet; cook and stir just until almonds are lightly browned. Stir in lemon juice; heat through. Spoon over chicken. **Yield:** 4 servings.

Ranch Potatoes

This golden crumb-topped casserole tastes like you spent hours preparing it, but actually it takes just minutes. I
occasionally substitute creamy Italian dressing in place of ranch for a more robust flavor. —Claire Darby
New Castle, Delaware

4 medium baking potatoes, peeled and cut into 1/4-inch slices
1 cup ranch salad dressing
1 teaspoon salt
1/4 teaspoon pepper
1/3 cup dry bread crumbs

Toss potatoes with dressing, salt and pepper. Place in a greased 13-in. x 9-in. x 2-in. baking pan. Sprinkle with bread crumbs. Cover and bake at 375° for 30 minutes. Uncover and bake 20 minutes longer or until potatoes are tender. **Yield:** 4-6 servings.

Cran-Raspberry Gelatin

(Pictured at right)

You'll love the sweet-tart flavor and beautiful ruby-red color of this chunky fruit salad. It's great served with a Thanksgiving turkey or with most any kind of meat.
—Kathy Jarvis, Bear Creek, Wisconsin

✓ **Nutritional Analysis included**

1 package (3 ounces) raspberry gelatin
1-1/2 cups boiling water
1 cup fresh *or* frozen cranberries
1/2 cup raspberry jam *or* spreadable fruit
1 can (8 ounces) crushed pineapple, undrained

In a bowl, dissolve gelatin in water. Place cranberries, jam and gelatin mixture in a blender or food processor; cover and process until the cranberries are coarsely chopped. Transfer to a bowl; stir in pineapple. Refrigerate until set. **Yield:** 8 servings. **Nutritional Analysis:** One 1/2-cup serving (prepared with sugar-free gelatin and spreadable fruit) equals 58 calories, 30 mg sodium, 0 cholesterol, 14 gm carbohydrate, 1 gm protein, trace fat. **Diabetic Exchange:** 1 fruit.

Fruited Sweet Potatoes

(Pictured below)

Dress up convenient canned sweet potatoes and apricot halves with brown sugar and cinnamon. This fast-to-fix side dish is delicious with a ham dinner.

—Nancy Zimmerman
Cape May Court House, New Jersey

☑ **Nutritional Analysis included**

2 cans (15 ounces *each*) cut sweet potatoes
1 can (15-1/4 ounces) apricot halves
3 tablespoons brown sugar
1 tablespoon cornstarch
1/8 teaspoon ground cinnamon

Drain sweet potatoes and apricots, reserving 1/2 cup syrup from each. If desired, cut apricots into fourths. Place potatoes and apricots in a greased 1-1/2-qt. baking dish. In a saucepan, combine brown sugar, cornstarch, cinnamon and reserved syrup; stir until smooth. Bring to a boil over medium-high heat. Remove from the heat; pour over the potatoes and apricots. Bake, uncovered, at 350° for 25 minutes or until bubbly. **Yield:** 6 servings. **Nutritional Analysis:** One 1/2-cup serving (prepared with light apricot halves) equals 192 calories, 68 mg sodium, 0 cholesterol, 46 gm carbohydrate, 2 gm protein, trace fat. **Diabetic Exchanges:** 2 starch, 1 fruit.

Curried Cashews

Curry powder is the key to these tasty cashews, perfect as a party snack or hostess gift. These unusual nuts were served at an open house I attended. I tracked down the recipe and now make them often for friends.

—Gertrude Wood, *Ellicottville, New York*

1/4 cup butter *or* margarine
1 can (10 ounces) salted cashews
2 tablespoons curry powder
1/2 teaspoon salt

In a skillet, melt butter. Add cashews; cook and stir over medium heat until lightly browned, about 10 minutes. Remove to paper towels to drain. Sprinkle with curry powder and salt. **Yield:** 2 cups.

Cran-Raspberry Gelatin
Almond-Topped Chicken
Fruited Sweet Potatoes

SOME DAYS when you're running behind schedule, a mere 10 minutes is just about all the time you have to get a home-made-tasting meal on the table.

So the next time you're hungry, hurried and truly "down to the wire" on feeding your family, take a deep breath and count to 10. Then turn to this one-of-a-kind chapter.

You will quickly uncover a mouth-watering variety of full-flavored dishes that can be table-ready in just 10 minutes. Folks will think you were in the kitchen all day long!

ON-THE-RUN RECIPES. Clockwise from upper left: Honey-Mustard Pork Scallopini (p. 76), Cheesy Squash (p. 73), Sweet 'n' Spicy Chicken (p. 74) and Chocolate Berry Parfaits (p. 79).

Parmesan Noodles

(Pictured at right)

This is an excellent side dish that even kids love. It's perfect when you don't have time to peel potatoes. —Ruth Dirks
Ravensdale, Washington

1 package (8 ounces) medium
  egg noodles
3 tablespoons chopped green
  onions
2 tablespoons butter *or*
  margarine
1/2 cup grated Parmesan cheese
Garlic salt and pepper to taste

Cook noodles according to package directions; drain. Toss with onions, butter, Parmesan cheese, garlic salt and pepper. **Yield:** 4 servings.

Garlic Broccoli Spears

Looking for an effortless way to liven up fresh broccoli? I toss cooked spears with garlic and lemon juice for simple, savory results. —Shirley Glaab
Hattiesburg, Mississippi

1 pound fresh broccoli, cut into spears
2 tablespoons olive *or* vegetable oil
1 tablespoon lemon juice
1 garlic clove, minced
1/4 teaspoon salt
1/8 teaspoon pepper

Place the broccoli in a saucepan with a small amount of water; cover and cook until crisp-tender. Meanwhile, combine remaining ingredients. Drain broccoli and place in a serving dish; add lemon mixture and toss to coat. Serve immediately. **Yield:** 4-6 servings.

Fast Fudge Sundaes

(Pictured above right)

For big chocolate taste, I treat my family to this thick ice cream topping. It's a snap to make the fudgy sauce. And we like it better than the store-bought kind.
—Sue Gronholz, Columbus, Wisconsin

1/2 cup semisweet chocolate chips
1 square (1 ounce) unsweetened chocolate
3 tablespoons butter *or* margarine
1 cup confectioners' sugar
1 can (5 ounces) evaporated milk
1/2 teaspoon vanilla extract
Ice cream

Place the chocolate and butter in a microwave-safe dish. Microwave, uncovered, on medium-high for 1 to 1-1/2 minutes. Stir in the sugar, milk and vanilla; beat until smooth. Microwave, uncovered, on medium for 5-6

**Tuna Burgers
Parmesan Noodles
Fast Fudge Sundaes**

minutes or until bubbly. Serve over ice cream. **Yield:** 1-1/4 cups. **Editor's Note:** This recipe was tested in a 700-watt microwave.

Tuna Burgers

(Pictured above)

When I fix these burgers, my husband likes his topped with melted Swiss cheese and Dijon mustard. You can also substitute salmon for the tuna. —Joann Brasington
Sumter, South Carolina

1 can (6 ounces) tuna, drained and flaked
1 egg
1/2 cup seasoned bread crumbs
1/3 cup finely chopped onion
1/4 cup chopped celery
1/4 cup chopped sweet red pepper
1/4 cup mayonnaise
2 tablespoons chili sauce
1/2 teaspoon dill weed
1/4 teaspoon salt
1/8 teaspoon pepper
Dash hot pepper sauce
Dash Worcestershire sauce
4 hamburger buns, split
Tomato slices and lettuce leaves, optional

In a bowl, combine the first 13 ingredients; mix well. Shape into four patties (mixture will be soft). Coat a skillet with nonstick cooking spray; fry patties for 3-4 minutes on each side or until cooked through. Serve on buns with tomato and lettuce if desired. **Yield:** 4 servings.

Maple Baked Beans

I came up with this recipe in a pinch after running out of baked beans at our oldest daughter's birthday party. I dressed up canned beans with maple syrup and a few other ingredients to produce this sweet, saucy version that tastes like homemade. —Brenda Tetreault
Newport Center, Vermont

1 medium onion, chopped
1 to 2 tablespoons vegetable oil
3 cans (28 ounces *each*) baked beans
1-1/2 teaspoons ground mustard
1 teaspoon garlic salt
3/4 to 1 cup maple syrup

In a Dutch oven or large kettle, saute onion in oil until tender. Add the beans, mustard and garlic salt. Cook over medium heat until bubbly, stirring occasionally. Add maple syrup; heat through, stirring occasionally. **Yield:** 8-10 servings.

Creole Rice

I've found a fast and fantastic way to turn leftover rice into a spectacular side dish. I give it a boost of flavor with Creole seasoning and pepper, then sprinkle it with paprika for color. —Sundra Lewis, Bogalusa, Louisiana

1/4 cup butter *or* margarine
1 teaspoon Creole seasoning*
1/8 teaspoon pepper
2 cups cooked long grain rice

In a saucepan, melt butter; add Creole seasoning and pepper. Cook over medium heat for 3 minutes. Stir in rice. Cover and heat through. **Yield:** 4 servings. ***Editor's Note:** The following spices may be substituted for the Creole seasoning—1/2 teaspoon *each* paprika and garlic powder, and a pinch *each* cayenne pepper, dried thyme and ground cumin.

Cheesy Squash

(Pictured on page 71)

I'm a retired police officer and now a deputy sheriff who loves to cook. But with my busy schedule, I must rely on speedy side dishes like this one. The squash retains its fresh taste and cooks to a perfect tender-crispness. You can give this cheesy treatment to other fresh veggies, too. It's so quick that I make some variation of it a few times a week. —Randy Lawrence, Clinton, Mississippi

1 small zucchini
1 small yellow summer squash
Salt and pepper to taste
1 cup (4 ounces) shredded mozzarella cheese
1/4 cup grated Parmesan cheese

Cut zucchini and yellow squash into 1/4-in. slices. Place in a greased shallow 1-qt. baking dish. Sprinkle with salt and pepper. Top with cheeses. Broil 4 in. from the heat for 7-10 minutes or until the squash is crisp-tender and cheese is bubbly. Serve immediately. **Yield:** 2 servings.

Onion Rye Breadsticks

(Pictured below)

An envelope of onion soup mix provides the fast flavor you'll find in these rye snacks. They're an easy accompaniment to soup or salad when time's at a premium. The buttery mixture is terrific on multi-grain bread, too. —Barbara Brown, Kentwood, Michigan

1/2 cup butter *or* margarine, softened
1 envelope onion soup mix
14 slices rye bread

Combine butter and soup mix; spread over bread. Cut each slice into 3/4-in. strips and place on ungreased baking sheets. Bake at 350° for 5-6 minutes or until butter is melted and breadsticks are crisp. **Yield:** about 7 dozen.

Broccoli Potato Soup

(Pictured below)

I rely on a few handy ingredients to make canned soup taste just like homemade. The creamy mixture that results is hearty with chunks of broccoli and potato. —Barbara Baker, Valparaiso, Indiana

2 cups broccoli florets
1 small onion, thinly sliced
1 tablespoon butter *or* margarine
1 can (10-3/4 ounces) condensed cream of potato soup, undiluted
1 cup milk
1/2 cup water
3/4 teaspoon minced fresh basil *or* 1/4 teaspoon dried basil
1/4 teaspoon pepper
1/3 cup shredded cheddar cheese

In a large saucepan, saute broccoli and onion in butter until tender. Stir in soup, milk, water, basil and pepper; heat through. Add cheese; stir until melted. **Yield:** 4 servings.

Broccoli Potato Soup
Onion Rye Breadsticks

Barbecued Ham Buns

The recipe for these hot ham sandwiches came from a best friend's mother. I often prepare them as a quick lunch for my husband and me. The versatile recipe can be increased and prepared in the oven or slow cooker to feed a crowd.
—*Janet Gregory, Spring Creek, Pennsylvania*

1/3 cup ketchup
1/3 cup water
3 tablespoons brown sugar
3 tablespoons sweet pickle relish
1 tablespoon prepared mustard
1 tablespoon vinegar
1 pound thinly sliced fully cooked ham
6 hamburger buns, split

In a large microwave-safe dish, combine the first six ingredients; mix well. Stir in ham. Cover and microwave on high for 2 minutes. Stir. Microwave 1-2 minutes longer or until heated through. Serve on buns. **Yield: 6 servings. Editor's Note:** This recipe was tested in an 850-watt microwave.

Curried Tuna Sandwiches

(Pictured below)

If you're looking for a change from traditional tuna sandwiches, try this recipe I developed. It includes my favorite ingredients from a few different tuna salad recipes, including apples, raisins and curry. The first time I combined them, I loved the results! —*Lorene Corbett Tryon, Nebraska*

☑ Nutritional Analysis included

1 can (6 ounces) tuna, drained and flaked
1/4 cup chopped apple
2 tablespoons raisins
2 tablespoons mayonnaise *or* salad dressing
1/4 teaspoon onion salt
1/8 teaspoon curry powder

Curried Tuna Sandwiches

2 sandwich rolls, split
Additional mayonnaise, optional
Lettuce leaves

In a bowl, combine the first six ingredients; mix well. Spread rolls with additional mayonnaise if desired; top each with 1/2 cup tuna mixture and lettuce. **Yield: 2 servings. Nutritional Analysis:** One serving (prepared with low-sodium tuna and fat-free mayonnaise; calculated without roll) equals 170 calories, 375 mg sodium, 15 mg cholesterol, 15 gm carbohydrate, 26 gm protein, 1 gm fat. **Diabetic Exchanges:** 3 very lean meat, 1 fruit.

Three-Fruit Salad

Nothing could be easier than stirring up this refreshing salad. The tangy honey mustard salad dressing is a wonderful complement to the different fruit flavors.
—*Ruth Andrewson, Leavenworth, Washington*

☑ Nutritional Analysis included

2 medium ripe bananas, sliced
1 cup pineapple chunks
1 cup seedless grapes, halved
3 tablespoons honey mustard salad dressing

In a bowl, combine the fruit. Add dressing and toss to coat. Cover and refrigerate until serving. **Yield: 4-6 servings. Nutritional Analysis:** One 1/2-cup serving (prepared with fat-free salad dressing) equals 79 calories, 39 mg sodium, 0 cholesterol, 20 gm carbohydrate, 1 gm protein, trace fat. **Diabetic Exchange:** 1 fruit.

Sweet 'n' Spicy Chicken

(Pictured on page 71)

My husband and three children love this tender chicken in a spicy sauce. Peach preserves add just a touch of sweetness, while taco seasoning and salsa give this dish some kick. To make it even zippier, add more taco seasoning and use spicier salsa. —*Sheri White, Higley, Arizona*

☑ Nutritional Analysis included

1 pound boneless skinless chicken breasts, cut into 1/2-inch cubes
3 tablespoons taco seasoning
1 to 2 tablespoons vegetable oil
1 jar (11 ounces) chunky salsa
1/2 cup peach preserves
Hot cooked rice

Place the chicken in a large resealable plastic bag; add taco seasoning and toss to coat. In a skillet, brown chicken in oil. Combine salsa and preserves; stir into skillet. Bring to a boil. Reduce heat; cover and simmer for 2-3 minutes or until meat juices run clear. Serve over rice. **Yield: 4 servings. Nutritional Analysis:** One serving (prepared with 1 tablespoon oil and sugar-free preserves; calculated without rice) equals 210 calories, 591 mg sodium, 63 mg cholesterol, 17 gm carbohydrate, 23 gm protein, 6 gm fat. **Diabetic Exchanges:** 3 very lean meat, 1 fruit, 1/2 fat.

Roast Beef Roll-Ups
Applesauce Sandwiches

Tangy Poppy Seed Dressing

My sister-in-law was kind enough to share her recipe for this deliciously tangy salad dressing. A super homemade mixture, it stirs up in a jiffy. —Michele Prendergast
Kingston, New York

  1/2 cup vegetable oil
  1/4 cup cider *or* white wine vinegar
    1 tablespoon honey
    1 teaspoon Dijon mustard
    1 teaspoon poppy seeds
  1/8 teaspoon garlic powder
  1/8 teaspoon salt
Mixed salad greens

In a jar with tight-fitting lid, combine the first seven ingredients and shake well. Serve over salad greens. **Yield:** 3/4 cup.

Applesauce Sandwiches

(Pictured above)

Cinnamon and sugar spice up the fun sandwiches that I make for breakfast or a snack. Since we have plenty of apple trees, I often use homemade applesauce. But the store-bought kind tastes almost as good.
—Eunice Bralley, Thornville, Ohio

  1 cup applesauce
  8 slices bread

  1/4 cup butter *or* margarine, softened
    1 tablespoon sugar
  1/4 teaspoon ground cinnamon

Spread the applesauce on four slices of bread; top with remaining bread. Lightly butter the outsides of sandwiches. Toast on a hot griddle for 3-4 minutes on each side or until golden brown. Combine sugar and cinnamon; sprinkle over hot sandwiches. Serve immediately. **Yield:** 4 servings.

Roast Beef Roll-Ups

(Pictured above)

You can't beat these flavorful sandwiches seasoned with salsa. Serve them with a green salad and tortilla chips for a cool dinner on a warm evening. —Susan Scott
Asheville, North Carolina

  1/2 cup sour cream
  1/4 cup mayonnaise
  1/4 cup salsa
  10 flour tortillas (8 inches)
    1 pound thinly sliced cooked roast beef
  10 large lettuce leaves
Additional salsa

Combine sour cream, mayonnaise and salsa; spread over tortillas. Top with roast beef and lettuce. Roll up tightly and secure with toothpicks; cut in half. Serve with salsa. **Yield:** 10 servings.

Ranch Chicken Salad

Ranch Chicken Salad

(Pictured above)

My weeknights are busy, so I rely on quick meals like this flavorful main-dish salad. With seasoned chicken strips, cheese and corn chips, it is one hurry-up meal the whole family enjoys. —Valerie Leist, Bulverde, Texas

    1 pound boneless skinless chicken breasts, cut
      into 1/4-inch strips
    2 teaspoons chili powder
    1 tablespoon vegetable oil
    1 package (16 ounces) ready-to-serve salad
    1 cup (4 ounces) shredded cheddar cheese
  3/4 cup ranch salad dressing
  3/4 cup salsa
  1/2 cup corn chips *or crushed tortilla chips*

Sprinkle chicken with chili powder. In a skillet, cook chicken in oil for 6 minutes or until the juices run clear. Meanwhile, place salad greens in a large bowl or on individual plates. Top with cheese and chicken. Combine salad dressing and salsa; drizzle over chicken. Top with chips. **Yield:** 8 servings.

Honey-Mustard Pork Scallopini

(Pictured on page 70)

This is one of the quickest main-dish entrees I have… and one of the most delicious. My family loves honey and mustard. Pounding the boneless chops tenderizes them and makes them cook quickly. —Stephanie Moon
Green Bay, Wisconsin

    4 boneless pork chops (about 4 ounces *each*),
      trimmed
    2 tablespoons honey
    2 tablespoons spicy brown mustard
  1/3 cup crushed butter-flavored crackers (about 8
      crackers)
  1/3 cup dry bread crumbs

    1 tablespoon vegetable oil
    1 tablespoon butter *or margarine*

Flatten pork to 1/8-in. thickness. Combine honey and mustard; brush over both sides of pork. In a shallow bowl, combine cracker and bread crumbs; add pork and turn to coat. In a skillet, heat oil and butter. Fry pork for 2-3 minutes on each side or until crisp and juices run clear. **Yield:** 4 servings.

Tuna Alfredo

For quick comfort, use a packaged noodles and sauce mix to make this old-fashioned-tasting tuna casserole. When it's just my husband and me for dinner, I rely on this fast favorite. —Vicki Didier, Machesney Park, Illinois

    1 package (4.4 ounces) quick-cooking Alfredo
      noodles and sauce mix*
    1 can (6 ounces) tuna, drained and flaked
    1 tablespoon chopped green onion

Prepare the noodles and sauce mix according to package directions. Stir in tuna and onion. Serve immediately. **Yield:** 2-3 servings. ***Editor's Note:** This recipe was tested with Lipton Alfredo Mix.

Quick Elephant Ears

(Pictured below)

I fry flour tortillas for a few seconds in oil, then have all eight children help sprinkle them with cinnamon and sugar. They're fun to make for a large group. —Terry Lynn Ayers, Anderson, Indiana

  1-1/2 cups sugar
      2 teaspoons ground cinnamon
  Oil for frying
      10 flour tortillas (7 inches)

Combine sugar and cinnamon in a shallow bowl or large plate; set aside. In a skillet, heat 1/2 in. of oil. Place one tortilla at a time in skillet. Cook for 5 seconds; turn and cook 10 seconds longer or until browned. Place in sugar mixture and turn to coat. Serve immediately. **Yield:** 10 servings.

Quick Elephant Ears

Creamy Dill Dressing

This refreshing, easy-to-mix salad dressing scores big with my family and friends. The creamy blend adds big dill flavor to garden-fresh salads, yet it's thick enough to use as a lively dip for raw veggies. —Kathryn Anderson
Wallkill, New York

    1 cup mayonnaise
  1/3 cup sour cream
    3 tablespoons half-and-half cream
    1 tablespoon dill weed
1-1/2 teaspoons sugar
  3/4 teaspoon lemon juice
  1/4 teaspoon garlic powder
  1/4 teaspoon Worcestershire sauce

In a small bowl, combine all of the ingredients; stir until smooth. Cover and chill. Serve over salad greens or as a dip for raw vegetables. Store in the refrigerator. **Yield:** 1-1/4 cups.

Flavorful Mac and Cheese

(Pictured below right)

It's a snap to stir together this zesty macaroni and cheese dish, thanks to the Mexican-seasoned process cheese sauce. If your family prefers a little less zip, use the original flavor for equally satisfying results. —Sandy Buchanan
Lake Alfred, Florida

    1 package (7 ounces) elbow macaroni
    1 jar (8 ounces) mild Mexican-
      seasoned *or* plain process
      cheese sauce
1-1/2 cups chopped fully cooked
      ham
    1 can (8 ounces) crushed
      pineapple, drained
  1/2 cup chopped green pepper
  1/4 cup finely chopped onion

Cook macaroni according to package directions; drain. Stir in the cheese sauce until combined. Add remaining ingredients. Transfer to a serving bowl; serve immediately. **Yield:** 4 servings.

In-a-Hurry Curry Soup

Curry makes this speedy soup so delicious. I just open a few cans, and I have a quick hearty meal in minutes. The wonderful aroma brings my family to the table so quickly that I don't even have a chance to call them first. —Denise Elder
Hanover, Ontario

    1 cup chopped onion
  3/4 teaspoon curry powder
    2 tablespoons butter *or*
      margarine
    2 chicken bouillon cubes
    1 cup hot water

    1 can (14-1/2 ounces) diced tomatoes,
      undrained
    1 can (10-3/4 ounces) condensed cream of
      celery soup, undiluted
    1 cup half-and-half cream
    1 can (5 ounces) white chicken, drained

In a 3-qt. saucepan, saute onion and curry powder in butter until onion is tender. Dissolve bouillon in water; add to the pan. Stir in remaining ingredients and heat through. **Yield:** about 5 servings.

Tropical Stuffed Pears

I fill pear halves with a sweet and creamy concoction of pineapple, coconut and pecans. This tempting dessert is special enough for guests but so easy to make. You can serve it after a quick lunch or dinner. —Deborah Reno
Central City, Kentucky

    1 cup (8 ounces) sour cream
    1 can (8 ounces) crushed pineapple, drained
    1 cup miniature marshmallows
    1 cup flaked coconut
  1/2 cup chopped pecans
    1 can (29 ounces) pear halves, drained
Lettuce leaves, optional

In a bowl, combine the sour cream, pineapple, marshmallows, coconut and pecans. Place pears on lettuce if desired; spoon pineapple mixture into the center of each. **Yield:** 6-7 servings.

Flavorful Mac and Cheese

Parmesan Chicken

(Pictured at right)

People can't believe it when I tell them how little time it takes to fix this delicious chicken. It's very moist inside and so pretty to serve with its lovely basil-flecked coating. —Mollie Hall, San Ramon, California

**4 boneless skinless chicken breast halves
(1 pound)**
1/2 cup seasoned bread crumbs
1/4 cup grated Parmesan cheese
1/2 teaspoon dried basil
1 egg
1 tablespoon butter *or* margarine
1 tablespoon vegetable oil

Flatten chicken to 1/4-in. thickness. In a shallow bowl, combine bread crumbs, Parmesan cheese and basil. In another bowl, beat the egg. Dip chicken into egg, then coat with crumb mixture. In a large skillet, brown chicken in butter and oil over medium heat for 3-5 minutes on each side or until juices run clear. **Yield: 4 servings.**

Italian Vegetable Saute

(Pictured at right)

This speedy side dish was the result of an abundant crop of green peppers my parents grew. —Kenda Nicholson, Honey Grove, Texas

✓ Nutritional Analysis included

2 medium green peppers, sliced
1 garlic clove, minced
1 teaspoon Italian seasoning
1 tablespoon butter *or* margarine
1 cup cherry tomatoes, halved
1/2 cup seasoned croutons, optional

In a skillet, saute the peppers, garlic and Italian seasoning in butter until peppers are crisp-tender, about 5 minutes. Add tomatoes; cook for 1-2 minutes or until heated through. Sprinkle with croutons if desired. **Yield: 4 servings. Nutritional Analysis:** One 1/2-cup serving (prepared with margarine and without croutons) equals 52 calories, 38 mg sodium, 0 cholesterol, 6 gm carbohydrate, 1 gm protein, 3 gm fat. **Diabetic Exchanges:** 1 vegetable, 1/2 fat.

Candy Store Pudding

(Pictured above right)

For variety, substitute miniature chocolate chips, pecans, gumdrops or whatever else you have on hand for the peanuts and mini marshmallows. —Sue Thomas Casa Grande, Arizona

1 cup cold milk
1 package (3.9 ounces) instant chocolate pudding mix
1 cup whipping cream, whipped

Candy Store Pudding
Italian Vegetable Saute
Parmesan Chicken

1/2 to 1 cup miniature marshmallows
1/4 to 1/2 cup chopped salted peanuts

In a bowl, whisk milk and pudding mix for 2 minutes. Fold in whipped cream, marshmallows and peanuts. Spoon into individual dessert dishes. Refrigerate until serving. **Yield: 4 servings.**

Tangy Broccoli

For years, my family has spiced up vegetable side dishes with this tangy sauce. Even my dad, who doesn't care much for broccoli, will eat it when it's topped with this bright fast-to-fix sauce. —Kristi Wise, Linwood, Kansas

✓ Nutritional Analysis included

1 cup fresh *or* frozen broccoli florets
3 tablespoons mayonnaise *or* salad dressing
2 tablespoons prepared mustard
1 teaspoon prepared horseradish

Place the broccoli and a small amount of water in a saucepan; cover and cook for 5-8 minutes or until crisp-tender. Meanwhile, combine remaining ingredients. Drain broccoli; top with sauce. **Yield: 2 servings** (about 1/3 cup sauce). **Nutritional Analysis:** One serving (1/2 cup broccoli with 2 tablespoons sauce, prepared with fat-free mayonnaise) equals 34 calories, 296 mg sodium, 0 cholesterol, 6 gm carbohydrate, 2 gm protein, 1 gm fat. **Diabetic Exchange:** 1 vegetable.

Fluffy Hot Chocolate

Melted marshmallows provide the frothy texture that you'll savor in this sweet and speedy warm beverage. They're also what makes this hot chocolate different from (and better than) the instant kind you make from a store-bought mix. Chocolaty and comforting, it's our daughter's favorite.
    —Jo Ann Schimcek, Weimar, Texas

  8 teaspoons sugar
  4 teaspoons baking cocoa
  4 cups milk
1-1/2 cups miniature marshmallows
  1 teaspoon vanilla extract

In a saucepan, combine the first four ingredients. Cook and stir over medium heat until the marshmallows are melted, about 8 minutes. Remove from the heat; stir in vanilla. Ladle into mugs. **Yield:** 4 servings.

Sausage Bean Stew

(Pictured below)

I made this colorful, robust stew often when our three kids were living at home. Since it calls for lots of canned vegetables, it stirs up in a jiffy. It's versatile, too—you can substitute cubed cooked turkey, chicken, ham or beef for the sausage.
    —Barb Schutz, Pandora, Ohio

  1 pound fully cooked smoked sausage, halved and cut into 1/4-inch slices
  2 cans (10 ounces *each*) diced tomatoes and green chilies, undrained
  1 can (15-1/2 ounces) great northern beans, rinsed and drained
  1 can (15-1/4 ounces) whole kernel corn, drained
  1 can (15 ounces) black beans, rinsed and drained

Sausage Bean Stew

  1 can (15 ounces) lima beans, drained
  1/2 teaspoon salt
  1/8 teaspoon pepper
Hot cooked rice, optional

In a large saucepan, combine the first eight ingredients. Heat through. Serve in bowls over rice if desired. **Yield:** 6-8 servings (2 quarts).

Chicken Mushroom Fettuccine

I depend on this recipe when I get home late from work and my hungry family wants something rich and delicious for dinner. It's quick, too, because it uses canned chicken and fresh mushrooms that I buy presliced.
    —Susanne Stevens, Cedar City, Utah

  1 package (16 ounces) fettuccine
  1 pound fresh mushrooms, sliced
  4 garlic cloves, minced
  1/4 cup butter *or* margarine
  2 cans (5 ounces *each*) chunk white chicken, drained
  1/2 cup milk
1-1/3 cups grated Parmesan cheese

Cook fettuccine according to package directions. Meanwhile, in a skillet, saute mushrooms and garlic in butter for 2-3 minutes. Add chicken and milk; cook for 5-7 minutes or until heated through. Drain fettuccine; add to the skillet. Sprinkle with Parmesan cheese and toss to coat. **Yield:** 6 servings.

Chocolate Berry Parfaits

(Pictured page 70)

This creamy dessert is easy to make for weekday dinners, yet pretty enough for company. Instant chocolate pudding is layered with a mixture of pureed strawberries and whipped cream to create yummy parfaits.
    —Lynn McAllister, Mount Ulla, North Carolina

  2 cups cold milk
  1 package (3.9 ounces) instant chocolate pudding mix
  1 package (10 ounces) frozen sweetened strawberries, thawed
  1 cup whipping cream
  1/4 cup confectioners' sugar
Sliced fresh strawberries, optional

In a mixing bowl, beat the milk and pudding mix until thick and smooth, about 2 minutes; set aside. Drain strawberries (discard the juice or save for another use); place the berries in a blender. Cover and process until smooth; set aside. In a mixing bowl, beat cream and sugar until stiff peaks form. Gently fold in the strawberry puree. Divide half of the chocolate pudding among four or six parfait glasses or bowls. Top with half of the strawberry mixture. Repeat layers. Garnish with a strawberry slice if desired. **Yield:** 4-6 servings. **Editor's Note:** 2 cups of whipped topping may be substituted for the whipping cream and sugar.

Chapter 6

GOOD EATING doesn't require a lot of extra effort or running around. By relying on a wide range of packaged convenience foods available on your grocer's shelves, you can come up with fast fixes to your dining dilemmas. So you can put together a mouth-watering meal pronto!

Or save yourself the shopping time—and money, too—by making your own. This chapter also offers an appealing assortment of homemade mix recipes that are quick to assemble in advance and get you started on menu planning.

HOMEMADE MAGIC. Hawaiian Cake (p. 95).

Fast Fixes With Mixes

WHEN the clock starts ticking closer to dinnertime and you're at a loss for what you ought to make, just peek into your pantry! You can have a tasty home-prepared meal ready in minutes by simply dressing up a boxed mix or combining canned soups.

Pantry Shortcuts Save Time

DOES stocking a pantry summon up images of Grandma's groaning shelves of sugar, flour and salt? Not anymore!

Today's busy cooks are discovering that—in addition to those traditional basics—keeping a variety of flavorful new-generation staples in their cupboards, refrigerator and freezer can greatly simplify meal planning and preparation. Here are some examples of what you might want to have on hand:

- ❏ Bouillon cubes or granules
- ❏ Bread crumbs
- ❏ Brownie, cake and pudding mixes
- ❏ Canned frostings
- ❏ Canned meats and seafood
- ❏ Canned mushrooms
- ❏ Canned pie filling
- ❏ Canned pumpkin
- ❏ Canned soups and dried soup mixes
- ❏ Canned vegetables
- ❏ Chocolate chips
- ❏ Corn bread mix
- ❏ Croutons
- ❏ Diced plain or seasoned tomatoes
- ❏ Evaporated and sweetened condensed milk
- ❏ Flour and corn tortillas
- ❏ Frozen vegetables
- ❏ Frozen whipped topping
- ❏ Fruit—canned and dried
- ❏ Grated and shredded cheese
- ❏ Honey
- ❏ Hot pepper sauce
- ❏ Ketchup and mustard
- ❏ Nuts for baking and snacking
- ❏ Pasta and pasta sauces
- ❏ Peanut butter
- ❏ Pickles and olives
- ❏ Pita bread
- ❏ Pizza crust mix
- ❏ Prepared pie shells
- ❏ Refrigerated pastry dough
- ❏ Rice, potato and stuffing mixes
- ❏ Salsa
- ❏ Soy sauce
- ❏ Taco and chili seasoning mixes

Chicken Tortilla Soup

(Pictured at right)

A few additions to canned cream of chicken soup provide the comforting flavor found in my mock chicken dumpling soup. The chunks of chicken are nice and tender. And you can't tell that the dumplings are actually tortilla strips.
—*Carolyn Griffin, Macon, Georgia*

✓ Nutritional Analysis included

> 1 can (10-3/4 ounces) condensed cream of chicken soup, undiluted
> 4 cups water
> 2 cups cubed cooked chicken
> 4 flour tortillas (7 inches), cut into 2-1/2-inch strips
> Minced fresh parsley

In a 3-qt. saucepan, bring the soup and water to a boil. Stir in the chicken and tortilla strips; reduce heat to medium-low. Cook, uncovered, for 25-30 minutes, stirring occasionally. Sprinkle with parsley. **Yield:** 6 servings. **Nutritional Analysis:** One 1-cup serving (prepared with low-fat soup and fat-free tortillas) equals 149 calories, 426 mg sodium, 32 mg cholesterol, 21 gm carbohydrate, 10 gm protein, 2 gm fat. **Diabetic Exchanges:** 1 starch, 1 lean meat.

Beefy Rice Dinner

I turn a boxed rice mix into a complete meal by adding ground beef, celery and green pepper. It's so quick to fix and makes a flavorful, filling main dish. —*Mildred Sherrer Bay City, Texas*

> 1 package (6.8 ounces) beef-flavored rice mix
> 1/2 pound lean ground beef
> 1/3 cup chopped celery
> 1/3 cup chopped green pepper
> 1/8 to 1/4 teaspoon salt
> 1/8 teaspoon pepper
> 1/3 cup shredded cheddar cheese

Prepare rice according to package directions. Meanwhile, in a large skillet, cook the beef, celery and green pepper until the meat is browned and vegetables are tender; drain. Add rice, salt and pepper. Transfer to a greased 2-qt. baking dish. Sprinkle with cheese. Bake, uncovered, at 350° for 10-15 minutes or until heated through and cheese is melted. **Yield:** 4-6 servings.

Cheesy Broccoli Pie

Biscuit mix is the secret to the no-fuss crust in this tasty broccoli dish. There's no need to roll out a crust—it makes its own as it bakes. I keep one pie in the freezer to thaw and warm up in a jiffy. —*Judy Siegrist Albuquerque, New Mexico*

> 2 packages (10 ounces *each*) frozen chopped broccoli, thawed
> 3 cups (12 ounces) shredded cheddar cheese, *divided*

Chicken Tortilla Soup
Simple Taco Soup

2/3 cup chopped onion
3 eggs
1-1/3 cups milk
3/4 cup biscuit/baking mix
1/2 teaspoon salt
1/4 teaspoon pepper

In a large bowl, combine broccoli, 2 cups cheese and onion. In another bowl, combine eggs, milk, biscuit mix, salt and pepper; mix well. Pour over broccoli mixture; toss gently. Pour into two greased 9-in. pie plates. Bake at 400° for 25-30 minutes or until a knife inserted near the center comes out clean. Sprinkle with the remaining cheese; return to the oven for 1-2 minutes or until melted. Let stand 5-10 minutes before cutting. **Yield:** 2 pies (6 servings each). **Editor's Note:** Baked pies may be frozen after cooling completely. To reheat, thaw and bake at 400° for 15-20 minutes or until heated through.

Simple Taco Soup

(Pictured above)

We first sampled this chili-like soup at a church dinner.

It's a warming dish on a cold day, and since it uses packaged seasonings and several cans of vegetables, it's a snap to prepare. —Glenda Taylor, Sand Springs, Oklahoma

2 pounds ground beef
1 envelope taco seasoning
1-1/2 cups water
1 can (15-3/4 ounces) mild chili beans
1 can (15-1/4 ounces) whole kernel corn, drained
1 can (15 ounces) pinto beans, rinsed and drained
1 can (14-1/2 ounces) stewed tomatoes
1 can (10 ounces) diced tomatoes and green chilies, undrained
1 can (4 ounces) chopped green chilies, optional
1 envelope ranch salad dressing mix

In a Dutch oven or large kettle, brown beef; drain. Add taco seasoning and mix well. Stir in remaining ingredients. Simmer, uncovered, for 15 minutes or until heated through, stirring occasionally. **Yield:** 6-8 servings (about 2 quarts).

Nacho Potato Soup

(Pictured below)

This soup is super easy to make! Since it starts with a box of au gratin potatoes, you don't have to peel or slice them. A co-worker recommended the recipe to me. Now my husband requests it often. —Sherry Dickerson
Sebastopol, Mississippi

    1 package (5-1/4 ounces) au gratin potatoes
    1 can (11 ounces) whole kernel corn, drained
    1 can (10 ounces) diced tomatoes and green
       chilies, undrained
    2 cups water
    2 cups milk
    2 cups cubed process American cheese
Dash hot pepper sauce, optional
Minced fresh parsley, optional

In a 3-qt. saucepan, combine the potatoes and sauce mix, corn, tomatoes and water; mix well. Bring to a boil. Reduce heat; cover and simmer for 15-18 minutes or until the potatoes are tender. Add milk, cheese and hot pepper sauce if desired; cook and stir until the cheese is melted. Garnish with parsley if desired. **Yield:** 6-8 servings (2 quarts).

Cheeseburger 'n' Fries Casserole

(Pictured below)

Believe it or not, there are only four ingredients in this quick recipe—and you're likely to have them all on hand. Kids love it because, as the name suggests, it combines two of their favorite fast foods. —Karen Owen
Rising Sun, Indiana

Cheeseburger 'n' Fries Casserole
Nacho Potato Soup

2 pounds lean ground beef
1 can (10-3/4 ounces) condensed golden mushroom soup, undiluted
1 can (10-3/4 ounces) condensed cheddar cheese soup, undiluted
1 package (20 ounces) frozen crinkle-cut French fries

In a skillet, brown the beef; drain. Stir in soups. Pour into a greased 13-in. x 9-in. x 2-in. baking dish. Arrange French fries on top. Bake, uncovered, at 350° for 50-55 minutes or until the fries are golden brown. **Yield:** 6-8 servings.

Chicken Can-Can

This fast-to-assemble recipe combines six cans of handy pantry ingredients. Just heat and serve! You can substitute any kind of noodles for the chow mein noodles.
—Carla Hodenfield, Mandan, North Dakota

1 can (12 ounces) evaporated milk
1 can (10-3/4 ounces) condensed cream of celery soup, undiluted
1 can (10-3/4 ounces) condensed cream of chicken soup, undiluted
1 can (10-3/4 ounces) condensed chicken noodle soup, undiluted
1/4 cup all-purpose flour
1 can (10 ounces) chunk white chicken, drained
1 can (5 ounces) chow mein noodles

In a large skillet, combine the first five ingredients. Bring to a boil. Cook and stir for 2 minutes or until thickened. Add the chicken; heat through. Serve over chow mein noodles. **Yield:** 5 servings.

Double Chocolate Bars

A friend brought these fudgy bars a few years ago to tempt me with yet another chocolate treat. Because you prepare them in the microwave, they are simple to make...and cleanup is a breeze! They're very rich, though, so be sure to cut them into bite-size pieces. —Nancy Clark
Zeigler, Illinois

1 package (16 ounces) cream-filled chocolate sandwich cookies, crushed
3/4 cup butter *or* margarine, melted
1 can (14 ounces) sweetened condensed milk
2 cups (12 ounces) miniature semisweet chocolate chips, *divided*

Combine cookie crumbs and butter; pat onto the bottom of an ungreased 13-in. x 9-in. x 2-in. baking pan. Combine milk and 1 cup of chocolate chips in a microwave-safe bowl. Cover and microwave on high for 1 minute or until chips are melted; stir until smooth. Pour over the crust. Sprinkle with remaining chips. Bake at 350° for 10-12 minutes or until the chips are melted. Cool. **Yield:** about 4 dozen. **Editor's Note:** This recipe was tested in a 700-watt microwave.

Peanut Crunch Cake

Peanut Crunch Cake

(Pictured above)

Here's a reliable recipe that quickly dresses up a plain old boxed cake mix. Peanut butter, chocolate chips and nuts add fun, yummy flavor to this moist yellow cake. When you need to feed a bunch, you can't go wrong with this crowd-pleasing recipe. —Sue Smith
Norwalk, Connecticut

1 package (18-1/4 ounces) yellow cake mix
1 cup peanut butter
1/2 cup packed brown sugar
1 cup water
3 eggs
1/4 cup vegetable oil
1/2 to 3/4 cup semisweet chocolate chips, *divided*
1/2 to 3/4 cup peanut butter chips, *divided*
1/2 cup chopped peanuts

In a mixing bowl, beat cake mix, peanut butter and brown sugar on low speed until crumbly. Set aside 1/2 cup. Add water, eggs and oil to remaining crumb mixture; blend on low until moistened. Beat on high for 2 minutes. Stir in 1/4 cup each of chocolate and peanut butter chips. Pour into a greased 13-in. x 9-in. x 2-in. baking pan. Combine peanuts, reserved crumb mixture and the remaining chips; sprinkle over batter. Bake at 350° for 40-45 minutes or until a toothpick inserted near the center comes out clean. Cool completely. **Yield:** 12-16 servings.

Spanish Sausage Supper

(Pictured below)

A pastor's wife shared her recipe for this colorful all-in-one skillet meal that she frequently brings to church dinners. Hearty chunks of smoked sausage and canned tomatoes with chilies add just the right amount of zip to a packaged rice mix.   —Gene Pitts
Wilsonville, Alabama

1/2 cup chopped green pepper
1/3 cup chopped celery
1/4 cup chopped onion
  1 tablespoon vegetable oil
  1 pound fully cooked smoked sausage, sliced
  2 cups water
  1 can (10 ounces) diced tomatoes and green chilies, undrained
  1 package (6.8 ounces) Spanish rice and vermicelli mix
1/4 cup sliced stuffed olives
1/8 teaspoon pepper

In a large skillet, saute green pepper, celery and onion in oil until tender. Add remaining ingredients; mix well. Cover and simmer for 15-20 minutes or until the rice is tender and the liquid is absorbed, stirring occasionally. **Yield:** 4 servings.

Campfire Stew

This speedy single-pan meal revives comforting memories from my childhood. The recipe goes back many years to my days at Girl Scout camp. It's so fun and flavorful it became an instant hit with my family.   —Eva Knight
Nashua, New Hampshire

  1 pound ground beef
  1 can (15 ounces) mixed vegetables, drained
  1 can (10-3/4 ounces) condensed tomato soup, undiluted
  1 can (10-1/2 ounces) condensed vegetable beef soup, undiluted
1/4 cup water
1/4 teaspoon garlic powder
1/4 teaspoon onion powder
1/4 teaspoon salt
1/8 teaspoon pepper

In a large saucepan over medium heat, brown beef; drain. Add the remaining ingredients and mix well. Bring to a boil. Reduce heat; cover and simmer for 8-10 minutes or until heated through. **Yield:** 4 servings.

Hearty Tortellini Soup

I modified a soup recipe to suit my family's tastes while taking advantage of convenience foods. Once you brown the sausage, it's a snap to throw in the other ingredients and let them simmer. Frozen tortellini is added minutes before serving for a savory soup that tastes like you spent hours making it.   —Diana Lauhon, Minerva, Ohio

  3 uncooked Italian sausage links (1/2 to 3/4 pound)
  1 quart water
  2 cans (14-1/2 ounces *each*) Italian stewed tomatoes
  1 can (10-1/2 ounces) condensed French onion soup, undiluted
  2 cups broccoli coleslaw mix
  1 cup frozen cut green beans
  2 cups frozen cheese tortellini
Grated Parmesan cheese, optional

Cut sausage into 3/4-in. pieces; brown in a Dutch oven or soup kettle. Drain. Add water, tomatoes, soup, coleslaw mix and beans; bring to a boil. Reduce heat; cover and simmer for 20-25 minutes or until the vegetables are tender. Uncover; add tortellini. Cook for 3-5 minutes or until pasta is tender. Garnish with Parmesan cheese if desired. **Yield:** 10-12 servings (about 3 quarts). **Editor's Note:** 3 cups cooked pasta of any kind may be substituted for the tortellini. Broccoli coleslaw mix may be found in the produce section of most grocery stores.

Spanish Sausage Supper

Chocolate Bundt Cake

Speedy Mealtime Solutions

WITH convenient ingredients like those right in your "pantry", you greatly increase your quick-cooking options. Consider ideas like these:

- Salsa can be a zippy low-fat substitute for creamy dressings and sauces. Use it as a sauce on grilled fish or meat. Combine salsa with mushrooms, cheese and olives for a zesty omelet topping. A spoonful of salsa on cottage cheese, in a bowl of tomato-based soup or added to a sandwich spread sparks the taste.
- Thin pasta like angel hair and tiny forms like bow ties cook quickly and create delicious meals with the addition of chicken or fish, vegetables and walnuts.
- Adding fast flavor is easy with the range of ethnic bottled sauces now available. They also make marvelous marinades. For example, try brushing fish or pork chops with pesto for super flavor.
- Add your own fresh ingredients like mushrooms, garlic and additional seasonings to make ready-made pasta and tomato sauces taste homemade.

When Minutes Matter

- Always make double batches of staples like rice and pasta, which can be simply reheated.
- Have a flexible meal plan and select recipes with a limited number of ingredients and short, simple directions.
- Rely on oven meals and casseroles in which all parts of the meal cook together.
- Do "weekend cooking" with the idea of leftovers that can stretch into quick, imaginative weekday meals. For instance, grilled salmon can become the basis for a cold pasta salad, a stir-fry and a seafood frittata. (For other similar ideas, turn to page 102.)
- Use the microwave whenever possible.

Chocolate Bundt Cake

(Pictured above)

I know how to satisfy a chocolate craving in a hurry. This moist, taste-tempting treat relies on pudding and cake mixes, so it can be stirred up in a jiffy. My neighbors can't wait to get this cake for their birthdays each year.
—Jeanine Gould-Kostka, Rockville, Maryland

    1 package (18-1/4 ounces) chocolate cake mix
    1 package (3.9 ounces) instant chocolate
       pudding mix
    3 tablespoons baking cocoa
1-3/4 cups milk
    2 eggs
    2 cups (12 ounces) semisweet chocolate chips
Confectioners' sugar

In a mixing bowl, combine cake and pudding mixes, cocoa, milk and eggs. Beat on low speed until moistened. Beat on medium for 2 minutes. Stir in chocolate chips. Pour into a greased and floured 10-in. fluted tube pan. Bake at 350° for 55-60 minutes or until a toothpick inserted near the center comes out clean. Cool for 10 minutes; remove from pan to a wire rack to cool completely. Dust with confectioners' sugar if desired. **Yield:** 12-15 servings.

Taco Pickup Sticks

Looking for something a bit different to munch on? Try this zesty snack mix. We enjoy the extra kick our taste buds get from the spices. One batch is never enough to satisfy my crew. —Kathy Hunt, Dallas, Texas

    3 cans (7 ounces *each*) potato sticks
    2 cans (6 ounces *each*) french-fried onions
    1 can (12 ounces) salted peanuts
    1/3 cup butter *or* margarine, melted
    1 envelope taco seasoning

In a large bowl, combine the potato sticks, onions and peanuts. Combine butter and taco seasoning; mix well. Pour over potato stick mixture and toss to coat. Place in three ungreased 15-in. x 10-in. x 1-in. baking pans. Bake, uncovered, at 250° for 45 minutes, stirring every 15 minutes. Store in airtight containers. **Yield:** 24 cups.

Hopscotch Treats

When the mood for something sweet strikes, I turn to these crunchy snacks packed with butterscotch flavor. I usually have all the ingredients on hand, and they're so easy to make. Our toddler likes to help mix the dry ingredients and lick the bowl. —Gayle Becker, Mt. Clemens, Michigan

    1 cup (6 ounces) butterscotch chips
    1/2 cup crunchy peanut butter
    2 cups miniature marshmallows
    1 can (3 ounces) chow mein noodles

In a saucepan over low heat, cook and stir butterscotch chips and peanut butter until chips are melted. In a large bowl, combine marshmallows and chow mein noodles. Add the butterscotch mixture and stir to coat. Drop by rounded tablespoonfuls onto waxed paper-lined baking sheets. Refrigerate until set, about 10 minutes. **Yield:** 2-1/2 dozen.

Macaroni Tuna Casserole

This dish is so easy to fix, and the flavor is better than any tuna helper I've ever tried. It was a staple when I was in college since a box of macaroni and cheese and a can of tuna cost so little. —Suzanne Zick, Osceola, Arkansas

    1 package (7-1/4 ounces) macaroni and cheese
    1 can (10-3/4 ounces) condensed cream of
      celery soup, undiluted
    1 can (6 ounces) tuna, drained and flaked
    1/2 cup milk
    1 cup (4 ounces) shredded cheddar cheese
Minced fresh parsley, optional

Prepare macaroni and cheese according to package directions. Stir in soup, tuna and milk. Pour into a greased 2-qt. baking dish. Sprinkle with cheese and parsley if desired. Bake, uncovered, at 350° for 20 minutes or until the cheese is melted. **Yield:** 4 servings.

Hash Brown Potato Salad

(Pictured at right)

Frozen hash browns pare down prep time for this quick potato salad. It's so easy to make in a hurry because you don't have to peel any potatoes. —Myra Innes
Auburn, Kansas

    1 quart water
    2 to 3 teaspoons salt
    1 package (16 ounces) frozen cubed hash
      brown potatoes

Keep Basic Ingredients on Hand to Spice Up Meals in a Snap

A WELL-STOCKED spice rack can be one of the quickest (and least expensive) ways to add distinctive flavor to everyday dishes. With a dash here and a pinch there, dried herbs, spices and seasonings add zest to most any meal while enhancing its natural flavors.

For premium flavor, keep spices and dried herbs in tightly closed containers. It's best to store them in a cool dry place away from the stove or other heat. Most will keep for a year before they begin to lose their flavor.

To substitute fresh herbs when a recipe calls for dried herbs, triple the amount listed. For example, substitute 1 tablespoon fresh thyme if 1 teaspoon dried thyme is listed in the recipe.

Here are some common herbs, spices and seasonings you may want to keep on hand:

❏ Basil
❏ Bay leaf
❏ Cinnamon (ground)
❏ Cloves (ground and whole)
❏ Cumin (ground)
❏ Dill weed
❏ Garlic cloves
❏ Ginger (ground)
❏ Italian seasoning
❏ Lemon-pepper seasoning
❏ Marjoram
❏ Minced onion
❏ Mustard (ground)
❏ Nutmeg (ground)
❏ Oregano
❏ Paprika
❏ Parsley flakes
❏ Peppers—black, cayenne and white
❏ Pickling spices
❏ Powders—chili, curry, garlic and onion
❏ Pumpkin pie spice
❏ Red pepper flakes (crushed)
❏ Rosemary
❏ Rubbed sage
❏ Salts—celery, garlic, plain or iodized and seasoned
❏ Seeds—caraway, celery, poppy and sesame
❏ Tarragon
❏ Thyme

Hash Brown Potato Salad
Frosted Gelatin Salad

2 hard-cooked eggs, chopped
1/4 cup mayonnaise
1/4 cup sour cream
1/4 cup chopped celery
3 tablespoons sweet pickle relish
2 tablespoons chopped green onions
1-1/2 teaspoons prepared mustard
1 teaspoon salt
1/8 teaspoon pepper

In a large saucepan, bring water and salt to a boil. Add the hash browns; cook for 3-4 minutes or until tender. Drain thoroughly. Combine remaining ingredients in a bowl; add hash browns and stir gently. Cover and chill until serving. Refrigerate leftovers. **Yield:** 4-6 servings.

Frosted Gelatin Salad

(Pictured above)

A sweet, creamy topping frosts this extra-fruity gelatin that is chock-full of canned apricots and crushed pineapple. It's a colorful salad to serve at potluck dinners. Everyone loves the combination of flavors.
—Bertha Johnson, Indianapolis, Indiana

1 package (6 ounces) orange gelatin
2 cups boiling water
3/4 cup miniature marshmallows
2 cans (17 ounces *each*) apricot halves, undrained
1 can (20 ounces) crushed pineapple, drained
1/2 cup sugar
3 tablespoons all-purpose flour
1 egg, beaten
1 teaspoon vanilla extract
2 envelopes whipped topping mix
1/4 cup finely shredded cheddar cheese

In a bowl, dissolve gelatin in boiling water. Add marshmallows; stir until melted. Drain apricots, reserving 1 cup juice; set juice aside. Chop apricots; add to gelatin with pineapple. Pour into an 11-in. x 7-in. x 2-in. pan. Chill until firm. Meanwhile, in a saucepan, combine the sugar and flour. Whisk in egg, vanilla and reserved apricot juice until smooth. Bring to a boil; boil and stir for 2 minutes. Cool completely. Prepare whipped topping according to package directions; fold in cooled juice mixture. Spread over gelatin. Sprinkle with cheese. Chill for 1 hour. **Yield:** 12 servings.

Dinner in a Bag

(Pictured below)

When it comes to convenience, this dinner is in the bag. Measure dry noodles and a mixture of spices into separate plastic bags, then store them in a paper bag with canned stewed tomatoes. This "pantry kit" gives a head start on a hearty meal. Since I work late occasionally, my family just has to brown ground beef, and soon dinner is simmering. —Darlene Markel, Sublimity, Oregon

  1 pound ground beef
  2 cans (14-1/2 ounces *each*) stewed tomatoes
1/4 cup dried minced onion
  1 teaspoon salt
  1 teaspoon chili powder
1/4 to 1/2 teaspoon pepper
1/4 teaspoon sugar
  1 cup uncooked elbow macaroni

In a skillet, brown beef; drain. Add tomatoes and seasonings; bring to a boil. Reduce heat and simmer for 5 minutes. Stir in macaroni; cover and simmer for 15 minutes. Uncover; simmer until macaroni is tender and sauce is thickened. **Yield:** 4 servings.

Wild Rice Soup

I tasted this thick and hearty soup at a food fair I helped judge. It didn't earn a ribbon, but I thought it was a real winner. The original recipe called for uncooked wild rice, but I use a quick-cooking rice blend instead.
                —Kathy Herink, Gladbrook, Iowa

1 pound ground beef
2 cups chopped celery
2 cups chopped onion
3 cups water
1 can (14-1/2 ounces) chicken broth
1 can (10-3/4 ounces) condensed cream of mushroom soup, undiluted
1 package (6.75 ounces) quick-cooking long grain and wild rice mix
5 bacon strips, cooked and crumbled

In a 3-qt. saucepan, cook beef, celery and onion until beef is browned and vegetables are tender; drain. Add water, broth, soup and rice with contents of the seasoning packet. Bring to a boil. Reduce heat; cover and simmer for 5 minutes. Garnish with bacon. **Yield:** 8 servings (about 2 quarts).

Dinner in a Bag

Banana Fudge Cake

(Pictured at right)

You'll love the banana flavor throughout this moist, fudgy cake and fluffy frosting. This recipe was given to me by my mother-in-law. It's a favorite at family gatherings. —Jan Gregory, Bethel, Ohio

    1 package (18-1/4 ounces) chocolate
        fudge cake mix
    1 large ripe banana, mashed
FROSTING:
    1/2 cup butter *or* margarine
    1/4 cup water
  5-1/2 cups confectioners' sugar, *divided*
    1/4 cup baking cocoa
    1 small ripe banana, mashed
    1/2 teaspoon vanilla extract

In a mixing bowl, prepare cake mix according to package directions, omitting 1/4 cup of the water. Beat on low speed until moistened. Add banana; beat on high for 2 minutes. Pour into a greased 13-in. x 9-in. x 2-in. baking pan. Bake at 350° for 35-40 minutes or until a toothpick inserted near the center comes out clean. Cool completely. In a saucepan, heat butter and water until butter is melted; set aside. In a mixing bowl, combine 4 cups confectioners' sugar and cocoa. Add butter mixture, banana and vanilla; beat until smooth. Add enough remaining sugar until frosting reaches desired spreading consistency. Frost the cake. **Yield:** 12-15 servings.

Coconut Chip Cookies
Banana Fudge Cake

Bean Salad Medley

Forget to plan a dish for the neighborhood potluck? Here's a speedy solution from the pantry that's sure to be a crowd-pleaser. Additional veggies give traditional bean salad an extra boost of flavor. It tastes just as good when made a day or two ahead of time. —Heather Molzan
Edmonton, Alberta

 Nutritional Analysis included

    1 can (16 ounces) kidney beans, rinsed and
        drained
    1 can (15-1/4 ounces) whole kernel corn,
        drained
    1 can (15-1/4 ounces) lima beans, rinsed and
        drained
    1 can (14-1/2 ounces) cut green beans, drained
    1 can (14-1/2 ounces) wax beans, drained
    2 jars (4-1/2 ounces *each*) whole mushrooms,
        drained
    1 medium green pepper, julienned
    1 medium onion, chopped
  3/4 cup vegetable oil
  3/4 cup vinegar
  3/4 cup sugar
    1 teaspoon pepper
  3/4 teaspoon salt

In a large bowl, combine the first eight ingredients. In a small bowl, combine remaining ingredients; mix well. Pour over vegetables and toss to coat. Cover and refrigerate until serving. Serve with a slotted spoon. **Yield:** 24 servings. **Nutritional Analysis:** One 1/2-cup serving equals 173 calories, 285 mg sodium, trace cholesterol, 26 gm carbohydrate, 3 gm protein, 7 gm fat. **Diabetic Exchanges:** 1-1/2 starch, 1-1/2 fat.

Coconut Chip Cookies

(Pictured above)

I easily transform a boxed white cake mix into a big batch of tasty cookies that are filled with coconut, nuts and chocolate chips. This recipe requires just six ingredients, so you can mix up the batter in a jiffy. —Flora Alers
Clinton, Maryland

    1 package (18-1/4 ounces) white cake mix
    2 eggs
  1/3 cup vegetable oil
    1 cup flaked coconut
  1/2 cup semisweet chocolate chips
  1/4 cup chopped macadamia nuts *or* almonds

In a mixing bowl, beat dry cake mix, eggs and oil (batter will be very stiff). Stir in coconut, chips and nuts. Roll into 1-in. balls. Place on lightly greased baking sheets. Bake at 350° for 10 minutes or until a slight indentation remains when lightly touched. Cool for 2 minutes; remove to a wire rack to cool completely. **Yield:** 3-1/2 dozen.

ABC Muffins

The ABC stands for Applesauce, Bran and Cinnamon. These moist bran muffins are an absolute favorite at our house. In fact, my husband asks for them instead of birthday cake! —Susan Smith, Newark, Ohio

    3 eggs
    3/4 cup vegetable oil
    1/2 cup applesauce
    1/4 cup honey
    1 package (18-1/4 ounces) yellow cake mix
1-1/2 cups wheat bran
    2 teaspoons ground cinnamon

In a mixing bowl, beat eggs, oil, applesauce and honey. Combine the dry cake mix, bran and cinnamon; add to egg mixture. Mix just until blended. Fill greased or paper-lined muffin cups two-thirds full. Bake at 350° for 20-25 minutes or until the muffins test done. **Yield:** 1-1/2 dozen.

Taco Stovetop Supper

(Pictured below)

You can serve a crowd with this quick-to-fix skillet supper that gets zip from taco seasoning mix. The recipe makes a lot, but I think the leftovers taste even better the next day. —Barbara Inglis, Addy, Washington

    2 pounds lean ground beef
    2 cans (15-1/2 ounces *each*) hot chili beans, undrained
    2 cans (10 ounces *each*) diced tomatoes and green chilies, undrained
    1 can (11-1/2 ounces) picante V-8 juice
    1 can (11 ounces) Mexicorn, drained
    2 envelopes taco seasoning
Optional garnishes: tortillas, shredded cheddar cheese, chopped onion, shredded lettuce *and/or* taco sauce

In a Dutch oven, brown the beef; drain. Stir in beans, tomatoes, V-8 juice, corn and taco seasoning. Simmer, uncovered, for 15-20 minutes or until heated through. Garnish as desired. **Yield:** 10-12 servings.

Taco Stovetop Supper

Zesty Cheese Soup

My husband and I are retired, but I still look for shortcut recipes like the one I received from a great-niece. You'll likely have the majority of ingredients for this colorful soup in your pantry. To save time, I start warming the canned ingredients on the stove while I cube the cheese.

—Modie Phillips, Lubbock, Texas

    1 can (15-1/4 ounces) whole kernel corn, drained
    1 can (15 ounces) pinto beans, rinsed and drained
    1 can (14-1/2 ounces) chicken broth
    1 can (10 ounces) diced tomatoes and green chilies, undrained
    1 can (10 ounces) premium chunk white chicken, drained
    1 can (4-1/2 ounces) chopped green chilies
    1 pound process American cheese, cubed
Crushed tortilla chips, optional

In a 3-qt. saucepan, combine the first seven ingredients. Cook and stir until cheese is melted. Garnish with tortilla chips if desired. **Yield:** 6-8 servings (2 quarts).

Pumpkin Cheesecake

(Pictured above right)

It takes mere minutes to add holiday flair to a no-bake cheesecake. I use canned pumpkin and spices to dress up the mix with thick, creamy results. —Leila Flavell
Bulyea, Saskatchewan

    1 package (11.1 ounces) no-bake cheesecake mix
    1/3 cup butter *or* margarine, melted
    2 tablespoons sugar
    3/4 cup milk
    3/4 cup canned *or* cooked pumpkin
    1 teaspoon ground cinnamon
    1/4 teaspoon ground cloves
Whipped topping
Additional cinnamon, optional

Brownie Alpine Biscotti
Pumpkin Cheesecake

Set aside filling mix packet from cheesecake. Combine the contents of the crust mix packet with butter and sugar. Press onto the bottom and up the sides of a 9-in. pie plate. Refrigerate for 10 minutes. Meanwhile, in a mixing bowl, combine contents of filling mix packet, milk, pumpkin, cinnamon and cloves. Beat on medium speed for 3 minutes. Pour into the crust. Chill for at least 1 hour. Garnish with whipped topping and sprinkle with cinnamon if desired. **Yield:** 6-8 servings.

Brownie Alpine Biscotti

(Pictured above)

I love visiting with friends over a pot of coffee, so I developed these crisp, chocolaty cookies to munch along with each cup. Brownie mix makes them easy to stir up, and a white chocolate and almond topping adds a special touch.
—Jeanie Williams, Minnetonka, Minnesota

  1 package fudge brownie mix (13-inch x
     9-inch size)
3/4 cup ground almonds

1/2 cup all-purpose flour
3/4 teaspoon baking powder
  1 egg plus 3 egg whites
  1 teaspoon almond extract
1/4 cup sliced almonds, optional
    3 squares (1 ounce *each*) white baking
     chocolate, melted, optional

In a large bowl, combine dry brownie mix, ground almonds, flour and baking powder; mix well. In a small bowl, whisk egg, egg whites and extract. Add to brownie mixture; stir until combined. Divide dough into thirds. On a greased baking sheet and using greased hands, shape each portion of dough into a 7-in. x 3-1/2-in. rectangle. Bake at 350° for 24 minutes. Remove from the oven; cool on baking sheet for 5 minutes. Transfer to a cutting board; cut diagonally with a serrated knife into 3/4-in. slices. Place cut side down on greased baking sheets. Bake 12-14 minutes longer or until firm. Cool on wire racks. If desired, sprinkle with sliced almonds and drizzle with chocolate. Let stand until chocolate is completely set. Store in an airtight container. **Yield:** 2-1/2 dozen.

Chicken Noodle Stir-Fry

(Pictured above)

Rely on Ramen noodles to stretch this appealing stir-fry. You can use whatever vegetables you happen to have on hand. The dish is different every time I make it.
—*Darlene Markel, Sublimity, Oregon*

- 1 package (3 ounces) chicken-flavored Ramen noodles
- 1 pound boneless skinless chicken breasts, cut into strips
- 1 tablespoon vegetable oil
- 1 cup broccoli florets
- 1 cup cauliflowerets
- 1 cup sliced celery
- 1 cup coarsely chopped cabbage
- 2 medium carrots, thinly sliced
- 1 medium onion, thinly sliced
- 1/2 cup fresh *or* canned bean sprouts
- 1/2 cup teriyaki *or* soy sauce

Set aside seasoning packet from noodles. Cook noodles according to package directions. Meanwhile, in a large skillet or wok, stir-fry chicken in oil for 5-6 minutes or un-til no longer pink. Add vegetables; stir-fry for 3-4 minutes or until crisp-tender. Drain noodles; add to the pan with contents of seasoning packet and the teriyaki sauce. Stir well. Serve immediately. **Yield:** 4 servings.

Rich 'n' Buttery Bars

You'll keep a cake mix on hand just to make these deliciously rich bars. They're fancy enough to serve company, yet easy enough to stir up for a bake sale. And they always disappear quickly.
—*Ann Horst*
Boonsboro, Maryland

- 1/2 cup cold butter *or* margarine
- 1 package (18-1/4 ounces) yellow cake mix
- 1 egg, beaten

FILLING:

- 1 package (8 ounces) cream cheese, softened
- 2 cups confectioners' sugar
- 2 eggs
- 1 teaspoon vanilla extract

Additional confectioners' sugar

In a bowl, cut butter into cake mix until crumbly. Add egg and mix well. Press into a greased 13-in. x 9-in. x

2-in. baking pan. In a mixing bowl, beat cream cheese and sugar. Add eggs and vanilla; beat until smooth. Spread evenly over the crust. Bake at 350° for 30 minutes. Reduce heat to 325°; bake 10 minutes longer. Dust with confectioners' sugar while warm. Cool to room temperature before cutting. **Yield:** 4 dozen.

Yogurt Fruit Dressing

This lightly sweet dressing tastes great over fruit or in a Waldorf salad. Best of all, it takes just seconds to stir up.
—*Fran Roberts, Hessel, Michigan*

✓ Nutritional Analysis included

1 carton (8 ounces) low-fat apple-cinnamon
yogurt
1/4 cup milk

In a bowl, stir yogurt; gradually stir in milk. Serve over fresh fruit or use in a fruit salad. **Yield:** about 1 cup. **Nutritional Analysis:** 2 tablespoons of dressing (prepared with skim milk) equals 27 calories, 17 mg sodium, 1 mg cholesterol, 5 gm carbohydrate, 1 gm protein, trace fat. **Diabetic Exchange:** 1/2 fruit.

Hawaiian Cake

(Pictured below right and on page 80)

I dress up a boxed yellow cake mix with pineapple, coconut and a delightful blend of instant pudding, cream cheese and whipped topping. This is a favorite dessert that suits any occasion. Try it once and you're sure to make it again.
—*Estella Traeger, Milwaukee, Wisconsin*

1 package (18-1/4 ounces)
yellow cake mix
2 cups cold milk
2 packages (3.4 ounces *each*)
instant vanilla pudding mix
1 package (8 ounces) cream
cheese, softened
1 carton (8 ounces) frozen
whipped topping, thawed
1 can (20 ounces) crushed
pineapple, drained
1/2 cup chopped maraschino
cherries, drained
1/2 cup flaked coconut
1/2 cup chopped walnuts

Prepare cake mix according to package directions, using a greased 15-in. x 10-in. x 1-in. baking pan. Bake at 350° for 20-25 minutes or until cake tests done; cool completely. In a mixing bowl, combine milk and pudding mixes; beat in cream cheese until smooth. Fold in whipped topping. Spread over cooled cake. Top with pineapple, cherries, coconut and walnuts. Refrigerate until serving. **Yield:** 16-20 servings.

Add Fun Flavor to Cake Mixes

HAVE a boxed cake mix in your cupboard? Create a new taste sensation by adding a simple ingredient or two!

Pillsbury shares the following fun variations that can be used with any of its Moist Supreme cake mixes.

For example, add rich flavor to a white cake mix with your favorite extract...mix coffee instead of water into chocolate cake mix for a mouth-watering mocha variation...or fold flaked coconut into a yellow cake batter for a tasty change of pace.

The sky's the limit, so be creative! The taste-tempting treats that result are sure to have your family asking for seconds.

Before mixing the cake batter, try one of the following variations:
- Substitute coffee or your favorite carbonated beverage for the water.
- Add 1 tablespoon of grated lemon or orange peel.
- Add 1 teaspoon ground cinnamon, 1/2 teaspoon ground nutmeg and 1/2 teaspoon ground cloves.
- Add 2 to 3 teaspoons of vanilla, almond, orange, lemon, coconut, peppermint or rum extract, or butter or maple flavoring.

After mixing the batter, stir in one of the following ingredients:
- 2 to 4 ounces of finely chopped semisweet or milk chocolate.
- 1 cup finely chopped nuts.
- 1 cup coarsely crushed cookies.
- 1 cup flaked coconut.
- 1/2 cup almond brickle baking chips or English toffee bits.
- 2 tablespoons poppy seeds.

Hawaiian Cake

Homemade Mixes

HANDY homemade mixes deliver all the great taste of the popular specialty products offered today but for far less cost. You'll find they're convenient to have on hand as a head start to any fast meal.

White Sauce Mix

I keep this mix handy in my fridge. I've never had a lumpy white sauce using this recipe.
—Joan Baskin
Black Creek, British Columbia

> 2 cups instant nonfat dry milk powder
> 1 cup all-purpose flour
> 2 teaspoons salt
> 1 cup cold butter *or* margarine
> **ADDITIONAL INGREDIENT:**
> 1 cup water

Combine dry milk, flour and salt; mix well. Cut in butter until mixture resembles fine crumbs. Store in an airtight container in the refrigerator for up to 3 months. **Yield:** Number of batches varies depending on thickness of sauce (4-2/3 cups total). **To prepare white sauce:** For a thin white sauce, combine 1/3 cup mix and 1 cup water in a saucepan. For a medium white sauce, use 1/2 cup mix. For a thick white sauce, use 3/4 cup of mix. Bring to a boil over medium heat; cook and stir for 2 minutes. **Yield:** 1 cup of sauce per batch.

Lemon Ice Tea Mix

A friend who has a large family and does a lot of entertaining created this mix. It's inexpensive and makes a tasty, refreshing batch of tea.
—Linda Fox, Soldotna, Alaska

> 7-1/2 cups sugar
> 2 cups unsweetened instant tea
> 5 envelopes (.23 ounce *each*) unsweetened lemonade soft drink mix
> **ADDITIONAL INGREDIENTS:**
> 1 cup warm water
> Cold water

Combine sugar, tea and drink mix. Store in an airtight container in a cool dry place. **Yield:** 5 batches (8-1/2 cups total). **To prepare tea:** Dissolve about 1-2/3 cups tea mix in 1 cup warm water. Place in a gallon container. Add cold water to measure 1 gallon. Cover and chill. **Yield:** about 16 (1-cup) servings per batch.

Pancake and Waffle Mix

(Pictured below)

This terrific blend provides the ease of a boxed pancake mix with the homemade goodness of light, fluffy pancakes and waffles made from scratch. It uses a terrific buttermilk powder.
—Deb Poitz, Fort Morgan, Colorado

> 8 cups all-purpose flour
> 2 cups buttermilk blend powder*
> 1/2 cup sugar
> 8 teaspoons baking powder
> 4 teaspoons baking soda
> 2 teaspoons salt
> **ADDITIONAL INGREDIENTS FOR PANCAKES:**
> 1 egg
> 1 cup water
> 2 tablespoons vegetable oil
> **ADDITIONAL INGREDIENTS FOR WAFFLES:**
> 3 eggs, *separated*
> 2 cups water
> 1/4 cup vegetable oil

In a large bowl, combine the first six ingredients with a wire whisk. Store in an airtight container in the refrigerator for up to 6 months. **Yield:** about 7 batches of pancakes or about 4 batches of waffles (11 cups total). **To prepare pancakes:** In a medium bowl, beat egg, water and oil. Whisk in 1-1/2 cups pancake/waffle mix. Let stand for 5 minutes. Pour batter by 1/3 cupfuls onto a lightly greased hot griddle; turn when bubbles form on top of pancakes. Cook until the second side is golden brown. **Yield:** about 6 pancakes per batch. **To prepare waffles:** In a large bowl, beat egg yolks, water and oil.

Pancake and Waffle Mix

Stir in 2-1/2 cups of pancake/waffle mix just until moistened. In a mixing bowl, beat the egg whites until stiff peaks form; fold into the batter. Bake in a preheated waffle iron according to manufacturer's directions until golden brown. **Yield:** 13 waffles (about 4 inches) per batch. ***Editor's Note:** Look for buttermilk blend powder in the powdered milk section of your grocery store.

Rice Seasoning Mix

With rice and this mix on hand, you can whip up a tasty side dish whenever you need one. —Linnea Rein, Topeka, Kansas

   1 cup sliced almonds, coarsely chopped
1/2 cup chicken bouillon granules
1/2 cup dried parsley flakes
   1 tablespoon dried basil
   1 tablespoon dill weed
   1 tablespoon dried minced onion
   1 teaspoon seasoned salt
   1 teaspoon garlic powder
   1 teaspoon lemon-pepper seasoning
ADDITIONAL INGREDIENTS:
   1 cup uncooked long grain rice
   2 cups water

Combine the first nine ingredients. Store in an airtight container. **Yield:** 10 batches (2 cups total). **To prepare rice:** Combine 3 tablespoons seasoning mix, rice and water in a saucepan. Bring to a boil. Reduce heat; cover and simmer for 20 minutes or until the water is absorbed. **Yield:** 4-6 servings per batch.

Versatile Coating Mix

(Pictured above right)

This mild blend of spices is good to keep on hand. It's so versatile—you can use it to coat chicken, pork or even fish.
   —Darlene Markel, Sublimity, Oregon

3/4 cup dry bread crumbs
3/4 cup grated Parmesan cheese
1/2 cup all-purpose flour
1/4 cup dried parsley flakes
   3 tablespoons cornmeal
   1 tablespoon dried minced onion
3/4 teaspoon garlic powder
1/2 teaspoon crushed red pepper flakes
1/2 teaspoon salt
1/2 teaspoon pepper
   3 tablespoons shortening
ADDITIONAL INGREDIENT:
   4 bone-in chicken breast halves

Combine the first 10 ingredients in a bowl; cut in shortening until mixture resembles fine crumbs. Store in an airtight container in a cool dry place or freeze for up to 6 months. **Yield:** 6 batches (3 cups total). **To prepare**

Versatile Coating Mix
French Salad Dressing Mix

chicken: Place 1/2 cup coating mix in shallow bowl or large resealable plastic bag. Add chicken and toss to coat. Place in an ungreased 13-in. x 9-in. x 2-in. baking dish. Bake, uncovered, at 400° for 40-45 minutes or until juices run clear. **Yield:** 4 servings per batch.

French Salad Dressing Mix

(Pictured above)

This tangy homemade salad dressing is more economical than store-bought, and we prefer the taste. The dressing keeps well in the fridge.
   —Darlene Markel

☑ Nutritional Analysis included

   4 teaspoons dried parsley flakes
   1 tablespoon sugar
1-1/2 teaspoons ground mustard
1-1/2 teaspoons onion powder
1-1/2 teaspoons paprika
1-1/2 teaspoons salt
   3/4 teaspoon pepper
   3/4 teaspoon garlic powder
ADDITIONAL INGREDIENTS:
   3/4 cup vegetable oil
   1/4 cup vinegar
   2 tablespoons water

Combine the first eight ingredients in a resealable plastic bag. Store in a cool dry place. **Yield:** 3 batches (6 tablespoons total). **To prepare dressing:** Combine 2 tablespoons dressing mix, oil, vinegar and water in a jar with tight-fitting lid; shake well. Refrigerate for at least 30 minutes. **Yield:** about 1 cup dressing per batch. **Nutritional Analysis:** 2 tablespoons of prepared salad dressing equals 93 calories, 73 mg sodium, 0 cholesterol, 1 gm carbohydrate, trace protein, 10 gm fat.

Spicy Chili Seasoning Mix
Corn Bread Mix

4 tablespoons chili powder
2-1/2 teaspoons ground coriander
2-1/2 teaspoons ground cumin
1-1/2 teaspoons garlic powder
1 teaspoon dried oregano
1/2 teaspoon cayenne pepper
ADDITIONAL INGREDIENTS:
1 pound boneless round steak,
cut into 1-inch pieces
2 teaspoons vegetable oil
1 pound lean ground beef
1 medium onion, chopped
1 can (28 ounces) diced
tomatoes, undrained
2 cans (15 ounces *each*) chili
beans, *divided*

Combine the first six ingredients. Store in an airtight container in a cool dry place. **Yield:** 4 batches (20 teaspoons total). **To prepare chili:** Lightly brown steak in oil in a Dutch oven; add 3 teaspoons of the seasoning mix and toss to coat. Add ground beef; cook until meat is no longer pink. Add onion; cook until tender. Add tomatoes and 2 more teaspoons of mix. Stir in one can of chili beans. Place the other can in a blender; cover and process until smooth. Add to chili. Cook on low for 30-40 minutes or until meat is tender. **Yield:** 10 servings (2-1/2 quarts) per batch.

Corn Bread Mix

(Pictured above)

I always keep a plastic bag of this corn bread mix in my freezer. Then I just add egg and milk for great, light-textured corn bread. —Donna Smith, Victor, New York

4-1/4 cups all-purpose flour
4 cups cornmeal
3/4 cup sugar
1/4 cup baking powder
1 to 2 teaspoons salt
1 cup shortening
ADDITIONAL INGREDIENTS:
1 egg
1 cup milk

In a bowl, combine the dry ingredients; cut in shortening until crumbly. Store in an airtight container in a cool dry place or in the freezer for up to 6 months. **Yield:** 5 batches (11-2/3 cups total). **To prepare corn bread:** In a bowl, beat egg; add milk and mix well. Stir in 2-1/3 cups corn bread mix just until moistened (the batter will be lumpy). Pour into a greased 8-in. square baking pan. Bake at 425° for 20-25 minutes or until bread tests done. **Yield:** 9 servings per batch.

Spicy Chili Seasoning Mix

(Pictured above)

Having the seasonings mixed up in advance makes stirring up a batch of chili a breeze. It's a bold but pleasant blend. I like the round steak and ground beef combination. —Mary Henderson, Opelika, Alabama

Oatmeal Cookie Mix

This easy cookie mix was a standby when we needed something quick for lunches on the Nebraska farm where I grew up. —Mary Jane Cantrell, Turlock, California

3 cups all-purpose flour
2-1/2 cups sugar
2 teaspoons salt
1 teaspoon baking soda
1 teaspoon baking powder
1 cup shortening
3 cups quick-cooking oats
ADDITIONAL INGREDIENTS:
1 egg
1 tablespoon milk
1 teaspoon vanilla extract
1/2 cup semisweet chocolate chips
1/2 cup chopped pecans, optional

Combine the first five ingredients; cut in shortening until crumbly. Add oats and mix well. Store in an airtight container in a cool dry place for up to 6 months. **Yield:** 5 batches (10 cups total). **To prepare cookies:** In a mixing bowl, combine 2 cups cookie mix, egg, milk and vanilla; mix well. Fold in chocolate chips and pecans if desired. Drop by tablespoonfuls 2 in. apart onto greased baking sheets. Bake at 375° for 10-12 minutes or until golden brown. Remove to wire racks to cool. **Yield:** about 2-1/2 dozen per batch.

Cinnamon Hot Chocolate Mix

(Pictured below right)

When our children left for college, they each insisted on taking a large container of this cinnamony cocoa mix with them to the dorm.
—*Linda Nilsen, Anoka, Minnesota*

☑ Nutritional Analysis included

1-3/4 cups instant nonfat dry milk powder
  1 cup confectioners' sugar
  1/2 cup nondairy creamer
  1/2 cup baking cocoa
  1/2 teaspoon ground cinnamon
  1 cup miniature marshmallows
ADDITIONAL INGREDIENTS:
  3/4 cup hot milk

In a bowl, combine milk powder, sugar, creamer, cocoa and cinnamon. Add the marshmallows; mix well. Store in an airtight container in a cool dry place for up to 3 months. **Yield:** 18-19 batches (about 3-1/2 cups total). **To prepare hot chocolate:** Dissolve about 3 tablespoons hot chocolate mix in hot milk. **Yield:** 1 serving per batch. **Nutritional Analysis:** One 3/4-cup serving (prepared with skim milk) equals 141 calories, 133 mg sodium, 5 mg cholesterol, 24 gm carbohydrate, 9 gm protein, 1 gm fat. **Diabetic Exchanges:** 1 skim milk, 1 fruit.

Classic Cream Soup Mix

With this easy-to-fix mix, you can make cream soup to enjoy or to use as a substitute for condensed cream soup in a recipe. —*DeAnn Alleva, Hudson, Wisconsin*

  2 cups instant nonfat dry milk powder
  1/2 cup plus 2 tablespoons cornstarch
  1/2 cup mashed potato flakes
  1/4 cup chicken bouillon granules
  2 tablespoons dried vegetable flakes
  1 teaspoon onion powder
  1/2 teaspoon dried marjoram
  1/4 teaspoon garlic powder
  1/8 teaspoon white pepper

In a food processor or blender, combine all ingredients; cover and process until the vegetable flakes are finely chopped. Store in an airtight container in a cool dry place for up to 1 year. **Yield:** 9 batches (3 cups total). **For a condensed cream soup substitute:** In a 1-qt. saucepan or microwave-safe bowl, combine 1/3 cup of soup mix and 1-1/4 cups water. Bring to a boil or microwave on high for 2 to 2-1/2 minutes, stirring occasionally. Cool or chill. Use as a substitute for one 10-3/4-ounce can of condensed cream of chicken, mushroom or celery soup. **For 1-1/2 cups of cream soup:** In a 1-qt. saucepan or microwave-safe bowl, combine 1/3 cup of soup mix and 1-1/2 cups water. Bring to a boil or microwave on high for 2 to 2-1/2 minutes, stirring occasionally. **Editor's Note:** This recipe was tested in an 850-watt microwave.

Molasses Cookie Mix

(Pictured at right)

For holiday gift-giving, I put a batch of this cookie mix in an attractive basket along with the recipe and a festive tea towel. —*Barbara Stewart Portland, Connecticut*

  6 cups all-purpose flour
  3 cups sugar
  1 tablespoon baking soda
  1 tablespoon baking powder
  1 tablespoon ground ginger
  1 tablespoon ground cinnamon
1-1/2 teaspoons ground nutmeg
  3/4 teaspoon ground cloves
  1/2 teaspoon ground allspice
ADDITIONAL INGREDIENTS:
  3/4 cup butter *or* margarine, softened
  1 egg
  1/4 cup molasses
Additional sugar

In a bowl, combine the first nine ingredients; mix well. Store in an airtight container in a cool dry place for up to 6 months. **Yield:** 3 batches (9 cups total). **To prepare cookies:** In a mixing bowl, cream butter. Add egg and molasses; mix well. Add 3 cups cookie mix; beat until smooth. Shape into 1-in. balls and roll in sugar. Place 2 in. apart on ungreased baking sheets. Bake at 375° for 9-11 minutes or until the edges are firm and the surface cracks. Cool on wire racks. **Yield:** about 4 dozen per batch.

Cinnamon Hot Chocolate Mix
Molasses Cookie Mix

Split Pea Soup Mix

My mother sent me some of this pretty dry blend along with the recipe. This hearty soup is thick with lentils, barley and peas, and chicken is a nice change from the usual ham. —Susan Ruckert, Tangent, Oregon

☑ Nutritional Analysis included

 1 package (16 ounces) dry green split peas
 1 package (16 ounces) dry yellow split peas
 1 package (16 ounces) dry lentils
 1 package (16 ounces) pearl barley
 1 package (12 ounces) alphabet pasta
 1 jar (1/2 ounce) dried celery flakes
 1/2 cup dried parsley flakes
ADDITIONAL INGREDIENTS:
 1 quart chicken broth
 1/4 teaspoon pepper
 1 cup cubed cooked chicken, optional

Combine the first seven ingredients. Store in airtight containers in a cool dry place for up to 1 year. **Yield:** 13 batches (13 cups total). **To prepare soup:** In a large saucepan, combine 1 cup soup mix, broth, pepper and chicken if desired. Bring to a boil. Reduce heat; cover and simmer for 60-70 minutes or until peas and lentils are tender. **Yield:** about 4 servings per batch. **Nutritional Analysis:** One 1-cup serving (prepared with chicken and low-sodium broth) equals 158 calories, 117 mg sodium, 7 mg cholesterol, 26 gm carbohydrate, 11 gm protein, 3 gm fat. **Diabetic Exchanges:** 1-1/2 starch, 1 lean meat.

Spaghetti Sauce Mix

(Pictured below)

Keep this blend of seasonings on hand so you can stir up speedy spaghetti sauce. All you need to add is browned

Spaghetti Sauce Mix

ground beef, tomato paste and water to create a mild, pleasantly flavored sauce. —Betty Claycomb
Alverton, Pennsylvania

 1/4 cup cornstarch
 1/4 cup dried minced onion
 1/4 cup dried parsley flakes
 3 tablespoons dried vegetable *or* sweet pepper flakes
 2 tablespoons Italian seasoning
 4 teaspoons salt
 4 teaspoons sugar
 2 teaspoons dried minced garlic
ADDITIONAL INGREDIENTS:
 1 pound ground beef
 2 cups water
 1 can (6 ounces) tomato paste

Combine the first eight ingredients. Store in an airtight container in a cool dry place up to 1 year. **Yield:** 4 batches (1 cup total). **To prepare spaghetti sauce:** In a skillet, brown beef; drain. Stir in 1/4 cup spaghetti sauce mix, water and tomato paste. Bring to a boil; boil and stir for 2 minutes. Reduce heat; cover and simmer for 20 minutes. **Yield:** about 3 cups sauce per batch.

Streusel Coffee Cake Mix

I prepare two mixes—one for the cake and one for the topping—to make this sweet breakfast treat. I often give these mixes as fun holiday gifts along with a cake pan, wooden spoon and festive dish towel. —Barbara Stewart
Portland, Connecticut

COFFEE CAKE MIX:
 4-1/2 cups all-purpose flour
 2-1/4 cups sugar
 2 tablespoons baking powder
 1-1/2 teaspoons salt
STREUSEL MIX:
 3/4 cup packed brown sugar
 3 tablespoons all-purpose flour
 1 tablespoon ground cinnamon
 1/4 teaspoon ground nutmeg
 1-1/2 cups chopped pecans
ADDITIONAL INGREDIENTS:
 1 egg, beaten
 1/2 cup milk
 1/4 cup vegetable oil
 1 tablespoon butter *or* margarine, melted

Combine the cake mix ingredients; set aside. Combine the first four streusel ingredients; add pecans. Store both mixes in separate airtight containers in a cool dry place for up to 6 months. **Yield:** 3 batches (6 cups of cake mix, 2-1/4 cups of streusel). **To prepare coffee cake:** In a mixing bowl, combine 2 cups of cake mix, egg, milk and oil; mix well. Pour into a greased 9-in. square baking pan. Combine 3/4 cup streusel mix and butter; sprinkle over batter. Bake at 375° for 25-30 minutes or until a toothpick inserted near the center comes out clean. Serve warm. **Yield:** 9 servings per batch.

Taco Seasoning Mix

I create my own taco seasoning for spicing up Mexican dishes. It's handy and less expensive than buying envelopes of prepared mix.
— *Karen Owen*
Rising Sun, Indiana

1/4 cup dried minced onion
1/4 cup chili powder
3 tablespoons salt
4 teaspoons cornstarch
1 tablespoon dried minced garlic
1 tablespoon ground cumin
1 tablespoon crushed red pepper flakes
2 teaspoons beef bouillon granules
1-1/2 teaspoons dried oregano
ADDITIONAL INGREDIENTS:
1 pound ground beef
1/3 to 1/2 cup water

Homemade Muffin Mix

Combine the first nine ingredients. Store in an airtight container in a cool dry place for up to 1 year. **Yield:** 6-7 batches (about 3/4 cup total). **To prepare tacos:** In a skillet, brown beef; drain. Add 2 tablespoons taco seasoning mix and water. Bring to a boil; cook and stir for 2 minutes. **Yield:** 4 servings per batch.

Homemade Muffin Mix

(Pictured above right)

Whether your family prefers sweet or savory muffins, you can satisfy them with this versatile muffin mix. You can prepare plain, cheddar and cinnamon-raisin muffins.
— *Audrey Thibodeau, Mesa, Arizona*

8 cups all-purpose flour
1 cup sugar
1/3 cup baking powder
1 tablespoon salt
1 cup shortening
ADDITIONAL INGREDIENTS:
1 egg
1 cup milk
FOR CHEDDAR MUFFINS:
3/4 cup shredded cheddar cheese
1/4 cup crumbled cooked bacon
2 tablespoons snipped fresh *or* dried chives
FOR CINNAMON-RAISIN MUFFINS:
1/2 cup raisins
1/4 teaspoon ground cinnamon

In a large bowl, combine flour, sugar, baking powder and salt. Cut in shortening until the mixture resembles coarse crumbs. Store in airtight containers in a cool dry place or in the freezer for up to 6 months. **Yield:** 4 batches (10 cups). **To prepare plain muffins:** Place 2-1/2 cups muffin mix in a bowl. Whisk egg and milk; stir into dry ingredients just until moistened. Fill greased or paper-lined muffin cups two-thirds full. Bake at 425° for 15-20 minutes or until muffins test done. Let stand for 10 minutes before removing to a wire rack. **To prepare cheddar muffins:** In a bowl, combine 2-1/2 cups muffin mix, cheese, bacon and chives. Whisk egg and milk; stir into cheese mixture just until moistened. Fill muffin cups and bake as directed for plain muffins. **To prepare cinnamon-raisin muffins:** In a bowl, combine 2-1/2 cups muffin mix, raisins and cinnamon. Whisk egg and milk; stir into raisin mixture just until moistened. Fill muffin cups and bake as directed for plain muffins. **Yield:** 1 dozen per batch.

Fruity Rice Mix

Dried apricots and golden raisins lend sweetness and pretty color to this flavorful rice mix dotted with almonds. I usually serve this special side dish with fish or chicken.
— *Emily Chaney, Penobscot, Maine*

11 cups uncooked long grain rice
4-1/2 cups diced dried apricots
2-1/2 cups golden raisins
1-1/2 cups slivered almonds
1 cup chicken bouillon granules
3 tablespoons brown sugar
ADDITIONAL INGREDIENTS:
2 cups water
1 tablespoon butter *or* margarine

In a bowl, combine the first six ingredients and mix well. Store in airtight containers in a cool dry place for up to 6 months. **Yield:** 21 batches (21 cups total). **To prepare rice:** In a saucepan, combine 1 cup rice mix, water and butter. Bring to a boil. Reduce heat; cover and simmer for 25-30 minutes or until the water is absorbed. **Yield:** 4 servings per batch.

Chapter 7

THIS chapter pleasantly proves that leftovers can make for quick and easy meals—without looking or tasting the same the second (or even third) time around!

The key is to first cook up a hearty dish on the weekend and then use the "planned leftovers" in a whole different dish or two during the middle of the week.

For example, start by treating your family to Turkey Breast with Gravy on the next page (like all the weekend dishes that supply the main ingredient for the weekday ones, its title is highlighted in a color box). Later, surprise them with such lively leftovers as Turkey Florentine and Saucy Turkey.

Your family will never again look at leftovers the same way!

TWICE AS TASTY. Top to bottom: Roasted Chicken and Chicken Enchiladas (recipes on p. 108).

Turkey Breast with Gravy

An herb rub is my tried-and-true secret for savory roast turkey. It seasons the meat nicely and makes a wonderful gravy. Depending on the size of your family, you may want to cook two turkey breasts to ensure leftovers!
—Emily Chaney, Penobscot, Maine

1 bone-in turkey breast (5 to 6 pounds)
1 medium onion, quartered
2 celery ribs, sliced
1 tablespoon lemon-pepper seasoning
1-1/2 teaspoons garlic powder
1-1/2 teaspoons onion powder
1 teaspoon rubbed sage
1 teaspoon paprika
2 tablespoons all-purpose flour
1 cup water
1 chicken bouillon cube

Place turkey breast in a shallow baking pan; coat the outside of the turkey with nonstick cooking spray. Tuck the onion and celery underneath in the breast cavity. Combine seasonings; rub over turkey. Bake, uncovered, at 325° for 2-1/2 to 3 hours or until a meat thermometer reads 185°, basting every 30 minutes. Remove turkey and keep warm. For gravy, combine flour and water in a saucepan until smooth. Add pan drippings and bouillon. Bring to a boil over medium heat, stirring constantly; boil for 2 minutes. Slice turkey; serve with the gravy. **Yield:** 6 servings.

Turkey Florentine

This creamy dish is one of my family's favorite ways to use up leftover turkey and gravy. The addition of spinach and noodles make it a hearty meal-in-one.
—Emily Chaney

1 package (10 ounces) frozen chopped spinach
2 tablespoons butter *or* margarine
2 cups cooked noodles
1-1/2 cups diced cooked turkey
1 cup turkey *or* chicken gravy
1 carton (8 ounces) sour cream onion dip
1/2 teaspoon onion salt
2 tablespoons grated Parmesan cheese

Cook spinach according to package directions; drain. Stir in butter. Place noodles in a greased 11-in. x 7-in. x 2-in. baking dish; top with spinach. Combine turkey, gravy, onion dip and onion salt; spoon over spinach. Sprinkle with Parmesan cheese. Bake, uncovered, at 325° for 25 minutes or until bubbly. **Yield:** 6 servings.

Saucy Turkey

The spicy sauce in this speedy dish is so quick to stir together because it uses convenience foods such as mustard, ketchup and hot pepper sauce.
—Mrs. Johnnye Masters, Rayville, Louisiana

2 tablespoons butter *or* margarine
1 small onion, chopped
1 small green pepper, chopped
1-1/2 cups ketchup
1/2 cup chicken broth
1-1/2 teaspoons Worcestershire sauce
1 teaspoon prepared mustard
1/4 to 1/2 teaspoon hot pepper sauce
1/4 teaspoon pepper
3 cups cubed cooked turkey
Hot cooked rice *or* sandwich rolls

In a large saucepan, melt butter; saute onion and green pepper until tender. Stir in ketchup, broth, Worcestershire sauce, mustard, hot pepper sauce and pepper. Add turkey. Simmer, uncovered, for 20 minutes or until heated through. Serve over rice or on rolls. **Yield:** 4 servings.

Favorite Pot Roast
(Pictured at right)

I love cooking a pot roast on the weekend because it can simmer for hours while I'm doing other things. This hearty beef roast with potatoes and carrots makes enough for a family of four with plenty left over.
—Leona Therou, Overland Park, Kansas

1 boneless rump roast (4 pounds)
2 tablespoons vegetable oil
2 teaspoons salt
1/2 teaspoon pepper
1/2 teaspoon dried thyme
1 bay leaf
3 cups water, *divided*
8 medium potatoes, peeled and quartered
8 large carrots
1 pound small onions, peeled
1/2 cup all-purpose flour
1/2 teaspoon browning sauce, optional
Additional salt and pepper to taste

In a Dutch oven, brown the roast in oil. Combine salt, pepper and thyme; sprinkle over meat. Add bay leaf and 2 cups of water; bring to a boil. Reduce heat; cover and simmer for 2-1/2 hours. Add potatoes, carrots and onions. Cover and simmer 45 minutes longer or until the meat and vegetables are tender. Remove the roast and vegetables to a serving platter; keep warm. Discard bay leaf. Skim fat from pan juices; add water to measure 2 cups. Mix flour and remaining water until smooth; stir into juices. Cook and stir until thickened and bubbly; cook and stir 1 minute longer. Stir in browning sauce if desired. Season with salt and pepper. Slice roast; serve with vegetables and gravy. **Yield:** 8 servings.

Beef Pasties
(Pictured above right)

We had lots of leftovers when we sampled Leona's pot roast in our test kitchen, so our staff came up with this

Beef Pasties
Favorite Pot Roast

recipe for fast-to-fix pasties. Just tuck the cooked roast beef, carrots, potatoes and onion into pie pastry—your family will be amazed at the tender and flaky results!

    2 cups cubed cooked roast beef (1/4-inch
        pieces)
1-1/2 cups cubed cooked potatoes
    1 cup beef gravy
    1/2 cup diced cooked carrots
    1/2 cup diced cooked onion
    1 tablespoon chopped fresh parsley
    1/4 teaspoon dried thyme
    1/2 teaspoon salt
    1/8 to 1/4 teaspoon pepper
Pastry for double-crust pie* (9 inches)
Half-and-half cream

In a bowl, combine the first nine ingredients; set aside. On a lightly floured surface, roll out one-fourth of the pastry into an 8-in. circle. Mound 1 cup filling on half of circle. Moisten edges with water; fold dough over filling and press the edges with a fork to seal. Place on an ungreased baking sheet. Repeat with remaining pastry and filling. Cut slits in top of each; brush with cream. Bake at 450° for 20-25 minutes or until golden brown. **Yield:** 4 servings. ***Editor's Note:** If using purchased pre-rolled pastry, cut each circle in half. Mound filling on half of the pastry; fold pastry over, forming a wedge.

Barbecued Beef Sandwiches

With only three ingredients, you can assemble these sandwiches in short order, our food staff confirms. Use store-bought barbecue sauce to flavor your leftover beef if you like. (This recipe works fine with deli roast beef, too.)

    2 cups shredded cooked roast beef
    1 bottle (18 ounces) barbecue sauce
    5 kaiser rolls, split

In a saucepan, combine beef and barbecue sauce; heat through. Serve on rolls. **Yield:** 5 servings.

Fried Potatoes

Don't forget fried potatoes—they're a wonderful way to use up leftovers, remind our test kitchen cooks. Ready in just seconds, they taste great with breakfast or as a side dish for supper.

    3 cups diced cooked potatoes
    1/2 cup diced cooked onion
    2 tablespoons butter *or* margarine
Salt and pepper to taste

In a skillet, cook the potatoes and onion in butter until golden brown, about 10 minutes. Season with salt and pepper. **Yield:** 3-4 servings.

Three-Meat Sauce

(Pictured below)

This authentic Italian spaghetti sauce recipe is a long-time family favorite. Very hearty with lots of meat and a zippy flavor, it's wonderful over a plateful of your favorite pasta.
—Lillian Di Senso
Lake Havasu City, Arizona

  1 boneless chuck roast (2-1/2 to 3 pounds), trimmed and cut into 1-inch cubes
  1 pork shoulder roast (2 to 2-1/2 pounds), trimmed and cut into 1-inch cubes
  1 pound fresh Italian sausage links, cut into 1-inch slices
  3 tablespoons olive *or* vegetable oil
  3 large onions, chopped
  5 cans (15 ounces *each*) tomato sauce
  3 cans (6 ounces *each*) tomato paste
  1 cup water
1/2 cup minced fresh parsley *or* 3 tablespoons dried parsley flakes
1/2 cup minced fresh oregano *or* 3 tablespoons dried oregano
  5 teaspoons salt
  2 teaspoons pepper

In a large Dutch oven or soup kettle, brown beef, pork and sausage in oil; drain. Add onions; cook until tender. Add tomato sauce and paste, water, parsley, oregano, salt and pepper; mix well. Bring to a boil. Reduce heat; cover and simmer for 2-1/2 to 3 hours or until the meat is tender. For 4-6 people, serve 4 cups of the meat sauce over 1 pound of cooked and drained spaghetti. Refrigerate or freeze remaining sauce (may be frozen up to 3 months). **Yield:** 18 cups.

Easy Lasagna

(Pictured below)

For a supper to please a crowd, I layer lasagna noodles with meat sauce and a tasty cottage cheese mixture to make this speedy version of a traditional favorite.
—Pam Beerens, Evart, Michigan

  1 carton (12 ounces) cottage cheese
  1 egg
1/4 cup grated Parmesan cheese
  1 tablespoon minced fresh parsley *or* 1 teaspoon dried parsley flakes

Easy Lasagna
Three-Meat Sauce

1/2 teaspoon dried oregano
1/4 teaspoon dried basil
9 lasagna noodles, cooked, rinsed and drained
4 cups Three-Meat Sauce* (recipe on previous page)
2 cups (8 ounces) shredded mozzarella cheese

In a bowl, combine the cottage cheese, egg, Parmesan cheese, parsley, oregano and basil; mix well. In a greased 13-in. x 9-in. x 2-in. baking dish, layer a third of the noodles, meat sauce, cottage cheese mixture and mozzarella. Repeat layers. Cover and bake at 350° for 30 minutes; uncover and bake 15-20 minutes longer or until bubbly. Let stand 15 minutes before cutting. **Yield:** 12 servings. *Editor's Note:* 1 pound of browned ground beef and one 26-1/2-ounce can of spaghetti sauce may be substituted for the Three-Meat Sauce.

Quick Calzones

Our kitchen staff came up with a delicious way to use up leftover meat sauce—calzones that taste made from scratch. Frozen bread dough makes them easy to assemble.

1 loaf (1 pound) frozen bread dough, thawed
1 cup Three-Meat Sauce (recipe on previous page)
1/4 cup shredded mozzarella cheese
1 to 2 tablespoons milk
1 tablespoon grated Parmesan cheese
1/2 teaspoon Italian seasoning

Divide bread dough into four portions; roll each into a 6-in. circle. Spoon 1/4 cup of meat sauce on half of each circle to within 1/2 in. of edges. Sprinkle each with 1 tablespoon of mozzarella cheese. Fold dough over the filling and press edges firmly to seal. Brush with milk. Combine Parmesan cheese and Italian seasoning; sprinkle over the calzones. Place on a greased baking sheet. Bake at 350° for 20 minutes or until golden brown. **Yield:** 4 servings.

Steak with Mushroom Sauce

I saute mushrooms with sliced onions and minced garlic, then create an unforgettable sauce that perfectly complements my pan-fried steaks. —Gloria Holmdahl
Spokane, Washington

4 boneless top loin *or* strip steaks* (about 2 pounds)
1/4 cup all-purpose flour
2 tablespoons vegetable oil
1 pound fresh mushrooms, sliced
2 medium onions, sliced
2 garlic cloves, minced
1/3 cup white wine *or* beef broth
1 can (14-1/2 ounces) beef broth
Salt and pepper to taste

Sprinkle both sides of steaks with flour. In a large skillet, cook steaks in oil to desired doneness (for rare, a meat thermometer should read 140°; medium, 160°; well-done,

170°). Remove and keep warm. In the same skillet, saute mushrooms, onions and garlic until tender, adding additional oil if necessary. Stir in wine. Bring to a boil; boil for 1 minute. Add broth, salt and pepper. Bring to a boil; boil for 6 minutes or until sauce is reduced by half. For 2 people, serve two steaks with 1-1/2 cups sauce. Save the remaining steaks and sauce for Steak and Mushroom Soup and Steak Hash (recipes below). **Yield:** 4 steaks (3 cups sauce). *Editor's Note:* Steak may be known as strip steak, Kansas City steak, New York Strip steak, Ambassador Steak or boneless Club Steak in your region.

Steak and Mushroom Soup

I transform the sauce and one of the remaining steaks into this soup, which I serve with a tossed salad and fresh-baked rolls. Topped with Swiss cheese and croutons, the nicely seasoned soup can't be beat. —Gloria Holmdahl

1 cooked steak, diced (about 1 cup)
1-1/2 cups Mushroom Sauce (recipe on this page)
1 can (14-1/2 ounces) chicken broth
1 can (14-1/2 ounces) beef broth
1 cup water
1/4 to 1/2 teaspoon celery seed
1/4 teaspoon pepper
2 drops hot pepper sauce
Herb-flavored croutons
Shredded Swiss cheese

In a soup kettle or Dutch oven, combine the first eight ingredients; bring to a boil. Reduce heat and simmer, uncovered, for 30-40 minutes. Top servings with croutons and cheese. **Yield:** 4 servings.

Steak Hash

Give leftover steak and baked potatoes a flavorful face-lift. Green pepper, onion and garlic powder lend just enough seasoning to this brunch dish. It's so hearty it can also be served for supper. —Barbara Nowakowski
North Tonawanda, New York

1 medium green pepper, chopped
1 small onion, chopped
2 tablespoons vegetable oil
3 medium potatoes (about 1 pound), peeled, cooked and diced
1 cooked steak, diced (about 1 cup)
1/4 to 1/2 teaspoon garlic powder
Salt and pepper to taste
1/4 cup shredded Monterey Jack cheese
4 eggs

In a skillet, saute the green pepper and onion in oil until tender. Stir in potatoes. Reduce heat; cover and cook over low heat for 10 minutes or until the potatoes are heated through, stirring occasionally. Add steak, garlic powder, salt and pepper. Sprinkle with cheese. Cover and cook on low for 5 minutes until heated through and cheese is melted; keep warm. Prepare eggs as desired. Divide hash between four plates and top with an egg. **Yield:** 4 servings.

Roasted Chicken
Chicken Enchiladas

Roasted Chicken

(Pictured above and on page 102)

This moist and tender chicken is a real time-saver on a busy weekend. A simple blend of seasonings makes it a snap to prepare, and it smells heavenly as it roasts. —Marian Platt
Sequim, Washington

2 roasting chickens (about 5 pounds each)
1 teaspoon *each* salt, seasoned salt, celery salt and onion salt
1/2 teaspoon pepper

Wash chickens and pat dry. Place with breast side up in an ungreased 13-in. x 9-in. x 2-in. baking pan. Combine seasonings; rub over and inside chickens. Cover tightly and bake at 400° for 1 hour. Uncover and bake 30 minutes longer or until a meat thermometer reads 180°. Serve one chicken immediately. Cool the second chicken; debone and cube the meat and refrigerate or freeze (may be frozen for up to 3 months). **Yield:** 8-12 servings (4-6 servings per chicken).

Chicken Enchiladas

(Pictured above and on page 102)

I use leftover chicken to create a rich and creamy meal-in-one. This colorful dish has zippy flavor, and it's a nice change of pace from beef enchiladas. —Julie Moutray
Wichita, Kansas

1 can (16 ounces) refried beans
10 flour tortillas (6 to 8 inches)
1 can (10-3/4 ounces) condensed cream of chicken soup, undiluted

1 cup (8 ounces) sour cream
3 to 4 cups cubed roasted *or* cooked chicken
3 cups (12 ounces) shredded cheddar cheese,
 divided
1 can (15 ounces) enchilada sauce
1/4 cup sliced green onions
1/4 cup sliced ripe olives
Shredded lettuce, optional

Spread about 2 tablespoons of beans on each tortilla. Combine soup and sour cream; stir in chicken. Spoon 1/3 to 1/2 cup down the center of each tortilla; top with 1 tablespoon cheese. Roll up and place seam side down in a greased 13-in. x 9-in. x 2-in. baking dish. Pour enchilada sauce over the top; sprinkle with onions, olives and remaining cheese. Bake, uncovered, at 350° for 35 minutes or until heated through. Just before serving, sprinkle lettuce around enchiladas if desired. **Yield:** 4-6 servings.

Fast Chicken Divan

Frozen broccoli and leftover chicken get an easy—but elegant—treatment in this dish. I dress them up with a saucy blend of cream soup and mayonnaise, then cover it all with a golden, cheesy crumb topping.
—Bertille Cooper, St. Inigoes, Maryland

2 packages (10 ounces *each*) frozen broccoli
 florets *or* chopped broccoli
3 cups cubed roasted *or* cooked chicken
2 cans (10-3/4 ounces *each*) condensed cream
 of chicken soup, undiluted
1 cup mayonnaise
1 teaspoon lemon juice
1 cup (4 ounces) shredded sharp cheddar
 cheese
3/4 cup dry bread crumbs
3 tablespoons butter *or* margarine, melted
1 tablespoon sliced pimientos, optional

Cook the broccoli in boiling water for 1 minute; drain. Transfer to a greased 11-in. x 7-in. x 2-in. baking dish; top with the chicken. Combine soup, mayonnaise and lemon juice; spread over chicken. Sprinkle with cheese. Combine bread crumbs and butter; sprinkle over top. Bake, uncovered, at 325° for 30 minutes or until heated through. Let stand for 10 minutes before serving. Garnish with pimientos if desired. **Yield:** 4-6 servings.

Herbed Pork Roast

A combination of dry herbs gives pork an out-of-this-world flavor! This wonderful, moist roast is a family favorite—and it makes great company fare, too.   —Carolyn Pope
Mason City, Iowa

2 tablespoons sugar
2 teaspoons dried marjoram
2 teaspoons rubbed sage
1 teaspoon salt

1/2 teaspoon celery seed
1/2 teaspoon ground mustard
1/8 teaspoon pepper
1 boneless pork loin roast (5 pounds)

Combine the first seven ingredients; rub over roast. Cover and refrigerate for 4 hours or overnight. Place roast on a rack in a shallow roasting pan. Bake, uncovered, at 325° for 2-1/2 hours or until a meat thermometer reads 160°-170°. Let stand for 15 minutes before slicing. Refrigerate or freeze remaining pork (may be frozen for up to 3 months). **Yield:** 12-14 servings.

Pork Noodle Casserole

I learned to make this hearty pork, corn and noodle dish from my grandmother. We never have a family get-together without it. It's a great addition to a buffet and makes a filling meal with the addition of warm rolls.
—Barbara Beyer, Two Rivers, Wisconsin

3 cups cubed cooked pork
1 cup chicken broth
1 can (14-3/4 ounces) cream-style corn
1 can (4 ounces) whole mushrooms, drained
2/3 cup chopped green pepper
2/3 cup chopped onion
4 ounces process American cheese, diced
2 tablespoons diced pimientos
1/2 teaspoon salt
1/4 teaspoon pepper
8 ounces uncooked medium noodles

In a large bowl, combine the first 10 ingredients; fold in noodles. Spoon into a greased deep 2-1/2-qt. baking dish. Cover tightly and bake at 325° for 1 hour or until noodles are tender, stirring every 20 minutes. **Yield:** 6 servings.

Spicy Pork Sandwiches

This flavorful sandwich spread is a fun alternative to standard mustard or mayo. It adds interest to leftover pork or most any sandwich meat, including turkey and roast beef.
—Myra Innes, Auburn, Kansas

1/2 cup mayonnaise
1-1/2 teaspoons finely chopped onion
1-1/2 teaspoons minced fresh parsley
1-1/2 teaspoons finely chopped celery
1-1/2 teaspoons picante sauce
1-1/2 teaspoons Dijon mustard
1/4 teaspoon salt
1/4 teaspoon pepper
10 slices whole wheat bread
5 slices cooked pork
Lettuce leaves

In a small bowl, combine the first eight ingredients. Spread about 1 tablespoonful on each slice of bread. Top five slices with pork and lettuce; top with remaining bread. Refrigerate any leftover spread. **Yield:** 5 sandwiches.

Prairie Meat Loaf

You can't top a hearty helping of meat loaf with creamy mashed potatoes on the side. This tender, moist meat loaf with a hint of cheese is a big hit at our house. The addition of oats boosts its nutritional value.
—Karen Laubman, Spruce Grove, Alberta

　2 eggs
1/2 cup ketchup
　2 tablespoons prepared mustard
　3 cups old-fashioned oats
　2 teaspoons salt
　1 teaspoon garlic powder
　1 teaspoon dried thyme
　1 teaspoon dried basil
1-1/2 cups beef broth
1-1/2 cups finely chopped onion
1-1/2 cups finely chopped celery
2-1/2 cups (10 ounces) shredded cheddar cheese,
　　divided
　4 pounds lean ground beef

In a large bowl, beat eggs; stir in ketchup, mustard, oats, salt, garlic powder, thyme and basil. In a small saucepan, bring broth to a boil; add to oat mixture and mix well. Stir in onion, celery and 2 cups of cheese. Add beef and mix well. Press into two ungreased 9-in. x 5-in. x 3-in. loaf pans. Bake at 375° for 1-1/4 hours or until a meat thermometer reads 170° and juices run clear; drain. Sprinkle with remaining cheese; let stand until melted. **Yield:** 2 loaves (6-8 servings each).

Southwest Stuffed Peppers

Looking for a great way to give leftover meat loaf a whole new taste? Try this simple stuffed peppers variation. The tasty filling in these tender peppers gets its zip from salsa and cumin.
—Greg Greinke
Round Rock, Texas

　4 medium green *or* sweet red peppers
1/2 cup chopped onion
　1 garlic clove, minced
　2 teaspoons vegetable oil
　2 cups cubed cooked meat loaf
1-1/2 cups cooked rice
　1 cup salsa
1/4 cup minced fresh cilantro *or* parsley
　1 teaspoon ground cumin
1/4 teaspoon salt
Pinch pepper
1/2 cup shredded Monterey Jack *or* cheddar
　　cheese

Cut tops off peppers; remove seeds. In a large saucepan, cook peppers in boiling water for 3 minutes. Drain and rinse in cold water; set aside. In a skillet, saute onion and garlic in oil until tender. Remove from the heat; add meat loaf, rice, salsa, cilantro and cumin. Sprinkle inside of peppers with salt and pepper. Stuff with meat loaf mix-

ture. Place in an ungreased 8-in. square baking dish. Bake, uncovered, at 350° for 20 minutes. Sprinkle with cheese; bake 5 minutes longer or until cheese is melted. **Yield:** 4 servings.

Meat Loaf Sandwiches

Dijon mustard provides the lively flavor in these hot open-faced sandwiches. Because they're so easy to prepare, you can have a hot meal ready in minutes.
—Wendy Moylan, Chicago, Illinois

　1 jar (12 ounces) beef gravy
　4 slices bread
　2 teaspoons butter *or* margarine
　2 teaspoons Dijon mustard
　4 slices cooked meat loaf, warmed

In a small saucepan, heat the gravy. Toast bread if desired; spread with butter and mustard. Top with meat loaf slices. Serve with gravy. **Yield:** 4 sandwiches.

Baked Salmon
(Pictured at right)

I often make this very moist and flavorful salmon for company because I can have it ready in less than half an hour. I like to serve it with rice, a green vegetable and a tossed salad.
—Emily Chaney, Penobscot, Maine

✓ **Nutritional Analysis included**

　1 salmon fillet (2 pounds)
　2 tablespoons butter *or* margarine, softened
1/4 cup white wine *or* chicken broth
　2 tablespoons lemon juice
1/2 teaspoon pepper
1/2 teaspoon dried tarragon

Pat salmon dry. Place in a greased 13-in. x 9-in. x 2-in. baking dish. Brush with butter. Combine remaining ingredients; pour over salmon. Bake, uncovered, at 425° for 20-25 minutes or until fish flakes easily with a fork. **Yield:** 8 servings. **To grill salmon:** Place fillet skin side down on the grill; cook, uncovered, over medium heat for 5 minutes. Brush with butter. Combine remaining ingredients. Grill salmon 15-20 minutes longer or until fish flakes easily with a fork, basting occasionally with wine mixture. **Nutritional Analysis:** One 1/4-pound serving (prepared with margarine and low-sodium broth) equals 192 calories, 132 mg sodium, 74 mg cholesterol, 1 gm carbohydrate, 28 gm protein, 8 gm fat. **Diabetic Exchanges:** 4 very lean meat, 1 fat.

Dilled Salmon Pasta Salad
(Pictured above right)

This pretty pasta salad for two calls for just a cup of leftover salmon. It's nicely seasoned with dill and makes a cool, light lunch.
—Elaine Williams
Sebastopol, California

Baked Salmon
Dilled Salmon Pasta Salad

✓ Nutritional Analysis included

1-1/2 cups tricolored spiral pasta
 1/2 cup sour cream
 1/2 cup mayonnaise
 1/4 cup chopped green pepper
 1/4 cup chopped sweet red pepper
 2 tablespoons chopped onion
 2 tablespoons minced fresh dill *or* 2 teaspoons
  dill weed
 1 cup fully cooked salmon chunks *or* 1 can
  (7-1/2 ounces) salmon, drained, bones and
  skin removed
Mixed salad greens

Cook pasta according to package directions. Meanwhile, combine the next six ingredients in a bowl. Drain and rinse pasta in cold water; add to sour cream mixture. Stir in the salmon. Cover and refrigerate. Serve over salad greens. **Yield:** 2 servings. **Nutritional Analysis:** One 1-1/2-cup serving (prepared with nonfat sour cream and fat-free mayonnaise) equals 353 calories, 500 mg sodium, 42 mg cholesterol, 51 gm carbohydrate, 21 gm protein, 5 gm fat. **Diabetic Exchanges:** 3 starch, 1-1/2 lean meat, 1 vegetable.

Salmon Puffs

Convenient pastry shells make this entree elegant. You'd never guess it is a second-day dish. —Carolyn Moseley
Mt. Pleasant, South Carolina

 2 frozen puff pastry shells *or* 2 slices toast
 1/2 cup apricot preserves
 1 tablespoon prepared horseradish
 2 teaspoons vinegar
 1 cup fully cooked salmon chunks *or* 1 can
  (7-1/2 ounces) salmon, drained, bones and
  skin removed

Bake pastry shells according to package directions. Meanwhile, combine the preserves, horseradish and vinegar in a saucepan. Cook over medium heat for 5 minutes or until heated through. Stir in salmon and heat through. Spoon into pastry shells or over toast; serve immediately. **Yield:** 2 servings.

Look Ahead for Lively Leftovers **111**

Ratatouille with Sausage

(Pictured below right)

I concocted this recipe when we lived on a farm and had lots of fresh veggies and sausage available. Prepared spaghetti sauce can be used in place of the fresh tomatoes.
—*Diane Halferty, Tucson, Arizona*

1 medium eggplant, peeled
4 small zucchini, cut into 1/2-inch slices
1/3 cup all-purpose flour
3 to 4 tablespoons olive *or* vegetable oil, *divided*
2 large onions, sliced
3 garlic cloves, minced
8 uncooked Italian sausage links (about 2 pounds)
4 medium green peppers, julienned
4 medium tomatoes, coarsely chopped
1/4 cup water
1/2 cup minced fresh basil *or* 8 teaspoons dried basil
2 tablespoons minced fresh oregano *or* 2 teaspoons dried oregano
2 tablespoons minced fresh thyme *or* 2 teaspoons dried thyme
1 teaspoon salt
1/4 teaspoon pepper
1 cup (4 ounces) shredded mozzarella cheese

Cut eggplant into 2-in. x 1/2-in. strips; place in a bowl. Add zucchini and flour; toss to coat. In a large skillet, heat 1 tablespoon of oil over medium heat; cook eggplant and zucchini in small batches until lightly browned, adding oil as needed. Transfer vegetables to a greased shallow 3-qt. baking dish. In the same skillet, saute onions and garlic until tender; spoon over eggplant mixture. Brown sausage in the skillet; drain. Cover and cook over low heat for 15-20 minutes or until no longer pink. Meanwhile, in another skillet, saute green peppers for 3 minutes. Add tomatoes, water and seasonings; cook on high for 2 minutes. Reduce heat; cover and simmer for 5 minutes. Drain sausage; place over onions. Top with the green pepper mixture. Bake, uncovered, at 350° for 20 minutes. Sprinkle with cheese; bake 10 minutes longer or until cheese is melted. **Yield:** 8 cups ratatouille and 8 sausages.

Sausage Spinach Casserole

This casserole can use leftover sausage to help create a light main or hearty side dish. It's delicious with lots of spinach and beans. —*Lynn Salsbury, Herington, Kansas*

2 packages (10 ounces *each*) frozen chopped spinach, thawed and drained
1 can (15 ounces) great northern beans, rinsed and drained
2 cooked Italian sausage links, sliced
1 can (12 ounces) evaporated milk
3/4 cup chopped onion
1/2 cup grated Parmesan cheese, *divided*
1 tablespoon lemon juice
1 teaspoon grated lemon peel
1/4 teaspoon ground nutmeg
1/8 teaspoon pepper
2 garlic cloves, minced
4 teaspoons butter *or* margarine
1/3 cup dry bread crumbs

In a bowl, combine the first five ingredients. Stir in 1/4 cup cheese, lemon juice and peel, nutmeg and pepper. Transfer to a greased 2-qt. baking dish. In a skillet, saute garlic in butter until tender. Remove from the heat; stir in bread crumbs and remaining cheese. Sprinkle over the

Ratatouille Frittata
Ratatouille with Sausage

spinach mixture. Bake, uncovered, at 375° for 30 minutes or until heated through. **Yield:** 4 servings.

Ratatouille Frittata

(Pictured below left)

The fluffy eggs in this dish pick up wonderful flavor from spicy chunks of sausage.
—*Anne Michalski, De Pere, Wisconsin*

2 cups frozen cubed hash brown potatoes
2 tablespoons olive *or* vegetable oil
2 cooked Italian sausage links, diced
2 cups cooked ratatouille* (from the Ratatouille with Sausage recipe on the previous page)
6 eggs
1/4 cup milk
1/4 teaspoon salt
1/8 teaspoon pepper

In a 10-in. or 12-in. ovenproof skillet, cook hash browns in oil until browned. Stir in sausage and ratatouille. In a bowl, beat eggs, milk, salt and pepper; pour over vegetables. Cover and cook over medium-low heat until eggs are nearly set, about 10 minutes. Uncover; broil 6 in. from the heat for 2-3 minutes or until eggs are completely set and top is lightly browned. **Yield:** 4 servings.
*Editor's Note: 2 cups of any vegetables may be substituted for the ratatouille.

Delicate Chocolate Cake

This cake has a light cocoa flavor, and the frosting is rich. Because you frost and serve just half the cake, you can use the remainder to make other scrumptious desserts later in the week. —*Annette Foster, Taylors, South Carolina*

1 cup vegetable oil
1 cup water
1/2 cup butter *or* margarine
1/4 cup baking cocoa
2 cups self-rising flour*
2 cups sugar
1/2 cup buttermilk
2 eggs
FROSTING (for the layer cake):
1/2 cup butter *or* margarine
1/4 cup baking cocoa
1/4 cup milk
4 to 4-1/2 cups confectioners' sugar
1 teaspoon vanilla extract

In a saucepan, combine oil, water, butter and cocoa. Bring to a boil over medium heat; boil for 1 minute. Remove from the heat. In a mixing bowl, combine flour and sugar; gradually add cocoa mixture, beating well. Add buttermilk and eggs; mix well. Pour into a greased 15-in. x 10-in. x 1-in. baking pan. Bake at 350° for 28-30 minutes or until a toothpick inserted near the center comes out clean. Cool on a wire rack. Cut cake into four 7-1/2-in. x 5-in. rectangles. Wrap two of the rectangles separately in foil; refrigerate or freeze. Set the other two rectangles aside. For frosting, combine butter, cocoa and milk in a saucepan. Bring to a boil; boil for 1 minute (mixture will appear curdled). Pour into a mixing bowl. Gradually add sugar and vanilla; beat until frosting is cooled and reaches desired spreading consistency. Frost the top of one cake rectangle; top with the second rectangle. Frost top and sides of cake. **Yield:** 1 two-layer cake (6-8 servings) plus 2 plain cake portions.
*Editor's Note: As a substitute for *each cup* of self-rising flour, place 1-1/2 teaspoons baking powder and 1/2 teaspoon salt in a measuring cup. Add all-purpose flour to equal 1 cup.

Butterscotch Banana Dessert

Butter and brown sugar combine to create this yummy sauce that's terrific served warm over cake or ice cream. This family favorite keeps well tightly covered in the fridge.
—*Carol Haugen, Fargo, North Dakota*

2/3 cup packed brown sugar
1/3 cup corn syrup
1/4 cup butter *or* margarine
1/4 cup water
1 egg yolk, beaten
One portion chocolate cake (7-1/2-inch x 5-inch rectangle) from the Delicate Chocolate Cake recipe on this page, cut into four pieces
2 medium firm bananas, sliced

In a heavy saucepan, combine the first five ingredients. Cook over low heat, stirring frequently, until mixture thickens slightly and a thermometer reads 180°, about 20 minutes. Place cake on serving plates; cover with bananas. Top with warm butterscotch sauce. Sauce may be stored in the refrigerator for up to 3 days. To reheat, heat in the microwave until simmering; whisk before serving. **Yield:** 4 servings (about 1 cup sauce).

Raspberry Chocolate Trifle

Guests will think you slaved over this impressive-looking dessert, but it's really a snap to assemble. —*Karena Bauman Minneapolis, Minnesota*

1 package (3 ounces) cream cheese, softened
2 tablespoons sugar
2 tablespoons milk
1-1/2 cups whipped topping
One portion chocolate cake (7-1/2-inch x 5-inch rectangle) from the Delicate Chocolate Cake recipe on this page, cut into 1/2-inch cubes (2 cups cubes)
2 cups unsweetened raspberries
1/4 cup slivered almonds, toasted

In a mixing bowl, combine cream cheese, sugar and milk; beat until smooth. Fold in whipped topping. In a 1- to 1-1/2-qt. trifle bowl, layer half of the cake cubes, raspberries, cream cheese mixture and almonds. Repeat layers. Refrigerate for at least 15 minutes. **Yield:** 4-6 servings.

Traditional Mashed Potatoes

Mashed potatoes make a wonderful accompaniment to most any meal, so keep this recipe handy.

    6 medium russet potatoes (about 2 pounds), peeled and cubed
1/2 cup warm milk
1/4 cup butter *or* margarine
3/4 teaspoon salt
Dash pepper

Place potatoes in a saucepan and cover with water. Cover and bring to a boil; cook for 20-25 minutes or until very tender. Drain well. Add milk, butter, salt and pepper; mash until light and fluffy. **Yield:** 6 servings (about 5 cups).

Potato Puff Casserole

You'd never guess leftover mashed potatoes are the main ingredient in this delightful casserole. This dish is perfect for everyday meals, yet nice enough for company.

    1 small onion, chopped
2 tablespoons butter *or* margarine
1/2 cup milk
1/2 teaspoon ground mustard
1/4 teaspoon salt
1/8 teaspoon pepper
2 cups mashed potatoes (prepared with milk and butter)
2 eggs, *separated*
1 cup (4 ounces) shredded cheddar cheese, optional

In a skillet, saute onion in butter until tender. Stir in milk, mustard, salt and pepper; bring to a boil. Remove from the heat; stir in potatoes and mix well. Stir in egg yolks until smooth. Cool at room temperature for 15 minutes. Stir in the cheese if desired. In a small mixing bowl, beat egg whites until soft peaks form. Fold into the potato mixture. Spoon into a greased 1-qt. baking dish. Bake at 350° for 40-45 minutes or until puffed and lightly browned. **Yield:** 6 servings.

Mashed Potato Soup

Topped with chives, this soup uses up mashed potatoes and is especially good on chilly evenings.
—Dorothy Bateman, Carver, Massachusetts

✓ Nutritional Analysis included

    1 tablespoon chopped onion
1 tablespoon butter *or* margarine
2 cups milk
1-1/2 cups mashed potatoes (prepared with butter and milk)
1/2 teaspoon salt, optional
1/8 teaspoon celery salt, optional
1/8 teaspoon pepper
1 tablespoon minced fresh *or* dried chives

In a saucepan, saute the onion in butter until tender. Add milk, potatoes, salt and celery salt if desired and pepper; heat through. Garnish with chives. **Yield:** 3 servings. **Nutritional Analysis:** One 1-cup serving (prepared with margarine and skim milk and without salt and celery salt) equals 192 calories, 401 mg sodium, 5 mg cholesterol, 28 gm carbohydrate, 8 gm protein, 6 gm fat. **Diabetic Exchanges:** 1 skim milk, 1 fat, 1 starch.

Simple Stuffed Potatoes

I created this recipe to use up leftovers. It tastes just like stuffed potatoes, but it's easier to make.
—Delorus Krizan, Dallas, South Dakota

    1 teaspoon butter *or* margarine
2 cups mashed potatoes (prepared with milk and butter)
1 cup cubed fully cooked ham
1/2 cup shredded cheddar cheese

In a skillet, melt butter. Stir in potatoes and ham; heat through. Sprinkle with cheese. Reduce heat; cover and cook for 3-5 minutes or until the cheese is melted. **Yield:** 2 servings.

Ham with Cherry Sauce
(Pictured at right)

The recipe for this tangy sauce was given to me by a friend. I usually serve the ham with sweet potatoes, coleslaw or applesauce and rolls.   *—Joan Laurenzo, Johnstown, Ohio*

    1/2 fully cooked bone-in ham (6 to 7 pounds)
1 jar (12 ounces) cherry preserves
1/4 cup cider *or* red wine vinegar
2 tablespoons light corn syrup
1/4 teaspoon *each* ground cloves, cinnamon and nutmeg
3 tablespoons slivered almonds

Place ham on a rack in a shallow roasting pan. If desired, remove skin from ham and score the surface with shallow diagonal cuts, making diamond shapes. Bake, uncovered, at 325° for 1-1/2 to 2 hours or until a meat thermometer reads 140°. In a saucepan, combine the preserves, vinegar, corn syrup, cloves, cinnamon and nutmeg. Bring to a boil, stirring often. Reduce heat; simmer, uncovered, for 2 minutes. Remove from the heat; stir in almonds. Serve with the ham. **Yield:** 10-12 servings (1-1/2 cups sauce).

Pretty Ham Primavera
(Pictured at right)

I use this mild cream sauce to give leftover ham fresh flavor and a colorful new look.   *—Joan Laurenzo*

    1/2 pound fresh mushrooms, sliced
1 small onion, chopped
2 tablespoons olive *or* vegetable oil
2 tablespoons all-purpose flour

2 teaspoons Italian seasoning
2 teaspoons chicken bouillon granules
1/2 teaspoon salt
1/8 teaspoon pepper
2 cups milk
1 package (7 ounces) thin spaghetti, cooked and drained
2 cups cubed fully cooked ham (1 pound)
1 package (10 ounces) frozen peas, thawed
Grated Parmesan cheese

In a large skillet, saute mushrooms and onion in oil until tender. Stir in flour, Italian seasoning, bouillon, salt and pepper until smooth. Gradually add milk, stirring constantly. Bring to a boil; boil and stir for 2 minutes. Stir in the spaghetti, ham and peas; heat through. Sprinkle with Parmesan cheese. **Yield:** 4 servings.

Plantation Ham Pie

Pretty parsley pinwheels top this hearty casserole filled with a saucy mixture of broccoli, ham and onion.
—*Sharon White, Morden, Manitoba*

4 cups cubed fully cooked ham (2 pounds)
1 medium onion, chopped
2 tablespoons butter *or* margarine
2 cans (10-3/4 ounces *each*) condensed cream of chicken soup, undiluted
1 cup milk
2 cups fresh *or* frozen broccoli florets, cooked and drained
2 cups biscuit/baking mix
1/2 cup water
1/2 cup minced fresh parsley

In a large skillet, saute ham and onion in butter until the onion is tender. Combine soup and milk; stir into ham mixture. Add broccoli; heat through. Pour into an ungreased shallow 2-1/2-qt. baking dish. Combine biscuit mix and water until a soft dough forms. On a lightly floured surface, knead dough 10 times. Roll out into a 12-in. square; sprinkle with parsley. Roll up jelly-roll style. Cut into 12 pieces; place over the ham mixture. Bake, uncovered, at 425° for 20-25 minutes or until biscuits are golden and the ham mixture is bubbly. **Yield:** 6 servings.

Ham with Cherry Sauce
Pretty Ham Primavera

THERE'S no better way to end the day than with a home-cooked meal—even when you don't have the energy to do much more than open up the freezer door and switch on the stove.

With just a little planning on your more leisurely days, you can create delicious time-easing and appetite-appeasing dishes you can simply pop into your freezer for fast, no-fuss future meals.

This selection of "cool" make-ahead recipes and host of helpful hints for stocking your freezer will hurriedly give hunger the cold shoulder!

THE BIG CHILL. Top to bottom: Cheese Sticks (p. 120), Frosty Freeze Pie (p. 121) and Hearty Ham Loaves (p. 120).

Make-Ahead Meatballs

My husband and I have company often. Keeping a supply of these frozen meatballs on hand means I can easily prepare a quick, satisfying meal. I start with a versatile meatball mix that makes about 12 dozen meatballs, then freeze them in batches for future use. I've included three serving variations here.
— *Ruth Andrewson, Leavenworth, Washington*

✓ Nutritional Analysis included

    4 eggs
    2 cups dry bread crumbs
    1/2 cup finely chopped onion
    1 tablespoon salt
    2 teaspoons Worcestershire sauce
    1/2 teaspoon white pepper
    4 pounds lean ground beef

In a large bowl, beat eggs. Add the next five ingredients. Add beef; mix well. Shape into 1-in. balls, about 12 dozen. Place in single layers in ungreased 15-in. x 10-in. x 1-in. baking pans. Bake at 400° for 10-15 minutes or until no longer pink, turning often; drain. Cool. Place about 30 meatballs each into freezer containers. May be frozen for up to 3 months. **Yield:** 5 batches (about 30 meatballs per batch). **Nutritional Analysis:** One serving of 5 meatballs (prepared with egg substitute) equals 139 calories, 357 mg sodium, 22 mg cholesterol, 6 gm carbohydrate, 14 gm protein, 6 gm fat. **Diabetic Exchanges:** 2 lean meat, 1/2 starch.

Spaghetti 'n' Meatballs

(Pictured at far right)

My handy meatballs can dress up any purchased spaghetti sauce for a fast supper with real homemade appeal and very little effort. — *Ruth Andrewson*

    1 package (12 ounces) spaghetti
    1 jar (28 ounces) spaghetti sauce
    1 batch of 30 meatballs (frozen *or* thawed)
Grated Parmesan cheese, optional

Cook spaghetti according to package directions. Meanwhile, in a saucepan, combine spaghetti sauce and meatballs; cover and simmer for 15-20 minutes or until the meatballs are heated through. Serve over spaghetti; top with Parmesan cheese if desired. **Yield:** 6 servings.

Meatball Sandwiches

(Pictured at far right)

These sandwiches are so yummy no one will guess frozen meatballs are your secret ingredient! They also make easy appetizers if unexpected guests stop by.
— *Ruth Andrewson*

    1 batch of 30 meatballs (frozen *or* thawed)
    1 cup ketchup
    3/4 cup packed brown sugar
    1/4 to 1/2 cup chopped onion

    1/4 teaspoon garlic powder
    1/8 teaspoon liquid smoke, optional
    6 sandwich rolls, split

Place meatballs in an ungreased 1-qt. baking dish. Combine the next five ingredients; pour over meatballs. Cover and bake at 350° for 1 hour. Serve on rolls. **Yield:** 6 servings. **Editor's Note:** These meatballs may be served as an appetizer with toothpicks instead of on rolls.

Sweet-and-Sour Meatballs

(Pictured at right)

A tangy sauce, combined with green pepper and pineapple, transforms pre-made meatballs into a delightful main dish served over rice. — *Ruth Andrewson*

    1 can (20 ounces) pineapple chunks
    1/3 cup water
    3 tablespoons vinegar
    1 tablespoon soy sauce
    1/2 cup packed brown sugar
    3 tablespoons cornstarch
    1 batch of 30 meatballs (frozen *or* thawed)
    1 large green pepper, cut into 1-inch pieces
Hot cooked rice

Drain pineapple, reserving juice. Set pineapple aside. Add water to juice if needed to measure 1 cup; pour into a large skillet. Add 1/3 cup water, vinegar, soy sauce, brown sugar and cornstarch; stir until smooth. Cook over medium heat until thick, stirring constantly. Add pineapple, meatballs and green pepper. Simmer, uncovered, for 20 minutes or until heated through. Serve over rice. **Yield:** 6 servings.

Out in the Cold on Freezing Foods?

ARE YOU unsure about how to stock your freezer? Don't get cold feet! Just follow these simple guidelines.

- Put cooked food in the freezer with the temperature set to 0° as soon as possible after preparing it. Food that is very hot should be cooled first, so it won't raise the temperature in the freezer and possibly cause other foods to start thawing.

- To cool food quickly and evenly, transfer it to a shallower pan or divide it among several small shallow containers. Or place the hot pan in the sink on a cooling rack with cool water running underneath it. Help hot liquids like soups and sauces cool by stirring them frequently.

- Freeze food in an airtight, moisture-resistant package to retain best quality and avoid freezer burn. Press down carefully on foil to remove air bubbles.

- Use combination wrapping. For example, wrap first in heavy-duty foil, then in a resealable plastic freezer bag. If you're using a rigid plastic container, first line it with a freezer bag to make it airtight.

- Properly wrapped, fresh ground beef can be kept in the freezer at 0°. For best quality, use within 3 months. Ground beef wrapped and frozen flat will stack easily and make best use of freezer space. These packages also thaw quicker. Be sure not to stack packages until they're completely frozen.

Spaghetti 'n' Meatballs
Sweet-and-Sour Meatballs
Meatball Sandwiches

Time-to-Spare Spuds

These creamy pre-filled potato shells can be quickly thawed, then baked as a side dish to go with a steak or any meat. —Dorothy Bateman, Carver, Massachusetts

    6 large potatoes, baked
    1 cup (8 ounces) sour cream
    1 cup (4 ounces) shredded cheddar cheese
    1 green onion, chopped
  1/4 cup milk
    2 tablespoons butter *or* margarine, melted
    1 tablespoon chopped fresh parsley
    1 teaspoon salt
  Additional melted butter *or* margarine

Cut hot potatoes in half lengthwise; carefully scoop out pulp, leaving a thin shell. In a bowl, mash pulp until smooth. Beat in sour cream, cheese, onion, milk, butter, parsley and salt. Fill shells; brush with butter. Cover and refrigerate. Wrap shells individually in plastic wrap; place in freezer containers. Freeze. To serve, thaw and place in an ungreased shallow baking dish. Bake, uncovered, at 400° for 20-25 minutes or until golden and heated through. May be frozen for up to 1 month. **Yield:** 12 servings.

Cheese Sticks
Frosty Freeze Pie
Hearty Ham Loaves

Cheese Sticks

(Pictured above and on page 117)

When our children were young, I'd pop these scrumptious cheesy snacks in the oven shortly before they'd get home from school. There's no need to thaw them, so they're ready to munch in less than 15 minutes.
—Ruth Peterson, Jenison, Michigan

> 1 jar (5 ounces) sharp American cheese spread
> 1/2 cup butter *or* margarine, softened
> 1 egg white
> 1 loaf unsliced bread (1 pound)

In a mixing bowl, beat cheese spread, butter and egg white until fluffy. Cut crust from bread. Slice bread 1 in. thick; cut each slice into 1-in. strips. Spread the cheese mixture on all sides of each strip and place 2 in. apart on greased baking sheets. Bake at 350° for 12-15 minutes or until lightly browned. Serve warm. Unbaked cheese sticks may be frozen for up to 4 months. Bake as directed (they do not need to be thawed first). **Yield:** 9 servings.

Hearty Ham Loaves

(Pictured above and on page 117)

This is a great way to use leftover baked ham. I serve one of these loaves right away and store the other in the freezer for later. They're so nicely flavored with a variety of seasonings that everyone loves 'em!
—Audrey Thibodeau, Mesa, Arizona

> 1 cup crushed butter-flavored crackers (about 25 crackers)
> 2/3 cup finely chopped onion
> 1/2 cup finely chopped green pepper
> 2 eggs, beaten

2 tablespoons lemon juice
1 teaspoon ground mustard
1 teaspoon ground ginger
1 teaspoon Worcestershire sauce
1/4 teaspoon pepper
Dash ground nutmeg
Dash paprika
1-1/3 pounds finely ground fully cooked ham
1 pound bulk pork sausage
GLAZE:
1/2 cup packed brown sugar
1/4 cup cider vinegar
1/4 cup water
1 teaspoon ground mustard

In a large bowl, combine the first 11 ingredients. Add ham and sausage; mix well. Shape into two loaves. Place in ungreased 9-in. x 5-in. x 3-in. loaf pans. Bake one loaf at 350° for 1 hour. Meanwhile, combine glaze ingredients in a small saucepan. Bring to a boil; boil for 2 minutes. Remove loaf from the oven; drain. Baste with half of the glaze. Bake 30-40 minutes longer or until a meat thermometer reads 160°-170°, basting occasionally. Cover and freeze the remaining loaf and glaze for up to 2 months. To prepare, thaw in the refrigerator overnight and bake as directed. **Yield:** 2 loaves (6-8 servings each).

Frosty Freeze Pie

(Pictured at left and on page 116)

This pretty pie can be whipped up in no time. But it tastes so sweet and creamy people will think you fussed. My family likes it best when it's made with orange sherbet. It's especially refreshing on a warm day.
—Sue Blow, Lititz, Pennsylvania

1 package (8 ounces) cream cheese, softened
1 jar (7 ounces) marshmallow creme
2 cups raspberry, orange *or* lime sherbet, softened
2 to 3 cups whipped topping
1 graham cracker crust (9 *or* 10 inches)

In a mixing bowl, beat cream cheese and marshmallow creme until smooth. Stir in sherbet. Fold in whipped topping. Pour into crust. Freeze until firm. Remove from the freezer 10 minutes before serving. Pie may be frozen for up to 3 months. **Yield:** 8-10 servings.

Hot Dog Sandwiches

These kid-pleasing sandwiches taste just like hot dogs smothered in mustard and relish. Drop the frozen sandwiches in lunch bags before school in the morning. By noon, they'll be thawed and ready to eat.   —Iola Egle
McCook, Nebraska

6 hot dogs, minced
1/2 cup dill pickle relish
1/4 cup chili sauce
2 tablespoons prepared mustard
12 slices bread

In a small bowl, combine hot dogs, relish, chili sauce and mustard; mix well. Spread on six slices of bread; top with the remaining bread. Freeze for up to 2 months. Remove from the freezer at least 4 hours before serving. **Yield:** 6 servings.

Nutty Marmalade Sandwiches

I make batches of fun-filled sandwiches to freeze for a few weeks' worth of brown-bag lunches. They taste so fresh you would never know they were ever frozen.   —Iola Egle

1/2 cup peanut butter
1/4 cup orange marmalade
1/4 cup shredded sharp cheddar cheese
1 to 2 teaspoons lemon juice
6 slices bread

In a small bowl, combine peanut butter, marmalade, cheese and lemon juice; mix well. Spread on three slices of bread; top with remaining bread. Freeze for up to 4 months. Remove from the freezer at least 4 hours before serving. **Yield:** 3 servings.

Consider Your Freezer a 'Frozen Pantry'

STOCKING your freezer is a great way to keep the ingredients for fast-to-fix meals on hand. Whether you store make-ahead main dishes or convenient packaged side dishes, follow these helpful freezer hints. They're sure to help you keep your cool!

• When preparing dishes to keep in the freezer and bake later, save space by storing just the food and not the container. (This also allows you to continue using well-liked baking dishes.) To do this, line your baking dish with foil, add the food, cover with foil and freeze.

   Once it has frozen, remove the foil-wrapped food and place it in a freezer bag before returning it to the freezer. When it's time to cook the dish, remove the foil and place the food in its original container for baking.

• When buying bags of frozen vegetables, examine the packages for signs that they've been thawed and refrozen. Steer clear of bagged vegetables that are frozen in blocks or large chunks. If the packages are transparent, check for crystallization. Both indicate thawing and refreezing, which can diminish quality.

• When your groceries are being packed at the checkout line, be sure frozen items are bagged together to help keep them cold. Put them in the freezer as soon as you get home.

• When scooping ice cream from the carton, do so quickly and return the unused portion to the freezer as soon as possible, since thawing and refreezing causes ice crystals to form on the surface. It's also a good idea to store ice cream in the coldest part of the freezer, away from the door.

Freeze Your Backyard Bounty

THERE'S NOTHING like the taste of fresh fruits and just-picked vegetables...but if your backyard garden produces more than your family can eat, freeze some of the abundance.

Properly prepared, much of your garden produce may be stored in labeled heavy-duty plastic bags or freezer containers.

Vegetables

- Blanching the vegetables (putting them in boiling water for a short time) helps them keep their bright color, fresh taste and natural crunch. It also helps them retain vitamins. Check cookbooks or call your county Extension agent for blanching times for specific vegetables.
- Blanch vegetables as soon as possible after harvesting. Then cool them quickly before freezing.

Fruits

- A variety of fresh fruits can be frozen whole or sliced with no need for blanching. While some can be frozen alone, others fare better when coated with sugar syrup or honey.
- For fruits that tend to turn brown, such as apples, pears and peaches, lemon juice or thawed orange juice can be added with the sugar or honey.
- Washed, drained berries like strawberries and blueberries can be frozen whole on a cookie sheet until solid. Then place the berries in heavy-duty plastic bags for storage.

Herbs

- Many fresh herbs will keep in the freezer if blanched first. Try freezing basil, chives, dill and thyme. It's best to submerge them in boiling water for a few seconds, then cool quickly before freezing.
- A simple way to freeze herbs in small quantities is to place chopped herbs or a few sprigs in ice cube trays and then fill them with water. When the cubes are frozen, place them in a labeled bag. Later, add a few cubes to soups and stews.

Shepherd's Pie

If I know my day will be hectic, I'll pull the meat mixture for this convenient, family-pleasing pie out of the freezer to thaw. And if you use frozen or instant mashed potatoes to top the pie, it's even quicker to fix.
—Paula Zsiray, Logan, Utah

    2 pounds ground beef
    2 cans (10-1/4 ounces *each*) beef gravy
    2 cups frozen corn
    2 cups frozen peas and carrots
    2 teaspoons dried minced onion
ADDITIONAL INGREDIENTS (for each casserole):
    2 to 3 cups mashed potatoes
    2 tablespoons butter *or* margarine, melted
Paprika

In a skillet, brown beef; drain. Add gravy, vegetables and onion. Spoon half into a greased 11-in. x 7-in. x 2-in. baking dish. Spread mashed potatoes evenly over the top. Drizzle with butter and sprinkle with paprika. Bake,

uncovered, at 350° for 30-35 minutes or until heated through. Place the remaining beef mixture in a freezer container and freeze for up to 3 months. To prepare, thaw in the refrigerator; transfer to a greased 11-in. x 7-in. x 2-in. baking dish. Top with potatoes, butter and paprika; bake as directed. **Yield:** 2 casseroles (4 servings each).

Beef Chimichangas

(Pictured below right)

A spicy sauce sparks up these hearty beef- and bean-filled tortillas. I often double the recipe and freeze the chimichangas individually to take out as needed. I serve them with shredded lettuce and sour cream.
—Schelby Thompson, Dover, Delaware

    1 pound ground beef
    1/2 cup finely chopped onion
    1 can (16 ounces) refried beans
    3 cans (8 ounces *each*) tomato sauce, *divided*
    2 teaspoons chili powder
    2 garlic cloves, minced
    1/2 teaspoon ground cumin
    12 flour tortillas (10 inches)
Melted butter *or* margarine
    1 can (4 ounces) chopped green chilies
    1 can (4 ounces) chopped jalapeno peppers
Vegetable oil for frying
1-1/2 cups (6 ounces) shredded cheddar cheese

In a skillet, brown the beef; drain. Stir in onion, beans, 1/2 cup tomato sauce, chili powder, garlic and cumin. Brush one side of the tortillas with melted butter. Spoon about 1/3 cup of beef mixture off-center on the unbuttered side of tortillas. Fold edge nearest filling up and over to cover. Fold in both sides and roll up. Fasten with toothpicks; place in a freezer container. For sauce, combine chilies, peppers and remaining tomato sauce in a saucepan; heat through. Cool and transfer to a freezer container. Sauce and chimichangas may be frozen for up to 3 months. To prepare, thaw sauce and chimichangas in the refrigerator. In an electric skillet or deep-fat fryer, heat 1 in. of oil to 375°. Fry the chimichangas for 1-1/2 to 2 minutes on each side or until browned. Drain on paper towels. Warm the sauce; serve over chimichangas. Top with cheese. **Yield:** 12 chimichangas. **Editor's Note:** Chimichangas may be baked instead of fried. Brush with melted butter and bake at 350° for 25-30 minutes or until golden brown (if frozen, thaw before baking).

Chocolate Mint Dessert

(Pictured at right)

A rich fudge layer plus crunchy nuts and coconut makes this dessert perfect for when you want to serve something special without last-minute fuss. It's easy to make the day before and freeze overnight. *—Barb Seibenaler*
Random Lake, Wisconsin

    1 cup butter *or* margarine, *divided*

1 package (10 ounces) shredded coconut
1/4 cup packed brown sugar
1/4 cup chopped pecans
4 squares (1 ounce *each*) unsweetened chocolate
1-1/2 cups sugar
1 can (12 ounces) evaporated milk
1 teaspoon vanilla extract
2 quarts mint chocolate chip ice cream, softened

In a skillet, melt 1/2 cup butter. Add coconut; cook and stir until golden brown. Remove from the heat. Stir in brown sugar and pecans; mix well. Set aside 1 cup. Press remaining coconut mixture onto the bottom and up the sides of a greased 13-in. x 9-in. x 2-in. dish. In a saucepan over medium heat, melt the chocolate and remaining butter. Add sugar and milk. Bring to a slow boil; cook for 5 minutes. Remove from the heat; stir in vanilla. Cool; pour over coconut mixture. Spread ice cream over top. Sprinkle with the reserved coconut mixture. Freeze for 6-8 hours or overnight. Remove from the freezer 15 minutes before serving. Dessert may be frozen for up to 2 months. **Yield:** 16-20 servings.

Frosty Fruit Cups

With just four ingredients, it's a snap to blend together these refreshing fruit cups. They're ideal for parties because they can be made ahead. Frozen in muffin cups for individual servings, they're a fun way to get kids to eat fruit.
—*Beth Litzenberger, Gothenburg, Nebraska*

 Nutritional Analysis included

2 cans (8 ounces *each*) crushed pineapple, undrained
3 medium firm bananas, sliced
1 package (16 ounces) frozen sweetened strawberries, thawed, undrained
1/4 cup chopped walnuts

Place pineapple in a blender or food processor; cover and process until smooth. Add bananas and strawberries; blend well. Pour 1/3 cup each into paper- or foil-lined muffin cups; sprinkle with walnuts. Freeze for at least 2 hours. May be frozen for up to 1 month. **Yield:** 16 servings. **Nutritional Analysis:** One serving equals 79 calories, 1 mg sodium, 0 cholesterol, 18 gm carbohydrate, 1 gm protein, 1 gm fat. **Diabetic Exchange:** 1-1/2 fruit.

Chocolate Mint Dessert
Beef Chimichangas

Breaded Chicken Patties

(Pictured below)

As a mother of three, I like to make a few batches of these patties at one time and freeze the extras for another meal. I remember helping my mother make big batches, too—there were 11 of us, so it took a lot of food to fill us up! —Brenda Martin, Lititz, Pennsylvania

1/4 cup finely chopped onion
1/4 cup finely chopped celery
   6 tablespoons butter *or* margarine, *divided*
   3 tablespoons all-purpose flour
1-1/3 cups milk, *divided*
   2 tablespoons minced fresh parsley
   1 teaspoon salt
   1 teaspoon onion salt
1/2 teaspoon celery salt
1/4 teaspoon pepper
   2 cups finely chopped cooked chicken
   1 cup dry bread crumbs
Sandwich rolls, split
Lettuce leaves and tomato slices, optional

In a medium saucepan, saute onion and celery in 3 tablespoons butter until tender. Stir in flour until smooth. Add 1 cup milk; mix well. Bring to a boil; cook and stir for 2 minutes. Add parsley, seasonings and chicken. Re-

Milk Chocolate Pie
Freezer Vegetable Soup
Breaded Chicken Patties

move from the heat; chill until completely cooled. Shape into six patties, using about 1/3 cup mixture for each. Roll in crumbs, then dip into remaining milk; roll again in crumbs. In a skillet, cook patties in remaining butter for 3 minutes on each side. Serve on rolls with lettuce and tomato if desired. Uncooked patties may be frozen for up to 3 months. **To use frozen patties:** Cook in butter for 5-6 minutes on each side or until golden and heated through. **Yield:** 6 servings.

Freezer Vegetable Soup

(Pictured at left)

This flavorful soup tastes so fresh you'll never know it's been frozen. You can easily double the recipe when tomatoes are plentiful or toss in extra vegetables from your garden. For heartier fare, beef it up with ground beef, sausage or meatballs. —Elizabeth Moore
Frankfort, Kentucky

☑ **Nutritional Analysis included**

SOUP BASE:
    1 quart chopped fresh tomatoes
    1 cup diced celery
    1 cup diced carrots
    1 cup diced onion
    1 teaspoon sugar
    1/2 teaspoon salt, optional
    1/4 teaspoon pepper
    1/4 teaspoon dill weed
ADDITIONAL INGREDIENTS (for each batch):
    2 cups diced cooked potatoes
    2 cups water

Combine soup base ingredients in a kettle or Dutch oven; bring to a boil over medium heat. Reduce heat; cover and simmer for 45 minutes. Cool. Place 2 cups each into freezer containers. May be frozen for up to 3 months. **Yield:** 2 batches (4 cups total). **To prepare soup:** Thaw soup base in the refrigerator. Transfer to a kettle or Dutch oven. Add potatoes and water; simmer for 30-40 minutes. **Yield:** 4 servings per batch. **Nutritional Analysis:** One 1-cup serving (prepared without salt) equals 108 calories, 31 mg sodium, 0 cholesterol, 25 gm carbohydrate, 3 gm protein, trace fat. **Diabetic Exchanges:** 1 starch, 1 vegetable.

Milk Chocolate Pie

(Pictured at left)

This is the best chocolate pie I've ever had. It's cool, rich and melts in your mouth. Best of all, it takes just 10 minutes to whip up and pop in the freezer. —Kathy Crow
Payson, Arizona

    1 cup milk chocolate chips
    1/2 cup milk, *divided*
    1 package (3 ounces) cream cheese, softened
    1 carton (8 ounces) frozen whipped topping, thawed
    1 chocolate crumb crust (9 inches)

Milk chocolate kisses and additional whipped topping, optional

In a microwave or double boiler, combine chocolate chips and 1/4 cup milk. Cook until chips are melted; stir until smooth. In a mixing bowl, beat cream cheese and remaining milk until smooth. Gradually beat in the chocolate mixture. Fold in whipped topping. Pour into crust. Freeze for 4-6 hours or overnight. May be frozen for up to 3 months. Remove from the freezer 5-10 minutes before serving. Garnish with kisses and whipped topping if desired. **Yield:** 6-8 servings.

Cookies 'n' Cream Pie

This creamy make-ahead dessert is perfect for company. Convenience foods—including instant pudding, frozen whipped topping, cookies and a prepared crust—make it a treat for the cook, too. —Julie Sterchi, Flora, Illinois

1-1/2 cups half-and-half cream
    1 package (3.4 ounces) instant vanilla pudding mix
    1 carton (8 ounces) frozen whipped topping, thawed
    1 cup crushed cream-filled chocolate sandwich cookies (about 11 cookies)
    1 chocolate crumb crust (9 inches)

In a mixing bowl, combine the cream and pudding mix; beat on medium speed for 1 minute. Let stand for 5 minutes. Fold in whipped topping and cookies. Spoon into crust. Freeze until firm, about 6 hours or overnight. May be frozen for up to 3 months. Remove from the freezer 10 minutes before serving. **Yield:** 6-8 servings.

Make-Ahead Sandwiches

I developed these "fun buns" about 20 years ago when our four children were preteens. Once they started high school, I kept some in the freezer for quick suppers when after-school activities kept them from eating with the rest of the family. —Marie Hass, Madison, Wisconsin

1-1/2 pounds ground beef
    3/4 cup chopped onion
    3/4 cup ketchup
    3/4 cup chopped dill *or* sweet pickles
1-1/2 teaspoons salt
    1/4 to 1/2 teaspoon pepper
    1/4 to 1/2 teaspoon garlic powder
    1/8 teaspoon hot pepper sauce
1-1/2 cups (6 ounces) shredded mozzarella cheese
    12 hot dog buns, split

In a saucepan, cook the beef and onion until meat is no longer pink; drain. Stir in ketchup, pickles, salt, pepper, garlic powder and hot pepper sauce; heat through. Stir in the cheese. Place about 1/3 cupful on six buns; serve immediately. Cover and refrigerate remaining meat mixture until cool. Fill the remaining buns; wrap individually in heavy-duty foil and seal tightly. Freeze for up to 3 months. **To use frozen sandwiches:** Bake in foil at 400° for 30-35 minutes or until heated through. **Yield:** 1 dozen.

Turkey Noodle Casserole

(Pictured at far right)

Celery, water chestnuts and mushrooms add texture and crunch to this hearty casserole that is full of ground turkey. I'll fix two and serve one with a salad to make a complete meal. I keep the second one in the freezer to bake when company's coming. —Georgia Hennings
Alliance, Nebraska

2 pounds ground turkey
2 cups chopped celery
1/4 cup chopped green pepper
1/4 cup chopped onion
  1 can (10-3/4 ounces) condensed cream of mushroom soup, undiluted
  1 can (8 ounces) sliced water chestnuts, drained
  1 jar (4-1/2 ounces) sliced mushrooms, drained
  1 jar (4 ounces) diced pimientos, drained
1/4 cup soy sauce
1/2 teaspoon salt
1/2 teaspoon lemon-pepper seasoning
  1 cup (8 ounces) sour cream
  8 ounces wide egg noodles, cooked and drained

In a large skillet over medium heat, brown the turkey. Add celery, green pepper and onion; cook until tender. Stir in soup, water chestnuts, mushrooms, pimientos, soy sauce, salt and lemon pepper. Reduce heat; simmer for 20 minutes. Remove from the heat; add sour cream and noodles. Spoon half into a freezer container; cover and freeze for up to 3 months. Place remaining mixture in a greased 2-qt. baking dish. Cover and bake at 350° for 30-35 minutes or until heated through. **To use the** **frozen casserole:** Thaw in the refrigerator. Transfer to a greased 2-qt. baking dish and bake as directed. **Yield:** 2 casseroles (6 servings each).

Hearty Meat Pie

(Pictured at right)

Prepared pie crust speeds preparation of this homemade meat and vegetable pie topped with a tasty mushroom gravy. It takes a little longer to make two pies. But the reward comes when you pull the extra pie out of the freezer later and pop it into the oven. —Twila Burkholder
Middleburg, Pennsylvania

Pastry for two double-crust pies
  2 cups grated peeled potatoes
1-1/4 cups diced celery
  1 cup grated carrots
1/4 cup chopped onion
  2 tablespoons Worcestershire sauce
  1 teaspoon salt
1/4 teaspoon pepper
3/4 pound uncooked lean ground beef
MUSHROOM GRAVY (for each pie):
  1 can (4 ounces) mushroom stems and pieces
  2 tablespoons all-purpose flour
  2 tablespoons vegetable oil
  1 teaspoon beef bouillon granules
  4 drops browning sauce, optional

Divide pastry into fourths. On a lightly floured surface, roll out one portion to fit a 9-in. pie plate. In a bowl, combine the next seven ingredients; add beef and mix well. Spoon half into crust. Roll out another portion of pastry to fit top of pie; place over filling and seal edges. Cut vents in top pastry. Repeat with remaining pastry and filling. Cover

---

Freezer's the Key to Easy Grill Bread

WHEN it comes to new ideas, the folks at Rhodes Bake-N-Serv are on a roll. The company, whose frozen dough products are available in the frozen food section of most grocery stores, has come up with a clever new way to use their frozen Texas rolls to make Grill Bread.

This fun round bread is tender, tasty and can be used much the same way you'd use flour tortillas or pita bread.

Grill Bread

4 frozen Texas rolls (2 ounces *each*), thawed
2 garlic cloves, minced
2 tablespoons olive *or* vegetable oil
1/2 pound fresh mushrooms, sliced
  1 small onion, cut into thin wedges
  1 medium green pepper, sliced
  1 medium sweet yellow pepper, sliced
  1 medium sweet red pepper, sliced
1/2 cup fresh snow peas
3/4 teaspoon salt
1/8 teaspoon pepper
1/2 teaspoon dried oregano

On a lightly floured surface, roll out each roll into an 8-in. to 10-in. circle, turning dough frequently; set aside. In a large skillet, saute garlic in oil until tender. Add mushrooms; saute for 2-3 minutes. Add onion, peppers, peas, salt, pepper and oregano; stir-fry until vegetables are crisp-tender, about 3 minutes. Meanwhile, grill bread, uncovered, over medium-high heat for 30-45 seconds on each side or until lightly browned. Fill with vegetable mixture and serve immediately. The bread can be reheated in the microwave. **Yield:** 4 servings.

Turkey Noodle Casserole
Hearty Meat Pie

and freeze one pie for up to 3 months. Bake second pie at 375° for 15 minutes. Reduce heat; bake at 350° for 1 hour. Meanwhile, drain mushrooms, reserving liquid. Add water to liquid to measure 1 cup; set aside. In a saucepan, cook mushrooms and flour in oil until bubbly. Remove from the heat; stir in bouillon and reserved mushroom liquid. Bring to a boil; cook and stir for 1 minute. Stir in browning sauce if desired. Serve with pie. **To use frozen pie:** Bake at 375° for 70 minutes. Make gravy as directed. **Yield:** 2 pies (6-8 servings each).

Orange Whip

It takes mere minutes to blend together this cool, silky smooth treat. Yogurt adds tang to the light orange-flavored dessert. —Sue Ross, Casa Grande, Arizona

☑ Nutritional Analysis included

   1 can (11 ounces) mandarin oranges, drained
   1 cup (8 ounces) vanilla yogurt
   2 tablespoons orange juice concentrate
   2 cups whipped topping

In a bowl, combine the oranges, yogurt and orange juice concentrate. Fold in the whipped topping. Spoon into serving dishes. Cover and freeze until firm. Remove from the freezer 20 minutes before serving. May be frozen for up to 1 month. **Yield:** 4 servings. **Nutritional Analysis:**

One 3/4-cup serving (prepared with light yogurt and light whipped topping) equals 145 calories, 39 mg sodium, 1 mg cholesterol, 22 gm carbohydrate, 3 gm protein, 4 gm fat. **Diabetic Exchanges:** 1 fruit, 1 fat, 1/2 skim milk.

Apricot-Almond Antarctica

Almonds add nutty crunch to the cookie crumb layers in this ice cream dessert. A friend brought us this special treat when she and her husband came over for dinner. The combination of almonds and apricots remains a family favorite. —Marcy McReynolds, Nixa, Missouri

   1 package (12 ounces) vanilla wafers, crushed
1-1/3 cups slivered almonds, toasted
   1/2 cup butter *or* margarine, melted
   1 tablespoon almond extract
   6 cups vanilla ice cream, softened
   1 jar (18 ounces) apricot preserves

In a bowl, combine wafer crumbs, almonds, butter and extract. Pat a third into an ungreased 13-in. x 9-in. x 2-in. pan. Freeze for 15 minutes. Carefully spread half of the ice cream over crust. Spoon half of the preserves over the ice cream. Sprinkle with half of the remaining crumb mixture. Freeze for 20-30 minutes. Repeat layers. Freeze. May be frozen for up to 2 months. Remove from the freezer 10 minutes before serving. **Yield:** 16-20 servings.

Colorful Chicken Casserole
Butter Pecan Ice Cream Roll

Colorful Chicken Casserole

(Pictured above)

This all-in-one entree is a nice change of pace from the usual creamy casseroles. I make one for dinner and keep the other in the freezer for unexpected company.
—*Bernice Morris, Marshfield, Missouri*

✓ Nutritional Analysis included

   1 cup chopped green pepper
   1 cup chopped celery
3/4 cup chopped onion
   2 tablespoons butter *or* margarine
   1 cup chicken broth
   1 cup frozen peas
   1 cup frozen corn
   1 teaspoon salt, optional
1/4 teaspoon pepper
   3 cups cubed cooked chicken
   1 package (7 ounces) ready-cut spaghetti *or* elbow macaroni, cooked and drained
   1 jar (4-1/2 ounces) sliced mushrooms, drained
   1 cup (4 ounces) shredded cheddar cheese

In a large skillet, saute green pepper, celery and onion in butter until tender. Add broth, peas, corn, salt if desired and pepper; heat through. Stir in chicken and spaghetti. Divide between two greased 8-in. square baking pans. Top with the mushrooms and cheese. Cover and freeze one casserole for up to 3 months. Cover and bake the second casserole at 350° for 20 minutes; uncover and bake 10 minutes longer. **To use frozen casserole:** Cover and bake at 350° for 35 minutes; uncover and bake 15 minutes longer. **Yield:** 2 casseroles (4 servings each). **Nutritional Analysis:** One 1-cup serving (prepared with margarine, low-sodium broth and reduced-fat cheese and without salt) equals 248 calories, 232 mg sodium, 35 mg cholesterol, 30 gm carbohydrate, 18 gm protein, 6 gm fat. **Diabetic Exchanges:** 2 starch, 2 lean meat.

Beef 'n' Olive Sandwiches

I blend dried beef, olives and walnuts into a rich and creamy sandwich filling. Cut into quarters, these sand-

wiches are sophisticated enough to serve at parties. And they freeze beautifully.   —Iola Egle, McCook, Nebraska

> 1 package (8 ounces) cream cheese, softened
> 2 tablespoons whipping cream
> 1/2 teaspoon white pepper
> 1/4 cup chopped dried beef
> 3 tablespoons sliced stuffed olives
> 3 tablespoons chopped walnuts
> 8 slices bread

In a mixing bowl, combine the cream cheese, cream and pepper; mix well. Stir in beef, olives and walnuts. Spread on four slices of bread; top with remaining bread. Freeze. Remove from the freezer at least 4 hours before serving. May be frozen for up to 2 months. **Yield:** 4 servings.

Seven-Layer Cake

Even if you can't bake, you can still impress guests with this easy make-ahead dessert. Assemble it when you have time to let the layers freeze, then store it in the freezer until you're ready to show off the colorful results.
—Diane Thompson, Nutrioso, Arizona

> 4 cups graham cracker crumbs (about 32 squares)
> 1/2 cup sugar
> 1/2 cup butter *or* margarine, melted
> 1 pint vanilla ice cream, softened
> 1 pint chocolate ice cream, softened
> 1 pint strawberry ice cream, softened

Line the bottom and sides of a 9-in. x 5-in. x 3-in. loaf pan with heavy-duty aluminum foil. Combine graham cracker crumbs, sugar and butter; press one-fourth of the mixture into the pan. Freeze for 15 minutes. Spread vanilla ice cream over crumbs. Sprinkle with another fourth of the crumbs; press down gently. Freeze for 45-60 minutes or until firm. Spread with chocolate ice cream. Sprinkle with another fourth of the crumbs; press down gently. Freeze until firm. Spread with the strawberry ice cream, then top with remaining crumbs (pan will be very full). Cover and freeze for several hours or overnight. May be frozen for up to 2 months. Remove from the freezer 10 minutes before serving. Using the foil, lift cake from pan; discard foil. Cut cake with a serrated knife. **Yield:** 10-12 servings.

Butter Pecan Ice Cream Roll

(Pictured above left)

An active mother of four young sons, I rely on recipes that keep entertaining simple. This cake roll can be chilling in the freezer long before guests arrive. Try varying the flavor of the ice cream to suit different tastes.
—Elaine Hefner, Elida, Ohio

☑ Nutritional Analysis included

> 4 eggs
> 2 teaspoons baking powder

Creating a Cake Roll

1 After the cake has cooled in the pan for 5 minutes, turn it out onto a kitchen towel dusted with confectioners' sugar. Gently peel off the waxed paper. Beginning with a short side, roll up the cake in the towel. Place on a wire rack until completely cooled.

2 When cool, carefully unroll the cake on a flat surface. Spread filling over cake to within 1 inch of edges.

3 Beginning at a short side, loosely roll up the cake, pulling away the towel as you roll. Place with seam side down on a serving platter, or refrigerate or freeze until serving.

> 1/2 teaspoon salt
> 1 cup sugar
> 1/4 cup water
> 2 teaspoons vanilla extract
> 1 cup all-purpose flour
> 1-1/2 quarts butter pecan ice cream, softened
> Confectioners' sugar and pecan halves, optional

In a mixing bowl, beat eggs, baking powder and salt until thick and lemon-colored. Gradually add sugar, beating until thickened. Beat in water and vanilla. Gradually add the flour. Spread into a greased and waxed paper-lined 15-in. x 10-in. x 1-in. baking pan. Bake at 375° for 12-14 minutes or until cake is lightly browned. Cool for 5 minutes; turn onto a kitchen towel dusted with confectioners' sugar. Peel off waxed paper and roll up jelly-roll style, starting with a short side; cool on a wire rack. When cool, unroll cake. Spread with ice cream to within 1 in. of edges. Reroll; cover and freeze until firm. May be frozen for up to 2 months. If desired, dust with confectioners' sugar and decorate with pecans before serving. **Yield:** 10 servings. **Nutritional Analysis:** One serving (prepared with egg substitute and reduced-fat ice cream and without pecans) equals 291 calories, 331 mg sodium, 3 mg cholesterol, 56 gm carbohydrate, 8 gm protein, 3 gm fat.

Chapter 9

GET GOING—that's what many people say they must do each morning. Unfortunately, rushing to get ready for work, school and other activities often means there's little time to fix and eat a good breakfast. Folks either forgo a morning meal altogether or head to the nearest fast-food drive-thru.

But offering your family wholesome, hearty breakfasts is a snap with these rise-and-shine selections that are perfect for families on the go.

From waffles, pancakes and French toast to egg dishes, breakfast beverages and fruit, you can get your family's day off to a delicious start—pronto!

COUNTRY BREAKFASTS. Clockwise from upper left: Hash Brown Egg Bake (p. 135), Hearty Scrambled Eggs (p. 142), Ham 'n' Cheddar Cups (p. 134) and Chocolate French Toast (p. 140).

Country Brunch Skillet

(Pictured at far right)

Frozen hash browns and packaged shredded cheese shave minutes off preparation of this skillet breakfast. It's an appealing meal-in-one that you can do in about 30 minutes.
—*Elvira Brunnquell, Port Washington, Wisconsin*

> 6 bacon strips
> 6 cups frozen cubed hash brown potatoes
> 3/4 cup chopped green pepper
> 1/2 cup chopped onion
> 1 teaspoon salt
> 1/4 teaspoon pepper
> 6 eggs
> 1/2 cup shredded cheddar cheese

In a large skillet over medium heat, cook bacon until crisp. Remove bacon; crumble and set aside. Drain, reserving 2 tablespoons of drippings. Add potatoes, green pepper, onion, salt and pepper to drippings; cook and stir for 2 minutes. Cover and cook, stirring occasionally, until potatoes are browned and tender, about 15 minutes. Make six wells in the potato mixture; break one egg into each well. Cover and cook on low heat for 8-10 minutes or until the eggs are completely set. Sprinkle with cheese and bacon. **Yield:** 6 servings.

Tutti-Frutti Waffles

(Pictured below)

Pineapple and pecans are the "secret" ingredients that give these light waffles their fruity flavor and nice nutty crunch. It takes just minutes to mix up the batter, then bake in a waffle iron. —*Bev Uken, Raymond, Minnesota*

> 2 cups biscuit/baking mix
> 2 eggs, lightly beaten
> 1/2 cup vegetable oil
> 1-1/3 cups club soda
> 1/4 cup crushed pineapple, drained
> 1/4 cup chopped pecans
> 1 pint fresh raspberries, optional
> 2 medium ripe bananas, sliced, optional

Tutti-Frutti Waffles

In a mixing bowl, combine biscuit mix, eggs and oil. Add soda and stir until smooth. Gently fold in the pineapple and pecans. Bake in a preheated waffle iron according to manufacturer's directions until golden brown. Top with raspberries and bananas if desired. **Yield:** 6-7 waffles (about 6-3/4 inches).

Bacon and Cheese Waffles

(Pictured at right)

Pancake mix gives a jump-start to this hearty hurry-up breakfast. Including bacon and cheese in the waffle batter makes an all-in-one breakfast flavor. Freeze extras to reheat another day. —*MarGenne Rowley, Oasis, Utah*

> 1 egg
> 1 cup milk
> 1 cup (8 ounces) sour cream
> 1 tablespoon butter *or* margarine, melted
> 2 cups pancake *or* biscuit/baking mix
> 6 to 8 bacon strips, cooked and crumbled
> 1 cup (4 ounces) shredded cheddar cheese

In a medium bowl, beat egg; add milk, sour cream and butter. Stir in pancake mix; mix well. Fold in bacon and cheese. Bake in a preheated waffle iron according to the manufacturer's directions until golden brown. **Yield:** 12 waffles (4-inch square).

Frothy Orange Drink

(Pictured at right)

A teaching friend blended this sunny slush in a wink at school early one morning. The sweet drink put a little "zip" in my day! —*Sue Ellen Bumpus, Lampasas, Texas*

> 1 can (6 ounces) frozen orange juice
>   concentrate, unthawed
> 1 cup water
> 1 cup milk
> 1/2 cup sugar
> 1 teaspoon vanilla extract
> 8 to 10 ice cubes

Combine all ingredients in a blender; cover and process until drink is thick and slushy. **Yield:** 4 cups.

Fruit Medley

Straight from the pantry comes a super-simple, colorful and pleasant-tasting fruit dish. Pie filling dresses up this combination of canned fruits. —*Margaret Anders Helena, Montana*

> 1 can (21 ounces) peach *or* apricot pie filling
> 2 cans (15 ounces *each*) fruit cocktail, drained
> 1 can (20 ounces) pineapple chunks, drained
> 1 can (15 ounces) mandarin oranges, drained
> 2 medium firm bananas, sliced

In a large bowl, combine pie filling and canned fruits. Cover and refrigerate. Stir in bananas just before serving. **Yield:** 12-14 servings.

Bacon and Cheese Waffles
Frothy Orange Drink
Country Brunch Skillet

Pancakes on the Go

Pancakes on the Go

(Pictured above)

Is your family tired of the same old breakfast pancakes? If so, try this recipe! Brown sugar wakes up your taste buds while oats add stick-to-your-ribs texture to carry you through to lunchtime. These pancakes are so nicely sweet they don't need syrup...and they're a fun way to get kids to eat oats. —Karen Ann Bland, Gove, Kansas

    1/2 cup all-purpose flour
    1/2 cup whole wheat flour
    1/2 cup plus 2 tablespoons quick-cooking oats
    1/3 cup packed brown sugar
    1/2 teaspoon baking soda
    1/2 teaspoon salt
      1 egg
  1-1/3 cups buttermilk
      2 tablespoons vegetable oil

In a mixing bowl, combine the first six ingredients. In another bowl, beat egg, buttermilk and oil; stir into dry ingredients and mix well. Pour batter by 1/3 cupfuls onto a lightly greased hot griddle; turn when bubbles form on top of pancakes. Cook until the second side is golden brown. **Yield:** about 9 pancakes.

Ham 'n' Cheddar Cups

(Pictured on page 131)

Start your day out right with these delicious muffins. Studded with ham, cheddar cheese and bacon, they're a meal in one—and a handy breakfast on the run.
—Carla Hodenfield, Mandan, North Dakota

      2 cups all-purpose flour
    1/4 cup sugar
      2 teaspoons baking powder
      1 teaspoon salt
    1/4 teaspoon pepper
      6 eggs
      1 cup milk
    1/2 pound fully cooked ham, cubed
    1/2 pound cheddar cheese, diced *or* shredded
    1/2 pound sliced bacon, cooked and crumbled
      1 small onion, finely chopped

In a bowl, combine the flour, sugar, baking powder, salt and pepper. Beat eggs and milk; stir into dry ingredients until well mixed. Stir in ham, cheese, bacon and onion. Fill well-greased muffin cups three-fourths full. Bake at 350° for 45 minutes or until a toothpick inserted near the center comes out clean. Cool for 10 minutes before removing to a wire rack. **Yield:** about 20 cups. **Editor's Note:** Paper-lined muffin cups are not recommended for this recipe.

Biscuit Breakfast Sandwiches

You can eat these hearty, satisfying sandwiches at home or on the go. While the biscuits bake, I ready the egg, ham and cheese filling. —Giovanna Garver
Paonia, Colorado

  1-1/2 cups all-purpose flour
      1 tablespoon baking powder
      1 tablespoon sugar
      1 teaspoon salt
    1/4 cup shortening
    3/4 cup milk
      6 eggs
      1 tablespoon butter *or* margarine
      6 slices process American cheese
      6 slices fully cooked ham

In a bowl, combine dry ingredients; cut in shortening until crumbly. Stir in milk just until moistened. Turn onto a lightly floured surface; knead five to six times. Roll to 1/2-in. thickness; cut with a 2-3/4-in. biscuit cutter. Place on an ungreased baking sheet. Bake at 450° for 12-15 minutes or until light golden brown; cool slightly. In a skillet over medium heat, fry eggs in butter until completely set. Split the biscuits; place cheese, hot eggs and ham on bottoms. Replace tops. Serve immediately. **Yield:** 6 servings.

No-Turn Omelet

(Pictured below)

I like to make this colorful casserole a day ahead, then refrigerate it and bake it the next morning. With ingredients such as sausage, eggs, cheese and peppers, it tastes like a strata. —Helen Clem, Creston, Iowa

No-Turn Omelet

8 eggs, beaten
2 cups cooked crumbled sausage *or* cubed
  fully cooked ham
2 cups cubed process American cheese
2 cups milk
1 cup crushed saltines (about 24 crackers)
1/4 cup chopped onion
1/4 cup chopped green pepper
1/4 cup chopped sweet red pepper
1/2 to 1 teaspoon salt

Combine all ingredients in a large bowl; pour into a greased shallow 3-qt. or 13-in. x 9-in. x 2-in. baking dish. Bake, uncovered, at 350° for 45 minutes or until a knife inserted near the center comes out clean. Let stand for 5 minutes before serving. **Yield:** 8-10 servings. **Editor's Note:** This dish may be prepared in advance, covered and refrigerated overnight. Remove from the refrigerator 30 minutes before baking.

Hash Brown Egg Bake

(Pictured on page 130)

Frozen hash browns make this recipe simple to prepare. You can even make it the night before, keep in the fridge and bake the next morning—so convenient!
—Cheryl Johnson, Plymouth, Minnesota

1 package (32 ounces) frozen cubed hash
  brown potatoes, thawed
1 pound sliced bacon, cooked and crumbled
1 cup (4 ounces) shredded cheddar cheese,
  divided
1/4 to 1/2 teaspoon salt
8 eggs
2 cups milk
Dash paprika

In a large bowl, combine hash browns, bacon, 1/2 cup cheese and salt. Spoon into a greased 13-in. x 9-in. x 2-in. baking dish. In a bowl, beat eggs and milk until smooth; pour over hash brown mixture. Sprinkle with paprika. Bake, uncovered, at 350° for 45-50 minutes or until golden. Top with the remaining cheese. **Yield:** 8 servings. **Editor's Note:** This dish may be prepared in advance, covered and refrigerated overnight. Remove from the refrigerator 30 minutes before baking.

Bacon Avocado Burritos

(Pictured above right)

These hand-held breakfast bundles are quick to make and fun to take when you're on the go. I set out a variety of filling ingredients and toppings and let everyone assemble their own. *—Cleo Gossett, Ephrata, Washington*

4 eggs
8 flour tortillas (7 inches)
1 to 2 tablespoons vegetable oil
1-1/2 cups (6 ounces) shredded cheddar cheese
1 large ripe avocado, thinly sliced
1-1/2 cups chopped green onions
1 pound sliced bacon, cooked and crumbled

Bacon Avocado Burritos

Salsa, ranch salad dressing *or* sour cream

In a bowl, beat the eggs. Dip one tortilla in eggs. In a large skillet, cook tortilla in oil just until egg sets; turn to cook other side. Remove and place between paper towels to drain; keep warm. Repeat with remaining tortillas, adding more oil if needed. Place cheese, avocado, onions and bacon down the center of tortillas; top with salsa, salad dressing or sour cream. Fold ends and sides over filling. If desired, filled burritos may be warmed in the microwave just before serving. **Yield:** 8 burritos.

Fresh Fruit Bowl

The light dressing on this summery salad lets the fruit's fresh flavor through. The pretty mixture's so easy to put together that I feel guilty when I get compliments on it!
—Norma Pippin, Bourbon, Missouri

✓ Nutritional Analysis included

3 medium peaches, cubed
2 cups cubed cantaloupe
1 cup halved green grapes
1 cup halved strawberries
1/2 cup sour cream
1 tablespoon honey
1 tablespoon orange juice

In a large bowl, combine peaches, cantaloupe, grapes and strawberries. In a small bowl, combine sour cream, honey and orange juice; pour over fruit and toss to coat. Serve immediately. **Yield:** 8-10 servings. **Nutritional Analysis:** One 3/4-cup serving (prepared with nonfat sour cream) equals 77 calories, 17 mg sodium, 1 mg cholesterol, 18 gm carbohydrate, 2 gm protein, trace fat. **Diabetic Exchange:** 1 fruit.

**Egg Biscuit Bake
Nutty French Toast**

Nutty French Toast

(Pictured below left)

This sweet breakfast treat is a cross of caramel rolls and French toast. It's easy to begin the night before. In the morning, just spread on the nutty topping and bake.
—Mavis Diment, Marcus, Iowa

12 slices French bread (1 inch thick)
8 eggs
2 cups milk
2 teaspoons vanilla extract
1/2 teaspoon ground cinnamon
3/4 cup butter *or* margarine, softened
1-1/3 cups packed brown sugar
3 tablespoons dark corn syrup
1 cup chopped walnuts

Place bread in a greased 13-in. x 9-in. x 2-in. baking dish. In a large bowl, beat eggs, milk, vanilla and cinnamon; pour over the bread. Cover and refrigerate overnight. Remove from the refrigerator 30 minutes before baking. Meanwhile, in a mixing bowl, cream the butter, brown sugar and syrup until smooth; spread over bread. Sprinkle with nuts. Bake, uncovered, at 350° for 1 hour or until golden brown. **Yield:** 6-8 servings.

Egg Biscuit Bake

(Pictured at left)

Convenient refrigerated biscuits create a golden border around this all-in-one brunch dish. It's a variation of a simple egg-cheese combination my mother used to make.
—Alice Le Duc, Cedarburg, Wisconsin

1 can (5 ounces) evaporated milk
8 ounces process American cheese, cubed
1 teaspoon prepared mustard
3/4 cup cubed fully cooked ham
1/2 cup frozen peas
2 tablespoons butter *or* margarine
10 eggs, beaten
1 tube (12 ounces) refrigerated buttermilk biscuits

In a saucepan, combine the milk, cheese and mustard; cook over low heat until smooth, stirring constantly. Stir in ham and peas. Melt butter in a large skillet; add eggs. Cook and stir over medium heat until the eggs are set. Add cheese sauce and stir gently. Spoon into an ungreased shallow 2-qt. baking dish. Separate the biscuits and cut in half. Place with cut side down around outer edge of dish. Bake, uncovered, at 375° for 15-20 minutes or until the biscuits are golden brown. **Yield:** 4-6 servings.

Tater Surprise

If your clan likes Tater Tots, they'll love this versatile skillet breakfast. We enjoy it with ham, but you can use any breakfast meat you choose. It's so filling I sometimes substitute chicken to make a hearty dinner.
—Paula West, St. Louis, Missouri

2-1/2 cups frozen Tater Tots *or* cubed hash brown potatoes
1 cup chopped fully cooked ham
1/4 cup chopped onion
1/4 cup chopped green pepper
2 tablespoons vegetable oil
4 eggs, beaten
Salt and pepper to taste

In a large skillet, cook potatoes, ham, onion and green pepper in oil over medium heat for 8-10 minutes or until browned, stirring constantly. (If using Tater Tots, break apart with a spatula; mix well.) Add eggs; cook and stir until eggs are completely set. Season with salt and pepper. **Yield:** 4 servings.

Breakfast Pita Pockets

At home or on the go, pita halves make handy holders for this flavorful mixture of sausage, scrambled eggs and Swiss cheese. I don't know where I found this recipe, but I do know everybody likes it. Once the pockets are filled, they can be kept warm in the oven until the whole family is fed.
—Mrs. James Kell, Ocala, Florida

1 pound bulk pork sausage
5 pita breads, halved
5 eggs
1/4 cup milk
1/2 teaspoon dried oregano
1/8 to 1/4 teaspoon salt
1/4 teaspoon pepper
5 slices Swiss cheese, halved

In a skillet, cook sausage until no longer pink. Drain and set aside. Place the pita halves in an ungreased 11-in. x 7-in. x 2-in. baking pan. Bake at 300° for 5 minutes. In a bowl, beat eggs, milk, oregano, salt and pepper. Pour into a lightly greased skillet. Cook and stir gently over medium heat until the eggs are completely set. Stir in sausage. Place a half slice of cheese in each pita half; spoon about 1/3 cup of egg mixture into each. Serve warm. **Yield:** 10 servings.

Herbed Cheese Omelet

One bite of this cheesy omelet and you'll notice its fresh flavor from a blend of different herbs. I serve it with bacon or ham, whatever I have on hand. *—Shirley LeFevre*
Lancaster, Pennsylvania

6 eggs
1/2 teaspoon onion powder
1/2 teaspoon dried basil
1/4 teaspoon dried parsley flakes
1/4 teaspoon celery seed
1 tablespoon butter *or* margarine
2 slices process American cheese

In a bowl, beat eggs and seasonings. Melt butter in a skillet. Add egg mixture; cook over medium heat. As eggs set, lift edges, letting uncooked portion flow underneath. When eggs are completely set, remove from the heat. Place cheese over half of the eggs. Fold in half and transfer to a warm platter. **Yield:** 2 servings.

Sausage Cheese Puffs

Sausage Cheese Puffs

(Pictured above)

People are always surprised when I tell them there are only four ingredients in these tasty bite-size puffs. Cheesy and spicy, the golden morsels are a fun novelty at a breakfast or brunch. —Della Moore, Troy, New York

1 pound bulk Italian sausage
3 cups biscuit/baking mix
4 cups (16 ounces) shredded cheddar cheese
3/4 cup water

In a skillet, cook and crumble sausage until no longer pink; drain. In a bowl, combine biscuit mix and cheese; stir in sausage. Add water and toss with a fork until moistened. Shape into 1-1/2-in. balls. Place 2 in. apart on ungreased baking sheets. Bake at 400° for 12-15 minutes or until puffed and golden brown. Cool on wire racks. **Yield:** about 4 dozen. **Editor's Note:** Baked puffs may be frozen; reheat at 400° for 7-9 minutes or until heated through (they do not need to be thawed first).

Daddy's Omelet

(Pictured at far right)

Omelets are one of my husband's specialties. His fast-to-fix filling of fresh-tasting vegetables and cheese adds a one-of-a-kind taste the whole family enjoys. —Glenn Powell Havana, Florida

1/4 cup *each* diced green pepper, onion and mushrooms
1 to 2 tablespoons butter *or* margarine
2 eggs
1/8 teaspoon salt
Pinch pepper
1/4 cup shredded cheddar cheese

In an 8-in. skillet, saute green pepper, onion and mushrooms in butter until tender. Remove with a slotted spoon and set aside. In a small bowl, beat eggs, salt and pepper. Pour into the skillet. Cook over medium heat; as eggs set, lift edges, letting uncooked portion flow underneath. When the eggs are set, spoon vegetables and cheese over one side; fold omelet over filling. Cover and let stand for 1-2 minutes or until cheese is melted. **Yield:** 1 serving.

Chocolate Chip Pancakes

(Pictured at right)

Chocolate lovers in my household rush to breakfast when these fluffy pancakes are on the menu. I use chocolate milk and miniature chocolate chips in the batter. Topped with butter and fruit, they're our daughter's all-time favorite. —Laura Rader, Fergus Falls, Minnesota

1 cup all-purpose flour
1 tablespoon sugar
2 teaspoons baking powder
1/4 teaspoon salt
1 egg
1 cup chocolate milk
2 tablespoons vegetable oil
1/2 teaspoon vanilla extract
1/4 cup miniature semisweet chocolate chips
Sliced strawberries and bananas

In a bowl, combine flour, sugar, baking powder and salt. In another bowl, beat the egg, milk, oil, vanilla and chocolate chips. Add to dry ingredients and mix well. Pour batter by 1/4 cupfuls onto a lightly greased hot griddle (stir the batter before pouring each batch). Turn when bubbles form on top of pancakes. Cook until the second side is brown. Top with strawberries and bananas. **Yield:** about 8 pancakes.

Sparkling Grape Punch

I rely on this lovely mauve-colored punch for quenching the thirst of my brunch guests. It's bubbly, fruity and simple to stir up for a crowd. —Arlyn Kramer Dumas, Arkansas

2 cups water
1 cup sugar
2 cups grape juice, chilled
1 cup orange juice, chilled
2 liters ginger ale, chilled

In a saucepan, combine water and sugar. Bring to a boil; boil for 3 minutes. Cool. Transfer to a punch bowl. Add juices and mix well. Stir in ginger ale just before serving. **Yield:** about 5-1/2 quarts.

Cinnamon Cream Syrup

Are you looking for a change of pace from maple syrup? Try this special topping. It jazzes up pancakes, waffles or French toast. —Mrs. Hamilton Myers Jr. Charlottesville, Virginia

1 cup sugar
1/2 cup light corn syrup
1/4 cup water
3/4 teaspoon ground cinnamon
1/2 cup evaporated milk

In a saucepan, combine the sugar, corn syrup, water and cinnamon; bring to a boil over medium heat. Boil for 2 minutes or until thickened. Remove from the heat; cool for 5 minutes. Stir in milk. Serve warm over pancakes, waffles or French toast. **Yield:** 1-1/2 cups.

Chocolate Chip Pancakes
Daddy's Omelet

Baked Brunch Sandwiches

(Pictured at right)

Serving brunch to your bunch is a breeze when you prepare these sandwiches the night before. They combine the flavor of grilled ham and cheese with the texture of French toast. —Carolyn Herfkens Crysler, Ontario

> 3 tablespoons Dijon mustard
> 12 slices bread
> 6 slices fully cooked ham
> 12 slices cheddar *or* Swiss cheese
> 1 medium tomato, thinly sliced
> 3 tablespoons butter *or* margarine, softened
> 4 eggs
> 1/4 cup milk
> 1/4 teaspoon pepper

Spread mustard on one side of six slices of bread. Layer ham, cheese and tomato over mustard; top with remaining bread. Butter the outsides of the sandwiches; cut in half. Arrange in a greased 13-in. x 9-in. x 2-in. baking dish. Beat eggs, milk and pepper; pour over sandwiches. Cover and refrigerate overnight. Remove from the refrigerator 30 minutes before baking. Bake, uncovered, at 375° for 30 minutes or until the sandwiches are golden brown and the cheese is melted. **Yield:** 6 servings.

Baked Brunch Sandwiches

French-Toasted English Muffins

This is an easy method for dressing up ordinary English muffins. I often serve these scrumptious muffins with maple syrup, seasonal fruit and pork sausage patties or links. —Aurora Denney, Spencer, Wisconsin

> 4 eggs
> 1/2 cup half-and-half cream
> 2 tablespoons sugar
> 1/2 teaspoon vanilla extract
> 6 English muffins, split
> 1/4 cup butter *or* margarine
> Maple syrup

In a small mixing bowl, beat eggs. Add cream, sugar and vanilla; mix well. Soak muffins, cut side down, in egg mixture for 1 minute; turn and dip the other side just until moistened. In a large skillet, melt butter. Fry muffins, cut side down, for 2-3 minutes or until golden brown. Turn and cook 2-3 minutes longer or until golden brown. Serve with syrup. **Yield:** 6 servings.

Maple-Bacon Oven Pancake

For years, my mother has served this tasty baked pancake for dinner. But it's so quick and easy I like to make it for breakfast, too. Leftovers taste just as good the next day warmed up in the microwave. —Kari Caven, Moscow, Idaho

> 1-1/2 cups biscuit/baking mix
> 1 tablespoon sugar
> 3/4 cup milk
> 2 eggs
> 1/4 cup maple syrup

> 1-1/2 cups (6 ounces) shredded cheddar cheese, *divided*
> 1/2 pound sliced bacon, cooked and crumbled
> Additional syrup, optional

In a mixing bowl, combine biscuit mix, sugar, milk, eggs, syrup and 1/2 cup cheese; mix well. Pour into a greased 13-in. x 9-in. x 2-in. baking dish. Bake, uncovered, at 425° for 10-15 minutes or until a toothpick inserted near the center comes out clean. Sprinkle with bacon and remaining cheese. Bake 3-5 minutes longer or until the cheese is melted. Serve with syrup if desired. **Yield:** 12 servings.

Chocolate French Toast

(Pictured on page 130)

Try this yummy treat for a special breakfast or brunch. The layer of chocolate hidden inside makes a wonderful flavor combination that appeals to kids of all ages. —Pat Habiger, Spearville, Kansas

> 3 eggs
> 1 cup milk
> 1 teaspoon sugar
> 1 teaspoon vanilla extract
> 1/4 teaspoon salt
> 12 slices day-old bread, crusts removed
> 3 milk chocolate candy bars* (1.55 ounces *each*), halved
> 2 tablespoons butter *or* margarine
> Confectioners' sugar

In a bowl, beat eggs, milk, sugar, vanilla and salt. Pour half into an ungreased 13-in. x 9-in. x 2-in. baking dish.

Arrange six slices of bread in a single layer over the egg mixture. Place one piece of chocolate in the center of each piece of bread. Top with remaining bread; pour remaining egg mixture over all. Let stand for 5 minutes. In a large nonstick skillet, melt butter over medium heat. Fry sandwiches until golden brown on both sides. Dust with confectioners' sugar. Cut sandwiches diagonally; serve warm. **Yield:** 6 servings. ***Editor's Note:** Six 1-ounce squares of bittersweet or semisweet chocolate may be substituted for the milk chocolate candy bars. Heat squares in the microwave for 10 seconds before cutting into smaller pieces to place on the bread.

Baked Cinnamon French Toast

There's no last-minute preparation and you can serve several people at once with this casserole. The guests at my bed-and-breakfast love the smooth, custardy bottom layer topped with thick slices of cinnamon bread.
—Lo Ann Brennock, Cloverdale, California

```
12 slices cinnamon bread
1/4 cup butter or margarine, softened
 9 eggs
 1 quart milk
 2 cups whipping cream
 1 cup sugar
4-1/2 teaspoons vanilla extract
Warmed blackberry preserves, optional
Whipped cream, optional
```

Line the bottom of a greased 13-in. x 9-in. x 2-in. baking dish with six slices of bread. Butter the remaining bread; place with butter side up over bread in pan. In a mixing bowl, beat eggs. Add milk, cream, sugar and vanilla; mix well. Pour over bread; let stand for 15 minutes. Place the dish in a larger baking pan. Pour boiling water into larger pan to a depth of 1 in. Bake, uncovered, at 375° for 40 minutes or until a knife inserted near the center comes out clean. Let stand for 10 minutes before serving. Top with preserves and whipped cream if desired. **Yield:** 6 servings.

Vegetarian Burritos

Our daughter loves to help out in the kitchen, so I try to choose recipes that are easy to follow. Just six ingredients, including convenient salsa, create the zippy filling in these speedy burritos.   —Ruth Behm, Defiance, Ohio

☑ Nutritional Analysis included

```
10 eggs
1/2 teaspoon salt, optional
1/8 teaspoon pepper
 1 cup salsa
1/4 cup chopped onion
 1 cup (4 ounces) shredded cheddar cheese
 8 flour tortillas (6 to 7 inches), warmed
```

In a bowl, beat the eggs, salt if desired and pepper. Pour into a skillet that has been coated with nonstick cooking spray. Cook and stir over medium heat until eggs are partially set. Add salsa and onion; cook and stir until eggs are completely set. Sprinkle with cheese. Spoon about 1/2 cup down the center of each tortilla; fold ends and sides over filling. Serve immediately. **Yield:** 8 servings. **Nutritional Analysis:** One serving (prepared with egg substitute, reduced-fat cheese and fat-free tortillas and without salt) equals 240 calories, 826 mg sodium, 269 mg cholesterol, 27 gm carbohydrate, 14 gm protein, 7 gm fat. **Diabetic Exchanges:** 1-1/2 starch, 1 vegetable, 1 meat, 1/2 fat.

Sunday Brunch Eggs

(Pictured below)

This recipe is special enough to consider when company comes, and it's a convenient way to serve eggs to a group. Nestled on top of Canadian bacon and Swiss cheese, the eggs are drizzled with rich cream. For a pretty presentation, cut around each egg and serve on toast.
—Judy Wells, Phoenix, Arizona

```
12 slices Canadian bacon
12 slices Swiss cheese
12 eggs
 1 cup whipping cream
1/3 cup grated Parmesan cheese
12 slices toast, optional
```

Place Canadian bacon in a greased 13-in. x 9-in. x 2-in. baking dish; top with Swiss cheese. Carefully break an egg over each piece of cheese. Pour cream over eggs and sprinkle with Parmesan cheese. Bake, uncovered, at 375° for 20-25 minutes or until the eggs reach desired doneness. Let stand for 5 minutes. Cut between each egg; serve on toast if desired. **Yield:** 6 servings.

Sunday Brunch Eggs

Rosy Citrus Drink

(Pictured at far right)

Cranberry juice gets a boost from fresh-tasting citrus juices and a hint of spice in this warm beverage. It's an awesome alternative to coffee and tea at brunches.
—*Patricia Kile, Greentown, Pennsylvania*

2 cups cranberry juice
1 cup unsweetened grapefruit juice
1 cup orange juice
1/2 cup sugar
1/4 teaspoon ground allspice
Apple slices and cinnamon sticks, optional

In a saucepan, combine juices, sugar and allspice; bring to a boil. Serve in mugs. Garnish with apple slices and cinnamon sticks if desired. **Yield:** 4 servings.

Stuffed French Toast

(Pictured at far right)

French toast gets special treatment in this recipe. I stuff each thick slice with Swiss cheese and sizzling sausage for a satisfying meal-in-one. —*Edna Hoffman Hebron, Indiana*

8 slices French bread (1-1/2 inches thick)
2 tablespoons butter *or* margarine, softened
1 package (8 ounces) brown-and-serve sausage patties, cooked
1 cup (4 ounces) shredded Swiss cheese
2 eggs
1/2 cup milk
1-1/2 teaspoons sugar
1/4 teaspoon ground cinnamon
Maple syrup, optional

Cut a pocket in the crust of each slice of bread. Butter the inside of pocket. Cut sausage into bite-size pieces; toss with cheese. Stuff into pockets. In a shallow bowl, beat eggs, milk, sugar and cinnamon; dip both sides of bread. Cook on a greased hot griddle until golden brown on both sides. Serve with syrup if desired. **Yield:** 4 servings.

Spiced Hot Fruit

(Pictured at far right)

This recipe for a crowd-pleasing compote takes advantage of convenient canned fruit. Its sweet, buttery sauce, spiced with ginger and cinnamon, makes a warm and wonderful addition to any breakfast buffet.
—*Irene Howard, Shenandoah, Iowa*

✓ Nutritional Analysis included

2 cans (one 20 ounces, one 8 ounces) pineapple chunks
2 cans (15-1/4 ounces *each*) apricots, drained and quartered
1 can (29 ounces) sliced peaches, drained
1 can (29 ounces) pear halves, drained and quartered

3/4 cup packed brown sugar
1/4 cup butter *or* margarine
2 cinnamon sticks (3 inches)
1/2 teaspoon ground ginger

Drain pineapple, reserving juice. In an ungreased shallow 3-1/2-qt. baking dish, combine the pineapple, apricots, peaches and pears; set aside. In a saucepan, combine brown sugar, butter, cinnamon, ginger and reserved pineapple juice; bring to a boil. Reduce heat; simmer for 5 minutes. Discard cinnamon sticks. Pour over fruit. Bake, uncovered, at 350° for 30 minutes or until heated through. **Yield:** 10 cups. **Nutritional Analysis:** One 1/2-cup serving (prepared with margarine) equals 131 calories, 38 mg sodium, 0 cholesterol, 29 gm carbohydrate, 1 gm protein, 2 gm fat. **Diabetic Exchanges:** 2 fruit, 1/2 fat.

Speedy Huevos Rancheros

Canned chilies, Mexican-style tomatoes, onion and bacon add plenty of zippy flavor to this hearty poached egg dish. I often make it when we go camping, because one skilletful provides a hearty breakfast for the whole family. —*Therese Langolf, Piru, California*

8 bacon strips, diced
3 cans (14-1/2 ounces *each*) Mexican diced tomatoes
1 medium onion, chopped
1 can (4 ounces) chopped green chilies, drained
10 eggs
1/2 cup shredded Colby cheese
Flour *or* corn tortillas, warmed, optional

In a skillet, cook bacon until crisp; drain. Stir in tomatoes, onion and chilies. Simmer, uncovered, until the onion is tender. With a spoon, make 10 wells in the tomato mixture; break an egg into each. Cover and cook over low heat for 15-20 minutes or until eggs are set. Sprinkle with cheese; cover and cook until the cheese is melted, about 1 minute. Serve with tortillas if desired. **Yield:** 5 servings.

Hearty Scrambled Eggs

(Pictured on page 131)

This breakfast dish includes classic omelet ingredients in a fun egg scramble that's quick to whip up! The eggs pick up plenty of flavor from the mushrooms, onion and cheese.
—*Carole Anhalt, Manitowoc, Wisconsin*

8 eggs
1-1/4 cups diced fully cooked ham
3/4 cup diced cheddar cheese
1/2 cup chopped fresh mushrooms
1/4 cup chopped onion
2 to 3 tablespoons butter *or* margarine

In a bowl, beat eggs. Add ham, cheese, mushrooms and onion. Melt butter in a skillet; add egg mixture. Cook and stir over medium heat until eggs are completely set and cheese is melted. **Yield:** 4 servings.

**Spiced Hot Fruit
Rosy Citrus Drink
Stuffed French Toast**

Curried Crab Quiche
Coconut Toast
Maple-Glazed Sausages

Curried Crab Quiche

(Pictured at left)

Curry and crab complement each other perfectly in this fuss-free quiche. With a sunny color and a rich taste, it's special enough for a holiday breakfast or brunch.
— *Kathy Kittell, Lenexa, Kansas*

    1 unbaked pastry shell (9 inches)
    6 to 8 ounces canned *or* frozen crabmeat,
        thawed, drained and cartilage removed
    3/4 cup shredded Swiss cheese
    3 eggs
1-1/2 cups whipping cream
    1/2 to 1 teaspoon curry powder
    1/2 teaspoon salt
Dash pepper

Line unpricked pastry shell with a double thickness of heavy-duty foil. Bake at 450° for 5 minutes. Remove foil; bake 5 minutes longer. Remove from the oven; reduce heat to 375°. Sprinkle crab and cheese into shell. In a bowl, beat eggs. Add cream, curry, salt and pepper; pour over cheese. Cover edges of pastry with foil; bake for 30-35 minutes or until a knife inserted near the center comes out clean. **Yield:** 6-8 servings.

Coconut Toast

(Pictured at left)

This toasty bread has a wonderfully sweet and buttery coconut topping that's simply scrumptious. It's easy to make and so yummy. Enjoy it with a cup of coffee at breakfast or for a snack anytime of day. — *Betty Checkett St. Louis, Missouri*

    1 cup flaked coconut
    1 cup sugar
    1/2 cup butter *or* margarine, melted
    1 egg, beaten
    1 teaspoon vanilla extract
    11 to 12 slices white bread

In a bowl, combine the coconut, sugar, butter, egg and vanilla; mix well. Spread over each slice of bread; place on ungreased baking sheets. Bake at 350° for 15-20 minutes or until lightly browned. **Yield:** 11-12 servings.

Maple-Glazed Sausages

(Pictured at left)

It's a breeze to simmer up this cinnamony syrup that nicely coats a skillet full of breakfast sausages. I often serve them to guests along with French toast and fruit compote. — *Trudie Hagen, Roggen, Colorado*

    2 packages (8 ounces *each*) brown-and-serve
        sausage links
    1 cup maple syrup
    1/2 cup packed brown sugar
    1 teaspoon ground cinnamon

In a large skillet, cook sausage links until browned; drain. Combine syrup, brown sugar and cinnamon; stir into

skillet. Bring to a boil; cook and stir until sausages are glazed. **Yield:** 6-8 servings.

Wake-Up Casserole

You'll find everything you want for breakfast—potatoes, eggs, cheese and ham—in this satisfying casserole. It can be made the night before and kept in the refrigerator. I frequently make it for church potlucks and for company. Everybody loves it. — *Iris Frank, Eureka, Illinois*

    8 frozen hash brown patties
    4 cups (16 ounces) shredded cheddar cheese
    1 pound cubed fully cooked ham (2 cups)
    7 eggs
    1 cup milk
    1/2 teaspoon salt
    1/2 teaspoon ground mustard

Place hash brown patties in a single layer in a greased 13-in. x 9-in. x 2-in. baking dish. Sprinkle with cheese and ham. In a bowl, beat eggs, milk, salt and mustard. Pour over ham. Cover and bake at 350° for 1 hour. Uncover; bake 15 minutes longer or until edges are golden brown and a knife inserted near the center comes out clean. **Yield:** 8 servings.

Blueberry Breakfast Sauce

(Pictured below)

This fresh-tasting sauce tastes great served over pancakes, French toast, waffles or even ice cream. Whether you use fresh or frozen blueberries, the flavor is fantastic. — *Ellen Benninger, Stoneboro, Pennsylvania*

    1/2 cup sugar
    1 tablespoon cornstarch
    1/3 cup water
    2 cups fresh *or* frozen blueberries

In a 2-qt. saucepan, combine sugar and cornstarch; gradually stir in water. Add blueberries; bring to a boil over medium heat, stirring constantly. Boil for 1 minute, stirring occasionally. Serve warm or cold over French toast, pancakes or waffles. **Yield:** about 2 cups.

Blueberry
Breakfast
Sauce

Chapter 10

⏱ *Casseroles and Skillet Suppers*

WHEN it comes to filling up your hungry family with true comfort food, nothing satisfies quite like a hearty casserole. Just quickly assemble it, pop it into the oven and forget it.

And when your time's at a premium, you'll appreciate this chapter's slew of skillet suppers that require just a single pan and only a few minutes to make. (Cleanup's a breeze, too!)

So whether it's an all-in-one meal highlighting seasonal produce, cleverly disguising leftovers or featuring classic meat-and-potato combinations, convenient casseroles and skillet suppers are sure to please!

ONE-DISH WONDER. Apricot Almond Chicken (p. 152).

Catchall Casseroles

YOU'LL welcome these hearty and hot dishes that are proven favorites with other families. Just toss the ingredients together and turn on the oven. (Most of these casseroles can be ready in an hour or under!)

Baked Fish and Rice

(Pictured below)

I just recently tried this simple-to-fix meal, and it was an instant hit at our house. Fish and rice are a tasty change of pace from traditional meat-and-potato fare. —*Jo Groth Plainfield, Iowa*

  1-1/2 cups boiling chicken broth
    1/2 cup uncooked long grain rice
    1/4 teaspoon Italian seasoning
    1/4 teaspoon garlic powder
      1 package (10 ounces) frozen chopped
        broccoli, thawed and drained
      1 tablespoon grated Parmesan cheese
      1 can (2.8 ounces) french-fried onions, *divided*
      1 pound fresh *or* frozen fish fillets, thawed
Dash paprika
    1/2 cup shredded cheddar cheese

In a greased 11-in. x 7-in. x 2-in. baking dish, combine the broth, rice, Italian seasoning and garlic powder. Cover and bake at 375° for 10 minutes. Add the broccoli, Parmesan cheese and half of the onions. Top with fish fillets; sprinkle with paprika. Cover and bake 20-25 minutes longer or until the fish flakes easily with a fork. Uncover; sprinkle with cheddar cheese and remaining onions. Return to the oven for 3 minutes or until cheese is melted. **Yield:** 4 servings.

Baked Fish and Rice

Spinach Beef Bake

Everyone loves the mild flavor and cheesy topping of this crowd-pleasing casserole. I usually round out this hearty meal with a tossed salad. —*LaVerne Schultz Greenfield, Wisconsin*

    1 pound ground beef
    1 jar (4-1/2 ounces) sliced mushrooms, drained
    1 medium onion, chopped
    2 garlic cloves, minced
 1-1/2 teaspoons dried oregano
 1-1/4 teaspoons salt
    1/4 teaspoon pepper
    2 packages (10 ounces *each*) frozen chopped
      spinach, thawed and squeezed dry
    1 can (10-3/4 ounces) condensed cream of
      celery soup, undiluted
    1 cup (8 ounces) sour cream
    1 cup uncooked long grain rice
    1 cup (4 ounces) shredded mozzarella cheese

In a skillet, brown beef; drain. Add mushrooms, onion, garlic, oregano, salt and pepper. Add spinach, soup, sour cream and rice; mix well. Transfer to a greased 2-1/2-qt. baking dish. Sprinkle with mozzarella cheese. Cover and bake at 350° for 45-50 minutes or until the rice is tender. **Yield:** 6-8 servings.

Wild Rice Turkey Dish

This rich, flavorful main dish has been one of my favorite meals to serve company. Made in one easy step, it's a real time-saver. Plus, it's a great way to use up leftover turkey. —*Clara Sawlaw, Paris, Illinois*

    6 cups cooked wild rice
    3 cups cubed cooked turkey
    1 can (10-3/4 ounces) condensed cream of
      mushroom soup, undiluted
    3 celery ribs, sliced
 1-1/3 cups sliced fresh mushrooms
    1 medium onion, chopped
    1 cup (8 ounces) sour cream
    1/2 cup butter *or* margarine, melted
    1 teaspoon salt
    1/4 teaspoon pepper

In a large bowl, combine all of the ingredients. Pour into a greased 13-in. x 9-in. x 2-in. baking dish. Cover and bake at 350° for 45 minutes. Uncover and bake 15 minutes longer or until lightly browned. **Yield:** 10 servings.

Company Chicken Casserole

Searching for an entree that's special enough for company, yet easy on the cook? Try this memorable make-ahead meal. It features chunks of tender chicken, mushrooms and water chestnuts in a cheesy sauce. —*Harriett McKay Cathedral City, California*

    6 slices bread, crusts removed
    4 cups cubed cooked chicken
    1/2 pound fresh mushrooms, sliced

6 tablespoons butter *or* margarine, *divided*
1 can (8 ounces) water chestnuts, drained
    and chopped
1/2 cup mayonnaise
6 slices Monterey Jack cheese
4 slices process American cheese
3 eggs
1-1/2 cups milk
1 can (10-3/4 ounces) condensed cream of
    mushroom soup, undiluted
1 can (10-3/4 ounces) condensed cream of
    chicken soup, undiluted
2/3 cup dry bread crumbs

Place bread in a greased 13-in. x 9-in. x 2-in. baking dish. Top with chicken. In a skillet, saute mushrooms in 2 tablespoons butter until tender. Using a slotted spoon, place mushrooms over the chicken. Combine water chestnuts and mayonnaise; spoon over mushrooms. Top with cheeses. Beat eggs and milk; pour over cheese. Combine soups; spread over top. Cover and refrigerate overnight. Remove from the refrigerator 30 minutes before baking. Bake, uncovered, at 350° for 1 hour. Melt the remaining butter; toss with bread crumbs. Sprinkle over the casserole; bake 10 minutes longer. **Yield:** 10-12 servings.

Zippy Beef Bake

Pork Sauerkraut Casserole

I get lots of compliments on this tangy pork dish, so I fix it often. To speed preparation, I use frozen hash browns instead of peeling and slicing potatoes. —Anne Yaeger
Houston, Texas

1 can (27 ounces) sauerkraut, drained
4 cups frozen cubed hash brown potatoes,
    thawed
6 pork chops (1 inch thick)
1 can (10-3/4 ounces) condensed tomato soup,
    undiluted
1 medium onion, chopped
1/2 cup water
1/4 cup packed brown sugar
2 tablespoons vinegar

In an ungreased 13-in. x 9-in. x 2-in. baking dish, combine sauerkraut and hash browns. Top with pork chops. Combine soup, onion, water, brown sugar and vinegar; pour over chops. Bake, uncovered, at 350° for 1-1/2 hours. **Yield:** 6 servings.

Sausage Rice Casserole

Spicy sausage provides just the right amount of zip in this satisfying dish. It's pretty, too, with three colors of peppers peeking through the rice mixture. —Delene Durham
Campbellsville, Kentucky

1 pound bulk hot pork sausage
1 medium onion, chopped
3 cups cooked rice
1 *each* medium green, sweet red and yellow
    pepper, diced

1 can (10-3/4 ounces) condensed cream of
    mushroom soup, undiluted
1 can (10-1/2 ounces) condensed French onion
    soup, undiluted

In a large skillet over medium heat, cook sausage and onion until the sausage is browned and onion is tender; drain. Add the rice, peppers and soups; mix well. Transfer to an ungreased 13-in. x 9-in. x 2-in. baking dish. Bake, uncovered, at 350° for 30-35 minutes or until bubbly. **Yield:** 6-8 servings.

Zippy Beef Bake

(Pictured above)

With its south-of-the-border flavor, this filling meal-in-one is a much-requested recipe in our home. In fact, we like it so much we have it about once a week! —Gay Kelley
Tucson, Arizona

3/4 pound ground beef
1 tablespoon butter *or* margarine
2 medium zucchini, thinly sliced
1/4 pound fresh mushrooms, sliced
2 tablespoons sliced green onions
1-1/2 teaspoons chili powder
1 teaspoon salt
1/8 teaspoon garlic powder
1-1/2 cups cooked rice
1 can (4 ounces) chopped green chilies
1/2 cup sour cream
1 cup (4 ounces) shredded Monterey Jack
    cheese, *divided*

In a large skillet over medium heat, cook beef until no longer pink. Add butter, zucchini, mushrooms and onions; cook and stir until the vegetables are tender. Drain. Stir in chili powder, salt and garlic powder. Add rice, chilies, sour cream and half of the cheese. Transfer to a greased 2-qt. baking dish; top with remaining cheese. Bake, uncovered, at 350° for 20 minutes or until cheese is melted. **Yield:** 4 servings.

Ham 'n' Noodle Hot Dish

(Pictured at right)

Frozen green peas add lovely color to this comforting meal-in-one. The easy, cheesy dish is a great way to use up leftover ham.
—Renee Schwebach, Dumont, Minnesota

> **3 tablespoons butter *or* margarine,** *divided*
> **2 tablespoons all-purpose flour**
> **1 cup milk**
> **1 cup (4 ounces) shredded process American cheese**
> **1/2 teaspoon salt**
> **2 cups diced fully cooked ham**
> **1-1/2 cups medium noodles, cooked and drained**
> **1 cup frozen peas, thawed**
> **1/4 cup dry bread crumbs**
> **1/2 teaspoon dried parsley flakes**

In a saucepan, melt 2 tablespoons butter; stir in flour until smooth. Gradually add milk. Bring to a boil over medium heat; cook and stir for 2 minutes. Remove from the heat; stir in cheese and salt until cheese is melted. Add the ham, noodles and peas. Pour into a greased 1-qt. baking dish. Melt remaining butter; add bread crumbs and parsley. Sprinkle over casserole. Bake, uncovered, at 350° for 30 minutes or until heated through. **Yield:** 4 servings.

Ham 'n' Noodle Hot Dish

Ham and Swiss Casserole

When I prepare this noodle casserole for church gatherings, it's always a hit. It can easily be doubled or tripled for a crowd.
—Doris Barb, El Dorado, Kansas

> **1 package (8 ounces) medium noodles, cooked and drained**
> **2 cups cubed fully cooked ham**
> **2 cups (8 ounces) shredded Swiss cheese**
> **1 can (10-3/4 ounces) condensed cream of celery soup, undiluted**
> **1 cup (8 ounces) sour cream**
> **1/2 cup chopped green pepper**
> **1/2 cup chopped onion**

In a greased 13-in. x 9-in. x 2-in. baking dish, layer a third of the noodles, ham and cheese. In a small bowl, combine soup, sour cream, green pepper and onion; spread half over the top. Repeat layers. Bake, uncovered, at 350° for 40-45 minutes or until heated through. **Yield:** 6-8 servings.

Golden Chicken Casserole

My sister and I developed this colorful, creamy casserole from two or three others we had tried. The whole family likes the hearty layers of chicken, Tater Tots, vegetables and cheese. —Ione Senn, Salt Lake City, Utah

> **1 can (10-3/4 ounces) condensed cream of chicken soup, undiluted**
> **1 can (10-3/4 ounces) condensed cream of celery soup, undiluted**
> **1/2 cup water**
> **1/4 to 1/2 teaspoon salt**
> **1 package (32 ounces) frozen Tater Tots**
> **1 package (16 ounces) frozen mixed vegetables**
> **2 cups cubed cooked chicken**
> **1 cup (4 ounces) shredded cheddar cheese**

Combine the soups, water and salt; mix well. In a greased 13-in. x 9-in. x 2-in. baking dish, layer a third of the soup mixture, half of the Tater Tots, half of the vegetables and half of the chicken. Repeat layers. Top with remaining soup mixture. Sprinkle with cheese. Cover and bake at 350° for 60-70 minutes or until bubbly. Uncover; bake 5-10 minutes longer or until browned and heated through. **Yield:** 6-8 servings.

Crunchy Curried Chicken

If you have leftover ham and chicken (or turkey) on hand, try this. It's a great potluck dish because it can be made a day ahead. —Eleanor Doering
Stoughton, Wisconsin

> **4-1/2 cups cooked long grain rice**
> **1 cup cubed cooked chicken**
> **1 cup cubed fully cooked ham**
> **1 can (8 ounces) water chestnuts, drained and chopped**
> **1 can (10-3/4 ounces) condensed cream of chicken soup, undiluted**
> **1-1/4 cups milk**

1/2 cup mayonnaise
1/4 cup minced fresh parsley
3/4 teaspoon salt
1/8 to 1/4 teaspoon curry powder
1/3 cup sliced almonds

Place rice in a greased 13-in. x 9-in. x 2-in. baking dish. Sprinkle with chicken, ham and water chestnuts. Combine the next six ingredients; pour over chicken mixture. Bake, uncovered, at 350° for 30-35 minutes or until bubbly. Sprinkle with almonds; bake 5 minutes longer. **Yield:** 6-8 servings.

Taco Pie

Crushed corn chips offer a lively crunch to this yummy main dish. Cut into neat wedges, this pie is a fun, fuss-free way of serving tacos without the mess.
—Margery Bryan, Royal City, Washington

1-1/2 pounds ground beef
1 envelope taco seasoning
1/2 cup water
1 can (2-1/4 ounces) sliced ripe olives, drained
2 cups corn chips, crushed, *divided*
1 unbaked pastry shell (9 inches)
1 cup (8 ounces) sour cream
1 cup (4 ounces) shredded cheddar cheese
Shredded lettuce and sliced avocado, optional

In a skillet, brown beef; drain. Stir in taco seasoning, water and olives. Simmer, uncovered, for 5 minutes, stirring frequently. Sprinkle half of the corn chips into pie shell. Top with meat mixture, sour cream and cheese. Cover with remaining corn chips. Bake at 375° for 20-25 minutes or until crust is golden brown. Cut into wedges. Top with lettuce and avocado if desired. **Yield:** 6 servings.

Chili Beef Bake

We served this zesty casserole at a fund-raising luncheon for a local college. The students went crazy for it and came back for seconds and thirds. Some even asked for the recipe, which relies on convenient canned beans, soup and tomatoes. —*Martha Huffman, Monticello, Arkansas*

2 pounds ground beef
1 medium onion, chopped
1 garlic clove, minced
1 teaspoon chili powder
1 teaspoon salt
1/4 teaspoon pepper
12 flour tortillas (6 inches)
2 cans (15 ounces *each*) pinto beans, rinsed and drained
6 slices process American cheese
2 cans (10-3/4 ounces *each*) condensed cream of chicken soup, undiluted
1 can (10 ounces) diced tomatoes and green chilies, undrained

In a skillet, brown beef; drain. Add onion and garlic; cook until tender. Remove from the heat; add chili powder, salt and pepper. Place six tortillas in a greased 13-in. x 9-

in. x 2-in. baking dish, overlapping slightly. Top with half of the meat mixture. Layer with beans, remaining meat mixture, cheese and remaining tortillas. Combine soup and tomatoes; pour over tortillas (dish will be full). Bake, uncovered, at 350° for 30 minutes or until bubbly and heated through. **Yield:** 8 servings.

Baked Beef Stew

(Pictured below)

This is such an easy way to make a wonderful beef stew. You don't need to brown the meat first—just combine it with hearty chunks of carrots, potatoes and celery...and let it all cook together in a flavorful gravy. My daughter Karen came up with the recipe for her busy family.
—Doris Sleeth, Naples, Florida

1 can (14-1/2 ounces) diced tomatoes, undrained
1 cup water
3 tablespoons quick-cooking tapioca
2 teaspoons sugar
1-1/2 teaspoons salt
1/2 teaspoon pepper
2 pounds lean beef stew meat, cut into 1-inch cubes
4 medium carrots, cut into 1-inch chunks
3 medium potatoes, peeled and quartered
2 celery ribs, cut into 3/4-inch chunks
1 medium onion, cut into chunks
1 slice bread, cubed

In a large bowl, combine the tomatoes, water, tapioca, sugar, salt and pepper. Add remaining ingredients; mix well. Pour into a greased 13-in. x 9-in. x 2-in. or 3-qt. baking dish. Cover and bake at 375° for 1-3/4 to 2 hours or until meat and vegetables are tender. Serve in bowls. **Yield:** 6-8 servings.

Baked Beef Stew

Beefy Noodle Bake

Cream-style corn adds a touch of sweetness to the overall spicy flavor of this filling and flavorful ground beef casserole. Use whatever amount of chili powder suits your family's tastes. —Edith Betz, Ethel, Louisiana

1-1/2 pounds ground beef
  1 cup chopped onion
  1/4 cup chopped green onions
  2 garlic cloves, minced
  1 can (17 ounces) peas, drained
  1 can (15 ounces) tomato sauce
  1 can (14-3/4 ounces) cream-style corn
  1 tablespoon chili powder
  1 teaspoon salt
  1/4 teaspoon pepper
  6 cups cooked wide egg noodles

In a skillet over medium heat, brown beef; drain. Add onions and garlic; saute until tender. Remove from the heat. Add remaining ingredients; stir until combined. Spoon into a greased 3-qt. baking dish. Cover and bake at 350° for 40 minutes or until heated through. **Yield:** 6-8 servings.

Apricot Almond Chicken

(Pictured on page 146)

This tender chicken topped with sweet apricot preserves and crunchy almonds is special enough for guests, yet requires no complicated cooking. The hearty brown rice, with colorful flecks of red and green pepper, makes a pretty accompaniment. —Betty Due, Mendota, Illinois

✓ Nutritional Analysis included

2-1/4 cups chicken broth
  1 cup uncooked long grain brown rice
  1 small onion, chopped
  1/4 cup chopped green pepper
  1/4 cup chopped sweet red pepper
  1 teaspoon salt, optional
  1/4 teaspoon dried thyme
  1/4 teaspoon dried marjoram
  4 boneless skinless chicken breast halves
    (1 pound)
  4 tablespoons apricot preserves
  1/3 cup sliced almonds, toasted

Combine the first eight ingredients in a greased 13-in. x 9-in. x 2-in. baking dish; mix well. Top with chicken. Cover and bake at 350° for 55-60 minutes or until rice is tender. Uncover and stir the rice. Place 1 tablespoonful of preserves on each chicken breast. Bake, uncovered, 5 minutes longer. Sprinkle with almonds. Bake 5 minutes more or until meat juices run clear. Let stand for 5 minutes before serving. **Yield:** 4 servings. **Nutritional Analysis:** One serving (prepared with low-sodium broth and without salt) equals 456 calories, 143 mg sodium, 76 mg cholesterol, 54 gm carbohydrate, 35 gm protein, 11 gm fat. **Diabetic Exchanges:** 3 starch, 3 lean meat, 1 vegetable, 1/2 fat.

Mozzarella Tomatoes

I received the recipe for this rich bread-and-tomato dish from a relative. We especially enjoy it when tomatoes from our garden are plentiful. It's a favorite at potlucks, too. —Gloria Bisek, Deerwood, Minnesota

4 medium tomatoes, sliced
8 cups soft bread cubes
3 cups (12 ounces) shredded mozzarella
  cheese, *divided*
4 bacon strips, cooked and crumbled
1/2 cup butter *or* margarine, melted
1/2 cup chopped celery
1/2 cup chopped onion
2 eggs, beaten
1/2 teaspoon garlic salt
1/2 teaspoon dried oregano

Place a single layer of tomatoes in a greased 13-in. x 9-in. x 2-in. baking dish; set aside. In a large bowl, combine the bread cubes, 2 cups of cheese, bacon, butter, celery, onion, eggs, garlic salt and oregano; mix well. Spoon over the tomatoes. Top with remaining tomatoes; sprinkle with remaining cheese. Bake, uncovered, at 350° for 30 minutes or until heated through. **Yield:** 6-8 servings.

Sausage Rice Pilaf

I serve this nicely seasoned rice casserole with a fresh green salad and some crusty bread or rolls. It's one of our favorite sausage recipes. My family likes freshly grated Parmesan cheese on their helpings. —Deborah Downing, Goshen, Indiana

2 pounds bulk Italian sausage
1 large onion, chopped
1 jar (6 ounces) sliced mushrooms, drained
2 cups uncooked long grain rice
2 cans (10-1/2 ounces *each*) condensed beef
  consomme, undiluted
2 cups water
2 teaspoons dried oregano
Grated Parmesan cheese, optional

In a large skillet over medium heat, brown sausage; drain. Add onion and mushrooms; saute until onion is tender. Add rice, consomme, water and oregano; mix well. Transfer to an ungreased 13-in. x 9-in. x 2-in. baking dish. Cover and bake at 350° for 55-60 minutes or until rice is tender, stirring once. Sprinkle with Parmesan cheese if desired. **Yield:** 8 servings.

Fiesta Chicken

Chili powder and picante sauce add just the right dash of zip to this hearty main dish. It's a snap to assemble since it uses convenience foods. —Teresa Peterson, Kasson, Minnesota

1 can (10-3/4 ounces) condensed cream of
  chicken soup, undiluted
1 can (10-3/4 ounces) condensed cream of
  mushroom soup, undiluted

2 small tomatoes, chopped
1/3 cup picante sauce
1 medium green pepper, chopped
1 small onion, chopped
2 to 3 teaspoons chili powder
12 corn tortillas (6 inches), cut into 1-inch strips
3 cups cubed cooked chicken
1 cup (4 ounces) shredded Colby cheese

In a bowl, combine the soups, tomatoes, picante sauce, green pepper, onion and chili powder. In a greased 13-in. x 9-in. x 2-in. baking dish, layer half of the tortilla strips, chicken, soup mixture and cheese. Repeat layers. Cover and bake at 350° for 40-50 minutes or until bubbly. **Yield:** 6-8 servings.

Italian Chicken and Rice

I combined the best of three different recipes to come up with this tender and tasty chicken-rice combination. It's become my family's way to eat chicken. —Cathee Bethel Lebanon, Oregon

✓ **Nutritional Analysis included**

2/3 cup biscuit/baking mix
1/3 cup grated Parmesan cheese
2 teaspoons Italian seasoning
1 teaspoon paprika
1 can (5 ounces) evaporated milk, *divided*

6 boneless skinless chicken breast halves (1-1/2 pounds)
2 cups boiling water
2 cups uncooked instant rice
1 teaspoon salt, optional
2 tablespoons butter *or* margarine, melted

In a large resealable plastic bag or shallow bowl, combine the first four ingredients. Place 1/3 cup milk in another bowl. Dip chicken in milk, then coat with the cheese mixture. In a greased 13-in. x 9-in. x 2-in. baking dish, combine water, rice, salt if desired and remaining milk; mix well. Top with chicken. Drizzle with butter. Bake, uncovered, at 425° for 25-30 minutes or until the rice is tender and chicken juices run clear. **Yield:** 6 servings. **Nutritional Analysis:** One serving (prepared with evaporated skim milk and margarine and without salt) equals 288 calories, 410 mg sodium, 78 mg cholesterol, 14 gm carbohydrate, 32 gm protein, 11 gm fat. **Diabetic Exchanges:** 4 lean meat, 1 starch.

Chicken 'n' Biscuits

(Pictured below left)

This cheesy chicken casserole gets its vibrant color from frozen vegetables and its unique flavor from crumbled bacon. The biscuit-topped dish has become a regular at our dinner table since my sister-in-law shared it with us after the birth of our son.
—Debbie Vannette Zeeland, Michigan

Chicken 'n' Biscuits

1 package (16 ounces) frozen mixed vegetables
2-1/2 cups cubed cooked chicken
1 can (10-3/4 ounces) condensed cream of chicken soup, undiluted
3/4 cup milk
1-1/2 cups (6 ounces) shredded cheddar cheese, *divided*
8 bacon strips, cooked and crumbled, optional
BISCUITS:
1-1/2 cups biscuit/baking mix
2/3 cup milk
1 can (2.8 ounces) french-fried onions

In a large bowl, combine the vegetables, chicken, soup, milk, 1 cup cheese and bacon if desired. Pour into an ungreased 13-in. x 9-in. x 2-in. baking dish. Cover and bake at 400° for 15 minutes. Meanwhile, in another bowl, combine biscuit mix and milk. Drop the batter by tablespoonfuls onto the chicken mixture. Bake, uncovered, for 20-22 minutes or until biscuits are golden brown. Top with the onions and remaining cheese. Bake 3-4 minutes longer or until the cheese is melted. **Yield:** 6 servings.

Dash in the Pan

Colorful Kielbasa

YOU'VE come to the right place if "going steady" with your stovetop doesn't fit into your—or your family's—active lifestyle. File these speedy skillet suppers under "F" for filling, flavorful...and flat-out fast!

Colorful Kielbasa

(Pictured at right)

This stick-to-your-ribs dish is sure to satisfy even the heartiest appetite. You can take it from stovetop to table in about half an hour. —Schelby Thompson
Dover, Delaware

        1 can (10-3/4 ounces) condensed cream of
          celery soup, undiluted
    3/4 cup water
        1 tablespoon butter *or* margarine
        1 pound smoked kielbasa, cut into 1/2-inch
          pieces
    3/4 cup uncooked long grain rice
        1 package (10 ounces) frozen peas
        1 jar (4-1/2 ounces) sliced mushrooms, drained
        1 cup (4 ounces) shredded cheddar cheese

In a skillet, combine soup, water and butter; bring to a boil. Add kielbasa and rice. Reduce heat; cover and simmer for 15-18 minutes or until rice is almost tender. Stir in peas and mushrooms. Cover and simmer for 15 minutes or until the rice is tender and the peas are heated through. Sprinkle with cheese; cover and let stand until melted. **Yield:** 4-6 servings.

Pork Chop Skillet Meal

My delicious meal-in-one is so colorful, with corn and tomatoes topping off the pork chops. The rice cooks right along with everything else. —Linda Andersen
Sheldon, Iowa

        6 pork chops (1/2 inch thick)
        2 tablespoons vegetable oil
    1-1/4 cups water
    2/3 cup uncooked long grain rice
    1/2 cup chopped onion
        1 teaspoon salt, *divided*
        1 can (11 ounces) whole kernel corn, drained
        1 can (14-1/2 ounces) diced tomatoes,
          undrained
    1/4 teaspoon pepper

In a large skillet, brown pork chops in oil; drain. Remove chops. Combine water, rice, onion and 1/2 teaspoon salt in the skillet. Place pork chops over rice mixture; top with corn and tomatoes. Sprinkle with pepper and remaining salt. Bring to a boil. Reduce heat; cover and simmer for 20-25 minutes or until pork and rice are tender. Let stand 5 minutes before serving. **Yield:** 6 servings.

Mexican Beef and Dumplings

My husband and I love this spicy ground beef concoction seasoned with chili powder. The cornmeal dumplings—which are a little "heavier" than typical dumplings—are a fun variation, and they can be stirred up in no time.
—Sue Gronholz, Columbus, Wisconsin

        2 pounds ground beef
        1 can (15-1/4 ounces) whole kernel corn,
          undrained
        1 can (14-1/2 ounces) diced tomatoes,
          undrained
        1 can (14-1/2 ounces) tomato sauce
        1 small onion, chopped
    1/2 cup chopped celery
    1/4 cup chopped green pepper
        1 tablespoon chili powder
    1-1/2 teaspoons salt
    DUMPLINGS:
        1 cup all-purpose flour
        1 cup cornmeal
        2 teaspoons baking powder
    Pinch salt
        1 cup milk

In a Dutch oven or large kettle, brown beef; drain. Stir in the next eight ingredients. Cover and simmer for 15 minutes. For the dumplings, combine flour, cornmeal, baking powder and salt; stir in milk. Drop into eight mounds onto boiling mixture. Reduce heat; cover and simmer for 12-15 minutes or until the dumplings test done. (Do not lift the cover while simmering.) **Yield:** 8 servings.

Italian Sausage Stew

I warm up my family with this satisfying stew. Add a green salad and hot Italian bread for a great meal on a cool day. Leftovers are terrific, too. —Cnora Cooper
North Syracuse, New York

1-1/2 pounds bulk Italian sausage
    1 cup water, *divided*
    1 can (14-1/2 ounces) stewed tomatoes
    1 can (10-1/2 ounces) condensed French onion soup, undiluted
    3 medium potatoes, diced
  1/2 teaspoon Worcestershire sauce
    1 package (10 ounces) frozen peas and pearl onions
    1 can (4 ounces) mushroom stems and pieces, drained
    3 tablespoons all-purpose flour
Grated Parmesan cheese, optional

In a Dutch oven or large kettle over low heat, cook sausage in 1/2 cup of water until no longer pink; drain. Add tomatoes, soup, potatoes and Worcestershire sauce; bring to a boil. Reduce heat; cover and simmer for 10 minutes. Stir in peas and mushrooms; cover and simmer for 15 minutes or until vegetables are tender. Combine flour and remaining water to form a smooth paste; stir into stew. Bring to a boil; cook and stir for 2 minutes over medium heat. Sprinkle servings with Parmesan cheese if desired. **Yield:** 6-8 servings.

Santa Fe Chicken

(Pictured below)

My day is busy from start to finish. So this quick and meaty main dish is one of my menu mainstays. With its lovely golden color, it's pretty enough to serve to company or as a special Sunday dinner. —Debra Cook
Pampa, Texas

    1 large onion, chopped
    1 tablespoon butter *or* margarine
1-1/4 cups chicken broth
    1 cup salsa
    1 cup uncooked long grain rice

Santa Fe Chicken

  1/8 teaspoon garlic powder
    4 boneless skinless chicken breast halves (about 1 pound)
  3/4 cup shredded cheddar cheese
Chopped fresh cilantro *or* parsley, optional

In a large skillet, saute onion in butter until tender. Add broth and salsa; bring to a boil. Stir in rice and garlic powder. Place chicken over rice; cover and simmer for 10 minutes. Turn chicken; cook 10-15 minutes longer or until meat juices run clear. Remove from the heat. Sprinkle with cheese; cover and let stand for 5 minutes. Garnish with cilantro if desired. **Yield:** 4 servings.

Curried Shrimp Stir-Fry

Tired taste buds, don't despair! This shrimp main dish proves that a satisfying, well-seasoned supper can be fixed with little fuss and mess. —Frances Riebe
Foster, Rhode Island

    1 cup chopped peeled tart apple
  1/2 to 3/4 cup chopped onion
  1/2 cup sliced celery
  1/4 cup butter *or* margarine
    3 tablespoons all-purpose flour
    1 teaspoon curry powder
  1/2 teaspoon salt
  1/4 teaspoon ground ginger
  1/8 teaspoon pepper
1-1/2 cups chicken broth
  1/2 cup milk
    1 teaspoon Worcestershire sauce
  3/4 pound cooked shrimp, peeled and deveined
Hot cooked rice

In a large skillet or wok, stir-fry apple, onion and celery in butter for 10 minutes or until tender. Combine flour, curry powder, salt, ginger and pepper; add to apple mixture and mix well. Gradually stir in the broth, milk and Worcestershire sauce. Bring to a boil; boil for 2 minutes, stirring constantly. Add shrimp and heat through. Serve over rice. **Yield:** 4 servings.

Hamburger Fry Pan Supper

This fast-to-fix main dish is easy to prepare since there are so few ingredients. Once the ground beef is browned, just add the vegetables and simmer 'til tender.
—Lucinda Walker, Somerset, Pennsylvania

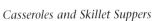

    1 pound ground beef
    1 medium onion, chopped
    2 medium unpeeled red potatoes, julienned
    2 cups shredded cabbage
    2 cups thinly sliced celery
  1/2 cup water
Salt and pepper to taste

In a large skillet, brown beef and onion; drain. Add remaining ingredients. Cover and simmer for 20 minutes or until vegetables are tender, stirring occasionally. **Yield:** 6 servings.

Steak Stir-Fry

(Pictured below)

No one would guess this elegant entree is a snap to prepare at the last minute. To save even more prep time, use frozen mixed veggies instead of fresh. Sometimes I substitute chicken, chicken bouillon and curry for the beef, beef bouillon and ginger. —Janis Plourde
Smooth Rock Falls, Ontario

   1 teaspoon beef bouillon granules
   1 cup boiling water
   2 tablespoons cornstarch
1/3 cup soy sauce
   1 pound boneless sirloin steak, cut into thin strips
   1 garlic clove, minced
   1 teaspoon ground ginger
1/4 teaspoon pepper
   2 tablespoons vegetable oil, *divided*
   1 large green pepper, julienned
   1 cup sliced carrots *or* celery
   5 green onions, cut into 1-inch pieces
Hot cooked rice

Dissolve bouillon in water. Combine the cornstarch and soy sauce until smooth; add to bouillon. Set aside. Toss beef with garlic, ginger and pepper. In a large skillet or wok over medium-high heat, stir-fry beef in 1 tablespoon oil until cooked as desired; remove and keep warm. Heat remaining oil; stir-fry vegetables until crisp-tender. Stir soy sauce mixture and add to the skillet; bring to a boil. Cook and stir for 2 minutes. Return meat to pan and heat through. Serve over rice. **Yield:** 4 servings.

Skillet Meat Loaf

Meat loaf that cooks in less than half an hour? It's true —with this speedy stovetop recipe. This is the best and fastest meat loaf I've ever tasted. The moist, mild slices are great served with mashed potatoes. —Becky Bolte
Jewell, Kansas

   2 eggs, beaten
1/2 cup ketchup
   1 tablespoon Worcestershire sauce
   1 teaspoon prepared mustard
1/4 teaspoon salt
1/4 teaspoon pepper
   2 cups crushed saltines (about 40 crackers)
   1 small onion, chopped
1/2 cup thinly sliced celery
1/2 cup thinly sliced carrot
   2 pounds lean ground beef
Additional ketchup and mustard, optional

In a large bowl, combine the first six ingredients. Add saltines, onion, celery and carrot. Add beef and mix well. Pat into a 10-in. skillet. Top with ketchup and mustard if desired. Cover and cook over medium heat for 8 minutes. Reduce heat to low; cover and cook 15-20 minutes longer or until meat is no longer pink and a meat thermometer reads 160°. Drain. Let stand a few minutes before serving. **Yield:** 8 servings.

Five-Vegetable Stir-Fry

We love the fresh taste and eye-catching color of this easy stir-fry. It's especially good in summer when the ingredients come from my garden. —Rose Norton
Sandusky, Michigan

✓ Nutritional Analysis included

   4 cups broccoli florets
   2 tablespoons vegetable oil
   2 medium yellow summer squash, cut into 1/4-inch slices
   2 medium zucchini, cut into 1/4-inch slices
   1 large sweet red pepper, cut into 3/4-inch pieces
   1 green onion, chopped
   2 garlic cloves, minced
   1 cup chicken broth
   1 tablespoon cornstarch
   2 teaspoons sugar
1/4 teaspoon ground ginger
1/4 teaspoon salt, optional
1/8 teaspoon cayenne pepper
   1 tablespoon minced fresh cilantro *or* parsley
Hot cooked rice, optional

In a large skillet or wok, stir-fry broccoli in oil for 3-4 minutes or until crisp-tender. Add the squash, zucchini, red pepper, onion and garlic; stir-fry for 2-3 minutes or until crisp-tender. In a small bowl, combine broth, corn-

Steak Stir-Fry

starch, sugar, ginger, salt if desired and cayenne; stir until smooth. Add to skillet. Bring to a boil and boil for 1 minute, stirring constantly. Sprinkle with cilantro. Serve over rice if desired. **Yield:** 7 servings. **Nutritional Analysis:** One 1-cup serving (prepared with low-sodium broth and without salt; calculated without rice) equals 82 calories, 31 mg sodium, 0 cholesterol, 10 gm carbohydrate, 3 gm protein, 5 gm fat. **Diabetic Exchanges:** 1-1/2 vegetable, 1 fat.

Pesto Pepper Tortellini
(Pictured at right)

This is a shortcut version of a rich, creamy pasta dish I enjoyed on a vacation trip. It's versatile, too—serve it as an awesome meatless entree or a special side dish. —Mickie Taft, Milwaukee, Wisconsin

    1 package (19 ounces) frozen cheese
      tortellini
1/2 cup julienned sweet red pepper
    3 garlic cloves, minced
1/2 cup butter *or* margarine
    2 cups whipping cream
1/4 cup ground walnuts
    2 tablespoons minced fresh basil *or* 2
      teaspoons dried basil
    1 tablespoon chopped green onion *or* chives

Prepare tortellini according to package directions. Meanwhile, in a skillet, saute red pepper and garlic in butter until pepper is crisp-tender. Stir in cream; cook for 8-10 minutes or until slightly thickened. Add walnuts, basil and onion; heat through. Drain tortellini; add to sauce and toss to coat. **Yield:** 4 servings.

Sausage Stir-Fry

Convenient frozen veggies and canned broth shorten prep time for this deliciously different stir-fry. Smoked kielbasa provides the hearty change of pace. —Nykii Chouteau, Clermont, Florida

 Nutritional Analysis included

    1 medium onion, thinly sliced
    2 garlic cloves, minced
    1 to 2 tablespoons vegetable oil
    1 pound fully cooked kielbasa *or* Polish
      sausage, halved lengthwise and sliced
    1 package (16 ounces) frozen stir-fry
      vegetables, thawed
    1 can (8 ounces) bamboo shoots, optional
    2 tablespoons cornstarch
1/2 teaspoon cayenne pepper
    1 can (14-1/2 ounces) beef broth
    2 tablespoons soy sauce
Hot cooked rice

In a large skillet or wok, stir-fry onion and garlic in oil until tender. Add sausage, vegetables and bamboo shoots if desired; stir-fry until heated through. Combine corn-

Pesto Pepper Tortellini

starch, cayenne, broth and soy sauce until smooth; add to the pan. Bring to a boil; cook and stir for 2 minutes. Serve over rice. **Yield:** 6 servings. **Nutritional Analysis:** One 1-cup serving (prepared with low-fat smoked turkey sausage, low-sodium broth and light soy sauce; calculated without rice) equals 182 calories, 885 mg sodium, 51 mg cholesterol, 12 gm carbohydrate, 15 gm protein, 9 gm fat. **Diabetic Exchanges:** 2 meat, 2 vegetable.

Potato Pepperoni Dish

Here's a way to get that popular pizza taste into an everyday menu. The potatoes cook up quickly when thinly sliced—and are nicely flavored by the tomato sauce and pepperoni. —Marlene Muckenhirn, Delano, Minnesota

    2 to 4 tablespoons butter *or* margarine
    5 large unpeeled potatoes, cut into 1/8-inch
      slices
    1 small onion, chopped
1/2 teaspoon salt
1/8 teaspoon pepper
    2 cups (8 ounces) shredded mozzarella cheese
    1 can (8 ounces) tomato sauce
    1 package (3-1/2 ounces) sliced pepperoni
    2 large tomatoes, diced

In a 12-in. nonstick skillet, melt butter; remove from the heat. Arrange potatoes on the bottom and up the sides of skillet; sprinkle with onion, salt and pepper. Cover and cook over low heat until the potatoes are tender, about 20 minutes. Sprinkle with cheese; layer with half of the tomato sauce, all of the pepperoni and tomatoes, and the remaining tomato sauce. Cover and cook on low until the cheese is melted and the tomatoes are heated through. **Yield:** 6 servings.

Turkey Bow Tie Skillet

(Pictured at right)

I came up with this satisfying stovetop dish after modifying a recipe printed on a ground turkey package. Our grandchildren love it and ask for seconds.
—Ruth Peterson, Jenison, Michigan

☑ Nutritional Analysis included

Turkey Bow Tie Skillet

  1/2 pound ground turkey breast
1-1/2 teaspoons vegetable oil
  3/4 cup chopped celery
  1/2 cup chopped onion
  1/2 cup chopped green pepper
    1 garlic clove, minced
    1 can (14-1/2 ounces) chicken broth
    2 cups uncooked bow tie pasta
    1 can (14-1/2 ounces) stewed tomatoes
    1 tablespoon vinegar
  3/4 teaspoon sugar
  1/2 teaspoon chili powder
  1/2 teaspoon garlic salt, optional
    2 tablespoons grated Parmesan cheese
    1 tablespoon minced fresh parsley

In a large skillet or Dutch oven, brown turkey in oil. Add celery, onion, green pepper and garlic; cook until vegetables are tender. Remove the turkey and vegetables with a slotted spoon and keep warm. Add broth to the pan; bring to a boil. Add pasta; cook for 10 minutes or until tender. Reduce heat; stir in the tomatoes, vinegar, sugar, chili powder, garlic salt if desired and turkey mixture. Simmer for 10 minutes or until heated through. Sprinkle with Parmesan cheese and parsley. **Yield:** 6 servings. **Nutritional Analysis:** One 1-cup serving (prepared with low-sodium broth and no-salt-added stewed tomatoes and without garlic salt) equals 208 calories, 128 mg sodium, 22 mg cholesterol, 30 gm carbohydrate, 15 gm protein, 3 gm fat. **Diabetic Exchanges:** 2 starch, 1 meat.

Herbed Pork and Potatoes

With red tomatoes and green parsley, this hearty combination of pork, stuffing and vegetables is a colorful meal.
—Evelyn Harzbecker, Charlestown, Massachusetts

  1/2 cup butter *or* margarine, *divided*
    3 cups cubed red potatoes (1-inch pieces)
    1 pound boneless pork loin, cut into 1-inch cubes
  1/2 teaspoon dried rosemary, crushed
  1/2 teaspoon rubbed sage
  1/2 teaspoon salt
  1/2 teaspoon pepper
    1 garlic clove, minced
    2 cups crushed herb-seasoned stuffing
    1 cup sliced celery
    1 cup chopped onion
  1/2 cup apple juice
    3 medium tomatoes, chopped
  1/4 cup minced fresh parsley

In a large skillet, melt 1/4 cup butter. Add potatoes; cook over medium heat, stirring occasionally, until lightly browned. Add pork, rosemary, sage, salt, pepper and garlic. Cook and stir until pork is browned, about 12 minutes. Add the stuffing, celery, onion, apple juice and remaining butter; stir well. Cover and cook for 7 minutes or until heated through. Stir in tomatoes and parsley. Remove from the heat; cover and let stand for 2 minutes. **Yield:** 4 servings.

Mexican Stir-Fry

Not only have I prepared this skillet meal for everyday meals, but also for potlucks and family get-togethers.
—Becky Taaffe, San Jose, California

  1/2 cup chopped onion
    2 garlic cloves, minced
    2 teaspoons vegetable oil
  1/2 cup finely chopped green pepper
  1/2 cup finely chopped sweet red pepper
    2 tablespoons minced jalapeno pepper*
  3/4 cup water
  1/2 cup tomato puree
  1/2 teaspoon chili powder
  1/2 teaspoon chicken bouillon granules
  1/4 teaspoon salt
Pinch cayenne pepper
1-1/3 cups diced cooked chicken
  2/3 cup canned kidney beans, rinsed and drained
    1 cup cooked rice
  1/2 cup shredded cheddar cheese

In a large skillet, saute onion and garlic in oil for 3 minutes. Add peppers; saute until crisp-tender, about 2 minutes. Stir in water, tomato puree, chili powder, bouillon, salt and cayenne; bring to a boil. Reduce heat; simmer, uncovered, for 5 minutes. Add chicken, beans and rice; heat through. Sprinkle with cheese. **Yield:** 2-4 servings. ***Editor's Note:** When cutting or seeding hot peppers, use rubber or plastic gloves to protect your hands. Avoid touching your face.

Speedy Ham and Macaroni

I came up with this recipe on a day I needed to get supper ready fast. Cook the broccoli along with the macaroni to save time. —Vicky Hartel, Caledonia, Wisconsin

2 cups uncooked elbow macaroni
1 package (10 ounces) frozen chopped broccoli, thawed
1 can (10-3/4 ounces) condensed cream of mushroom soup, undiluted
1/2 cup milk
1 tablespoon butter *or* margarine
1/2 teaspoon ground nutmeg
1/8 teaspoon garlic powder
1/8 teaspoon pepper
2 cups cubed fully cooked ham
Grated Parmesan cheese, optional

In a large saucepan, cook macaroni in boiling water for 5 minutes. Add broccoli; return to a boil. Cook for 2-3 minutes or until the macaroni is tender; drain. Return to the pan. Combine soup, milk, butter, nutmeg, garlic powder and pepper; add to macaroni mixture with ham. Mix well; heat through. Garnish with Parmesan cheese if desired. **Yield:** 4-6 servings.

Franks 'n' Beans Supper

Your hungry clan will clean their plates when you serve this creamy concoction. —Marlene Muckenhirn, Delano, Minnesota

2 bacon slices, diced
6 hot dogs, cut into thirds
1 small onion, chopped
1 can (10-3/4 ounces) condensed cream of chicken soup, undiluted
1/2 cup water
1/4 teaspoon dried thyme
1/8 to 1/4 teaspoon pepper
3 cups sliced cooked potatoes
1 cup frozen cut green beans, thawed

In a skillet, cook bacon until crisp. Remove with a slotted spoon and set aside; drain, reserving 1 tablespoon drippings. Saute hot dogs and onion in drippings until onion is tender. Combine soup, water, thyme and pepper; add to skillet with potatoes and beans. Mix well; bring to a boil. Reduce heat; cover and simmer for 10 minutes or until heated through. Top with bacon. **Yield:** 4-6 servings.

Almost Stuffed Peppers

For a quick way to enjoy an old favorite, stir up stuffed green pepper makings in a skillet. This easy one-pan meal is requested so often that I even make it when I'm not in a hurry. —Jan Roat, Red Lodge, Montana

1 pound ground beef
2 cups water
1 can (14-1/2 ounces) diced tomatoes, undrained
1 large green pepper, cut into 1/4-inch slices
1 medium onion, thinly sliced
1-1/2 teaspoons salt
1/2 teaspoon Italian seasoning
1/2 teaspoon pepper
1-1/2 cups uncooked instant rice

In a large skillet, brown beef; drain. Set beef aside and keep warm. In the same skillet, combine water, tomatoes, green pepper, onion and seasonings; bring to a boil. Reduce heat; simmer, uncovered, until vegetables are tender. Stir in rice; cover and remove from the heat. Let stand for 5 minutes. Stir in beef; return to the stove and heat through. **Yield:** 4-6 servings.

Bacon and Pepper Pasta

(Pictured below)

I serve this snappy combination as either a main dish or a side dish. It gets its fresh flavor and pretty color from onions, peppers and tomatoes. —Teri Rasey-Bolf, Cadillac, Michigan

1/2 pound sliced bacon, diced
2 medium onions, halved and sliced
2 garlic cloves, minced
1 medium green pepper, julienned
1 medium sweet red pepper, julienned
1 small jalapeno pepper, seeded and minced*
1 can (14-1/2 ounces) stewed tomatoes
1 pound linguini *or* pasta of your choice, cooked and drained

In a large skillet, cook bacon until crisp. Remove with a slotted spoon and set aside; reserve drippings. Saute onions and garlic in drippings for 3 minutes. Add peppers; cook and stir for 3 minutes. Stir in tomatoes; heat through. Add bacon and mix well. Serve over pasta. **Yield:** 4 servings. ***Editor's Note:** When cutting and seeding hot peppers, use rubber or plastic gloves to protect your hands. Avoid touching your face.

Bacon and Pepper Pasta

Chapter 11

TENDER breads...moist muffins...fluffy biscuits. You can enjoy the home-baked goodness of items like these without spending hours in the kitchen.

With no yeast or rising time required, quick breads are a boon to the busy cook.

Just mix the batter, fill the pan and pop it into the oven. Soon, the irresistible aroma of home-baked bread will be wafting through your kitchen.

And thanks to today's bread machines, old-fashioned home-made yeast breads can be easy, too. They promise fresh-from-the-oven flavor without all the work.

These fast-to-fix recipes will help you round out any meal.

A BOUNTY OF BISCUITS. Top to bottom: Garlic Cheese Biscuits and Iced Cinnamon Biscuits (both recipes on p. 168).

Oven-Fresh Quick Breads

YOU need not worry about kneading—or spending hours in the kitchen—when you make these quick loaves, muffins, sweet rolls and biscuits. Whether you want sweet or savory, you're sure to find a recipe to suit your taste and time.

Pecan Sticky Muffins

These are so much quicker and easier to make than traditional raised sticky buns. Everyone just loves them! They are great for a Sunday brunch. —Dorothy Bateman
Carver, Massachusetts

    2 cups all-purpose flour
    1 tablespoon baking powder
    1 teaspoon ground cinnamon
    1/4 teaspoon salt
    2 eggs
    1 cup milk
    1/4 cup vegetable oil
    1/2 cup packed brown sugar
    1 teaspoon vanilla extract
TOPPING:
    1/4 cup butter *or* margarine, melted
    1/4 cup packed brown sugar
    1 cup chopped pecans

In a large bowl, combine flour, baking powder, cinnamon and salt. In another bowl, beat the eggs, milk, oil, sugar and vanilla until smooth. Stir into dry ingredients just until moistened. Into each greased muffin cup, spoon 1 teaspoon butter, 1 teaspoon brown sugar and 1 heaping tablespoon of pecans. Top each with 1/4 cup of batter. Bake at 350° for 25-30 minutes or until muffins test done. Invert pan onto a piece of foil. Let stand for 2 minutes; remove pan. Serve warm. **Yield:** 1 dozen.

Frozen Blueberry Muffins

(Pictured above right)

I keep frozen berries on hand to make these moist muffins. It's so convenient to be able to fold them unthawed into the muffin batter. —Ardyce Piehl
Wisconsin Dells, Wisconsin

    4 cups all-purpose flour
    4 teaspoons baking powder
    1/2 teaspoon salt
    1 cup butter *or* margarine, softened
    2 cups sugar
    4 eggs
    1 cup milk

    2 teaspoons vanilla extract
    2 cups frozen blueberries, unthawed
TOPPING:
    2 tablespoons sugar
    1/2 teaspoon ground nutmeg

In a large bowl, combine the flour, baking powder and salt. In a mixing bowl, cream butter and sugar. Add eggs, milk and vanilla; mix well. Stir in the dry ingredients just until moistened. Fold in frozen blueberries. Fill greased or paper-lined muffin cups two-thirds full. Combine sugar and nutmeg; sprinkle over muffins. Bake at 375° for 20-25 minutes or until muffins test done. Cool in pan for 10 minutes before removing to a wire rack. **Yield:** about 2 dozen. **Editor's Note:** Fresh blueberries may be substituted for frozen.

Coffee Shop Corn Muffins

These are so quick to stir up, and they bake in just 15 minutes! They come out oh-so-tender but don't crumble like many corn muffins do. —Clare Masyada
Woodbridge, New Jersey

    1-1/4 cups cornmeal
    1 cup all-purpose flour
    1/3 cup packed brown sugar
    1/3 cup sugar
    1 teaspoon baking soda
    1/2 teaspoon salt
    1 egg
    1 cup buttermilk
    3/4 cup vegetable oil

In a bowl, combine cornmeal, flour, sugars, baking soda and salt. In another bowl, beat egg, buttermilk and oil; stir into dry ingredients just until moistened. Fill greased or paper-lined muffin cups three-fourths full. Bake at 425° for 12-15 minutes or until muffins test done. Cool in pan for 10 minutes before removing to a wire rack. **Yield:** 1 dozen.

Orange Nut Bread

(Pictured above right)

This bread is delicious for breakfast or with a salad. A friend shared the recipe years ago, and it has withstood the test of time. —Helen Luksa, Las Vegas, Nevada

    4-1/2 cups all-purpose flour
    1-3/4 cups sugar
    4 teaspoons baking powder
    1-1/2 teaspoons salt
    1 teaspoon baking soda
    1-1/2 cups chopped walnuts
    2 tablespoons grated orange peel
    2 eggs
    1 cup milk
    1 cup orange juice
    1/4 cup butter *or* margarine, melted

In a large bowl, combine flour, sugar, baking powder, salt and baking soda. Stir in nuts and orange peel. In a small bowl, beat eggs, milk, orange juice and butter until

Frozen Blueberry Muffins
Orange Nut Bread

smooth. Stir into dry ingredients just until moistened. Pour into two greased 8-in. x 4-in. x 2-in. loaf pans. Bake at 350° for 50-60 minutes or until a toothpick inserted near the center comes out clean. Cool in pans for 10 minutes before removing to a wire rack. **Yield:** 2 loaves.

Ham 'n' Cheese Wedges

Baking mix is a shortcut in this savory round loaf. We enjoy it for breakfast, and I like to serve big wedges with a bowl of soup.
—*Marietta Slater, Augusta, Kansas*

2 cups biscuit/baking mix
2 eggs
2/3 cup milk
2 tablespoons finely chopped onion
1 tablespoon vegetable oil
1/2 teaspoon prepared mustard
1-1/4 cups (5 ounces) shredded cheddar cheese, *divided*
1 cup cubed fully cooked ham
1 tablespoon butter *or* margarine, melted
2 tablespoons sesame seeds

In a mixing bowl, combine the first six ingredients; mix well. Stir in 1 cup of cheese and the ham. Spread into a greased 10-in. quiche dish or pie plate. Brush with butter; sprinkle with sesame seeds. Bake at 350° for 30-35 minutes or until set and lightly browned. Sprinkle with remaining cheese. Bake 5-10 minutes longer or until the

cheese is melted. Let stand for 5 minutes before cutting. Serve warm. **Yield:** 6-8 servings.

Buttermilk Cinnamon Bread

Nuts and cinnamon swirled through the batter give this bread its pretty pattern. It looks so fancy yet is very simple. —*Aloma Robinson, Clarkston, Michigan*

4 cups all-purpose flour
2 teaspoons baking soda
1 teaspoon salt
1/2 cup vegetable oil
2-1/2 cups sugar, *divided*
2 cups buttermilk
2 eggs
1 tablespoon ground cinnamon
1 to 2 tablespoons finely chopped walnuts

In a mixing bowl, combine flour, baking soda and salt. In a small bowl, combine oil and 1-1/2 cups sugar. Add buttermilk and eggs; mix well. Stir into dry ingredients just until moistened. Fill two greased 8-in. x 4-in. x 2-in. or five 5-3/4-in. x 3-in. x 2-in. loaf pans about one-third full. Combine cinnamon and remaining sugar; sprinkle half over the batter. Top with remaining batter and cinnamon-sugar. Swirl batter with a knife. Sprinkle with nuts. Bake at 350° for 45-55 minutes or until a toothpick inserted near the center comes out clean. Cool in pans for 10 minutes before removing to a wire rack. **Yield:** 2 loaves or 5 mini loaves.

Crispy Garlic Breadsticks
Parmesan Herb Bread

Parmesan Herb Bread

(Pictured above)

Wedges of this delicious cheese-topped bread go great with spaghetti and other Italian dishes. They also taste special when dressed up with one of the flavorful spreads.
—*Diane Hixon, Niceville, Florida*

1-1/2 cups biscuit/baking mix
1 egg, beaten
1/4 cup apple juice
1/4 cup milk
1 tablespoon dried minced onion
1 tablespoon sugar
1/2 teaspoon dried oregano
1/4 cup grated Parmesan cheese
HERB BUTTER:
1/2 cup butter, softened
1 garlic clove, minced
2 tablespoons minced fresh parsley *or 2 teaspoons dried parsley flakes*
1 teaspoon dried basil
TOMATO BUTTER:
1/2 cup butter, softened
4 teaspoons tomato paste
Dash cayenne pepper

In a mixing bowl, combine the first seven ingredients just until blended. Spoon into a greased 9-in. round cake pan. Sprinkle with Parmesan cheese. Bake at 400° for 18-20 minutes or until golden brown. In separate small mixing bowls, combine herb butter and tomato butter ingredients; beat until smooth. Serve with warm bread. **Yield:** 6-8 servings.

Buttermilk Biscuits

Buttermilk is the key to these tender, fluffy biscuits. Your family will devour them fresh from the oven or topped with creamy butter or a favorite jam. —*Bonita Coleman Camarillo, California*

2 cups all-purpose flour
2-1/2 teaspoons baking powder
1/8 teaspoon salt
1/3 cup butter-flavored shortening
3/4 cup buttermilk

In a bowl, combine flour, baking powder and salt. Cut in shortening until crumbly. Stir in buttermilk just until moistened. Knead on a floured surface for 1 minute. Roll out to 1/2-in. thickness; cut with a 2-1/2-in. biscuit cutter. Place on a greased baking sheet. Bake at 450° for 10-12 minutes or until golden brown. **Yield:** 10 biscuits.

Crispy Garlic Breadsticks

(Pictured at left)

This is a surprisingly tasty way to use day-old hot dog buns. Thanks to the mild garlic flavor, they're a nice accompaniment to a meal or a crunchy snack. For a kid-pleasing treat, substitute cinnamon and sugar for the garlic powder.
—Linda Rainey, Monahans, Texas

4 day-old hot dog buns
1/2 cup butter *or* margarine, melted
1/2 teaspoon garlic powder

Split buns in half; cut each half lengthwise. Combine butter and garlic; brush over breadsticks. Place on a greased 15-in. x 10-in. x 1-in. baking pan. Bake at 325° for 25-30 minutes or until golden brown. **Yield:** 8-10 servings. **Editor's Note:** Breadsticks may also be baked at 250° for 60-70 minutes.

Honey Wheat Muffins

Mix these up in a wink for a tender-textured treat with sweet honey taste. You can sample them close to half an hour after starting. —Carolyn Deming, Miami, Arizona

1 cup all-purpose flour
1/2 cup whole wheat flour
2 teaspoons baking powder
1/2 teaspoon salt
1 egg
1/2 cup honey
1/2 cup milk
1/4 cup vegetable oil
1 teaspoon grated lemon peel

In a large bowl, combine flours, baking powder and salt. In another bowl, beat egg, honey, milk, oil and lemon peel; stir into the dry ingredients just until moistened. Fill greased muffin cups three-fourths full. Bake at 375° for 18-20 minutes or until muffins test done. Cool in the pan for 10 minutes before removing to a wire rack. **Yield:** 6 muffins.

Poppy Seed Bread

Preparation time's kept to a minimum for this seeded treat. It's a bread that you can make a day ahead of time, and then warm in the microwave moments prior to serving for just-baked appeal. —Rosemarie Surwillo
Lake St. Louis, Missouri

3 cups all-purpose flour
2-1/4 cups sugar
1 tablespoon poppy seeds
1-1/2 teaspoons baking powder
1-1/2 teaspoons salt
3 eggs
1-1/2 cups milk
1 cup vegetable oil
1-1/2 teaspoons almond extract
1-1/2 teaspoons butter flavor *or* vanilla extract

In a bowl, combine the first five ingredients. In another bowl, beat eggs, milk, oil and extracts. Stir into dry ingredients just until moistened. Pour into two greased 8-in. x 4-in. x 2-in. loaf pans. Bake at 350° for 55-60 minutes or until a toothpick inserted near the center comes out clean. Cool in pans for 10 minutes before removing to a wire rack. **Yield:** 2 loaves.

Banana Chip Muffins

These moist muffins showcase bananas and mini chocolate chips. After the original recipe flopped, I experimented with different ingredients and measurements until I came up with this winning combination. —Joanne Shields
Olds, Alberta

1 egg
1/3 cup vegetable oil
3/4 cup sugar
3 medium ripe bananas, mashed
2 cups all-purpose flour
1/2 cup old-fashioned oats
1 teaspoon baking powder
1 teaspoon baking soda
1/2 teaspoon salt
3/4 cup miniature semisweet chocolate chips

In a mixing bowl, beat egg, oil and sugar until smooth. Stir in bananas. Combine dry ingredients; stir into the banana mixture just until moistened. Stir in chocolate chips. Fill greased muffin cups three-fourths full. Bake at 375° for 18-20 minutes or until muffins test done. **Yield:** 1 dozen.

Moist Nut Bread

The unexpected ingredient in these moist, convenient loaves is baby food! A neighbor shared the recipe years ago when we both had small children—and many jars of baby food. This bread has remained a favorite.
—Judi Oudekerk, St. Michael, Minnesota

3-1/3 cups all-purpose flour
3 cups sugar
2 teaspoons baking soda
1 teaspoon salt
1 teaspoon ground cinnamon
4 eggs
2 jars (6 ounces *each*) strained apricot baby food
1 cup vegetable oil
2/3 cup water
1 tablespoon vanilla extract
1 cup chopped walnuts

In a large bowl, combine dry ingredients. In another bowl, combine eggs, baby food, oil, water and vanilla. Stir into dry ingredients; mix until well blended. Stir in nuts. Pour into two greased 9-in. x 5-in. x 3-in. loaf pans. Bake at 350° for 50-60 minutes or until a toothpick inserted near the center comes out clean. Cool in pans for 15 minutes before removing to a wire rack to cool completely. **Yield:** 2 loaves.

Corn Bread Strips

I discovered this recipe over 30 years ago and have used it ever since. With just three ingredients, the corn-flavored strips couldn't be simpler. Toasty from the oven, they are wonderful with a soup or salad.
—Patricia Kile, Greentown, Pennsylvania

2 cups biscuit/baking mix
1 can (8-1/2 ounces) cream-style corn
3 tablespoons butter *or* margarine, melted

In a bowl, combine biscuit mix and corn until mixture forms a ball. Turn onto a lightly floured surface and knead 10-12 times. Pat into a 10-in. x 6-in. rectangle. Cut into 3-in. x 1-in. strips; roll in butter. Place in a greased 15-in. x 10-in. x 1-in. baking pan. Bake at 450° for 12-14 minutes or until golden brown. Serve warm. **Yield:** 20 strips.

Rhubarb Coffee Cake

My family's roots go back to Lebanon County in Pennsylvania, so we pride ourselves on our Pennsylvania Dutch cooking. My husband and three boys love the old-fashioned flavor of this tart rhubarb cake topped with a sweet vanilla glaze.   —Kathy Shafer, Upland, California

1/2 cup butter *or* margarine, softened
1-1/2 cups sugar
1 egg
2-1/2 cups all-purpose flour
1 teaspoon baking soda
1/2 teaspoon salt
1 cup buttermilk
3 cups sliced fresh *or* frozen rhubarb, thawed and drained
1 teaspoon vanilla extract
1 cup packed brown sugar
1/2 cup chopped walnuts
GLAZE:
1 cup sugar
1/2 cup butter *or* margarine
3 tablespoons milk
1 teaspoon vanilla extract

In a mixing bowl, cream butter and sugar. Beat in egg. Combine flour, baking soda and salt; add alternately to the creamed mixture with buttermilk. Mix well. Stir in rhubarb and vanilla. Pour into a greased 13-in. x 9-in. x 2-in. baking pan. Sprinkle with brown sugar and nuts. Bake at 350° for 45 minutes or until a toothpick inserted near the center comes out clean. Meanwhile, in a saucepan, combine the sugar, butter and milk; bring to a boil. Remove from the heat and stir in vanilla. Pour over hot cake. Serve immediately. **Yield:** 12 servings.

Orange Streusel Muffins

These tender muffins have a fresh taste I'm sure you'll enjoy. The recipe doesn't call for much sugar, but the streusel topping and marmalade filling add just the right sweetness.   —Donna Smith, Victor, New York

1-3/4 cups all-purpose flour
1/4 cup sugar
2-1/2 teaspoons baking powder
1/2 teaspoon salt
1 egg
3/4 cup milk
1/3 cup vegetable oil
1/4 cup orange marmalade
STREUSEL:
2 tablespoons all-purpose flour
2 tablespoons brown sugar
1 teaspoon ground cinnamon
1 tablespoon cold butter *or* margarine

In a bowl, combine flour, sugar, baking powder and salt. In another bowl, beat egg, milk and oil. Stir into dry ingredients just until moistened. Fill eight greased or paper-lined muffin cups half full. Spoon 1 teaspoon of marmalade over each. Top with the remaining batter. For streusel, combine flour, brown sugar and cinnamon in a small bowl. Cut in butter until crumbly; sprinkle over batter. Bake at 400° for 20-25 minutes or until muffins test done. **Yield:** 8 muffins.

Ranch Garlic Bread

I've worked as a manager of a fast-food restaurant for 12 years. At home, I like to cook up different things using everyday ingredients. I give a buttery loaf of French bread plenty of flavor simply with salad dressing mix and garlic powder.   —John Palmer
Cottonwood, California

1 cup butter *or* margarine, softened
2 to 3 tablespoons ranch salad dressing mix
2 teaspoons garlic powder
1 loaf (1 pound) French bread, halved lengthwise

In a small mixing bowl, combine butter, dressing mix and garlic powder; beat until combined. Spread over cut sides of bread. Place on a baking sheet. Broil 4-6 in. from the heat for 3-4 minutes or until golden brown. **Yield:** 8 servings.

Apple Pinwheels

(Pictured at right)

I swirl convenient crescent roll dough with a spiced apple filling for homemade appeal. The apple flavor is simply wonderful. For an extra-special touch, drizzle the rolls with a confectioners' sugar glaze.   —Christine Campos
Scottsdale, Arizona

1/3 cup water
1/3 cup butter *or* margarine
1-1/3 cups sugar, *divided*
2 tubes (8 ounces *each*) refrigerated crescent rolls
3 cups finely chopped peeled tart apples
1 teaspoon apple pie spice

In a saucepan, combine water, butter and 1 cup sugar;

cook over medium heat until the butter is melted and the sugar is dissolved. Set aside. Unroll crescent roll dough into one long rectangle; seal seams and perforations. Combine the apples, apple pie spice and remaining sugar; sprinkle over dough to within 1 in. of edges. Roll up, jelly-roll style, starting with a long side. Cut into 1-in. rolls; place in a greased 15-in. x 10-in. x 1-in. baking pan. Pour reserved syrup over rolls. Bake at 350° for 40-45 minutes or until golden brown. Serve warm. **Yield:** 2 dozen.

Raspberry Coffee Cake

(Pictured below)

Raspberries are abundant at our summer home on nearby Aziscohos Lake. So I developed this recipe to share the bounty with our guests. The fruity flavor of this pretty crumb-topped cake really shines through.
—Marian Cummings, West Paris, Maine

1 cup plus 3 tablespoons sugar, *divided*
1/4 cup cornstarch

3 cups fresh *or* frozen unsweetened raspberries
2 cups biscuit/baking mix
2/3 cup milk
2 eggs
2 tablespoons vegetable oil
TOPPING:
1 package (3.4 ounces) instant vanilla pudding mix
1/2 cup sugar
1/4 cup cold butter *or* margarine

In a saucepan, combine 1 cup of sugar and cornstarch. Add raspberries; bring to a boil over medium heat. Boil for 2 minutes, stirring constantly. Remove from the heat; allow to cool. Meanwhile, in a mixing bowl, combine the biscuit mix, milk, eggs, oil and remaining sugar; mix well. Spread two-thirds of the batter into a greased 13-in. x 9-in. x 2-in. baking pan. Spread with raspberry mixture. Spoon remaining batter over the top. For topping, combine pudding mix and sugar. Cut in butter until crumbly; sprinkle over batter. Bake at 350° for 35-40 minutes. **Yield:** 12 servings.

Raspberry Coffee Cake
Apple Pinwheels

Iced Cinnamon Biscuits

1 pound bulk pork sausage
4 cups biscuit/baking mix
3/4 cup milk
1/2 cup water
1 can (4 ounces) diced green chilies, undrained
1 egg, beaten
1 can (11 ounces) whole kernel corn, drained

In a skillet over medium heat, brown sausage. Drain and set aside. In a large bowl, combine biscuit mix, milk, water, chilies and egg; mix well. Stir in the corn and sausage. Fill greased or paper-lined muffin cups two-thirds full. Bake at 425° for 16-18 minutes or until golden brown. Cool for 5 minutes; remove from pan and serve warm. **Yield:** 2 dozen.

Garlic Cheese Biscuits

(Pictured on page 160)

This is a savory variation on my favorite buttermilk biscuit recipe. Shredded cheddar cheese adds nice color, and a tasty butter mixture brushed on top of these drop biscuits provides a burst of garlic flavor. —Gayle Becker
Mt. Clemens, Michigan

2 cups all-purpose flour
4 teaspoons baking powder
3 teaspoons garlic powder, *divided*
1/2 teaspoon baking soda
1 teaspoon chicken bouillon granules, *divided*
1/2 cup butter-flavored shortening
3/4 cup shredded cheddar cheese
1 cup buttermilk
3 tablespoons butter *or* margarine, melted

In a bowl, combine flour, baking powder, 2 teaspoons garlic powder, baking soda and 1/2 teaspoon bouillon; cut in shortening until mixture resembles coarse crumbs. Add cheese. Stir in buttermilk just until moistened. Drop by heaping tablespoonfuls onto a greased baking sheet. Bake at 450° for 10 minutes. Combine the butter with the remaining garlic powder and bouillon; brush over biscuits. Bake 4 minutes longer or until golden brown. Serve warm. **Yield:** about 1 dozen.

Bacon Cheddar Muffins

Bacon and cheddar cheese add hearty breakfast flavor to these tasty muffins. Calling for just six ingredients, they're quick to stir up and handy to eat on the run.
—Suzanne McKinley, Lyons, Georgia

Iced Cinnamon Biscuits

(Pictured above and on page 161)

Serve these biscuits oven-fresh for breakfast or brunch. They are wonderfully light and have an appealing cinnamon flavor. The plump raisins and simple icing add the right touch of sweetness. —Wendy Masters
Grand Valley, Ontario

2 cups all-purpose flour
1/4 cup sugar
1 tablespoon baking powder
1 teaspoon salt
1 teaspoon ground cinnamon
1/4 teaspoon baking soda
1/3 cup shortening
1/2 cup raisins
3/4 cup buttermilk
ICING:
1/3 cup confectioners' sugar
1 to 2 teaspoons milk

In a bowl, combine the first six ingredients; cut in the shortening until mixture resembles coarse crumbs. Stir in raisins. Add buttermilk; stir just until moistened. Turn onto a lightly floured surface; knead 4-5 times. Roll to 1/2-in. thickness; cut with a 2-1/2-in. biscuit cutter. Place with sides barely touching on a greased baking sheet. Bake at 425° for 12-17 minutes or until golden brown. Combine the icing ingredients; drizzle over biscuits. Serve warm. **Yield:** about 1 dozen.

Sausage Brunch Muffins

I'm glad to share this recipe for zippy muffins chock-full of sausage. They've become a Sunday-morning standard whenever the family gathers. They also make a hearty hurry-up breakfast. —Beverly Borges
Rockland, Massachusetts

Tips for Better Biscuits

- For more tender biscuits, be careful not to overmix or overknead the dough.
- Bake biscuits until they are golden brown on the top and bottom. The sides will always be a little lighter.
- If you don't have the right size biscuit cutter, roll the dough into a square or rectangle and cut into 2-1/2-inch squares, rectangles or diamonds. Cut each biscuit the same size for even baking.

Biscuits in a Snap

1 Turn dough onto a lightly floured surface and knead gently with your fingers for as many times as the recipe directs.

2 Roll dough evenly to 1/2-in. thickness. Cut with a floured biscuit cutter, using a straight downward motion; do not twist the cutter.

3 For drop biscuits, drop dough from a tablespoon onto a greased baking sheet, using a rubber spatula or knife to push the dough off the spoon.

    2 cups biscuit/baking mix
  2/3 cup milk
  1/4 cup vegetable oil
    1 egg
    1 cup (4 ounces) finely shredded sharp cheddar cheese
    8 bacon strips, cooked and crumbled

In a bowl, combine biscuit mix, milk, oil and egg just until moistened. Fold in cheese and bacon. Fill greased muffin cups three-fourths full. Bake at 375° for 20 minutes or until golden brown. Cool for 10 minutes; remove from pan to a wire rack. **Yield:** about 1 dozen.

Fiesta Bread

A neighbor gave me this quick-and-easy recipe more than 25 years ago, when my children were small. You can use your favorite seasoning mix in this bread, so it's very versatile. It makes a tasty accompaniment to most any meal.
—Helen Carpenter, Highland Haven, Texas

    2 cups biscuit/baking mix
  2/3 cup milk
4-1/2 teaspoons chili seasoning mix*
    2 tablespoons butter *or* margarine, melted

In a bowl, combine the biscuit mix, milk and seasoning mix; mix well. Pat into a greased 8-in. baking pan; drizzle with butter. Bake at 425° for 15-17 minutes or until

a toothpick inserted near the center comes out clean. **Yield:** 9 servings. *****Editor's Note:** Italian or ranch salad dressing mix, taco seasoning or onion soup mix may be substituted for the chili seasoning mix.

Apple Cider Biscuits

My family enjoys these tender, flaky biscuits warm from the oven. We have a lot of apple trees, so we're always looking for apple recipes. This is a tasty way to use some of our cider. —Harriet Stichter, Milford, Indiana

    2 cups all-purpose flour
    1 tablespoon baking powder
    2 teaspoons sugar
  1/2 teaspoon salt
  1/3 cup cold butter *or* margarine
  3/4 cup apple cider
  1/8 teaspoon ground cinnamon

In a bowl, combine flour, baking powder, sugar and salt. Cut in butter until mixture resembles coarse crumbs. Stir in cider just until moistened. Turn onto a lightly floured surface and knead 8-10 times. Roll out to 1/2-in. thickness; cut with a 2-1/2-in. biscuit cutter. Place on ungreased baking sheets. Sprinkle with cinnamon; pierce tops of biscuits with a fork. Bake at 425° for 12-14 minutes or until golden brown. Serve warm. **Yield:** about 1 dozen.

Heart Biscuits

Mom always made heart-shaped biscuits for Valentine's Day. When I realized how easy they were, I continued the tradition! They're great anytime of year served warm with a honey or cinnamon spread. —Tina Christensen Addison, Illinois

    2 cups all-purpose flour
    1 tablespoon baking powder
    1 teaspoon salt
  1/2 cup cold butter *or* margarine
  3/4 cup milk
HONEY SPREAD:
  1/2 cup butter *or* margarine, softened
  1/4 cup honey
CINNAMON SPREAD:
  1/2 cup butter *or* margarine, softened
  3/4 cup sugar
    1 tablespoon ground cinnamon

In a bowl, combine dry ingredients. Cut in butter until the mixture resembles coarse crumbs. With a fork, stir in milk until the mixture forms a ball. Turn onto a lightly floured surface; knead 5-6 times. Roll to 1/2-in. thickness; cut with a 2-in. heart-shaped cookie or biscuit cutter. Place on an ungreased baking sheet. Bake at 450° for 10-12 minutes or until golden brown. Meanwhile, for the honey spread, combine butter and honey in a mixing bowl; beat until smooth. For the cinnamon spread, combine butter, sugar and cinnamon in a mixing bowl; beat until smooth. Serve with the warm biscuits. **Yield:** about 1 dozen.

Nutmeg Muffins

A pretty brown sugar topping adds a pleasant sweetness to these tender breakfast treats. The nutmeg provides a nice change of pace from other muffins that are seasoned with cinnamon. —Sharon Evans, Rockwell, Iowa

        3 cups all-purpose flour, *divided*
1-1/2 cups packed brown sugar
    1/2 cup cold butter *or* margarine
        2 teaspoons baking powder
        1 to 2 teaspoons ground nutmeg
    1/2 teaspoon baking soda
    1/2 teaspoon salt
        2 eggs
        1 cup buttermilk

In a bowl, combine 2 cups flour and the brown sugar; cut in butter until crumbly. Reserve 3/4 cup for topping. To the remaining crumb mixture, add baking powder, nutmeg, baking soda, salt and remaining flour. Combine eggs and buttermilk; add to the crumb mixture just until moistened. Fill greased or paper-lined muffin cups two-thirds full. Sprinkle with reserved crumb mixture. Bake at 350° for 20-25 minutes or until muffins test done. Cool for 10 minutes; remove to a wire rack. **Yield:** 1-1/2 dozen.

Peanut Butter Muffins

Kids of all ages will love these delicious peanutty treats. Topped with your favorite jelly, the pretty muffins are sure to bring back sweet childhood memories. —Ann Janis, Tucson, Arizona

        2 cups all-purpose flour
    1/2 cup sugar
        1 tablespoon baking powder
    1/2 teaspoon salt
    1/2 cup peanut butter
        3 tablespoons cold butter *or* margarine, *divided*
        2 eggs
        1 cup milk
Cinnamon-sugar
Jelly, optional

In a large bowl, combine flour, sugar, baking powder and salt. Cut in peanut butter and 2 tablespoons butter until the mixture resembles coarse crumbs. Beat the eggs

Tips for Better Muffins

- For more tender muffins, do not overmix the batter. Muffin batter should be lumpy.
- Muffins should go into the oven as soon as the batter is mixed, unless otherwise directed.
- If your muffin recipe does not fill all the cups in your muffin pan, fill the empty ones with water. The muffins will bake more evenly.
- To check if muffins are done, insert a toothpick in the center of one of them. If it comes out clean, the muffins are done.

and milk; stir into the dry ingredients just until moistened. Fill greased or paper-lined muffin cups two-thirds full. Bake at 400° for 15-17 minutes or until muffins test done. Melt remaining butter; brush over the tops of muffins. Sprinkle with cinnamon-sugar. Cool for 10 minutes; remove to a wire rack. Serve with jelly if desired. **Yield:** 1 dozen.

Pecan Pear Bread

(Pictured at right)

We have almost 50 fruit trees on our country property, including five pear trees. I like to can most of the crop, but I make sure to save some for this moist, mildly spiced bread. —Margaret Slocum, Ridgefield, Washington

        1 cup sugar
    1/2 cup vegetable oil
        2 eggs
    1/4 cup sour cream
        1 teaspoon vanilla extract
        2 cups all-purpose flour
        1 teaspoon baking soda
    1/2 teaspoon salt
    1/4 to 1/2 teaspoon ground cardamom
    1/4 to 1/2 teaspoon ground cinnamon
1-1/2 cups chopped peeled pears
    2/3 cup chopped pecans
    1/2 teaspoon grated lemon peel

In a mixing bowl, combine sugar and oil. Add eggs, one at a time, beating well after each addition. Add sour cream and vanilla; mix well. Combine dry ingredients; add to sour cream mixture and mix well. Stir in pears, pecans and lemon peel. Spread into a greased 8-in. x 4-in. x 2-in. loaf pan. Bake at 350° for 65-75 minutes or until a toothpick inserted near the center comes out clean. Cool for 10 minutes; remove from pan to a wire rack to cool completely. **Yield:** 1 loaf.

Poppy Cheddar Muffins

(Pictured above right)

When I was a teenager, I adapted this recipe from a cookbook. Since we didn't have the caraway seeds called for in the original recipe, I substituted poppy seeds. We liked the savory cheese-topped muffins so well that I still make them this way. —Patricia Van Wyk
Newton, Iowa

1-3/4 cups all-purpose flour
        2 tablespoons sugar
2-1/2 teaspoons baking powder
        2 teaspoons poppy seeds
    3/4 teaspoon salt
        1 egg
    3/4 cup milk
    1/3 cup vegetable oil
        1 cup (4 ounces) shredded cheddar cheese

In a bowl, combine flour, sugar, baking powder, poppy seeds and salt. Combine egg, milk and oil; mix well.

Poppy Cheddar Muffins
Pecan Pear Bread

Stir into the dry ingredients just until moistened. Fold in cheese. Fill greased or paper-lined muffin cups two-thirds full. Bake at 400° for 25 minutes or until muffins test done. **Yield:** about 1 dozen.

Peach Muffins

When fresh peaches are in season, I often make these pretty peach muffins. With their delicate sour cream flavor and crunchy pecans, they disappear in no time.
—Mrs. Alton Michelson, Mondovi, Wisconsin

　1/2 cup butter *or* margarine, softened
　3/4 cup sugar
　　1 egg
　1/2 cup sour cream
　　1 teaspoon vanilla extract
1-1/2 cups all-purpose flour
1-1/2 teaspoons baking powder
　　1 cup chopped fresh *or* frozen peaches
　　1 cup chopped pecans

In a mixing bowl, cream butter and sugar. Add egg, sour cream and vanilla; mix well. Combine flour and baking powder; stir into creamed mixture just until moistened. Fold in peaches and pecans. Fill greased or paper-lined muffin cups three-fourths full. Bake at 400° for 20-25 minutes or until muffins test done. Cool for 10 minutes; remove from pan to a wire rack. **Yield:** 1 dozen.

Broccoli Quiche Muffins

I like to keep a batch of these quiche-like muffins in the freezer—it's handy to warm them in the microwave when time is short. These muffins are great for breakfast, lunch or a quick snack.　　　　　*—Cindy Hrychuk*
Gilbert Plains, Manitoba

　　1 package (10 ounces) frozen chopped
　　　　broccoli, thawed and drained
　　1 medium onion, chopped
　1/2 cup diced fully cooked ham
　1/2 cup grated Parmesan cheese
　　6 eggs
　1/2 cup vegetable oil
1-1/4 cups all-purpose flour
　　1 tablespoon baking powder
　　1 teaspoon dried oregano
　　1 teaspoon dried parsley flakes
　1/4 teaspoon garlic powder
　1/4 teaspoon salt
　1/4 teaspoon dried thyme

Combine the broccoli, onion, ham and cheese; set aside. In a mixing bowl, beat eggs until frothy. Add oil; mix well. Combine dry ingredients; add to the egg mixture just until moistened. Fold in broccoli mixture. Fill greased muffin cups two-thirds full. Bake at 375° for 18-22 minutes or until muffins test done. Cool for 10 minutes; remove from pan to a wire rack. **Yield:** 1-1/2 dozen.

Christmas Tree Rolls

(Pictured below)

Our kids love it when I bake these yummy rolls in the shape of a Christmas tree. Taking advantage of convenient crescent roll dough, I make this impressive addition to a special brunch without a lot of fuss. —Diedra Walker
Martin, Tennessee

   1 tube (8 ounces) refrigerated crescent rolls
   1 tablespoon butter *or* margarine, softened
   2 tablespoons sugar
 1/2 teaspoon ground cinnamon
 3/4 cup confectioners' sugar
   2 to 3 teaspoons milk
Red *and/or* green candied cherries, optional

Unroll crescent roll dough into a rectangle. Press seams and perforations to seal; roll lightly with a rolling pin. Spread butter over dough. Combine sugar and cinnamon; sprinkle over butter. Roll up, jelly-roll style, starting with a long side. Seal edge. Cut into 22 slices. To form a tree, place slices on a greased baking sheet with sides touching and cut side up. Place one slice in the top row and two slices in the second row. Repeat with remaining rolls, adding one slice per row, until the tree has six rows. Center the one remaining slice under the last row for a trunk. Bake at 350° for 16-20 minutes or until golden brown. Remove to a wire rack. Combine confectioners' sugar and milk; drizzle over warm rolls. Decorate with cherries if desired. **Yield:** 22 rolls.

Cinnamon Crescents

(Pictured below)

I've had the recipe for these crispy cinnamon-sugar roll-ups for years. They're one of my family's favorites and so easy to make. —Emily Engel, Quill Lake, Saskatchewan

2-1/2 cups all-purpose flour
   1 teaspoon baking powder
   1 cup cold butter *or* margarine
 1/2 cup milk
   1 egg, beaten
   1 cup sugar
   4 teaspoons ground cinnamon

Combine flour and baking powder in a large bowl; cut in butter until crumbly. Stir in milk and egg. Divide into three portions; shape each portion into a ball. Combine sugar and cinnamon; sprinkle a third over a pastry board or a surface. Roll one ball into a 12-in. circle; cut into 12 wedges. Roll up from wide edge. Repeat with the remaining dough and cinnamon-sugar. Place rolls with point side down on lightly greased baking sheets; form into crescent shapes. Bake at 350° for 16-18 minutes or until lightly browned (do not overbake). **Yield:** 3 dozen.

Gumdrop Bread
Christmas Tree Rolls
Cinnamon Crescents

Maple Corn Bread

It's not necessary to serve maple syrup with this moist corn bread. The maple flavor is baked into the loaf, providing a delicious change of pace from traditional corn bread.
—Dorothy Bateman, Carver, Massachusetts

1-1/4 cups all-purpose flour
1/4 cup cornmeal
1-1/2 teaspoons baking powder
1/2 teaspoon salt
1 egg
3/4 cup milk
1/2 cup maple syrup
3 tablespoons vegetable oil

In a bowl, combine flour, cornmeal, baking powder and salt. In another bowl, beat egg; add milk, syrup and oil. Stir into dry ingredients just until moistened. Pour into a greased 9-in. square baking pan. Bake at 400° for 20-22 minutes or until a toothpick inserted near the center comes out clean. Cool on a wire rack for 10 minutes; cut into squares. Serve warm. **Yield:** 9 servings.

Gumdrop Bread

(Pictured at left)

Colorful gumdrops make these fun miniature loaves just perfect for holiday gift-giving. I usually bake this moist bread at Christmas, but it's also requested at Easter.
—Linda Samaan, Fort Wayne, Indiana

3 cups biscuit/baking mix
2/3 cup sugar
1 egg
1-1/4 cups milk
1-1/2 cups chopped nuts
1 cup chopped gumdrops

In a bowl, combine biscuit mix and sugar. In another bowl, beat the egg and milk; add to dry ingredients and stir well. Add nuts and gumdrops; stir just until mixed. Pour into three greased 5-3/4-in. x 3-in. x 2-in. loaf pans. Bake at 350° for 35 minutes or until a toothpick inserted near the center comes out clean. Cool for 10 minutes; remove from pans to wire racks to cool completely. **Yield:** 3 mini loaves.

Fruited Mini Loaves

A lovely brown crust surrounds these miniature loaves packed with yummy goodies like pineapple, apricots, raisins and pecans. I make them ahead and freeze them for busy times.   —Suzanne McKinley, Lyons, Georgia

3/4 cup sugar
1/3 cup butter *or* margarine, melted
1 egg
1 can (8 ounces) crushed pineapple, undrained
1/4 cup milk
2-1/2 cups all-purpose flour
1-1/2 teaspoons baking powder
1/4 teaspoon salt
1/4 teaspoon baking soda
1 cup chopped pecans
1/2 cup chopped dried apricots
1/4 cup raisins

In a mixing bowl, combine sugar, butter and egg; mix well. Add pineapple and milk; mix well. Combine dry ingredients; add to butter mixture just until moistened. Stir in pecans, apricots and raisins. Pour into three greased 5-3/4-in. x 3-in. x 2-in. loaf pans. Bake at 350° for 45-55 minutes or until a toothpick inserted near the center comes out clean. Cool for 10 minutes; remove from pans to a wire rack to cool completely. **Yield:** 3 loaves.

Dutch Spice Bread

During the busy Christmas season, I make this moist, spicy bread often. I wrap it and allow it to "ripen" for a day before slicing. Serve it with cream cheese to enhance the old-fashioned gingerbread flavor.
—Gladys De Boer, Castleford, Idaho

1 cup dark corn syrup
1/2 cup packed brown sugar
1 egg
2-1/2 cups all-purpose flour
1-1/2 teaspoons baking soda
1 teaspoon ground cinnamon
1 teaspoon ground ginger
1/2 teaspoon ground cloves
1/2 teaspoon ground nutmeg
1/4 teaspoon salt
1 cup milk

In a bowl, combine corn syrup, brown sugar and egg; mix well. Combine dry ingredients; add to the egg mixture alternately with milk and mix well. Pour into a greased and waxed paper-lined 9-in. x 5-in. x 3-in. loaf pan. Bake at 325° for 80-90 minutes or until a toothpick inserted near the center comes out clean. Cool for 10 minutes; remove from pan to a wire rack to cool completely. Wrap and let stand for 24 hours before slicing. **Yield:** 1 loaf.

Sweet Corn Muffins

I love making corn bread and corn muffins, but often the results are not moist or sweet enough for my taste. So I experimented until I came up with these light, pleasantly sweet muffins.   —Patty Bourne, Owings, Maryland

1-1/2 cups all-purpose flour
1 cup sugar
3/4 cup cornmeal
1 tablespoon baking powder
1/2 teaspoon salt
2 eggs
1/2 cup shortening
1 cup milk, *divided*

In a mixing bowl, combine the dry ingredients. Add eggs, shortening and 1/2 cup of milk; beat for 1 minute. Add remaining milk; beat just until blended. Fill paper-lined muffin cups three-fourths full. Bake at 350° for 25-30 minutes or until muffins test done. **Yield:** 1 dozen.

Bread at the Touch of a Button

EVEN the best store-bought loaf can't compare with fresh homemade bread. But who has time anymore to bake it from scratch? You do!

Bread machines actually make it more convenient to bake bread at home than pick it up at the supermarket. As you'll see in these recipes, it takes only minutes to put your ingredients in the pan, flick a few switches and make a simple check. Then about all you need to do is wait for the aroma to fill the kitchen.

Editor's Note: All of these recipes were tested in a Regal brand bread machine *and* in a West Bend or Black & Decker bread machine.

Cranberry Yeast Bread

Cranberry Yeast Bread

(Pictured at right)

I adapted a raisin bread recipe to make this wonderful, slightly sweet loaf. The combination of tart dried cranberries and aromatic orange peel gives it fun flavor.
—*Sandy Hunt, Racine, Wisconsin*

    1 cup plus 3 tablespoons water (70° to 80°)
    2 tablespoons butter *or* margarine, softened
    3 tablespoons instant nonfat dry milk powder
    3 tablespoons sugar
    2 teaspoons salt
3-1/2 cups bread flour
2-1/2 teaspoons active dry yeast
    3/4 cup dried cranberries
    1 tablespoon grated orange peel

In bread machine pan, place the first seven ingredients in order suggested by manufacturer. Select basic bread setting. Choose crust color and loaf size if available. Bake according to bread machine directions (check dough after 5 minutes of mixing; add 1 to 2 tablespoons of water or flour if needed). Just before the final kneading (your machine may audibly signal this), add cranberries and orange peel. **Yield:** 1 loaf (2 pounds). **Editor's Note:** Use of the timer feature is not recommended for this recipe.

Macadamia Nut Bread

Crusty outside and chewy inside, this bread is chock-full of crunchy nuts. It tastes great toasted and topped with cream cheese...and the aroma is heavenly, too.
—*Darlene Markel, Sublimity, Oregon*

    1/2 cup pineapple juice (70° to 80°)
    1/4 cup water (70° to 80°)
    1 egg
    2 tablespoons butter *or* margarine, softened
    3 tablespoons sugar
    3/4 teaspoon salt
    3 cups bread flour
2-1/4 teaspoons active dry yeast
    3/4 cup macadamia nuts, chopped
    1/2 cup flaked coconut

In bread machine pan, place the first eight ingredients in order suggested by manufacturer. Select basic bread setting. Choose crust color and loaf size if available. Bake according to bread machine directions (check dough after 5 minutes of mixing; add 1 to 2 tablespoons of water or flour if needed). Just before the final kneading (your machine may audibly signal this), add nuts and coconut. **Yield:** 1 loaf (1-1/2 pounds). **Editor's Note:** Use of the timer feature is not recommended for this recipe.

Measuring Up

TO ASSURE the best results from bread machines, always measure accurately.

- Measure water by pouring it into a transparent liquid measuring cup; read the measurement at eye level.
- Measure flour by spooning it into a standard dry measuring cup; level with a straight-edged knife.
- Measure yeast, salt or spices by filling a standard measuring spoon to overflowing; level with a straight-edged knife.

Sweet Almond Bread

(Pictured below)

My niece shared this recipe with me a few years ago, and I adapted it to use the dough setting on my bread machine. It's delicious as a breakfast bread or served warm with ice cream. —Sally Ball, Gladwin, Michigan

DOUGH:
2/3 cup warm milk (70° to 80°)
1 egg yolk
1/4 cup butter *or* margarine, softened
1/4 cup applesauce, room temperature
1/3 cup sugar
1/2 teaspoon salt
2-3/4 cups bread flour
2-1/4 teaspoons active dry yeast
TOPPING:
1/4 cup butter *or* margarine
3 tablespoons sugar
1 tablespoon milk
1/4 teaspoon ground cinnamon
1/8 teaspoon salt
6 tablespoons sliced almonds

In bread machine pan, place dough ingredients in order suggested by manufacturer. Select dough setting (check dough after 5 minutes of mixing; add 1 to 2 tablespoons of water or flour if needed). When cycle is completed, turn dough onto a floured surface and punch down. Divide dough in half. Roll each portion into a 6-in. circle and place on greased baking sheets. Cover and let rise in a warm place until doubled, about 30 minutes. Meanwhile, for topping, combine butter, sugar, milk, cinnamon and salt in a small saucepan. Cook and stir over low heat until butter is melted. Simmer for 1 minute. Remove from the heat; cool for 5 minutes.

Sweet Almond Bread

For the Best Bread...

- Bread machines vary somewhat, depending on the manufacturer. It will be easier for you to use your machine if you first become very familiar with it. Before trying new recipes, make a variety of those provided in your manual—they were developed specifically for your machine.

- When trying any new recipe, be sure to stay within the limits of the maximum flour amounts listed in the recipes in your machine's manual.

- Canadian cooks should use 3 to 4 tablespoons less flour than called for in the bread recipes published in this chapter.

- Add the ingredients only in the order recommended by the manufacturer (which isn't always how they may appear in a recipe here).

- Your bread machine does the mixing and kneading for you. Because of that, you must learn to judge the bread with your eyes and ears to decide whether a recipe is right for your machine or needs a little adjusting.

- Listen to your bread machine as it's kneading the dough. If the machine sounds labored, the dough might be too dry. After 5 minutes of mixing, take a look at it. It should be forming a smooth satiny ball. If the dough looks dry or cracked, add 1 to 2 tablespoons of water. If the dough is flat and wet-looking, add 1 to 2 tablespoons of flour.

Make a 1/4-in. depression in the center of each loaf with the tip of a wooden spoon. Brush with butter mixture and sprinkle with almonds. Bake at 375° for 18-20 minutes or until golden brown. Cool for 10 minutes. Serve warm. **Yield:** 2 loaves. **Editor's Note:** Use of the timer feature is not recommended for this recipe.

Jim's Cheddar Bread

I've been using a bread machine for 4 years now and wonder how I ever got along without it. Flavorful slices of this mild cheese bread are great for sandwiches.
—Jim Bodle, Clockville, New York

1 cup water (70° to 80°)
1/4 cup buttermilk blend powder
1-1/2 cups (6 ounces) shredded sharp cheddar cheese
4-1/2 teaspoons sugar
1 teaspoon salt
1/2 teaspoon garlic salt
3 cups bread flour
1-1/2 teaspoons active dry yeast

In bread machine pan, place all ingredients in order suggested by manufacturer. Select the basic bread setting. Choose light crust color and loaf size if available. Bake according to bread machine directions (check dough after 5 minutes of mixing; add 1 to 2 tablespoons of water or flour if needed). **Yield:** 1 loaf (about 2 pounds). **Editor's Note:** Use of the timer feature is not recommended for this recipe.

Tarragon Carrot Bread

Tarragon Carrot Bread

(Pictured above)

As home economists, we develop bread machine recipes in our own test kitchen. We hope you try this moist, nicely textured loaf that's flecked with pretty carrot pieces.
—*Donna Washburn and Heather Butt*
Mallorytown, Ontario

✓ **Nutritional Analysis included**

> 1 cup plus 2 tablespoons water (70° to 80°)
> 2 tablespoons honey
> 1 tablespoon shortening
> 3/4 cup grated carrots
> 3 tablespoons instant nonfat dry milk powder
> 2 tablespoons dried tarragon
> 1-1/2 teaspoons grated orange peel
> 1-1/2 teaspoons salt
> 3/4 cup All-Bran
> 1 cup whole wheat flour
> 2-1/4 cups bread flour
> 1-1/4 teaspoons active dry yeast

In bread machine pan, place all ingredients in order suggested by manufacturer. Select the basic bread setting. Choose crust color and loaf size if available. Bake according to bread machine directions (check dough after 5 minutes of mixing; add 1 to 2 tablespoons of water or flour if needed). **Yield:** 1 loaf, 16 slices (about 2 pounds). **Nutritional Analysis:** One slice equals 128 calories, 271 mg sodium, trace cholesterol, 26 gm carbohydrate, 5 gm protein, 1 gm fat. **Diabetic Exchange:**

2 starch. **Editor's Note:** Use of the timer feature is not recommended for this recipe.

Crusty French Rolls

Save time by letting your bread machine knead the dough for these hearty, chewy rolls with a wonderful golden crust. They're best eaten the same day they're baked or frozen for later. —*Donna Washburn and Heather Butt*

✓ **Nutritional Analysis included**

> 1-1/4 cups water (70° to 80°)
> 2 teaspoons sugar
> 1 teaspoon salt
> 3-1/2 cups bread flour
> 1-1/4 teaspoons active dry yeast
> 1 tablespoon cornmeal
> 1 egg white
> 1 tablespoon water

In bread machine pan, place the first five ingredients in order suggested by manufacturer. Select dough setting (check dough after 5 minutes of mixing; add 1 to 2 tablespoons of water or flour if needed). When cycle is completed, turn dough onto a lightly floured surface. Divide into 18 portions; shape each into a round ball. Place on lightly greased baking sheets; sprinkle with cornmeal. Cover and let rise in a warm place until doubled, about 45 minutes. Beat egg white and water; brush over the dough. Bake at 375° for 15 minutes; brush again with egg white mixture. Bake 10 minutes longer or until golden brown. **Yield:** 1-1/2 dozen. **Nutritional Analysis:** One roll equals 101 calories, 133 mg sodium, 0 cholesterol, 20 gm carbohydrate, 4 gm protein, trace fat. **Diabetic Exchange:** 1-1/2 starch. **Editor's Note:** This recipe can be prepared in a 1-1/2- or 2-pound bread machine.

Sunflower Rye Bread

This wholesome, rustic-looking loaf is crusty outside and moist inside. We prefer to use unroasted, unsalted sunflower seeds without the shells.
—Donna Washburn and Heather Butt

1-1/2 cups water (70° to 80°)
   3 tablespoons instant nonfat dry milk powder
   2 tablespoons honey
   2 tablespoons molasses
   2 tablespoons shortening
1-1/2 teaspoons salt
  1/3 cup unsalted sunflower kernels
   2 cups bread flour
1-1/3 cups whole wheat flour
   1 cup rye flour
1-1/4 teaspoons active dry yeast

In bread machine pan, place all ingredients in order suggested by manufacturer. Select wheat bread setting.* Choose crust color and loaf size if available. Bake according to bread machine directions (check dough after 5 minutes of mixing; add 1 to 2 tablespoons of water or flour if needed). **Yield:** 1 loaf (2 pounds). ***Editor's Note:** If your bread machine does not have a wheat setting, follow the manufacturer's directions using the basic setting.

Country White Bread

This beautiful loaf of home-style white bread is simply wonderful. Its light texture makes it great for sandwiches or toast. *—Karen Kaloydis, Flushing, Michigan*

   1 cup plus 1 tablespoon water (70° to 80°)
   1 egg
4-1/2 teaspoons vegetable oil
3-1/4 cups bread flour
  1/4 cup sugar
1-1/2 teaspoons salt
2-1/4 teaspoons active dry yeast

In bread machine pan, place all ingredients in order suggested by manufacturer. Select the basic bread setting. Choose crust color and loaf size if available. Bake according to bread machine directions (check dough after 5 minutes of mixing; add 1 to 2 tablespoons of water or flour if needed). **Yield:** 1 loaf (about 2 pounds).

Maple Oatmeal Bread

(Pictured at right)

Maple syrup gives this soft, tender bread its delicate flavor and golden color. The pleasantly sweet slices taste terrific when toasted. *—Kathy Morin, Methuen, Massachusetts*

3/4 cup plus 2 tablespoons water (70° to 80°)
1/3 cup maple syrup

   1 tablespoon vegetable oil
   1 teaspoon salt
3/4 cup quick-cooking oats
2-1/2 cups bread flour
2-1/4 teaspoons active dry yeast

In bread machine pan, place all ingredients in order suggested by manufacturer. Select the basic bread setting. Choose crust color and loaf size if available. Bake according to bread machine directions (check dough after 5 minutes of mixing; add 1 to 2 tablespoons of water or flour if needed). **Yield:** 1 loaf (1-1/2 pounds).

Wild Rice Bread

Wild rice is abundant in our state, so I use it in many recipes. Combined with caraway, the wild rice lends an excellent flavor to this hearty bread. *—Dotty Egge*
Pelican Rapids, Minnesota

✓ Nutritional Analysis included

3/4 cup water (70° to 80°)
   1 tablespoon vegetable oil
   1 tablespoon molasses
   1 teaspoon salt
1-2/3 cups bread flour
  1/2 cup cooked wild rice, cooled
  1/2 cup whole wheat flour
   1 teaspoon caraway seeds
   1 teaspoon active dry yeast

In bread machine pan, place all ingredients in order suggested by manufacturer. Select the basic bread setting. Choose crust color and loaf size if available. Bake according to bread machine directions (check dough after 5 minutes of mixing; add 1 to 2 tablespoons of water or flour if needed). **Yield:** 1 loaf, 16 slices (1-1/2 pounds). **Nutritional Analysis:** One slice equals 82 calories, 147 mg sodium, 0 cholesterol, 15 gm carbohydrate, 3 gm protein, 1 gm fat. **Diabetic Exchange:** 1 starch. **Editor's Note:** Use of the timer feature is not recommended for this recipe.

Maple Oatmeal Bread

Flavorful Herb Bread

(Pictured below)

This bread is one of my favorites. It has a wonderful texture and slices beautifully. The flavor of the herbs really comes through. —Gerri Hamilton, Kingsville, Ontario

    1 cup warm milk (70° to 80°)
    1 egg
    2 tablespoons butter *or* margarine, softened
    1/4 cup dried minced onion
    2 tablespoons sugar
1-1/2 teaspoons salt
    2 tablespoons dried parsley flakes
    1 teaspoon dried oregano
3-1/2 cups bread flour
    2 teaspoons active dry yeast

In bread machine pan, place all ingredients in order suggested by manufacturer. Select the basic bread setting. Choose crust color and loaf size if available. Bake according to bread machine directions (check dough after 5 minutes of mixing; add 1 to 2 tablespoons of water or flour if needed). **Yield:** 1 loaf (2 pounds). **Editor's Note:** Use of the timer feature is not recommended for this recipe.

Sauerkraut Rye Bread

Caraway adds deliciously subtle flavor to this hearty bread, while sauerkraut makes it nice and moist. The loaf bakes up into a lovely brown rye color. —Mary Kelly Hopland, California

3/4 cup plus 1 tablespoon water (70° to 80°)
    2 tablespoons molasses
    2 tablespoons butter *or* margarine, softened
    1 cup sauerkraut, well drained and chopped
    1 tablespoon caraway seed
    2 tablespoons brown sugar
1-1/2 teaspoons salt
    1 cup rye flour
    2 cups bread flour
2-1/4 teaspoons active dry yeast

In bread machine pan, place all ingredients in order suggested by manufacturer. Select the basic bread setting. Choose light crust color and loaf size if available. Bake according to bread machine directions (check dough after 5 minutes of mixing; add 1 to 2 tablespoons of water or flour if needed). **Yield:** 1 loaf (2 pounds). **Editor's Note:** Use of the timer feature is not recommended for this recipe.

Flavorful Herb Bread

Honey Whole Wheat Bread

You'll appreciate the hearty whole wheat goodness in this tender bread. The recipe calls for a blend of whole wheat and white flours to produce a loaf that tastes just like Grandma used to make. —Diane Kahnk
Tecumseh, Nebraska

✓ Nutritional Analysis included

> 1 cup water (70° to 80°)
> 1/4 cup vegetable oil
> 2 tablespoons honey
> 1 teaspoon salt
> 2 cups bread flour
> 1 cup whole wheat flour
> 1 package (1/4 ounce) active dry yeast (2-1/4 teaspoons)

In bread machine pan, place all ingredients in order suggested by manufacturer. Select basic bread setting. Choose crust color and loaf size if available. Bake according to bread machine directions (check dough after 5 minutes of mixing; add 1 to 2 tablespoons of water or flour if needed). **Yield:** 1 loaf, 16 slices (1-1/2 pounds). **Nutritional Analysis:** One slice equals 127 calories, 146 mg sodium, 0 cholesterol, 20 gm carbohydrate, 3 gm protein, 4 gm fat. **Diabetic Exchanges:** 1 starch, 1 fat.

Anise Almond Loaf

Garlic Yeast Bread

I like to use slices of this tender garlic bread to make roast beef sandwiches. With its golden crust and wonderful Italian flavor, it's also a nice accompaniment to spaghetti and other pasta dishes. —Sharen Clark
Sunnyside, Washington

✓ Nutritional Analysis included

> 2/3 cup water (70° to 80°)
> 2 teaspoons butter *or* margarine, softened
> 1 garlic clove, minced
> 2 cups bread flour
> 1 tablespoon sugar
> 1 teaspoon salt
> 1/4 teaspoon dried rosemary, crushed
> 1/8 teaspoon dried thyme
> 1/8 teaspoon dried basil
> 1-3/4 teaspoons active dry yeast

In bread machine pan, place all ingredients in order suggested by manufacturer. Select the basic bread setting. Choose crust color and loaf size if available. Bake according to bread machine directions (check dough after 5 minutes of mixing; add 1 to 2 tablespoons of water or flour if needed). **Yield:** 1 loaf, 16 slices (1 pound). **Nutritional Analysis:** One slice (prepared with margarine) equals 71 calories, 152 mg sodium, 0 cholesterol, 13 gm carbohydrate, 2 gm protein, 1 gm fat. **Diabetic Exchange:** 1 starch.

Anise Almond Loaf

(Pictured above)

I own two bread machines and look forward to coming up with different recipes to try in them. This golden loaf, with its tasty combination of anise and almond flavors, is one I like to make often. It especially makes a nice gift to give during the holidays. —Diane Widmer
Blue Island, Illinois

> 3/4 cup water (70° to 80°)
> 1 egg
> 1/4 cup butter *or* margarine, softened
> 1/4 cup sugar
> 1/2 teaspoon salt
> 3 cups bread flour
> 1 teaspoon aniseed
> 2 teaspoons active dry yeast
> 1/2 cup chopped almonds

In bread machine pan, place the first eight ingredients in order suggested by manufacturer. Select the basic bread setting. Choose light crust color and loaf size if available. Bake according to bread machine directions (check dough after 5 minutes of mixing; add 1 to 2 tablespoons of water or flour if needed). Just before the final kneading (your machine may audibly signal this), add the almonds. **Yield:** 1 loaf (about 1-1/2 pounds). **Editor's Note:** Use of the timer feature is not recommended for this recipe.

Chapter 12

FOR folks on the go, a quick soup, salad and sandwich combination is often a mealtime mainstay. But don't depend on a drive-thru to give you delicious down-home flavor.

Any of this chapter's souped-up meals can be assembled in a snap in your own kitchen. So your family won't have to wait long to hear "Soup's on!"

You'll eagerly add these easy-to-prepare items to your recipe collection. And your family will like what they find at the table—hearty homemade dishes that will fill 'em up fast.

TASTE-TEMPTING TRIO. Top to bottom: Zesty Tomato Soup, Grilled Roast Beef Sandwiches and Summer Squash Slaw (all recipes on p. 193).

Shrimp Salad Bagels

Dill adds fresh taste to the shrimp and cream cheese topping to this spread. I usually prepare these open-faced sandwiches for a fast lunch. You can heat them quickly in the microwave or pop them under the broiler if you'd like crispy bagels. —*Angie Hansen, Gildford, Montana*

☑ **Nutritional Analysis included**

    1 package (3 ounces) cream cheese, softened
    3 tablespoons mayonnaise *or* salad dressing
    1 tablespoon lemon juice
    1/2 teaspoon dill weed
    1 can (6 ounces) small shrimp, rinsed and
        drained
    2 bagels, split and toasted
    1/4 cup shredded Swiss cheese

In a bowl, combine cream cheese, mayonnaise, lemon juice and dill. Stir in the shrimp; spread over bagels. Microwave, uncovered, on high for 1-1/2 to 2 minutes or broil 4 in. from the heat until hot and bubbly. Sprinkle with Swiss cheese. **Yield:** 4 servings. **Nutritional Analysis:** One serving (prepared with fat-free cream cheese, fat-free mayonnaise and reduced-fat Swiss cheese) equals 201 calories, 465 mg sodium, 80 mg cholesterol, 19 gm carbohydrate, 23 gm protein, 3 gm fat. **Diabetic Exchanges:** 2 very lean meat, 1-1/2 starch.

Thick 'n' Quick Clam Chowder

You'd never guess that this thick, rich soup is a blend of convenient canned ingredients. My husband and I love it during our busy harvest season...it's so simple to simmer up when time is tight. —*Betty Sitzman Wray, Colorado*

    1 can (10-3/4 ounces) condensed cream of
        celery soup, undiluted
    1 can (10-3/4 ounces) condensed cheddar
        cheese soup, undiluted
    1 can (10-3/4 ounces) condensed creamy onion
        soup, undiluted
    3 cups half-and-half cream
    2 cans (6-1/2 ounces *each*) chopped clams,
        drained

In a saucepan, combine the soups and cream; cook over medium heat until heated through. Add clams and heat through (do not boil). **Yield:** 6-8 servings.

Spicy Turkey Chili

(Pictured at far right)

This peppery chili is not for the faint of stomach. It's saucy and satisfying—according to my daughter, it's the one thing she can taste when she has a cold. It also freezes very well, so I always have some on hand.

—*Margaret Shauers, Great Bend, Kansas*

    2 pounds ground turkey *or* turkey sausage
    1 large onion, chopped

    4 garlic cloves, minced
    2 cans (15-3/4 ounces *each*) chili beans,
        undrained
    2 cans (15 ounces *each*) tomato sauce
    1 can (28 ounces) crushed tomatoes
1-1/2 cups beef broth *or* beer
    2 to 3 tablespoons chili powder
    2 teaspoons Italian seasoning
    1/4 to 1/2 teaspoon ground cinnamon
    1 jalapeno pepper, finely chopped*
Dash cayenne pepper

In a large kettle, brown turkey, onion and garlic; drain. Add the remaining ingredients. Bring to a boil; reduce heat. Simmer, uncovered, for 45 minutes, stirring occasionally. **Yield:** 12-14 servings (3-1/2 quarts). ***Editor's Note:** When cutting or seeding hot peppers, use rubber or plastic gloves to protect your hands. Avoid touching your face.

Sweet-Sour Lettuce Salad

(Pictured at right)

This super-quick salad dressing is a breeze to shake up when you're in a hurry. Its refreshing, slightly sweet flavor complements fresh lettuce and crisp bacon bits quite nicely.
—*Lois Fetting, Nelson, Wisconsin*

    1/2 cup sugar
    1/4 cup vinegar
    2 tablespoons water
    3/4 cup half-and-half cream
    8 cups torn salad greens
    6 bacon strips, cooked and crumbled

In a jar with tight-fitting lid, combine the sugar, vinegar and water; shake until sugar is dissolved. Add cream; shake well. Just before serving, toss greens, bacon and dressing in a large bowl. **Yield:** 8 servings.

Hot Turkey Sandwiches

(Pictured at right)

I was first served this hearty hot sandwich at a friend's home. I couldn't wait to get the recipe and make it myself. The cheesy sauce is a delicious disguise for leftover turkey or chicken. —*Charla Sackmann, Glidden, Iowa*

    2 cups cubed cooked turkey
    1 celery rib, chopped
    1/3 cup mayonnaise
    1 cup cubed process American cheese
Salt and pepper to taste
    6 hamburger buns, split

In a greased 1-1/2-qt. baking dish, combine the turkey, celery, mayonnaise, cheese, salt and pepper; stir well. Cover and bake at 450° for 35-40 minutes or until celery is tender, stirring occasionally. Toast the buns if desired. Serve about 1/2 cup of turkey mixture on each bun. **Yield:** 6 servings.

Sweet-Sour Lettuce Salad
Spicy Turkey Chili
Hot Turkey Sandwiches

30-Minute Minestrone
Lasagna Sandwiches
Crisp Side Salad

Lasagna Sandwiches

(Pictured at left)

These cheesy grilled sandwiches really taste like lasagna. They're perfect for a quick evening meal—our children loved them with vegetable soup and crunchy potato sticks.
—Gail Rotheiser, Highland Park, Illinois

1/4 cup sour cream
2 tablespoons chopped onion
1/2 teaspoon dried oregano
1/4 teaspoon seasoned salt
8 slices Italian *or* other white bread
8 bacon strips, halved and cooked
8 slices tomato
4 slices mozzarella cheese
2 to 3 tablespoons butter *or* margarine

Combine the first four ingredients; spread on four slices of bread. Top each with four bacon pieces, two tomato slices and a slice of cheese; top with remaining bread. In a skillet over medium heat, melt 2 tablespoons butter. Cook sandwiches on both sides until bread is lightly browned and cheese is melted, adding more butter if necessary. **Yield:** 4 servings.

Crisp Side Salad

(Pictured at left)

The light dressing over this crunchy combination of colorful salad fixings contains just a hint of sweetness. I like to make the dressing ahead to let the flavors blend.
—Craig Miller, Torrance, California

1/4 cup olive *or* vegetable oil
2 tablespoons cider vinegar
4 teaspoons sugar
1/2 teaspoon salt
1/4 teaspoon pepper
4 cups torn salad greens
3/4 cup sliced zucchini
2 medium carrots, sliced
2 celery ribs, sliced
2 green onions, sliced
1/4 cup seasoned croutons
1 tablespoon whole almonds, toasted
1 tablespoon sesame seeds, toasted

In a jar with tight-fitting lid, combine the first five ingredients and shake well. In a large salad bowl, combine greens, zucchini, carrots, celery and onions. Just before serving, add dressing and toss to coat. Top with croutons, almonds and sesame seeds. **Yield:** 4 servings.

30-Minute Minestrone

(Pictured at left)

This simple, chunky soup is low in calories. The broth's seasoned nicely, while the spinach adds a refreshing difference. —Betty Claycomb, Alverton, Pennsylvania

✓ **Nutritional Analysis included**

2 medium carrots, chopped

1 cup chopped cabbage
1 celery rib, thinly sliced
1 small onion, chopped
1 garlic clove, minced
2 teaspoons vegetable oil
3 cups water
1 can (14-1/2 ounces) Italian stewed *or* diced
   tomatoes, undrained
3 beef bouillon cubes
1 cup torn fresh spinach
2/3 cup cooked elbow macaroni
1/4 teaspoon pepper

In a 3-qt. saucepan, saute carrots, cabbage, celery, onion and garlic in oil for 5 minutes. Add water, tomatoes and bouillon; bring to a boil. Reduce heat. Simmer, uncovered, for 20-25 minutes or until vegetables are tender. Stir in spinach, macaroni and pepper; heat through. **Yield:** 5 servings. **Nutritional Analysis:** One 1-cup serving (prepared with low-sodium bouillon) equals 88 calories, 178 mg sodium, 0 cholesterol, 14 gm carbohydrate, 3 gm protein, 2 gm fat. **Diabetic Exchange:** 1 starch.

Turkey Meatball Soup

This speedy soup stars tasty meatballs made from ground turkey. Cook it up to feed a crowd…or freeze leftovers for future meals.
—Randal Robert Wilson, Bellevue, Kentucky

✓ **Nutritional Analysis included**

MEATBALLS:
1/4 cup cooked rice
1/4 cup finely chopped onion
1/4 cup finely chopped celery
2 tablespoons all-purpose flour
2 tablespoons water
1/2 teaspoon ground cumin
1/2 teaspoon salt, optional
1/8 teaspoon pepper
3/4 pound ground turkey breast
SOUP:
6 cups chicken broth
1 cup uncooked fine egg noodles
1/2 teaspoon pepper
1/4 teaspoon garlic salt, optional
1/8 teaspoon dill weed
1 tablespoon minced fresh parsley

In a bowl, combine the first eight ingredients. Add turkey; mix well. Shape into 1-in. balls and place on two baking sheets that have been coated with nonstick cooking spray. Bake, uncovered, at 450° for 15 minutes or until turkey is no longer pink. In a Dutch oven or large soup kettle, bring broth to a boil. Add meatballs, noodles, pepper, garlic salt if desired and dill; return to a boil. Reduce heat and simmer, uncovered, for 5 minutes or until noodles are tender. Stir in parsley. **Yield:** 12 servings (3 quarts). **Nutritional Analysis:** One 1-cup serving (prepared with low-sodium broth and without salt and garlic salt) equals 65 calories, 77 mg sodium, 19 mg cholesterol, 5 gm carbohydrate, 9 gm protein, 2 gm fat. **Diabetic Exchanges:** 1 very lean meat, 1/2 starch.

Creole Fish Soup

(Pictured at far right)

You can serve up a pot of this hearty soup in under an hour. The recipe calls for frozen mixed veggies, so there's not a lot of peeling and chopping.
—Ruby Williams
Bogalusa, Louisiana

✓ **Nutritional Analysis included**

  1 can (28 ounces) diced tomatoes, undrained
  1 can (15 ounces) tomato sauce
  1/2 cup chopped onion
  1/2 teaspoon garlic powder
  1/2 teaspoon celery salt
  1/4 teaspoon dried thyme
  1/8 to 1/4 teaspoon cayenne pepper
  2 bay leaves
  1 package (16 ounces) frozen mixed vegetables
  1 pound fresh *or* frozen cod, cut into 3/4-inch pieces

In a soup kettle, combine the first eight ingredients; cover and simmer for 10 minutes. Add vegetables; cover and simmer for 10 minutes. Add fish; cover and simmer for 8-10 minutes or until the fish flakes easily with a fork. Discard the bay leaves. **Yield:** 8 servings (2 quarts). **Nutritional Analysis:** One 1-cup serving equals 129 calories, 663 mg sodium, 27 mg cholesterol, 17 gm carbohydrate, 15 gm protein, 1 gm fat. **Diabetic Exchanges:** 2 very lean meat, 1 starch.

BLT Burritos

This fun variation on the traditional bacon, lettuce and tomato sandwich is a breeze to fix. Flour tortillas make them easy to eat on the run.
—Dorothy Anderson
Ottawa, Kansas

  3 cups shredded lettuce
1-1/2 cups diced fresh tomatoes
  12 bacon strips, cooked and crumbled
  1/4 cup mayonnaise
  1/8 teaspoon pepper
  4 flour tortillas (10 inches), warmed

In a large bowl, combine the first five ingredients; mix well. Spoon down the center of each tortilla; fold the ends and sides over filling and roll up. Serve immediately. **Yield:** 4 servings.

Italian-Style Pasta Toss

You can prepare this salad in a flash since it uses convenience foods. It's a lip-smacking sensation that stands out from ordinary pasta salads. Serve it warm or cold.

  1 can (14-1/2 ounces) diced tomatoes with garlic and onion, undrained
  1 bottle (8 ounces) Italian *or* Caesar salad dressing
  1 jar (6-1/2 ounces) marinated artichoke hearts, undrained

  1 can (6 ounces) pitted ripe olives, drained
  1 package (3 ounces) sliced pepperoni
  1 medium green pepper, chopped
  2 medium carrots, thinly sliced
  2 green onions, sliced
  4 cups cooked tortellini
Shredded Parmesan cheese

In a large bowl, combine the first eight ingredients. Add tortellini and toss to coat. Sprinkle with Parmesan cheese. Serve immediately with a slotted spoon or refrigerate. **Yield:** 4-6 servings.

Hot Bacon Asparagus Salad

(Pictured at right)

This meal-in-one salad is so easy to fix when I get home from work...but it looks like I spent an hour preparing it.
—Paulette Balda, Prophetstown, Illinois

  7 bacon strips, diced
  1 pound fresh asparagus, trimmed
  1/3 cup vinegar
  1 tablespoon sugar
  1/2 teaspoon ground mustard
  1/4 teaspoon pepper
  4 cups torn salad greens
  1/2 cup sliced almonds
  2 hard-cooked eggs, sliced

In a skillet, cook bacon until crisp; remove with a slotted spoon to paper towel. Drain, reserving 2-3 tablespoons drippings. Cut asparagus into 1-1/2-in. pieces; saute in drippings until crisp-tender. Add vinegar, sugar, mustard, pepper and bacon. Cook and stir for 1-2 minutes. In a large bowl, combine the salad greens and almonds. Add the asparagus mixture and toss gently. Top with eggs. Serve immediately. **Yield:** 6 servings.

Cajun Chicken Club

(Pictured at right)

It takes just minutes to assemble these sandwiches. Cajun seasoning gives them the right amount of zippy flavor.
—Mrs. J.M. Andrews, Marcellus, New York

  4 boneless skinless chicken breast halves (about 1 pound)
  1/2 to 1 teaspoon Cajun seasoning
  1 tablespoon vegetable oil
  4 slices Swiss cheese
  1/4 cup creamy Parmesan salad dressing
  4 sandwich rolls, split and toasted
  8 tomato slices
  8 bacon strips, cooked

Flatten the chicken to 3/8-in. thickness; sprinkle with Cajun seasoning. In a skillet, cook chicken in oil for 5 minutes on each side or until juices run clear. Place cheese over chicken. Remove from the heat; cover and let stand for 1 minute or until cheese begins to melt. Spread dressing over both halves of rolls. Layer bottom halves with two slices of tomato, chicken and two strips of bacon; replace tops. **Yield:** 4 servings.

Creole Fish Soup
Hot Bacon Asparagus Salad
Cajun Chicken Club

Superb Yellow Pepper Soup
Hot Hoagies
Steak and Potato Salad

Superb Yellow Pepper Soup

(Pictured at left)

I first tasted this sunny-looking soup at a luncheon hosted by a good friend. It's simple and superb when served warm with a dollop of sour cream...or you can chill it for a refreshing change of pace in summer. —Linda Nilsen
Anoka, Minnesota

✓ **Nutritional Analysis included**

    1 tablespoon olive *or* vegetable oil
    1 tablespoon butter *or* margarine, optional
    6 medium sweet yellow peppers, cut into
      1-inch pieces
    1 large onion, diced
    1 medium potato, peeled and quartered
    1 garlic clove, minced
    6 cups chicken broth
    1 bay leaf
    1/2 teaspoon salt, optional
    1/4 teaspoon pepper
    1 cup buttermilk
Sour cream and snipped chives, optional

Heat oil and butter if desired in a Dutch oven or soup kettle; saute the peppers, onion, potato and garlic until onion is tender, about 5 minutes. Add broth, bay leaf, salt if desired and pepper; bring to a boil. Reduce heat; cover and simmer for 20 minutes or until vegetables are tender. Discard bay leaf. Cool slightly; puree in batches in a blender. Return to pan. Stir in buttermilk; heat through. Serve hot or cold; garnish with sour cream and chives if desired. **Yield:** 12 servings (3 quarts). **Nutritional Analysis:** One 1-cup serving (prepared with low-sodium broth and without butter, salt and sour cream) equals 57 calories, 78 mg sodium, 3 mg cholesterol, 8 gm carbohydrate, 3 gm protein, 2 gm fat. **Diabetic Exchanges:** 1-1/2 vegetable, 1/2 fat.

Steak and Potato Salad

(Pictured at left)

After working all week, my husband and I like to spend a lot of time with our two kids on weekends instead of cooking in the kitchen. That's when this recipe comes in handy. We marinate the meat in the fridge overnight, then grill it quickly for a fast, filling meal. —Linda Emily Dow
Princeton Junction, New Jersey

    2 pounds boneless sirloin steak (1 inch thick)
    1/2 cup cider *or* red wine vinegar
    1/4 cup olive *or* vegetable oil
    1/4 cup soy sauce
    6 cups cubed cooked potatoes
    1 cup diced green pepper
    1/3 cup chopped green onions
    1/4 cup minced fresh parsley
    1/2 cup Caesar salad dressing
Lettuce leaves, optional

Place steak in a large resealable plastic bag or shallow glass container. Combine vinegar, oil and soy sauce; pour over the steak. Cover and refrigerate for 1 hour or over-

night. Drain, discarding marinade. Grill or broil steak for 8-10 minutes on each side or until meat reaches desired doneness (for rare, a meat thermometer should read 140°; medium, 160°; well-done, 170°). Slice into thin strips across the grain and place in a bowl. Add the potatoes, green pepper, onions, parsley and dressing; toss to coat. Serve on lettuce if desired. **Yield:** 8-10 servings.

Hot Hoagies

(Pictured at far left)

A convenient package of Italian salad dressing mix provides the yummy herb flavor in these broiled sandwiches that I assemble for my family of 10. I use their favorite combination of meats and cheeses, then serve the sandwiches with chips and pickles. They're a hit every time.
—Paula Hadley, Forest Hill, Louisiana

    3/4 cup butter *or* margarine, softened
    1 envelope Italian salad dressing mix
    6 hoagie buns, split
    12 to 16 ounces sliced luncheon meat (salami,
      ham *and/or* turkey)
    12 thin slices cheese (Swiss, cheddar *and/or* brick)

Combine butter and salad dressing mix; spread 1 tablespoonful inside each bun. On bottom of each bun, layer one slice of meat, two slices of cheese and another slice of meat; replace tops. Spread 1 tablespoon butter mixture over top of each bun. Place on a baking sheet. Broil 6 in. from the heat for 2-3 minutes or until tops are lightly browned. **Yield:** 6 servings.

Fruit 'n' Cheese Salad

Sweet dressing, tart grapefruit sections, toasted walnuts and pungent blue cheese come together in this unusual salad. The recipe showcases one of the citrus fruits my brother, Ed, and I grow at Peterson's Groves and Nursery.
—Fred Peterson, Vero Beach, Florida

✓ **Nutritional Analysis included**

    8 to 10 cups torn salad greens
    3 medium grapefruit, peeled and sectioned
    1 cup halved seedless red grapes
    3/4 cup crumbled blue cheese
    1/2 cup thinly sliced red onion
    1/4 cup chopped walnuts, toasted, optional
    1/4 cup cider *or* red wine vinegar
    2 tablespoons olive *or* vegetable oil
    2 tablespoons honey
    1 tablespoon Dijon mustard
    1/4 teaspoon salt, optional

In a large bowl, combine greens, fruit, cheese, onion and nuts if desired. In a small bowl, whisk vinegar, oil, honey, mustard and salt if desired. Pour over salad and toss to coat. **Yield:** 8-10 servings. **Nutritional Analysis:** One 1/2-cup serving (prepared without walnuts and salt) equals 126 calories, 195 mg sodium, 8 mg cholesterol, 16 gm carbohydrate, 4 gm protein, 6 gm fat. **Diabetic Exchanges:** 1 fruit, 1 fat, 1/2 meat.

Vegetable Stack-Up Salad

This colorful salad is great for family reunions or church get-togethers because it can be prepared the night before. Just sprinkle on the cheese and bacon before serving.
—Joan Snider, Celina, Ohio

    4 cups shredded salad greens
    1 small green pepper, chopped
    1 can (11 ounces) Mexicorn, drained
    2 small zucchini, sliced
    2 cups chopped fresh tomatoes
    1 cup sliced celery
    2 cups mayonnaise *or* salad dressing
    2 cups (8 ounces) shredded cheddar cheese
    6 bacon strips, cooked and crumbled

In a 2-1/2-qt. glass serving bowl, layer salad greens, green pepper, corn, zucchini, tomatoes and celery. Spread mayonnaise over all; seal to edges of bowl. Cover and refrigerate for several hours or overnight. Just before serving, sprinkle with cheese and bacon. **Yield:** 10-12 servings.

Chilled Potato Soup

It takes just minutes to blend together this unusual soup seasoned with basil. It's creamy, rich and so refreshing on a hot summer day.
—Sandi Pichon, Slidell, Louisiana

1-1/3 cups milk
    1 can (10-3/4 ounces) condensed cream of
        potato soup, undiluted
    3/4 teaspoon snipped fresh basil *or* 1/4 teaspoon
        dried basil
    1/4 teaspoon snipped fresh *or* dried chives
    1 cup (8 ounces) sour cream
    1/4 cup white wine *or* chicken broth

Place all the ingredients in a blender or food processor; cover and process until smooth. Transfer to a bowl; cover and chill until serving. **Yield:** 4 servings. **To serve soup warm:** Process milk, soup and herbs in a blender until smooth; transfer to a saucepan. Bring to a boil over medium heat, stirring constantly. Reduce heat. Add sour cream and wine or broth; heat through (do not boil).

Avocado Ham Sandwiches

(Pictured at far right)

An avocado spread adds mild flavor and delicate color to this ham and cheese sandwich. You also can toast or grill the bread.
—Toby Raymond, Springfield, Oregon

    1 medium ripe avocado, peeled and mashed
    2 tablespoons mayonnaise
Dash cayenne pepper
    12 slices whole wheat *or* sourdough bread
    6 slices fully cooked ham
    6 slices Swiss cheese
    6 tablespoons cream cheese, softened

In a small bowl, combine the first three ingredients;

spread on six slices of bread. Top with ham and Swiss. Spread cream cheese on remaining bread; place over Swiss cheese. **Yield:** 6 servings.

Zucchini Soup

(Pictured at right)

When there's an abundance of zucchini in our garden, I know it's time for this fresh-tasting soup.
—Mrs. R.C. Friend, Lynden, Washington

✓ Nutritional Analysis included

    1 cup chopped onion
    1 cup thinly sliced celery
    1 garlic clove, minced
    1/4 cup chopped green pepper
    1 tablespoon vegetable oil
    2 pounds zucchini, chopped
    2 medium tomatoes, chopped
    3 cups chicken broth
    1/2 teaspoon dried basil
    1/4 teaspoon dried thyme
    1 cup half-and-half cream *or* milk

In a large saucepan, saute onion, celery, garlic and green pepper in oil until tender. Add zucchini, tomatoes, broth, basil and thyme; bring to a boil. Reduce heat; simmer, uncovered, for 20-30 minutes or until the vegetables are tender. Stir in cream; heat through. Serve hot or cold. **Yield:** 8 servings (2 quarts). **Nutritional Analysis:** One 1-cup serving (prepared with low-sodium broth and skim milk) equals 70 calories, 77 mg sodium, 2 mg cholesterol, 9 gm carbohydrate, 4 gm protein, 3 gm fat. **Diabetic Exchanges:** 2 vegetable, 1/2 fat.

Tomatoes with Parsley Pesto

(Pictured at right)

You'll love the summery flavor of this pretty salad. It's a snap to whip up the pesto in the blender, then pour it over ripe tomato wedges.
—Donna Hackman Huddleston, Virginia

✓ Nutritional Analysis included

    1 cup packed fresh parsley
    1/4 cup snipped fresh chives
    1 garlic clove
    1/4 teaspoon salt, optional
Dash pepper
    3 tablespoons olive *or* vegetable oil
    2 tablespoons cider *or* red wine vinegar
    3 medium tomatoes, cut into wedges

In a blender or food processor, combine parsley, chives, garlic, salt if desired and pepper. Cover and process until finely chopped. Add oil and vinegar; mix well. Transfer to a bowl; cover and refrigerate. When ready to serve, add tomatoes and gently toss to coat. **Yield:** 6 servings. **Nutritional Analysis:** One 2-tablespoon serving of pesto (prepared without salt) equals 79 calories, 12 mg sodium, 0 cholesterol, 4 gm carbohydrate, 1 gm protein, 7 gm fat. **Diabetic Exchanges:** 1 fat, 1 vegetable.

Avocado Ham Sandwiches
Zucchini Soup
Tomatoes with Parsley Pesto

Zesty Tomato Soup
Grilled Roast Beef Sandwiches
Summer Squash Slaw

Zesty Tomato Soup

(Pictured at left and on page 180)

When some friends stopped by unexpectedly, my husband, Phil, came up with this fast-to-fix soup that tastes homemade. Two easy ingredients give canned soup just the right amount of zip. —*JoAnn Gunio, Franklin, North Carolina*

2 cans (10-3/4 ounces *each*) condensed tomato soup, undiluted
2-2/3 cups water
2 teaspoons chili powder
Oyster crackers *or* shredded Monterey Jack cheese, optional

In a saucepan, combine the first three ingredients; heat through. Garnish with crackers or cheese if desired. **Yield:** 4-5 servings.

Grilled Roast Beef Sandwiches

(Pictured at left and on page 180)

I first tasted a memorable combination of roast beef and green chilies at a local cafe. In this recipe, the chilies give the quick grilled sandwich a little bite. It's simple and delicious. —*Karen Ledbetter, Fort Collins, Colorado*

1 can (4 ounces) chopped green chilies, drained
2 tablespoons mayonnaise
1 tablespoon Dijon mustard
10 slices rye bread
5 slices Swiss cheese
10 thin slices cooked roast beef
2 tablespoons butter *or* margarine, softened
Salsa *or* picante sauce, optional

Combine chilies, mayonnaise and mustard; spread about 1 tablespoon on one side of each slice of bread. Top half of the bread with one slice of cheese and two slices of beef. Cover with remaining bread. Butter the outsides of bread. Grill sandwiches on a griddle or in a large skillet over medium heat until both sides are golden brown and the cheese is melted. Serve with salsa or picante sauce if desired. **Yield:** 5 servings.

Summer Squash Slaw

(Pictured at left and on page 181)

I often create this colorful medley of fresh zucchini, summer squash and red pepper. It's a flavorful way to use up my garden bounty, and the dill adds wonderful flavor. —*Mary Ann Kosmas, Minneapolis, Minnesota*

☑ **Nutritional Analysis included**

2 small yellow summer squash, julienned
2 small zucchini, julienned
1 small sweet red pepper, julienned
1/3 cup sliced onion
3 tablespoons vegetable oil
2 tablespoons cider *or* white wine vinegar
1 tablespoon mayonnaise
1 teaspoon sugar
1/2 teaspoon dill weed
1/2 teaspoon garlic salt
1/4 teaspoon celery salt
1/4 teaspoon pepper

In a large bowl, combine squash, zucchini, red pepper and onion. In a small bowl, combine remaining ingredients; mix well. Pour over squash mixture and toss to coat. Cover and refrigerate. Serve with a slotted spoon. **Yield:** 10 servings. **Nutritional Analysis:** One 1/2-cup serving (prepared with cider vinegar and fat-free mayonnaise) equals 52 calories, 140 mg sodium, 0 cholesterol, 4 gm carbohydrate, 1 gm protein, 4 gm fat. **Diabetic Exchanges:** 1 fat, 1/2 vegetable.

Colby Corn Chowder

This comforting, cheesy soup is perfect for a cold winter's night—and it doesn't have to simmer for hours. The creamed corn adds a nice touch of sweetness. My family enjoys it with dill pickle spears and crusty fresh-from-the-oven bread. —*Darlene Drane, Fayette, Missouri*

6 large potatoes, peeled and cubed
1 teaspoon salt
1 large onion, chopped
1/4 cup butter *or* margarine
2 cans (14-3/4 ounces *each*) cream-style corn
4 bacon strips, cooked and crumbled
3 cups milk
8 ounces Colby cheese, cubed

Place potatoes in a Dutch oven or soup kettle; sprinkle with salt and cover with water. Bring to a boil. Reduce heat; cover and simmer until potatoes are tender. Meanwhile, in a skillet, saute onion in butter until tender. Stir in corn and bacon; heat through. Drain potatoes. Add milk; heat through. Stir in corn mixture and cheese. Serve immediately. **Yield:** 12-14 servings (about 3 quarts).

Wild Rice and Turkey Salad

Serve this tasty main-dish salad for a colorful change of pace. Spinach and wild rice provide the refreshing difference. Plus, it's a great way to use leftover turkey. —*Ginny Schneider, Muenster, Texas*

☑ **Nutritional Analysis included**

4 cups torn fresh spinach
2 cups cubed cooked turkey breast
2 cups cooked wild rice
1 medium onion, chopped
1 cup sliced fresh mushrooms
2 medium tomatoes, chopped
1 jar (2 ounces) chopped pimientos, drained
1 bottle (8 ounces) Italian salad dressing

In a large bowl, combine the first seven ingredients. Add dressing just before serving; toss to coat. **Yield:** 9 servings. **Nutritional Analysis:** One 1-cup serving (prepared with fat-free dressing) equals 157 calories, 71 mg sodium, 10 mg cholesterol, 21 gm carbohydrate, 14 gm protein, 2 gm fat. **Diabetic Exchanges:** 1 starch, 1 meat, 1 vegetable.

Chapter 13

FOLKS will think you fussed when you serve a selection of these sweet treats. But these irresistible desserts are actually easy to prepare, so you can quickly whip them up for your family, unexpected company and even dinner guests.

Whether you're looking for a fantastic finale to serve at a special-occasion supper or for a tasty take-along treat to share at a potluck, you're sure to impress everyone with these delights that don't require a lot of time in the kitchen.

You'll soon have treats to share with time to spare!

SWEETS THAT SATISFY. Clockwise from upper right: Brown Sugar Shortbread (p. 198), Chocolate Mousse Pie (p. 202), Cherry Cheesecake (p. 202) and Layered Toffee Cake (p. 198).

Cinnamon Snack Mix
Picnic Bars

1 package (6 ounces)
  strawberry gelatin
1/2 cup sugar
2 cups miniature
  marshmallows
1 package (18-1/4 ounces)
  white *or* yellow cake mix
Whipped topping, optional

Place rhubarb in a greased 13-in. x 9-in. x 2-in. baking pan. Sprinkle with the gelatin, sugar and marshmallows. Prepare cake mix according to package directions; pour batter over marshmallows. Bake at 350° for 50-55 minutes or until a toothpick inserted near the center comes out clean. Cool for 10 minutes; invert cake onto a serving plate. Serve with whipped topping if desired. **Yield:** 12-16 servings.

Picnic Bars

(Pictured at left)

You'll score points with a crowd when you stir together these delicious fudge-like treats. They're very moist and rich. The chocolate chips and walnuts make a pretty topping. —Frank Bee, Eugene, Oregon

1-3/4 cups all-purpose flour
1 cup sugar
1/4 cup baking cocoa
1/2 cup cold butter *or* margarine
2 eggs
1 can (14 ounces) sweetened condensed milk
2 cups (12 ounces) semisweet chocolate chips, *divided*
1 cup chopped walnuts

In a bowl, combine flour, sugar and cocoa; cut in butter until mixture resembles coarse crumbs. Stir in eggs. Set aside 1-1/2 cups for topping. Press remaining crumb mixture into a greased 13-in. x 9-in. x 2-in. baking pan. Bake at 350° for 6-8 minutes or until set. Meanwhile, in a saucepan, combine the milk and 1 cup of chocolate chips; cook and stir over low heat until melted. Carefully spread over crust. Combine reserved crumb mixture with nuts and remaining chips. Sprinkle over chocolate layer. Bake for 15-20 minutes or until top is set (chips will not look melted). Cool before cutting. **Yield:** 3 dozen.

Cinnamon Snack Mix

(Pictured above)

The pleasant sweetness of this crisp, munchable mixture will surprise you. I've taken it to my children's schools for parties or as a special treat. I've also packaged it in bow-topped tins for special gifts. —Donna Scully
Newark, Delaware

11 whole cinnamon graham crackers, broken into bite-size pieces
1 package (17.9 ounces) Crispix cereal
1 cup miniature pretzels
1 cup pecan halves
2/3 cup butter *or* margarine, melted
1/2 cup honey
1 cup vanilla *or* butterscotch baking chips

In a large bowl, combine graham crackers, cereal, pretzels and pecans. Combine butter and honey; drizzle over graham cracker mixture and mix well. Transfer to two greased 15-in. x 10-in. x 1-in. baking pans. Bake at 350° for 12-15 minutes, stirring once. Cool completely. Stir in chips. **Yield:** about 6 quarts.

Rhubarb Upside-Down Cake

I like to prepare this colorful dessert when fresh rhubarb is abundant. When I take it to church potlucks, people really clean up the pan fast. —Bonnie Krogman
Thompson Falls, Montana

5 cups cut fresh *or* frozen rhubarb (1/2-inch pieces), thawed and drained

Potato Chip Cookies

A friend at work shared this wonderful recipe. Potato chips give these buttery cookies a unique flavor. They're simple to make and so good. —Irene Carey
Hansville, Washington

1 cup butter *or* margarine, softened
1/2 cup sugar

3/4 cup crushed ridged potato chips
1/2 cup ground pecans
1 teaspoon vanilla extract
2 cups all-purpose flour

In a mixing bowl, cream butter and sugar. Stir in potato chips and pecans. Add vanilla; mix well. Stir in flour just until dough pulls away from the sides of the bowl and forms a ball. Shape into 1-in. balls; place 2 in. apart on greased baking sheets. Flatten with a glass dipped in flour. Bake at 350° for 12-15 minutes or until lightly browned. **Yield:** about 5 dozen.

Chocolate Peanut Dream Pie

(Pictured below right)

I love the flavor of peanut butter cups, so I dreamed up this creamy, rich pie to serve to company. It's wonderfully simple to make and always gets rave reviews.
—*Rosanne Marshall, Depew, New York*

1 package (3.4 ounces) cook-and-serve chocolate pudding mix
1/2 cup creamy peanut butter
1 cup whipped topping
1 graham cracker crust (9 inches)
Peanuts and additional whipped topping, optional

Prepare pudding according to package directions. Remove from the heat; whisk in peanut butter. Place pan in a bowl of ice water for 5 minutes, stirring occasionally. Fold in whipped topping. Pour into the crust. Cover and refrigerate for 1 hour or until set. Garnish with peanuts and whipped topping if desired. **Yield:** 6-8 servings.

Chocolate Chip Butter Cookies

(Pictured at right)

At the downtown Chicago law firm where I work, we often bring in goodies for special occasions. When co-workers hear I've baked these melt-in-your-mouth cookies, they make a special trip to my floor to sample them. Best of all, these crisp, buttery treats can be made in no time.
—*Janis Gruca*
Mokena, Illinois

1 cup butter (no substitutes)
1/2 teaspoon vanilla extract
2 cups all-purpose flour
1 cup confectioners' sugar
1 cup (6 ounces) miniature semisweet chocolate chips

Melt butter in a microwave or double boiler; stir in vanilla. Cool completely. In a large bowl, combine flour and sugar; stir in butter mixture and chocolate chips (mixture will be crumbly). Shape into 1-in. balls. Place 2 in. apart on ungreased baking sheets; flatten slightly. Bake at 375° for 12 minutes or until edges begin to brown. Cool on wire racks. **Yield:** about 4 dozen.

Honey Cereal Bars

The honey sweetens and holds together these five-ingredient bars. The chocolate-topped cereal treats are great to make for an after-school snack.
—*Ellie Conlon*
Proctor, West Virginia

3/4 cup honey
3/4 cup peanut butter
1 teaspoon vanilla extract
3 cups Special K cereal
1 cup (6 ounces) semisweet chocolate chips, melted

In a large saucepan over medium heat, bring honey and peanut butter to a boil. Remove from the heat; stir in vanilla and cereal. Press into an ungreased 9-in. square pan. Spread chocolate over bars. Chill until firm. **Yield:** 20 bars.

Chocolate Peanut Dream Pie
Chocolate Chip Butter Cookies

Chocolate Coconut Bars

Chocolate Coconut Bars

(Pictured above)

With a middle layer of coconut, these sweet chocolaty treats taste similar to a Mounds candy bar! If time is short, don't wait for the bars to cool—just lay on several thin milk chocolate bars right after you take the pan from the oven and spread them as they melt. —Sharon Skildum
Maple Grove, Minnesota

    2 cups graham cracker crumbs
1/2 cup butter *or* margarine, melted
1/4 cup sugar
    2 cups flaked coconut
    1 can (14 ounces) sweetened condensed milk
1/2 cup chopped pecans
    1 plain chocolate candy bar (7 ounces)
    2 tablespoons creamy peanut butter

Combine the crumbs, butter and sugar. Press into a greased 13-in. x 9-in. x 2-in. baking pan. Bake at 350° for 10 minutes. Meanwhile, in a bowl, combine coconut, milk and pecans; spread over the crust. Bake at 350° for 15 minutes; cool completely. In a small saucepan, melt the candy bar and peanut butter over low heat; spread over bars. Cool until set. **Yield:** about 3 dozen.

Brown Sugar Shortbread

(Pictured on page 195)

These rich cookies have just three ingredients! They're a snap to make for a last-minute gift or when guests will be arriving on short notice. For best results, gradually stir the flour into the dough. —Shirley Gardiner
Clearwater, Manitoba

    1 cup butter (no substitutes), softened
1/2 cup packed brown sugar
2-1/4 cups all-purpose flour

In a mixing bowl, cream butter and brown sugar. Gradually stir in the flour. Turn onto a lightly floured surface

and knead until smooth, about 3 minutes. Pat into a 1/3-in.-thick rectangle measuring 11 in. x 8 in. Cut into 2-in. x 1-in. strips. Place 1 in. apart on ungreased baking sheets. Prick with a fork. Bake at 300° for 25 minutes or until bottom begins to brown. Cool for 5 minutes; remove to a wire rack. **Yield:** 3-1/2 dozen.

Layered Toffee Cake

(Pictured on page 194)

This is a quick and yummy way to dress up a purchased angel food cake. To keep the plate clean while assembling this pretty layered dessert, cut two half circles of waxed paper to place under the bottom layer and remove them after frosting the cake and sprinkling on the toffee.
—Pat Squire, Alexandria, Virginia

    2 cups whipping cream
1/2 cup caramel *or* butterscotch ice cream
      topping
1/2 teaspoon vanilla extract
    1 prepared angel food cake (16 ounces)
    9 Heath candy bars (1.4 ounces *each*), chopped

In a mixing bowl, beat cream just until it begins to thicken. Gradually add the ice cream topping and vanilla, beating until soft peaks form. Cut cake horizontally into three layers. Place the bottom layer on a serving plate; spread with 1 cup cream mixture and sprinkle with 1/2 cup candy bar. Repeat. Place top layer on cake; frost top and sides with remaining cream mixture and sprinkle with the remaining candy bar. Store in the refrigerator. **Yield:** 12-14 servings.

Chocolate Chip Snack Cake

Instant pudding mix and cake mix cut the preparation time for this delicious cake that is loaded with grated chocolate and miniature chocolate chips. I often make it for weekend guests and work luncheons. It always goes over well. —Karen Walker, Sterling, Virginia

    1 package (18-1/4) yellow cake mix
    1 package (3.4 ounces) instant vanilla pudding
      mix
    4 eggs
    1 cup water
1/2 cup vegetable oil
    1 package (12 ounces) miniature semisweet
      chocolate chips
    1 package (4 ounces) German sweet chocolate,
      grated, *divided*
Confectioners' sugar

In a mixing bowl, combine the first five ingredients; beat for 5 minutes. Stir in chocolate chips and half of the grated chocolate. Pour into a greased 13-in. x 9-in. x 2-in. baking pan. Bake at 350° for 45-50 minutes or until a toothpick inserted near the center comes out clean. Sprinkle with remaining grated chocolate while slightly warm. Cool completely. Dust with confectioners' sugar. **Yield:** 12-15 servings.

Quick Little Devils

Enjoy the classic combination of peanut butter and chocolate in these speedy squares. A short list of ingredients, including devil's food cake mix, yields results that are sure to satisfy any sweet tooth.
—Denise Smith
Lusk, Wyoming

1 package (18-1/4 ounces) devil's food cake
   mix
3/4 cup butter *or* margarine, melted
1/3 cup evaporated milk
1 jar (7 ounces) marshmallow creme
3/4 cup peanut butter

In a bowl, combine dry cake mix, butter and milk; mix well. Spread half into a greased 13-in. x 9-in. x 2-in. baking pan. Combine the marshmallow creme and peanut butter; carefully spread over cake mixture to within 1 in. of edge. Drop reserved cake mixture by teaspoonfuls over marshmallow mixture. Bake at 350° for 20-22 minutes or until edges are golden brown. Cool completely. Cut into squares. **Yield:** about 2-1/2 dozen.

Peanut Butter Fudge

Easy Mint Chip Ice Cream

(Pictured below)

You can whip up this easy homemade ice cream in just minutes. Pop it into the freezer overnight to set up—you don't need an ice cream freezer! The minty treat is the favorite of students in my home economics classes.
—Cynthia Kolberg, Syracuse, Indiana

1 can (14 ounces) sweetened condensed milk
2 tablespoons water
1/4 to 1/2 teaspoon peppermint extract
3 to 4 drops green food coloring
2 cups whipping cream, whipped
1 cup (6 ounces) miniature semisweet
   chocolate chips

In a large bowl, combine milk, water, extract and food coloring. Fold in whipped cream and chocolate chips. Pour into a foil-lined 9-in. x 5-in. x 3-in. loaf pan. Cover

and freeze for 6 hours or until firm. Lift out of the pan and remove foil; slice. **Yield:** 8 servings.

Peanut Butter Fudge

(Pictured above)

My sister shared the recipe for this unbelievably easy confection. I prefer using creamy peanut butter for the mouthwatering fudge, but the chunky style works just as well.
—Mrs. Kenneth Rummel, Linglestown, Pennsylvania

2 cups sugar
1/2 cup milk
1-1/3 cups peanut butter
1 jar (7 ounces) marshmallow creme

In a saucepan, bring sugar and milk to a boil; boil for 3 minutes. Add peanut butter and marshmallow creme; mix well. Quickly pour into a buttered 8-in. square pan; chill until set. Cut into squares. **Yield:** 3-4 dozen.

Pecan Pie Bars

I'm always on the lookout for recipes that are quick and easy to prepare. A neighbor shared this fast favorite with me. The chewy bars taste just like pecan pie.
—Kimberly Pearce, Amory, Mississippi

3 eggs
2-1/4 cups packed brown sugar
2 cups self-rising flour*
2 cups chopped pecans
1-1/2 teaspoons vanilla extract

In a mixing bowl, beat eggs. Add brown sugar. Stir in flour until smooth. Add pecans and vanilla (dough will be stiff). Spread into a greased 13-in. x 9-in. x 2-in. baking pan. Bake at 300° for 30-35 minutes or until a toothpick inserted near the center comes out clean. Cool before cutting. **Yield:** 2 dozen. ***Editor's Note:** As a substitute for *each cup* of self-rising flour, place 1-1/2 teaspoons baking powder and 1/2 teaspoon salt in a measuring cup. Add all-purpose flour to equal 1 cup.

Easy Mint Chip Ice Cream

Fancy Fuss-Free Torte
Shortcake Squares
Patriotic Frozen Delight

Patriotic Frozen Delight

(Pictured at left)

My husband and I pick lots of fruit at berry farms in the area and freeze it to enjoy all year long. This frozen dessert showcases both blueberries and strawberries and has a refreshing lemon flavor.
—Bernice Russ
Bladenboro, North Carolina

 ✓ Nutritional Analysis included

    1 can (14 ounces) sweetened condensed milk
1/3 cup lemon juice
    2 teaspoons grated lemon peel
    2 cups (16 ounces) plain yogurt
    2 cups miniature marshmallows
1/2 cup chopped pecans
    1 cup sliced fresh strawberries
    1 cup fresh blueberries

In a bowl, combine milk, lemon juice and peel. Stir in yogurt, marshmallows and pecans. Spread half into an ungreased 11-in. x 7-in. x 2-in. dish. Sprinkle with half of the strawberries and blueberries. Cover with the remaining yogurt mixture; top with remaining berries. Cover and freeze. Remove from the freezer 15-20 minutes before serving. **Yield:** 12 servings. **Nutritional Analysis:** One serving (prepared with fat-free sweetened condensed milk and nonfat yogurt) equals 185 calories, 71 mg sodium, 3 mg cholesterol, 34 gm carbohydrate, 6 gm protein, 4 gm fat. **Diabetic Exchanges:** 1 starch, 1 fruit, 1 fat.

Fancy Fuss-Free Torte

(Pictured at left)

This pretty torte relies on frozen pound cake and canned pie filling. I put toothpicks through the ends to hold the layers in place, then remove them before serving.
—Joan Causey, Greenwood, Arkansas

    1 loaf (10-3/4 ounces) frozen pound cake,
      thawed
    1 can (21 ounces) cherry pie filling *or* flavor of
      your choice
    1 carton (8 ounces) frozen whipped topping,
      thawed
1/2 cup chopped pecans

Split cake into three horizontal layers. Place bottom layer on a serving plate; top with half of the pie filling. Repeat layers. Top with the third cake layer. Frost top and sides with whipped topping. Sprinkle with pecans. Store in the refrigerator. **Yield:** 8-10 servings.

Shortcake Squares

(Pictured at left)

Homemade goodness abounds in this recipe from my aunt. And there isn't any need to shape individual cakes—just cut squares out of the pan and top them with fruit.
—Pat Walter, Pine Island, Minnesota

    2 cups all-purpose flour
    1 tablespoon baking powder
    1 tablespoon sugar
1/2 teaspoon salt
1/3 cup shortening
    1 egg
1/2 cup milk
    2 tablespoons butter *or* margarine, softened
Sweetened raspberries *or* fruit of your choice
Whipped cream

In a bowl, combine flour, baking powder, sugar and salt; cut in shortening until mixture resembles coarse crumbs. In a bowl, whisk the egg and milk until well blended; add to dry ingredients. Stir with a fork just until moistened. Pat into a greased 9-in. square baking pan. Bake at 375° for 18-20 minutes or until golden brown. Cool on a wire rack. Cut into squares. Split each square horizontally and butter the cut sides. Top with berries and whipped cream. **Yield:** 9 servings.

Speedy Brownies

(Pictured below)

Since you "dump" all the ingredients together for these brownies, they take very little time to prepare. There's no mistaking the homemade goodness of a freshly baked batch—they are rich and fudgy!
—Diane Heier
Harwood, North Dakota

    2 cups sugar
1-3/4 cups all-purpose flour
1/2 cup baking cocoa
    1 teaspoon salt
    5 eggs
    1 cup vegetable oil
    1 teaspoon vanilla extract
    1 cup (6 ounces) semisweet chocolate chips

In a mixing bowl, combine the first seven ingredients; beat until smooth. Pour into a greased 13-in. x 9-in. x 2-in. baking pan. Sprinkle with chocolate chips. Bake at 350° for 30 minutes or until a toothpick inserted near the center comes out clean. Cool in pan on a wire rack. **Yield:** about 3 dozen.

Speedy Brownies

Nutty Cracker Delights

(Pictured at right)

I always receive compliments when I serve these crispy snacks. Both sweet and salty, they're fun as appetizers or for munching. They freeze well, too, so you can make them ahead if you're planning a party. —Carla Lee
Devils Lake, North Dakota

  42 Club crackers (2-1/2 inches x 1 inch)
1/2 cup butter *or* margarine
1/2 cup sugar
  1 teaspoon vanilla extract
  1 cup slivered almonds

Place crackers in a single layer in a foil-lined 15-in. x 10-in. x 1-in. baking pan. In a saucepan over medium heat, melt butter. Add sugar; bring to a boil, stirring constantly. Boil for 2 minutes. Remove from the heat; add vanilla. Pour evenly over crackers; sprinkle with nuts. Bake at 350° for 10-12 minutes or until lightly browned. Immediately remove from the pan, cutting between crackers if necessary, and cool on wire racks. Store in an airtight container. **Yield:** 3-1/2 dozen.

Nutty Cracker Delights

Fudgy Buttons

(Pictured below)

Not all of Grandma's recipes are time-consuming—her fast fudge proves it! She stirred up a batch for us grandkids every time we visited. Now I'm carrying on the tasty tradition for my family whenever we want a quick chocolate treat with a peanut butter twist. —Ann August
Roscoe, Illinois

  2 tablespoons butter *or* margarine
1-1/2 teaspoons baking cocoa
1/2 cup confectioners' sugar
1/2 teaspoon milk
  2 tablespoons creamy peanut butter

In a small saucepan, melt the butter; remove from the heat. Add cocoa and mix well. Stir in sugar. Add milk and stir until smooth. Add peanut butter and mix well. Drop by teaspoonfuls onto waxed paper; flatten tops and shape into 1-in. patties. **Yield:** about 1-1/2 dozen.

Fudgy Buttons

Cherry Cheesecake

(Pictured on page 194)

When I worked full-time and needed a quick dessert to take to a potluck or a friend's home, this pie was always the answer. You can substitute a graham cracker crust or use another type of fruit pie filling for a change of pace. Even the chilling time is flexible if you're in a big hurry. —Mary Smith, Bradenton, Florida

  2 packages (one 8 ounces, one 3 ounces) cream cheese, softened
  1 cup confectioners' sugar
  1 carton (8 ounces) frozen whipped topping, thawed
  1 shortbread *or* graham cracker crust (8 *or* 9 inches)
  1 can (21 ounces) cherry pie filling

In a mixing bowl, beat the cream cheese and sugar until smooth. Fold in whipped topping; spoon into crust. Top with pie filling. Refrigerate until serving. **Yield:** 6-8 servings.

Chocolate Mousse Pie

(Pictured on page 195)

Sky-high and scrumptious, this fluffy chocolate delight is super to serve to company. You can put the pie together in a wink—and it'll disappear just as fast! —Lois Mulkey
Sublimity, Oregon

  1 milk chocolate candy bar with almonds (7 ounces)
 16 large marshmallows *or* 1-1/2 cups miniature marshmallows
1/2 cup milk
  2 cups whipping cream, whipped
  1 pastry shell, baked *or* graham cracker *or* chocolate crumb crust (8 or 9 inches)

Place the candy bar, marshmallows and milk in a heavy saucepan; cook over low heat, stirring constantly until chocolate is melted and mixture is smooth. Cool. Fold in whipped cream; pour into crust. Refrigerate for at least 3 hours. **Yield:** 6-8 servings.

Zucchini Chip Cupcakes

(Pictured below)

My three girls love these moist, nut-topped cupcakes even without frosting. They're a great way to use up zucchini, and they freeze well for a quick snack. —Debra Forshee
Stockton, Kansas

1/2 cup butter *or* margarine, softened
1/2 cup vegetable oil
1-3/4 cups sugar
2 eggs
1/2 cup milk
1 teaspoon vanilla extract
2-1/2 cups all-purpose flour
1/4 cup baking cocoa
1 teaspoon baking soda
1/2 teaspoon salt
1/2 teaspoon ground cinnamon
2 cups shredded zucchini
1/4 cup miniature semisweet chocolate chips
1/4 cup chopped pecans

In a mixing bowl, cream the butter, oil and sugar. Add eggs, milk and vanilla; mix well. Combine flour, cocoa, baking soda, salt and cinnamon; add to the creamed mixture. Fold in the zucchini and chocolate chips. Fill greased or paper-lined muffin cups two-thirds full. Top with pecans. Bake at 375° for 20-25 minutes or until top of cupcake springs back when lightly touched. **Yield:** about 2 dozen.

Chewy Peanut Bars

(Pictured below)

Kids will gobble up these chewy peanut-packed treats made with two kinds of crunchy cereal. The sweet coating contrasts nicely with the salty nuts to make these bars a family favorite. They travel well, too.
—Diane Eitreim, Garretson, South Dakota

5 cups cornflakes
3 cups crisp rice cereal
1 cup dry roasted peanuts
1 cup flaked coconut
1 cup light corn syrup
1/2 cup butter *or* margarine
1/2 cup half-and-half cream
1/2 cup sugar

In a large bowl, combine the first four ingredients; set aside. In a heavy saucepan, combine corn syrup, butter, cream and sugar; cook and stir over medium heat until sugar is dissolved. Cook until a candy thermometer reads 234° (soft-ball stage). Pour over cereal mixture and toss to coat. Pat into a greased 13-in. x 9-in. x 2-in. baking pan. Cool before cutting. **Yield:** 2 dozen.

Zucchini Chip Cupcakes
Chewy Peanut Bars

Colorful Popcorn Balls
White Brownies

Colorful Popcorn Balls

(Pictured above)

These easy-to-make, fruit-flavored snacks are a big hit with our four young sons. For extra fun, choose gelatin flavors that match your child's school colors. They're sure to become best-sellers, so it's fortunate this recipe can easily be doubled. —Mary Kay Morris
Cokato, Minnesota

9 cups popped popcorn
1/4 cup butter *or* margarine
1 package (10 ounces) large marshmallows
6 tablespoons fruit-flavored gelatin (any flavor)

Place popcorn in a large bowl; set aside. In a saucepan, melt butter and marshmallows over low heat. Stir in gelatin until dissolved. Pour over popcorn and toss to coat. When cool enough to handle, lightly butter hands and quickly shape mixture into balls. **Yield:** 1 dozen.

Five-Minute Blueberry Pie

If you like the taste of fresh blueberries, you'll love this pie. It's a breeze to whip up so I make it often, especially in summer. —Milda Anderson, Osceola, Wisconsin

1/2 cup sugar
2 tablespoons cornstarch
3/4 cup water
4 cups fresh *or* frozen blueberries, thawed
1 graham cracker crust (9 inches)
Whipped cream, optional

In a saucepan, combine sugar and cornstarch. Stir in wa-

ter until smooth. Bring to a boil over medium heat; cook and stir for 2 minutes. Add blueberries. Cook for 3 minutes, stirring occasionally. Pour into crust. Chill. Garnish with whipped cream if desired. **Yield:** 6-8 servings.

White Brownies

(Pictured above)

I use white chocolate and vanilla chips to give traditional brownies a delicious twist. These moist, chewy snacks will satisfy even the most avid chocolate lover.
—Geneva Mayer, Olney, Illinois

6 squares (1 ounce *each*) white baking
chocolate
1 cup butter *or* margarine
6 eggs
3 cups sugar
2 teaspoons vanilla extract
3 cups all-purpose flour
1 teaspoon baking powder
1/2 teaspoon salt
1 package (12 ounces) vanilla chips
1 cup chopped pecans

In a double boiler or microwave, melt chocolate and butter; cool for 20 minutes. In a mixing bowl, beat eggs and sugar until thick and lemon-colored, about 4 minutes. Gradually beat in melted chocolate and vanilla. Combine flour, baking powder and salt; add to chocolate mixture. Stir in chips and pecans. Pour into a greased 15-in. x 10-in. x 1-in. baking pan. Bake at 350° for 40-45 minutes or until golden brown. Cool on a wire rack. **Yield:** about 4 dozen.

Peanut Butter Squares

These rich bite-size squares taste creamier than store-bought peanut butter cups. Since they're made on the stove, there's no need to turn on the oven. —Val Worthing
Clio, Michigan

    2 cups creamy peanut butter
    1 cup butter *or* margarine, *divided*
    1 package (16 ounces) confectioners' sugar
    3 teaspoons vanilla extract, *divided*
    1 cup semisweet chocolate chips
    1 cup milk chocolate chips

In a saucepan over medium heat, cook and stir peanut butter and 3/4 cup butter until smooth. Remove from the heat; stir in sugar and 2 teaspoons vanilla (mixture will be very thick). Pat into a greased 13-in. x 9-in. x 2-in. baking pan. In a saucepan over low heat, combine chips and remaining butter; cook and stir until chips are melted and mixture is smooth. Remove from the heat; stir in the remaining vanilla. Spread over peanut butter layer. Chill until firm. **Yield:** about 6 dozen.

Caramel Nut Candy

(Pictured below)

You can stir up a batch of these coconut-coated peanut caramel logs in no time, since they're made in the microwave! Both of my sons-in-law rate these as their favorite homemade candies. —Adaline Crabtree
Silverdale, Washington

    28 caramels
    1/4 cup butter *or* margarine
    2 tablespoons half-and-half cream
    1-1/2 cups confectioners' sugar
    1 cup salted peanuts
    2 cups miniature marshmallows
    1 to 2 cups flaked coconut

Place caramels, butter and cream in a 2-qt. microwave-safe dish. Microwave, uncovered, on medium for 2 minutes; stir. Microwave 1-3 minutes more, stirring every minute, until smooth. Stir in sugar until smooth. Add

Caramel Nut Candy

peanuts. Gently fold in marshmallows. Sprinkle the coconut in a 10-in. x 5-in. strip onto two sheets of waxed paper; spoon caramel mixture down the center of coconut. Using the waxed paper, coat caramel with coconut and roll into two 10-in. logs. Discard waxed paper. Wrap logs in plastic wrap and chill for 4 hours. Remove plastic wrap. Cut logs into 1/2-in. slices. Store in an airtight container in the refrigerator. **Yield:** about 4 dozen. **Editor's Note:** This recipe was tested in a 700-watt microwave.

Coconut Chocolate Cake

This heavenly cake is so rich and gooey you wouldn't guess it starts with a boxed cake mix. Although I love making cakes from scratch, mixes are so convenient. It's fun to spruce them up with goodies like coconut, almonds and chocolate chips. —Elsie Shell, Topeka, Indiana

    1 package (18-1/4 ounces) chocolate cake mix
    1-1/2 cups evaporated milk, *divided*
    1-1/2 cups sugar, *divided*
    24 large marshmallows
    1 package (14 ounces) flaked coconut
    1/2 cup butter *or* margarine
    2 cups (12 ounces) semisweet chocolate chips
    1/2 cup slivered almonds, toasted

Mix cake according to package directions, using a 15-in. x 10-in. x 1-in. baking pan. Bake at 350° for 20 minutes or until a toothpick inserted near the center comes out clean. Meanwhile, in a large saucepan, combine 1 cup milk and 1 cup sugar; bring to a boil, stirring occasionally. Remove from the heat. Add marshmallows and stir until melted. Add coconut and mix well. Spread over cake immediately after baking. Cool for 30 minutes. In a small saucepan, combine butter and remaining milk and sugar; bring to a boil. Remove from the heat; stir in the chocolate chips until melted. Spread over coconut layer; sprinkle with almonds. **Yield:** 16-20 servings.

Fast Fruit Cocktail Cake

A convenient can of fruit cocktail is the key to this moist, down-home dessert. It's so comforting served warm with whipped cream or ice cream. —Karen Naramore
Gillette, Wyoming

    1 cup all-purpose flour
    1 cup sugar
    1 teaspoon baking soda
    1 teaspoon salt
    1 can (15-1/4 ounces) fruit cocktail, undrained
    1 egg, beaten
    1/2 cup packed brown sugar
    1/2 cup chopped walnuts
Whipped cream, optional

In a large bowl, combine the first six ingredients; stir until smooth. Pour into a greased 9-in. square baking pan. Combine brown sugar and nuts; sprinkle over top. Bake at 350° for 30-35 minutes or until a toothpick inserted near the center comes out clean. Serve with whipped cream if desired. **Yield:** 9 servings.

Apple Cream Cake

(Pictured at far right)

This is the first dessert Mom would make when apples were ready to pick. One bite of this old-fashioned country cake will have you coming back for more. A boxed cake mix makes it easy, but it tastes like it's made from scratch.
—Antoinette Kilhoffer, Ridgway, Pennsylvania

1 package (18-1/4 ounces) yellow cake mix
3 cups sliced peeled tart apples
1/2 cup chopped walnuts
1/4 cup sugar
1 teaspoon ground cinnamon
1 cup whipping cream
Whipped cream *or* vanilla ice cream, optional

Prepare cake batter according to package directions; pour into a greased 13-in. x 9-in. x 2-in. baking dish. Combine apples, walnuts, sugar and cinnamon; spoon over batter. Pour cream over the top. Bake at 350° for 60-70 minutes or until a toothpick inserted near the center comes out clean. Serve with whipped cream or ice cream if desired. **Yield:** 12-15 servings.

Quick Coconut Cream Pie

(Pictured below)

I've found a way to make coconut cream pie without a lot of fuss and still get terrific flavor. Using a convenient purchased crust, instant pudding and frozen whipped topping, I can enjoy an old-time dessert even when time is short.   —Betty Claycomb, Alverton, Pennsylvania

1 package (5.1 ounces) instant vanilla
    pudding mix
1-1/2 cups cold milk
1 carton (8 ounces) frozen whipped topping,
    thawed, *divided*
3/4 to 1 cup flaked coconut, toasted, *divided*
1 pastry shell, baked *or* graham cracker crust
    (8 *or* 9 inches)

In a mixing bowl, beat pudding and milk on low speed for 2 minutes. Fold in half of the whipped topping and 1/2 to 3/4 cup of coconut. Pour into crust. Spread with

Quick Coconut
Cream Pie

remaining whipped topping; sprinkle with remaining coconut. Chill. **Yield:** 6-8 servings.

Applescotch Sundaes

(Pictured at right)

We're always coming up with new and delicious ways to serve apples. The sweet sauce with tender chunks of apple is heavenly over ice cream, gingerbread or pound cake.   —Jayne Schilling, Salem, Oregon

1 cup packed brown sugar
1/4 cup all-purpose flour
1/4 cup water
1 tablespoon lemon juice
1/2 teaspoon salt
5 cups thinly sliced peeled tart apples
3 tablespoons butter *or* margarine
1 teaspoon vanilla extract
Vanilla ice cream

In a saucepan, combine brown sugar, flour, water, lemon juice and salt; stir until smooth. Bring to a boil; boil and stir for 2 minutes. Add apples; return to a boil. Reduce heat; cover and simmer for 10-12 minutes or until apples are tender. Remove from the heat; add butter and vanilla. Stir until butter is melted. Serve warm or at room temperature over ice cream. Topping can also be served over pound cake or gingerbread. **Yield:** 4-6 servings.

Chocolate Fondue

(Pictured at right)

I combine prepared chocolate frosting with sour cream to create a sweet dip that's perfect with fresh fruit. It's easy to keep the ingredients for this quick dessert on hand for company.   —Jane Franks, Spokane, Washington

1 can (16 ounces) chocolate frosting
1 cup (8 ounces) sour cream
Assorted fresh fruit

Combine the frosting and sour cream; spoon into a serving bowl. Serve with fruit for dipping. Refrigerate any leftovers. **Yield:** about 2-1/2 cups.

Strawberry Parfaits

I whip up this family-pleaser in no time. It forms two layers—a creamier bottom and foamier top—that make it look fancy. But it takes just minutes to blend together.
—Margaret McCoy, Uniontown, Pennsylvania

1 quart vanilla ice cream
1 package (6 ounces) strawberry gelatin
2 cups boiling water

Spoon ice cream into a large bowl. Dissolve gelatin in water; pour over the ice cream and blend well. Pour into parfait glasses. Refrigerate until set, about 1-1/2 hours. **Yield:** 8 servings. **Editor's Note:** An ungreased 11-in. x 7-in. x 2-in. pan may be used instead of the parfait glasses. Cut into squares to serve.

Chocolate Fondue
Apple Cream Cake
Applescotch Sundaes

No-Bake Bars
Peanut Butter Cookies

1 carton (8 ounces) frozen whipped topping, thawed
1 chocolate crumb crust (9 inches)

Melt the chocolate chips in a microwave or double boiler; stir until smooth. In a mixing bowl, beat cream cheese and sugar. Beat in melted chocolate and whipped topping at low speed. Pour into the crust. Cover and refrigerate for at least 4 hours. **Yield:** 6-8 servings.

Peanut Butter Cookies

(Pictured at left)

The old-fashioned taste of these crisp, peanut buttery cookies is irresistible. And they're as quick to make as they are to disappear. I often double the recipe.
—Jessie MacLeod, St. Stephen, New Brunswick

  1/2 cup butter *or* margarine, softened
  1/2 cup sugar
  1/2 cup packed brown sugar
  1/2 cup peanut butter
    1 egg
  1/2 teaspoon vanilla extract
1-1/4 cups all-purpose flour
  1/2 teaspoon baking soda
  1/2 teaspoon baking powder
Additional sugar

In a mixing bowl, cream butter and sugars. Add peanut butter, egg and vanilla; beat until smooth. Combine the flour, baking soda and baking powder; add to the creamed mixture and mix well. For easier shaping, chill the dough for 1 hour. Shape into 1-in. balls; place 2 in. apart on ungreased baking sheets. Flatten each ball by crisscrossing with the tines of a fork dipped in sugar. Bake at 375° for 10-12 minutes or until bottoms are lightly browned and cookies are set. **Yield:** about 4 dozen.

No-Bake Bars

(Pictured above)

This recipe for chewy treats is big on taste but needs little effort. They are handy to make when the weather is hot since the oven never has to be turned on.
—Susie Wingert, Panama, Iowa

  4 cups Cheerios
  2 cups crisp rice cereal
  2 cups dry roasted peanuts
  2 cups M&M's
  1 cup light corn syrup
  1 cup sugar
1-1/2 cups creamy peanut butter
  1 teaspoon vanilla extract

In a large bowl, combine the first four ingredients; set aside. In a saucepan, bring corn syrup and sugar to a boil, stirring frequently. Remove from the heat; stir in peanut butter and vanilla. Pour over cereal mixture and toss to coat evenly. Spread into a greased 15-in. x 10-in. x 1-in. baking pan. Cool. Cut into 3-in. x 3-in. bars. **Yield:** 15 bars.

Festive Fruit Pie

Fresh banana slices, canned pineapple tidbits and chopped pecans dress up the cherry filling in this fuss-free pie. For quicker results, you can substitute a prepared graham cracker crust for the baked pastry shell.
—Dorothy Smith, El Dorado, Arkansas

  1 cup sugar
1/4 cup all-purpose flour
  1 can (21 ounces) cherry pie filling
  1 can (14 ounces) pineapple tidbits, drained
  1 package (3 ounces) orange gelatin
  3 to 4 medium firm bananas, sliced
  1 cup chopped pecans
  2 pastry shells, baked (9 inches)
Whipped topping, optional

In a saucepan, combine sugar and flour. Stir in pie filling and pineapple. Bring to a boil over medium heat; cook and stir for 2 minutes or until thickened. Remove from the heat; stir in gelatin. Cool. Stir in the bananas and pecans. Pour into pie shells. Refrigerate for 3 hours.

No-Bake Chocolate Cheesecake

Cooking and collecting new recipes are my favorite hobbies. Since I discovered this one around 5 years ago, my family's requested it often. It's so creamy and rich you won't believe it has only five ingredients.
—Michelle Overton, Oak Ridge, Tennessee

1-1/2 cups (9 ounces) semisweet chocolate chips
  2 packages (one 8 ounces, one 3 ounces) cream cheese, softened
  1/4 cup sugar

Garnish with whipped topping if desired. **Yield:** 2 pies (6-8 servings each).

Monster Cookies

(Pictured below)

This recipe combines several favorite flavors—peanut butter, butterscotch and chocolate—in one big cookie. Before baking, I like to press a few extra M&M's on top for added color. —Patricia Schroedl, Jefferson, Wisconsin

 1 cup peanut butter
 1/2 cup butter *or* margarine, softened
1-1/4 cups packed brown sugar
 1 cup sugar
 3 eggs
 2 teaspoons baking soda
 1 teaspoon vanilla extract
 4 cups quick-cooking oats
 1 cup M&M's
 1 cup butterscotch chips
 1 cup salted peanuts
 2 cups all-purpose flour

In a large mixing bowl, cream peanut butter, butter and sugars. Add eggs, one at a time, beating well after each addition. Add baking soda and vanilla. Add oats, M&M's, butterscotch chips and peanuts; let stand for 10 minutes. Stir in flour (the dough will be crumbly). Shape 1/4 cupfuls into balls. Place on greased baking sheets, about nine cookies per sheet. Gently flatten cookies. Bake at 325° for 15-18 minutes or until the edges are lightly browned. Remove to wire racks. **Yield:** about 2-1/2 dozen.

Pizza Popcorn

(Pictured below)

Looking for something different—and not sweet—for a bake sale? Whip up this fun popcorn snack. It's lightly spiced with pizza seasonings and very munchable.
 —Sheri Warner, Louisville, Nebraska

2-1/2 quarts popped popcorn
 1/3 cup butter *or* margarine
 1/4 cup grated Parmesan cheese
 1/2 teaspoon garlic salt
 1/2 teaspoon dried oregano
 1/2 teaspoon dried basil
 1/4 teaspoon onion powder
 1/4 teaspoon salt

Place popcorn in an ungreased 13-in. x 9-in. x 2-in. baking pan. Melt butter in a small saucepan; add remaining ingredients. Pour over popcorn and mix well. Bake, uncovered, at 350° for 15 minutes. **Yield:** 2-1/2 quarts.

Pizza Popcorn
Monster Cookies

Brownie Cups
Fluffy Pineapple Pie

Fluffy Pineapple Pie

(Pictured at left)

Refreshing pineapple bits add tropical flair to this fluffy dessert. It is very light, and it isn't overly sweet. Plus it's easy to make. —Ozela Haynes, Emerson, Arkansas

    2 cans (8 ounces *each*) crushed pineapple
    24 large marshmallows
    2 cups whipped topping
    1 graham cracker crust (9 inches)
Maraschino cherries, optional

Drain pineapple, reserving 1/2 cup juice (discard the remaining juice or save for another use). Set the pineapple aside. In a large microwave-safe bowl, combine juice and marshmallows. Microwave on high for 1 minute; stir. Microwave 1 minute longer or until mixture is smooth. Refrigerate for 30 minutes or until slightly thickened and cooled, stirring occasionally. Fold in whipped topping and pineapple. Pour into the crust. Cover and refrigerate for 2 hours or until firm. Garnish with cherries if desired. **Yield:** 6-8 servings. **Editor's Note:** This recipe was tested in a 700-watt microwave.

Frozen Raspberry Pie

Guests' eyes will light up at the sight of this appealing make-ahead pie. The light raspberry flavor is accented by the pleasant crunch of almonds. It's especially refreshing in summer. —Dorothy Latta-McCarty
Lakewood, Colorado

    1 jar (7 ounces) marshmallow creme
    1 cup (8 ounces) raspberry yogurt
    1 cup raspberry sherbet, softened
    2 cups whipped topping
    1/2 cup chopped toasted slivered almonds
    1 graham cracker crust (9 inches)
Additional whipped topping and almonds, optional

Place marshmallow creme in a deep microwave-safe bowl. Microwave, uncovered, on high for 1 minute or until creme puffs and becomes smooth when stirred. Cool to room temperature, stirring several times. Stir in yogurt and sherbet. Fold in the whipped topping and almonds. Pour into the crust. Cover and freeze for 6 hours or overnight. Remove from the freezer 10-15 minutes before serving. Garnish with whipped topping and almonds if desired. **Yield:** 6-8 servings. **Editor's Note:** This recipe was tested in a 700-watt microwave.

Brownie Cups

(Pictured above)

These individual brownie-like cupcakes are studded with pecan pieces. The crinkly tops of these chewy treats are so pretty that they don't need frosting. —Merrill Powers
Spearville, Kansas

    1 cup butter *or* margarine
    1 cup (6 ounces) semisweet chocolate chips
    1 cup chopped pecans
    4 eggs
1-1/2 cups sugar
    1 cup all-purpose flour
    1 teaspoon vanilla extract

In a saucepan over low heat, melt the butter and chocolate chips, stirring until smooth. Cool. Add pecans; stir until well-coated. In a bowl, combine eggs, sugar, flour and vanilla. Fold in chocolate mixture. Fill paper-lined muffin cups two-thirds full. Bake at 325° for 35-38 minutes or until a toothpick inserted near the center comes out clean. **Yield:** about 1-1/2 dozen. **Editor's Note:** This recipe contains no leavening.

Out-of-This-World Pie

Whipped topping conceals a glorious blend of cherries, pineapple, bananas and pecans in this pie. This was one of my father's favorites. I also like to serve it to special company. —Louise Roth, Sterling, Kansas

    1 can (21 ounces) cherry pie filling
    1 can (20 ounces) crushed pineapple,
      undrained
3/4 cup sugar
    1 tablespoon cornstarch

1 package (3 ounces) raspberry gelatin
1/2 teaspoon red food coloring, optional
6 medium firm bananas, sliced
1 cup chopped pecans, toasted
2 pastry shells (9 inches), baked
1 carton (12 ounces) frozen whipped topping, thawed

In a saucepan, combine pie filling and pineapple. Combine sugar and cornstarch; add to fruit mixture. Cook and stir over medium heat until the mixture comes to a boil. Cook 1-2 minutes longer. Remove from the heat. Add the gelatin and food coloring if desired; mix well. Cool. Add bananas and pecans. Pour into the pie shells. Cover with whipped topping. Chill until serving. **Yield:** 2 pies (6-8 servings each).

Lazy-Day Grasshopper Pie

Dazzle dinner guests with this eye-pleasing pie. It's simple to put together the night before. It's light, cool and refreshing—with just the right amount of mint.
—*Carol Severson, Shelton, Washington*

1 jar (7 ounces) marshmallow creme
1/4 cup milk
6 to 8 drops peppermint extract
6 to 8 drops green food coloring
1 cup whipping cream, whipped
1 chocolate crumb crust (9 inches)
Shaved chocolate and additional whipped cream, optional

In a mixing bowl, beat marshmallow creme, milk, extract and food coloring until smooth. Fold in whipped cream. Spoon into the crust. Cover and freeze overnight or until firm. Remove from the freezer 20 minutes before serving. Garnish with shaved chocolate and whipped cream if desired. **Yield:** 6-8 servings.

Lemon Coconut Squares

The tangy lemon flavor of this no-fuss bar dessert is especially delicious on a warm day. It reminds me of selling lemonade on the sidewalk as a little girl.
—*Donna Biddle, Elmira, New York*

1-1/2 cups all-purpose flour
1/2 cup confectioners' sugar
3/4 cup cold butter *or* margarine
4 eggs
1-1/2 cups sugar
1/2 cup lemon juice
1 teaspoon baking powder
3/4 cup flaked coconut

In a bowl, combine flour and confectioners' sugar; cut in the butter until crumbly. Press onto the bottom of a lightly greased 13-in. x 9-in. x 2-in. baking pan. Bake at 350° for 15 minutes. Meanwhile, in a mixing bowl, beat the eggs, sugar, lemon juice and baking powder until well mixed. Pour over the crust; sprinkle coconut evenly over the top. Bake at 350° for 20-25 minutes or un-

til golden brown. Cool on a wire rack. Cut into bars. **Yield:** 4 dozen.

Licorice Cookie Strips

(Pictured below)

If you like the flavor of licorice, you'll love these crispy cookies. When our six children were young, I often made them for lunches or after-school snacks. Flattening the dough logs with a fork gives them a pretty look. Once they're baked, it's a breeze to cut them into strips.
—*Dolores Hurtt, Florence, Montana*

1 cup butter (no substitutes), softened
1 cup sugar
1 cup packed brown sugar
1 egg
2-1/2 cups all-purpose flour
2 teaspoons aniseed
1 teaspoon baking soda
1/2 teaspoon salt
1/2 teaspoon ground cinnamon
1/2 teaspoon ground nutmeg
1/2 cup chopped nuts

In a mixing bowl, cream butter and sugars. Beat in egg. Combine dry ingredients; add to creamed mixture and mix well. Stir in nuts. Divide dough into 10 portions; shape each into a 12-in. log. Place 3 in. apart on ungreased baking sheets. Flatten with a fork to 1/4-in. thickness. Bake at 350° for 8-10 minutes or until golden brown. Cool for 5 minutes; cut diagonally into 1-in. slices. Remove to wire racks to cool completely. **Yield:** about 8 dozen.

Licorice Cookie Strips

Walnut Apple Bundt Cake

At the campground where my husband and I have a trailer, the campers hold an auction of baked goods every Fourth of July. I donated this moist bundt cake one year, and it brought in the highest bid! —Donna Gonda
North Canton, Ohio

    3 eggs
    1 cup vegetable oil
    1 tablespoon vanilla extract
    2 cups shredded peeled tart apples
    2 cups sugar
    3 cups all-purpose flour
    1 tablespoon ground cinnamon
    1 teaspoon baking soda
    1 teaspoon salt
    3/4 teaspoon ground nutmeg
    1/2 teaspoon baking powder
    1 cup chopped walnuts
    2 tablespoons confectioners' sugar
    2 tablespoons brown sugar

In a mixing bowl, beat the eggs, oil and vanilla. Add apples and sugar; beat for 1 minute. Combine the flour, cinnamon, baking soda, salt, nutmeg and baking powder; add to apple mixture until blended. Stir in walnuts. Pour into a greased and floured 10-in. fluted tube pan. Bake at 325° for 50-60 minutes or until a toothpick inserted near the center comes out clean. Cool for 10 minutes; remove from pan to a wire rack to cool completely. Combine the confectioners' sugar and brown sugar; sprinkle over cake. **Yield:** 12-15 servings.

Chocolate Pretzel Rings

(Pictured at far right)

If you like chocolate-covered pretzels, you'll love these simple snacks. They're fun to make anytime of year because you can color-coordinate the M&M's to each holiday.
—Kim Scurio, Carol Stream, Illinois

    48 to 50 pretzel rings *or* mini twists
    1 package (8 ounces) milk chocolate kisses
    1/4 cup M&M's

Place the pretzels on greased baking sheets; place a chocolate kiss in the center of each pretzel. Bake at 275° for 2-3 minutes or until chocolate is softened. Remove from the oven. Place an M&M on each, pressing down slightly so chocolate fills the pretzel. Refrigerate for 5-10 minutes or until chocolate is firm. Store at room temperature. **Yield:** about 4 dozen.

Spiced Oranges

(Pictured at far right)

This refreshing fruit cup makes a delightfully different dessert. The orange sections, spiced with cloves and cinnamon, can be prepared ahead of time and kept in the fridge until serving. —Sue Ross, Casa Grande, Arizona

    1/4 cup red wine *or* grape juice
    3 tablespoons water

    2 tablespoons honey
    1 lemon slice
    1 small cinnamon stick (1 inch)
    1 whole clove
    2 medium oranges, peeled and sectioned
Fresh mint, optional

In a saucepan, combine the first six ingredients. Cook over medium heat until slightly thickened, about 15 minutes. Add the oranges; simmer for 1 minute. Pour into a bowl; refrigerate. Discard lemon, cinnamon and clove before serving. Garnish with mint if desired. **Yield:** 2 servings.

Microwave Truffles

(Pictured at right)

I love to entertain and try new recipes, so I couldn't wait to make these chocolaty confections for the holidays. They're smooth, rich and so pretty topped with pecans. No one will ever guess how easy they are to make.
—Joy Neustel, Jamestown, North Dakota

    1/3 cup finely chopped pecans, toasted, *divided*
    8 squares (1 ounce *each*) semisweet baking
      chocolate
    1/4 cup butter (no substitutes)
    1/4 cup whipping cream
    1/4 teaspoon almond extract

Place 24 small foil candy cups in miniature muffin cups or on a baking sheet. Spoon 1/2 teaspoon pecans into each; set cups and remaining pecans aside. In a 2-qt. microwave-safe bowl, combine chocolate and butter. Microwave at 50% power for 1-1/2 to 2 minutes or until melted. Stir in cream and extract. Beat with an electric mixer until slightly thickened, scraping sides of bowl occasionally. Immediately pour into prepared cups. Top with remaining pecans. Refrigerate until set. **Yield:** 2 dozen. **Editor's Note:** This recipe was tested in an 850-watt microwave.

Cherry Almond Bark

(Pictured at right)

Chock-full of colorful cherries and almonds, this fast-to-fix candy is a Christmas tradition at my home. It's one of my family's favorite munchies while decorating the tree and wrapping presents. —Rita Goshaw
South Milwaukee, Wisconsin

    1 pound white confectionery coating,* broken
      into pieces
    3/4 cup chopped candied cherries
    1/2 cup unblanched whole almonds

In a saucepan over medium-low heat, melt coating, stirring until smooth. Add cherries and almonds; mix well. Spread onto a foil-lined baking sheet. Refrigerate until firm. Break into pieces. **Yield:** about 1 pound. ***Editor's Note:** White confectionery coating is found in the baking section of most grocery stores. It is sometimes labeled "almond bark" or "candy coating" and is often sold in bulk packages of 1 to 1-1/2 pounds.

Chocolate Pretzel Rings
Spiced Oranges
Cherry Almond Bark
Microwave Truffles

Cookies 'n' Cream Fudge

(Pictured at right)

I invented this confection for a bake sale at our children's school. Boy, was it a hit! The crunchy chunks of sandwich cookie soften a bit as the mixture mellows. It's so sweet that one panful serves a crowd. —Laura Lane
Richmond, Virginia

16 chocolate cream-filled sandwich cookies, broken into chunks, *divided*
1 can (14 ounces) sweetened condensed milk
2 tablespoons butter *or* margarine
2-2/3 cups vanilla chips
1 teaspoon vanilla extract

Line an 8-in. square baking pan with aluminum foil; coat with nonstick cooking spray. Place half of the broken cookies in the pan. In a heavy saucepan, combine milk, butter and chips; cook and stir over low heat until chips are melted. Remove from the heat; stir in vanilla. Pour over cookies in pan. Sprinkle with remaining cookies. Cover and refrigerate for at least 1 hour. Cut into squares. **Yield:** 3 dozen.

Cookies 'n' Cream Fudge

Quick Peach Cobbler

This delightful dessert can be stirred up while your oven preheats, so it's a snap to make for unexpected visitors. Canned peaches make it even more convenient. —Linda Emery
Tuckerman, Arkansas

1/2 cup butter *or* margarine, melted
2 cans (15-1/4 ounces *each*) sliced peaches, undrained
1 cup self-rising flour*
1 cup sugar
1 cup milk
1/4 teaspoon ground nutmeg
Ice cream, optional

Pour butter into a 13-in. x 9-in. x 2-in. baking dish. Pour peaches with juice over butter. In a mixing bowl, combine the flour and sugar. Add milk and beat until smooth. Pour batter evenly over peaches. Sprinkle with nutmeg. Bake at 375° for 40 minutes or until golden brown. Serve warm with ice cream if desired. **Yield:** 10-12 servings. ***Editor's Note:** As a substitute for self-rising flour, place 1-1/2 teaspoons baking powder and 1/2 teaspoon salt in a measuring cup. Add all-purpose flour to equal 1 cup.

Blueberry Oat Bars

Oats add crunch to the tasty crust and crumbly topping of these fruity bars. I often bake them for church parties. —Deena Hubler, Jasper, Indiana

1-1/2 cups all-purpose flour
1-1/2 cups quick-cooking oats
1-1/2 cups sugar, *divided*
1/2 teaspoon baking soda
3/4 cup cold butter *or* margarine

2 cups fresh *or* frozen blueberries
2 tablespoons cornstarch
2 tablespoons lemon juice

In a bowl, combine flour, oats, 1 cup sugar and baking soda. Cut in butter until the mixture resembles coarse crumbs. Reserve 2 cups for topping. Press remaining crumb mixture into a greased 13-in. x 9-in. x 2-in. baking pan; set aside. In a saucepan, combine blueberries, cornstarch, lemon juice and remaining sugar. Bring to a boil; boil for 2 minutes, stirring constantly. Spread evenly over the crust. Sprinkle with the reserved crumb mixture. Bake at 375° for 25 minutes or until lightly browned. Cool before cutting. **Yield:** 2-1/2 to 3 dozen.

Crunchy Peanut Bark

Cereal and peanuts add the crunch to these sweet and peanut-buttery treats you can whip up in no time. One batch makes plenty for snacking and sharing. At Christmas, my sister and I add them to trays of homemade candies we give to the customers of the housecleaning service we run. We're often asked for the recipe. —Jan Thoele, Effingham, Illinois

2 pounds white confectionery coating*
1 cup peanut butter
3 cups crisp rice cereal
2 cups dry roasted peanuts
2 cups miniature marshmallows

Place confectionery coating in a large microwave-safe bowl; microwave at 50% power until melted, about 5 minutes. Stir in remaining ingredients. Drop by heaping tablespoonfuls onto waxed paper or divide between two greased 9-in. square pans. **Yield:** 10 dozen. ***Editor's Note:** White confectionery coating is found in the baking section of most grocery stores. It is sometimes labeled "almond bark" or "candy coating" and is often sold in bulk packages of 1 to 1-1/2 pounds. This recipe was tested in an 850-watt microwave.

Pinkston Photography

Chocolate Applesauce Cake

Applesauce adds moistness to this tender cake with a sweet chocolate and nut topping. It's a breeze to make and perfect for picnics.
—Sue Braunschweig, Delafield, Wisconsin

✓ Nutritional Analysis included

1/2 cup butter *or* margarine, softened
1-1/2 cups sugar
  2 eggs
  2 cups all-purpose flour
  2 tablespoons baking cocoa
1-1/2 teaspoons baking soda
  1/2 teaspoon salt
  1/2 teaspoon ground cinnamon
  2 cups unsweetened applesauce
TOPPING:
  1 cup (6 ounces) semisweet chocolate chips
  1/2 cup chopped pecans
  2 tablespoons sugar

In a mixing bowl, cream butter and sugar. Add the eggs, one at a time, beating well after each addition. Combine dry ingredients; add to the creamed mixture alternately with applesauce. Pour into a greased 13-in. x 9-in. x 2-in. baking pan. Combine topping ingredients; sprinkle over batter. Bake at 350° for 30-35 minutes or until a toothpick inserted near the center comes out clean. **Yield:** 16 servings. **Nutritional Analysis:** One serving (prepared with margarine and egg substitute) equals 283 calories, 274 mg sodium, trace cholesterol, 44 gm carbohydrate, 4 gm protein, 12 gm fat. **Diabetic Exchanges:** 2 starch, 2 fat, 1 fruit.

Berries 'n' Cream

This couldn't be a simpler or more delicious dessert. It's also versatile—you can drizzle the delightful dressing over strawberries or use it as a fruit dip for a summery snack.
—Lucille Terry, Frankfort, Kentucky

  1 cup (8 ounces) sour cream
  1/2 cup packed brown sugar
  2 pints fresh strawberries, hulled

In a small bowl, combine sour cream and brown sugar; stir until smooth. Chill until serving. Use as a dip for whole strawberries or drizzle over a bowl of sliced berries. Store in the refrigerator. **Yield:** 1-1/4 cups.

Chewy Date Nut Bars

You'll need just six ingredients to bake up these chewy bars chock-full of walnuts and dates. They are my husband's favorite snack, and he loves to take them to work.
—Linda Hutmacher, Teutopolis, Illinois

  1 package (18-1/4 ounces) yellow cake mix
  3/4 cup packed brown sugar
  3/4 cup butter *or* margarine, melted
  2 eggs
  2 cups chopped dates
  2 cups chopped walnuts

In a mixing bowl, combine dry cake mix and brown sugar. Add butter and eggs; beat on medium speed for 2 minutes. Combine dates and walnuts; stir into batter (the batter will be stiff). Spread into a greased 13-in. x 9-in. x 2-in. baking pan. Bake at 350° for 35-45 minutes or until edges are golden brown. Cool on a wire rack for 10 minutes. Run a knife around sides of pan to loosen; cool completely before cutting. **Yield:** 3 dozen.

Chocolate Caramel Cookies

(Pictured below)

This is my favorite recipe for bake sales and bazaars. Each delightfully sweet chocolate cookie has a fun caramel surprise in the middle, thanks to a Rolo candy. Dipped in pecans before baking, they look so nice that they sell in a hurry.
—Melissa Vannoy, Childress, Texas

  1 cup butter (no substitutes), softened
  1 cup plus 1 tablespoon sugar, *divided*
  1 cup packed brown sugar
  2 eggs
  2 teaspoons vanilla extract
2-1/2 cups all-purpose flour
  3/4 cup baking cocoa
  1 teaspoon baking soda
  1 cup chopped pecans, *divided*
  1 package (13 ounces) Rolo candies

In a mixing bowl, cream butter, 1 cup sugar and brown sugar. Add eggs and vanilla; mix well. Combine flour, cocoa and baking soda; add to the creamed mixture and beat just until combined. Stir in 1/2 cup pecans. Shape dough by tablespoonfuls around each candy. In a small bowl, combine remaining pecans and sugar; dip each cookie halfway. Place with nut side up on ungreased baking sheets. Bake at 375° for 7-10 minutes or until top is slightly cracked. Cool for 3 minutes; remove to wire racks to cool completely. **Yield:** about 5 dozen.

Chocolate Caramel Cookies

Sweet Tooth Treats

Sweet Tooth Treats

(Pictured above)

I remember Mom would have these yummy snacks waiting for us kids when we got home from school. Now I stir up these homemade treats for my husband and two daughters. They love the combination of peanut butter and chocolate...and I love that they don't keep me in the kitchen all day. —Tina Jacobs, Wantage, New Jersey

   1 cup peanut butter
1/2 cup light corn syrup
1/2 cup confectioners' sugar
1/4 cup shredded coconut
   2 cups Cheerios
   1 cup (6 ounces) semisweet chocolate chips
   1 tablespoon shortening

In a bowl, combine peanut butter, corn syrup, sugar and coconut until blended. Stir in cereal. Shape into 1-1/2-in. balls. In a small saucepan over medium heat, melt chocolate chips and shortening. Dip balls halfway into chocolate; place on waxed paper-lined baking sheets to harden. **Yield:** 2-1/2 dozen.

S'more Clusters

(Pictured at far right)

Our two sons love to help me break up the chocolate and graham crackers for these tasty treats—that way, they can tell their friends they made them! The chocolaty clusters taste just like s'mores, but without the gooey mess. It's difficult to eat just one. —Kathy Schmittler, Sterling Heights, Michigan

   6 milk chocolate candy bars (1.55 ounces *each*), broken into pieces
1-1/2 teaspoons vegetable oil
   2 cups miniature marshmallows
   8 whole graham crackers, broken into bite-size pieces

In a large microwave-safe bowl, toss chocolate and oil. Microwave, uncovered, at 50% power for 1-1/2 to 2 minutes or until chocolate is melted, stirring once. Stir in marshmallows and graham crackers. Spoon into paper-

lined muffin cups (about 1/3 cup each). Refrigerate for 1 hour or until firm. **Yield:** 1 dozen. **Editor's Note:** This recipe was tested in an 850-watt microwave.

Banana Pudding Dessert

I blend cream cheese, sweetened condensed milk and whipped topping into instant pudding, then layer this creamy concoction with vanilla wafers and sliced bananas. Served in a pretty glass bowl, the rich results make for a fancy yet fuss-free dessert. —Edna Perry, Rice, Texas

   1 package (8 ounces) cream cheese, softened
   1 can (14 ounces) sweetened condensed milk
   1 cup cold milk
   1 package (3.4 ounces) instant vanilla pudding mix
   1 carton (8 ounces) frozen whipped topping, thawed
52 vanilla wafers
   4 medium firm bananas, sliced

In a mixing bowl, beat the cream cheese until smooth. Beat in condensed milk; set aside. In another bowl, whisk milk and pudding mix; add to cream cheese mixture. Fold in whipped topping. Arrange a third of the vanilla wafers in a 2-1/2-qt. glass bowl. Top with a third of the bananas and pudding mixture. Repeat layers twice. Refrigerate until serving. **Yield:** 10-12 servings.

Dipped Peanut Butter Cookies

(Pictured at right)

Baking mix makes these soft, moist cookies a snap to stir up, yet they're pretty enough for parties. I'm often asked to bring them to wedding and baby showers, and they're popular around the holidays, too. —Stephanie DeLoach, Magnolia, Arkansas

   1 cup peanut butter
   1 can (14 ounces) sweetened condensed milk
   1 egg
   1 teaspoon vanilla extract
   2 cups biscuit/baking mix
3/4 to 1 pound milk chocolate confectionery coating*
   1 tablespoon shortening

In a mixing bowl, combine the peanut butter, milk, egg and vanilla; beat until smooth. Stir in biscuit mix; mix well. Cover and refrigerate for 1 hour. Shape into 1-in. balls and place 1 in. apart on ungreased baking sheets. Flatten each ball with the bottom of a glass. Bake at 350° for 8-10 minutes or until golden brown. Cool on wire racks. In a small saucepan over low heat, melt confectionery coating and shortening. Dip each cookie halfway into chocolate; shake off excess. Place on waxed paper-lined baking sheets to harden. **Yield:** about 5 dozen. ***Editor's Note:** Milk chocolate confectionery coating is found in the baking section of most grocery stores. It is sometimes labeled "candy coating" and is often sold in bulk packages of 1 to 1-1/2 pounds.

Nutmeg Sugar Crisps

(Pictured below)

My grandma shared her recipe for these old-fashioned sugar cookies. They are light, crunchy and so delicious.

—*Kristi Thorpe, Portland, Oregon*

    1 cup butter (no substitutes), softened
    3/4 cup sugar
    1/2 cup confectioners' sugar
    1 egg
    1 teaspoon vanilla extract
2-1/2 cups all-purpose flour
    1/2 teaspoon baking soda
    1/2 teaspoon cream of tartar
    1/4 to 1/2 teaspoon ground nutmeg
    1/8 teaspoon salt

In a mixing bowl, cream butter and sugars. Beat in egg and vanilla; mix well. Combine the flour, baking soda, cream of tartar, nutmeg and salt; add to the creamed mixture and mix well. Refrigerate for 1 hour. Shape into 3/4-in. balls; place 2 in. apart on greased baking sheets. Flatten with a glass dipped in sugar. Bake at 350° for 10-12 minutes or until lightly browned. Cool on wire racks. **Yield:** about 6 dozen.

Jewel Nut Bars

(Pictured below)

These colorful bars, with eye-catching candied cherries and the crunchy goodness of mixed nuts, are certain to become a holiday favorite. I get lots of compliments on the combination of sweet and salty flavors.

—*Joyce Fitt*
Listowel, Ontario

1-1/4 cups all-purpose flour
    2/3 cup packed brown sugar, *divided*
    3/4 cup cold butter *or* margarine
    1 egg
    1/2 teaspoon salt
1-1/2 cups salted mixed nuts
1-1/2 cups halved green and red candied cherries
    1 cup (6 ounces) semisweet chocolate chips

In a bowl, combine flour and 1/3 cup brown sugar; cut in butter until mixture resembles coarse crumbs. Press into a lightly greased 13-in. x 9-in. x 2-in. baking pan. Bake at 350° for 15 minutes. Meanwhile, in a mixing bowl, beat egg. Add salt and remaining brown sugar. Stir in the nuts, cherries and chocolate chips. Spoon evenly over crust. Bake at 350° for 20 minutes. Cool on a wire rack. Cut into bars. **Yield:** 3 dozen.

Nutmeg Sugar Crisps
Jewel Nut Bars
Dipped Peanut Butter Cookies
S'more Clusters

Chapter 14

⏱ *Fast, Delicious...and Nutritious*

IF you're counting calories or trying to reduce sugar or fat in your diet (and doing all this while keeping an eye on the clock), these fast-to-fix dishes will fit right in.

That's because each recipe is lower in fat, sugar and salt, making them perfect for today's healthy lifestyle. Plus, this chapter provides some helpful hints for making your favorite foods a little lighter.

Anyone on a special diet—and even those who aren't—will enjoy these delicious nutritious dishes.

(For a complete listing of dishes that are lower in fat, sugar and salt, refer to the Nutritional Analysis Recipes Index on page 354.)

GOOD FOOD FAST. Cinnamon Peaches (p. 223) and Chocolate Mousse Frosting (p. 222).

Fish and
Veggies Primavera

All recipes in this chapter
include Nutritional Analysis

Fish and Veggies Primavera

(Pictured above)

The most time-consuming thing about this recipe is chopping the vegetables—and that takes just seconds. Broccoli, cauliflower and carrots perk up the seafood entree, which goes from oven to table in less than half an hour. —Annette White, Whittier, California

    1 tablespoon margarine, melted
    4 fresh *or* frozen orange roughy fillets
      (6 ounces *each*), thawed
    2 tablespoons lemon juice
Pinch pepper
    1 garlic clove, minced
    1 tablespoon olive *or* vegetable oil
1-1/2 cups broccoli florets
    1 cup cauliflowerets
    1 cup julienned carrots
    1 cup sliced fresh mushrooms
  1/2 cup sliced celery
  1/4 teaspoon dried basil
  1/4 teaspoon salt
  1/4 cup grated Parmesan cheese

Place margarine in a 13-in. x 9-in. x 2-in. baking dish; add fish and turn to coat. Sprinkle with lemon juice and pepper. Bake, uncovered, at 450° for 5 minutes. Meanwhile, in a large skillet over medium heat, saute garlic in oil. Add the next seven ingredients; stir-fry until vegetables are crisp-tender, about 2-3 minutes. Spoon over the fish; sprinkle with cheese. Bake, uncovered, at 450° for 3-5 minutes or until fish flakes easily with a fork. **Yield:** 4 servings. **Nutritional Analysis:** One serving equals 232 calories, 434 mg sodium, 39 mg cholesterol, 7 gm carbohydrate, 29 gm protein, 10 gm fat. **Diabetic Exchanges:** 4 very lean meat, 1-1/2 vegetable, 1 fat. **Editor's Note:** Cod or haddock fillets may be substituted for the orange roughy.

Luncheon Salad

When our garden is producing lots of tomatoes and cucumbers, this refreshing main-dish salad is a favorite of ours. It's a real lifesaver on hot days when I don't want to turn on the oven. —Rhonda Burns, Hopkins, Michigan

    2 medium tomatoes, cubed
    1 medium cucumber, cubed
    1 cup cubed fully cooked low-fat ham
    1 cup cubed reduced-fat Swiss cheese
    4 green onions, sliced
    6 tablespoons fat-free ranch salad dressing

In a large bowl, combine the first five ingredients. Add dressing and toss. Serve immediately. **Yield:** 6 servings. **Nutritional Analysis:** One 1-cup serving equals 112 calories, 551 mg sodium, 19 mg cholesterol, 10 gm carbohydrate, 12 gm protein, 2 gm fat. **Diabetic Exchanges:** 2 vegetable, 1 lean meat.

Spinach Rice Casserole

This blend of spinach, mushrooms, brown rice and cottage cheese is hearty enough to serve as a main dish. The creamy casserole gets nice crunch from sunflower kernels sprinkled on top.
—Kathleen Taugher
East Troy, Wisconsin

2 cups sliced fresh mushrooms
1 cup chopped onion
1 garlic clove, minced
1 package (10 ounces) frozen chopped
   spinach, thawed and drained
1 tablespoon all-purpose flour
Egg substitute equivalent to 1 egg
2 cups low-fat cottage cheese
2 cups cooked instant brown rice
2 tablespoons grated Parmesan cheese, *divided*
1/2 teaspoon dried thyme

Good Food That's Good for You

WHEN TIME'S SHORT and your family's hungry, you want to put a tasty meal on the table fast. But you'd like it to be nutritious, too. You can do both, at any time of day.

Better Breakfasts
- Blend up a breakfast shake from fresh fruit, low-fat yogurt and skim milk.
- When you're cooking pancakes or French toast, nonstick cooking spray can be substituted for butter or oil. Serve with light syrup or spreadable fruit.
- Occasionally use egg substitute in a vegetable omelet, then top it with salsa for an eye-opening kick.

Lighter Lunches
- Vary sandwiches with meats that are lower in fat, such as grilled chicken, turkey breast and turkey ham. Add more lettuce, cucumbers, tomatoes and alfalfa sprouts for extra crunch.
- In tuna salad sandwiches, use tuna packed in water and either light or fat-free mayonnaise. (Fat-free ranch salad dressing also makes a tasty substitute for mayonnaise.) Add chopped celery or apple for a crunchy change of pace.

Sensible Suppers
- Consider low-fat cottage cheese and chives, low-fat canned chili and chopped onions, or black beans and salsa as a baked-potato topping.
- Grill colorful kabobs. On a skewer, alternate chunks of fresh vegetables (green peppers, mushrooms, onions, new potatoes) with shrimp, chunks of lean beef, chicken or other lean meats.
- Warm tortillas in the microwave and fill them with fat-free refried beans, salsa, shredded lettuce and tomato. Top with a dollop of nonfat sour cream or nonfat plain yogurt.

1/4 teaspoon pepper
2 tablespoons sunflower kernels

In a nonstick skillet that has been coated with nonstick cooking spray, saute mushrooms, onion and garlic until tender. Add spinach. In a large bowl, combine the flour and egg substitute until smooth. Stir in cottage cheese, rice, 1 tablespoon Parmesan cheese, thyme, pepper and mushroom mixture; mix well. Transfer to an 11-in. x 7-in. x 2-in. baking dish that has been coated with nonstick cooking spray. Sprinkle with sunflower kernels and remaining Parmesan cheese. Bake, uncovered, at 350° for 30 minutes or until heated through. **Yield:** 12 servings. **Nutritional Analysis:** One 1/2-cup serving equals 97 calories, 175 mg sodium, 6 mg cholesterol, 12 gm carbohydrate, 8 gm protein, 2 gm fat. **Diabetic Exchanges:** 1 starch, 1/2 meat.

Salt Substitute

I keep this nicely flavored blend in a salt shaker on the back of my stove. I use a teaspoon of it in almost everything I cook, from meat loaf to stew. It's perfect for people on restricted diets as well as those who are simply cutting back on salt.   —Myrta Sweet, Wildwood, Florida

1 tablespoon garlic powder
1 teaspoon *each* dried parsley flakes, basil,
   marjoram and thyme
1 teaspoon rubbed sage
1 teaspoon pepper
1 teaspoon onion powder
1/2 teaspoon ground mace
1/2 teaspoon cayenne pepper

In a small bowl, combine all ingredients. Use to season pork, chicken or fish. Store in an airtight container. **Yield:** 1/4 cup. **Nutritional Analysis:** 1/4 teaspoon equals 1 calorie, trace sodium, trace cholesterol, trace carbohydrate, trace protein, trace fat. **Diabetic Exchange:** Free.

Black-Eyed Pea Salad

A can of black-eyed peas is the main ingredient in this side dish that comes together fast. It tastes and looks fresh, thanks to the peppers, onions, tomato and celery.
—Carol Forcum, Marion, Illinois

1 can (15-1/2 ounces) black-eyed peas, rinsed
   and drained
1 cup chopped celery
1/2 cup chopped green pepper
1/2 cup chopped sweet red pepper
1/4 cup chopped green onions
1 large tomato, seeded and chopped
2 cups shredded lettuce
2/3 cup fat-free ranch salad dressing

In a large bowl, combine all ingredients; toss lightly. Serve immediately. **Yield:** 16 servings. **Nutritional Analysis:** One 1/2-cup serving equals 45 calories, 194 mg sodium, 0 cholesterol, 9 gm carbohydrate, 2 gm protein, trace fat. **Diabetic Exchanges:** 1/2 starch, 1/2 vegetable.

Black Beans and Rice

(Pictured below)

I often serve this quick skillet side dish to delighted guests. It tastes so delicious it's hard to believe it's good for you. And it's hearty enough to serve as a meatless main dish.
—*Bonnie Baumgardner, Sylva, North Carolina*

1 medium onion, chopped
1 medium green pepper, chopped
1 medium sweet red pepper, chopped
1 garlic clove, minced
1/2 teaspoon dried basil
1/4 teaspoon pepper
1 tablespoon tomato sauce
1 can (15 ounces) black beans, rinsed and drained
1 cup cooked long grain rice
1 tablespoon cider *or* red wine vinegar
1/4 cup shredded reduced-fat cheddar cheese

In a nonstick skillet that has been coated with nonstick cooking spray, saute the onion, green and red peppers, garlic, basil and pepper until tender. Stir in tomato sauce. Add beans, rice and vinegar; heat through. Transfer to a serving dish; sprinkle with cheese. **Yield:** 4 servings.

Nutritional Analysis: One 1-cup serving equals 175 calories, 396 mg sodium, 1 mg cholesterol, 32 gm carbohydrate, 10 gm protein, 2 gm fat. **Diabetic Exchanges:** 2 starch, 1 vegetable.

Light Carrot Cake

Allspice and cinnamon give wonderful spicy flavor to this appealing cake. It's so moist and delicious that it doesn't taste like it's good for you—but it is! —*Ruth Hastings Louisville, Illinois*

1/2 cup sugar
1/3 cup vegetable oil
1/3 cup orange juice concentrate
3 egg whites
1 cup all-purpose flour
1 teaspoon baking powder
1 teaspoon ground cinnamon
1/2 teaspoon ground allspice
1/4 teaspoon baking soda
1/8 teaspoon salt
1 cup grated carrots
2 teaspoons confectioners' sugar

In a mixing bowl, combine the first four ingredients; beat for 30 seconds. Combine flour, baking powder, cinnamon, allspice, baking soda and salt; add to the orange juice mixture and mix well. Stir in carrots. Pour into an 8-in. square baking pan that has been coated with nonstick cooking spray. Bake at 350° for 30 minutes or until a toothpick inserted near the center comes out clean. Cool; dust with confectioners' sugar. **Yield:** 9 servings. **Nutritional Analysis:** One serving equals 196 calories, 145 mg sodium, 0 cholesterol, 28 gm carbohydrate, 3 gm protein, 8 gm fat. **Diabetic Exchanges:** 2 starch, 1 fat.

Chocolate Mousse Frosting

(Pictured above right and on page 219)

This smooth, fluffy frosting is a real treat for cake lovers on a restricted diet—plus everybody else. Another way I like to serve it is layered in a parfait glass with cubed angel food cake or fresh fruit and topped with additional whipped topping. It makes a pretty dessert.
—*Kim Marie Van Rheenen, Mendota, Illinois*

1 cup cold skim milk
1 package (1.4 ounces) sugar-free instant chocolate fudge pudding mix
1 carton (8 ounces) frozen light whipped topping, thawed
1 prepared angel food cake

In a mixing bowl, beat milk and pudding mix on low speed for 2 minutes. Fold in whipped topping. Frost the cake. **Yield:** 3-1/2 cups. **Nutritional Analysis:** 1/4 cup of frosting equals 56 calories, 94 mg sodium, 0 cholesterol, 7 gm carbohydrate, 1 gm protein, 2 gm fat. **Diabetic Exchanges:** 1/2 starch, 1/2 fat. **Editor's Note:** The chocolate mousse would also make a good dip for fresh strawberries or other fruit.

Black Beans and Rice

Cinnamon Peaches
Chocolate Mousse Frosting

Cinnamon Peaches

(Pictured above and on page 218)

When time's at a premium, I just jazz up canned peaches with cinnamon and lemon juice. Still warm from the oven or chilled, the tangy results taste terrific as a side dish or a light and fruity dessert.
—Sue Ross, Casa Grande, Arizona

1 can (16 ounces) peach halves in natural juices
1 cinnamon stick (4 inches)
1 to 2 tablespoons lemon juice

Drain peaches, reserving 1/4 cup juice (discard remaining juice or save for another use). Place peaches with cut side down in an ungreased shallow 1-qt. baking dish. Cut a slit in each. Break cinnamon stick into pieces; place in slits. Combine the lemon juice and reserved peach juice; pour over peaches. Bake, uncovered, at 350° for 20-25 minutes or until heated through. **Yield:** 6 servings. **Nutritional Analysis:** One serving equals 34 calories, 3 mg sodium, 0 cholesterol, 9 gm carbohydrate, trace protein, trace fat. **Diabetic Exchange:** 1/2 fruit.

Trim Fat from Your Diet with Turkey

WATCHING your intake of fat? Turkey has fewer calories and less fat and cholesterol than equal amounts of chicken, beef, lamb or pork. So consider substituting it from time to time for the meat in favorite recipes.

Ground turkey, for example, is at least 50 percent lower in fat than other ground meats. It blends easily with spices and seasonings, so it works especially well in chili, stew, lasagna and Mexican dishes. (And see how ground turkey breast is used in the recipe for Pronto Pita Pizzas on page 232.)

The National Turkey Federation offers these additional ways to add diversity and new flavor to everyday meals while also trimming fat:

- Prepare turkey bacon or sausage as part of a hearty breakfast.
- Brown Italian or regular turkey sausage to use as a pizza topping.
- Use turkey breast when making fajitas, grilled kabobs and stir-fry dishes.
- Serve turkey franks in your children's favorite hot dog recipes.
- Layer deli-sliced turkey breast and turkey ham in sandwiches.

Salsa Tuna Salad

(Pictured at right)

Flavorful salsa perks up this fresh-tasting tuna salad. Bright corn and green pepper add pretty color to the mixture. Served on a bed of lettuce, it makes a great light lunch.
—Jennifer Harris, Skellytown, Texas

1/2 cup plain nonfat yogurt
1/4 cup salsa
1/4 teaspoon pepper
1 can (12 ounces) water-packed low-sodium tuna, drained
1 cup frozen corn, thawed
1 cup chopped green pepper
Lettuce leaves, optional

In a bowl, combine yogurt, salsa and pepper; mix well. Add tuna, corn and green pepper; toss to coat. Serve in a lettuce-lined bowl if desired. **Yield:** 6 servings. **Nutritional Analysis:** One 1/2-cup serving equals 122 calories, 153 mg sodium, 11 mg cholesterol, 10 gm carbohydrate, 19 gm protein, 1 gm fat. **Diabetic Exchanges:** 2 very lean meat, 1/2 starch, 1/2 vegetable.

Salsa Tuna Salad

Blender Bran Muffins

Bananas complement the hearty whole wheat flavor of these moist muffins. Using a blender to mix the ingredients makes them fun and fast. —Frances Ward
St. Louis, Missouri

2 medium ripe bananas
Egg substitute equivalent to 1 egg
3/4 cup whole wheat flour
1/2 cup skim milk
1/4 cup vegetable oil
1/4 cup apple juice concentrate
1 teaspoon baking soda
1/2 teaspoon vanilla extract
1-1/4 cups All-Bran
1/2 cup raisins, optional

Cut bananas into quarters; place in a blender. Add the next seven ingredients; cover and process until smooth. Blend in cereal. Stir in raisins if desired. Coat muffin cups with nonstick cooking spray; fill half full. Bake at 400° for 16-18 minutes or until muffins test done. **Yield:** 1 dozen. **Nutritional Analysis:** One muffin (prepared without raisins) equals 124 calories, 223 mg sodium, trace cholesterol, 20 gm carbohydrate, 4 gm protein, 5 gm fat. **Diabetic Exchanges:** 1 fat, 1 starch. **Editor's Note:** Paper-lined muffin cups are not recommended for this recipe.

Mexican Pizzas

When I need a quick and easy dinner, I make these satisfying pizzas that capture the flavor of Mexico. Piled high with zesty ingredients, the tortillas are a snap to prepare and taste great. —Katherine Jones, Renton, Washington

4 fat-free flour tortillas (12 inches)
1 can (16 ounces) fat-free refried beans
1 cup salsa
2 medium plum tomatoes, diced
1 can (4 ounces) chopped green chilies, drained
1/2 cup chopped green pepper
1/4 cup chopped onion
1 can (2-1/4 ounces) sliced ripe olives, drained
1 cup reduced-fat shredded cheddar cheese

Place tortillas on two ungreased baking sheets; spread with beans. Layer with salsa, tomatoes, chilies, green pepper, onion, olives and cheese. Bake at 350° for 10 minutes or until the cheese is melted. **Yield:** 4 servings. **Nutritional Analysis:** One serving equals 359 calories, 1,665 mg sodium, 20 mg cholesterol, 52 gm carbohydrate, 19 gm protein, 8 gm fat. **Diabetic Exchanges:** 3 starch, 1-1/2 meat, 1 vegetable.

Tropical Tuna Salad

Slice a few veggies, open a couple of cans and you can put together this hearty salad in just seconds. The oranges and pineapple add a hint of sweetness, while the water chestnuts add crunch. —Helen Myhre
Kailua-Kona, Hawaii

1 bunch romaine, torn
2 cups canned unsweetened pineapple chunks
1/2 cup sliced green onions
1 can (12 ounces) water-packed low-sodium tuna, drained

1 can (11 ounces) mandarin oranges in light
  syrup, drained
1 can (8 ounces) sliced water chestnuts,
  drained
1/2 cup fat-free mayonnaise
4 teaspoons light soy sauce
1/2 teaspoon lemon juice

In a large bowl, toss romaine, pineapple, onions, tuna, oranges and water chestnuts. In a small bowl, combine mayonnaise, soy sauce and lemon juice; pour over salad and toss. **Yield:** 6 servings. **Nutritional Analysis:** One serving equals 205 calories, 303 mg sodium, 10 mg cholesterol, 32 gm carbohydrate, 19 gm protein, 1 gm fat. **Diabetic Exchanges:** 2 very lean meat, 1-1/2 vegetable, 1-1/2 fruit.

Zippy Orange Chicken

Try one bite of this coated chicken—you'll taste the zesty orange flavor first, then the cayenne zip. The coating is simple to make, and it keeps the chicken moist and flavorful.
—Marie Hoyer, Hodgenville, Kentucky

4 boneless skinless chicken breast halves
  (1 pound)
2 tablespoons orange juice concentrate
1/3 cup seasoned bread crumbs
1/2 teaspoon paprika
1/2 teaspoon salt
1/8 teaspoon pepper
Pinch cayenne pepper *or* to taste

Prick chicken with a fork; brush with orange juice concentrate. Combine the remaining ingredients in a large resealable plastic bag; add chicken, one piece at a time, and shake to coat. Place chicken in an 11-in. x 7-in. x 2-in. baking dish that has been coated with nonstick cooking spray. Bake, uncovered, at 400° for 25-30 minutes or until juices run clear. **Yield:** 4 servings. **Nutritional Analysis:** One serving equals 193 calories, 620 mg sodium, 73 mg cholesterol, 11 gm carbohydrate, 28 gm protein, 3 gm fat. **Diabetic Exchanges:** 4 very lean meat, 1/2 starch.

Apple Butter French Toast

I give a special treatment to my baked French toast slices. For a pleasant sweetness and nutty crunch, I top them with cinnamony apple butter and toasted slivered almonds.
—Mavis Diment, Marcus, Iowa

6 slices French bread (1 inch thick)
Egg substitute equivalent to 3 eggs
2/3 cup skim milk
2 tablespoons apple juice concentrate
1/2 teaspoon vanilla extract
2 tablespoons slivered almonds, toasted
1/4 cup apple butter
1/8 teaspoon ground cinnamon

Place bread in a 9-in. square baking dish that has been coated with nonstick cooking spray. In a bowl, combine egg substitute, milk, apple juice concentrate and vanilla. Pour over bread and turn to coat. Cover and refrigerate for 2 hours or overnight. Remove from the refrigerator 30 minutes before baking. Bake, uncovered, at 350° for 30-35 minutes or until edges are golden brown. Sprinkle with almonds. Combine apple butter and cinnamon; serve with French toast. **Yield:** 6 servings. **Nutritional Analysis:** One serving equals 154 calories, 224 mg sodium, trace cholesterol, 23 gm carbohydrate, 8 gm protein, 3 gm fat. **Diabetic Exchanges:** 1-1/2 starch, 1 fat.

Sherbet Dessert

(Pictured below)

This refreshing summer dessert was served at a baby shower I attended. It was so delicious I asked the hostess to share her secret. I couldn't believe it was made with only three ingredients, and was low-fat as a bonus.
—Shirley Colvin, Tremonton, Utah

1/2 gallon orange sherbet *or* flavor of your
  choice,* softened
1 package (10 ounces) frozen sweetened
  raspberries, thawed
2 medium ripe bananas, mashed

Place the sherbet in a large bowl; stir in raspberries and bananas. Freeze until firm. **Yield:** 18 servings. **Nutritional Analysis:** One 1/2-cup serving equals 150 calories, 40 mg sodium, 4 mg cholesterol, 34 gm carbohydrate, 1 gm protein, 2 gm fat. **Diabetic Exchanges:** 1 starch, 1 fruit, 1/2 fat. *Editor's Note:** Rainbow sherbet is not recommended for this recipe.

Sherbet Dessert

Coconut Fruit Dip
Turkey Sloppy Joes
Buttermilk Salad Dressing

Buttermilk Salad Dressing

(Pictured above)

Serve this creamy ranch-style salad dressing on almost everything. Besides drizzling it over mixed greens, I use it as a dip for raw vegetables, a topper for baked potatoes and a sauce for roast beef sandwiches. —Iola Egle
McCook, Nebraska

    2 cups buttermilk
    2 cups fat-free mayonnaise
    1/2 cup minced fresh parsley
    1/2 teaspoon garlic powder *or* salt
    1/2 teaspoon onion powder *or* salt
    1 teaspoon coarsely ground *or* cracked pepper
Salad greens

In a bowl, combine the first six ingredients; whisk until smooth. Cover and chill until serving. Serve over salad greens. Store in the refrigerator. **Yield:** 4 cups. **Nutritional Analysis:** One 2-tablespoon serving of dressing (prepared with garlic and onion powder) equals 19 calories, 125 mg sodium, 1 mg cholesterol, 3 gm carbohydrate, 1 gm protein, trace fat. **Diabetic Exchange:** Free.

Turkey Sloppy Joes

(Pictured above)

This is a wonderful sandwich for family meals or parties. Once the meat is browned, the mixture simmers for just 10 minutes, so it's perfect for spur-of-the-moment backyard picnics. —Sue Ann O'Buck
Sinking Spring, Pennsylvania

    1 pound ground turkey breast

1/4 cup chopped onion
1/2 cup no-salt-added ketchup
3 tablespoons barbecue sauce
1 tablespoon prepared mustard
1 tablespoon vinegar
1-1/2 teaspoons Worcestershire sauce
1/2 teaspoon celery seed
1/4 teaspoon pepper
6 whole wheat hamburger buns, split

In a nonstick skillet, cook the turkey and onion for 5 minutes or until turkey is no longer pink. Add the next seven ingredients; simmer for 10 minutes, stirring occasionally. Serve on buns. **Yield:** 6 servings. **Nutritional Analysis:** One serving equals 236 calories, 364 mg sodium, 37 mg cholesterol, 29 gm carbohydrate, 23 gm protein, 3 gm fat. **Diabetic Exchanges:** 2-1/2 very lean meat, 2 starch.

Coconut Fruit Dip

(Pictured at left)

This fruit dip has a fun pineapple and coconut flavor. I usually serve it with melon slices, strawberries and grapes, but you could use whatever fruit you have on hand. It's a big hit whenever I make it. —Nancy Tanguay
Lakeville, Massachusetts

1 can (8 ounces) crushed unsweetened
    pineapple, undrained
3/4 cup skim milk
1/2 cup (4 ounces) nonfat sour cream
1 package (3.4 ounces) instant coconut cream
    pudding mix
Fresh pineapple, grapes and strawberries *or*
    other fruit

In a blender, combine the first four ingredients; cover and process for 1 minute or until smooth. Serve with fruit. Store in the refrigerator. **Yield:** 2 cups. **Nutritional Analysis:** One 2-tablespoon serving of dip equals 40 calories, 58 mg sodium, 1 mg cholesterol, 8 gm carbohydrate, 1 gm protein, trace fat. **Diabetic Exchange:** 1/2 starch.

Spicy Haddock

This is one of my favorite ways to serve fish. I'm originally from Louisiana, where much of the food is spicy. So I like the spark that the chili powder and green chilies give these good-for-you baked fillets. —Kathleen Plake
Fort Wayne, Indiana

2 pounds fresh *or* frozen haddock fillets,
    thawed
1 can (4 ounces) chopped green chilies
2 tablespoons vegetable oil
2 tablespoons soy sauce
2 tablespoons Worcestershire sauce
1 teaspoon paprika
1/2 teaspoon garlic powder
1/2 teaspoon chili powder
Dash hot pepper sauce

Place fillets in a 13-in. x 9-in. x 2-in. baking dish that has been coated with nonstick cooking spray. Combine remaining ingredients; spoon over fish. Bake, uncovered, at 350° for 20-25 minutes or until fish flakes easily with a fork. **Yield:** 8 servings. **Nutritional Analysis:** One 1/4-pound serving equals 139 calories, 501 mg sodium, 65 mg cholesterol, 2 gm carbohydrate, 22 gm protein, 4 gm fat. **Diabetic Exchanges:** 3 very lean meat, 1/2 vegetable.

Spanish Chicken and Rice

Using leftover chicken, this meaty tomato and rice meal-in-one bakes quickly.
—Patricia Rutherford, Winchester, Illinois

2/3 cup finely chopped onion
1/4 cup sliced fresh mushrooms
1-1/4 cups cubed cooked chicken breast
2 plum tomatoes, peeled and chopped
1/2 cup cooked long grain rice
1/2 cup low-sodium tomato juice
1/2 cup low-sodium chicken broth
1/3 cup frozen peas
1 tablespoon chopped pimientos
1/8 teaspoon dried tarragon
1/8 teaspoon dried savory
Pinch pepper

Lightly coat a skillet with nonstick cooking spray; saute onion and mushrooms until tender, about 4 minutes. Place in an ungreased 1-qt. casserole. Add remaining ingredients and mix well. Cover and bake at 375° for 15-20 minutes or until liquid is absorbed. **Yield:** 2 servings. **Nutritional Analysis:** One 1-1/2-cup serving equals 207 calories, 108 mg sodium, 54 mg cholesterol, 25 gm carbohydrate, 19 gm protein, 4 gm fat. **Diabetic Exchanges:** 2 very lean meat, 1 vegetable, 1/2 fat.

Here's the Skinny on Low-Fat Fixin's

YOU can reduce fat in many of your favorite recipes by keeping these few simple tips in mind.

- In a casserole that calls for whole milk, use skim. Even if you can't stand to drink "that blue stuff", it's difficult to tell the difference in a casserole.
- In casseroles that call for cream, use evaporated skim milk. Evaporation enriches the texture of the skim milk, making it a better substitute for cream—and significantly reducing the calories.
- In fruit salads or Stroganoff, replace some or all of the sour cream with plain nonfat yogurt. Afraid your family will notice the difference? Begin by substituting just a small amount, then increase it gradually. Also, use nonfat sour cream in dips that call for sour cream.
- Fat-free salad dressing (such as ranch) makes a good dip for vegetables and pretzels...and fat-free Italian or honey Dijon dressing can be used to marinate meat for grilling, baking or broiling.

—Sue Call, Beech Grove, Indiana

Linda's Lemon Fish
Low-Fat Tartar Sauce

1/2 cup nonfat plain yogurt
1/4 cup fat-free mayonnaise
1 tablespoon sweet pickle relish, drained
2 teaspoons dried minced onion
1 teaspoon dried parsley flakes
1 teaspoon Dijon mustard
2 drops hot pepper sauce

In a small bowl, combine all ingredients. Cover and refrigerate until serving. **Yield:** 1 cup. **Nutritional Analysis:** One 1-tablespoon serving equals 9 calories, 43 mg sodium, trace cholesterol, 2 gm carbohydrate, trace protein, trace fat. **Diabetic Exchange:** Free.

Sesame Apple Toss

Looking for a fun variation on a traditional Waldorf salad? Try this simple version. A colorful combination of apples and grapes is dressed in fruity yogurt and sprinkled with toasted sesame seeds. —Mary Patterson
Bethel, Connecticut

1 cup chopped red apple
1 cup halved green grapes
1 cup sliced celery
1/3 cup low-fat orange *or* lemon yogurt
Lettuce leaves, optional
2 teaspoons sesame seeds, toasted

In a bowl, combine the first three ingredients; add yogurt and toss to coat. Serve on lettuce if desired. Sprinkle with sesame seeds. **Yield:** 6 servings. **Nutritional Analysis:** One 1/2-cup serving equals 52 calories, 26 mg sodium, 1 mg cholesterol, 11 gm carbohydrate, 1 gm protein, 1 gm fat. **Diabetic Exchange:** 1 fruit.

Linda's Lemon Fish

(Pictured above)

I've used this fish recipe since I was about 15 years old. The zippy seasoning tastes great on almost any fish, but I prefer sole. Served with a salad and fresh hot wheat rolls, it is an excellent light meal. —Linda Gaido
New Brighton, Pennsylvania

1 pound whitefish *or* sole fillets
1/4 cup lemon juice
1 teaspoon olive *or* vegetable oil
1 to 2 teaspoons salt-free lemon-pepper seasoning
1 small onion, thinly sliced
1 teaspoon dried parsley flakes

Cut fish into serving-size pieces. Place in an ungreased 11-in. x 7-in. x 2-in. baking dish. Drizzle with lemon juice and oil; sprinkle with lemon pepper. Arrange onion over fish; sprinkle with parsley. Cover and let stand for 5 minutes. Bake at 350° for 20 minutes or until fish flakes easily with a fork. **Yield:** 4 servings. **Nutritional Analysis:** One serving equals 178 calories, 60 mg sodium, 70 mg cholesterol, 3 gm carbohydrate, 23 gm protein, 8 gm fat. **Diabetic Exchange:** 3 lean meat.

Low-Fat Tartar Sauce

(Pictured above)

I like to whip up a batch of this creamy tartar sauce whenever I plan to serve fish or seafood. You'll be delighted with its flavor. —Laura Letobar, Livonia, Michigan

Oven Swiss Steak

There's no need to brown the steak first, so you can get this meaty main course into the oven in short order. The fork-tender results are sure to remind you of the Swiss steak Grandma used to make, with lots of sauce left over for dipping. —Sue Call
Beech Grove, Indiana

2 pounds boneless round steak (1/2 inch thick)
1/4 teaspoon pepper
1 medium onion, thinly sliced
1 can (4 ounces) mushroom stems and pieces, drained
1 can (8 ounces) no-salt-added tomato sauce
Hot cooked noodles

Trim beef; cut into serving-size pieces. Place in a greased 13-in. x 9-in. x 2-in. baking dish. Sprinkle with pepper. Top with the onion, mushrooms and tomato sauce. Cover and bake at 325° for 1-3/4 to 2 hours or until meat is tender. Serve over noodles. **Yield:** 8 servings. **Nutritional**

Analysis: One serving (calculated without noodles) equals 209 calories, 112 mg sodium, 68 mg cholesterol, 4 gm carbohydrate, 26 gm protein, 10 gm fat. **Diabetic Exchanges:** 3 lean meat, 1 vegetable.

Hearty Red Beans and Rice

I adapted this recipe from a cookbook to eliminate time-consuming steps like browning the sausage and soaking and boiling the beans. Red pepper flakes add zest to this satisfying dish that's loaded with beans and sausage.
—Brenda Heidhoff Leonard, Missoula, Montana

   3 celery ribs, chopped
   1 medium onion, chopped
   6 green onions, thinly sliced
   2 garlic cloves, minced
1-3/4 cups water
   1 can (16 ounces) light red kidney beans, rinsed and drained
   1 can (16 ounces) dark red kidney beans, rinsed and drained
  1/2 teaspoon dried oregano
  1/2 teaspoon dried thyme
  1/4 teaspoon crushed red pepper flakes
  1/4 teaspoon pepper
  1/4 pound fully cooked smoked turkey sausage, halved and cut into 1/4-inch pieces
   4 cups hot cooked rice

In a large skillet that has been coated with nonstick cooking spray, saute celery, onions and garlic until tender. Add water, beans, oregano, thyme, red pepper flakes and pepper. Bring to a boil; reduce heat. Simmer, uncovered, for 10 minutes, stirring occasionally. Remove about 1-1/2 cups of bean mixture and mash with a fork. Return to skillet. Add sausage; bring to a boil. Boil for 5 minutes or until bean mixture reaches desired thickness. Serve over rice. **Yield:** 10 servings. **Nutritional Analysis:** One serving (1/2 cup bean mixture and 1/3 cup rice) equals 197 calories, 116 mg sodium, 7 mg cholesterol, 35 gm carbohydrate, 9 gm protein, 2 gm fat. **Diabetic Exchanges:** 2 starch, 1/2 meat, 1/2 vegetable.

Tangy Potato Salad

Bottled salad dressing is the secret to my quick and tangy side dish. It was inspired by traditional German-style potato salad with its vinegar dressing. My husband and I usually can't wait for it to chill, so we know it's good warm, too! —Mary Bilyeu, Ann Arbor, Michigan

   1 pound red potatoes, cooked and cubed
  1/2 cup sliced green onions
   1 bottle (8 ounces) fat-free Italian salad dressing
   3 tablespoons Dijon mustard

In a large bowl, combine potatoes and onions. Combine the salad dressing and mustard; pour 1/2 cup over potato mixture. Toss to coat. Cover and chill. Add remaining dressing just before serving. **Yield:** 4 servings. **Nutritional Analysis:** One 1/2-cup serving equals 88 calories, 559 mg sodium, 0 cholesterol, 18 gm carbohydrate, 3 gm protein, 1 gm fat. **Diabetic Exchange:** 1 starch.

Caramel Pineapple Cake

(Pictured below)

When I serve this cake, no one ever guesses it's low in fat. The lemon yogurt and pineapple add moistness missing in many reduced-fat cakes. It's scrumptious topped with caramel sauce. —Amanda Denton, Barre, Vermont

Egg substitute equivalent to 2 eggs
   2 cans (8 ounces *each*) crushed pineapple, undrained
   2 cups all-purpose flour
   1 cup sugar
   1 cup packed brown sugar
  1/2 cup nonfat lemon yogurt
   2 teaspoons baking soda
   1 teaspoon vanilla extract
  1/4 teaspoon ground ginger
   1 jar (12-1/4 ounces) fat-free caramel ice cream topping
   1 to 2 tablespoons pineapple juice

In a mixing bowl, combine egg substitute and pineapple; mix well. Add the next seven ingredients and mix well. Spread into a 13-in. x 9-in. x 2-in. baking pan that has been coated with nonstick cooking spray. Bake at 350° for 35 minutes or until golden brown. For sauce, combine caramel topping and pineapple juice in a saucepan; cook and stir over medium heat just until bubbly. Cool slightly. Serve warm over cake. **Yield:** 16 servings. **Nutritional Analysis:** One serving with 2 tablespoons of sauce equals 241 calories, 258 mg sodium, trace cholesterol, 59 gm carbohydrate, 3 gm protein, trace fat. **Diabetic Exchanges:** 3 fruit, 1 starch.

Caramel Pineapple Cake

Strawberry Lemon Trifle

(Pictured below)

This refreshingly fruity dessert is one of our favorites. It looks so beautiful layered in a glass bowl that people will think you fussed. The secret is starting with a purchased angel food cake.
—Lynn Marie Frucci
Pullman, Washington

    4 ounces fat-free cream cheese, softened
    1 cup nonfat lemon yogurt
    2 cups skim milk
    1 package (3.4 ounces) instant lemon pudding
      mix
    2 teaspoons grated lemon peel
2-1/2 cups sliced fresh strawberries, *divided*
    1 tablespoon white grape juice *or* water
    1 prepared angel food cake (10 inches)

In a mixing bowl, beat cream cheese and yogurt. Add the milk, pudding mix and lemon peel; beat until smooth. In a blender, process 1/2 cup strawberries and grape juice until smooth. Tear cake into 1-in. cubes; place a third in a trifle bowl or 3-qt. serving bowl. Top with a third of the pudding mixture and half of the remaining strawberries. Drizzle with half of the strawberry sauce. Repeat. Top with remaining cake and pudding mixture. Cover and refrigerate for at least 2 hours. **Yield:** 14 servings. **Nutritional Analysis:** One serving equals 180 calories, 378 mg sodium, 2 mg cholesterol, 39 gm carbohydrate, 6 gm protein, trace fat. **Diabetic Exchanges:** 2 starch, 1/2 fruit.

Strawberry Lemon Trifle

Corn-Stuffed Tomatoes

Team up canned corn with chopped green pepper and onion to create a fresh-tasting salad with light mayonnaise coating. The pretty mixture is especially appealing presented in a tomato shell.
—Hazel Holley
Samson, Alabama

    1 can (16 ounces) shoepeg corn, drained
    2 cans (7 ounces *each*) Mexicorn, drained
1/2 cup chopped onion
1/4 cup chopped green pepper
    2 tablespoons fat-free mayonnaise
1/8 teaspoon pepper
    8 medium tomatoes

In a bowl, combine the first four ingredients. Combine mayonnaise and pepper; mix well. Pour over the corn mixture and toss to coat. Cut the top off each tomato. Scoop out pulp, leaving a 1/2-in. shell (discard pulp). Spoon corn mixture into the tomatoes. Refrigerate until serving. **Yield:** 8 servings. **Nutritional Analysis:** One serving equals 134 calories, 480 mg sodium, 0 cholesterol, 28 gm carbohydrate, 4 gm protein, 1 gm fat. **Diabetic Exchanges:** 1-1/2 starch, 1 vegetable.

Easy Cocoa Mousse

This airy, melt-in-your-mouth mousse has a light cocoa flavor that's so good. It's simple to mix, then pop in the fridge while you're preparing the rest of your meal.
—Donna Brooks, Jefferson, Maine

    1 envelope unflavored gelatin
1/4 cup cold water
1-1/4 cups skim milk
Artificial sweetener equivalent to 1/3 cup sugar
1/4 cup baking cocoa
    1 teaspoon vanilla extract
1-3/4 cups light whipped topping, *divided*

In a small saucepan, sprinkle gelatin over water; let stand for 5 minutes. Cook over low heat until gelatin is dissolved. In a blender or food processor, combine milk, sweetener, cocoa and vanilla. Slowly add gelatin mixture. Fold in 1-1/2 cups whipped topping. Spoon into serving dishes. Cover and chill for at least 1 hour. Garnish with remaining topping. **Yield:** 6 servings. **Nutritional Analysis:** One 3/4-cup serving equals 81 calories, 29 mg sodium, 1 mg cholesterol, 10 gm carbohydrate, 3 gm protein, 3 gm fat. **Diabetic Exchanges:** 1 fat, 1/2 starch.

Cream of Broccoli Soup

Frozen vegetables make this a quick soup to stir up. Turkey ham lends a hearty flavor with less fat. —Eileen Claeys
Long Grove, Iowa

    1 package (10 ounces) frozen chopped broccoli
3/4 cup finely chopped cooked turkey ham
1/2 cup water
1/4 cup frozen cut green beans
    1 tablespoon chopped onion

Seasoned Turkey Burgers
Carrots with Dill

2 tablespoons all-purpose flour
1 cup skim milk
1/3 cup cubed light process American cheese

In a large saucepan, combine the first five ingredients; cover and cook over medium heat until vegetables are tender, about 5 minutes (do not drain). Combine flour and milk until smooth; gradually add to the vegetable mixture. Bring to a boil; boil for 1-2 minutes, stirring constantly. Remove from the heat. Stir in cheese; cover and let stand until melted, about 5 minutes. Stir before serving. **Yield:** 3 servings. **Nutritional Analysis:** One 1-cup serving equals 151 calories, 788 mg sodium, 23 mg cholesterol, 14 gm carbohydrate, 17 gm protein, 3 gm fat. **Diabetic Exchanges:** 1 meat, 1 vegetable, 1/2 skim milk.

Carrots with Dill

(Pictured above)

This is a great way to present sweet, tender carrots. I glaze the colorful coins with margarine and add dill just before serving for a simple, savory side dish.
—Dorothy Pritchett, Wills Point, Texas

1 pound carrots, sliced 1/8 inch thick
2 tablespoons water
4 teaspoons reduced-fat margarine
1 to 2 tablespoons snipped fresh dill *or* 1 to 2 teaspoons dill weed

Place carrots, water and margarine in a saucepan. Cover and bring to a boil over high heat. Reduce heat; sim-

mer for 8 minutes or until the carrots are crisp-tender. Uncover and simmer until liquid has evaporated. Stir in dill. **Yield:** 5 servings. **Nutritional Analysis:** One 1/2-cup serving equals 55 calories, 66 mg sodium, 0 cholesterol, 9 gm carbohydrate, 1 gm protein, 2 gm fat. **Diabetic Exchanges:** 1-1/2 vegetable, 1/2 fat.

Seasoned Turkey Burgers

(Pictured above)

This fun mixture of turkey and dressing tastes almost like Thanksgiving on a bun. These moist burgers are great alone, but my family likes them best with lettuce, onion, tomato and a dab of mayonnaise on a whole wheat bun. *—Vicki Engelhardt, Grand Rapids, Michigan*

1/2 cup herb-seasoned stuffing croutons
1 pound ground turkey breast
1 small onion, finely chopped
5 hamburger buns, split
Lettuce leaves, onion, tomato slices and fat-free mayonnaise, optional

Crush or process stuffing croutons into fine crumbs. In a bowl, combine crumbs, turkey and onion. Shape into four patties. Broil or grill over medium-hot heat for 8-10 minutes, turning once. Serve on buns with lettuce, onion, tomato and mayonnaise if desired. **Yield:** 5 servings. **Nutritional Analysis:** One serving (calculated without bun, lettuce, onion, tomato and mayonnaise) equals 124 calories, 163 mg sodium, 45 mg cholesterol, 5 gm carbohydrate, 23 gm protein, 1 gm fat. **Diabetic Exchanges:** 3 very lean meat, 1/2 starch.

Pronto Pita Pizzas

I call on pita bread as a terrific crust for my quick-to-fix individual pizzas. With the healthy ground turkey breast mixture on top, they can also be cut into quarters and served as appetizers.
—Debbi Smith
Crossett, Arkansas

    1 pound ground turkey breast
    1 cup sliced fresh mushrooms
    1/2 cup chopped onion
    2 garlic cloves, minced
    1 can (8 ounces) no-salt-added tomato sauce
    1/2 teaspoon fennel seed
    1/4 teaspoon dried oregano
    4 pita breads, warmed
    1/2 cup shredded reduced-fat mozzarella cheese

In a skillet, brown the turkey; drain. Add mushrooms, onion and garlic; cook until tender. Stir in tomato sauce, fennel seed and oregano. Cover and simmer for 10-15 minutes or until heated through. Spread 1 cup of meat mixture on each pita; sprinkle with cheese. Serve immediately. **Yield:** 4 servings. **Nutritional Analysis:** One serving equals 358 calories, 187 mg sodium, 63 mg cholesterol, 41 gm carbohydrate, 38 gm protein, 5 gm fat. **Diabetic Exchanges:** 4 very lean meat, 2 starch, 2 vegetable.

Raspberry Nut Bars

(Pictured at far right)

Raspberry jam adds sweetness to these pretty bars. I revised the original recipe to reduce fat and calories. The end result is a treat so delicious you'll never know it's good for you.   —Beth Ask, Ulster, Pennsylvania

    1/2 cup margarine
    1/4 cup reduced-fat margarine
    1/3 cup packed brown sugar
    1/4 cup sugar
    1 egg
    1 teaspoon vanilla extract
    2 cups all-purpose flour
    1 teaspoon baking powder
    1/4 teaspoon baking soda
    1/4 teaspoon salt
    3/4 cup chopped pecans, *divided*
    2/3 cup raspberry jam
    2 tablespoons lemon juice
GLAZE:
    1/2 cup confectioners' sugar
    2 teaspoons skim milk

In a mixing bowl, cream margarines and sugars. Beat in egg and vanilla. Combine flour, baking powder, baking soda and salt; add to creamed mixture and mix well. Stir in 1/2 cup pecans. Spread half of the dough into a 13-in. x 9-in. x 2-in. baking pan that has been coated with nonstick cooking spray. Combine jam and lemon juice; spread over dough. Dollop remaining dough over top. Sprinkle with remaining pecans. Bake at 325° for 30-35 minutes or until lightly browned. Cool. Combine glaze

ingredients; drizzle over bars. **Yield:** 3 dozen. **Nutritional Analysis:** One bar equals 107 calories, 88 mg sodium, 6 mg cholesterol, 15 gm carbohydrate, 1 gm protein, 5 gm fat. **Diabetic Exchanges:** 1 starch, 1 fat. **Editor's Note:** This recipe uses both regular margarine and reduced-fat margarine.

Iced Coffee

(Pictured at right)

When my sister introduced me to iced coffee, I didn't think I'd like it. Not only did I like it, I decided I could make my own. My fast-to-fix version is a refreshing alternative to hot coffee.   —Jenny Reece, Lowry, Minnesota

    4 teaspoons instant coffee granules
    1 cup boiling water
Artificial sweetener equivalent to 4 teaspoons
    sugar, optional
    1 cup skim milk
    4 teaspoons chocolate syrup
    1/8 teaspoon vanilla extract
Ice cubes

In a bowl, dissolve coffee in water. Add sweetener if desired. Stir in milk, chocolate syrup and vanilla; mix well. Serve over ice. **Yield:** 2 cups. **Nutritional Analysis:** One 1-cup serving (prepared without sweetener) equals 79 calories, 76 mg sodium, 2 mg cholesterol, 15 gm carbohydrate, 5 gm protein, trace fat. **Diabetic Exchanges:** 1/2 skim milk, 1/2 starch.

Tender Herbed Chicken

Whoever said that all chicken recipes taste the same just haven't experimented enough. For tender chicken with a refreshing herb flavor, marinate the meat overnight in this quick-to-fix yogurt mixture.   —Margaret Shauers
Great Bend, Kansas

    1 cup nonfat plain yogurt
    3 tablespoons lime juice
    2 tablespoons snipped fresh dill *or* 2 teaspoons
        dill weed
    1 garlic clove, minced
    1 teaspoon ground cumin
    1/2 teaspoon ground ginger
    1/4 to 1/2 teaspoon aniseed
    1/8 to 1/4 teaspoon cayenne pepper
    8 boneless skinless chicken breast halves (2
        pounds)

In a large resealable plastic bag or shallow glass container, combine the first eight ingredients; mix well. Add chicken and turn to coat. Cover and refrigerate overnight, turning once. Drain and discard marinade. Place chicken on a rack over a greased 15-in. x 10-in. x 1-in. baking pan. Bake, uncovered, at 350° for 25-30 minutes or until juices run clear. **Yield:** 8 servings. **Nutritional Analysis:** One serving equals 152 calories, 76 mg sodium, 73 mg cholesterol, 1 gm carbohydrate, 28 gm protein, 3 gm fat. **Diabetic Exchange:** 4 very lean meat.

Iced Coffee
Raspberry Nut Bars

Chapter 15

◉ *Centsible Foods—Fast and Frugal*

WHEN you're in a pinch, it's tempting to pick up store-bought packaged entrees and carryout restaurant meals. But while these fast foods save time, they don't always save money. As a matter of fact, they could quickly break the family's budget.

So if you're counting pennies as well as minutes, look here for "centsible" express-eating alternatives that are not only easy and economical, but appetizing as well.

Our test kitchen staff has figured the cost per serving for each dish. So these fast and frugal recipes are sure to result in prompt meals and a plumper pocketbook!

THE PRICE IS RIGHT. Vegetarian Chili (p. 240).

Pasta Shells and Peppers

4 bacon strips, diced
1/2 cup chopped onion
1/3 cup chopped green pepper
1/3 cup chopped celery
2 garlic cloves, minced
1 cup unsweetened pineapple juice
3/4 cup ketchup
1/4 teaspoon salt
1/4 teaspoon chili powder
1 package (1 pound) hot dogs, cut into bite-size pieces
5 cups hot cooked rice

In a saucepan over medium heat, cook bacon until crisp. Remove bacon to paper towels; set aside. Drain, reserving 1 tablespoon of drippings. Saute onion, green pepper, celery and garlic in the drippings until tender. Add pineapple juice, ketchup, salt and chili powder; mix well. Bring to a boil. Add hot dogs; return to a boil. Reduce heat; cover and simmer for 5-8 minutes or until heated through. Serve over rice. Sprinkle with bacon. **Yield: 8 servings.**

Pasta Shells and Peppers

(Pictured above)

Tomatoes and green peppers spooned over the top give this easy-to-prepare macaroni and cheese fresh homemade taste. The thrifty main dish costs just 94¢ per serving.
—*Sharon Ann Sluski, West Ossipee, New Hampshire*

1 package (1 pound) medium shell pasta
4 medium green peppers, cut into 1-inch chunks
1 tablespoon butter *or* margarine
1 can (28 ounces) crushed tomatoes, undrained
1-1/2 teaspoons sugar
1 teaspoon salt
1/4 teaspoon pepper
1 pound process American cheese, shredded
Fresh basil *and/or* oregano, optional

Cook pasta according to package directions. Meanwhile, in a skillet, saute peppers in butter for 2-3 minutes or until crisp-tender. Stir in tomatoes, sugar, salt and pepper; heat through. Drain pasta; stir in cheese until melted. Spoon into bowls; top with tomato mixture. Garnish with basil and/or oregano if desired. **Yield: 6 servings.**

Saucy Franks with Rice

Here is a fast, flavorful, simple way to dress up plain old hot dogs. This hearty, economical mainstay comes in at only 43¢ per serving. —*Roslyn Beal, Bremen, Georgia*

Salad Croutons

Homemade croutons are a delight to serve with your favorite mixed green salad—or as a crunchy snack. My well-seasoned salad toppers will set you back a mere 4¢ per serving! —*Fayne Lutz, Taos, New Mexico*

1 tablespoon vegetable *or* olive oil
1 garlic clove, minced
1 cup cubed day-old bread
Pinch onion salt

Pour the oil into an 8-in. square baking pan; add garlic. Bake at 325° until garlic is lightly browned, about 3-4 minutes. Add bread and onion salt; stir to coat. Bake 10-12 minutes longer or until the bread is lightly browned, stirring frequently. Store in an airtight container. **Yield: 6 (2-tablespoon) servings.**

Magic Apple Pie

This pie is unique—it forms its own crust on the top as it bakes and has a chewy cake-like consistency. It's just 13¢ per slice! —*Helen Hassler, Reinholds, Pennsylvania*

1 egg
3/4 cup sugar
1/2 cup all-purpose flour
1 teaspoon baking powder
Pinch salt
1 medium tart apple, peeled and diced
1/2 cup raisins
Whipped cream *or* ice cream, optional

In a mixing bowl, beat egg. Add sugar, flour, baking powder and salt. Stir in apple and raisins. Spread into a greased 9-in. pie plate. Bake at 350° for 25-30 minutes or until golden brown and a toothpick inserted near the center comes out clean. Serve with whipped cream or ice cream if desired. **Yield: 8 servings.**

Diane Cattau

Creamy Corn Casserole

Besides helping on our farm, I work as an environmental assistant for a power district. It's quite a challenge to put a good nutritious meal on the table and still have time for doing things with my family. My husband and our two girls enjoy this dish, which you can make for just 20¢ a serving.
—Denise Goedeken, Platte Center, Nebraska

    1 can (15-1/4 ounces) whole kernel corn,
      undrained
    1 can (15 ounces) cream-style corn
    1 cup uncooked elbow macaroni
    1 cup (4 ounces) diced process American
      cheese
1/2 cup butter *or* margarine, melted
    1 tablespoon finely chopped onion

In a large bowl, combine all of the ingredients. Pour into an ungreased 2-qt. baking dish. Cover and bake at 350° for 40 minutes. Uncover and bake 30 minutes longer. **Yield:** 10 servings.

Sausage Spaghetti Supper

Since I work, I look for recipes like this that are quick and easy and fit into our budget. At about 71¢ a serving, this dish fills the bill for me and my husband.
—Maria Costello, Monroe, North Carolina

    1 pound smoked kielbasa, thinly sliced and
      halved
    1 medium onion, chopped
1/2 cup sliced celery
    1 can (28 ounces) crushed tomatoes,
      undrained
    1 can (4 ounces) mushroom stems and pieces,
      drained
    1 teaspoon dried oregano
    1 teaspoon dried basil
1/2 teaspoon garlic salt
    4 cups hot cooked spaghetti
1/2 cup shredded cheddar cheese

In a large skillet, cook sausage, onion and celery over medium heat until vegetables are tender. Add tomatoes, mushrooms, oregano, basil and garlic salt; bring to a boil. Reduce heat and simmer for 2 minutes. Spoon over spaghetti; sprinkle with cheese. **Yield:** 6 servings.

Minestrone Macaroni

(Pictured at right)

This is by far the easiest, tastiest economical recipe I've found. It seems to taste even better as a leftover. The frugal dish costs just 78¢ per serving.
—Diane Varner
Elizabeth, Colorado

    1 pound ground beef
    2 cans (14-1/2 ounces *each*) Italian diced
      tomatoes, undrained

2-1/4 cups water
1-1/2 cups uncooked elbow macaroni
    2 beef bouillon cubes
    1 can (16 ounces) kidney beans, rinsed and
      drained
    1 can (15 ounces) garbanzo beans, rinsed and
      drained
    1 can (14-1/2 ounces) cut green beans, rinsed
      and drained

In a large skillet, brown beef; drain. Add the tomatoes, water, macaroni and bouillon; bring to a boil. Reduce heat; cover and simmer for 12-15 minutes or until macaroni is tender. Stir in beans and heat through. **Yield:** 6 servings.

Black Bean Salad

This salad goes wonderfully with chicken and Mexican main dishes and is great when you need something quick for a potluck. Make it for a mere 43¢ per serving.
—Peg Kenkel-Thomsen, Iowa City, Iowa

✓ Nutritional Analysis included

    2 cans (15 ounces *each*) black beans, rinsed
      and drained
1-1/2 cups salsa
    2 tablespoons minced fresh parsley *or* cilantro

Combine all ingredients in a bowl. Chill for 15 minutes. **Yield:** 8 servings. **Nutritional Analysis:** One 1/2-cup serving equals 93 calories, 453 mg sodium, 0 cholesterol, 16 gm carbohydrate, 6 gm protein, 1 gm fat. **Diabetic Exchange:** 1 starch.

Minestrone Macaroni

Garlic Angel Hair Pasta

(Pictured on front cover)

I add the garlic cloves to the noodles as they are cooking for fast and flavorful results. At only 11¢ a serving, this pasta is a thrifty accompaniment to most any lunch or dinner.
—Denise Baumert, Dalhart, Texas

☑ **Nutritional Analysis included**

- 8 ounces uncooked angel hair pasta
- 2 garlic cloves, peeled and halved
- 1/4 cup butter *or* margarine
- 1/4 cup grated Parmesan cheese
- 1 teaspoon snipped fresh *or* dried chives
- 1/2 teaspoon garlic salt, optional

Cook pasta according to package directions, adding garlic to the water. Drain; discard garlic. Place pasta in a serving bowl; add butter. Toss gently until butter is melted. Add Parmesan cheese, chives and garlic salt if desired; toss to coat. **Yield:** 8 servings. **Nutritional Analysis:** One 1/2-cup serving (prepared with reduced-fat margarine and nonfat Parmesan cheese and without garlic salt) equals 103 calories, 152 mg sodium, 2 mg cholesterol, 13 gm carbohydrate, 4 gm protein, 4 gm fat. **Diabetic Exchanges:** 1 starch, 1 fat.

Rise 'n' Shine Biscuits

These biscuits come out nice and sweet and fluffy—and they couldn't be easier! Adjust the sugar to your liking. You're sure to like the price of only 8¢ each. *—Diane Hixon Niceville, Florida*

- 1/3 cup club soda
- 1/3 cup sour cream
- 5 teaspoons sugar
- 2 cups biscuit/baking mix

In a bowl, combine the club soda, sour cream and sugar. Add biscuit mix, stirring just until moistened. Drop dough by 1/3 cupfuls 2 in. apart onto a greased baking sheet. Bake at 450° for 10-12 minutes or until golden brown. **Yield:** 9 biscuits.

Black Forest Mousse

If you like chocolate and cherries, you'll love this smooth, light dessert. Pantry staples such as instant pudding and canned pie filling make it quick to fix and inexpensive at 32¢ a serving. *—Deanna Richter, Elmore, Minnesota*

- 2 cups milk
- 1 package (3.9 ounces) instant chocolate pudding mix
- 1 can (21 ounces) cherry pie filling
- 2 cups whipped topping

In a bowl, beat the milk and pudding mix for 2 minutes or until smooth. Let stand until slightly thickened, about 2 minutes. Stir in pie filling. Gently fold in whipped topping. Spoon into individual dessert dishes; refrigerate until serving. **Yield:** 8 servings.

Like-Homemade Baked Beans

Looking for a speedy way to jazz up canned pork and beans? Give them homemade taste with bacon, onion, brown sugar and Worcestershire sauce. A pleaser at picnics, this dish is easy on your pocketbook at a mere 28¢ per serving. *—Sue Ross, Casa Grande, Arizona*

- 2 bacon strips, diced
- 1/2 cup chopped onion
- 1 can (16 ounces) pork and beans
- 2 tablespoons brown sugar
- 1-1/2 teaspoons Worcestershire sauce
- 1/2 teaspoon ground mustard

In a skillet, cook bacon until crisp. Add onion; cook until tender. Add the remaining ingredients. Reduce heat; simmer for 10-15 minutes or until heated through, stirring frequently. **Yield:** 3 servings.

Creamed Chicken Over Beans

(Pictured below)

This simple but tasty blend will surprise you. It uses leftover chicken and frozen green beans, so it's fast to fix for a brunch or light lunch. This reasonably priced main dish costs just 81¢ a serving. *—Louise Martin Denver, Pennsylvania*

- 1/4 cup butter *or* margarine
- 1/4 cup all-purpose flour
- 1/2 teaspoon salt
- 1/8 teaspoon pepper
- 1-1/2 cups water
- 1/4 cup milk
- 1 teaspoon chicken bouillon granules
- 2 cups cubed cooked chicken
- 1 package (16 ounces) frozen cut green beans, cooked and drained

Paprika, optional

In a saucepan, melt butter. Stir in flour, salt and pepper

Creamed Chicken Over Beans

Cheesy Zucchini Casserole

until smooth. Gradually add water, milk and bouillon. Bring to a boil; boil and stir for 2 minutes. Add the chicken and heat through. Serve over beans. Sprinkle with paprika if desired. **Yield:** 4 servings.

Pizza Mac Casserole

This is a tasty variation on a basic ground beef and noodle casserole. A satisfying main dish, it's simple to make because it uses convenient pizza sauce. And at 83¢ a helping, it's economical as well. —Trish Quinn
Marion, Indiana

 1 pound ground beef
 2 cups elbow macaroni, cooked and drained
 1/2 cup chopped onion
 1/2 cup chopped green pepper
 2 jars (14 ounces *each*) pizza sauce
 2 cups (8 ounces) shredded mozzarella cheese

In a skillet, brown beef; drain. Add the macaroni, onion, green pepper and pizza sauce. Pour into a greased 2-1/2-qt. baking dish. Cover and bake at 350° for 20 minutes. Uncover and sprinkle with cheese. Bake 10-15 minutes longer or until the cheese is melted. **Yield:** 6 servings.

Cheesy Zucchini Casserole

(Pictured above)

Tender cubed zucchini gets pleasant flavor from a cheesy sauce and cracker-crumb topping. This fast-to-fix side dish is a great way to use up a big crop of this common squash. At 35¢ a serving, it's an uncommon value.
—Kathi Grenier, Auburn, Maine

2-1/2 pounds zucchini, cut into 1/2-inch cubes

 1 cup diced process American cheese
 2 tablespoons butter *or* margarine
 1/2 teaspoon salt
 1/8 teaspoon pepper
 1/3 cup crushed saltines (about 10 crackers)

Place the zucchini in a saucepan and cover with water; cook over medium heat until tender, about 8 minutes. Drain well. Add cheese, butter, salt and pepper; stir until the cheese is melted. Transfer to a greased shallow 1-1/2-qt. baking dish. Sprinkle with cracker crumbs. Bake, uncovered, at 400° for 10-15 minutes or until lightly browned. **Yield:** 6 servings.

Open-Faced Tuna Melts

Mom used to make these quick-and-easy sandwiches for us using leftover hamburger buns and fresh tomatoes out of the garden. They're a nice warm change from the usual tuna sandwich. They're also a snap to assemble, easy to eat...and only 40¢ each. —Sandy McKenzie
Braham, Minnesota

 2 cans (6 ounces *each*) tuna, drained and flaked
 1/4 cup mayonnaise *or* salad dressing
 1 green onion, finely chopped
 1 medium dill pickle, finely chopped
 1 teaspoon horseradish sauce
 4 hamburger buns, split
 1 medium tomato, cut into 8 thin slices
 8 slices process American cheese

In a bowl, combine the first five ingredients. Place buns cut side up on a baking sheet. Spread tuna mixture evenly over buns; top with tomato. Bake at 350° for 5 minutes. Top with cheese. Bake 3-5 minutes longer or until cheese is melted. Serve warm. **Yield:** 8 servings.

Vegetarian Chili

Hamburger Hot Dish

With a tossed green salad, this ground beef casserole makes an easy and delightful meal. You won't mind when your family asks for seconds, because the satisfying supper dish costs a mere 87¢ per serving. —Dee Eastman
Fairfield Glade, Tennessee

    2 cups uncooked elbow macaroni
    2 pounds ground beef
    1 can (28 ounces) whole tomatoes, undrained
        and quartered
    1 can (15 ounces) tomato sauce
    1 jar (12 ounces) beef gravy
1/2 cup chopped onion
    1 teaspoon garlic powder

Cook macaroni according to package directions. Meanwhile, in a large skillet, brown beef; drain. Add tomatoes, tomato sauce, gravy, onion and garlic powder. Drain macaroni; add to beef mixture and mix well. Transfer to a greased shallow 3-qt. baking dish. Bake, uncovered, at 350° for 25-30 minutes or until heated through. **Yield:** 8 servings.

Vegetarian Chili

(Pictured above and on page 234)

Hominy and garbanzo beans are interesting additions to this zippy chili. I often serve it with corn bread or flour tortillas for a speedy meal. At 72¢ a serving, you can afford to also. —Karen Hunt, Bellvue, Colorado

✓ Nutritional Analysis included

    2 cans (15 ounces *each*) pinto beans, rinsed
        and drained
    1 can (28 ounces) crushed tomatoes
    1 can (16 ounces) kidney beans, rinsed and
        drained
    1 can (15-1/2 ounces) hominy, rinsed and
        drained
    1 can (15 ounces) garbanzo beans, rinsed and
        drained
    1 can (6 ounces) tomato paste
    1 can (4 ounces) chopped green chilies
    2 small zucchini, halved and thinly sliced
    1 medium onion, chopped
1-1/2 to 2 cups water
    1 to 2 tablespoons chili powder
    1 teaspoon ground cumin
    1 teaspoon salt, optional
1/2 teaspoon garlic powder
1/2 teaspoon sugar
1/2 cup shredded Monterey Jack cheese

In a large kettle or Dutch oven, combine the first 15 ingredients; mix well. Bring to a boil. Reduce heat; cover and simmer for 30-35 minutes. Sprinkle with cheese. **Yield:** 12 servings (about 3 quarts). **Nutritional Analysis:** One 1-cup serving (prepared with no-salt-added tomato paste and fat-free cheese and without salt) equals 217 calories, 507 mg sodium, trace cholesterol, 39 gm carbohydrate, 13 gm protein, 2 gm fat. **Diabetic Exchanges:** 2 starch, 1 lean meat, 1 vegetable.

Peanut Butter Drops

Shredded zucchini is the ingredient that sets these peanut butter cookies apart from others. The soft moist treats have a sweet price—just 5¢ a cookie. —Patricia Teller
Lewiston, Idaho

    1 cup shortening
    1 cup chunky peanut butter
    1 cup packed brown sugar
1/2 cup sugar
    2 eggs
    1 teaspoon vanilla extract
    1 cup shredded peeled zucchini
    3 cups all-purpose flour
    1 teaspoon salt
1/2 teaspoon baking powder
1/2 teaspoon baking soda

In a mixing bowl, cream the shortening, peanut butter and sugars. Beat in eggs and vanilla. Stir in zucchini. Combine dry ingredients; add to the zucchini mixture. Drop by rounded tablespoonfuls 2 in. apart onto greased baking sheets. Bake at 350° for 12-15 minutes or until lightly browned. Cool on wire racks. **Yield:** 5-1/2 dozen.

Apricot Round Steak

(Pictured at right)

Looking for a fun alternative to traditional steak sauce? I serve tender slices of round steak with a sweet apricot sauce that has a hint of pepper. The broiled entree is a snap to prepare and easy on the pocketbook, too, at only 53¢ a serving. —Bernadine Dirmeyer, Harpster, Ohio

1-3/4 pounds boneless top round steak (3/4 inch
        thick)
    3/4 cup apricot preserves
    1 tablespoon lemon juice

1/2 teaspoon salt
1/8 teaspoon hot pepper sauce

Place steak on broiler pan rack; broil for 6-8 minutes on each side. Meanwhile, in a saucepan or microwave-safe bowl, combine remaining ingredients. Cook until preserves are melted. Set aside 1/2 cup; brush remaining sauce over steak. Broil 2-3 minutes longer or until meat reaches desired doneness (for rare, a meat thermometer should read 140°; medium, 160°; well-done, 170°). Slice meat on the diagonal; serve with reserved apricot sauce. **Yield:** 8 servings.

Cabbage Salad

(Pictured below)

This crisp, fresh-tasting slaw keeps in the fridge for several days. It's a bargain besides: 13¢ a serving. We live about an hour from the nearest major city, so shopping trips can be few and far between. I often buy cabbage rather than lettuce for salads because it stores longer.
—*Deborah Moore-Dedenbach, Big Bay, Michigan*

☑ Nutritional Analysis included

1/4 cup vinegar
   2 tablespoons olive *or* vegetable oil
   2 teaspoons garlic salt, optional
   2 teaspoons sugar
1/2 teaspoon dried tarragon
   6 cups shredded cabbage

In a small bowl or jar with tight-fitting lid, combine vinegar, oil, garlic salt if desired, sugar and tarragon. Place the cabbage in a large bowl; add dressing and toss to coat. Cover and refrigerate for at least 2 hours. **Yield:** 7 servings. **Nutritional Analysis:** One 1/2-cup serving (prepared without garlic salt) equals 55 calories, 11 mg sodium, 0 cholesterol, 5 gm carbohydrate, 1 gm protein, 4 gm fat. **Diabetic Exchanges:** 1 vegetable, 1/2 fat.

Saucy Potatoes

(Pictured below)

Cream of chicken soup provides the comforting flavor in this pleasant potato dish. Each homey helping costs a mere 41¢.
—*Edna Hoffman, Hebron, Indiana*

☑ Nutritional Analysis included

   1 can (10-3/4 ounces) condensed cream of chicken soup, undiluted
1/4 cup chicken broth
   5 medium potatoes, peeled, cooked and cubed

In a saucepan, combine soup and broth; stir in potatoes. Cook over medium-low heat until mixture just begins to simmer and potatoes are heated through. **Yield:** 4 servings. **Nutritional Analysis:** One 3/4-cup serving (prepared with low-fat soup and low-sodium broth) equals 166 calories, 288 mg sodium, 5 mg cholesterol, 35 gm carbohydrate, 5 gm protein, 1 gm fat. **Diabetic Exchange:** 2-1/2 starch.

Apricot Round Steak
Saucy Potatoes
Cabbage Salad

Chapter 16

KIDS of all ages will jump at the chance to lend a hand with meal preparation when they see all of these fast, fun foods they can prepare.

From speedy snacks to hearty main dishes, younger children can mix and measure ingredients while older ones help you get a head start on dinner. (Toddlers can also help with the "cleanup" by licking the bowl!)

Your kids are sure to enjoy the hands-on learning, and you'll appreciate the quality time spent together. Best of all, the whole family will be pleased (and proud) to sit down to a family dinner that they helped create.

CHILD'S PLAY. Top to bottom: Chili Bread and Stuffed Celery Sticks (both recipes on p. 253).

Nutty Apple Wedges

A crunchy coating turns apples and peanut butter into a finger-licking snack. Kids have a blast putting them together. —Beatrice Richard, Posen, Michigan

1 medium unpeeled tart apple, cored
1/2 cup peanut butter
1 cup crushed cornflakes

Cut apple into 12 thin wedges. Spread peanut butter on cut sides; roll in cornflakes. **Yield:** 4-6 servings.

Quick Pea Soup

This brightly colored, fresh-tasting soup is one of our daughter's favorites. She purees it in the blender in just seconds, then "zaps" a mugful in the microwave until heated through. —Paula Zsiray, Logan, Utah

☑ Nutritional Analysis included

1-1/2 cups frozen peas, thawed
1-1/4 cups milk, *divided*
1/4 teaspoon salt, optional
1/8 teaspoon pepper

Place the peas and 1/4 cup of milk in a blender; cover and process until pureed. Pour into a saucepan; add salt if desired, pepper and remaining milk. Cook and stir for 5 minutes or until heated through. **Yield:** 2 servings. **Nutritional Analysis:** One 1-cup serving (prepared with skim milk and without salt) equals 137 calories, 200 mg sodium, 3 mg cholesterol, 22 gm carbohydrate, 11 gm protein, 1 gm fat. **Diabetic Exchanges:** 1 starch, 1 skim milk.

Caramel Corn Puffs

Both kids and adults find these sweet and crunchy puffs habit-forming. They make a perfect late-night snack and travel well when you're on the run. —Dawn Fagerstrom Warren, Minnesota

1 package (8 ounces) popped hulled popcorn*
2 cups packed brown sugar
1 cup butter *or* margarine
1/2 cup dark corn syrup
1 teaspoon vanilla extract
1/2 teaspoon baking soda

Place the popcorn in a large bowl and set aside. In a saucepan, combine brown sugar, butter and corn syrup; bring to a boil over medium heat, stirring constantly. Boil for 5 minutes, stirring occasionally. Remove from the heat. Stir in vanilla and baking soda; mix well. Pour over popcorn and mix until well coated. Pour into two greased 15-in. x 10-in. x 1-in. baking pans. Bake, uncovered, at 250° for 1 hour, stirring every 15 minutes. Cool completely. Store in airtight containers or plastic bags. **Yield:** about 4-1/2 quarts. ***Editor's Note:** Popped hulled popcorn can be found in the snack aisle of grocery stores. Regular popcorn can also be substituted.

Circle-O Skillet Supper

Circle-O Skillet Supper

(Pictured at left)

This quick-to-fix macaroni and hot dog combination will please kids of all ages. Our grandchildren love it, and I like it because we can make it together with things I have on hand. —Anna Mayer Fort Branch, Indiana

5 hot dogs, sliced*
1/4 cup chopped onion
1 tablespoon vegetable oil
1-1/2 cups water
1/2 cup chili sauce
1 tablespoon prepared mustard
1 tablespoon sugar
1-1/2 teaspoons cornstarch
1/2 teaspoon salt
Pinch pepper
1-1/4 cups elbow macaroni, cooked and drained

In a skillet, cook hot dogs and onion in oil until lightly browned. Combine the next seven ingredients; mix well. Stir into skillet; bring to a boil. Reduce heat; cook and stir for 2 minutes. Add macaroni; cook on low until heated through. **Yield:** 4-5 servings. ***Editor's Note:** If serving small children, cut the hot dog circles in half.

'Burgers and Fries' Are a Sweet Surprise

**Cookie Burgers
Peanutty Fries**

YOU may have to install a drive-thru window in your kitchen after family and friends sample these playful treats from the Hershey Kitchens!

Kids will have fun helping craft the look-alike "burgers and fries". (They're great for a birthday or school party.)

Made with a packaged sugar cookie mix and peanut butter chips, the "buns" hold a "patty" of deliciously creamy cocoa icing on a bed of green-tinted coconut "lettuce". The "fries" are cut from a quick peanut butter fudge and drizzled with red-tinted icing "ketchup".

Cookie Burgers

(Pictured above right)

DOUGH:
- 1 package (22.3 ounces) golden sugar cookie mix
- 2 eggs
- 1/3 cup vegetable oil
- 1 teaspoon water

- 1 package (10 ounces) peanut butter chips, chopped

TOPPING:
- 3/4 cup flaked coconut
- 5 to 6 drops green food coloring

FILLING:
- 1/2 cup butter *or* margarine, softened
- 2-2/3 cups confectioners' sugar
- 1/2 cup baking cocoa
- 1/4 cup milk
- 1 teaspoon vanilla extract

In a large bowl, combine cookie mix, eggs, oil and water; mix well. Stir in peanut butter chips. Shape into 1-1/4-in. balls; place 2 in. apart on ungreased baking sheets. Bake at 375° for 9-11 minutes or until lightly browned. Remove to wire racks to cool. Toss coconut and food coloring until coated; set aside. In a mixing bowl, cream butter. Add sugar, cocoa, milk and vanilla; beat until smooth. Frost the bottoms of 22 cookies; sprinkle with coconut. Top with remaining cookies and gently squeeze together. **Yield:** 22 sandwich cookies. **Editor's Note:** You may substitute your favorite sugar cookie recipe for the cookie mix, eggs, oil and water; just add the peanut butter chips.

Peanutty Fries

(Pictured above)

- 1 package (10 ounces) peanut butter chips
- 1 cup sweetened condensed milk
- Paper muffin cup liners (2-1/2-inch diameter)
- Red icing, optional

In a microwave or double boiler, melt peanut butter chips with milk; stir until smooth. Pour into a 9-in. baking pan lined with foil and greased. Cool completely at room temperature. Lift out of the pan and invert onto a cutting board. Remove foil; cut into 3-in. x 1/4-in. strips. Fold muffin cup liners in half, pressing out creases; fold in half again. Fold point under; use as holders for fries. Use icing for ketchup if desired. **Yield:** about 3-1/2 dozen.

Pint-Size Snackers Prize Pickles

HAVING a hard time getting kids to eat their vegetables? A survey conducted by Pickle Packers International reports that schoolkids from all across the country choose pickles as a favorite snack.

So it's nice to know that 1/8 cup of pickles counts as one of the five daily servings of fruits and vegetables recommended by the United States Department of Agriculture.

If you're in a pickle for after-school snack ideas, consider some of these suggestions provided by Pickle Packers International:

- Create a cool pickle pop by skewering a chilled large dill pickle on an ice cream stick. Young kids love them!
- Wrap a baby dill or sweet gherkin with a slice of lean ham or smoked turkey for a taste-tempting treat. For extra flavor, spread cream cheese on one side of the meat before wrapping.
- Make munchable pickle kabobs by threading wooden skewers with chunks of pickle, cheddar cheese, ham or salami. You could also add whole pepperoncinis and pitted olives for a pretty presentation.
- Boost the flavor of a grilled cheese sandwich by adding a layer of bread and butter pickles. After grilling, cut the sandwiches into triangles.

Busy Bodies Will Buzz Over Bite-Size Bees

Peanut Butter Honeybees

ADORABLE is the best way to describe these yummy peanut buttery treats from Heather Bazinet of Ingleside, Ontario.

"I was thrilled when a friend shared this clever recipe," she informs. "Children young and old find these snacks irresistible."

Even the youngest kitchen helpers can help out by crushing the graham crackers or measuring and mixing the ingredients.

They'll love getting their fingers sticky as they roll the soft and squishy dough into little bee bodies. (And we bet they'll sample a bit while they make 'em!)

Older kids can add the chocolate stripes while the younger set turns sliced almonds into crunchy wings.

It won't "bee" long before busy hands complete the sweet treats...and beg to make another batch.

Peanut Butter Honeybees

(Pictured above right)

1/2 cup creamy peanut butter
2 tablespoons butter or margarine, softened
1/2 cup confectioners' sugar
3/4 cup graham cracker crumbs (about 12 squares)

1 square (1 ounce) semisweet chocolate
1/3 cup sliced almonds, toasted

In a mixing bowl, cream peanut butter, butter and sugar until smooth. Add crumbs and mix well. Shape teaspoonfuls of dough into 1-1/4-in. ovals; place on a waxed paper-lined baking sheet. Place chocolate in a small microwave-safe bowl; microwave on high for 1 minute or until melted. Transfer melted chocolate to a resealable plastic bag; cut a small hole in corner of bag. Pipe three stripes on each bee. Insert two almonds into each bee for wings. Use a toothpick to poke holes for eyes. Store in the refrigerator. **Yield:** 4 dozen.

Use Your Noodle in the Kitchen

COOKING is a terrific way for parents and children to spend time together, learn about nutrition and create tasty meals. It also offers beginning cooks an opportunity to learn about safety in the kitchen.

The folks at Kellogg's have compiled the following tips to make your family's time in the kitchen both safe and satisfying:

- Tie back long hair, roll up loose sleeves and cover your clothes with an apron or smock.
- Never use wet hands to plug in or unplug electrical appliances.
- Read the entire recipe before you start cooking.
- Gather all the ingredients and utensils you need for the recipe before you begin.
- An adult should assist when the stove, oven or microwave is used. Parents should also help when hot pans, pots and bowls are handled...when electrical appliances such as can openers are used...and when knives are utilized for cutting food.
- Keep clean, dry oven mitts or hot pads nearby for safe handling of hot pans, pots or bowls.
- When cooking on the stove, point pot handles toward the back of the stove to prevent spills.
- Wash your hands with soap and water and dry them before handling food. Also thoroughly wash hands after touching uncooked foods like meat and poultry.
- Clean up spills on the floor immediately to prevent slipping.
- Always turn off the stove burners and the oven as soon as you're finished cooking.

Ham and Cheese Bagels

(Pictured below)

These fun bite-size bagel sandwiches are easy to fix for breakfast, lunch, snacks and family get-togethers.
—Kristin Dallum, Vancouver, Washington

    1 package (3 ounces) cream cheese, softened
    6 miniature bagels, split
    3 ounces thinly sliced fully cooked ham
    4 ounces cheddar cheese, thinly sliced
    6 thin slices tomato
    1 tablespoon chopped red onion
  1/4 cup pineapple tidbits
  1/4 teaspoon dried parsley flakes

Spread cream cheese over cut sides of bagels. Place on an ungreased baking sheet with cream cheese side up. Cut the ham and cheddar cheese into 2-in. squares; place over cream cheese. Top half of the bagels with tomato and onion and half with pineapple and parsley. Bake at 350° for 10 minutes or until cheese is melted. **Yield:** 1 dozen.

Peanut Butter 'n' Jelly Pie

(Pictured below)

This is a tempting twist on a traditional twosome. A chocolate crumb crust holds a rich peanut butter layer topped with strawberry preserves and whipped cream. The tasty make-ahead dessert is sure to appeal to the young... and the young at heart.
—Vikki Rebholz
West Chester, Ohio

    1 package (8 ounces) cream cheese, softened
  1/2 cup confectioners' sugar
  1/3 cup peanut butter
    1 chocolate crumb crust (9 inches)
  1/2 cup strawberry preserves
    2 cups whipped topping
Additional strawberry preserves, optional

In a mixing bowl, beat cream cheese, sugar and peanut butter until smooth. Spread into crust. Top with preserves and whipped topping. Cover and refrigerate for 4 hours or overnight. If desired, dollop additional preserves on top before serving. **Yield:** 8 servings.

Peanut Butter 'n' Jelly Pie
Ham and Cheese Bagels

Strawberry Banana Shakes
Breakfast Pizza

Breakfast Pizza

(Pictured above)

Pizza for breakfast? Kids of all ages will love making—and munching—this hearty meal-in-one made with convenient crescent rolls and frozen hash browns. It's great for brunch, camping or whenever you want to feed a lot of people at one time. —Rae Truax, Mattawa, Washington

  1 tube (8 ounces) refrigerated crescent rolls
  1 pound bulk pork sausage
  1 cup frozen shredded hash brown potatoes, thawed
  1 cup (4 ounces) shredded cheddar cheese
  3 eggs
1/4 cup milk
1/4 teaspoon pepper
1/4 cup grated Parmesan cheese

Unroll crescent dough and place on a greased 12-in. pizza pan; press seams together and press up sides of pan to form a crust. In a skillet, brown sausage over medium heat; drain and cool slightly. Sprinkle sausage, hash browns and cheddar cheese over crust. In a bowl, beat eggs, milk and pepper; pour over pizza. Sprinkle with Parmesan cheese. Bake at 375° for 28-30 minutes or until golden brown. Let stand 10 minutes before cutting. **Yield:** 6-8 servings.

Strawberry Banana Shakes

(Pictured above)

This very thick, not-too-sweet shake packs a big strawberry and banana taste. It's easy to mix together in the blender. I especially like it topped with whipped cream. —Grant Dixon, Roseburg, Oregon

1/4 cup milk
  1 cup strawberry ice cream
  1 medium firm banana, sliced
Whipped cream and two fresh strawberries, optional

Place milk, ice cream and banana in a blender; cover and process until smooth. Pour into glasses. Serve immediately. Garnish with whipped cream and a strawberry if desired. **Yield:** 2 servings.

Sweet Cereal Treats

It doesn't take long to mix up a batch of these yummy snacks since they have only four ingredients and don't need to bake. As a small child, I helped my grandma make them. Now my three children enjoy helping me. We all love this crunchy treat.
—Barri VanderHulst
Allegan, Michigan

5-1/3 cups Peanut Butter Captain Crunch cereal
1 cup dry roasted peanuts
1 package (12 ounces) vanilla baking chips
1 tablespoon butter (no substitutes)

In a large bowl, combine cereal and peanuts; set aside. In a microwave or double boiler, melt chips and butter; stir until smooth. Pour over cereal mixture and stir to coat. Drop by rounded tablespoonfuls onto waxed paper-lined baking sheets. Refrigerate until firm. **Yield:** about 5 dozen.

Katie's Sugar 'n' Spice

Orange peel gives an extra boost of flavor to this cinnamon-sugar mixture. It's so simple for youngsters to mix up. I use it when making cinnamon toast, French toast, cinnamon rolls, applesauce and peach or apple pies.
—Katie Koziolek, Hartland, Minnesota

2 cups sugar
1 tablespoon ground cinnamon
1-1/4 teaspoons dried orange peel
3/4 teaspoon ground nutmeg

Combine all ingredients; store in a shaker jar. Sprinkle on toast, French toast or applesauce, or use as you would plain cinnamon-sugar. **Yield:** 2 cups.

Gooey Peanut Treats

Youngsters need only a few easy ingredients to whip up a big panful of these chocolaty, peanut-packed squares. When they're served at our family reunions, it's not just the kids who rush to the dessert table. —Angela Wisdom
Athens, Alabama

2 cups (12 ounces) semisweet chocolate chips
1 can (14 ounces) sweetened condensed milk
1 jar (16 ounces) salted dry roasted peanuts
1 package (10-1/2 ounces) miniature marshmallows

In a microwave or saucepan over low heat, cook and stir chocolate chips and milk until smooth. Stir in the peanuts and marshmallows. Pat into a greased 13-in. x 9-in. x 2-in. pan. Cool completely before cutting. **Yield:** 2 to 2-1/2 dozen.

Teddies Will Tickle Your Taste Buds

Teddy Bear Biscuits

Teddy Bear Biscuits

(Pictured at left)

Refrigerated biscuit dough makes these cute cinnamony bears easy, convenient and fun!
—Catherine Berra Bleem, Walsh, Illinois

1 tube (7-1/2 ounces) refrigerated buttermilk biscuits (10 biscuits)
1 egg, beaten
2 tablespoons sugar
1/4 teaspoon ground cinnamon
9 miniature semisweet chocolate chips

For each bear, shape one biscuit into an oval for the body and place on a greased baking sheet. Cut one biscuit into four pieces; shape into balls for arms and legs. Place next to body. Cut one biscuit into two small pieces and one large piece; shape into head and ears and place above body. Brush with egg. Combine sugar and cinnamon; sprinkle over bears. Bake at 425° for 8-10 minutes (the one remaining biscuit can be baked with the bears). Place chocolate chips on head for eyes and nose while the biscuits are still warm. **Yield:** 3 bears.

Bubble Pizza

(Pictured below)

A top-ranked food with teens, pizza can quickly quell a growling tummy! This recipe has a no-fuss crust made from refrigerated biscuits. —*Jo Groth, Plainfield, Iowa*

1-1/2 pounds ground beef
   1 can (15 ounces) pizza sauce
   2 tubes (12 ounces *each*) refrigerated buttermilk biscuits
1-1/2 cups (6 ounces) shredded mozzarella cheese
   1 cup (4 ounces) shredded cheddar cheese

In a skillet, brown the beef; drain. Stir in pizza sauce. Quarter the biscuits; place in a greased 13-in. x 9-in. x 2-in. baking dish. Top with the beef mixture. Bake, uncovered, at 400° for 20-25 minutes. Sprinkle with the cheeses. Bake 5-10 minutes longer or until cheese is melted. Let stand for 5-10 minutes before serving. **Yield:** 6-8 servings.

Dogs in a Sweater

(Pictured below)

For a new twist on an old favorite, try these skewered hot dogs from the National Hot Dog and Sausage Council. They're fun to dip in ketchup, mustard or ranch dressing.

   1 package (11 ounces) refrigerated breadstick dough

8 hot dogs
8 Popsicle sticks
Ketchup, mustard *and/or* ranch dressing

Separate dough; roll each piece into a 15-in. rope. Insert sticks into hot dogs lengthwise. Starting at one end, wrap dough in a spiral around hot dog; pinch ends to seal. Place 1 in. apart on a baking sheet that has been coated with nonstick cooking spray. Bake at 350° for 18-20 minutes. Serve with toppings of your choice. **Yield:** 8 servings.

Fruit Cocktail Ice Pops

Even adults like these refreshing, fruity snacks. And they're so easy to make—kids can spoon the fruit cocktail into plastic cups in a jiffy. The hard part is waiting for them to freeze! —*Jeanie Beers, Montgomery, New York*

✓ Nutritional Analysis included

   1 can (29 ounces) fruit cocktail in extra light syrup, undrained
  12 Popsicle molds *or* 12 paper cups (3 ounces *each*) and Popsicle sticks

Fill molds or cups with about 1/4 cup fruit cocktail; top with holders or insert sticks into cups. Freeze. **Yield:** 1 dozen. **Nutritional Analysis:** One serving equals 31 calories, 3 mg sodium, 0 cholesterol, 8 gm carbohydrate, trace protein, trace fat. **Diabetic Exchange:** 1/2 fruit.

Dogs in a Sweater
Bubble Pizza

Savor Summer's Sweetness with Fun Watermelon Slices

WHEN she made Watermelon Cookies for her daughter's kindergarten class, they were an instant hit, shares Diane Hunt of Logansport, Indiana. "The students loved these frosted treats and gobbled them up!" she says.

Decorated to look like watermelon slices, the cute cookies are especially nice for summer picnics and family gatherings.

They're fun to make, too. Youngsters can help roll out the make-ahead dough and cut out circle shapes with a cookie cutter.

After the cookies are baked, kids can lend a hand by trimming the treats with tinted frosting to resemble a watermelon's green rind and pretty pink inside. (A convenient can of prepared frosting and a few drops of food coloring make this step a breeze.)

Then sprinkle mini chocolate chips on top for "seeds"—if you can keep your helpers from sampling them first!

Bunch Up for Brunch

THE CRUNCH of work, school and social calendars can interrupt family meals during the week. Leisurely weekend brunches at home are a fun way to make up for lost time.

The following tips from chef Francis Anthony and the Minute Maid Company will help you and your children make the most of this tasty time:

It's a Date. Schedule a brunch in advance. Make sure the whole family has the time and date on their calendars.

Creativity Is Key. Pick a theme focused on the season, a holiday or special family milestone. Reflect it in the menu and decorations.

Go Get It. A day or two before brunch, turn a trip to the grocery store into a treasure hunt. Give children a list of clues that will lead them to the items needed for the event.

Divide and Conquer. Involve all family members in preparing for the occasion. Have teens pick flowers and make a centerpiece. Let younger kids fold napkins and set the table.

Polish It Up. Break out the good dishes and glasses and eat in the dining room to create an elegant atmosphere.

Cheers! Whip up especially festive drinks. Making beverages can be a fun hands-on activity for children.

Mind Your Manners. Use brunch as a backdrop for teaching and practicing table manners, etiquette and the old-fashioned art of family conversation.

Smile! Capture your family cooks in action on home video or in photographs.

Watermelon Cookies

Watermelon Cookies

(Pictured above)

       1 cup butter (no substitutes), softened
1-1/2 cups sugar
       2 eggs
       1 teaspoon vanilla extract
       3 cups all-purpose flour
       1 teaspoon baking soda
    1/2 teaspoon salt
       1 cup (8 ounces) sour cream
       1 can (12 ounces) whipped vanilla frosting
Red and green food coloring
Miniature chocolate chips

In a mixing bowl, cream butter and sugar. Add eggs and vanilla; mix well. Combine flour, baking soda and salt; add to the creamed mixture alternately with the sour cream. Cover and refrigerate for 2 hours or overnight. On a heavily floured surface, roll out half of the dough at a time to 1/8-in. thickness. Cut with a 3-in. round cookie cutter; cut circles in half. Place on ungreased baking sheets. Bake at 375° for 9-10 minutes or until bottoms are lightly browned and cookies are set. Cool on wire racks. Place two-thirds of the frosting in a bowl; add red food coloring. Add green food coloring to the remaining frosting. Spread pink frosting on tops of cookies. Frost the edges with green frosting, using a pastry bag with a small star tip if desired. Place chocolate chips randomly over the pink frosting for seeds. **Yield:** about 8-1/2 dozen.

Cute Fruit Critters Are Fun To Decorate

Mousy Pear Salad

YOU won't mind if there's a mouse in the house when your kids help make their own Mousy Pear Salad.

"When our five children were small, they loved to make these fun fruit salads," states Marie Hoyer of Hodgenville, Kentucky.

The darling decorated pears are quick and easy for kids to assemble and made with ingredients they love.

"The youngsters gobbled up any leftover cheese and licorice as soon as the mice were assembled," Marie recalls. "And the salads were the first thing they'd dig into when we started supper."

Creative kids can come up with different animals using the pear half as a body. For example, with longer cheese ears and a mini-marshmallow tail, you have a bunny. Use your imagination!

Mousy Pear Salad

(Pictured above right)

✓ **Nutritional Analysis included**

> 2 cups shredded lettuce *or* lettuce leaves
> 1 can (15 ounces) pear halves, drained
> 24 raisins
> Black shoestring licorice—cut into four 3-inch pieces and sixteen 1-inch pieces
> 1 red maraschino cherry, quartered
> 1 slice process American cheese

On four salad plates, place lettuce and a pear half, cut side down. Insert two raisins at narrow end of pear for eyes. Tuck four raisins under pear for feet. Insert one 3-in. licorice piece into wide end of each pear for a tail. Insert four 1-in. pieces into each face for whiskers. Place a cherry piece under whiskers for nose. For ears, cut small teardrop-shaped pieces from cheese; place just above the eyes. **Yield:** 4 servings. **Nutritional Analysis:** One serving (prepared with light process American cheese) equals 150 calories, 126 mg sodium, 3 mg cholesterol, 36 gm carbohydrate, 2 gm protein, 1 gm fat. **Diabetic Exchanges:** 2 fruit, 1/2 starch.

Beware the Brown-Bag Blues

IT DOESN'T take long for lunch-toting schoolkids to get bored with the same lunch choices week after week. How can you give their noontime menu a quick pick-me-up? Just try a few of the following ideas.

Spice Up Sandwiches

- Replace good ol' white bread with fun alternatives such as tortillas, croissants, bagels, biscuits, English muffins, slices of raisin or nut bread or even hot dog or hamburger buns.
- Try a different sandwich filling or put a spin on an old favorite. Blend peanut butter with apple butter or grated carrots...combine cottage cheese with pineapple tidbits...add apple and almonds to a favorite chicken salad recipe.

Try Something New

- Instead of sandwiches, send along leftovers kids can eat with their hands like slices of cold pizza or quiche.
- Try salads with fun fixings like sliced cucumber, green pepper chunks, raw cauliflower, cherry tomatoes, shredded cheese, ripe olives, peanuts, sunflower kernels, croutons or orange sections. Be sure to send along a small plastic container of salad dressing, too.
- Prepare an assortment of crackers with cheese, sausage and deli meats cut into cracker-size pieces. Or add a small container of spreadable cheese.

Tuck in Extras

- Kids love to dip. Send along fresh veggies with a side of ranch dressing or dill dip, or mixed fresh fruit cubes with a container of fruit yogurt.
- Pick up handy portion-size containers of applesauce, fruit cocktail, gelatin, yogurt or pudding.
- Fill a resealable snack bag with raisins, dried apricots, banana chips, popcorn, peanuts, pretzels or granola.

Note: Be sure to refrigerate meat and dairy items or place in an insulated lunch bag with reusable ice pack. In general, keep cold foods cold and hot foods hot.

Mallow Fruit Cups

Instead of serving plain fruit cocktail, I toss in a few of my family's favorite ingredients to make this colorful concoction. I created the quick salad when our boys were younger, and it's been around ever since as a good hurry-up fill-in at meals. —Karen Coffman, Delphi, Indiana

✓ Nutritional Analysis included

    1 can (15 ounces) fruit cocktail, drained
    1 medium tart apple, diced
    1/2 cup miniature marshmallows
    1/2 cup whipped topping

In a bowl, combine all ingredients. Cover and refrigerate until serving. **Yield:** 4-6 servings. **Nutritional Analysis:** One 1/2-cup serving (prepared with light whipped topping) equals 91 calories, 6 mg sodium, 0 cholesterol, 21 gm carbohydrate, trace protein, 1 gm fat. **Diabetic Exchange:** 1-1/2 fruit.

Peppy Macaroni

I like to keep an extra box of macaroni and cheese on the pantry shelf to make this fun pizza-flavored casserole for unexpected guests. Because it's a snap to prepare, older kids could assemble it to give Mom and Dad a break from dinner duties. —Helen Cluts, Sioux Falls, South Dakota

    1 package (7-1/4 ounces) macaroni and cheese dinner
    2 eggs, lightly beaten
    1 jar (8 ounces) pizza sauce
    40 slices pepperoni (about 2-1/2 ounces)
    2 cups (8 ounces) shredded mozzarella cheese

Prepare macaroni and cheese according to package directions. Fold in eggs. Spread into a greased 13-in. x 9-in. x 2-in. baking dish. Top with pizza sauce, pepperoni and mozzarella. Bake, uncovered, at 350° for 30-35 minutes or until lightly browned and cheese is melted. Let stand for 5 minutes before serving. **Yield:** 4 servings.

Chili Bread

(Pictured at right and on page 243)

Dressed-up chili, sprinkled with colorful red tomatoes, green onions and mozzarella cheese, makes a tasty topping for a loaf of crusty French bread. This filling open-faced sandwich tastes terrific and can be made in minutes.
—Marian Dinwiddie
Roy, Washington

    1 loaf (1 pound) French bread
    1 can (16 ounces) kidney beans, rinsed and drained
    1 can (15 ounces) chili without beans

    3/4 to 1 cup spaghetti sauce
    1 garlic clove, minced
    1 medium tomato, chopped
    2 green onions, thinly sliced
    1 cup (4 ounces) shredded mozzarella cheese
    2 tablespoons grated Parmesan cheese

Cut bread in half lengthwise; place with cut side up on a foil-lined baking sheet. Combine beans, chili, spaghetti sauce and garlic; spread over the bread. Top with tomato and onions. Sprinkle with cheeses. Bake at 350° for 10-12 minutes or until the cheese is melted. **Yield:** 8 servings.

Stuffed Celery Sticks

(Pictured below and on page 242)

I mix cream cheese, soy sauce and peanut butter to give this stuffed celery a rich, unique flavor. The filling is easy to blend together, and kids will have a ball squeezing it into the celery sticks before they start crunching away.
—Opal Schmidt, Battle Creek, Iowa

    1 package (3 ounces) cream cheese, softened
    1/4 cup creamy peanut butter
    1 tablespoon milk
    2 teaspoons soy sauce
    4 celery ribs, cut into serving-size pieces

In a small mixing bowl, beat the cream cheese, peanut butter, milk and soy sauce until smooth. Transfer to a small resealable plastic bag. Cut a small hole in the corner of the bag; pipe mixture into celery pieces. **Yield:** 4 servings.

Chili Bread
Stuffed Celery Sticks

Turkey Treats Are Talk Of the Table

TURKEY at Thanksgiving is a timeless tradition. But you can give your meal a novel twist with these birds of a different feather.

The holiday treats are cute, sweet and made from all kinds of goodies youngsters love to nibble on.

"The kids and I had a ball making these tasty turkeys for Thanksgiving one year," shares Sue Gronholz of Columbus, Wisconsin.

"They loved forming the turkey bodies from the gooey cereal mixture and twisting the sandwich cookies apart," she reports. "But using chocolate frosting to 'glue' on the candy corn was their favorite part."

These festive fall treats also would make fun favors at each place setting on your Thanksgiving table.

Gobbler Goodies

(Pictured below)

> 1/4 cup butter *or* margarine
> 4 cups miniature marshmallows
> 6 cups crisp rice cereal
> 28 chocolate cream-filled sandwich cookies
> 1-1/2 cups chocolate frosting
> 1 package (12-1/2 ounces) candy corn

In a large saucepan, melt butter. Add marshmallows; stir over low heat until melted. Stir in the cereal. Cool for 10 minutes. With buttered hands, form cereal mixture into 1-1/2-in. balls. Twist apart sandwich cookies; spread frosting on the inside of cookies. Place 28 cookie halves under cereal balls to form the base for each turkey. Place three pieces of candy corn in a fan pattern on remaining cookie halves; press each half onto a cereal ball to form the tail. Attach remaining candy corn with frosting to form turkey's head. **Yield:** 28 servings.

Gobbler Goodies

Bacon Biscuit Wreath

(Pictured at right)

As a Girl Scout leader, I showed my troop how to make this pretty golden wreath. The girls (and even some of their parents) enjoyed making and sampling the cheesy appetizer. It's a snap to prepare with cheese spread and convenient refrigerated biscuits.
> —Kathy Kirkland, Denham Springs, Louisiana

> 1 jar (5 ounces) sharp American cheese spread
> 3 tablespoons butter-flavored shortening
> 1 tube (12 ounces) flaky biscuits
> 4 bacon strips, cooked and crumbled
> 2 tablespoons minced fresh parsley

In a small saucepan, melt the cheese spread and shortening; stir until blended. Pour into a well-greased 6-cup ovenproof ring mold or 9-in. fluted tube pan. Cut each biscuit into quarters and place over cheese mixture. Bake at 400° for 12-14 minutes or until golden brown. Immediately invert pan onto a serving platter and remove. Sprinkle with bacon and parsley. Serve warm. **Yield:** 10 servings.

Tender Chicken Nuggets

(Pictured at right)

I came up with this recipe for our son, who likes the fried chicken nuggets we get at a fast-food restaurant. These tender chunks of chicken with a tasty corn-flake crumb coating are fun to make—and eat.
> —Linda Keller, Jonesboro, Arkansas

> 1 cup crushed cornflakes
> 1/2 cup grated Parmesan cheese
> 1/2 teaspoon salt
> 1/4 teaspoon pepper
> 1/8 teaspoon garlic powder
> 1/4 cup prepared ranch salad dressing
> 1 pound boneless skinless chicken breasts, cut into 1-inch cubes
> Additional ranch dressing

In a shallow bowl, combine the first five ingredients. Place dressing in another bowl. Toss chicken cubes in dressing, then roll in the cornflake mixture. Place in a greased 11-in. x 7-in. x 2-in. baking pan. Bake, uncovered, at 400° for 12-15 minutes or until juices run clear. Serve with additional dressing for dipping. **Yield:** 4 servings.

Peanut Butter-Jelly Spread

With just five simple ingredients, kids of all ages can stir up this sweet peanut butter spread in a jiffy. It's wonderful slathered on warm biscuits for breakfast.
> —Connie Bell, Wagoner, Oklahoma

> 1 cup peanut butter
> 1/4 cup butter *or* margarine
> 3/4 cup strawberry jam *or* preserves
> 1/4 cup honey

Tender Chicken Nuggets
Bacon Biscuit Wreath

2 tablespoons maple syrup
Warm biscuits *or* toast

In a microwave-safe bowl, combine the peanut butter and butter. Microwave, uncovered, on high for 1 to 1-1/2 minutes or until melted. Stir until smooth. Add jam, honey and syrup; mix well. Serve on biscuits or toast. **Yield:** 2-1/2 cups. **Editor's Note:** This recipe was tested in an 850-watt microwave.

Cashew Candies

Salted nut rolls were my mother's favorite candy bar, so I always think of her when I make these sweet snacks. Youngsters can help knead and shape the marshmallow mixture and later roll the treats in nuts after they have been dipped in caramel.
—Darlene Markel
Sublimity, Oregon

3 cups confectioners' sugar
1 jar (7 ounces) marshmallow creme
1 teaspoon vanilla extract
1/4 teaspoon almond extract
1 package (14 ounces) caramels
3 tablespoons water
3 cups chopped salted cashews

In a bowl, combine the first four ingredients; knead until smooth (mixture will be dry). Shape into eight rolls 5 in. long x 1/2 in. in diameter (do not butter hands before shaping the mixture). Wrap in waxed paper and freeze until firm, about 2 hours. Place the caramels in a shallow microwave-safe dish; microwave, uncovered, on high until melted. Add water; stir until smooth. Carefully dip the frozen rolls into the caramel mixture, then roll in cashews. Wrap in waxed paper and refrigerate for 1 hour. Cut into 1/3-in. slices. **Yield:** 3-1/2 dozen.

Chapter 17

⏰ 'Makeovers' Make Favorites Faster

IT'S no wonder Grandma served such comforting, down-home dishes...she spent all day in the kitchen!

Now you can savor those old-fashioned foods once more and enjoy time to spare. With these "recipe redos", our home economists prove older recipes can be streamlined without sacrificing their satisfying great taste.

Readers shared family-favorite dishes and asked us to rework them into speedier forms. We then tested the revised recipes against the originals. The home-style flavors are so appealing you might even fool Grandma!

QUICK CHANGE. Top to bottom: Traditional Beef Potpie and Quicker Beef Potpie (recipes on p. 264).

Quicker Chicken and Dumplings

HOMEY "from-scratch" dishes like this are often just memories for today's busy cooks.

"My family really loves Chicken and Dumplings," confides Edna Hoffman of Hebron, Indiana. "But can you provide some shortcuts for preparing this time-consuming favorite?"

Our test kitchen promptly took up Edna's challenge by creating Quicker Chicken and Dumplings. Instead of making homemade broth, this revised recipe calls for frozen or canned broth. This dish is ready to eat in about a third the time, thanks to chicken breasts and purchased biscuit mix.

Chicken and Dumplings

✓ Nutritional Analysis included

  1 broiler/fryer chicken (2-1/2 to 3 pounds), cut up
  2 to 2-1/4 quarts water
1/2 cup sliced celery
1/2 cup sliced carrots
  2 fresh parsley sprigs
  1 bay leaf
  1 teaspoon salt
1/4 teaspoon pepper

DUMPLINGS:
  3/4 cup all-purpose flour
    1 tablespoon minced fresh parsley
    1 teaspoon baking powder
  1/4 teaspoon salt
Dash ground nutmeg
  1/3 cup milk
    1 egg, lightly beaten
    1 tablespoon vegetable oil
GRAVY:
  1/4 cup all-purpose flour
  1/2 cup water
  1/4 teaspoon salt
  1/8 teaspoon pepper

Place the first eight ingredients in a 5-qt. Dutch oven or kettle. Cover and bring to a boil; skim fat. Reduce heat; cover and simmer for 1-1/2 hours or until the chicken is tender. In a bowl, combine the first five dumpling ingredients; stir in milk, egg and oil. Drop by tablespoonfuls onto boiling broth. Cover and cook without lifting lid for 12-15 minutes or until dumplings are tender. Remove the dumplings and chicken with a slotted spoon to a serving dish; keep warm. Strain broth, reserving 2 cups for gravy (save remaining broth for another use). Place reserved broth in a saucepan; bring to a boil. Combine flour, water, salt and pepper until smooth; gradually stir into broth. Cook and stir over medium heat until thickened, about 2 minutes. Pour over chicken and dumplings. **Yield:** 4 servings. **Nutritional Analysis:** One serving equals 491 calories, 1,139 mg sodium, 162 mg cholesterol, 28 gm carbohydrate, 32 gm protein, 27 gm fat. **Diabetic Exchanges:** 3 meat, 3 fat, 2 starch.

Quicker Chicken and Dumplings

(Pictured at left)

✓ Nutritional Analysis included

    4 cups chicken broth
1/2 cup sliced celery
1/2 cup sliced carrots
    1 bay leaf
    1 teaspoon dried parsley flakes
DUMPLINGS:
    2 cups biscuit/baking mix
1/4 teaspoon dried thyme
Dash ground nutmeg
2/3 cup milk
1/2 teaspoon dried parsley flakes
    3 cups cubed cooked chicken breast

In a 5-qt. Dutch oven or kettle, combine the broth, celery, carrots, bay leaf and parsley; bring to a boil. For dumplings, combine biscuit mix, thyme and nutmeg; stir in milk and parsley just until moistened. Drop by tablespoonfuls onto the boiling broth. Cook, uncovered, for 10 minutes; cover and cook 10 minutes longer. With a slotted spoon, remove dumplings to a serving dish; keep warm. Bring broth to a boil. Reduce heat; add chicken and heat through. Remove bay leaf. Spoon over the dumplings. **Yield:** 4 servings. **Nutritional Analysis:** One serving (prepared with low-sodium broth, reduced-fat biscuit/baking mix and skim milk) equals 374 calories, 858 mg sodium, 69 mg cholesterol, 48 gm carbohydrate, 26 gm protein, 9 gm fat. **Diabetic Exchanges:** 3 starch, 3 very lean meat, 1 fat.

FROM Ulster, Pennsylvania, Beth Ask, a registered dietitian, sent a low-fat remake of a popular side dish—which we made faster.

"I swapped olives for sweet pickle relish and used one fewer egg," notes Beth. "Plus, I replaced the mayonnaise with a fat-free version."

Then, our kitchen crew substituted leftover baked potatoes to come up with Quicker Potato Salad.

Traditional Potato Salad

✓ Nutritional Analysis included

    3 medium potatoes (about 1-1/2 pounds)
    1 tablespoon cider vinegar
    1 teaspoon sugar
1/2 cup chopped celery
1/3 cup chopped onion
1/4 cup chopped stuffed olives
1/2 teaspoon salt
1/2 teaspoon celery seed

Time-Saving Kitchen Tips

TO SAVE even more precious minutes in the kitchen, try these hot hints from fellow cooks:

- Making shepherd's pie? Instead of fussing with mashed potatoes, combine a can of cream of celery soup with milk and frozen hash browns, then layer that mixture on top of your meat and vegetables.
    —Tanya Sheets, Stoney Creek, Ontario

- Bake your favorite meat loaf in muffins tins rather than a loaf pan to cut down on cooking time.
    —Doreen Kelly, Rosyln, Pennsylvania

- When making potato salad, I peel and cube the potatoes before boiling to reduce cooking time. I also put the eggs in the pan along with the boiling potatoes. In minutes, the potatoes *and* hard-cooked eggs are ready.
    —Connie Ericson Hutchinson, Minnesota

- Don't have time to make homemade frosting for a favorite sheet cake? I learned this trick from my sister: Mix a can of store-bought frosting (any flavor) with an 8-ounce container of whipped topping. The result is so soft, creamy and easy to spread that everyone will think you made a traditional cooked 7-minute frosting. *—Sheila Shipston Eleanor, West Virginia*

    3/4 cup mayonnaise
    2 hard-cooked eggs, chopped

In a saucepan, cook potatoes in boiling water until tender. Peel and cube; place in a medium bowl. Sprinkle with vinegar and sugar. Add celery, onion, olives, salt and celery seed. Fold in mayonnaise and eggs. Cover and refrigerate for at least 1 hour. **Yield:** 4 servings. **Nutritional Analysis:** One 1-cup serving equals 488 calories, 638 mg sodium, 136 mg cholesterol, 33 gm carbohydrate, 6 gm protein, 37 gm fat.

Quicker Potato Salad

✓ Nutritional Analysis included

    3 medium baked *or* cooked potatoes (about 1-1/2 pounds)
    1 tablespoon cider vinegar
    1 teaspoon sugar
1/2 cup chopped celery
1/3 cup chopped onion
    3 tablespoons sweet pickle relish
1/2 teaspoon celery seed
1/2 teaspoon salt
1/2 cup fat-free mayonnaise
    1 hard-cooked egg, chopped

Peel and cube the potatoes; place in a medium bowl. Sprinkle with vinegar and sugar. Add celery, onion, pickle relish, celery seed and salt. Fold in mayonnaise and egg. Cover and refrigerate for at least 1 hour. **Yield:** 4 servings. **Nutritional Analysis:** One 1-cup serving equals 194 calories, 629 mg sodium, 53 mg cholesterol, 41 gm carbohydrate, 5 gm protein, 2 gm fat. **Diabetic Exchanges:** 2 starch, 1 vegetable, 1/2 fat.

WHEN St. Patrick's Day rolls around each year, Joy Strasser's clan looks forward to a traditional hearty meal of corned beef and cabbage.

"Corned beef is a real treat in our family," shares the Mukwonago, Wisconsin cook. "And we love the savory flavor the vegetables pick up from simmering in the pickling spices.

"But working part-time, going to school and caring for three active boys leaves me little time in the kitchen. I'd be thrilled if you could come up with a recipe that fits my busy schedule, yet keeps this traditional dish's flavor."

Believe it or not, our kitchen crew's Quicker Boiled Dinner can be made in less than 45 minutes from start to finish.

The faster version relies on cooked corned beef from the deli to reduce cooking time. It also eliminates peeling and cutting vegetables by using frozen sliced carrots, convenient packaged coleslaw mix and small red potatoes that don't need to be peeled.

Traditional Boiled Dinner

1 corned beef brisket with spice packet
(3 pounds)
1 teaspoon whole black peppercorns
2 bay leaves
2 medium potatoes, peeled and quartered
3 medium carrots, quartered
1 medium onion, cut into 6 wedges
1 small head green cabbage, cut into 6 wedges
Prepared horseradish *or* mustard, optional

Place the brisket and contents of spice packet in a large kettle or Dutch oven. Add the peppercorns, bay leaves and enough water to cover; bring to a boil. Reduce heat; cover and simmer for 2 hours or until meat is almost tender. Add potatoes, carrots and onion; bring to a boil. Reduce heat; cover and simmer for 10 minutes. Add cabbage; cover and simmer for 15-20 minutes or until tender. Discard bay leaves and peppercorns. Thinly slice meat; serve with vegetables and horseradish or mustard if desired. **Yield:** 6 servings.

Quicker Boiled Dinner

(Pictured far right above)

1 pound unsliced cooked corned beef
4 small unpeeled red potatoes, quartered
3 cups water
1 to 2 tablespoons pickling spices
1 teaspoon dried minced onion
1 teaspoon garlic salt
1/8 teaspoon dried thyme
2 cups frozen sliced carrots
4 cups coleslaw mix
Prepared horseradish *or* mustard, optional

In a large kettle or Dutch oven, place corned beef, pota-

toes and water. Place pickling spices in a double thickness of cheesecloth; bring up corners of cloth and tie with string to form a bag. Add to kettle with onion, garlic salt and thyme. Bring to a boil. Reduce heat; cover and simmer for 10 minutes. Add carrots; cover and simmer for 10 minutes or until carrots are almost tender. Add coleslaw mix; bring to a boil. Cover and simmer 10 minutes longer or until vegetables are tender. Discard spice bag. Thinly slice the meat; serve with vegetables and horseradish or mustard if desired. **Yield:** 4 servings.

THE SUNNY FLAVOR of Linda Blaska's Lemon Angel Food Supreme has made it a crowd-pleaser for generations.

"This heavenly dessert has been in our family for years," reports the Dunwoody, Georgia cook. "Everyone loves wedges of this delicate angel food cake topped with a tart, creamy lemon sauce.

"Trouble is, it can be time-consuming to make. I'd like a quick alternative I can whip up in a flash...but I'd hate to sacrifice any from-scratch goodness. Can you help?"

Yes we can, Linda! Our test kitchen came up with several time-saving shortcuts when they created Quicker Lemon Angel Food Supreme.

Boxed angel food cake speeds prep time but retains the cake's home-baked taste. And the no-cook version of sauce uses handy prepared lemon pie filling and whipped topping for fuss-free fixing and old-fashioned results.

Lemon Angel Food Supreme

1 cup cake flour
1-1/2 cups plus 2 tablespoons sugar, *divided*
1-1/2 cups egg whites (about 10 eggs)
1-1/2 teaspoons cream of tartar
1-1/2 teaspoons vanilla extract
1/2 teaspoon lemon extract
1/4 teaspoon salt
LEMON SAUCE:
3 eggs

Zest Successfully

Shredded or grated lemon peel, also called lemon zest, can be made using a tool called a zester. Holding the lemon in one hand, firmly pull the zester over it to remove very thin strips of the outer yellow peel. Rotate the lemon in your hand and repeat, removing as much zest as needed.

Quicker Lemon Angel Food Supreme
Quicker Boiled Dinner

1 cup sugar
1/2 cup lemon juice
1/4 cup butter *or* margarine, melted
1 tablespoon grated lemon peel
1/2 cup whipping cream, whipped

Combine cake flour and 3/4 cup plus 2 tablespoons sugar; set aside. In a mixing bowl, beat egg whites, cream of tartar, extracts and salt until foamy. Add remaining sugar, 2 tablespoons at a time, beating until stiff peaks form. Gently fold in flour mixture, about a fourth at a time. Pour into an ungreased 10-in. tube pan. Using a metal spatula or knife, cut through batter to remove air pockets. Bake at 375° for 30-35 minutes or until top is golden brown and cracks feel dry. Immediately invert pan; cool completely. Loosen sides of cake from pan with a knife and remove. For sauce, beat eggs and sugar in a double boiler. Stir in the lemon juice, butter and lemon peel. Cook over simmering water until the mixture thickens and reaches 160°, about 15 minutes; chill. Fold in whipped cream. Serve with cake. Store sauce in the refrigerator. **Yield:** 12 servings.

Quicker Lemon Angel Food Supreme

(Pictured above)

1 package (16 ounces) one-step angel food cake mix
2 teaspoons grated lemon peel
1/2 teaspoon lemon extract
LEMON SAUCE:
1 can (15-3/4 ounces) lemon pie filling
3 to 4 tablespoons milk
1 tablespoon lemon juice
1/8 teaspoon lemon extract
1 cup whipped topping

Prepare cake batter according to package directions, adding the lemon peel and extract. Bake according to package directions. After baking, immediately invert pan and cool completely. For the sauce, combine pie filling, milk, lemon juice and extract in a mixing bowl; beat until smooth. Fold in whipped topping. Serve with cake. Store sauce in the refrigerator. **Yield:** 12 servings.

MEAT BUNS are a delicious meal in hand for Sharon Leno and her family. The Keansburg, New Jersey cook's homemade yeast rolls encase a flavorful combination of ground beef, cabbage and cheddar cheese.

"Everyone loves the golden, tender crust that surrounds the hearty filling...but making the dough from scratch can be time-consuming," Sharon admits.

On occasion, she uses her bread machine to do some of the work for her. But rolling the dough and filling the individual buns still take time.

"I'd serve these delicious sandwiches more often if they were quicker to make," she notes. "Can you help?"

Our test kitchen captured the flavor of Sharon's family favorite in a faster form when they created Meat Bun Bake. This satisfying entree shares many of the same ingredients as Meat Buns but bakes up in an easy-to-assemble casserole form.

Using biscuit mix is a speedy alternative to the original yeast dough, which requires kneading and rising.

It also eliminates the need to shape and fill each bun.

Once the biscuit mix is blended with milk and egg, it's a snap to pour it over the tasty beef mixture and pop the pan in the oven.

Meat Buns
(Pictured below)

DOUGH:
1-1/2 teaspoons active dry yeast
1/2 cup plus 1 tablespoon warm water (110° to 115°)
3 tablespoons sugar
1 egg
1/2 teaspoon salt
2 to 2-1/4 cups bread flour
FILLING:
1 pound ground beef
1-1/2 cups chopped cabbage
1/2 cup chopped onion
Salt and pepper to taste
1/2 cup shredded cheddar cheese
2 tablespoons butter *or* margarine, melted

Meat Buns
Meat Bun Bake

In a mixing bowl, dissolve yeast in water. Add sugar, egg, salt and 1 cup of flour; beat on low for 3 minutes. Add enough remaining flour to form a soft dough. Turn onto a floured surface; knead until smooth and elastic, about 6-8 minutes. Place in a greased bowl; turn once to grease top. Cover and let rise in a warm place until doubled, about 1 hour. Meanwhile, in a skillet, brown beef; drain. Add cabbage, onion, salt and pepper. Cover and cook over medium heat for 15 minutes or until vegetables are tender. Stir in cheese. Remove from the heat; set aside to cool. Punch dough down and divide into 12 pieces. Gently roll out and stretch each piece into a 5-in. circle. Top each with about 1/4 cup filling. Fold dough over filling to meet in the center; pinch edges to seal. Place seam side down on a greased baking sheet. Cover and let rise in a warm place until doubled, about 30 minutes. Brush with butter. Bake at 350° for 20 minutes or until golden brown. Serve warm. **Yield:** 1 dozen. **Editor's Note:** The dough may be prepared in a bread machine. Place dough ingredients (using water that is 70°-80° and only 2 cups of bread flour) in bread pan in order suggested by manufacturer. Select dough setting (check dough after 5 minutes of mixing; add 1 to 2 tablespoons of water or flour if needed). When cycle is completed, turn dough onto a floured surface and punch down. Prepare buns as directed.

Meat Bun Bake

(Pictured at left)

1-1/2 pounds ground beef
   2 cups chopped cabbage
  1/4 cup chopped onion
  1/2 teaspoon salt
  1/4 teaspoon pepper
  1/2 to 1 cup shredded cheddar cheese
1-1/2 cups biscuit/baking mix
   1 cup milk
   2 eggs

In a skillet, brown beef; drain. Add cabbage, onion, salt and pepper; cook over medium heat for 15 minutes or until the cabbage and onion are tender. Stir in cheese. Spoon into a greased 13-in. x 9-in. x 2-in. baking dish. In a bowl, blend biscuit mix, milk and eggs. Pour over beef mixture. Bake, uncovered, at 400° for 20-25 minutes or until golden brown. **Yield:** 6 servings.

WHENEVER she feels a "knead" for homemade bread, Teri Albrecht of Gaithersburg, Maryland sets a batch of her Potato Rolls to rising.

"These sweet, moist dinner rolls with their beautiful golden color are so special that I like to serve them when company comes—if I have the time to make them ahead," she confides.

"Preparation takes even longer than plain yeast rolls because the potatoes must be cooked and mashed first. Can you recommend a way to speed up the whole process?"

We certainly can, Teri, thanks in part to quick-rise yeast. A real boon to busy bakers, it cuts the time needed for bread and rolls to rise by about one-third.

Our version of Quicker Potato Rolls also uses instant mashed potatoes to help reduce the time it takes to make these tender, tasty rolls. Enjoy!

Potato Rolls

   1 package (1/4 ounce) active dry yeast
  1/2 cup warm water (110° to 115°)
  1/2 cup milk
  1/3 cup mashed potatoes (without added milk or
      butter), room temperature
  1/4 cup butter *or* margarine, melted
   2 eggs
   1 tablespoon sugar
   1 teaspoon salt
3-1/2 to 4 cups all-purpose flour

In a mixing bowl, dissolve yeast in water. Add milk, potatoes, butter, one egg, sugar, salt and 2 cups flour; beat until smooth. Add enough remaining flour to form a soft dough. Turn onto a floured surface; knead until smooth and elastic, about 6-8 minutes. Place in a greased bowl, turning once to grease top. Cover and let rise in a warm place until doubled, about 1 hour. Punch dough down. Divide into 12 pieces and shape each into a smooth ball. Place in a greased 13-in. x 9-in. x 2-in. baking pan. Cover and let rise in a warm place until doubled, about 30 minutes. Lightly beat remaining egg; brush over rolls. Bake at 375° for 20-25 minutes or until golden brown. Remove from pan to a wire rack. **Yield:** 1 dozen.

Quicker Potato Rolls

3-1/2 to 4 cups all-purpose flour, *divided*
   1 tablespoon sugar
   1 package (1/4 ounce) quick-rise yeast
   1 teaspoon salt
  3/4 cup warm water (120° to 130°)
  1/2 cup warm milk (120° to 130°)
  1/4 cup butter *or* margarine, melted
  1/4 cup mashed potato flakes
   2 eggs

In a mixing bowl, combine 1 cup flour, sugar, yeast and salt; set aside. In another bowl, combine water, milk and butter; stir in potato flakes. Let stand for 1 minute. Add to dry ingredients. Add one egg; beat until smooth. Add enough remaining flour to form a soft dough. Turn onto a floured surface and knead until smooth and elastic, about 4-6 minutes. Cover and let stand for 10 minutes. Divide dough into 12 pieces; shape each into a ball. Place in a greased 13-in. x 9-in. x 2-in. baking pan. Place a large shallow pan on the counter; fill half full with boiling water. Place baking pan containing rolls over the water-filled pan. Cover and let rise for 15 minutes. Lightly beat remaining egg; brush over rolls. Bake at 375° for 20-25 minutes or until golden brown. Remove from pan to a wire rack. **Yield:** 1 dozen.

WHEN Beth Armstrong's family in Milwaukee, Wisconsin is hungry, nothing satisfies like hearty servings of her mouth-watering Traditional Beef Potpie.

"I'd serve it more often if it didn't take so long to make—over 1-1/2 hours from start to finish. Is there a faster way to prepare my potpie?" she asks.

Our kitchen crew set to work and soon came up with a Quicker Beef Potpie—one that can be on the table in about 30 minutes!

This faster version uses a purchased pastry crust, frozen vegetables and a jar of gravy to reduce prep time...and the filling is prepared speedily on the stove instead of baked in the oven.

Even so, you'll be amazed at how good our quicker version tastes! Serving it in soup bowls gives it a pretty and different look on your dinner table.

Traditional Beef Potpie

(Pictured on page 256)

CRUST:
1-1/2 cups all-purpose flour
   2/3 cup shredded cheddar cheese
   1/2 teaspoon salt
   1/4 teaspoon pepper
   1/8 teaspoon dried thyme
   1/2 cup shortening
   5 to 6 tablespoons cold water
FILLING:
1-1/2 pounds boneless round steak, cut into 1-inch cubes
   1 medium onion, chopped
   1 tablespoon vegetable oil
1-1/2 cups sliced fresh mushrooms
   2 cups beef broth, *divided*
   3/4 teaspoon salt
   1/2 teaspoon dried thyme
   1/4 teaspoon garlic powder
   1/8 teaspoon pepper
1-1/2 cups cubed peeled potatoes
   1 cup sliced carrots
   3/4 cup sliced celery
   1/3 cup all-purpose flour
   1/2 teaspoon browning sauce, optional

In a bowl, combine the flour, cheese, salt, pepper and thyme; cut in shortening until the mixture resembles coarse crumbs. Stir in water just until moistened. Form into a ball. Cover and refrigerate. Meanwhile, in a large saucepan or Dutch oven, brown beef and onion in oil. Add mushrooms; saute for 1 minute. Add 1 cup broth, salt, thyme, garlic powder and pepper; bring to a boil. Reduce heat; cover and simmer for 30 minutes. Add potatoes, carrots and celery; cover and simmer 20 minutes longer or until meat is tender and vegetables are crisp-tender. Combine flour and remaining broth until smooth; gradually add to beef mixture. Bring to a boil; cook and stir for 2 minutes. Stir in browning sauce if desired. Reduce heat; keep warm. Roll two-thirds of the dough into a 14-in. x 10-in. rectangle; place in an un-

greased 11-in. x 7-in. x 2-in. baking dish, lining the bottom and sides. Roll remaining pastry into a 6-in. circle; cut into six wedges. Spoon beef mixture into crust. Place pastry wedges on top. Bake, uncovered, at 450° for 10 minutes. Reduce heat to 350°; bake 30 minutes longer or until pastry is golden brown. **Yield:** 6 servings.

Quicker Beef Potpie

(Pictured on page 256)

Pastry for a single-crust pie (9 inches)
   1 tablespoon water
   1/3 cup shredded cheddar cheese
   3/4 teaspoon dried thyme, *divided*
   1 pound boneless sirloin *or* top round steak, cut into thin strips
   1 tablespoon vegetable oil
   1 package (16 ounces) frozen vegetables for stew
   1 jar (12 ounces) beef gravy
   1 can (4 ounces) mushroom stems and pieces, drained
   1/2 teaspoon garlic salt
   1/8 teaspoon pepper

On a floured surface, roll pastry to 1/8-in. thickness. Brush with water. Sprinkle with cheese and 1/4 teaspoon of thyme; press lightly. Using a 3-in. biscuit cutter, cut four 3-in. circles. Place circles and remaining pastry on ungreased baking sheets. Bake at 450° for 8-10 minutes or until golden brown; set aside. In a skillet over medium-high heat, brown beef in oil for 5 minutes or until no longer pink; drain. Stir in vegetables, gravy, mushrooms, garlic salt, pepper and remaining thyme; bring to a boil. Reduce heat; cover and simmer for 15 minutes or until the vegetables are tender. Set pastry circles aside. Break remaining pastry into 2-in. pieces; place in soup bowls. Fill bowls with beef mixture; top each with a pastry circle. Serve immediately. **Yield:** 4 servings.

WHEN Jessie Barnes of Atchison, Kansas shared her family recipe for Traditional Stollen, it sounded so yummy we couldn't wait to try it.

Our test kitchen staff eagerly baked up a batch of the buttery holiday bread that gets a festive flavor from candied fruit, chewy raisins and crunchy almonds.

"The recipe came from my grandmother and was originally written in German," Jessie relates.

The results are definitely worth the extra time needed to make the yeast dough, but we didn't want busy *Quick Cooking* readers to miss out on this classic Christmas treat.

So our home economists found a way to cut the preparation time in half without sacrificing the bread's rich flavor. Quicker Stollen tastes like the real thing but uses a convenient box of hot roll mix from the grocery store shelf.

This speedy method eliminates the traditional first

Quicker Stollen

rise that yeast breads require. It also shortens the dough's final resting time.

Traditional Stollen

     1 package (1/4 ounce) active dry yeast
     2 tablespoons warm water (110° to 115°)
     1 cup warm milk (110° to 115°)
  3/4 cup butter *or* margarine, softened
  1/2 cup sugar
     2 eggs, beaten
1-1/2 teaspoons grated lemon peel
  1/2 teaspoon salt
4-3/4 to 5-1/4 cups all-purpose flour
  3/4 cup raisins
  1/2 cup mixed candied fruit
  1/2 cup chopped almonds
GLAZE:
1-1/2 cups confectioners' sugar
     2 to 3 tablespoons milk
Candied cherries and sliced almonds, optional

In a mixing bowl, dissolve yeast in water. Add milk, butter, sugar, eggs, lemon peel, salt and 3 cups flour. Add raisins, candied fruit and almonds. Add enough remaining flour to form a soft dough. Turn onto a floured surface; knead until smooth and elastic, about 6-8 minutes. Place in a greased bowl, turning once to grease top. Cover and let rise in a warm place until doubled, about 1-1/2 hours. Punch dough down and divide in half; cover and let rest for 10 minutes. Roll or press each half into a 12-in. x 7-in. oval. Fold a long side over to within 1 in. of opposite side; press edge lightly to seal. Place on greased baking sheets; curve ends slightly. Cover and let rise until nearly doubled, about 1 hour. Bake at 375° for 25-30 minutes or until golden brown. Cool on wire racks.

Combine confectioners' sugar and milk; spread over stollen. Decorate with cherries and almonds if desired. **Yield:** 2 loaves.

Quicker Stollen

(Pictured above)

     1 package (16 ounces) hot roll mix
  1/4 cup sugar
     1 cup warm water (120° to 130°)
     2 tablespoons butter *or* margarine
     1 egg, beaten
  3/4 teaspoon grated lemon peel
  1/4 teaspoon almond extract
  1/3 cup raisins
  1/4 cup mixed candied fruit
  1/4 cup chopped almonds
GLAZE:
  3/4 cup confectioners' sugar
     1 to 2 tablespoons milk
Candied cherries and sliced almonds, optional

In a mixing bowl, combine contents of hot roll package and yeast envelope with sugar; mix well. Stir in water, butter, egg, lemon peel and extract to form a soft dough. Turn onto a floured surface. Knead in raisins, candied fruit and almonds, about 5 minutes. Cover and let rest for 5 minutes. Roll or press dough into a 12-in. x 7-in. oval. Fold a long side over to within 1 in. of opposite side; press edge lightly to seal. Place on a greased baking sheet; curve ends slightly. Cover and let rise until nearly doubled, about 20-30 minutes. Bake at 375° for 20 minutes or until golden brown. Cool on a wire rack. Combine confectioners' sugar and milk; spread over stollen. Decorate with cherries and almonds if desired. **Yield:** 1 loaf.

Chapter 18

WHEN a full schedule keeps you away from the kitchen, put your slow cooker, grill and microwave to work making wholesome, hearty meals.

With just a few minutes of preparation, you can assemble all the ingredients in your slow cooker. Then simply put on the lid...switch on the pot...and go!

Capture outdoor flavor the whole year—fast and fuss-free—by firing up the grill for a selection of sizzling favorites. You'll agree that grilling is "hot"—no matter the season.

And when it comes to putting all types of appetizing food on the table in a jiffy, nothing can compare to a microwave's quick convenience.

SWITCH AND GO. Clockwise from lower right: Meat Loaf Burgers (p. 274), Cheesy Creamed Corn (p. 275) and Lemon Red Potatoes (p. 275).

Slow-Cooked Specialties

EVEN THOUGH it simmers foods ever so slowly, a slow cooker can be an indispensable time-saver. After a busy day, a "from-scratch" meal can be cooked to perfection when you walk in the door.

Chicken-Fried Chops

It takes only a few minutes to brown the meat before assembling this savory meal. The pork chops simmer all day in a flavorful sauce until they're tender.
—Connie Slocum, Brunswick, Georgia

```
1/2 cup all-purpose flour
  2 teaspoons salt
1-1/2 teaspoons ground mustard
1/2 teaspoon garlic powder
  6 pork loin chops (3/4 inch thick), trimmed
  2 tablespoons vegetable oil
  1 can (10-3/4 ounces) condensed cream of
      chicken soup, undiluted
1/3 cup water
```

In a shallow bowl, combine flour, salt, mustard and garlic powder; dredge pork chops. In a skillet, brown chops on both sides in oil. Place in a slow cooker. Combine soup and water; pour over chops. Cover and cook on low for 6-8 hours or until meat is tender. If desired, thicken pan juices and serve with the chops. **Yield:** 6 servings.

Hot Caramel Apples

This old-time favorite goes together quickly...and it's such a treat to come home to the aroma of cinnamony baked apples just like Mom used to make! —Pat Sparks
St. Charles, Missouri

```
  4 large tart apples, cored
1/2 cup apple juice
  8 tablespoons brown sugar
 12 red-hot candies
  4 tablespoons butter or margarine
  8 caramels
1/4 teaspoon ground cinnamon
Whipped cream, optional
```

Peel about 3/4 in. off the top of each apple; place in a slow cooker. Pour juice over apples. Fill the center of each apple with 2 tablespoons of sugar, three red-hots, 1 tablespoon of butter and two caramels. Sprinkle with cinnamon. Cover and cook on low for 4-6 hours or until the apples are tender. Serve immediately with whipped cream if desired. **Yield:** 4 servings.

Beef in Mushroom Gravy

This is one of the best and easiest meals I've ever made. It has only four ingredients, and they all go into the pot at once. The meat is nicely seasoned and makes its own gravy—it tastes wonderful when you serve it over mashed potatoes. —Margery Bryan, Royal City, Washington

```
  2 to 2-1/2 pounds boneless round steak
  1 to 2 envelopes dry onion soup mix
  1 can (10-3/4 ounces) condensed cream of
      mushroom soup, undiluted
1/2 cup water
Mashed potatoes, optional
```

Cut steak into six serving-size pieces; place in a slow cooker. Combine soup mix, soup and water; pour over beef. Cover and cook on low for 7-8 hours or until the meat is tender. Serve with mashed potatoes if desired. **Yield:** 6 servings.

Hearty Italian Sandwiches

This sweet and spicy sandwich filling smells as good as it tastes! It's a great reward after a day working or playing. —Elaine Krupsky, Las Vegas, Nevada

```
1-1/2 pounds lean ground beef
1-1/2 pounds bulk Italian sausage
  2 large onions, sliced
  2 large green peppers, sliced
  2 large sweet red peppers, sliced
  1 teaspoon salt
  1 teaspoon pepper
1/4 teaspoon crushed red pepper flakes
  8 sandwich rolls, split
Shredded Monterey Jack cheese, optional
```

In a skillet, brown beef and sausage; drain. Place a third of the onions and peppers in a slow cooker; top with half of the meat mixture. Repeat layers of vegetables and meat, then top with remaining vegetables. Sprinkle with salt, pepper and pepper flakes. Cover and cook on low for 6 hours or until vegetables are tender. With a slotted spoon, serve about 1 cup of meat and vegetables on each roll. Top with cheese if desired. Use pan juices for dipping if desired. **Yield:** 8 servings.

No-Fuss Potato Soup

(Pictured above right)

For a busy-day supper, my family loves to have big steaming, delicious bowls of this soup, along with fresh bread. —Dotty Egge
Pelican Rapids, Minnesota

☑ **Nutritional Analysis included**

```
  6 cups cubed peeled potatoes
  5 cups water
  2 cups chopped onion
1/2 cup chopped celery
1/2 cup thinly sliced carrots
1/4 cup butter or margarine
```

Tender 'n' Tangy Ribs
No-Fuss Potato Soup

4 teaspoons chicken bouillon granules
2 teaspoons salt
1/4 teaspoon pepper
1 can (12 ounces) evaporated milk
3 tablespoons chopped fresh parsley
Snipped chives, optional

In a large slow cooker, combine the first nine ingredients. Cover and cook on high for 7 hours or until the vegetables are tender. Add milk and parsley; mix well. Cover and cook 30-60 minutes longer or until heated through. Garnish with chives if desired. **Yield:** 8-10 servings (about 3 quarts). **Nutritional Analysis:** One 1-cup serving (prepared with margarine) equals 190 calories, 827 mg sodium, 12 mg cholesterol, 26 gm carbohydrate, 5 gm protein, 7 gm fat. **Diabetic Exchanges:** 1-1/2 starch, 1-1/2 fat, 1 vegetable.

Tender 'n' Tangy Ribs

(Pictured above)

These ribs are so simple to prepare. Just brown them, then combine with the sauce ingredients in your slow cooker. —Denise Hathaway Valasek, Perrysburg, Ohio

3/4 to 1 cup vinegar
1/2 cup ketchup
2 tablespoons sugar
2 tablespoons Worcestershire sauce
1 garlic clove, minced
1 teaspoon ground mustard
1 teaspoon paprika
1/2 to 1 teaspoon salt
1/8 teaspoon pepper

2 pounds pork spareribs
1 tablespoon vegetable oil

Combine the first nine ingredients in a slow cooker. Cut ribs into serving-size pieces; brown in a skillet in oil. Transfer to slow cooker. Cover and cook on low for 4-6 hours or until tender. **Yield:** 2-3 servings.

Slow-Cooked Flank Steak

My slow cooker gets lots of use, especially during the hectic summer months. I can fix this flank steak in the morning and forget about it until dinnertime.
—Michelle Armistead, Keyport, New Jersey

1 flank steak (about 1-1/2 pounds), cut in half
1 tablespoon vegetable oil
1 large onion, sliced
1/3 cup water
1 can (4 ounces) chopped green chilies
2 tablespoons vinegar
1-1/4 teaspoons chili powder
1 teaspoon garlic powder
1/2 teaspoon sugar
1/2 teaspoon salt
1/8 teaspoon pepper

In a skillet, brown steak in oil; transfer to a slow cooker. In the same skillet, saute onion for 1 minute. Gradually add water, stirring to loosen browned bits from pan. Add remaining ingredients; bring to a boil. Pour over the flank steak. Cover and cook on low for 7-8 hours or until the meat is tender. Slice the meat; serve with onion and pan juices. **Yield:** 4-6 servings.

Slow-Cooked Meat Loaf
Turkey Enchiladas

Slow-Cooked Meat Loaf

(Pictured above)

This meat loaf retains its shape in the slow cooker and slices beautifully. Because potatoes and carrots cook along with it, the entire dinner is ready at the same time.
—Marna Heitz, Farley, Iowa

    1 egg
1/4 cup milk
    2 slices day-old bread, cubed
1/4 cup finely chopped onion
    2 tablespoons finely chopped green pepper
    1 teaspoon salt
1/4 teaspoon pepper
1-1/2 pounds lean ground beef
1/4 cup ketchup
    8 medium carrots, cut into 1-inch chunks
    8 small red potatoes

In a bowl, beat egg and milk. Stir in the bread cubes, onion, green pepper, salt and pepper. Add the beef and mix well. Shape into a round loaf. Place in a 5-qt. slow cooker. Spread ketchup on top of loaf. Arrange carrots around loaf. Peel a strip around the center of each potato; place potatoes over carrots. Cover and cook on high for 1 hour. Reduce heat to low; cover and cook 7-8 hours longer or until the meat is no longer pink and the vegetables are tender. **Yield:** 4 servings.

Turkey Enchiladas

(Pictured above)

Here's a different way to serve an economical cut of meat. Simmer turkey thighs with tomato sauce, green chilies and seasonings until they're tender and flavorful. Then shred the turkey and serve it in tortillas with other fresh fixings.
—Stella Schams, Tempe, Arizona

    2 turkey thighs *or* drumsticks (about 2 pounds)
    1 can (8 ounces) tomato sauce
    1 can (4 ounces) chopped green chilies
1/3 cup chopped onion
    2 tablespoons Worcestershire sauce
    1 to 2 tablespoons chili powder

1/4 teaspoon garlic powder
8 flour tortillas (7 inches)
Optional toppings: chopped green onions, sliced ripe olives, chopped tomatoes, shredded cheddar cheese, sour cream *and/or* shredded lettuce

Remove skin from turkey. Place in a 5-qt. slow cooker. Combine tomato sauce, chilies, onion, Worcestershire sauce, chili powder and garlic powder; pour over turkey. Cover and cook on low for 6-8 hours or until turkey is tender. Remove turkey; shred meat with a fork and return to the slow cooker. Heat through. Spoon about 1/2 cup of turkey mixture down the center of each tortilla. Fold bottom of tortilla over filling and roll up. Add toppings of your choice. **Yield:** 4 servings.

Beef and Beans

This deliciously spicy steak and beans over rice will have family and friends asking for more. It's a favorite in my recipe collection. —Marie Leadmon, Bethesda, Maryland

✓ Nutritional Analysis included

1-1/2 pounds boneless round steak
   1 tablespoon prepared mustard
   1 tablespoon chili powder
1/2 teaspoon salt, optional
1/4 teaspoon pepper
   1 garlic clove, minced
   2 cans (14-1/2 ounces *each*) diced tomatoes, undrained
   1 medium onion, chopped
   1 beef bouillon cube, crushed
   1 can (16 ounces) kidney beans, rinsed and drained
Hot cooked rice

Cut steak into thin strips. Combine mustard, chili powder, salt if desired, pepper and garlic in a bowl; add steak and toss to coat. Transfer to a slow cooker; add tomatoes, onion and bouillon. Cover and cook on low for 6-8 hours. Stir in beans; cook 30 minutes longer. Serve over rice. **Yield:** 8 servings. **Nutritional Analysis:** One 1-cup serving (prepared with no-salt-added tomatoes and low-sodium bouillon and without salt; calculated without rice) equals 215 calories, 116 mg sodium, 53 mg cholesterol, 20 gm carbohydrate, 25 gm protein, 4 gm fat. **Diabetic Exchanges:** 2 lean meat, 1 starch, 1 vegetable.

Golden Chicken and Noodles

This tender chicken cooks up in a golden sauce that is nicely flavored with basil. It's great for taking to a potluck supper, especially if you work and don't have time to cook during the day. —Charlotte McDaniel
Anniston, Alabama

✓ Nutritional Analysis included

   6 boneless skinless chicken breast halves (1-1/2 pounds)

   2 cans (10-3/4 ounces *each*) condensed broccoli cheese soup, undiluted
   2 cups milk
   1 small onion, chopped
1/2 to 1 teaspoon salt, optional
1/2 to 1 teaspoon dried basil
1/8 teaspoon pepper
Hot cooked noodles

Cut chicken pieces in half; place in a 5-qt. slow cooker. Combine the soup, milk, onion, salt if desired, basil and pepper; pour over chicken. Cover and cook on high for 1 hour. Reduce heat to low; cover and cook 5-6 hours longer or until the meat juices run clear. Serve over noodles. **Yield:** 6 servings. **Nutritional Analysis:** One serving (prepared with low-fat soup and skim milk and without salt; calculated without noodles) equals 232 calories, 499 mg sodium, 76 mg cholesterol, 12 gm carbohydrate, 31 gm protein, 5 gm fat. **Diabetic Exchanges:** 3 lean meat, 1 starch.

Pineapple Baked Beans

Sweet and tangy pineapple dresses up these hearty baked beans. Brown the beef while you open cans and chop the vegetables, and it won't take long to get this ready for the slow cooker. —Gladys De Boer, Castleford, Idaho

   1 pound ground beef
   1 can (28 ounces) baked beans
   1 can (8 ounces) pineapple tidbits, drained
   1 jar (4-1/2 ounces) sliced mushrooms, drained
   1 large onion, chopped
   1 large green pepper, chopped
1/2 cup barbecue sauce
   2 tablespoons soy sauce
   1 garlic clove, minced
1/2 teaspoon salt
1/4 teaspoon pepper

In a skillet, brown beef; drain. Transfer to a 5-qt. slow cooker. Add remaining ingredients and mix well. Cover and cook on low for 4-8 hours or until bubbly. Serve in bowls. **Yield:** 6-8 main-dish or 12-16 side-dish servings.

Tender Pork Roast

This melt-in-your-mouth fall-apart-tender pork roast is wonderful to serve to company because it never fails to please. With five ingredients, it couldn't be easier. —LuVerne Peterson, Minneapolis, Minnesota

   1 boneless pork roast (about 3 pounds)
   1 can (8 ounces) tomato sauce
3/4 cup soy sauce
1/2 cup sugar
   2 teaspoons ground mustard

Cut roast in half; place in a 5-qt. slow cooker. Combine remaining ingredients; pour over roast. Cover and cook on low for 8-9 hours or until a meat thermometer reads 160°-170°. Remove roast to a serving platter and keep warm. If desired, skim fat from pan juices and thicken for gravy. **Yield:** 8 servings.

Green Chili Stew

This stew is much heartier than most—and very tasty, too. Men especially enjoy the zippy broth and the generous amounts of tender beef. They frequently request second helpings.
—Jacqueline Thompson Graves
Lawrenceville, Georgia

✓ **Nutritional Analysis included**

- 2 pounds beef stew meat, cut into 1-inch cubes
- 2 medium onions, chopped
- 2 tablespoons vegetable oil
- 1 can (15 ounces) pinto beans, rinsed and drained
- 1 can (14-1/2 ounces) diced tomatoes, undrained
- 2 cans (4 ounces *each*) chopped green chilies
- 1 cup water
- 3 beef bouillon cubes
- 1 garlic clove, minced
- 1 teaspoon sugar
- 1/2 teaspoon salt, optional
- 1/4 teaspoon pepper
- Shredded cheddar *or* Monterey Jack cheese, optional

In a skillet, brown beef and onions in oil; drain. Transfer to a 5-qt. slow cooker. Combine beans, tomatoes, chilies, water, bouillon, garlic, sugar, salt if desired and pepper; pour over beef. Cover and cook on low for 7-8 hours or until beef is tender. Sprinkle with cheese if desired. **Yield:** 8 servings. **Nutritional Analysis:** One 1-cup serving (prepared with low-sodium bouillon and without salt and cheese) equals 259 calories, 363 mg sodium, 70 mg cholesterol, 12 gm carbohydrate, 25 gm protein, 12 gm fat. **Diabetic Exchanges:** 2-1/2 meat, 1 starch.

Slow-Cooked Vegetables

I simmer an assortment of garden-fresh vegetables into a satisfying side dish. My sister-in-law shared this recipe with me. It's a favorite at holiday gatherings and potlucks.
—Kathy Westendorf, Westgate, Iowa

✓ **Nutritional Analysis included**

- 4 celery ribs, cut into 1-inch pieces
- 4 small carrots, cut into 1-inch pieces
- 2 medium tomatoes, cut into chunks
- 2 medium onions, thinly sliced
- 2 cups cut fresh green beans (1-inch pieces)
- 1 medium green pepper, cut into 1-inch pieces
- 1/4 cup butter *or* margarine, melted
- 3 tablespoons quick-cooking tapioca
- 1 tablespoon sugar
- 2 teaspoons salt, optional
- 1/8 teaspoon pepper

Place the vegetables in a slow cooker. Combine butter, tapioca, sugar, salt if desired and pepper; pour over vegetables and stir well. Cover and cook on low for 7-8 hours or until vegetables are tender. Serve with a slotted spoon. **Yield:** 8 servings. **Nutritional Analysis:** One 1-cup serving (prepared with margarine and without salt) equals 118 calories, 99 mg sodium, 0 cholesterol, 16 gm carbohydrate, 2 gm protein, 6 gm fat. **Diabetic Exchanges:** 2 vegetable, 1 fat.

Chicken in a Pot

It takes just minutes to get this supper ready for the slow cooker. And at the end of a busy day, your family will appreciate the simple goodness of tender chicken and vegetables.
—Alpha Wilson, Roswell, New Mexico

- 3 medium carrots, cut into 3/4-inch pieces
- 2 celery ribs with leaves, cut into 3/4-inch pieces
- 2 medium onions, sliced
- 1 broiler/fryer chicken (3 to 4 pounds), cut up
- 1/2 cup chicken broth
- 1-1/2 teaspoons salt
- 1 teaspoon dried basil
- 1/2 teaspoon pepper

In a 5-qt. slow cooker, place carrots, celery and onions. Top with chicken. Combine remaining ingredients; pour over chicken. Cover and cook on low for 7-9 hours or until chicken juices run clear and vegetables are tender. Serve with a slotted spoon. **Yield:** 6 servings.

Saucy Scalloped Potatoes

For old-fashioned flavor, try these scalloped potatoes. They cook up tender, creamy and comforting. Chopped ham adds a hearty touch.
—Elaine Kane, Keizer, Oregon

- 4 cups thinly sliced peeled potatoes (about 2 pounds)
- 1 can (10-3/4 ounces) cream of celery *or* mushroom soup, undiluted
- 1 can (12 ounces) evaporated milk
- 1 large onion, sliced
- 2 tablespoons butter *or* margarine
- 1/2 teaspoon salt
- 1/4 teaspoon pepper
- 1-1/2 cups chopped fully cooked ham

In a slow cooker, combine the first seven ingredients; mix well. Cover and cook on high for 1 hour. Stir in ham. Reduce heat to low; cook 6-8 hours longer or until the potatoes are tender. **Yield:** 4-6 main-dish or 8-12 side-dish servings.

Fruit Salsa

(Pictured at right)

I serve this fruity salsa anywhere I'd use ordinary salsa. My son and I experimented with different ingredients to find the combination we liked best.
—Florence Buchkowsky, Prince Albert, Saskatchewan

- 1 can (11 ounces) mandarin oranges, undrained
- 1 can (8-1/2 ounces) sliced peaches, undrained
- 1 can (8 ounces) pineapple tidbits, undrained
- 1 medium onion, chopped

1/2 *each* medium green, sweet red and yellow
    pepper, chopped
  3 garlic cloves, minced
  3 tablespoons cornstarch
  4 teaspoons vinegar
Tortilla chips

In a slow cooker, combine the fruit, onion, peppers, garlic, cornstarch and vinegar; stir well. Cover and cook on high for 2 hours or until thickened and heated through, stirring occasionally. Serve with tortilla chips. **Yield:** 4 cups.

Marinated Chicken Wings

(Pictured below)

I have made these nicely flavored chicken wings many times for get-togethers. They're so moist and tender...I always get lots of compliments and many requests for the recipe. —Janie Botting, Sultan, Washington

20 whole chicken wings* (about 4 pounds)

  2 cups soy sauce
1/2 cup white wine *or* chicken broth
1/2 cup vegetable oil
  2 to 3 garlic cloves, minced
  2 tablespoons sugar
  2 teaspoons ground ginger

Cut chicken wings into three sections; discard wing tips. Place wings in a large resealable heavy-duty plastic bag or 13-in. x 9-in. x 2-in. baking dish. In a bowl, combine remaining ingredients; mix well. Pour half of the sauce over chicken; turn to coat. Seal or cover the chicken and remaining sauce; refrigerate overnight. Drain chicken, discarding the marinade. Place chicken in a 5-qt. slow cooker; top with reserved sauce. Cover and cook on low for 3-1/2 to 4 hours or until chicken juices run clear. Transfer the wings to a serving dish; discard cooking juices. **Yield:** 18-20 servings. ***Editor's Note:** 4 pounds of uncooked chicken wing sections may be substituted for the whole chicken wings. Omit the first step of the recipe.

Fruit Salsa
Marinated Chicken Wings

Sesame Pork Roast

Marinate a boneless cut of pork in a tangy sauce overnight before cooking it slowly the next day. The result is a tasty roast that's fall-apart tender. —Sue Brown
San Miguel, California

- 1 boneless pork shoulder roast (4 pounds), trimmed
- 2 cups water
- 1/2 cup soy sauce
- 1/4 cup sesame seeds, toasted
- 1/4 cup molasses
- 1/4 cup cider *or* white wine vinegar
- 4 green onions, sliced
- 2 teaspoons garlic powder
- 1/4 teaspoon cayenne pepper
- 3 tablespoons cornstarch
- 1/4 cup cold water

Cut roast in half; place in a large resealable plastic bag or glass dish. In a bowl, combine the water, soy sauce, sesame seeds, molasses, vinegar, onions, garlic powder and cayenne. Pour half over the roast. Cover the pork and remaining marinade; refrigerate overnight. Drain pork, discarding marinade. Place roast in a 5-qt. slow cooker; add the reserved marinade. Cover and cook on high for 1 hour. Reduce temperature to low; cook 8-9 hours longer or until meat is tender. Remove the roast and keep warm. In a saucepan, combine cornstarch and cold water until smooth; stir in cooking juices. Bring to a boil; boil and stir for 2 minutes. Serve with the roast. **Yield:** 8 servings.

Summer's Bounty Soup

Lots of wonderfully fresh-tasting vegetables are showcased in this chunky soup. It's a great way to use up summer's excess produce. And it's so versatile—you can add or delete just about any vegetable. —Victoria Zmarzley-Hahn
Northampton, Pennsylvania

✓ Nutritional Analysis included

- 4 medium tomatoes, chopped
- 2 medium potatoes, peeled and cubed
- 2 cups halved fresh green beans
- 2 small zucchini, cubed
- 1 medium yellow summer squash, cubed
- 4 small carrots, thinly sliced
- 2 celery ribs, thinly sliced
- 1 cup cubed peeled eggplant
- 1 cup sliced fresh mushrooms
- 1 small onion, chopped
- 1 tablespoon minced fresh parsley
- 1 tablespoon salt-free garlic and herb seasoning
- 4 cups V-8 juice

Combine all ingredients in a 5-qt. slow cooker. Cover and cook on low for 7-8 hours or until the vegetables are tender. **Yield:** 12-14 servings (about 3-1/2 quarts). **Nutritional Analysis:** One 1-cup serving (prepared with low-sodium V-8) equals 60 calories, 59 mg sodium, 0 cholesterol, 13 gm carbohydrate, 2 gm protein, trace fat. **Diabetic Exchange:** 2 vegetable.

Mandarin Chicken

Oranges and olives are elegantly paired in this different but delicious dish. The chicken is marinated, then cooked slowly in a flavorful sauce, so it stays moist. To trim prep time, ask your butcher to cut up and skin the chicken for you. —Aney Chatterton, Soda Springs, Idaho

- 1 broiler/fryer chicken (3 to 3-1/2 pounds), cut up and skin removed
- 2 cups water
- 1 cup ketchup
- 1/4 cup packed brown sugar
- 1/4 cup soy sauce
- 1/4 cup orange juice concentrate
- 2 teaspoons ground mustard
- 2 teaspoons salt
- 1 teaspoon pepper
- 1 teaspoon ground ginger
- 1 teaspoon garlic salt
- 3 tablespoons cornstarch
- 1/2 cup cold water
- 1 can (11 ounces) mandarin oranges, drained
- 1/2 cup whole pitted ripe olives
- 2 tablespoons chopped green pepper

Hot cooked rice

Place chicken in a large resealable plastic bag or glass dish. In a bowl, combine the water, ketchup, brown sugar, soy sauce, orange juice concentrate, mustard, salt, pepper, ginger and garlic salt. Pour half over the chicken. Cover chicken and remaining marinade; refrigerate for 8 hours or overnight. Drain chicken, discarding marinade. Place chicken in a slow cooker; add reserved marinade. Cover and cook on low for 7-8 hours. Combine cornstarch and cold water until smooth; stir into the chicken mixture. Add oranges, olives and green pepper. Cover and cook on high for 30-45 minutes or until thickened. Serve over rice. **Yield:** 4-6 servings.

Meat Loaf Burgers

(Pictured above right and on page 267)

These hearty sandwiches are great for potluck dinners. Served on hamburger buns, the beefy patties get extra flavor when topped with the seasoned tomato sauce. —Peggy Burdick
Burlington, Michigan

- 1 large onion, sliced
- 1 celery rib, chopped
- 2 pounds lean ground beef
- 1-1/2 teaspoons salt, *divided*
- 1/4 teaspoon pepper
- 2 cups tomato juice
- 4 garlic cloves, minced
- 1 tablespoon ketchup
- 1 bay leaf
- 1 teaspoon Italian seasoning
- 6 hamburger buns, split

Place onion and celery in a slow cooker. Combine beef, 1 teaspoon of salt and pepper; shape into six patties. Place over onion mixture. Combine tomato juice, gar-

Lemon Red Potatoes
Cheesy Creamed Corn
Meat Loaf Burgers

lic, ketchup, bay leaf, Italian seasoning and remaining salt. Pour over the patties. Cover and cook on low for 7-9 hours or until meat is tender. Discard bay leaf. Separate patties with a spatula if necessary; serve on buns. **Yield:** 6 servings.

Lemon Red Potatoes

(Pictured above and on page 266)

Butter, lemon juice, parsley and chives enhance this simple side dish. I usually prepare these potatoes when I'm having company. Since they cook in the slow cooker, there's plenty of room on the stove for other dishes.
—Tara Branham, Cedar Park, Texas

1-1/2 pounds medium red potatoes
  1/4 cup water
  1/4 cup butter *or* margarine, melted
    1 tablespoon lemon juice
    3 tablespoons snipped fresh parsley
    1 tablespoon snipped fresh chives
Salt and pepper to taste

Cut a strip of peel from around the middle of each potato. Place the potatoes and water in a slow cooker. Cover and cook on high for 2-1/2 to 3 hours or until tender (do not overcook); drain. Combine butter, lemon juice, parsley and chives; mix well. Pour over the potatoes and toss to coat. Season with salt and pepper. **Yield:** 6 servings.

Cheesy Creamed Corn

(Pictured above and on page 266)

My family really likes this creamy, cheesy side dish—and it's so easy to make. Even those who usually don't eat much corn will ask for a second helping.
—Mary Ann Truitt, Wichita, Kansas

  3 packages (16 ounces *each*) frozen corn
  2 packages (one 8 ounces, one 3 ounces) cream cheese, cubed
1/4 cup butter *or* margarine, cubed
  3 tablespoons water
  3 tablespoons milk
  2 tablespoons sugar
  6 slices process American cheese, cut into small pieces

Combine all ingredients in a slow cooker; mix well. Cover and cook on low for 4 hours or until heated through and the cheese is melted. Stir well before serving. **Yield:** 12 servings.

Sausage Sauerkraut Supper

(Pictured above)

With big, tender chunks of sausage, potatoes and carrots, this meal-in-one has old-world flavor that will satisfy the heartiest of appetites. A co-worker often made a big pot of this for our office staff, and it always disappeared in a hurry. —Joalyce Graham, St. Petersburg, Florida

    4 cups carrot chunks (2-inch pieces)
    4 cups red potato chunks
    2 cans (14 ounces *each*) sauerkraut, rinsed and
       drained
2-1/2 pounds fresh Polish sausage, cut into 3-inch
       pieces
    1 medium onion, thinly sliced
    3 garlic cloves, minced
1-1/2 cups dry white wine *or* chicken broth
    1 teaspoon pepper
    1/2 teaspoon caraway seed

In a 5-qt. slow cooker, layer carrots, potatoes and sauerkraut. In a skillet, brown the sausage; transfer to the slow cooker (slow cooker will be full). Reserve 1 tablespoon drippings in skillet; saute onion and garlic until tender. Gradually add wine or broth. Bring to a boil; stir to loosen browned bits. Stir in pepper and caraway. Pour over sausage. Cover and cook on low for 8-9 hours or until vegetables are tender and sausage is no longer pink. **Yield:** 10-12 servings.

Chocolate Pudding Cake

This rich, fudgy dessert is a cross between pudding and cake. I like to serve it warm with a scoop of vanilla ice cream. Whenever I take it to parties, everybody wants the recipe. —Paige Arnette, Lawrenceville, Georgia

    1 package (18-1/4 ounces) chocolate cake mix
    1 package (3.9 ounces) instant chocolate
       pudding mix

2 cups (16 ounces) sour cream
4 eggs
1 cup water
3/4 cup vegetable oil
1 cup (6 ounces) semisweet chocolate chips
Whipped cream *or* ice cream, optional

In a mixing bowl, combine the first six ingredients. Beat on medium speed for 2 minutes. Stir in chocolate chips. Pour into a 5-qt. slow cooker that has been coated with nonstick cooking spray. Cover and cook on low for 6-7 hours or until a toothpick inserted near the center comes out with moist crumbs. Serve in bowls with whipped cream or ice cream if desired. **Yield:** 10-12 servings.

Curried Lentil Soup

(Pictured at left)

Curry gives a different taste sensation to this chili-like soup. It's delicious with a dollop of sour cream. My family welcomes it with open arms...and watering mouths.
—Christina Till, South Haven, Michigan

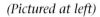 Nutritional Analysis included

4 cups hot water
1 can (28 ounces) crushed tomatoes
3 medium potatoes, peeled and diced
3 medium carrots, thinly sliced
1 large onion, chopped
1 celery rib, chopped
1 cup dry lentils
2 garlic cloves, minced
2 bay leaves
4 teaspoons curry powder
1-1/2 teaspoons salt, optional

In a slow cooker, combine all ingredients; stir well. Cover and cook on low for 8 hours or until vegetables and lentils are tender. Discard the bay leaves before serving. **Yield:** 10 servings (2-1/2 quarts). **Nutritional Analysis:** One 1-cup serving (prepared without salt) equals 169 calories, 150 mg sodium, 0 cholesterol, 34 gm carbohydrate, 9 gm protein, 1 gm fat. **Diabetic Exchanges:** 2 starch, 1 vegetable.

Sweet Potato Stuffing

Mom likes to make sure there will be enough stuffing to satisfy our large family. For our holiday gatherings, she slow-cooks this tasty sweet potato dressing in addition to the traditional stuffing cooked inside the turkey.
—Kelly Pollock, London, Ontario

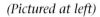 Nutritional Analysis included

1/2 cup chopped celery
1/2 cup chopped onion
1/4 cup butter *or* margarine
6 cups dry bread cubes
1 large sweet potato, cooked, peeled and finely chopped
1/2 cup chicken broth

1/4 cup chopped pecans
1/2 teaspoon poultry seasoning
1/2 teaspoon rubbed sage
1/2 teaspoon salt, optional
1/2 teaspoon pepper

In a skillet, saute celery and onion in butter until tender. Add the remaining ingredients; toss gently. Transfer to a greased slow cooker. Cover and cook on low for 4 hours or until bread and vegetables are soft. **Yield:** 10 servings. **Nutritional Analysis:** One 1-cup serving (prepared with margarine and low-sodium broth and without salt) equals 343 calories, 625 mg sodium, trace cholesterol, 53 gm carbohydrate, 9 gm protein, 10 gm fat. **Diabetic Exchanges:** 3-1/2 starch, 2 fat.

Southwestern Chicken

Prepared salsa and convenient canned corn and beans add fun color, texture and flavor to this tender chicken dish. I usually serve it with salad and rice. Our children love it.
—Karen Waters, Laurel, Maryland

2 cans (15-1/4 ounces *each*) whole kernel corn, drained
1 can (15 ounces) black beans, rinsed and drained
1 jar (16 ounces) chunky salsa, *divided*
6 boneless skinless chicken breast halves
1 cup (4 ounces) shredded cheddar cheese

Combine the corn, black beans and 1/2 cup of salsa in a slow cooker. Top with chicken; pour the remaining salsa over chicken. Cover and cook on high for 3-4 hours or on low for 7-8 hours or until meat juices run clear. Sprinkle with cheese; cover until cheese is melted, about 5 minutes. **Yield:** 6 servings.

Chili Casserole

Even people who try to bypass casseroles can't stay away from this zesty meat-and-rice dish. The seasonings make it irresistible. —Marietta Slater, Augusta, Kansas

1 pound bulk pork sausage
2 cups water
1 can (15-1/2 ounces) chili beans, undrained
1 can (14-1/2 ounces) diced tomatoes, undrained
3/4 cup uncooked long grain rice
1/4 cup chopped onion
1 tablespoon chili powder
1 teaspoon Worcestershire sauce
1 teaspoon prepared mustard
3/4 teaspoon salt
1/8 teaspoon garlic powder
1 cup (4 ounces) shredded cheddar cheese

In a skillet, cook sausage until no longer pink; drain. Transfer to a slow cooker. Add the next 10 ingredients; stir well. Cover and cook on low for 7 hours or until rice is tender. Stir in cheese during the last 10 minutes of cooking time. **Yield:** 6 servings.

Italian Meatball Subs

This is one of those recipes you always come back to. A flavorful tomato sauce and mildly spiced meatballs make a hearty sandwich filling, or they can be served over pasta. I broil the meatballs first to quickly brown them. —Jean Glacken, Elkton, Maryland

2 eggs, beaten
1/4 cup milk
1/2 cup dry bread crumbs
2 tablespoons grated Parmesan cheese
1 teaspoon salt
1/4 teaspoon pepper
1/8 teaspoon garlic powder
1 pound ground beef
1/2 pound bulk Italian sausage
SAUCE:
1 can (15 ounces) tomato sauce
1 can (6 ounces) tomato paste
1 small onion, chopped
1/2 cup chopped green pepper
1/2 cup red wine *or* beef broth
1/3 cup water
2 garlic cloves, minced
1 teaspoon dried oregano
1 teaspoon salt
1/2 teaspoon sugar
1/2 teaspoon pepper
6 to 7 Italian rolls, split
Additional Parmesan cheese, optional

In a bowl, combine eggs and milk; add bread crumbs, Parmesan cheese, salt, pepper and garlic powder. Add beef and sausage; mix well. Shape into 1-in. balls. Broil 4 in. from the heat for 4 minutes; turn and broil 3 minutes longer. Transfer to a slow cooker. Combine tomato sauce and paste, onion, green pepper, wine or broth, water and seasonings; pour over meatballs. Cover and cook on low for 4-5 hours. Serve on rolls. Sprinkle with cheese if desired. **Yield:** 6-7 servings.

Cheesy Hash Brown Potatoes

I adapted this recipe for my slow cooker so I could bring these cheesy potatoes to a potluck picnic. Canned soup and frozen hash browns make them easy to assemble. Everyone agrees they're irresistible. —Becky Weseman
Becker, Minnesota

2 cans (10-3/4 ounces *each*) condensed
   cheddar cheese soup, undiluted
1-1/3 cups buttermilk
2 tablespoons butter *or* margarine, melted
1/2 teaspoon seasoned salt
1/4 teaspoon garlic powder
1/4 teaspoon pepper
1 package (32 ounces) frozen cubed hash
   brown potatoes
1/4 cup grated Parmesan cheese
1 teaspoon paprika

In a slow cooker, combine the first six ingredients; stir in hash browns. Sprinkle with Parmesan cheese and pa-

prika. Cover and cook on low for 4 to 4-1/2 hours or until potatoes are tender. **Yield:** 6-8 servings.

Peachy Spiced Cider

Welcome guests with the inviting aroma of this warm beverage. I served the spiced cider at a cookie exchange and received so many compliments. Everyone enjoys its subtle peach flavor. —Rose Harman, Hays, Kansas

4 cans (5-1/2 ounces *each*) peach *or* apricot
   nectar
2 cups apple juice
1/4 to 1/2 teaspoon ground ginger
1/4 teaspoon ground cinnamon
1/4 teaspoon ground nutmeg
4 fresh orange slices (1/4 inch thick), halved

Combine the first five ingredients in a slow cooker. Top with the orange slices. Cover and cook on low for 4-6 hours or until heated through. Stir before serving. **Yield:** about 1 quart.

Hearty Broccoli Dip

You'll need just five ingredients to stir up this no-fuss appetizer. People often ask me to bring my creamy dip to potlucks and parties. I never leave with leftovers. —Sue Call, Beech Grove, Indiana

1 pound ground beef
1 pound process American cheese, cubed
1 can (10-3/4 ounces) condensed cream of
   mushroom soup, undiluted
1 package (10 ounces) frozen chopped
   broccoli, thawed
2 tablespoons salsa
Tortilla chips

In a skillet, brown beef; drain. Transfer to a slow cooker. Add cheese, soup, broccoli and salsa; mix well. Cover and cook on low for 2-3 hours or until heated through, stirring after 1 hour. Serve with tortilla chips. **Yield:** 5-1/2 cups.

Stuffed Flank Steak

(Pictured at right)

This elegant slow-cooked meal is nice for family as well as for company. I like to make it on special occasions. The tasty tender steak cuts easily into appetizing spirals for serving, and extra stuffing cooks conveniently in a foil packet on top of the steak. —Diane Hixon
Niceville, Florida

1 package (8 ounces) crushed corn bread
   stuffing
1 cup chopped onion
1 cup chopped celery
1/4 cup minced fresh parsley
2 eggs
1-1/4 cups beef broth
1/3 cup butter *or* margarine, melted
1/2 teaspoon seasoned salt

1/2 teaspoon pepper
1-1/2 pounds flank steak

In a large bowl, combine stuffing, onion, celery and parsley. In a small bowl, beat the eggs; stir in broth and butter. Pour over stuffing mixture. Sprinkle with seasoned salt and pepper; stir well. Pound steak to 1/2-in. thickness. Spread 1-1/2 cups stuffing mixture over steak. Roll up, starting with a short side; tie with string. Place in a 5-qt. slow cooker. Remaining stuffing can be wrapped tightly in foil and placed over the rolled steak. Cover and cook on low for 6-8 hours or until a meat thermometer inserted in stuffing reads 165°. Remove string before slicing. **Yield:** 6 servings. **Editor's Note:** No liquid is added to the slow cooker. The moisture comes from the meat.

Shrimp Marinara

(Pictured below)

This flavorful marinara sauce simmers for most of the day. Then shortly before mealtime, I simply add cooked shrimp, which merely require being heated through. Served over spaghetti, it makes a delicious dressed-up main dish. —Sue Mackey
Galesburg, Illinois

 ✓ **Nutritional Analysis included**

1 can (14-1/2 ounces) Italian diced tomatoes, undrained
1 can (6 ounces) tomato paste
1/2 to 1 cup water
2 garlic cloves, minced
2 tablespoons minced fresh parsley
1 teaspoon salt, optional
1 teaspoon dried oregano
1/2 teaspoon dried basil
1/4 teaspoon pepper
1 pound fresh *or* frozen shrimp, cooked, peeled and deveined
1 pound spaghetti, cooked and drained
Shredded Parmesan cheese, optional

In a slow cooker, combine the first nine ingredients. Cover and cook on low for 3-4 hours. Stir in shrimp. Cover and cook 20 minutes longer or just until shrimp are heated through. Serve over spaghetti. Garnish with Parmesan cheese if desired. **Yield:** 6 servings. **Nutritional Analysis:** One serving (prepared with no-salt-added tomato paste and without salt and Parmesan cheese) equals 383 calories, 256 mg sodium, 90 mg cholesterol, 68 gm carbohydrate, 21 gm protein, 2 gm fat. **Diabetic Exchanges:** 4 starch, 2 very lean meat, 1 vegetable.

Shrimp Marinara
Stuffed Flank Steak

Great Grilling Recipes

In a small saucepan, combine the first six ingredients. Cook and stir until sugar is dissolved. Meanwhile, grill salmon, covered, over medium-hot heat for 5 minutes. Turn salmon; baste with the butter sauce. Grill 7-9 minutes longer, turning and basting occasionally, or until the salmon flakes easily with a fork. **Yield:** 4 servings.

Teriyaki Kabobs

(Pictured below)

It takes just seconds to stir up this delicious marinade, which flavors the beef and veggies wonderfully. Marinate the meat a few hours or overnight—whatever suits your schedule. —Candy VanderWaal, Elkhart Lake, Wisconsin

☑ Nutritional Analysis included

WANT to spend a lot less time in the kitchen? Step outdoors anytime of year and fix a meal on the grill! It's easy to cook an entire menu at once…plus there's less mess and cleanup.

Barbecued Alaskan Salmon

(Pictured below)

We eat salmon all summer long, and this is our favorite way to fix it. The mild sauce—brushed on as the fish grills—really enhances the taste. —Janis Smoke
King Salmon, Alaska

      2 tablespoons butter *or* margarine
      2 tablespoons brown sugar
      1 to 2 garlic cloves, minced
      1 tablespoon lemon juice
      2 teaspoons soy sauce
  1/2 teaspoon pepper
      4 salmon steaks (1 inch thick)

  1/3 cup soy sauce
      2 tablespoons vegetable oil
      1 tablespoon brown sugar
      1 garlic clove, minced
      1 teaspoon ground ginger
      1 teaspoon seasoned salt
1-1/2 pounds boneless sirloin steak, cut into 1-1/4-inch cubes
    12 whole fresh mushrooms
      1 large green pepper, cut into 1-1/2-inch pieces
      1 large onion, cut into wedges
    12 cherry tomatoes
Hot cooked rice, optional

Teriyaki Kabobs
Barbecued Alaskan Salmon

In a bowl, combine soy sauce, oil, brown sugar, garlic, ginger and salt; mix well. Pour half of the marinade into a large resealable plastic bag or shallow glass container; add beef and turn to coat. Seal or cover; refrigerate for 4-8 hours, turning occasionally. Cover and refrigerate remaining marinade. Drain meat, discarding marinade. On metal or soaked bamboo skewers, alternate meat, mushrooms, green pepper, onion and tomatoes. Grill, uncovered, over medium heat for 3 minutes on each side. ~~~ with reserved marinade. Continue turning ar~~~ for 8-10 minutes or until meat reaches ~~~ss (for rare, a meat thermometer sh~~~ ~~~dium, 160°; well-done, 170°). Se~~~ ~~~ver rice if desired. **Yield:** 6 se~~~ ~~~ysis: One serving (calculated without ~~~ calories, 690 mg sodium, 77 mg cholesterol, 10 gm carbohydrate, 29 gm protein, 10 gm fat. **Diabetic Exchanges:** 3-1/2 lean meat, 2 vegetable.

Potatoes Plus

On our busy farm, meals need to be ready fast. These herb-seasoned potatoes and vegetables wrapped in foil packets cook in only half an hour. They're excellent with steak or chicken. —Jill Jellett, Leduc, Alberta

> 4 medium red potatoes, cubed
> 1 medium onion, cubed
> 1 medium sweet red pepper, cubed
> 1/2 teaspoon seasoned salt
> 1/4 teaspoon garlic powder
> 1/4 teaspoon *each* dried basil, dill weed and parsley flakes
> 1/4 cup butter *or* margarine

Combine vegetables and seasonings; divide between four pieces of heavy-duty foil (about 12 in. x 12 in.). Dot with butter. Fold foil around vegetables and seal tightly. Grill, covered, over medium heat for 25-30 minutes. Open foil carefully to allow steam to escape. **Yield:** 4 servings.

Oriental Pork Chops

My family really likes pork. I experimented with a poultry marinade until I came up with this nicely seasoned version for chops. —Annie Arnold, Plymouth, Minnesota

☑ **Nutritional Analysis included**

> 3 tablespoons soy sauce
> 3 tablespoons honey
> 1 tablespoon lemon juice
> 1 tablespoon olive *or* vegetable oil
> 3 garlic cloves, minced
> 1/2 teaspoon ground ginger
> 4 boneless pork chops (1/2 to 3/4 inch thick)

In a large resealable plastic bag or shallow glass container, combine the first six ingredients. Add pork and turn to coat. Seal or cover; refrigerate for 4-8 hours. Grill, uncovered, over medium heat for 10-12 minutes or until juices run clear, turning once. **Yield:** 4 servings. **Nutritional Analysis:** One serving (prepared with light soy sauce) equals 225 calories, 420 mg sodium, 55 mg cholesterol, 16 gm carbohydrate, 21 gm protein, 9 gm fat. **Diabetic Exchanges:** 3 lean meat, 2 starch.

Blues Burgers

If you like blue cheese, you'll love the flavorful surprise inside these moist hamburgers. They're so filling that just a serving of coleslaw on the side makes for a hearty meal. —Dee Dee Mitchell, Longmont, Colorado

> 1/2 pound fresh mushrooms, sliced
> 2 tablespoons butter *or* margarine
> 1-1/2 pounds lean ground beef
> 1/2 teaspoon ground cumin
> 1/2 teaspoon paprika
> 1/4 teaspoon chili powder
> 1/4 teaspoon salt
> 1/4 teaspoon pepper
> Pinch cayenne pepper
> 2 ounces crumbled blue cheese
> 2/3 cup barbecue sauce
> 4 onion rolls *or* hamburger buns, split

In a skillet, saute mushrooms in butter for 2-3 minutes or until tender. Set aside and keep warm. In a bowl, combine the beef and seasonings just until well mixed. Shape into eight thin patties. Sprinkle half of the patties with blue cheese. Place remaining patties on top and press edges firmly to seal. Grill, uncovered, over medium-hot heat for 3 minutes on each side. Brush with barbecue sauce. Grill 10-12 minutes longer or until juices run clear, basting and turning occasionally. Drain the mushrooms. Serve burgers on rolls topped with mushrooms. **Yield:** 4 servings.

Maple Mustard Chicken

For make-ahead convenience, I marinate these chicken breasts overnight. Their sweet and mustardy flavor goes well with baked potatoes and a tossed salad. They'd make delightful chicken sandwiches, too. —Lynda Ebel Medicine Hat, Alberta

> 1/2 cup maple syrup
> 3 tablespoons cider *or* red wine vinegar
> 2 tablespoons Dijon mustard
> 1 tablespoon vegetable oil
> 2 garlic cloves, minced
> 3/4 to 1 teaspoon pepper
> 6 boneless skinless chicken breast halves (about 1-1/2 pounds)

In a bowl, combine the first six ingredients; mix well. Reserve 1/4 cup for basting; cover and refrigerate. Pour remaining marinade into a large resealable plastic bag or shallow glass container; add chicken and turn to coat. Seal or cover; refrigerate for 4-8 hours, turning occasionally. Drain and discard marinade. Grill, uncovered, over medium heat for 3 minutes on each side. Grill 6-8 minutes longer or until juices run clear, basting with the reserved marinade and turning occasionally. **Yield:** 6 servings.

Sirloin Caesar Salad

Sirloin Caesar Salad

(Pictured above)

A tangy sauce that combines bottled salad dressing, lemon juice and Dijon mustard flavors this filling main-dish salad. You save on cleanup time because both the steak and bread are cooked on the grill. —Carol Sinclair
St. Elmo, Illinois

✓ Nutritional Analysis included

    1 boneless top sirloin steak (1 pound)
    1 cup Caesar salad dressing
  1/4 cup Dijon mustard
  1/4 cup lemon juice
    6 slices French bread (1 inch thick)
  12 cups torn romaine
    1 medium tomato, chopped

Place steak in a large resealable plastic bag or shallow glass container. In a bowl, combine the salad dressing, mustard and lemon juice; set aside 3/4 cup. Pour remaining dressing mixture over the steak. Seal or cover and refrigerate for 1 hour, turning occasionally. Brush both sides of bread with 1/4 cup of the reserved dressing mixture. Grill bread, uncovered, over medium heat for 1-2 minutes on each side or until lightly toasted. Wrap in foil and set aside. Drain steak, discarding mari-nade. Grill, covered, for 5-8 minutes on each side or until meat reaches desired doneness (for rare, a meat thermometer should read 140°; medium, 160°; well-done, 170°). Place romaine and tomato on a serving platter. Slice steak diagonally; arrange over salad. Serve with the bread and remaining dressing. **Yield:** 6 servings. **Nutritional Analysis:** One serving (prepared with fat-free dressing) equals 214 calories, 586 mg sodium, 50 mg cholesterol, 18 gm carbohydrate, 22 gm protein, 6 gm fat. **Diabetic Exchanges:** 2 lean meat, 1 starch, 1 vegetable.

Grilled Sweet Corn

Since we have plenty of fresh sweet corn available in our area, we use this recipe often in summer. Parsley, chili powder and cumin accent the corn's just-picked flavor.
—Connie Lou Hollister, Lake Odessa, Michigan

    8 large ears sweet corn in husks
    6 tablespoons butter *or* margarine, softened
    1 tablespoon minced fresh parsley
    1 to 2 teaspoons chili powder
    1 teaspoon garlic salt
  1/2 to 1 teaspoon ground cumin

Carefully peel back husks from corn to within 1 in. of bottom; remove silk. Combine the remaining ingredients; spread over corn. Rewrap corn in husks and secure with string. Place in a large kettle; cover with cold water. Soak for 20 minutes; drain. Grill corn, covered, over medium heat, for 10-15 minutes or until tender, turning often. **Yield:** 8 servings.

Citrus Steak

The mild citrus flavor of this marinade offers a nice change of pace from usual steak seasonings. It's easy to prepare the steak the night before, then throw it on the grill before dinner. —Carol Towey, Pasadena, California

  2 medium unpeeled lemons, quartered
  1 medium unpeeled orange, quartered
1/2 cup vegetable oil
  1 garlic clove, minced
  1 boneless sirloin steak (about 2-1/2 pounds
    and 1-3/4 inches thick)

In a skillet, cook the lemon and orange wedges in oil over medium heat for 10-15 minutes, stirring often. Add garlic; cook and stir 1-2 minutes longer. Place steak in a shallow glass baking dish; pierce meat every inch with a fork. Pour citrus mixture over meat; turn to coat. Cover and refrigerate overnight, turning three or four times. Drain and discard marinade. On a covered grill over medium-hot heat, cook steak for 9-10 minutes on each side or until meat reaches desired doneness (for rare, a meat thermometer should read 140°; medium, 160°; well-done, 170°). **Yield:** 6-8 servings.

Grilled Jalapenos

When barbecuing with friends, I also use the grill to serve up hot appetizers. These crowd-pleasing stuffed peppers have a bit of bite. They were concocted by my son. —Catherine Hollie, Cleveland, Texas

24 fresh jalapeno peppers*
12 ounces bulk pork sausage
12 bacon strips, halved

Wash peppers and remove stems. Cut a slit along one side of each pepper. Remove seeds; rinse and dry peppers. In a skillet over medium heat, cook sausage until no longer pink; drain. Stuff peppers with sausage and wrap with bacon; secure with a toothpick. On an uncovered grill over medium heat, grill peppers for about 15 minutes or until tender and bacon is crisp, turning frequently. **Yield:** 2 dozen. ***Editor's Note:** When handling jalapeno peppers, use rubber gloves and avoid touching your face.

Marinated Ham Steaks

It's a snap to combine this zippy marinade…and you can vary the marinating time to fit your day's activities. The steaks cook up quickly and are always a hit! —Maribeth Edwards, Follansbee, West Virginia

1-1/2 cups pineapple juice

1/4 cup packed brown sugar
  2 tablespoons butter *or* margarine, melted
  1 to 2 tablespoons ground mustard
  1 garlic clove, minced
1/4 teaspoon paprika
  2 fully cooked ham steaks (1 pound *each*)

In a large resealable plastic bag or shallow glass container, combine the first six ingredients; mix well. Add ham and turn to coat. Seal or cover; refrigerate for at least 2 hours, turning occasionally. Drain and reserve marinade. Grill ham, uncovered, over medium-hot heat for 3-4 minutes on each side, basting frequently with reserved marinade. **Yield:** 6 servings.

Tummy Dogs

Looking for a fun and flavorful way to jazz up hot dogs? Try these bacon-wrapped versions with zippy Dijon mustard. They don't take long to fix, and your tummy will thank you. —Myra Innes, Auburn, Kansas

8 bacon strips
8 hot dogs
4 ounces Monterey Jack cheese, cut into strips
1/4 cup butter *or* margarine, softened
1/4 cup Dijon mustard
8 hot dog buns
1 small onion, thinly sliced, optional
1 can (4 ounces) diced green chilies, optional

Partially cook bacon; drain on paper towels. Cut a 1/4-in. lengthwise slit in each hot dog; place cheese in each slit. Starting at one end, wrap bacon in a spiral around hot dog; secure with toothpicks. Split buns just halfway. Combine butter and mustard; spread inside buns. Set aside. On a covered grill over medium heat, cook hot dogs with cheese side down for 2 minutes. Turn and grill 3-4 minutes longer or until bacon is crisp and cheese is melted. Place buns on grill with cut side down; grill until lightly toasted. Remove toothpicks from the hot dogs; serve in buns with onion and chilies if desired. **Yield:** 8 sandwiches.

Baked Apples on the Grill

Sweet coconut provides the delicious difference in this fun grilled treat. Our two children enjoy helping me stuff the yummy filling into the apples. It's so easy that sometimes we don't even bother to do the measuring! —Jodi Rugg, Aurora, Illinois

4 medium tart apples, cored
1/3 cup raisins
1/3 cup flaked coconut
1/4 cup packed brown sugar
1/2 teaspoon ground cinnamon

Place each apple on a 12-in.-square piece of heavy-duty foil. Combine remaining ingredients; spoon into center of apples. Fold foil over apples and seal tightly. Grill, covered, over medium heat for 20-25 minutes or until apples are tender. **Yield:** 4 servings.

Tangy Barbecue Sauce

This sweet and tangy basting sauce came from my husband's family. With just four ingredients, it's simple to stir up. A speedy alternative to bottled sauce, it can be brushed on chicken, ribs, pork or even turkey. —Jenine Schmidt
Stoughton, Wisconsin

　　1 cup ketchup
　2/3 cup packed brown sugar
　　2 teaspoons prepared mustard
　1/2 teaspoon ground nutmeg

In a bowl, combine all ingredients. Use as a basting sauce for grilled meat. **Yield:** 1-1/3 cups.

Grilled Sweet Potatoes

I love trying new recipes, so my son-in-law suggested we grill sweet potatoes. Served with steak, they're a great change of pace from traditional baked potatoes...and pretty, too. —Lillian Neer, Long Eddy, New York

✓ Nutritional Analysis included

　　2 large sweet potatoes, halved lengthwise
　　2 tablespoons butter *or* margarine, softened
Garlic salt and pepper to taste
　　2 teaspoons honey

Cut two pieces of heavy-duty foil (about 18 in. x 12 in.); place a potato half on each. Spread cut side with butter. Sprinkle with garlic salt and pepper. Top each potato with another half. Fold foil over potatoes and seal tightly. Grill, covered, over medium-hot heat for 30 minutes or until tender, turning once. To serve, fluff potatoes with a fork and drizzle with honey. **Yield:** 4 servings. **Nutritional Analysis:** One serving (prepared with margarine and without garlic salt) equals 123 calories, 73 mg sodium, 0 cholesterol, 16 gm carbohydrate, 1 gm protein, 6 gm fat. **Diabetic Exchanges:** 1 starch, 1 fat.

T-Bones with Onions

Steak gets a dressy treatment when topped with tasty onion slices flavored with honey and mustard. I found this recipe on a bag of charcoal more than 10 years ago. It's terrific with green beans or corn. —Sheree Quate
Cave Junction, Oregon

　　3 large onions, cut into 1/4-inch-thick slices
　　2 tablespoons honey
　1/2 teaspoon salt
　1/2 teaspoon pepper
　1/2 teaspoon ground mustard
　1/2 teaspoon paprika
　　4 T-bone steaks

Place onions in the center of a piece of heavy-duty foil (about 20 in. x 18 in.). Drizzle with honey; sprinkle with salt, pepper, mustard and paprika. Fold foil over onions and seal tightly. Grill, uncovered, over medium-hot heat for 20-25 minutes or until tender, turning once. Grill the steaks, uncovered, over medium-hot heat for 12-26 minutes, turning once, or until meat reaches desired doneness (for rare, a meat thermometer should read 140°; medium, 160°; well-done, 170°). Serve with onions. **Yield:** 4 servings.

Harvest Vegetables

(Pictured at right)

This colorful combination includes so many different vegetables that there's something to please everyone. Cleanup's a snap because there are no dishes to wash. —Linda Farni, Durango, Iowa

✓ Nutritional Analysis included

　　1 small cabbage, cored
　　2 tablespoons butter *or* margarine, softened
　1/2 to 1 teaspoon onion salt, optional
　1/8 to 1/4 teaspoon pepper
　　4 medium carrots, cut into 1-inch pieces
　　2 celery ribs, cut into 1-inch pieces
　　1 small onion, cut into wedges
　1/2 pound whole fresh mushrooms
　　1 small green pepper, cut into pieces
　　4 bacon strips, cooked and crumbled, optional

Cut cabbage into six wedges; spread butter on cut sides. Place cabbage on a piece of heavy-duty foil (about 24 in. x 18 in.). Sprinkle with onion salt if desired and pepper. Arrange remaining vegetables and bacon if desired around cabbage. Seal foil tightly. Grill, covered, over medium-hot heat for 30 minutes or until vegetables are tender, turning occasionally. **Yield:** 6 servings. **Nutritional Analysis:** One serving (prepared with margarine and without onion salt and bacon) equals 110 calories, 102 mg sodium, 0 cholesterol, 17 gm carbohydrate, 4 gm protein, 4 gm fat. **Diabetic Exchanges:** 1 starch, 1 fat.

Dessert from the Grill

(Pictured at right)

A grilled meal isn't complete without this light, refreshing dessert. By the time we're done eating, the coals have cooled to the right temperature. I brush slices of pineapple and pound cake with a sweet sauce, toast them on the grill and top them with ice cream and convenient caramel sauce. —Becky Gillespie, Boulder, Colorado

　　1 can (20 ounces) sliced pineapple
　　1 tablespoon butter *or* margarine
　1/2 teaspoon brown sugar
　1/4 teaspoon vanilla extract
　1/8 teaspoon ground cinnamon
　1/8 teaspoon ground nutmeg
　　6 slices pound cake
Vanilla ice cream
Caramel ice cream topping

Drain pineapple, reserving 1/3 cup juice and six pineapple rings (save remaining juice and pineapple for another use). In a microwave-safe dish, combine butter, brown sugar, vanilla, cinnamon, nutmeg and reserved pineapple juice. Microwave, uncovered, on high for 1-2 minutes or until bubbly. Brush half of the mixture on both

Dessert from the Grill
Zesty Grilled Chops
Harvest Vegetables

sides of pineapple rings and cake slices. On an uncovered grill over medium heat, cook pineapple and cake for 1-2 minutes on each side or until golden brown, brushing occasionally with remaining pineapple juice mixture. Top each slice of cake with a pineapple ring and scoop of ice cream; drizzle with caramel topping. Serve immediately. **Yield:** 6 servings.

Zesty Grilled Chops

(Pictured above)

My sister gave me the recipe for this easy five-ingredient marinade. It keeps the meat so moist and tasty...now it's the only way my husband wants his pork chops prepared.
—Bernice Germann, Napoleon, Ohio

3/4 cup soy sauce
1/4 cup lemon juice
  1 tablespoon chili sauce
  1 tablespoon brown sugar
1/4 teaspoon garlic powder
  6 rib *or* loin pork chops (3/4 inch thick)

In a large resealable plastic bag or shallow glass container, combine the first five ingredients; mix well. Remove 1/4 cup for basting and refrigerate. Add pork chops to the remaining marinade and turn to coat. Cover and refrigerate for 3 hours or overnight, turning once. Drain chops, discarding marinade. Grill, covered, over medium-hot heat for 4 minutes. Turn; baste with reserved marinade. Grill 4-7 minutes longer or until juices run clear. **Yield:** 6 servings.

Microwave Magic

TRY the made-in-minutes microwave recipes here and you'll never again use your "zapper" just for heating up coffee or warming leftovers.

Editor's Note: All of these recipes were tested in an 850-watt microwave.

Stuffed Green Pepper Cups

You can make this delicious main dish from start to finish in about half an hour. I like the way the garden-fresh peppers keep their bright green color and crunchy texture.
—Merrill Powers, Spearville, Kansas

    1 pound ground beef
    1/3 cup finely chopped onion
    1 can (15 ounces) tomato sauce, *divided*
    1/4 cup water
    3 tablespoons grated Parmesan cheese, *divided*
    1 teaspoon salt
    1/8 teaspoon pepper
    1/2 cup uncooked instant rice
    4 medium green peppers

Crumble beef into a 1-1/2-qt. microwave-safe bowl; add the onion. Cover and microwave on high for 3 to 4-1/2 minutes or until meat is browned; drain. Stir in 1-1/2 cups of tomato sauce, water, 1 tablespoon of Parmesan cheese, salt and pepper. Cover and microwave on high for 2-3 minutes. Stir in rice; cover and let stand for 5 minutes. Remove tops and seeds from the peppers; cut in half lengthwise. Stuff with meat mixture; place in an ungreased microwave-safe shallow 3-qt. or 13-in. x 9-in. x 2-in. baking dish. Spoon the remaining tomato sauce over peppers; sprinkle with remaining cheese. Cover and microwave on high for 10-12 minutes or until peppers are tender. Let stand for 5 minutes before serving. **Yield:** 4 servings.

Catfish in Ginger Sauce

Whenever I want to serve fish in a flash, I turn to this recipe. The fillets always turn out moist, tender and tasty. For even more flavor, spoon extra sauce over the fish before serving. —Mary Dixon, Decatur, Alabama

    1/2 cup chopped green onions
    1 tablespoon vegetable oil
    1/4 teaspoon ground ginger
    1 teaspoon cornstarch
    2 tablespoons water
    1 cup chicken broth
    1 tablespoon soy sauce
    1 tablespoon white wine vinegar

    1/8 teaspoon cayenne pepper
    4 catfish fillets (6 ounces each)

In a 2-cup microwave-safe bowl, combine onions, oil and ginger. Microwave, uncovered, on high for 1 to 1-1/2 minutes or until the onions are tender. In small bowl, combine the cornstarch and water until smooth. Add broth, soy sauce, vinegar and cayenne; mix well. Stir into onion mixture. Microwave, uncovered, at 70% power for 3-4 minutes, stirring after each minute, until sauce comes to a boil. Place catfish in a microwave-safe 3-qt. casserole; pour sauce over the fish. Cover and microwave on high for 5-1/2 to 7 minutes or until the fish flakes easily with a fork. **Yield:** 4 servings.

Microwave Snack Mix

The peanuts and pretzels come out so crisp and munchy you'd think they were oven-baked. —Priscilla Weaver
Hagerstown, Maryland

    1/2 cup butter *or* margarine
    2 teaspoons chili powder
    1 teaspoon ground cumin
    1/2 teaspoon garlic powder
    5 cups oyster crackers
    3 cups miniature pretzels
2-1/2 cups salted peanuts
    2 tablespoons Parmesan cheese

In a small microwave-safe bowl, combine butter, chili powder, cumin and garlic powder. Cover and microwave on high for 45-60 seconds or until butter is melted. In a 3-qt. microwave-safe dish, combine crackers, pretzels and peanuts. Add butter mixture and mix lightly. Sprinkle with Parmesan cheese; toss to coat. Microwave, uncovered, on high for 7-8 minutes or until mixture begins to toast, carefully stirring every 2 minutes. Cool. Store in an airtight container. **Yield:** 10 cups.

Tamale Pie

(Pictured at right)

My family really enjoys Mexican food. When I'm in a hurry, I make this zippy deep-dish pie. It always satisfies their appetites. —Nancy Roberts, Cave City, Arkansas

    1 pound ground beef
    1/4 pound bulk pork sausage
    1/4 cup chopped onion
    1 garlic clove, minced
    1 can (14-1/2 ounces) stewed tomatoes, drained
    1 can (11 ounces) whole kernel corn, drained
    1 can (6 ounces) tomato paste
    1/4 cup sliced ripe olives
1-1/2 teaspoons chili powder
    1/2 teaspoon salt
    1 egg
    1/3 cup milk
    1 package (8-1/2 ounces) corn bread/muffin mix
Paprika
    1/2 cup shredded cheddar cheese

In a 2-1/2-qt. microwave-safe dish, combine the beef, sausage, onion and garlic. Cover and microwave on high for 5 to 5-1/2 minutes, stirring once to crumble meat. Drain. Add the tomatoes, corn, tomato paste, olives, chili powder and salt; mix well. Cover and microwave on high for 5-7 minutes or until heated through. In a bowl, beat egg; add milk and corn bread mix. Stir just until moistened. Spoon over meat mixture; sprinkle with paprika. Microwave, uncovered, on high for 9-10 minutes or until a toothpick inserted near the center of the corn bread comes out clean. Sprinkle with cheese. **Yield:** 6 servings.

In a large microwave-safe bowl, combine the marshmallows, peanut butter, chocolate chips and butter. Cover and microwave on high for 2 to 2-1/2 minutes. Stir until well blended (the mixture will be lumpy). Add cereal and peanuts; stir until well coated. Spread into a greased 13-in. x 9-in. x 2-in. pan. For the frosting, combine chocolate chips, butter and milk in another microwave-safe bowl. Cover and microwave on high for 1 to 1-1/2 minutes or until melted; mix well. Add confectioners' sugar and vanilla. With an electric mixer, beat frosting until smooth. Spread over the cereal mixture. Cover and refrigerate for 2 hours or until firm. Cut into squares. **Yield:** about 4 dozen.

Crispy Chocolate Squares

(Pictured below)

Folks will think you slaved away on these fast and fudgy treats. People are surprised to find out how easy they are to make. —Karen Speidel, Wheeling, Illinois

- 1 package (10-1/2 ounces) miniature marshmallows
- 1 cup peanut butter
- 1 cup (6 ounces) semisweet chocolate chips
- 1/2 cup butter *or* margarine
- 2 cups crisp rice cereal
- 1 cup salted peanuts

FROSTING:
- 1 cup (6 ounces) semisweet chocolate chips
- 1/4 cup butter *or* margarine
- 1/4 cup milk
- 2 cups confectioners' sugar
- 1 teaspoon vanilla extract

Lemon Asparagus

(Pictured on front cover)

I live in the heart of asparagus country, so I'm always on the lookout for new ways to serve it. Lemon and a touch of tarragon make this a quick elegant side dish. —Clarice Scheeringa, Ripon, California

- 1 pound fresh asparagus, cut into 1-inch pieces
- 2 tablespoons water
- 2 tablespoons butter *or* margarine, melted
- 1 to 2 teaspoons lemon juice

Pinch dried tarragon
Salt and pepper to taste

Place asparagus and water in a 1-1/2-qt. microwave-safe bowl. Cover and microwave on high for 6-1/2 to 8 minutes or until crisp-tender; drain. Add butter, lemon juice and tarragon; toss to coat. Sprinkle with salt and pepper. **Yield:** 4-6 servings.

Tamale Pie
Crispy Chocolate Squares

Microwave Stir-Fry

Microwave Stir-Fry

(Pictured above)

After working all day, rely on this fast-to-fix main dish that's similar to a stir-fry but made in the microwave.
—*Nancy Johnson, Connersville, Indiana*

✓ Nutritional Analysis included

  1/4 cup all-purpose flour
    2 teaspoons salt, optional
  1/4 teaspoon pepper
  1/4 teaspoon ground cumin
    1 pound boneless sirloin steak, cut into
      1/8-inch strips
    1 tablespoon vegetable oil
    1 can (14-1/2 ounces) diced tomatoes
    3 medium carrots, julienned
  1/2 cup finely chopped onion
  1/2 teaspoon dried basil
  1/4 teaspoon dried oregano
    1 cup julienned zucchini
1-1/2 cups sliced fresh mushrooms
Hot cooked rice

In a shallow dish or resealable plastic bag, combine the first four ingredients. Add meat and toss to coat. Pour oil into a shallow 2-qt. microwave-safe dish; arrange meat evenly in dish. Cover and microwave at 50% power for 6 minutes, stirring once; set aside. Drain tomatoes, reserving juice; set tomatoes aside. In a microwave-safe bowl, combine tomato juice, carrots, onion, basil and oregano. Cover and microwave on high for 4 minutes, stirring once. Pour over meat; add the tomatoes, zucchini and mushrooms. Cover and microwave at 50% power for 12 minutes, stirring several times. Let stand for 3 minutes. Serve over rice. **Yield:** 5 servings. **Nutritional Analysis:** One serving (prepared without salt; calculated without rice) equals 237 calories, 203 mg sodium, 61 mg cholesterol, 16 gm carbohydrate, 24 gm protein, 9 gm fat. **Diabetic Exchanges:** 3 lean meat, 1 starch.

Cinnamon Bread Pudding

This dessert is different and delicious. I've used this recipe for more than 10 years with much success.
—*Emma Magielda, Amsterdam, New York*

12 slices cinnamon bread, crusts removed
  3 squares (1 ounce *each*) semisweet chocolate,
    melted
  2 cups half-and-half cream

1 cup milk
4 eggs
3/4 cup sugar
1-1/2 teaspoons vanilla extract

Cut bread in half diagonally. Arrange half of the slices in a single layer, overlapping if necessary, in an ungreased shallow 2-qt. microwave-safe dish. Drizzle with half of the chocolate; top with the remaining bread. In a 1-qt. microwave-safe bowl, combine the cream and milk; microwave, uncovered, on high for 4-6 minutes or until hot but not boiling. In a small bowl, beat eggs; add sugar. Add a small amount of cream mixture; mix well. Return all to the larger bowl; stir in vanilla. Pour over bread; drizzle with the remaining chocolate. Cover and microwave at 50% power for 14-15 minutes or until a knife inserted near the center comes out clean, rotating a half-turn once (mixture will puff up during cooking). Uncover and let stand for 5 minutes. Serve warm or cold. Refrigerate leftovers. **Yield:** 6-8 servings.

Broccoli-Rice Side Dish

This creamy side dish cooks in about 15 minutes, so it's easy to put together before church on potluck Sundays.
— *Faye Hintz, Springfield, Missouri*

1 can (10-3/4 ounces) condensed cream of chicken soup, undiluted
1 jar (8 ounces) process cheese spread
1 cup uncooked instant rice
1/2 cup milk
Dash pepper
1 package (10 ounces) frozen chopped broccoli
1/2 cup chopped onion
1/2 cup chopped celery
1 can (2.8 ounces) french-fried onions

In a microwave-safe 2-qt. casserole, combine the soup, cheese spread, rice, milk and pepper. Microwave, uncovered, on high for 2-3 minutes or until cheese is melted. Stir in broccoli, onion and celery. Microwave, uncovered, on high for 12-14 minutes, rotating a half-turn once. Sprinkle onions over the top; microwave on high for 1 minute. **Yield:** 8-10 servings.

Microwave Cherry Crisp

(Pictured on front cover)

Our family loves this pretty, tasty dessert. It uses convenient pie filling, so you can make it in no time—and it takes just a few minutes to heat in the microwave.
—*Laurie Todd, Columbus, Mississippi*

1 can (21 ounces) cherry pie filling
1 teaspoon lemon juice
1 cup all-purpose flour
1/4 cup packed brown sugar
3/4 teaspoon ground cinnamon
1/4 teaspoon ground allspice
1/3 cup cold butter *or* margarine
1/2 cup chopped walnuts
Vanilla ice cream

Combine the pie filling and lemon juice in an ungreased 1-1/2-qt. microwave-safe dish; set aside. In a small bowl, combine flour, brown sugar, cinnamon and allspice; cut in butter until mixture resembles coarse crumbs. Add walnuts. Sprinkle over filling. Microwave, uncovered, on high for 5-6 minutes or until bubbly. Serve warm with ice cream. **Yield:** 4 servings.

Chocolate Chip Bars

People are always surprised when I tell them these sweet treats come from the microwave. Chock-full of chocolate chips, the bars are especially good served with a big glass of cold milk.
—*Shirley Glaab*
Hattiesburg, Mississippi

1/2 cup butter *or* margarine, softened
3/4 cup packed brown sugar
1 egg
1 tablespoon milk
1 teaspoon vanilla extract
1-1/4 cups all-purpose flour
1/2 teaspoon baking powder
1/8 teaspoon salt
1 cup (6 ounces) semisweet chocolate chips, *divided*
1/2 cup chopped walnuts

In a mixing bowl, cream butter and brown sugar. Add egg, milk and vanilla; mix well. Combine flour, baking powder and salt; add to creamed mixture. Stir in 1/2 cup chocolate chips and walnuts. Spread into a greased 8-in. square microwave-safe dish. Sprinkle with the remaining chocolate chips. Microwave, uncovered, on high for 5 minutes or until bars test done, rotating a quarter-turn every minute. Cool before cutting. **Yield:** about 1-1/2 dozen.

Overnight Tuna Casserole

This is an update of an old-time favorite—comforting tuna casserole. It may be the easiest tuna macaroni casserole ever. I prepare it the night before, then just pop it in the microwave. There's no need to precook the macaroni, so there's really no fuss.
—*Shirley Glaab*

1 can (10-3/4 ounces) condensed cream of celery soup, undiluted
1 cup milk
1 can (6 ounces) tuna, drained
1 cup uncooked elbow macaroni
1 cup frozen peas
1/2 cup chopped green onions
1 cup (4 ounces) shredded cheddar cheese, *divided*

In a bowl, combine soup and milk until smooth. Add the tuna, macaroni, peas, onions and 3/4 cup cheese; mix well. Pour into a greased 2-qt. microwave-safe dish. Cover and refrigerate overnight. Microwave, covered, on high for 14-16 minutes or until bubbly. Uncover; sprinkle with remaining cheese and let stand for 5 minutes or until melted. **Yield:** 4 servings.

Pistachio Brittle

This crunchy nut brittle is a favorite in my family. It's a snap to prepare so I don't mind making a batch whenever they ask. Tucked inside a festive holiday tin, it also makes a nice last-minute gift at Christmas. Be careful moving it in and out of the microwave, though, because the syrup gets very hot.
—Cheryl Brungardt
Wheat Ridge, Colorado

 1 cup sugar
 1/2 cup light corn syrup
 1/8 teaspoon salt
 1 teaspoon butter (no substitutes)
 1/2 cup shelled natural pistachios
 1 teaspoon baking soda
 1 teaspoon vanilla extract

In a 2-qt. microwave-safe bowl, combine sugar, corn syrup and salt. Microwave, uncovered, on high for 4 minutes. Stir. Microwave 3 minutes longer. Stir in butter and pistachios. Microwave on high for 30-60 seconds or until mixture turns a light amber (it will be very hot). Quickly stir in baking soda and vanilla until light and foamy. Immediately pour onto a greased baking sheet and spread out. Refrigerate for 20 minutes or until firm; break into small pieces. Store in an airtight container. **Yield:** 3/4 pound.

Gingerbread with Lemon Sauce

An old-fashioned-tasting lemon sauce tops this very moist spiced cake. The simple dessert is incredibly quick to make, so it's perfect for drop-in guests.
—Lucile Proctor
Panguitch, Utah

 1/4 cup shortening
 1 tablespoon sugar
 1 egg
 1/2 cup molasses
 1/2 cup boiling water
1-1/4 cups all-purpose flour
 1 teaspoon ground cinnamon
 1/2 teaspoon baking soda
 1/2 teaspoon ground ginger
 1/4 teaspoon salt
LEMON SAUCE:
 1 cup sugar
 1/2 cup butter *or* margarine
 1/4 cup water
 1 egg, beaten
 2 to 3 tablespoons lemon juice
 1 tablespoon grated lemon peel

In a mixing bowl, cream shortening and sugar. Add egg, molasses and water; mix well. Combine flour, cinnamon, baking soda, ginger and salt; add to creamed mixture. Pour into a greased 9-in. microwave-safe pie plate. Microwave, uncovered, on high for 7-8 minutes, rotating a quarter-turn every 2 minutes, or until a toothpick inserted near the center comes out clean. Cover with waxed paper; let stand for 5 minutes. Remove waxed paper and invert onto a serving plate. In a 1-qt. microwave-safe bowl, combine sugar, butter and water. Microwave,

uncovered, on high for 2-3 minutes or until butter is melted and mixture begins to boil; stir. Add a small amount to egg; beat well. Return all to the bowl. Microwave on high for 1 minute. Stir in lemon juice and peel. Cook 1 minute longer or until slightly thickened. Serve with the gingerbread. **Yield:** 6-8 servings.

Tangy Cauliflower

Our children never liked cauliflower until I started serving it this way. They love the colorful mustard sauce—there are never any leftovers.
—Stephanie Myers
Mobile, Alabama

 1 medium head cauliflower
 1 tablespoon water
 1/2 cup mayonnaise
1-1/2 teaspoons prepared mustard
 1/2 teaspoon ground mustard
 1/2 cup shredded sharp cheddar cheese

Place cauliflower in a microwave-safe dish. Add water. Cover and microwave on high for 12-14 minutes or until tender. Combine the mayonnaise, prepared mustard and ground mustard; spread over cauliflower. Sprinkle with cheese. Microwave, uncovered, on high for 1 minute or until the cheese is melted. **Yield:** 6-8 servings.

Chicken Primavera

(Pictured at right)

This fantastic chicken dish is a variation on a recipe from one of my microwave cookbooks. No one can resist the tender chicken and mushrooms in a creamy white sauce. Just toss together a salad, and your family can sit down to a satisfying meal in minutes.
—Karen Badger
Mahomet, Illinois

 1 pound boneless skinless chicken breasts
 2 tablespoons butter *or* margarine
 2 tablespoons all-purpose flour
 3/4 cup chicken broth
 1/4 cup white wine *or* additional chicken broth
 1/8 teaspoon pepper
 2 cups sliced fresh mushrooms
 1 cup frozen peas
 1/2 cup shredded mozzarella cheese
Hot cooked linguine

Cut chicken into 1/2-in. strips; place in a 2-qt. microwave-safe dish. Cover and microwave on high for 3 minutes. Turn chicken and move center pieces to the outside of the dish. Cover and microwave on high 3 minutes longer. Drain; set aside and keep warm. In another microwave-safe bowl, cover and microwave butter on high for 45 seconds or until melted. Stir in the flour until smooth. Gradually stir in the broth, wine and pepper; mix well. Add mushrooms and peas. Microwave, uncovered, on high for 5-7 minutes or until the vegetables are tender, stirring once. Stir in chicken; sprinkle with cheese. Microwave, uncovered, on high for 1-2 minutes or until the cheese is melted. Serve over linguine. **Yield:** 4 servings.

Thick Chocolate Pudding
Chicken Primavera

Bread 'n' Butter Dressing

This moist stuffing is a speedy way to stretch a meal. With yummy herb flavor from sage and thyme, it's tastier than the boxed stuffing mixes you buy at the store.
—Myra Innes, Auburn, Kansas

    8 slices bread
    6 tablespoons butter *or* margarine, *divided*
3/4 cup chicken broth
1/4 cup chopped onion
1/2 teaspoon rubbed sage
1/4 teaspoon dried thyme
1/4 teaspoon salt
1/4 teaspoon pepper

Toast bread and spread with 2 tablespoons of butter; cut into 3/4-in. cubes. Place in a 1-qt. microwave-safe dish; set aside. Place remaining butter in a microwave-safe bowl; cover and microwave on high for 50-60 seconds. Stir in broth, onion and seasonings. Pour over bread cubes and toss to coat. Microwave, uncovered, on high for 6 minutes, stirring once. **Yield:** 4 servings.

Thick Chocolate Pudding

(Pictured above)

Smooth and chocolaty, this pudding tastes old-fashioned but stirs up in a jiffy. It's much faster than cooking it on the stovetop and so easy that even older kids can make it.
—Myra Innes

1/3 cup sugar
1/4 cup baking cocoa
    3 tablespoons cornstarch
1/8 teaspoon salt
    2 cups milk
    1 teaspoon vanilla extract
Whipped topping, optional

In a 1-qt. microwave-safe bowl, combine the first four ingredients. Stir in milk until smooth. Microwave, uncovered, on high for 3 minutes; stir. Microwave 4-6 minutes longer or until thickened, stirring after each minute. Stir in vanilla. Pour into individual serving dishes; cool. Refrigerate. Garnish with whipped topping if desired. **Yield:** 4 servings.

Chapter 19

HERE'S a collection of reliable theme-related recipes that are tops for taste *and* time-saving.

We've rounded up favorite recipes for preparing meaty mainstays such as ground beef and leftover turkey as well as garden-fresh tomatoes, "spuds", pumpkins and blueberries.

Creative cooks will appreciate the tortilla wraps stuffed with enticing fillings and the suggestions for seasoning foods with herbs and honey.

And next time you need a family dessert, school party snack or team treat, cupcakes can't be beat.

CREATIVE CROP. Top to bottom: Fruited Pumpkin Bread and Pumpkin Soup (both recipes on p. 298).

Tempting Tater Toppers

WITH just a few ingredients, you can transform baked potatoes into a savory side dish or a complete meal.

Baked Potatoes

While the potatoes bake, you can whip up one of the pleasing toppings on this page.

4 medium baking potatoes (about 1-1/3 pounds)

Oven: Scrub and pierce potatoes. Bake at 400° for 40-60 minutes or until tender. **Microwave:** Scrub and pierce potatoes; place on a microwave-safe plate. Microwave, uncovered, on high for 12-14 minutes or until tender, turning once. **Yield:** 4 servings.

Tangy Cheese-Topped Spuds

Horseradish provides the zing in this creamy potato topper. —Letha Burdette, Greer, South Carolina

**1 package (8 ounces) cream cheese, softened
1 cup (8 ounces) sour cream
1/4 cup finely chopped onion
2 tablespoons prepared horseradish
1 to 2 tablespoons lemon juice
2 tablespoons minced fresh parsley
1/2 teaspoon salt
4 hot baked potatoes
1/2 cup shredded sharp cheddar cheese**

In a mixing bowl, blend cream cheese and sour cream until smooth. Add onion, horseradish, lemon juice, parsley and salt; mix well. With a sharp knife, cut an X in the top of each potato; fluff pulp with a fork. Top with cream cheese mixture; sprinkle with cheese. **Yield:** 4 servings.

Idaho Tacos

Chicken Ranch Potatoes

You'll get rave reviews on this one. Ranch salad dressing is a tasty change from the usual sour cream. —Edie DeSpain, Logan, Utah

**2-1/2 cups cubed cooked chicken
1 package (10 ounces) frozen mixed vegetables
Salt and pepper to taste
3/4 cup ranch salad dressing
4 hot baked potatoes**

Place chicken and vegetables in a 2-qt. microwave-safe dish; cover and microwave on high for 6-7 minutes, stirring once. Add salt and pepper. Let stand for 2 minutes. Fold in salad dressing. With a sharp knife, cut an X in the top of each potato; fluff pulp with a fork. Top with chicken mixture. **Yield:** 4 servings.

Potatoes with Crab Sauce

A mild sauce allows the delicate flavor of crab to shine through. This combination tastes great on leftover pasta, too. —Corene Thorsen, Oconomowoc, Wisconsin

**1 cup chicken broth
1/4 cup all-purpose flour
2 tablespoons butter *or* margarine, softened
1 package (3 ounces) cream cheese, cut into 1-inch cubes
1/2 pound process American cheese, cut into 1-inch cubes
3 to 4 drops hot pepper sauce
Pinch onion powder
1 package (6 ounces) imitation crabmeat, flaked
4 hot baked potatoes**

In a blender, combine the first seven ingredients. Cover and process until smooth. Pour into a saucepan; cook and stir over medium heat until thickened. Reduce heat to low; add crab. With a sharp knife, cut an X in the top of each potato; fluff pulp with a fork. Top with crab sauce. **Yield:** 4 servings.

Idaho Tacos

(Pictured at left)

These potatoes are almost a meal by themselves. I serve them with breadsticks, a green salad and dessert. —Kaleta Shepperson, Ozona, Texas

**1 pound ground beef
1 envelope taco seasoning
4 hot baked potatoes
1 cup (4 ounces) shredded sharp cheddar cheese
1 cup chopped green onions
Salsa, optional**

In a skillet, brown beef; drain. Add taco seasoning; prepare according to package directions. With a sharp knife, cut an X in the top of each potato; fluff pulp with a fork. Top with the taco meat, cheese and onions. Serve with salsa if desired. **Yield:** 4 servings.

Tangy Citrus Chicken
Veggie Ribbons

Honey Gives a Sweet Boost

BUSY AS A BEE? With today's active lifestyles, cooking with honey makes good sense. Honey is an instant energy booster, plus its beautiful golden color and delightful sweetness bring out the best in so many foods.

These recipes shared by the National Honey Board will surely make your fast and furious days a little sweeter.

Tangy Citrus Chicken

(Pictured above)

In just over 30 minutes, you can enjoy chicken breasts topped with a light, refreshing sauce that combines honey with lemonade, mustard and herbs.

✓ **Nutritional Analysis included**

> 8 boneless skinless chicken breast halves (2-1/2 pounds)
> 1 can (6 ounces) frozen lemonade concentrate, thawed
> 1/2 cup honey
> 1 teaspoon rubbed sage
> 1/2 teaspoon ground mustard
> 1/2 teaspoon dried thyme
> 1/2 teaspoon lemon juice

Place chicken breasts in a 13-in. x 9-in. x 2-in. baking dish coated with nonstick cooking spray. In a small bowl, combine remaining ingredients; mix well. Pour half over the chicken. Bake, uncovered, at 350° for 20 minutes. Turn chicken; pour remaining sauce on top. Bake 15-20 minutes longer or until meat juices run clear. **Yield:** 8 servings. **Nutritional Analysis:** One serving equals 268 calories, 70 mg sodium, 78 mg cholesterol, 31 gm car-

bohydrate, 29 gm protein, 4 gm fat. **Diabetic Exchanges:** 4 very lean meat, 2 fruit.

Salad with Honey Dressing

No one will ever guess how quickly you put together this pretty, fresh-tasting salad with its simple dressing.

✓ **Nutritional Analysis included**

> 6 cups torn Boston *or* Bibb lettuce
> 2 cups torn red leaf lettuce
> 2 medium oranges, peeled and sectioned
> 1/4 cup water
> 1/4 cup tarragon white wine vinegar
> 1/4 cup honey

Divide greens among six plates. Top with orange segments. Combine water, vinegar and honey in a jar with tight-fitting lid; shake well. Drizzle over salads. **Yield:** 6 servings. **Nutritional Analysis:** One serving with 2 tablespoons dressing equals 77 calories, 5 mg sodium, 0 cholesterol, 19 gm carbohydrate, 1 gm protein, trace fat. **Diabetic Exchanges:** 1 vegetable, 1 fruit.

Honey Berry Milk Shakes

For sipping with breakfast or as a snack, this thick, smooth and creamy milk shake is a "honey" of a treat that requires only four ingredients.

✓ **Nutritional Analysis included**

> 1 pint vanilla ice cream *or* frozen yogurt
> 2-1/2 cups sliced fresh strawberries
> 1/2 cup milk
> 1/4 cup honey

In a blender, combine the ice cream, berries, milk and honey; cover and process until smooth. Pour into glasses. **Yield:** 4 servings. **Nutritional Analysis:** One 1-cup serving (prepared with fat-free frozen yogurt and skim milk) equals 202 calories, 82 mg sodium, 2 mg cholesterol, 45 gm carbohydrate, 7 gm protein, 1 gm fat. **Diabetic Exchanges:** 1-1/2 starch, 1-1/2 fruit.

Making Veggie Ribbons

These vegetable ribbons (pictured above left) are a breeze to create using a potato or carrot peeler. With firm pressure, make even strokes down the length of a carrot or zucchini. The pieces will be wider as you reach the center of the vegetable. Steam or saute the vegetables until cooked as desired; arrange attractively on the plate.

Coconut Orange Cupcakes
Chocolate Cherry Cupcakes

Cupcakes Are Speedy Sweets

VERSATILE, fun-to-eat cupcakes are an ideal dessert when time's at a premium. Most cupcakes freeze well, so you can stash a few to pull out on a busy day.

Cream Cheese Cupcakes

It's hard to believe these cupcakes can taste so delicious, yet be so easy.   —Nancy Reichert, Thomasville, Georgia

> 1 package (3 ounces) cream cheese, softened
> 1 package (18-1/4 ounces) yellow cake mix
> 1-1/4 cups water
> 1/2 cup butter *or* margarine, melted
> 3 eggs
> Chocolate frosting, optional

In a mixing bowl, beat cream cheese until smooth. Add cake mix, water, butter and eggs; mix well. Spoon batter by 1/4 cupfuls into paper-lined muffin cups. Bake at 350° for 25 minutes or until golden brown. Remove to a wire rack to cool completely. Frost if desired. **Yield:** 2 dozen.

Coconut Orange Cupcakes

(Pictured above)

This recipe features the delicate tastes of orange, white chocolate and coconut.   —Donna Justin, Sparta, Wisconsin

> 1 cup sugar
> 2/3 cup vegetable oil
> 2 eggs
> 1 cup orange juice
> 3 cups all-purpose flour
> 1 tablespoon baking powder
> 1 teaspoon baking soda
> 3/4 teaspoon salt

> 1 can (11 ounces) mandarin oranges, drained
> 1 cup vanilla chips
> TOPPING:
> 1 cup flaked coconut
> 1/3 cup sugar
> 2 tablespoons butter *or* margarine, melted

In a mixing bowl, combine the sugar, oil, eggs and orange juice; mix well. Combine dry ingredients; stir into orange juice mixture just until moistened. Fold in the oranges and chips. Fill greased or paper-lined muffin cups two-thirds full. Combine topping ingredients; sprinkle over cupcakes. Bake at 375° for 15-20 minutes or until golden brown. **Yield:** 2 dozen.

Chocolate Cherry Cupcakes

(Pictured at left)

*Inside each of these cupcakes is a fruity surprise! I start with a convenient cake mix to produce the special treats.
—Bertille Cooper, St. Inigoes, Maryland*

> 1 package (18-1/4 ounces) chocolate cake mix
> 1-1/3 cups water
> 1/2 cup vegetable oil
> 3 eggs
> 1 can (21 ounces) cherry pie filling
> 1 can (16 ounces) vanilla frosting

In a mixing bowl, combine cake mix, water, oil and eggs; mix well. Spoon batter by 1/4 cupfuls into paper-lined muffin cups. Spoon a rounded teaspoon of pie filling onto the center of each cupcake. Set remaining pie filling aside. Bake at 350° for 20-25 minutes or until a toothpick inserted on an angle toward the center comes out clean. Remove to a wire rack to cool completely. Frost cupcakes; top with one cherry from pie filling. Serve additional pie filling with cupcakes or refrigerate for another use. **Yield:** 2 dozen.

Rosy Rhubarb Cupcakes

If you're in a big hurry, these cupcakes are delicious without frosting. —Sharon Nichols, Brookings, South Dakota

> 1/2 cup shortening
> 1 cup packed brown sugar
> 1/2 cup sugar
> 1 egg
> 2 cups all-purpose flour
> 1 teaspoon baking soda
> 1/4 teaspoon ground nutmeg
> 1 cup buttermilk
> 1-1/2 cups finely chopped fresh *or* frozen rhubarb, thawed
> Cream cheese frosting, optional

In a mixing bowl, cream shortening and sugars. Add egg and mix well. Combine flour, baking soda and nutmeg; add to creamed mixture alternately with buttermilk. Fold in the rhubarb. Fill paper-lined muffin cups two-thirds full. Bake at 350° for 30-35 minutes or until a toothpick inserted near the center comes out clean. Frost if desired. **Yield:** about 1-1/2 dozen.

Tortillas Enfold Fillings

WITH flour tortillas on hand, you can have a meal or snack *in hand* in a jiffy. Just bundle up favorite ingredients, and it's a "wrap"!

These convenient recipes from the American Dairy Association and *Quick Cooking's* kitchen staff will get you on a roll to creating other delicious fillings to please your family.

South of the Border Wraps

This easy recipe brings the taste of the Southwest into your kitchen, no matter where you live.

    1/2 cup black beans, rinsed and drained
    2 tablespoons chunky salsa
    1 tablespoon chopped green onions
    1 tablespoon minced fresh cilantro *or* parsley
    4 flour tortillas (7 inches)
    1 medium tomato, chopped
    1 cup (4 ounces) shredded Monterey Jack
      cheese
    2 to 4 tablespoons butter *or* margarine

In a bowl, mash beans slightly. Add salsa, onions and cilantro. Spread over tortillas. Sprinkle with tomato and cheese. Roll up tightly. Melt butter in a large skillet. Add tortillas, seam side down; cook until golden on all

Turkey Ranch Wraps

sides, adding additional butter if necessary. Serve immediately. **Yield:** 4 servings.

Pretty Ham Pinwheels

Plan ahead to slice party-perfect appetizers from these zippy rolls. They're easy to assemble and sure to be a hit.

    1 package (3 ounces) cream cheese, softened
    1 garlic clove, minced
    1/4 teaspoon curry powder
    1/4 teaspoon ground mustard
    1 cup shredded peeled tart apple
    4 flour tortillas (7 inches)
    1/4 cup chopped sweet red pepper
    2 green onions, thinly sliced
    4 thin slices fully cooked ham

In a mixing bowl, beat the cream cheese, garlic, curry powder and mustard. Stir in apple. Spread about 2 tablespoons over each tortilla. Layer with the red pepper, onions and ham. Roll up tightly and wrap in plastic wrap. Refrigerate for at least 2 hours. Cut into 1-in. slices. **Yield:** about 2 dozen.

Rich Chocolate Wraps

Never thought of using a tortilla to wrap something sweet? This novel treat will make a believer out of everyone.

    1/2 cup miniature semisweet chocolate chips
    2 teaspoons butter *or* margarine
    1 cup (8 ounces) sour cream
    1 tablespoon confectioners' sugar
    1/4 to 1/2 teaspoon ground cinnamon
    6 flour tortillas (7 inches)
Baking cocoa

In a microwave or double boiler, melt the chocolate chips and butter; cool slightly. In a small mixing bowl, combine sour cream, sugar and cinnamon; stir in melted chocolate. Spread about 3 tablespoonfuls over each tortilla. Roll up tightly and wrap in plastic wrap. Refrigerate for 1 hour. Sprinkle with cocoa before serving. **Yield:** 6 servings.

Turkey Ranch Wraps

(Pictured at left)

Here's a terrific use for deli turkey. Add lettuce, tomato, green pepper, cheese and dressing for a flavorful blend.

    8 thin slices cooked turkey
    4 flour tortillas (7 inches)
    1 large tomato, thinly sliced
    1 medium green pepper, cut into thin strips
    1 cup shredded lettuce
    1 cup (4 ounces) shredded cheddar cheese
    1/3 cup ranch salad dressing

Place two slices of turkey on each tortilla. Layer with tomato, green pepper, lettuce and cheese. Drizzle with salad dressing. Roll up tightly and serve immediately. **Yield:** 4 servings.

American Dairy Association

Pick of the Pumpkin Patch

Fruited Pumpkin Bread
Pumpkin Soup

PUMPKIN adds moistness, mild flavor and a lovely golden hue to meals and baked treats. And when you don't have time to cook your own, convenient canned pumpkin does the trick quickly. (For easy conversion in recipes, a 15-ounce can of solid-pack pumpkin is equal to 1-3/4 cups cooked pumpkin.)

Here's a handful of handy recipes we harvested that highlight this seasonal squash.

Pumpkin Soup

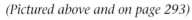

(Pictured above and on page 293)

While it looks elegant and is an appealing addition to a holiday meal, this creamy soup is so simple to make.
—Elizabeth Montgomery
Taylorville, Illinois

        1/2 cup finely chopped onion
          2 tablespoons butter *or* margarine
          1 tablespoon all-purpose flour
          2 cans (14-1/2 ounces *each*) chicken broth
          1 can (15 ounces) solid-pack pumpkin
          1 teaspoon brown sugar
        1/4 teaspoon salt
        1/8 teaspoon pepper
        1/8 teaspoon ground nutmeg
          1 cup whipping cream

In a large saucepan, saute onion in butter until tender. Remove from the heat; stir in flour until smooth. Gradually stir in the broth, pumpkin, brown sugar, salt, pepper and nutmeg; bring to a boil. Reduce heat and simmer for 5 minutes. Add cream; cook for 2 minutes or until heated through. **Yield:** 6 servings.

Fruited Pumpkin Bread

(Pictured at left and on page 292)

This quick bread is chock-full of yummy goodies, including walnuts, dates and apricots. The blend of spices comes through nicely.
—Rose Mower, Chugiak, Alaska

          2 eggs
          1 cup sugar
          1 cup canned *or* cooked pumpkin
        1/2 cup vegetable oil
        1/2 cup orange juice
          2 cups all-purpose flour
          1 teaspoon baking soda
        1/2 teaspoon baking powder
        1/2 teaspoon *each* ground cinnamon,
            cloves, ginger and nutmeg
        1/2 cup chopped dates
        1/2 cup chopped walnuts
        1/4 cup chopped dried apricots

In a mixing bowl, combine the first five ingredients; mix well. Combine the flour, baking soda, baking powder, cinnamon, cloves, ginger and nutmeg; add to the pumpkin mixture and mix well. Fold in dates, walnuts and apricots. Pour into a greased 9-in. x 5-in. x 3-in. loaf pan. Bake at 350° for 1 hour and 15 minutes or until a toothpick inserted near the center comes out clean. Cool for 10 minutes; remove from pan to a wire rack to cool completely. **Yield:** 1 loaf.

Frozen Pumpkin Pie

As a rule, I don't like pumpkin. But this light, melt-in-your-mouth pie is an exception! —Diane Hixon
Niceville, Florida

          3 cups vanilla ice cream, softened
          1 cup cooked *or* canned pumpkin
        1/2 cup packed brown sugar
        1/4 teaspoon salt
        1/4 teaspoon *each* ground cinnamon, ginger and
            nutmeg
          1 graham cracker crust (9 inches)

In a mixing bowl, combine ice cream, pumpkin, brown sugar, salt, cinnamon, ginger and nutmeg; mix well. Pour into crust. Freeze for 4 hours or until firm. **Yield:** 6-8 servings.

The Best 'Berried' Treasures

BLUE because you have little time to spend making yummy blueberry treats? Cheer up! You can still enjoy this luscious lineup of goodies featuring delicious plump blueberries!

Blueberry Delight

(Pictured at right)

Prepared angel food cake makes this impressive dessert a breeze to assemble. Plus, it can be put together ahead of time.
    —Christine Halandras, Meeker, Colorado

Blueberry Delight
Blueberry Kuchen

    1 package (8 ounces) cream cheese, softened
1/2 cup confectioners' sugar
    1 can (14 ounces) sweetened condensed milk
    1 package (3.4 ounces) instant vanilla pudding mix
    1 carton (12 ounces) frozen whipped topping, thawed, *divided*
    1 angel food cake (10 inches), cut into 1-inch cubes
    1 quart fresh *or* frozen blueberries, thawed
Additional blueberries, optional

In a mixing bowl, beat cream cheese and confectioners' sugar. Add milk and pudding mix; mix well. Fold in 1-1/2 cups of whipped topping. Place half of the cake cubes in a 3-qt. glass bowl. Layer with half of the berries and pudding mixture. Cover with remaining cake cubes. Layer with the remaining berries and pudding mixture. Spread remaining whipped topping over top. Garnish with additional berries if desired. Store leftovers in the refrigerator. **Yield:** 12-14 servings.

Blueberry Kuchen

(Pictured above right)

Our local peat bogs are known around the world for their beautiful blueberries. I can prepare this dessert quick as a wink.   —Anne Krueger, Richmond, British Columbia

1-1/2 cups all-purpose flour
    3/4 cup sugar
    2 teaspoons baking powder
1-1/2 teaspoons grated lemon peel
    1/2 teaspoon ground nutmeg
    1/4 teaspoon salt
    2/3 cup milk
    1/4 cup butter *or* margarine, melted
    1 egg, beaten
    1 teaspoon vanilla extract
    2 cups fresh *or* frozen blueberries

TOPPING:
    3/4 cup sugar
    1/2 cup all-purpose flour
    1/4 cup butter *or* margarine, melted

In a mixing bowl, combine the first six ingredients. Add the milk, butter, egg and vanilla. Beat for 2 minutes or until well blended. Pour into a greased 13-in. x 9-in. x 2-in. baking pan. Sprinkle with blueberries. In a bowl, combine sugar and flour; add butter. Toss with a fork until crumbly; sprinkle over blueberries. Bake at 350° for 40 minutes or until lightly browned. **Yield:** 12 servings.

Blueberry Coffee Cake

My mother often baked this on Sunday mornings, and the aroma always got me and my brother up out of bed early.   —Joy McGhee, Gilbert, Arizona

    2 cups all-purpose flour
    1 cup sugar
    1 tablespoon baking powder
    1/4 teaspoon salt
    1/2 cup shortening
    2 eggs
    1 cup milk
    2 cups fresh *or* frozen blueberries
1-1/3 cups flaked coconut

In a bowl, combine flour, sugar, baking powder and salt. Cut in shortening until crumbly. In a small bowl, combine eggs and milk; stir into crumb mixture just until moistened. Fold in blueberries. Pour the batter into two greased 9-in. round baking pans. Sprinkle with coconut. Bake at 375° for 25 minutes or until a toothpick inserted near the center comes out clean. Serve warm. **Yield:** 2 coffee cakes (8 servings each).

Herbs Add Savory Flavor

WHEN an action-packed schedule leaves you short on time, use fresh or dried herbs to season fast-to-fix dishes that are long on flavor.

Creamy Thyme Spread

(Pictured below right)

This make-ahead cracker spread showcases thyme and garlic. A neighbor who has an herb garden gave me the recipe. It's simple to stir up and makes a special appetizer for company. It's also fun to serve at a party.
—Mary Steiner, West Bend, Wisconsin

1 package (8 ounces) cream cheese, softened
1 tablespoon minced fresh thyme *or* 1
    teaspoon dried thyme
1 tablespoon minced fresh parsley *or* 1
    teaspoon dried parsley flakes
1 garlic clove, minced
Assorted crackers

In a bowl, combine the cream cheese, thyme, parsley and garlic; mix well. Cover and refrigerate until serving. Serve with crackers. **Yield:** about 1 cup.

Rosemary Carrots

(Pictured at right)

You'll really enjoy the bold rosemary flavor in each bite of this pretty side dish. The sliced carrots get added sweetness from a bit of brown sugar.
—Jacqueline Thompson Graves, Lawrenceville, Georgia

✓ Nutritional Analysis included

2-1/4 cups thinly sliced carrots
    1/2 cup water
        1 tablespoon snipped fresh *or* dried chives
        1 tablespoon brown sugar
        1 teaspoon chicken bouillon granules
    1/2 teaspoon snipped fresh rosemary *or* pinch
        dried rosemary, crushed
    1/8 teaspoon pepper

Place carrots and water in a saucepan; cover and cook over medium heat for 8-9 minutes or until crisp-tender. Drain, reserving 2 tablespoons cooking liquid. Transfer carrots to a serving bowl and keep warm. In the same pan, combine chives, brown sugar, bouillon, rosemary, pepper and reserved cooking liquid. Bring to a boil; stir until bouillon is dissolved. Pour over the carrots and toss to coat. **Yield:** 4 servings. **Nutritional Analysis:** One

1/2-cup serving (prepared with low-sodium bouillon) equals 44 calories, 27 mg sodium, 0 cholesterol, 11 gm carbohydrate, 1 gm protein, trace fat. **Diabetic Exchange:** 2 vegetable.

Chive Cucumber Salad

Mother always made this refreshing salad when we had Sunday guests. It has a light, pleasant dressing and looks lovely served in a pretty glass bowl. —Ruth Andrewson
Leavenworth, Washington

✓ Nutritional Analysis included

2 large cucumbers, peeled and thinly sliced
1/2 cup sour cream
    3 tablespoons snipped fresh *or* dried chives
    2 tablespoons vinegar
    1 tablespoon water
    1 tablespoon chopped green onion
1/4 teaspoon garlic powder
1/4 teaspoon salt, optional
1/8 teaspoon pepper

In a bowl, combine cucumbers and sour cream. Cover and refrigerate for at least 1 hour. Stir in the remaining ingredients just before serving. **Yield:** 4 servings. **Nutritional Analysis:** One 1/2-cup serving (prepared with nonfat sour cream and without salt) equals 50 calories, 27 mg sodium, 3 mg cholesterol, 9 gm carbohydrate, 3 gm protein, trace fat. **Diabetic Exchange:** 2 vegetable.

Creamy Thyme Spread
Rosemary Carrots

Red, Ripe and Ready to Go!

Crisscross Salad
Tempting Tomato Cups

FRESH, juicy and still warm from the garden, tomatoes are an irresistible addition to meals. In an instant, they add bright color and robust flavor to all kinds of dishes from appetizers to salads to casseroles.

Crisscross Salad

(Pictured at right)

This colorful confetti salad tastes even better when it's made ahead of time and chilled overnight. —Linda Dow
Bradford, Pennsylvania

✓ **Nutritional Analysis included**

> 1 pound fresh broccoli, chopped
> 1 can (16 ounces) kidney beans, rinsed and drained
> 2 large tomatoes, chopped
> 1 medium red onion, chopped
> 1 cup (4 ounces) shredded cheddar cheese
> 1 bottle (16 ounces) Italian salad dressing

In a large bowl, combine the first five ingredients. Add dressing and toss to coat. Serve immediately or refrigerate for 4 hours or overnight, stirring occasionally. **Yield:** 10 servings. **Nutritional Analysis:** One 3/4-cup serving (prepared with fat-free cheese and salad dressing) equals 103 calories, 520 mg sodium, 1 mg cholesterol, 17 gm carbohydrate, 8 gm protein, trace fat. **Diabetic Exchanges:** 1 starch, 1 very lean meat.

Scalloped Tomatoes

The tomato wedges in this delicious dish get a special treatment from a mushroom-and-crumb topping.
—Ruth Pyles, Temple Hills, Maryland

> 1 garlic clove, minced
> 4 tablespoons butter *or* margarine, melted, *divided*
> 1 cup finely chopped fresh *or* canned mushrooms
> 1 cup crushed butter-flavored crackers (about 25 crackers)
> 2 tablespoons minced fresh parsley *or* 2 teaspoons dried parsley flakes
> 1/2 teaspoon salt
> 1/8 teaspoon pepper
> 6 medium tomatoes, quartered

In a skillet, saute garlic in 2 tablespoons butter for 2 minutes. Add mushrooms; cook until heated through. Remove from the heat. Add cracker crumbs, parsley, salt, pepper and remaining butter; mix well. Place tomatoes in a greased 8-in. square baking dish. Top with the mushroom mixture. Bake, uncovered, at 400° for 20 minutes or until heated through. **Yield:** 6 servings.

Tempting Tomato Cups

(Pictured above)

Brimming with a crunchy filling, this makes a wonderful light lunch or can replace a green salad at dinner.
—Carla Browning, Fort Walton Beach, Florida

✓ **Nutritional Analysis included**

> 3 large tomatoes
> 1/2 cup crushed saltines (about 15 crackers)
> 1/3 cup chopped celery
> 1/3 cup chopped green pepper
> 1/4 cup chopped onion
> 1/4 cup mayonnaise
> 1/2 teaspoon garlic salt, optional
> 1/8 teaspoon pepper
> Sliced ripe olives, optional

Cut a thin slice from the top of each tomato. Leaving a 1/4-in.-thick shell, scoop out pulp (discard pulp or save for another use). Invert tomatoes onto paper towels to drain. In a bowl, combine cracker crumbs, celery, green pepper, onion, mayonnaise, garlic salt if desired and pepper; mix well. Spoon into tomatoes. Refrigerate until serving. Garnish with olives if desired. **Yield:** 3 servings. **Nutritional Analysis:** One serving (prepared with low-sodium saltines and fat-free mayonnaise and without garlic salt and olives) equals 129 calories, 284 mg sodium, 0 cholesterol, 25 gm carbohydrate, 3 gm protein, 2 gm fat. **Diabetic Exchanges:** 1 starch, 1 vegetable, 1/2 fat.

Turkey Nachos
Turkey Pita Tacos

1 garlic clove, minced
1 cup (4 ounces) shredded cheddar cheese
5 pita breads (6 inches), halved

In a small bowl, combine the first six ingredients; set aside. In a large bowl, combine the turkey, peppers, tomato, salsa, onions, olives and garlic. Stir the oil mixture; pour over the turkey mixture and mix well. Stir in cheese. On a lightly greased griddle, heat pita breads on both sides. Spoon about 1/2 cup of turkey mixture into each half. **Yield:** 5 servings.

Turkey Nachos

(Pictured at left)

Chunks of leftover turkey are a tasty addition to this cheesy dip. You'd never guess it has just three ingredients. —Gayle Lewis, Winston, Oregon

1 can (10-3/4 ounces) condensed cheddar
    cheese soup, undiluted
3/4 cup salsa
1 cup cubed cooked turkey *or* chicken
Tortilla chips

Combine soup and salsa in a saucepan or microwave-safe bowl. Stir in turkey; cook until heated through. Serve warm with tortilla chips. **Yield:** about 2 cups.

After Thanksgiving Salad

I serve this on a bed of lettuce, as a sandwich or in a croissant for a special occasion. —Ruthe Holmberg, Louisville, Kentucky

1 hard-cooked egg
4 cups shredded cooked turkey *or* chicken
3/4 cup mayonnaise
1 tablespoon sweet pickle relish
1/2 cup chopped pecans

In a bowl, mash the egg with a fork. Add turkey, mayonnaise and relish. Cover and refrigerate until serving. Stir in pecans just before serving. **Yield:** 4 servings.

A New Take On Turkey

THANKSGIVING wouldn't be the same without the traditional turkey dinner...or the inevitable turkey surplus. Bypass the usual turkey sandwiches this year. Instead, give your leftovers new life by whipping up one or more of these speedy second-day dishes.

Turkey Pita Tacos

(Pictured above)

In addition to garden-fresh vegetables, this recipe calls for time-saving ingredients such as salsa, olives and shredded cheese. —Ann Bergstrom, Warrenville, Illinois

1 tablespoon vegetable oil
1 tablespoon cider *or* red wine vinegar
1 teaspoon chili powder
1 teaspoon ground cumin
1/4 teaspoon salt
1/4 teaspoon pepper
1 cup cubed cooked turkey *or* chicken
1 medium green pepper, chopped
1 medium sweet red pepper, chopped
1 small tomato, chopped
1 cup chunky salsa
3 green onions, thinly sliced
1 can (2-1/4 ounces) sliced ripe olives, drained

Turkey Asparagus Casserole

Convenient frozen asparagus lends bright color and garden flavor while a sprinkling of french-fried onion rings provides a yummy crunch. —Cheryl Schut, Grand Rapids, Michigan

1 package (8 ounces) frozen chopped asparagus
2 cups cubed cooked turkey *or* chicken
1 can (10-3/4 ounces) condensed cream of
    chicken soup, undiluted
1/4 cup water
1 can (2.8 ounces) french-fried onions

In a small saucepan, cook asparagus in a small amount of water for 2 minutes; drain. Place in a greased 11-in. x 7-in. x 2-in. baking dish. Top with turkey. Combine soup and water; spoon over turkey. Bake, uncovered, at 350° for 25-30 minutes. Sprinkle with onions. Bake 5 minutes longer or until golden brown. **Yield:** 4 servings.

Ground Beef's A Fast Favorite

GROUND BEEF is a mainstay of many down-home dishes, and no wonder—it's tasty, inexpensive and can be used in a variety of ways. Best of all, ground beef cooks quickly so meal preparation is a breeze.

For speedy meal preparation, brown several pounds of ground beef ahead of time (with chopped onion and minced garlic if you like) and freeze it in heavy-duty plastic bags or freezer containers for up to 3 months. (Use the chart below to package cooked ground beef in appropriate amounts.)

Soupy Joes

(Pictured below right)

A can of vegetable soup dresses up these sloppy joes. When our children were growing up, I often served these quick-to-fix sandwiches. —Patricia Novak, Mesa, Arizona

    1 pound ground beef
    1 medium onion, chopped
    1 can (10-1/2 ounces) condensed vegetable
      soup, undiluted
    1 tablespoon ketchup
    1 teaspoon prepared mustard
    1/2 teaspoon salt
    1/4 teaspoon pepper
    6 hamburger buns, split and toasted

In a saucepan over medium heat, cook beef and onion until beef is no longer pink; drain. Add soup, ketchup, mustard, salt and pepper; mix well. Simmer, uncovered, for 5-10 minutes. Serve on buns. **Yield:** 6 sandwiches.

Hash Brown Beef Pie

(Pictured at right)

Convenient frozen hash browns and shredded cheddar cheese top this hearty mixture of vegetables and ground beef. —Mina Dyck, Boissevain, Manitoba

    1 pound ground beef
    1 medium onion, chopped
    1 garlic clove, minced
    1 can (14-1/2 ounces) diced tomatoes, drained

    1 teaspoon chili powder
    1 teaspoon dried oregano
    1/2 teaspoon salt
    1/4 teaspoon pepper
  1-1/2 cups frozen mixed vegetables
TOPPING:
    3 cups frozen shredded hash brown potatoes,
      thawed and drained
    1 cup (8 ounces) shredded cheddar cheese
    1 egg
    1/8 teaspoon salt
    1/8 teaspoon pepper

In a large skillet, cook beef, onion and garlic until beef is no longer pink; drain. Stir in the tomatoes, chili powder, oregano, salt and pepper; bring to a boil. Reduce heat; simmer, uncovered, for 10 minutes. Stir in the vegetables. Pour into a greased 9-in. pie plate. Combine topping ingredients; spoon evenly over the meat mixture. Bake, uncovered, at 400° for 30 minutes. **Yield:** 6-8 servings.

Beefy Vegetable Stew

This is my family's favorite budget meal. It's not only inexpensive, but quick and tasty, too! —Theresa Stone
Bakersfield, California

    1 pound ground beef
    1 can (28 ounces) stewed tomatoes, cut up
    1 can (15 ounces) tomato sauce
    1 package (16 ounces) frozen California blend
      vegetables
    1 package (8 ounces) frozen corn
    1 package (8 ounces) frozen broccoli cuts
    2 cups water
    1 tablespoon beef bouillon granules
    1/2 teaspoon salt
    1/4 teaspoon pepper
    1/4 teaspoon garlic powder

In a large kettle or Dutch oven, cook the beef until no longer pink; drain. Add remaining ingredients. Cover and simmer for 40-45 minutes, stirring occasionally. **Yield:** 10-12 servings.

Hash Brown Beef Pie
Soupy Joes

Ground Beef Yields		
Uncooked Weight	Approximate Cooked Weight	Cooked Cup Amount (loosely packed)
1 pound ground beef	11 ounces	2-1/2 to 3 cups
4 pounds ground beef	3 pounds	10 to 12 cups

NO TIME for entertaining? Think again! An elaborate meal can have time-easing elements that make entertaining easier ...and a lot more fun. You can even treat unexpected visitors to a memorable meal on a moment's notice.

All of these practical step-saving recipes allow you to spend more time visiting with your dinner company, instead of slaving away in the kitchen. So you'll feel like a guest at your own party!

Plus, effortless garnishes and simple table decorations provide special touches without a lot of fuss.

SPECIAL SUPPER. Clockwise from upper right: Company Carrots, Spinach-Stuffed Pork Roast and Apricot Barley Casserole (all recipes on p. 307).

YOU'LL proudly serve this impressive meal that has convenience built in—the main and side dishes bake together to eliminate stovetop fuss. (Turn to page 318 to add special touches to your table.)

Spinach-Stuffed Pork Roast

This beautiful, moist pork roast is my family's favorite special-occasion entree. —Lila Crowley, Jefferson, Iowa

    1/4 cup chopped fresh mushrooms
    1/4 cup chopped onion
      1 tablespoon vegetable oil
      1 package (10 ounces) frozen chopped
        spinach, thawed and well drained
      1 cup soft bread crumbs
    1/2 teaspoon salt
    1/2 teaspoon pepper
    1/4 teaspoon garlic powder
    1/4 teaspoon rubbed sage
      1 boneless pork loin roast (4 to 5 pounds), tied

In a skillet, saute mushrooms and onion in oil until tender. Stir in spinach, bread crumbs, salt, pepper, garlic powder and sage. Untie pork roast and separate the loins. Spread stuffing over one loin to within 1 in. of the edges. Top with the remaining loin; retie securely with heavy string. Place in an ungreased shallow baking pan. Bake, uncovered, at 325° for 2-1/2 hours or until a meat thermometer reads 160°-170°. Let stand for 15 minutes before slicing. **Yield:** 8 servings.

Company Carrots

These savory carrots add color to any meal—and do it with just five ingredients. —Lee Ann Arey, Scarborough, Maine

      2 pounds baby carrots *or* medium carrots,
        quartered
    1/4 cup water
    1/4 cup butter *or* margarine
      1 teaspoon dried oregano
    1/2 teaspoon salt

Place the carrots in an ungreased 9-in. square baking dish. Add water; dot with butter. Sprinkle with oregano and salt. Cover and bake at 325° for 1-1/4 hours or until tender. **Yield:** 8-10 servings.

Golden Fruit Punch

(Not pictured)

This light, fruity punch is a breeze to serve—I make it ahead and store it in the freezer. —Margaret Wagner Allen Abingdon, Virginia

      1 can (30 ounces) fruit cocktail, undrained
      1 can (29 ounces) peaches, undrained
      1 can (20 ounces) crushed pineapple, undrained
      4 medium bananas
      2 cups sugar
      2 cups water
      1 can (12 ounces) frozen orange juice
        concentrate, thawed

      2 tablespoons lemon juice
Lemon-lime soda, chilled

Place fruit cocktail in a blender; cover and process until smooth. Pour into a large freezer container. Repeat with peaches and pineapple. Place bananas, sugar and water in the blender; process until smooth. Add to the pureed fruit with orange juice concentrate and lemon juice; mix well. Cover and freeze. Remove from the freezer 2 hours before serving. Just before serving, mash mixture with a potato masher or large spoon. For each serving, combine 1/4 cup fruit slush with 3/4 cup soda. **Yield:** 64 (1-cup) servings.

Apricot Barley Casserole

My mother often served this to the threshers during harvesttime. —Diane Swink, Signal Mountain, Tennessee

    2/3 cup pine nuts *or* slivered almonds
    1/4 cup butter *or* margarine, *divided*
      2 cups pearl barley
      1 cup sliced green onions
      7 cups chicken broth
    2/3 cup diced dried apricots
    1/2 cup golden raisins

In a skillet, saute nuts in 2 tablespoons of butter until lightly browned; remove and set aside. In the same skillet, saute the barley and onions in remaining butter until onions are tender. Add broth; bring to a boil. Stir in the apricots, raisins and nuts. Pour into a greased 13-in. x 9-in. x 2-in. baking dish. Bake, uncovered, at 325° for 1-1/4 hours or until barley is tender. **Yield:** 8-10 servings.

Chocolate Praline Torte

No one will know this fancy dessert started with a boxed cake mix. —Sandra Castillo, Watertown, Wisconsin

      1 cup packed brown sugar
    1/2 cup butter (no substitutes)
    1/4 cup whipping cream
    3/4 cup coarsely chopped pecans
      1 package (18-1/4 ounces) devil's food cake mix
TOPPING:
1-3/4 cups whipping cream
    1/4 cup confectioners' sugar
    1/4 teaspoon vanilla extract
Chocolate curls (see page 318), optional

In a saucepan, combine brown sugar, butter and cream. Stir over low heat until butter is melted. Pour into two greased 9-in. round cake pans. Sprinkle with pecans; set aside. Prepare cake mix according to package directions. Carefully pour batter over pecans. Bake at 325° for 35-45 minutes or until a toothpick comes out clean. Cool in pans for 10 minutes; invert onto wire racks to cool completely. For the topping, beat cream in a mixing bowl until soft peaks form. Add sugar and vanilla; beat until stiff. Place one cake layer, pecan side up, on a serving plate. Spread with half of the topping. Top with second cake layer and remaining topping. Garnish with chocolate curls if desired. Store in the refrigerator. **Yield:** 8-10 servings.

'Brisk'-et
Makes for
No-Fuss Meal

WITH a little preparation, you can easily entertain. In this meal, the broccoli is the only last-minute dish—and it won't take you more than 10 minutes to cook it. (See page 319 for table decorating ideas.)

Marinated Beef Brisket

This tender brisket cooks a long time, but it's so easy to prepare. —*Janet Parham, Cibolo, Texas*

      1 tablespoon all-purpose flour
      1 large *or* turkey-size oven bag
      4 teaspoons Worcestershire sauce
      2 teaspoons garlic salt
      2 teaspoons onion salt
      2 teaspoons pepper
      1 to 3 tablespoons liquid smoke, optional
      1 fresh beef brisket* (about 4 pounds)
      1 cup ketchup
      3 tablespoons brown sugar
      2 tablespoons lemon juice
      2 teaspoons ground mustard
      3 drops hot pepper sauce

Shake flour in the oven bag; place in an ungreased 13-in. x 9-in. x 2-in. baking pan. Combine the Worcestershire sauce, garlic salt, onion salt, pepper and liquid smoke if desired; rub over both sides of brisket. Place in the oven bag. Close with tie and refrigerate for 8 hours or overnight, turning occasionally. Combine ketchup, brown sugar, lemon juice, mustard and hot pepper sauce; spread over brisket. Close oven bag with nylon tie; cut six 1/2-in. slits in top of bag. Return to pan. Bake at 325° for 3-4 hours or until beef is tender. If desired, thicken pan juices to serve with beef. **Yield:** 6-8 servings. **Editor's Note:** This is a fresh beef brisket, not corned beef.

Cool Cucumber Dip

(Not pictured)

You can whip up this creamy dip in your food processor in no time, then chill it 'til company comes.
—*Gail Rhoades, Denver, Colorado*

    1/2 small cucumber, peeled, seeded and cubed
      1 small onion, chopped
      1 package (8 ounces) cream cheese, cubed
    1/2 cup mayonnaise
    1/2 to 1 teaspoon celery seed
    1/2 teaspoon garlic salt
      2 to 3 tablespoons Western salad dressing

Combine all ingredients in a blender or food processor; cover and process until smooth. Chill until serving. Serve with raw vegetables. **Yield:** 2 cups.

Scalloped Potatoes and Onions

You can prepare this in the morning, then put it in the oven later. —*Dorothy Bateman, Carver, Massachusetts*

      5 large potatoes, peeled and thinly sliced
    3/4 cup chopped onion
      3 tablespoons butter *or* margarine

    1/4 cup all-purpose flour
1-3/4 cups chicken broth
      2 tablespoons mayonnaise
    3/4 teaspoon salt
    1/8 teaspoon pepper
Paprika

In a greased 2-1/2-qt. baking dish, layer potatoes and onion. In a saucepan, melt the butter; stir in flour until smooth. Gradually add broth, mayonnaise, salt and pepper; cook and stir for 2 minutes or until thick and bubbly. Pour over potatoes. Sprinkle with paprika. Cover and bake at 325° for 2 hours or until tender. **Yield:** 6 servings.

Zesty Broccoli

These sauteed florets stay bright green, and the garlic and pepper add flavor. —*Myra Innes, Auburn, Kansas*

☑ **Nutritional Analysis included**

      1 garlic clove, minced
Pinch crushed red pepper flakes
      2 tablespoons olive *or* vegetable oil
      1 large bunch fresh broccoli, cut into florets
         (3-1/2 cups)
    1/4 to 1/2 teaspoon salt, optional

In a large skillet, saute garlic and pepper flakes in oil. Add broccoli and toss to coat; saute for 8 minutes or until crisp-tender. Sprinkle with salt if desired. **Yield:** 6 servings. **Nutritional Analysis:** One serving (prepared without salt) equals 60 calories, 19 mg sodium, 0 cholesterol, 4 gm carbohydrate, 2 gm protein, 5 gm fat. **Diabetic Exchanges:** 1 vegetable, 1 fat.

Brownie Swirl Cheesecake

It may look fancy, but this cheesecake is so simple. The secret is the speedy crust—it's from a packaged brownie mix!
—*Janet Brunner, Burlington, Kentucky*

      1 package (8 ounces) brownie mix
      2 packages (8 ounces *each*) cream cheese,
         softened
    1/2 cup sugar
      1 teaspoon vanilla extract
      2 eggs
      1 cup milk chocolate chips, melted
**Whipped cream and miniature chocolate kisses,
    optional**

Prepare brownie mix according to package directions for chewy fudge brownies. Spread into a greased 9-in. springform pan. Bake at 350° for 15 minutes (brownies will not test done). Cool for 10 minutes on a wire rack. Meanwhile, in a mixing bowl, combine cream cheese, sugar and vanilla; mix well. Add eggs, one at a time, beating well after each addition. Pour over the brownie crust. Top with melted chocolate; cut through batter with a knife to swirl the chocolate. Bake at 350° for 35-40 minutes or until center is almost set. Run a knife around edge of pan to loosen; cool completely. Remove sides of pan; refrigerate for at least 3 hours. Garnish with whipped cream and chocolate kisses if desired. **Yield:** 8-10 servings.

Don't Dread Drop-in Guests

KNOCK-KNOCK! Sometimes that's the only warning you get when company drops by unexpectedly. Don't be shy—invite 'em in, even if it's near dinnertime.

A simple menu with versatile recipes is the key to enjoying these occasions. (And see the effortless garnishes and table decorations on page 320.)

For example, Tortellini Toss gives you a choice of items you likely have in your freezer right now. If you don't have pork tenderloin, substitute chicken. No sugar snap peas? Chances are you have broccoli or colorful mixed vegetables in your freezer. Even the tortellini can be replaced with whatever pasta you have in your pantry.

But watch out...an impromptu dinner like this might encourage your guests to "drop in" again!

Tortellini Toss

Basil, marjoram and Parmesan cheese nicely season this satisfying main dish. I saute the meat while the pasta is cooking, so it takes just minutes to make. —Polly Lynam
Mequon, Wisconsin

      1 small onion, chopped
      1 garlic clove, minced
  1/4 cup butter *or* margarine
1-1/2 pounds pork tenderloin *or* boneless skinless
         chicken breasts, cut into 3-inch strips
      1 teaspoon salt
      1 teaspoon dried basil
  1/2 teaspoon lemon-pepper seasoning
  1/4 teaspoon dried marjoram
      1 package (14 ounces) frozen sugar snap peas
         or vegetable of your choice, partially thawed
      1 package (19 ounces) frozen cheese tortellini,*
         cooked and drained
  1/4 to 1/2 cup grated Parmesan cheese

In a large skillet, saute onion and garlic in butter until tender. Add meat and seasonings; cook and stir for 5-7 minutes or until meat is no longer pink. Add vegetables; reduce heat. Cover and simmer for 2-3 minutes or until heated through. Add the tortellini and Parmesan cheese; toss to coat. **Yield:** 6 servings. ***Editor's Note:** 4 cups of any cooked pasta may be substituted for the tortellini.

Celery Seed Dressing

This wonderfully versatile dressing is a snap to whisk together. It adds refreshing flavor when drizzled over a seasonal fruit assortment. And it's equally tasty if you serve it over lettuce or spinach. —Jane Veliky
Harrisburg, Pennsylvania

  1/2 cup sugar
      1 teaspoon celery seed
      1 teaspoon ground mustard
      1 teaspoon paprika
      1 teaspoon salt
  1/4 cup cider vinegar
  1/4 teaspoon dried minced onion
      1 cup vegetable oil

In a small bowl, combine the first five ingredients. Stir in vinegar and onion. Slowly add oil, whisking constantly until combined. Refrigerate until ready to serve. Serve over fresh fruit or salad greens. **Yield:** 1-1/2 cups.

Brownie Caramel Parfaits

Brownies, ice cream and caramel topping are easily transformed into this tempting treat. Layers of toasted coconut and nuts add nice crunch and make this dessert seem fancy. But it really couldn't be simpler to put together.
—Chris Schnittka, Charlottesville, Virginia

  1/2 cup chopped pecans
  1/2 cup shredded coconut
      1 package brownie mix (8-inch x 8-inch pan
         size)
      1 pint vanilla ice cream
      1 jar (12-1/4 ounces) caramel ice cream
         topping

Place pecans and coconut in an ungreased baking pan. Bake at 350° for 10-12 minutes or until toasted, stirring frequently. Meanwhile, prepare brownies according to package directions. Cool; cut into small squares. When ready to serve, layer the brownies, ice cream, caramel topping and pecan mixture in parfait or dessert glasses; repeat layers one or two times. **Yield:** 6 servings. **Editor's Note:** Any type of nuts, ice cream or topping may be used in these parfaits.

Make Festive Strawberry Fans

1 Place firm ripe berries with stem down on a cutting board. With a sharp knife, make cuts 1/8 inch apart through the strawberry to within 1/8 inch of the stem.

2 With your fingers, gently spread apart the slices to form a fan.

3 If it's available, fresh mint can add further appeal. After carefully removing the strawberry leaves with the knife point, replace them with a sprig of mint.

Grilling in the
Great Outdoors

THIS MENU is perfect for a casual summer get-together. You won't heat up the kitchen to prepare it either, since all the dishes that require cooking are made on the grill. And cleanup is a breeze!

The main dish—a huge stuffed burger that feeds six—can be quickly assembled to cut down on last-minute fuss.

The light, lemony dessert can be made ahead of time and then kept in the freezer until minutes before serving. For an easy and elegant ending to the meal, present scoops of this refreshing ice cream in lovely lemon boats. (Turn to page 321 for tips on preparing them—and for other ways to dress up your table.)

Giant Stuffed Picnic Burger

Guests will be delighted when they sink their teeth into juicy wedges of this full-flavored burger. The moist filling is chock-full of mushrooms, onion and parsley. It's a great alternative to regular burgers. —Helen Hudson Brockville, Ontario

 2 pounds ground beef
 1 teaspoon salt
 1 teaspoon Worcestershire sauce
 3/4 cup crushed seasoned stuffing mix
 1 can (4 ounces) mushroom stems and pieces, drained
 1/4 cup beef broth
 1/4 cup minced fresh parsley
 1/4 cup sliced green onions
 1 egg, beaten
 1 tablespoon butter *or* margarine, melted
 1 teaspoon lemon juice

Combine beef, salt and Worcestershire sauce. Divide in half; pat each half into an 8-in. circle on waxed paper. Combine the remaining ingredients; spoon over one patty to within 1 in. of the edge. Top with second patty; press edges to seal. Grill, covered, over medium heat for 12-13 minutes on each side or until the juices run clear. Cut into wedges. **Yield: 6 servings. Editor's Note:** Stuffed burger may be placed directly on the grill or in a well-greased wire grill basket.

Cheddar Herb Bread

This crunchy, delicious bread is a hit with my husband and children. It's a fun accompaniment to any meal you make on the grill—the garlic flavor really comes through. —Ann Jacobsen, Oakland, Michigan

 1 cup (4 ounces) finely shredded cheddar cheese
 1/2 cup butter *or* margarine, softened
 1/4 cup minced fresh parsley
 1 garlic clove, minced
 1/2 teaspoon garlic powder
 1/2 teaspoon paprika
 1 loaf (1 pound) French bread, sliced

In a mixing bowl, combine the first six ingredients; beat until smooth. Spread on both sides of each slice of bread; reassemble the loaf. Wrap in a large piece of heavy-duty foil (about 28 in. x 18 in.); seal tightly. Grill, covered, over medium heat for 15-20 minutes or until heated through, turning once. **Yield: 10-12 servings. Editor's Note:** Bread may also be heated in a 375° oven for 15-20 minutes.

Veggies on the Grill

I like to experiment a bit with marinades and sauces that combine different spices and herbs. This particular mix of seasonings really perks up garden-fresh vegetables.
— H. Ross Njaa, Salinas, California

 1/3 cup vegetable oil
 1-1/2 teaspoons garlic powder
 1/2 teaspoon salt
 1/4 teaspoon pepper
 1/8 teaspoon cayenne pepper
 3 medium carrots, halved lengthwise
 3 large potatoes, quartered lengthwise
 3 medium zucchini, quartered lengthwise

In a small bowl, combine oil, garlic powder, salt, pepper and cayenne. Brush over vegetables. Grill carrots and potatoes, covered, over medium heat for 10 minutes. Baste. Add the zucchini. Cover and grill 10-15 minutes longer, basting and turning every 5 minutes or until vegetables are tender. **Yield: 6 servings.**

Refreshing Lemon Cream

Fresh lemon juice provides the tangy flavor in this smooth, rich ice cream recipe from Sunkist. The refreshing make-ahead treat can be prepared without an ice cream maker and looks splendid and summery when served in individual cups made from lemon halves.

 2 cups whipping cream
 1 cup sugar
 1/3 cup lemon juice
 1 tablespoon grated lemon peel
Lemon boats (see page 321), optional
Fresh mint and shredded lemon peel, optional

In a bowl, stir cream and sugar until sugar is dissolved. Stir in lemon juice and peel (mixture will thicken slightly). Cover and freeze until firm, about 4 hours. Remove from the freezer 15 minutes before serving. Serve in lemon boats or individual dishes. Garnish with mint and lemon peel if desired. **Yield: 6 servings. Editor's Note:** 1/2 cup mashed strawberries may be added to the lemon mixture before freezing.

Timely Kitchen Tip

WHEN unpacking groceries, I repackage cuts of meat and poultry I've purchased for grilling into freezer bags, add my favorite marinade and freeze.

When I plan to barbecue, I just pull the bag out of the freezer. As the meat thaws, the marinade flavors it.
—Amy Watson, Elmendorf Air Force Base, Alaska

Festive
Foods Fit
For the
Harvest

YOU'LL harvest a bushel of compliments with this mouth-watering meal featuring make-ahead dishes.

The prep work for the stuffed chicken and squash side dish can be completed before your dinner guests arrive. (Turn to page 322 for tips on stuffing the chicken breasts and other special table touches.)

For an appetizer, the meatballs can be shaped and baked ahead of time. When your company comes, all you need to do is reheat the meatballs in the glaze.

The dessert can be put together the night before.

Spinach-Stuffed Chicken

A mixture of spinach, spices and three kinds of cheese tucked into these chicken breasts makes them extra special. They bake to a golden brown and look lovely on the plate, too.   —Barbara Eitemiller, Churchville, Maryland

    2 packages (10 ounces *each*) frozen chopped
       spinach, thawed and squeezed dry
    1 cup (4 ounces) shredded Swiss cheese
    3/4 cup ricotta cheese
    1/3 cup grated Parmesan cheese
    3 tablespoons finely chopped onion
    1 garlic clove, minced
    1/4 teaspoon salt
    1/4 teaspoon pepper
    1/4 teaspoon ground nutmeg
    6 bone-in chicken breast halves
    2 tablespoons olive *or* vegetable oil
    1 teaspoon paprika
    1/2 teaspoon dried oregano
    1/2 teaspoon dried thyme
Additional paprika, optional

Combine the first nine ingredients; gently stuff 1/2 cupful under the skin of each chicken breast (see page 322). Place in a greased 15-in. x 10-in. x 1-in. baking pan. Combine oil, paprika, oregano and thyme; brush over chicken. Sprinkle with additional paprika if desired. Bake at 350° for 1 to 1-1/4 hours or until juices run clear. **Yield:** 6 servings.

Savory Butternut Squash

The recipe for this tender squash came from Russia. It's especially hearty when served over rice. —Natasha Kearns Philadelphia, Pennsylvania

✓ Nutritional Analysis included

    1 medium onion, chopped
    2 to 3 garlic cloves, minced
    2 tablespoons olive *or* vegetable oil
    4 cups cubed peeled butternut squash
    2 cans (14-1/2 ounces *each*) Italian diced
       tomatoes, undrained
    1 cup shredded carrots
    1 teaspoon *each* chopped fresh oregano, basil
       and parsley *or* 1/4 teaspoon *each* dried
       oregano, basil and parsley flakes
    1 teaspoon salt, optional
    1/4 teaspoon pepper
Hot cooked rice

In a skillet, saute onion and garlic in oil until tender. Add the squash, tomatoes, carrots and seasonings; stir well. Pour into a greased 2-qt. baking dish. Cover and bake at 350° for 60-70 minutes or until squash is tender. Serve over rice. **Yield:** 8 servings. **Nutritional Analysis:** One serving (prepared without salt; calculated without rice) equals 84 calories, 196 mg sodium, 0 cholesterol, 15 gm carbohydrate, 2 gm protein, 2 gm fat. **Diabetic Exchange:** 1 starch.

Appetizer Meatballs

(Not pictured)

I blend a can of crushed pineapple into my meatballs to create a taste-tempting treat. The sweet and tangy glaze is irresistible.   —Karen Mellinger Baker, Dover, Ohio

    1 can (8 ounces) crushed pineapple
    1 egg
    1/4 cup dry bread crumbs
    1/8 teaspoon pepper
    1/2 pound bulk pork sausage
    1/2 pound ground beef
GLAZE:
    1/4 cup packed brown sugar
    1/4 cup ketchup
    1/4 cup vinegar
    1/4 cup water
    2 tablespoons Dijon-mayonnaise blend

Drain pineapple, reserving juice. Place pineapple and 2 tablespoons juice in a bowl (set the remaining juice aside for glaze). Add the egg, bread crumbs and pepper to pineapple; mix well. Add sausage and beef; mix well. Shape into 1-in. balls; place in a greased 15-in. x 10-in. x 1-in. baking pan. Bake, uncovered, at 450° for 12-15 minutes or until no longer pink; drain. In a large skillet, combine glaze ingredients and reserved pineapple juice. Add meatballs. Bring to a boil over medium heat. Reduce heat; simmer and stir for 5-10 minutes or until heated through. **Yield:** 4 dozen.

Ladyfinger Trifle

During the busy holiday season, you'll want to stock your pantry with the ingredients for this fast and festive dessert. It looks so pretty in a glass bowl—people will think you fussed.   —Gloria Aegerter, Summerfield, Florida

    2 packages (one 8 ounces, one 3 ounces) cream
       cheese, softened
    1 cup confectioners' sugar
    2 cups whipping cream, whipped
    1 package (3 ounces) ladyfingers
    1 can (21 ounces) dark cherry pie filling *or*
       filling of your choice

In a mixing bowl, beat cream cheese and sugar until smooth. Fold in whipped cream. Split ladyfingers; arrange upright around the edge and over the bottom of a 2-qt. serving bowl (about 8-in. diameter). Pour cream cheese mixture into bowl. Cover and refrigerate for 4 hours or overnight. Just before serving, spoon pie filling over cream cheese mixture. **Yield:** 8-10 servings.

Fine Dining
With Flair

EVEN during the hectic holidays, you can entertain effortlessly with a time-easing menu like this one. (Turn to page 323 for festive table decorating ideas.)

Fully cooked ham slices hurry along the preparation when warmed with a quick-to-fix cranberry coating.

To cut down on last-minute fuss, both the appetizer and delightful dessert can be made ahead. The rest of the meal can be cooked on the stovetop while guests snack on the colorful cracker spread.

Holiday Ham Slices

My family loves this dressy treatment for ham, so I keep extra cranberry sauce on hand at holiday time.
—Marilou Robinson, Portland, Oregon

    3/4 cup whole-berry cranberry sauce
    4 to 6 green onions, finely chopped
    3 tablespoons water
    1 tablespoon Dijon mustard
    1 tablespoon butter *or* margarine, melted
    1 teaspoon brown sugar
    1/4 teaspoon ground ginger
    4 slices (6 to 8 ounces *each*) fully cooked ham

In a large skillet, combine the first seven ingredients. Cook over medium heat, stirring constantly. Add ham; cook for 3-4 minutes or until heated through. Spoon sauce over ham to serve. **Yield:** 4-6 servings.

Dijon-Dill Brussels Sprouts

I added my own touches, including crunchy water chestnuts, to this recipe from a friend. The tender brussels sprouts get winning flavor from lemon, dill and Dijon mustard. —Audrey Thibodeau, Mesa, Arizona

1-1/2 pounds fresh brussels sprouts, halved
    3 tablespoons butter *or* margarine, melted
    2 teaspoons Dijon mustard
    2 teaspoons lemon juice
    1 teaspoon dill weed
1/4 to 1/2 teaspoon salt
1/8 teaspoon pepper
    1 can (8 ounces) sliced water chestnuts,
       drained and halved

Place brussels sprouts in a saucepan with a small amount of water; cover and steam until tender, about 12-14 minutes. Combine butter, mustard, lemon juice, dill, salt and pepper. Drain brussels sprouts; add butter mixture and water chestnuts. Mix well. **Yield:** 4-6 servings.

Rosemary Rice

The aroma of this light and lemony rice dish flecked with pretty carrot shreds is heavenly. I have an herb garden, so I prepare this with fresh rosemary in summer.
—Mary Ann Kosmas, Minneapolis, Minnesota

✓ **Nutritional Analysis included**

    2 cups chicken broth
    1 cup uncooked long grain rice
    1 medium onion, chopped

    1 small carrot, shredded
1/2 to 1 teaspoon grated lemon peel
    2 garlic cloves, minced
    1 teaspoon dried rosemary, crushed
1/2 teaspoon salt, optional

Combine all ingredients in a medium saucepan. Bring to a boil. Reduce heat; cover and simmer for 20 minutes or until liquid is absorbed. **Yield:** 6-8 servings. **Nutritional Analysis:** One 1/2-cup serving (prepared with low-sodium broth and without salt) equals 222 calories, 63 mg sodium, 3 mg cholesterol, 46 gm carbohydrate, 6 gm protein, 1 gm fat. **Diabetic Exchange:** 3 starch.

Spruced-Up Cheese Spread

(Not pictured)

A neighbor gave me this recipe. It's easy to shape into a Christmas tree for a festive occasion (see page 323).
—Judy Grimes, Brandon, Mississippi

    1 jar (4 ounces) diced pimientos, drained,
       divided
    1 small onion, grated
    1 cup mayonnaise
    1 to 2 tablespoons prepared mustard
    1 tablespoon Worcestershire sauce
    1 teaspoon celery seed
1/2 teaspoon paprika
1/4 teaspoon garlic salt
    3 cups (12 ounces) finely shredded sharp
       cheddar cheese
    2 tablespoons finely chopped pecans
1/3 cup minced fresh parsley

Set aside 2 tablespoons pimientos for topping. In a bowl, combine remaining pimientos and the next seven ingredients. Stir in cheese. Transfer to a serving bowl; sprinkle with pecans, parsley and reserved pimientos. **Yield:** 4 cups.

Magic Mousse

Dishes of this delightfully sweet dessert are a breeze to whip up ahead of time, yet they taste like you fussed.

    2 tablespoons cold water
    1 envelope unflavored gelatin
1/4 cup boiling water
    1 cup sugar
1/2 cup baking cocoa
    2 cups whipping cream
    2 teaspoons vanilla extract
English toffee bits

In a small bowl, combine cold water and gelatin; let stand for 2 minutes. Add boiling water; stir until gelatin is dissolved. Cool slightly. In a mixing bowl, combine sugar and cocoa. Add the cream and vanilla; beat on medium speed until stiff peaks form. Add gelatin mixture; beat just until blended. Spoon into dessert dishes. Chill for at least 30 minutes. Garnish with toffee bits. Store leftovers in the refrigerator. **Yield:** 8 servings.

Topping Your Table for Company

FOR a special meal, you can add the perfect finishing touches with tasteful table toppers, pretty folded napkins and colorful food garnishes. Our kitchen staff came up with these eye-pleasing inexpensive ideas.

Straight Story on Chocolate Curls

TRY a sweet twist—garnishing your dessert with chocolate curls!

If you have a solid block of chocolate, simply use a vegetable peeler to peel off curls, allowing them to fall gently onto a plate or piece of waxed paper in a single layer. (If you get only shavings, try warming the chocolate just slightly.)

Otherwise, begin by melting chocolate chips, chocolate confectionery coating or chocolate bars. (The amount used depends on the number of curls needed.)

Pour the melted chocolate onto the back of an inverted cookie sheet and spread to a smooth, thin layer. Let cool until firm and pliable but not brittle.

With a cheese slicer, metal spatula or pancake turner, scrape up a thin layer of chocolate using even pressure. The chocolate will curl as you go. The slower you scrape, the wider your curls will be.

Slide a toothpick or wooden skewer through each curl to carefully lift it onto the cake and arrange as desired.

Take Hold of Napkin Folding

FOLDED NAPKINS are a fun, easy way to dress up your table. Best of all, you can do the folding days in advance! You needn't be an expert to make a "standing fan". Here's how:

1. Fold an open square cloth or paper napkin in half like a book. (If necessary, starch cloth napkins for crisp folds.) Be-

ginning at the bottom edge, form 1-inch accordion-pleats until 4 inches remain.

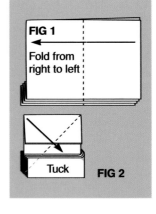

2. Turn the napkin over so the pleats you just made are under the bottom edge and the flat side without pleats faces you. See Fig. 1. Fold the napkin in half from right to left so half of the pleats are now on top.

3. Fold the top down to form a 1-1/2-inch hem. See Fig. 2. Fold the top left corner down diagonally and tuck it under the pleats.

4. Pull open the pleats so the napkin forms a fan and it stands upright on the plate.

Centerpiece Stems from Simplicity

FLOWERS add such a fresh and welcoming look to the table. If you are a gardener, you'll likely find the key "ingredients" right at hand.

To make a horizontal arrangement like the one pictured below, line a shallow oblong basket (ours was 10 inches long, 5 inches wide and 3 inches high) with plastic wrap. Cut floral foam to fit basket. Immerse foam in water, then set it in basket.

1 Push stems of greens such as fern, ivy, hosta leaves, etc. (myrtle is pictured) into the top perimeter of the foam almost horizontally so they drape over the edge of the basket. Use longer greens at the ends and shorter ones along the sides.

2 Insert stems of large anchor flowers almost upright but leaning a bit out of the basket in all directions—taller stems in the middle and shorter ones along the edges. Keep the tallest part of your topper under 10 inches so guests can see over it.

3 Fill the gaps with small accent flowers and additional greens until foam is hidden and arrangement looks full. Consider baby's breath, statice, flowering herbs or any small flowers. (We used alstroemeria and white monte casino.)

Our arrangement measures 27 inches long and 9 inches high. Add water to foam as needed to keep flowers fresh. The centerpiece can be made a day in advance if desired.

Braided Napkin Ring Ties Up Look

NAPKINS held in creative napkin rings give polish to a place setting.

Braided raffia napkin rings (like the one shown above) give country charm to a casual dinner. (Raffia is a natural-colored crafter's straw sold in bundles at craft stores.) They can be made in advance and are easy to assemble.

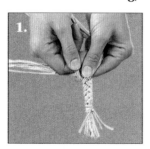

1. For each ring, cut 21 strands of raffia 19 inches long. Secure one end of the bunch by wrapping and tying another piece of raffia around it, forming a tassel about 1-1/2 inches long.

Divide the strands into three sections of seven strands each. Braid down the length of the raffia until about 1-1/2 inches remain.

Wrap and tie the end with another piece of raffia, forming a second tassel.

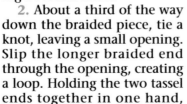

2. About a third of the way down the braided piece, tie a knot, leaving a small opening. Slip the longer braided end through the opening, creating a loop. Holding the two tassel ends together in one hand, pull the loop to open it and tighten the knot.

3. Fold a square napkin in half, then in half again, creating a square one-fourth the size of the original. Roll two opposite corners toward the center until they meet. Fold one of the remaining pointy corners over the rolls about a third of the way down.

Easy Onion Garnish

GIVE plates sparkle with an impressive garnish like green onion tassels (see photo on page 308). They aren't tricky, so you won't shed a tear making them!

1. Trim the root end of each green onion. Cut the onion into a 2- to 3-inch piece. Discard tops.

2. Using a small scissors or sharp knife, cut lengthwise slits, 1/8 to 1/4 inch apart and 1 to 2 inches long, opposite the root end.

3. Immediately place onions in a bowl of ice water so they open and curl. If you make green onion tassels early in the day to use in the evening, store them in ice water in the refrigerator. Remove just before garnishing.

Turn the napkin over; push the folded end through the loop of the braided raffia ring so the knot is on top of the napkin. Pull the knot snug with the tassels pointed in the direction of the unfolded end of the napkin (see photo at top left).

Pretty Place Markers

SIMPLE flowers in simple containers can make your guests feel welcome and relaxed at your casual dinner.

For memorable place markers, put a few favorite short-stemmed flowers in small glass jelly or canning jars filled with water. Add an adhesive label with a guest's name on each jar (see photo at top left).

Consider any pretty seasonal blooms. White daisies look fresh and don't have an overpowering scent.

To finish off this decorative table topper, loop a couple strands of raffia around the neck of each jar and tie them in a bow.

For a centerpiece, use a larger glass jar or vase also tied with raffia and filled with longer-stemmed flowers similar to those in your place-marker jars. Be sure the centerpiece stands less than 12 inches tall so guests can see over it. A few marbles in the jar help keep the stems in place.

Speedy Way to Slice Fresh Melons

WHEN you don't have a lot of time, scooping out melon balls can be a hassle. Here's a fast method for removing the rind from cantaloupe and honeydew melons, then quickly slicing the fruit for pretty presentation on a platter.

1 Halve melon widthwise. Use a large spoon to scoop out seeds and discard.

2 Place melon, cut side down, on a cutting board. With a single motion, cut off a thin slice of the rind, starting at the top and continuing down the side of the melon. Remove remaining rind this way. Repeat with other melon half.

3 Cut melon half in two and slice into even-sized pieces. Arrange them in pleasing patterns on platter. Garnish with other fresh fruits like raspberries or strawberry fans (see page 310).

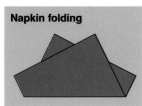

Fast Floral Centerpiece

THIS floral centerpiece is so quick and easy you may find yourself putting one together even when you don't have guests over for dinner.

You need merely three things—a shallow bowl, some water and a few pretty flowers to float in the water.

While you're preparing dinner, enlist the help of your kids. Send them into the backyard to pick a handful of daisies from your flower patch.

A variety of blooms will work, but those that have "heads" (such as dahlias, mums and zinnias) will float better than others. We used gerbera daisies (see photo above).

Since this centerpiece doesn't require any long-stemmed blooms, it's okay if the kids happen to break the stems off close to the flower heads while picking.

If you don't have a flower garden, try floating several small flowers from a blooming houseplant like an African violet or a hanging plant like a begonia.

What's great about this centerpiece is you don't need a whole bouquet to make a statement. Depending on the size of your bowl and the size of your flowers, you can float one or several. (A single rose, its petals fully open, can look very elegant.)

Experiment with what you have on hand. Add a few leaves or ferns for contrast. If you'd like a more dramatic look, add a few drops of food coloring to tint the water.

Place Settings Get Summery Look

SIMPLE TOUCHES like an ordinary napkin ring and a casual fold can perk up a plain cloth napkin and jazz up an individual place setting.

You can continue to visit with your guests while you ready these napkins, because there's no complicated folding involved.

In fact, this napkin fold is so simple it's hardly a fold at all. To achieve this casual look, lay the napkin flat. Hold two adjacent corners, one in each hand, and begin to fold the napkin in half. Rather than matching the corners, place them slightly askew as illustrated at right.

Napkin folding

Then grab the center of the fold and pull it through a cheery colored napkin ring. It's that simple.

For a summery touch at each plate, tuck the stem of a single flower through the napkin ring, using the same blooms featured in your centerpiece.

Paper Napkins Tie Look Together

WHILE cloth napkins add elegance to special occasions, paper napkins have their place at the table, too.

They're especially handy for casual get-togethers because they're disposable and sold in many bright colors.

For a special touch, use paper napkins to bundle each guest's utensils. Secure the neat packages with a length of coordinating ribbon, twine, paper twist, decorative cord or raffia.

Brilliant Paper Lanterns

DURING THE DAY, festive paper lanterns add a bright spot of color to your outdoor dinner table. As the sun sets and the candles are lit, they contribute a warm, welcoming glow that won't be extinguished by an evening breeze.

These effortless and eye-catching lanterns are simply candles set in canning jars that have been wrapped with decorative paper.

Pint- and quart-size jars offer plenty of space for a candle. Votives, tea lights or other short candles are suggested, because you don't want the flame reaching the top of the jar.

To cover the jars, we used gift wrap. With a variety of colors and patterns available, you can select one that coordinates with your dinnerware. Be sure to pick paper that's light-colored and not too thick so the candle's light can shine through.

Lanterns made with unfolded wrapping paper are very quick to put together—simply cut the paper so it fits snugly around the jar and reaches no more than 1 inch above the top.

Trim the top edge with a pinking shears. If you'd like to let more light through, use a paper punch to create holes along the top and bottom edges of the paper.

For folded lanterns, cut a length of paper twice the circumference of the jar and, again, no more than 1 inch taller than the jar.

1. For pint- and quart-size jars, fold the paper accordion-style, starting with a short side. We made the folds about 1 inch wide.

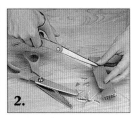

2. Once the paper is folded, snip off one end with a pinking shears to create a pretty top edge. Use a regular scissors or pinking shears to cut triangle shapes on one or both folded sides.

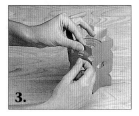

3. After placing the candle in the jar, loosely wrap the folded paper around the outside and tape it together.

Light the candle with a long match or taper, being careful not to ignite the paper wrap. For safety, never leave lit candles unattended and keep them out of children's reach.

Lemon Boats Add Zest to Meals

SUNNY LEMONS may taste tart, but they make sweet garnishes at special summer meals. Desserts and fruit salads look especially pretty when presented in lovely lemon boats.

1 Cut a large lemon in half lengthwise. With pulp side down, cut a thin slice of peel from the top of each half so the lemon shell will sit level on a plate. Gently squeeze the juice from each half. Discard or save for another use. With a small scissors or sharp knife, cut the membrane at each end to loosen pulp from shell.

2 Using fingertips, pull membrane and pulp away from the shell. Place lemon shells upside down on a moistened paper towel and refrigerate until serving. Fill with the Refreshing Lemon Cream on page 313, ice cream, sherbet or fruit.

Harvest Centerpiece

AN ASSORTMENT of fall produce makes an effortless arrangement for your dinner table. It's fast to fix, too—a simple, seasonal centerpiece like the one shown below takes just minutes to assemble.

First, choose an appropriate container to hold your arrangement. Try an antique wooden tray, woven basket or rustic-looking bowl. Its size will depend on the size and number of items you plan to put into it.

Then fill the container with most any type of colorful fall produce—gather it straight from your garden or pick some up at a local farmer's market, roadside stand or grocery store.

Good choices are seasonal squash and gourds of different colors and shapes, a few ears of Indian corn, a collection of cute mini pumpkins, shiny red, yellow and green apples or pretty pears.

Make a statement with just one type of fruit or vegetable, or mix and match a few different kinds.

To continue the fall theme, especially if you combine it with the leaf tablecloth idea on this page, tuck a few autumn leaves into your centerpiece for added interest.

Stuffing Chicken Breasts

TRANSFORM ordinary baked chicken into a special-occasion entree by dressing it up with savory stuffing.

Stuffed chicken breasts look difficult to prepare, but they're really quite simple. Fancy enough for company, they're so easy to make that you'll find yourself serving them at weekday dinners.

Start with bone-in chicken breasts that have skin, and almost any type of moist stuffing...the Spinach-Stuffed Chicken recipe on page 315 has a flavorful spinach and cheese filling.

1 Work fingers underneath each chicken breast's skin to form a pocket, leaving the skin attached at the ends and one side.

2 Gently stuff each pocket with 1/2 cup of filling, allowing it to peek out of the open side. Be sure not to overfill the pocket or the skin may become unattached.

Tablecloth Has Autumn Covered

DESIGN your own tablecloth that captures the glorious colors of fall. It takes only a few minutes and a few items to create this eye-catching tabletop.

You will need a plain tablecloth, some bright autumn leaves from your backyard and a length of sheer fabric the same size as your tablecloth.

To begin, cover your table with a white, pastel or other light-colored tablecloth. (We chose a pretty gold one.)

Then enlist the help of your kids to collect brilliant red, orange and gold fall leaves from your yard. Have them look for the prettiest and most colorful ones they can find.

Leaves that have just fallen and have not had time to curl and dry will work best. (If you don't have access to real leaves, you can use silk leaves like we did.)

1. Arrange the leaves on top of the tablecloth, using as many or as few as you'd like. Space them randomly over the length of the table so color peeks out here and there from underneath your dishes.

Another possibility is to encircle the centerpiece or individual place settings with a ring of leaves to draw attention to them as shown in the photo above left.

2. Carefully place the sheer fabric over the leaves. This helps keep the leaves in place while allowing their natural beauty to show through. Materials such as net or tulle work great because they're relatively inexpensive and they don't need to be hemmed (which saves lots of time).

If you can't get either of these fabrics, consider sheer voile or organdy. (But they cost more and will need to be hemmed.)

What's nice about this idea is that you can adapt it to use whatever you have on hand. Instead of fall leaves, fresh fern fronds would look pretty in spring while bright green leaves would be attractive in summer.

Ornaments Brighten Table

TO MAKE a sparkling centerpiece like the one pictured above, gather a few pine boughs about a foot long. We used fresh-cut branches, but you can use real or artificial garlands, branches or swags.

Napkin Fold Adds Elegance

YOU can learn to create the classy fold shown above in no time. To begin, place an ironed cloth napkin open on a flat surface. Fold the napkin in half diagonally by bringing two opposite corners together to form a triangle.

1 Bring two points created by the fold together to meet at the open point of the napkin. This will form a square.

2 Now fold the closed point about one-third of the way underneath the napkin.

3 Take one of the side points and fold it past the center line. Repeat with the remaining side point, tucking it into the small flap to secure it.

Turn the napkin over and place it flat on a plate as shown in the photo above.

We used floral wire to tie the cut ends together at the center. Then we wired a few smaller sprays at the center to fill out the arrangement.

Now nestle ornaments throughout the arrangement. Both metallic plastic balls and glass balls look lovely.

For the final touch, add a simple ribbon bow, winding the ends through the greens.

Additional Christmas tree balls can serve as pretty place markers. Use a gold marker to write each dinner guest's name on an ornament.

Place a ball into the water glass at each setting to display the name (left). At the end of the evening, guests can take their ornament home as a memento.

Festive Cheese Spread

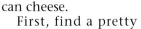

THE Spruced-Up Cheese Spread recipe on page 317 can easily be transformed into an appetizing tree (right).

The only extra ingredients needed are 1/4 cup of softened cream cheese, 2 teaspoons of milk and a slice of process American cheese.

First, find a pretty serving tray or cover a board (about 15 x 15 inches) with aluminum foil or bright wrapping paper and plastic wrap.

Then make the spread as directed, reserving the pecans, parsley and pimientos for garnish.

1. Drop spoonfuls in mounds. To speed the process, use a miniature ice cream or cookie scoop (#30) that holds 2 tablespoons.

Begin with one mound for treetop. In the second row, drop three mounds. Follow with rows of two mounds, four mounds, three mounds and five mounds. Center the remaining cheese spread (about two mounds) below the tree for a trunk.

2. Carefully spread the cheese mixture with an icing knife to form a tree.

3. Decorate it by sprinkling parsley and pimiento "ornaments" over the branches and pecans over the trunk.

To make the "garland", beat the cream cheese and milk in a bowl. Cut a small hole in the corner of a plastic bag and insert an open star tip #20. Fill the bag with the cream cheese mixture and pipe it across the tree.

Using a small star cookie cutter, cut a star from the cheese slice; attach it to the treetop with a small amount of cream cheese mixture.

Chapter 21

DURING the week, most folks barely have an extra moment to sit and relax—much less head to the kitchen and cook something that requires a bit more time.

So on those more leisurely weekend days when you do have a few minutes to spare, why not take some time out to cook with these special recipes and tips?

From homemade frosting, sticky buns, cinnamon rolls and elegant cheesecakes to old-fashioned ice cream, from-scratch soup and roasted turkey, you'll surely sharpen your culinary skills in a snap!

While these recipes take a little longer to make, one taste and you'll agree they're worth the extra effort.

SWEET RESULTS. Chocolate Mint Ice Cream (p. 332).

Cover Your Cakes With Incredible Spreadables

1/3 cup water
1/4 teaspoon cream of tartar
1 teaspoon vanilla extract

In a heavy saucepan or double boiler, combine sugar, egg whites, water and cream of tartar. With a portable mixer, beat mixture on low speed for 1 minute. Continue beating on low speed over low heat until frosting reaches 160°, about 8-10 minutes. Pour into a large mixing bowl; add vanilla. Beat on high speed until frosting forms stiff peaks, about 7 minutes. **Yield:** about 5 cups. **Editor's Note:** A stand mixer is recommended for beating the frosting after it reaches 160°.

Buttercream Frosting

(Pictured at right)

This basic buttery frosting has unmatchable homemade taste. With a few simple variations, you can come up with different colors and flavors. —Diana Wilson, Denver, Colorado

**1 cup butter (no substitutes), softened
8 cups confectioners' sugar
2 teaspoons vanilla extract
1/2 to 3/4 cup milk**

In a mixing bowl, cream butter. Beat in sugar and vanilla. Add milk until frosting reaches desired consistency. **Yield:** about 4 cups. **For Chocolate Frosting:** Substitute 1/2 cup baking cocoa for 1/2 cup of the confectioners' sugar. **For Peanut Butter Frosting:** Substitute peanut butter for butter. **For Lemon- or Orange-Flavored Frosting:** Substitute lemon or orange juice for milk and add 1 teaspoon grated lemon or orange peel. **For Almond- or Peppermint-Flavored Frosting:** Substitute almond or peppermint extract for the vanilla. Liquid or paste food coloring may be added to match flavoring (green for mint, for example) or for contrast when decorating.

Fluffy White Frosting

IT'S actually easy and inexpensive to make your own irresistible icing and turn out a cake as pretty as a picture!

Even if you've never done so before, you'll be collecting compliments after frosting your favorite cake with one of these tempting toppers.

Fluffy White Frosting

(Pictured above)

For a heavenly light and fluffy frosting, you can't top this cooked version. You'll definitely want to lick the beaters after whipping up this modern variation of the classic 7-minute frosting. —Georgie Bohmann West Allis, Wisconsin

**1-1/2 cups sugar
2 egg whites**

Creamy Chocolate Frosting

Whisking up a batch of smooth-as-silk fudgy chocolate icing is a snap using this short recipe and your favorite flavor of baking chips. —Jeannette Mack Rushville, New York

**2 cups whipping cream
2 cups (12 ounces) semisweet chocolate, milk chocolate or vanilla baking chips
3 to 3-1/2 cups confectioners' sugar**

In a medium saucepan, bring cream to a simmer, about 160°; remove from the heat. Stir in chips until melted. Place pan in a bowl of ice water; stir constantly until cooled. Gradually whisk in sugar until smooth and thick. **Yield:** 4 cups.

Frosting Amounts for Buttercream Frosting

For cooked fluffy frostings, such as 7-minute, double the amounts needed.
Plan on an extra 1/2 to 1 cup frosting to use for decorating.

Pan Size and Shape	Between Each Layer	Sides	Top	Total
8- or 9-inch round, two layers	1/2 cup	1-1/4 cups	3/4 cup	2-1/2 cups
8- or 9-inch square, one layer	—	1 cup	3/4 cup	1-3/4 cups
8- or 9-inch square, two layers	3/4 cup	1-1/2 cups	3/4 cup	3 cups
13- x 9-inch rectangle	—	1 cup	1-1/4 cups	2-1/4 cups
10-inch tube pan (angel food)	—	1-1/2 cups	3/4 cup	2-1/4 cups
10-inch fluted tube pan (bundt) or 24 cupcakes	—	—	2-1/4 cups	2-1/4 cups

Buttercream Frosting

Frosting the Cake

- To keep the serving plate free of frosting, arrange narrow strips of waxed paper around the edges of the plate, then position the cake on top, centering it on the plate. When the cake is frosted, carefully slide out the paper strips.

- Use a flexible metal pastry spatula or wide-bladed knife to spread the icing. For fudgy or butter-based frostings such as buttercream or creamy chocolate, dip the spatula in cold water occasionally to keep the frosting from sticking. For confectioners' sugar or cooked frostings such as 7-minute frosting, dip the knife into hot water before spreading.

- If your cake filling is different from the frosting, it might spill out the edges and discolor the frosting. To prevent this, spread a 1/2-inch strip of icing around the edge of each layer before spreading the filling in the center. This acts as a barrier to keep the filling inside.

- Once the layers are assembled, spread a paper-thin coating of icing over the entire surface of the cake to seal in any crumbs and keep them from showing on your finished cake. Then apply a second, generous layer of frosting to the side, swirling it up to make a 1/2-inch ridge above the rim of the cake. Finally, frost the top of the cake, swirling the frosting or leaving it smooth.

- Can't get the frosting smooth on top of your cake? Mist it lightly with water and, using a feather-light touch, smooth over the surface with your spatula.

Decorating the Cake

- Give white frosting a lovely pastel tint with food coloring. Or for rich dark colors, tint the frosting with food coloring paste (available at kitchen and cake decorating supply stores).

- A pastry bag and decorating tips can have you decorating cakes like a professional. Don't own a pastry bag? Buy decorating tips and slip one inside a snipped-off corner of a resealable plastic bag.

- Wrap masking tape around the outside to reinforce the seal between the opening in the bag and the tip (see photo at right). Or purchase inexpensive plastic couplers that hold the tips on the bag and allow you to change them without changing  bags. For very simple decorations, just snip the corner off a heavy-duty resealable plastic bag and pipe frosting that way.

- Before creating a design or writing on cake frosting, use a toothpick to draw the pattern. If you make a mistake, just smooth the frosting and start over. Once the pattern is completed, pipe over the lines with tinted icing.

- For fun and easy patterns, trace around cookie cutters on the top of the cake.

- An easy way to make a dramatic design on the top or sides of your cake is to pipe a thin continuous line of icing (see photo above left). Curve it up, down and around so the new sections of the squiggly line never touch the sections already piped.

- For a pretty effect, or if you're not that happy with your frosting job, pat chopped nuts or colored or chocolate sprinkles around the sides and top of the cake.

- To flatten or touch up a frosting decoration, simply dip your finger in cornstarch and smooth out the desired area.

- To prevent icing from drying out while decorating a cake, cover the reserved amount with a damp cloth or paper towel until you're ready to use it.

- To prevent plastic wrap from sticking to frosting, spray the wrap with nonstick cooking spray.

With Finger-Licking Treats, It's Easy To Get on a Roll

Sticky Buns

EVEN if you've never attempted to make sweet yeast rolls from scratch, you'll rise to the occasion with the straightforward recipes here. Plus, shortcuts using a bread machine or frozen bread dough are options if you need to shave off some prep time.

Sticky Buns

(Pictured above)

It's impossible to eat just one of these soft, yummy sticky buns—they have wonderful old-fashioned goodness. Use the conventional method or your bread machine to make the dough. —Dorothy Showalter, Broadway, Virginia

DOUGH:
- 2 teaspoons active dry yeast
- 1-1/4 cups warm water (110° to 115°)
- 3 tablespoons butter *or* margarine, softened
- 3 tablespoons sugar
- 2 tablespoons instant nonfat dry milk powder
- 1 teaspoon salt
- 3 to 3-1/4 cups bread flour

FILLING:
- 1/3 cup butter *or* margarine, softened
- 1 tablespoon sugar
- 1 teaspoon ground cinnamon

SAUCE:
- 1/2 cup packed brown sugar
- 1/4 cup butter *or* margarine
- 1/4 cup corn syrup
- 1/2 cup chopped pecans

In a mixing bowl, dissolve yeast in water; let stand for 5 minutes. Add butter, sugar, milk powder, salt and 2 cups flour; beat on low for 3 minutes. Stir in enough remaining flour to form a soft dough. Turn onto a floured surface; knead until smooth and elastic, about 6-8 minutes. Place in a greased bowl; turn once to grease top. Cover and let rise in a warm place until doubled, about 1 hour. Punch dough down. **To prepare buns:** Roll the dough into a 16-in. x 10-in. rectangle. Spread with butter; sprinkle with sugar and cinnamon. Roll up from a long side; pinch seam to seal. Cut into 12 slices; set aside. In a saucepan, combine brown sugar, butter and corn syrup; cook over medium heat until the sugar is dissolved. Stir in pecans. Pour into a greased 13-in. x 9-in. x 2-in. baking pan. Place buns with cut side down over sauce. Cover and let rise until doubled, about 1 hour. Bake at 375° for 20-25 minutes or until golden brown. Cool in pan for 3 minutes. Invert onto a serving platter. **Yield:** 1 dozen. **Editor's Note:** The dough may be prepared in a bread machine. Place dough ingredients (using water that is 70°-80° and only 3 cups of bread flour) in bread pan in order suggested by manufacturer. Select dough setting (check dough after 5 minutes of mixing; add 1-2 tablespoons of water or flour if needed). When cycle is completed, turn dough onto a floured surface and punch down. Prepare buns as directed.

Mother's Cinnamon Rolls

(Pictured at right)

I'm a busy wife, mother and nurse, but I love to cook and bake when I can. It's a thrill to serve these scrumptious rolls to my family and guests. For quicker preparation, substitute frozen bread dough.
—Deanitta Clemmons, Brownsville, Indiana

- 2 packages (1/4 ounce *each*) active dry yeast
- 1/2 cup warm water (110° to 115°)
- 1-1/2 cups warm milk (110° to 115°)
- 1/2 cup butter *or* margarine, softened
- 1/2 cup sugar
- 1 teaspoon salt
- 2 eggs
- 6 to 6-1/2 cups all-purpose flour

FILLING:
    1/4 cup butter *or* margarine, softened
    1/2 cup sugar
    4 teaspoons ground cinnamon
    1/2 cup raisins, optional
    1/2 cup chopped walnuts, optional
ICING:
    2 cups confectioners' sugar
    2 to 3 tablespoons milk
    1 teaspoon vanilla extract

In a mixing bowl, dissolve yeast in water; let stand for 5 minutes. Add milk, butter, sugar, salt, eggs and 2 cups flour; beat on low for 3 minutes. Stir in enough remaining flour to form a soft dough. Turn onto a floured surface; knead until smooth and elastic, about 6-8 minutes. Place in a greased bowl, turning once to grease top. Cover and let rise in a warm place until doubled, about 1 hour. Punch dough down; divide in half. Turn onto a lightly floured surface; roll out each half into a 12-in. x 8-in. rectangle. Spread with butter. Combine remaining filling ingredients; sprinkle over butter. Roll up from a long side; pinch seam to seal. Cut into 12 slices; place with cut side down in a greased 13-in. x 9-in. x 2-in. baking pan. Cover and let rise until doubled, about 30 minutes. Bake at 350° for 25-30 minutes or until gold-

en brown. Cool in pan on a wire rack. Combine the icing ingredients and drizzle over warm rolls. **Yield:** 2 dozen. **Editor's Note:** Two loaves of frozen bread dough may be used with this filling and icing.

Tips for Rolls That Are Tops

- After punching down the dough, allow it to rest for 10 minutes for easier rolling.

- Be sure to roll up the dough tightly and firmly to avoid big gaps in the rolls once they're baked.

- A simple way to cut the dough into rolls is to place a piece of dental floss or heavy-duty thread under the rolled dough, 1 inch from the end. Bring the ends of the floss or thread up around the dough, cross them over at the top and pull, cutting through the dough and filling. Repeat every inch.

- Evenly space the cut rolls in the pan, leaving room around each to allow for the final rising.

- It's easy to create tasty variations on the standard cinnamon roll. Change the flavor of the icing by replacing the vanilla with almond extract or maple flavoring. Substitute dried cranberries for raisins and orange extract for vanilla. Or use a different kind of nut.

Mother's Cinnamon Rolls

Cheesecakes Never Fail to Impress

Mocha Chip Cheesecake
Luscious Lemon Cheesecake

chocolate chips contrast nicely with the creamy coffee filling.
—*Renee Gastineau*
Seattle, Washington

CRUST:
2 cups chocolate wafer
  crumbs (about 32 wafers)
1/2 cup sugar
1/2 cup butter *or* margarine,
  melted
FILLING:
3 packages (8 ounces *each*)
  cream cheese, softened
1 cup sugar
3 tablespoons all-purpose
  flour
4 eggs
1/3 cup whipping cream
1 tablespoon instant coffee
  granules
1 teaspoon vanilla extract
1 cup (6 ounces) miniature
  semisweet chocolate
  chips, *divided*

In a bowl, combine crumbs and sugar; stir in butter. Press onto the bottom and 2 in. up the sides of a greased 9-in. springform pan; set aside. In a mixing bowl, beat cream cheese and sugar until smooth. Add flour and beat well. Add eggs, beating on low speed just until combined. In a small bowl, combine cream and coffee; let stand for 1 minute. Add to cream cheese mixture with vanilla; beat just until mixed. Stir in 3/4 cup chocolate chips. Pour into crust. Sprinkle with remaining chocolate chips. Bake at 325° for 50-55 minutes or until center is almost set. Cool on a wire rack for 1 hour. Refrigerate overnight. Remove sides of pan. Let stand at room temperature for 30 minutes before slicing.
Yield: 12-14 servings.

WHEN you want to "wow" special guests, nothing beats the sumptuous flavor and palate-pleasing texture of a homemade cheesecake.

True, making one can be a bit tricky...but we've compiled pointers to help you avoid common pitfalls associated with this yummy baked dessert.

Try your hand at one of these sensational specialties. You and your guests will be impressed with the dazzling results.

Mocha Chip Cheesecake

(Pictured above)

Two favorite flavors—coffee and chocolate—combine in this treat. The chocolate crumb crust and sprinkling of

Luscious Lemon Cheesecake

(Pictured above left)

I'm always greeted with oohs and aahs when I bring out this exquisite dessert. It has a wonderful lemony flavor, silky texture and rich sour cream topping. The nuts in the crust make it delectable. —*Kaaren Jurack, Virginia Beach, Virginia*

CRUST:
1-1/4 cups graham cracker crumbs (about 20
  squares)

3/4 cup finely chopped nuts
1/4 cup sugar
1/3 cup butter *or* margarine, melted
FILLING:
    4 packages (8 ounces *each*) cream cheese, softened
1-1/4 cups sugar
    4 eggs
    1 tablespoon lemon juice
    2 teaspoons grated lemon peel
    1 teaspoon vanilla extract
TOPPING:
    2 cups (16 ounces) sour cream
    1/4 cup sugar
    1 teaspoon grated lemon peel
    1 teaspoon vanilla extract

In a bowl, combine crumbs, nuts and sugar; stir in butter. Press onto the bottom of a greased 10-in. springform pan; set aside. In a mixing bowl, beat cream cheese and sugar until smooth. Add eggs, beating on low speed just until combined. Add lemon juice, peel and vanilla; beat just until blended. Pour into crust. Bake at 350° for 55 minutes or until center is almost set. Remove from the oven; let stand for 5 minutes. Combine topping ingredients; spread over filling. Return to the oven for 5 minutes. Cool on a wire rack for 10 minutes. Carefully run a knife around edge of pan to loosen; cool 1 hour longer. Refrigerate overnight. Remove sides of pan. Let stand at room temperature for 30 minutes before slicing. **Yield:** 12-14 servings.

Making a Crumb Crust

1 Place cookies or crackers in a heavy-duty resealable plastic bag. Seal bag, pushing out as much air as possible. Press a rolling pin over the bag, crushing the cookies or crackers to fine crumbs.

2 Use a flat-bottomed glass or a measuring cup to firmly press the prepared crumb mixture onto the bottom (and up the sides if recipe directs) of a springform pan.

3 For the best results, the springform pan should not be warped and should seal tightly. To prevent butter in the crust from leaking out, lightly wrap heavy-duty foil around the outside of the springform pan.

Preparing Perfect Cheesecakes

EVEN experienced bakers often end up with a "cracked" cheesecake.

Listed below are several steps you can take to help prevent the top from splitting open. If cracks appear despite your efforts, don't despair—your cheesecake will still taste wonderful as it disappears into smiling mouths.

But if you'd like, you can use a topping such as slightly sweetened sour cream, whipped cream, fresh fruit or preserves to hide any cracks.

Prevent Overmixing

- When mixing, be sure that the cream cheese has softened and the other ingredients are at room temperature.

- Before adding the eggs, beat other ingredients until smooth, scraping the sides of the mixing bowl often to eliminate lumps. Then beat eggs into the mixture on low speed just until blended. (If too much air is beaten into the mixture, it will puff during baking, then collapse and split when cooled.)

Grease Sides of Pan

- Grease the sides of the springform pan to help prevent the filling from cracking when the cheesecake cools. (It will naturally pull away from the sides.)

Watch Time and Temperature

- Place the rack at the middle level of the oven.

- Check the accuracy of your oven temperature with an oven thermometer. Cheesecake generally requires moderate temperatures (from 325° to 350°).

- Open the oven door as seldom as possible during baking, particularly during the first 30 minutes. Drafts can cause a cheesecake to crack.

- Do not use a knife to test for doneness in cheesecake because it may create a crack in the top. The center of a cheesecake (about the size of a walnut) should not be completely set and will jiggle slightly when removed from the oven. The retained heat will continue to cook the cheesecake, and it will become firm throughout.

Cool Properly

- Cool the cheesecake for 10 minutes on a wire rack. Then run a sharp knife around the inside edge of the pan to loosen the cheesecake. Do not remove the sides of the pan.

- Cool the cheesecake on a wire rack in a draft-free location for 1 hour, then refrigerate it. When completely cool, cover with foil or plastic wrap and refrigerate for at least 6 hours or overnight before serving. This allows the cheesecake to set and will make it easier to cut. It also mellows the flavors and gives a creamier texture to the cheesecake.

- Before serving, unlatch the springform pan and carefully remove the sides. Let the cheesecake stand at room temperature for 30 minutes before slicing and serving.

Bring Back Warm Memories with A Cool Treat

Chocolate Mint Ice Cream

The Scoop on Ice Cream Makers

ICE CREAM LOVERS can use one of several types of ice cream freezers to make their favorite dessert.

If you don't have an old ice cream maker stored in your basement, you may want to look for a motorized type at a yard sale or pick up a new state-of-the-art model at your local hardware or department store.

No matter which type you choose, follow the manufacturer's directions for the best results.

Salt and Ice Needed

Most people recall the old-fashioned wooden bucket model with the inner metal canister. After crushed ice and rock salt are layered around the metal canister inside the bucket, eager helpers take their turn at the crank.

The crank rotates the canister, which has a vertical paddle called a dasher inside. As the canister is rotated, the dasher stirs the ice cream mixture, aerating it and keeping it smooth by preventing ice crystals from forming while it freezes.

While hand-cranking is a fun activity, especially for a group, it can be tiring for young arms. Some bucket models have an electric motor that sits on top to turn the crank—eliminating fatigue. More recent countertop models have a motor beneath the canister and accommodate ice cubes and table salt.

All these models need to be churned continuously, with additional ice and salt added as the ice melts.

Container Is Pre-Chilled

Another type of ice cream maker eliminates the use of ice and salt altogether. Often called a Donvier type after the company that invented it, it relies on a double-sided cylinder with a special coolant sealed inside its walls.

Before it's used, the cylinder's placed in the freezer for several hours to chill the coolant. Then the ice cream mixture is poured into the cylinder and, depending on the model, the dasher is rotated by hand or by an electric motor.

This type of ice cream maker does not require continuous churning, and it will freeze the ice cream more quickly than models that use ice and salt.

Refrigerated Unit

A more expensive type of maker has a built-in refrigeration unit, so it doesn't require ice and salt or a cylinder chilled ahead of time.

This countertop model has freezing coils wrapped around the canister and a motorized dasher that stirs the ice cream mixture as it freezes.

Once the mixture is poured into the cylinder, you just turn on the machine and let it do all the work.

FEW THINGS can bring back sweet memories like the cold, creamy taste of old-fashioned hand-cranked ice cream.

With most any type of ice cream freezer, you can travel back to the good ol' days and enjoy a family activity that's sure to warm your spirit and melt your heart. (Even without an ice cream maker, you can re-create that homemade taste in your kitchen freezer with the Chocolate Mint Ice Cream recipe below.)

So when you find you have "time out to cook", why not try your hand at one of the delicious desserts featured here? You and your family will have a memorable time making—and eating—the fun and frosty results.

Chocolate Mint Ice Cream

(Pictured above and on page 324)

When the weather gets hot, my family really enjoys this cool combination of chocolate and mint. It doesn't require an ice cream maker—all that you need is an ordinary freezer. My ice cream's versatile, too. We've used crushed Heath bars, Oreo cookies and miniature chocolate chips in place of the Andes candies. —Fran Skaff
Egg Harbor, Wisconsin

>   1 can (14 ounces) sweetened condensed milk
> 1/2 cup chocolate syrup
>   2 cups whipping cream
>   1 package (4.67 ounces) mint Andes candies
>   (28 pieces), chopped

In a small bowl, combine the milk and chocolate syrup; set aside. In a mixing bowl, beat cream until stiff peaks form. Fold in chocolate mixture and candies. Transfer to a freezer-proof container; cover and freeze for 5 hours or until firm. Remove from the freezer 10 minutes before serving. **Yield:** 1-1/2 quarts.

Raspberry Ice Cream

(Pictured below right)

When local farmers have an abundance of raspberries, we know it's time to make this fruity frozen dessert. It's super in the summertime…and a treat throughout the year made with frozen raspberries. —Diana Leskauskas
Chatham, New Jersey

> **2 cups fresh *or* frozen raspberries**
> **2 cups whipping cream**
> **1 cup half-and-half cream**
> **1 cup sugar**
> **2 teaspoons vanilla extract**

Place the raspberries in a blender; cover and process on medium-high speed until chopped. Combine all ingredients in the cylinder of an ice cream freezer. Stir until sugar is dissolved. Freeze according to manufacturer's directions. **Yield:** about 1-1/2 quarts.

Creamy Vanilla Ice Cream

(Pictured below right)

A traditional cooked custard base is the key to this creamy ice cream with rich vanilla flavor. It is a treasured family favorite that has been handed down and enjoyed for generations. Whenever we serve this delicious treat, we get lots of requests for the recipe. —Mary Thompson
Minneapolis, Minnesota

> **2 eggs**
> **1 cup sugar**
> **1/4 teaspoon salt**
> **2-1/2 cups whipping cream**
> **2 cups half-and-half cream**
> **2-1/4 teaspoons vanilla extract**

In a heavy saucepan, combine the first five ingredients. Cook over medium-low heat, stirring constantly, until the mixture is thick enough to coat a metal spoon and reaches at least 160°. Remove from the heat; cool quickly by setting the pan in ice and stirring the mixture. Cover and refrigerate overnight or freeze immediately. When ready to freeze, pour custard and vanilla into the cylinder of an ice cream freezer. Freeze according to the manufacturer's directions. **Yield:** about 1-1/2 quarts.

Sandwich Your Ice Cream

1 Place 1/2 cup of ice cream on the flat side of a 3-inch cookie.

2 Top with a second cookie; gently press cookies together until ice cream is even with the edges.

3 Place toppings (such as miniature chocolate chips, chopped nuts, chocolate sprinkles, etc.) in pie plate. Roll edges of the sandwich in toppings until covered. Serve immediately or wrap in plastic wrap and freeze.

Raspberry Ice Cream
Creamy Vanilla Ice Cream

Homemade Broth Is Secret to Spirit-Warming Soups

FOR SOUPS with old-fashioned goodness, you can't beat the flavor you get when you start with homemade broth—or "stock", as it's sometimes called.

The home economists in our test kitchen share basic chicken and beef broth recipes, plus some pointers to help you make a better broth and two quick soup recipes that use homemade stock.

Homemade Chicken Broth

Rich in chicken flavor, this traditional broth is lightly seasoned with herbs. Besides making wonderful chicken soups, it can be used in casseroles, rice dishes and other recipes that call for chicken broth.

    2-1/2 pounds bony chicken pieces
        2 celery ribs with leaves, cut into chunks
        2 medium carrots, cut into chunks
        2 medium onions, quartered
        2 bay leaves
    1/2 teaspoon dried rosemary, crushed
    1/2 teaspoon dried thyme
        8 to 10 whole peppercorns
        2 quarts cold water

Place all ingredients in a soup kettle or Dutch oven. Slowly bring to a boil; reduce heat. Skim foam. Cover and simmer for 2 hours. Set chicken aside until cool enough to handle. Remove meat from bones. Discard bones; save meat for another use. Strain broth, discarding vegetables and seasonings. Refrigerate for 8 hours or overnight. Skim fat from surface. **Yield:** about 6 cups.

Chunky Chicken Noodle Soup

Chunky Chicken Noodle Soup

(Pictured above left)

Marjoram and thyme come through nicely in this old-fashioned soup that tastes just like Grandma used to make. You can modify the recipe to include vegetables your family enjoys.

    1/2 cup diced carrot
    1/4 cup diced celery
    1/4 cup chopped onion
        1 teaspoon butter *or* margarine
        6 cups chicken broth
    1-1/2 cups diced cooked chicken
        1 teaspoon salt
    1/2 teaspoon dried marjoram
    1/2 teaspoon dried thyme
    1/8 teaspoon pepper
    1-1/4 cups uncooked medium egg noodles
        1 tablespoon minced fresh parsley

In a large saucepan or Dutch oven, saute carrot, celery and onion in butter until tender. Add broth, chicken and seasonings; bring to a boil. Reduce heat. Add noodles; cook for 10 minutes or until tender. Add parsley. **Yield:** 6 servings.

Simmer a Better Broth

THERE ARE several "secrets" to successful homemade beef or chicken stock. As you prepare yours, keep these tips from our test kitchen in mind:

- For a more flavorful broth, use a high proportion of meat/bones and vegetables to water.
- Be sure to use cold water when starting to make stock.
- Bring the broth mixture to a boil slowly to help release more meat juices. An initial rapid boil tends to seal the juices into the meat.
- Feel free to use additional seasonings in the broth such as basil, dill, sage, turmeric, cloves or lemon peel.
- Do not add starchy vegetables like potatoes to the broth mixture.
- During cooking time, if necessary, add just enough hot water to keep meat and vegetables covered.
- If cheesecloth is not available to strain stock, use dampened paper towels or a large coffee filter.
- It's best not to press the meat and vegetables when straining.
- Broth can be refrigerated for 1 to 2 days or frozen in freezer containers for 6 months.

Homemade Beef Broth

Roasting soup bones in the oven first gives hearty beef flavor to this basic stock. In addition to soups, use the beefy broth to provide extra flavor in stews, gravies, sauces and vegetable dishes.

4 pounds meaty beef soup bones (beef shanks *or* short ribs)
3 medium carrots, cut into chunks
3 celery ribs, cut into chunks
2 medium onions, quartered
1/2 cup warm water
3 bay leaves
3 garlic cloves
8 to 10 whole peppercorns
3 to 4 sprigs fresh parsley
1 teaspoon *each* dried thyme, marjoram and oregano
3 quarts cold water

Place soup bones in a large roasting pan. Bake, uncovered, at 450° for 30 minutes. Add carrots, celery and onions. Bake 30 minutes longer; drain fat. With a slotted spoon, transfer the bones and vegetables to a soup kettle. Add warm water to the roasting pan; stir to loosen browned bits from pan. Transfer pan juices to kettle. Add seasonings and enough cold water just to cover. Slowly bring to a boil, about 30 minutes. Reduce heat; simmer, uncovered, for 4-5 hours, skimming the surface as

Beef Barley Soup

foam rises. If necessary, add hot water during the first 2 hours to keep the ingredients covered. Set beef bones aside until cool enough to handle. Remove meat from bones; discard bones and save meat for another use. Strain broth, discarding vegetables and seasonings. Refrigerate for 8 hours or overnight. Skim fat from surface. **Yield:** about 2-1/2 quarts.

Beef Barley Soup

(Pictured above)

Senior Recipe Editor Sue Jurack shares her recipe for a delicious soup brimming with tasty and colorful ingredients. It's so comforting on a crisp autumn day.

1/2 cup *each* chopped carrot, celery and onion
1 tablespoon butter *or* margarine
4 cups beef broth
4 cups water
2 cups chopped cooked roast beef
1 can (14-1/2 ounces) diced tomatoes, undrained
1 cup quick-cooking barley
1-1/2 teaspoons salt
1/2 teaspoon pepper
1/2 teaspoon dried basil
1/2 teaspoon dried oregano
1/2 cup frozen peas

In a soup kettle or Dutch oven, saute carrot, celery and onion in butter until tender, about 5 minutes. Add the broth, water, beef, tomatoes, barley, salt, pepper, basil and oregano; bring to a boil. Reduce heat; cover and simmer for 20 minutes, stirring occasionally. Add the peas. Simmer, uncovered, for 5 minutes. **Yield:** 12 servings (3 quarts).

Preparing Broth

1 While the broth simmers (chicken is shown here), use a slotted spoon to skim foam from the surface. Skim frequently during the first 30 minutes, then as needed or every hour as the broth cooks.

2 To strain broth, line a colander with two layers of cheesecloth and place in a large heat-resistant bowl. Gradually pour broth mixture into colander. Slowly lift the colander from the bowl, letting broth drain.

3 When ready to use the broth (beef is shown here), take chilled mixture from refrigerator and use a spoon to remove the hardened fat from the broth's surface. Discard fat.

Classic Stuffed Turkey

Prepare a Picture-Perfect Turkey

ROASTING a whole turkey—the highlight of a traditional Thanksgiving feast—can be intimidating, especially to novice cooks. But it needn't be with these tried-and-true techniques compiled by our test kitchen that simplfy the process from beginning to end.

Classic Stuffed Turkey
(Pictured at left)

For years, my mother has stuffed a holiday turkey with this moist dressing featuring fresh mushrooms. Now I do the

Getting a Turkey Ready for Roasting

1 Combine stuffing ingredients according to the recipe directions. Spoon the stuffing loosely into the neck cavity just before baking. Pull the neck skin over the stuffing and under the turkey. Secure with a skewer.

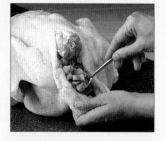

2 Tuck the wing tips under the body to avoid overbrowning.

3 Loosely spoon stuffing into the body cavity. (Bake any extra stuffing separately.) To truss the turkey, position skewers and lace shut using kitchen string.

4 Tie drumsticks together with kitchen string.

5 Place turkey breast side up on a rack in a shallow roasting pan. Insert an ovenproof meat thermometer into the thick portion of the inner thigh area (do not touch the bone). Or an instant-read thermometer may be used instead toward the end of the roasting time.

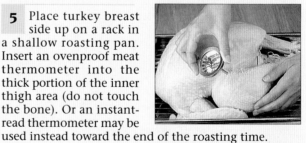

6 When the breast area has browned, loosely cover with foil to prevent excess browning. Continue roasting until the thermometer reads 180° for the turkey and 165° in the center of the stuffing.

same. Its special flavor nicely complements the tender, juicy slices of oven-roasted turkey. —*Kathi Graham*
Naperville, Illinois

2 large onions, chopped
2 celery ribs, chopped
1/2 pound fresh mushrooms, sliced
1/2 cup butter *or* margarine
1 can (14-1/2 ounces) chicken broth
1/3 cup minced fresh parsley
2 teaspoons rubbed sage
1 teaspoon poultry seasoning
1 teaspoon salt
1/2 teaspoon pepper
12 cups unseasoned stuffing croutons *or* dry
   bread cubes
Warm water
1 turkey (14 to 16 pounds)
Melted butter *or* margarine

In a large skillet, saute onions, celery and mushrooms in butter until tender. Add broth and seasonings; mix well. Place bread cubes in a large bowl; add mushroom mixture and toss to coat. Stir in enough warm water to reach desired moistness. Loosely stuff the turkey just before baking. Skewer openings; tie drumsticks together. Place breast side up on a rack in a roasting pan. Brush with butter. Bake, uncovered, at 325° for 4-1/4 to 4-1/2 hours or until a meat thermometer reads 180° for turkey and 165° for stuffing. Baste occasionally with pan drippings. When turkey begins to brown, cover lightly with foil. Cover and let stand 20 minutes before removing the stuffing and carving the turkey. If desired, thicken pan drippings for gravy. **Yield:** 12-14 servings (10 cups stuffing). **Editor's Note:** Stuffing may be prepared as directed and baked separately in a 3-qt. baking dish. Cover and bake at 325° for 10 minutes; uncover and bake 10 minutes longer or until lightly browned.

Herbed Turkey Rub

A simple-to-prepare rub, like this three-ingredient blend, easily adds a wonderful flavor and beautiful color to the turkey's skin.

2 tablespoons butter *or* margarine, melted
1/2 teaspoon paprika
1/2 teaspoon poultry seasoning

Combine all ingredients; brush over turkey skin before roasting. **Yield:** enough for a 14- to 16-pound turkey.

Turkey Carving Basics

AFTER removing the roasted turkey from the oven, allow it to stand for 10-20 minutes. Remove all stuffing to a serving bowl; cover with foil to keep warm. Then follow these simple steps to carve the bird like an expert!

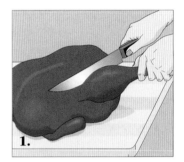

1. Remove the trussing strings and skewers; spoon stuffing into an ovenproof serving dish. Cover stuffing and return to the warm oven. Pull the leg away from the body until the thigh bone pops out of its socket. Cut between the thigh joint and the body to remove the entire leg. Repeat with the other leg. Separate the drumstick and the thigh by cutting through the ball joint. Hold each part by the bone and cut off 1/4-inch slices.

2. Hold the turkey with a meat fork and make a deep cut into the breast meat just above the wing area. This marks the end of each breast meat slice.

3. Slice down from the breast into the cut made in Step 2. Slice meat 1/4 inch thick.

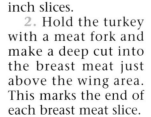

Timely Tips for Terrific Turkey

AS YOU PLAN your holiday feast, keep in mind these helpful hints from our test kitchen:

● When buying a bird, purchase 3/4 to 1 pound per person for whole turkeys that weigh 6 to 12 pounds. For larger whole turkeys (over 12 pounds), purchase 1/2 to 3/4 pound per person.

● The best way to thaw a frozen turkey is to place it breast side up in the refrigerator in its unopened wrapper for 2 to 3 days.

● Be sure to remove neck and giblets from the body and neck cavities before stuffing. Always stuff a turkey just before baking.

● An unstuffed turkey cooks more quickly than a stuffed one. If short on time, bake stuffing separately.

● Roast turkey at a temperature of 325° or higher, basting occasionally to keep skin moist.

● If the dark meat has reached 180° and the stuffing has not reached 165°, scoop stuffing into a greased baking dish and continue to bake while the turkey stands before carving.

● Tying or trussing a turkey keeps the stuffing in place and produces a more rounded, beautiful result. Some turkeys come with the legs held together by a metal clip, which serves the same purpose as trussing.

● If you let the turkey stand before carving, the meat will firm up and the slices will hold together better.

● Remove stuffing and carve the meat off the bones within 2 hours of roasting. Leftover turkey stored in the refrigerator should be used within 3 days. Properly wrapped or placed in a freezer container, cooked turkey will keep for 2 months in the freezer.

General Recipe Index

This handy index lists every recipe by food category and/or major ingredient.

CHOCOLATE
Snacks (continued)
   Gobbler Goodies, 254
   Gooey Peanut Treats, 249
   Peanut Butter Honeybees, 246

COCONUT
Baked Apples on the Grill, 283
Brownie Caramel Parfaits, 311
Caramel Nut Candy, 205
Chewy Macaroons, 60
Chewy Peanut Bars, 203
Chocolate Coconut Bars, 198
Chocolate Mint Dessert, 122
Coconut Chip Cookies, 91
Coconut Chocolate Cake, 205
Coconut Fruit Dip, 227
Coconut Orange Cupcakes, 296
Coconut Toast, 145
Cookie Burgers, 245
Hawaiian Cake, 95
Lemon Coconut Squares, 211
Nutty Peach Crisp, 59
Peter Rabbit Cake, 45
Quick Coconut Cream Pie, 206
Sweet Tooth Treats, 216
Tropical Bananas, 56
Tropical Stuffed Pears, 77

COFFEE CAKES
Blueberry Coffee Cake, 299
Raspberry Coffee Cake, 167
Rhubarb Coffee Cake, 166
Streusel Coffee Cake Mix, 100

CONDIMENTS (also see Salads & Salad Dressing; Sauces)
Fruit Salsa, 272
Herbed Turkey Rub, 337
Katie's Sugar 'n' Spice, 249
Salt Substitute, 221
Versatile Coating Mix, 97

COOKIES (also see Bars & Brownies)
Cutout
   Moonbeam Munchies, 43
   Watermelon Cookies, 251
Drop
   Chewy Macaroons, 60
   Oatmeal Cookie Mix, 98
   Peanut Butter Drops, 240
Shaped
   Chocolate Caramel Cookies, 215
   Chocolate Chip Butter
      Cookies, 197
   Coconut Chip Cookies, 91
   Dipped Peanut Butter
      Cookies, 216
   Licorice Cookie Strips, 211
   Molasses Cookie Mix, 99
   Monster Cookies, 209
   Nutmeg Sugar Cookies, 217
   Peanut Butter Cookies, 208
   Potato Chip Cookies, 196
   Scandinavian Pecan Cookies, 67
Specialty
   Mexican Cookies, 34

Brownie Almond Biscotti, 93
Brown Sugar Shortbread, 198
Cookie Burgers, 245

CORN
Cheesy Creamed Corn, 275
Colby Corn Chowder, 193
Corn Bread Casserole, 25
Corn Bread Strips, 166
Corn-Stuffed Tomatoes, 230
Creamy Corn Casserole, 237
Grilled Sweet Corn, 282
Skillet Steak and Corn, 12

CORN BREAD & CORNMEAL
Coffee Shop Corn Muffins, 162
Corn Bread Casserole, 25
Corn Bread Mix, 98
Maple Corn Bread, 173
Sweet Corn Muffins, 173
Tamale Pie, 286

CRANBERRIES
Cran-Apple Salad, 68
Cran-Raspberry Gelatin, 68
Cranberry Yeast Bread, 174
Holiday Ham Slices, 317

CUCUMBERS
Chive Cucumber Salad, 300
Cool Cucumber Dip, 309
Dressed-Up Cucumbers, 17

CUPCAKES
Black Cat Cupcakes, 51
Brownie Cups, 210
Chocolate Cherry Cupcakes, 296
Coconut Orange Cupcakes, 296
Cream Cheese Cupcakes, 296
Rosy Rhubarb Cupcakes, 296
Zucchini Chip Cupcakes, 203

DATES (see Raisins & Dates)

DESSERTS (also see specific kinds)
Ambrosia Fruit Cups, 31
Apple Delight, 32
Applescotch Sundaes, 206
Apricot-Almond Antarctica, 127
Banana Pudding Dessert, 216
Berries 'n' Cream, 215
Black Forest Mousse, 238
Blueberry Delight, 299
Blueberry Kuchen, 299
Brownie Caramel Parfaits, 311
Butterscotch Banana Dessert, 113
Chocolate Fondue, 206
Chocolate Mint Dessert, 122
Cinnamon Peaches, 223
Dessert from the Grill, 284
Easy Cocoa Mousse, 230
Easy Mint Chip Ice Cream, 199
Hot Caramel Apples, 268
Ladyfinger Trifle, 315
Magic Mousse, 317
Microwave Cherry Crisp, 289
Nutty Peach Crisp, 59

Orange Whip, 127
Patriotic Frozen Delight, 201
Quick Peach Cobbler, 214
Raspberry Chocolate Trifle, 113
Refreshing Lemon Cream, 313
Rich Chocolate Wraps, 297
Sherbet Dessert, 225
Spiced Oranges, 212
Strawberry Lemon Trifle, 230
Strawberry Parfaits, 206
Strawberry Sponge Cake, 13
Sweet Snowman, 53
Tropical Bananas, 56
Tropical Stuffed Pears, 77
Vanilla Fruit Dessert, 29

DIPS
Coconut Fruit Dip, 227
Cool Cucumber Dip, 309
Creamy Fruit Dip, 58
Hearty Broccoli Dip, 278
Little Dippers, 43
Peanut Butter Apple Dip, 56
Southwestern Cheese Dip, 10

DRESSING (see Stuffing & Dressing)

DUMPLINGS
Chicken and Dumplings/Quicker
   Chicken and Dumplings, 258
   and 259
Mexican Beef and Dumplings, 154

EGGS
Bacon Avocado Burritos, 135
Baked Brunch Sandwiches, 140
Biscuit Breakfast Sandwiches, 134
Breakfast Pita Pockets, 137
Breakfast Pizza, 248
Cheesy Broccoli Pie, 82
Country Brunch Skillet, 132
Curried Crab Quiche, 145
Daddy's Omelet, 138
Dilly Scrambled Eggs, 31
Egg Biscuit Bake, 137
Great Pumpkin Sandwiches, 51
Hash Brown Egg Bake, 135
Hearty Scrambled Eggs, 142
Herbed Cheese Omelet, 137
No-Turn Omelet, 134
Ratatouille Frittata, 113
Speedy Huevos Rancheros, 142
Steak Hash, 107
Sunday Brunch Eggs, 141
Tater Surprise, 137
Tie-Dyed Easter Eggs, 45
Vegetarian Burritos, 141
Wake-Up Casserole, 145

FISH & SEAFOOD
Main Dishes
   Baked Fish and Rice, 148
   Baked Salmon, 110
   Barbecued Alaskan Salmon, 280
   Catch-of-the-Day Fish, 47
   Catfish in Ginger Sauce, 286
   Curried Crab Quiche, 145

NUTS (*also see Peanut Butter*)
Almond Currant Rice, 27
Almond Ice Cream Cups, 15
Almond Rice Pilaf, 56
Almond-Topped Chicken, 68
Anise Almond Loaf, 179
Apricot Almond Chicken, 152
Apricot-Almond Antarctica, 127
Broccoli Cashew Salad, 35
Brownie Almond Biscotti, 93
Caramel Nut Candy, 205
Cashew Candies, 255
Cherry Almond Bark, 212
Chewy Date Nut Bars, 215
Chewy Peanut Bars, 203
Chocolate Praline Torte, 307
Crunchy Peanut Bark, 214
Crunchy Raisin Treats, 61
Curried Cashews, 69
Gooey Peanut Treats, 249
Green Beans with Almonds, 67
Jewel Nut Bars, 217
Macadamia Nut Bread, 174
Microwave Snack Mix, 286
Moist Nut Bread, 165
Nutty Cracker Delights, 202
Nutty French Toast, 137
Nutty Peach Crisp, 59
Orange Nut Bread, 162
Peanut Crunch Cake, 85
Pecan Pear Bread, 170
Pecan Pie Bars, 199
Pecan Sticky Muffins, 162
Pistachio Brittle, 290
Praline Grahams, 33
Praline Parfaits, 62
Raspberry Nut Bars, 232
Rocky Road Fudge, 57
Scandinavian Pecan Cookies, 67
Snackers, 62
Sweet Almond Bread, 175
Walnut Apple Bundt Cake, 212
Walnut Brownies, 17

OATS
Blueberry Oat Bars, 214
Maple Oatmeal Bread, 177
Monster Cookies, 209
Oatmeal Cookie Mix, 98

ONIONS
Onion Rye Breadsticks, 73
Scalloped Potatoes and Onions, 309
T-Bones with Onions, 284

ORANGE
Citrus Steak, 283
Coconut Orange Cupcakes, 296
Frothy Orange Drink, 132
Fruity Orange Gelatin, 67
Katie's Sugar 'n' Spice, 249
Mandarin Chicken, 274
Nutty Marmalade Sandwiches, 121
Orange Blossom Lamb, 27
Orange Nut Bread, 162
Orange Streusel Muffins, 166
Orange-Topped Chops, 56

Orange Whip, 127
Spiced Oranges, 212
Tropical Tuna Salad, 224
Zippy Orange Chicken, 225

PASTA & NOODLES
Main Dishes
Bacon and Pepper Pasta, 159
Beefy Noodle Bake, 152
Chicken Mushroom
   Fettuccine, 79
Chicken Noodle Stir-Fry, 94
Chicken Primavera, 290
Circle-O Skillet Supper, 244
Colorful Chicken Casserole, 128
Dinner in a Bag, 90
Easy Lasagna, 106
Easy Pasta Alfredo, 62
Flavorful Mac and Cheese, 77
Golden Chicken and
   Noodles, 271
Ham 'n' Noodle Hot Dish, 150
Ham and Swiss Casserole, 150
Hamburger Hot Dish, 240
Lasagna Casserole, 20
Macaroni Tuna Casserole, 88
Minestrone Macaroni, 237
Oven Swiss Steak, 228
Overnight Tuna Casserole, 289
Pasta Shells and Peppers, 236
Peppy Macaroni, 253
Pesto Pepper Tortellini, 157
Pizza Mac Casserole, 239
Pork Noodle Casserole, 109
Pretty Ham Primavera, 114
Ravioli Casserole, 63
Sausage Spaghetti Supper, 237
Seafood Fettuccine, 35
Shrimp Marinara, 279
Spaghetti 'n' Meatballs, 118
Speedy Ham and Macaroni, 159
Swiss Tuna Bake, 58
Tortellini Toss, 311
Tuna Alfredo, 76
Turkey Bow Tie Skillet, 158
Turkey Florentine, 104
Turkey Linguine, 38
Turkey Noodle Casserole, 126
Salads
Italian-Style Pasta Toss, 186
Salmon Pasta Salad, 110
Seashell Salad, 49
Side Dishes
Creamy Corn Casserole, 237
Garlic Angel Hair Pasta, 238
Parmesan Noodles, 72
Soups
Chunky Chicken Noodle
   Soup, 334
Hearty Tortellini Soup, 86
Split Pea Soup Mix, 100
30-Minute Minestrone, 185
Turkey Meatball Soup, 185

PEACHES
Cinnamon Peaches, 223
Nutty Peach Crisp, 59

Peach Cake, 24
Peach Mallow Pie, 19
Peach Muffins, 171
Peachy Spiced Cider, 278
Quick Peach Cobbler, 214

PEANUT BUTTER
Chocolate Peanut Dream Pie, 197
Cookie Burgers, 245
Crispy Chocolate Squares, 287
Crunchy Peanut Bark, 214
Dipped Peanut Butter Cookies, 216
Honey Cereal Bars, 197
Hopscotch Treats, 88
Monster Cookies, 209
No-Bake Bars, 208
Nutty Apple Wedges, 244
Nutty Marmalade Sandwiches, 121
Peanut Butter 'n' Jelly Pie, 247
Peanut Butter Apple Dip, 56
Peanut Butter Cookies, 208
Peanut Butter Drops, 240
Peanut Butter Fudge, 199
Peanut Butter Honeybees, 246
Peanut Butter-Jelly Spread, 254
Peanut Butter Muffins, 170
Peanut Butter Squares, 205
Peanut Crunch Cake, 85
Peanutty Fries, 245
Quick Little Devils, 199
Snackers, 62
Stuffed Celery Sticks, 253
Sweet Cereal Treats, 249
Sweet Tooth Treats, 216

PEARS
Mousy Pear Salad, 252
Pecan Pear Bread, 170
Tropical Stuffed Pears, 77

PEAS
Black-Eyed Pea Salad, 221
Dilly Sweet Peas, 27
Quick Pea Soup, 244
Split Pea Soup Mix, 100

PEPPERS
Almost Stuffed Peppers, 159
Bacon and Pepper Pasta, 159
Grilled Jalapenos, 283
Italian Vegetable Saute, 78
Pasta Shells and Peppers, 236
Pesto Pepper Tortellini, 157
Southwest Stuffed Peppers, 110
Stuffed Green Pepper Cups, 286
Superb Yellow Pepper Soup, 189

PIES
Berry Special Pie, 30
Chocolate Mousse Pie, 202
Chocolate Peanut Dream Pie, 197
Cookies 'n' Cream Pie, 125
Festive Fruit Pie, 208
Five-Minute Blueberry Pie, 204
Fluffy Pineapple Pie, 210
Frosty Freeze Pie, 121

Alphabetical Index

*This handy index lists every recipe in alphabetical order
so you can easily find your favorite recipes.*

F

Fancy Fuss-Free Torte, 201
Fast Baked Fish, 18
Fast Chicken Divan, 109
Fast Fruit Cocktail Cake, 205
Fast Fudge Sundaes, 72
Favorite Meat Loaf Cups, 38
Favorite Pot Roast, 104
Festive Fruit Pie, 208
Feta Pitas, 65
Fiesta Bread, 169
Fiesta Chicken, 152
Fish and Veggies Primavera, 220
Fish Nuggets, 67
Five-Minute Blueberry Pie, 204
Five-Vegetable Stir-Fry, 156
Flavorful Herb Bread, 178
Flavorful Mac and Cheese, 77
Fluffy Hot Chocolate, 79
Fluffy Pineapple Pie, 210
Fluffy White Frosting, 326
Flying Saucers, 43
Frankenstein Salads, 51
Franks 'n' Beans Supper, 159
Freezer Vegetable Soup, 125
French Salad Dressing Mix, 97
French-Toasted English Muffins, 140
Fresh Fruit Bowl, 135
Fried Potatoes, 105
Frosted Gelatin Salad, 89
Frosty Freeze Pie, 121
Frosty Fruit Cups, 123
Frothy Orange Drink, 132
Frozen Blueberry Muffins, 162
Frozen Pumpkin Pie, 298
Frozen Raspberry Pie, 210
Fruit 'n' Cheese Salad, 189
Fruit Cocktail Ice Pops, 250
Fruit Medley, 132
Fruit Salsa, 272
Fruited Lettuce Salad, 12
Fruited Mini Loaves, 173
Fruited Pumpkin Bread, 298
Fruited Sweet Potatoes, 69
Fruity Orange Gelatin, 67
Fruity Rice Mix, 101
Fudgy Buttons, 202

G

Garlic Angel Hair Pasta, 238
Garlic Broccoli Spears, 72
Garlic Cheese Biscuits, 168
Garlic Yeast Bread, 179
Giant Stuffed Picnic Burger, 313
Gingerbread with Lemon
  Sauce, 290
Gobbler Goodies, 254
Golden Chicken and Noodles, 271
Golden Chicken Casserole, 150
Golden Fruit Punch, 307
Gooey Peanut Treats, 249
Great Pumpkin Sandwiches, 51
Green Beans with Almonds, 67

Green Chili Burritos, 34
Green Chili Stew, 272
Greens with Herb Vinaigrette, 61
Grill Bread, 126
Grilled Jalapenos, 283
Grilled Roast Beef Sandwiches, 193
Grilled Sweet Corn, 282
Grilled Sweet Potatoes, 284
Gumdrop Bread, 173

H

Ham 'n' Cheddar Cups, 134
Ham and Cheese Bagels, 247
Ham 'n' Cheese Wedges, 163
Ham 'n' Noodle Hot Dish, 150
Ham and Swiss Casserole, 150
Ham with Cherry Sauce, 114
Hamburger Fry Pan Supper, 155
Hamburger Hot Dish, 240
Harvest Vegetables, 284
Hash Brown Beef Pie, 303
Hash Brown Egg Bake, 135
Hash Brown Potato Salad, 88
Hawaiian Cake, 95
Heart Biscuits, 169
Hearty Broccoli Dip, 278
Hearty Ham Loaves, 120
Hearty Hamburger Supper, 36
Hearty Italian Sandwiches, 268
Hearty Meat Pie, 126
Hearty Red Beans and Rice, 229
Hearty Scrambled Eggs, 142
Hearty Tortellini Soup, 86
Herbed Cheese Omelet, 137
Herbed Pork and Potatoes, 158
Herbed Pork Roast, 109
Herbed Tossed Salad, 21
Herbed Turkey Rub, 337
Holiday Ham Slices, 317
Homemade Beef Broth, 335
Homemade Chicken Broth, 334
Homemade Chocolate Pudding, 25
Homemade Muffin Mix, 101
Honey Berry Milk Shakes, 295
Honey Cereal Bars, 197
Honey-Glazed Carrots, 18
Honey-Mustard Pork Scallopini, 76
Honey Wheat Muffins, 165
Honey Whole Wheat Bread, 179
Hook, Line 'n' Sinker Mix, 47
Hopscotch Treats, 88
Hot Bacon Asparagus Salad, 186
Hot Caramel Apples, 268
Hot Dog Sandwiches, 121
Hot Hoagies, 189
Hot Turkey Sandwiches, 182

I

Iced Cinnamon Biscuits, 168
Iced Coffee, 232
Idaho Tacos, 294
In-a-Hurry Curry Soup, 77
Italian Chicken and Rice, 153

Italian Meatball Subs, 278
Italian Sausage Skillet, 30
Italian Sausage Stew, 155
Italian-Style Pasta Toss, 186
Italian Vegetable Saute, 78

J

Jewel Nut Bars, 217
Jim's Cheddar Bread, 175

K

Katie's Sugar 'n' Spice, 249

L

Ladyfinger Trifle, 315
Lasagna Casserole, 20
Lasagna Sandwiches, 185
Layered Toffee Cake, 198
Lazy-Day Grasshopper Pie, 211
Lemon Angel Food
Supreme/Quicker Lemon Angel
  Food Supreme, 260 and 261
Lemon Asparagus, 287
Lemon Coconut Squares, 211
Lemon Ice Tea Mix, 96
Lemon Red Potatoes, 275
Licorice Cookie Strips, 211
Light Carrot Cake, 222
Like-Homemade Baked Beans, 238
Linda's Lemon Fish, 228
Little Dippers, 43
Low-Fat Tartar Sauce, 228
Luncheon Salad, 220
Luscious Lemon Cheesecake, 330

M

Macadamia Nut Bread, 174
Macaroni Tuna Casserole, 88
Magic Apple Pie, 236
Magic Mousse, 317
Make-Ahead Meatballs, 118
Make-Ahead Sandwiches, 125
Mallow Fruit Cups, 253
Mandarin Chicken, 274
Maple-Bacon Oven Pancake, 140
Maple Baked Beans, 73
Maple Corn Bread, 173
Maple-Glazed Sausages, 145
Maple Mustard Chicken, 281
Maple Oatmeal Bread, 177
Marinated Beef Brisket, 309
Marinated Chicken Wings, 273
Marinated Ham Steaks, 283
Mashed Potato Soup, 114
Meat Buns/Meat Bun Bake, 262
  and 263
Meat Loaf Burgers, 274

Nutritional Analysis Recipes Index

Refer to this index when you're looking for a recipe that uses less sugar, salt and fat and includes Nutritional Analysis and Diabetic Exchanges. These fast, delicious and nutritious recipes are marked with a ✓ throughout the book.